TO
BELANNA, ARIEL AND ANNIKA
JACQUELINE AND REBECCA
CATHERINE, NICHOLAS AND PETER

micro

PRINCIPLES OF MICROECONOMICS

JOSHUA GANS
STEPHEN KING
GREGORY MANKIW

5e

CENGAGE Learning

Principles of Microeconomics
5th Edition
Joshua Gans
Stephen King
N. Gregory Mankiw

Publishing manager: Dorothy Chiu
Senior publishing editor: Michelle Aarons
Developmental editor: Kylie McInnes
Senior project editor: Ronald Chung
Permissions research manager: Corrina Tauschke
Cover designer: Leigh Ashforth
Text designer: Olga Lavecchia
Editor: Greg Alford
Proofreader: Craig MacKenzie
Indexer: Russell Brooks
Reprint: Katherine Fullagar
Cover: Masterfile
Typeset by S4 Carlisle Publishing Services

First Australian edition published in 1999 by Harcourt Australia Pty Limited
Second edition published in 2002 by Cengage Learning Australia
Third edition published in 2005
Fourth edition published in 2009
Fifth edition published in 2012

National Library of Australia Cataloguing-in-Publication Data
Author: Gans, Joshua S.
Title: Principles of microeconomics / Joshua S. Gans; Stephen P. King; N. Gregory Mankiw.
Edition: 5th ed.
ISBN: 9780170191708 (pbk.)
Notes: Includes index.
Previous ed: 2009.
Subjects: Microeconomics--Textbooks.
Other Authors/Contributors:
King, Stephen P.
Mankiw, N. Gregory
Dewey Number: 338.5

Cengage Learning Australia
Level 7, 80 Dorcas Street
South Melbourne, Victoria Australia 3205

Cengage Learning New Zealand
Unit 4B Rosedale Office Park
331 Rosedale Road, Albany, North Shore 0632, NZ

For learning solutions, visit **cengage.com.au**

Printed in China by China Translation & Printing Services.
5 6 7 8 9 10 11 18 17 16 15 14

Brief Contents

Contents

Preface to this edition

Studying economics should invigorate and enthral. It should challenge students' preconceptions and provide them with a powerful, coherent framework for analysing the world they live in. Yet, all too often, economics textbooks are dry and confusing. Rather than highlighting the important foundations of economic analysis, these books focus on the 'ifs' and 'buts'. The motto underlying this book is that it is 'the rule, not the exception' that is important. Our aim is to show the power of economic tools and the importance of economic ideas.

This book has been designed particularly for students in Australia and New Zealand. However, we are keenly aware of the diverse mix of students studying in these countries. When choosing examples and applications, we have kept an international focus. Whether the issue is sauce tariffs in the EU, rent control in Mumbai, DVD prices in the USA or the gas industry in Australia, examples have been chosen for their relevance and to highlight that the same economic questions are being asked in many countries. The specific context in which economics is applied may vary, but the lessons and insights offered by the economic way of thinking are universal.

To boil economics down to its essentials, we had to consider what is truly important for students to learn in their first course in economics. As a result, this book differs from others not only in its length but also in its orientation.

It is tempting for professional economists writing a textbook to take the economist's point of view and to emphasise those topics that fascinate them and other economists. We have done our best to avoid that temptation. We have tried to put ourselves in the position of students seeing economics for the first time. Our goal is to emphasise the material that students should and do find interesting about the study of the economy.

One result is that more of this book is devoted to applications and policy, and less is devoted to formal economic theory, than is the case with many other books written for the principles course. For example, after students learn about the market forces of supply and demand in chapters 4 to 6, they immediately apply these tools in chapters 7 to 9 to consider three important questions facing our society: Why is the free market a good way to organise economic activity? How does taxation interfere with the market mechanism? Who are the winners and losers from international trade? These kinds of questions resonate with the concerns and interests that students hear about in the news and bring from their own lives.

Throughout this book we have tried to return to applications and policy questions as often as possible. Most chapters include case studies illustrating how the principles of economics are applied. In addition, 'In the news' boxes offer excerpts from newspaper and magazine articles showing how economic ideas shed light on the current issues facing society. It is our hope that after students finish their first course in economics, they will think about news stories from a new perspective and with greater insight.

To write a brief and student-friendly book, we had to consider new ways to organise the material. This book includes all the topics that are central to a first course in economics, but the topics are not always arranged in the traditional order. What follows is a whirlwind tour of this text. This tour will, we hope, give instructors some sense of how the pieces fit together.

Chapter 1, 'Ten lessons from economics', introduces students to the economist's view of the world. It previews some of the big ideas that recur throughout economics, such as opportunity cost, marginal decision making, the role of incentives, the gains from trade and the efficiency of market allocations. Throughout the book, we refer regularly to the Ten Lessons from Economics in chapter 1 to remind students that these lessons are the foundation for most economic analysis. A key icon in the margin calls attention to these references.

Chapter 2, 'Thinking like an economist', examines how economists approach their field of study. It discusses the role of assumptions in developing a theory and introduces the concept of an economic model. It also discusses the role of economists in making policy. The appendix to this chapter offers a brief refresher course on how graphs are used and how they can be abused.

Chapter 3, 'Interdependence and the gains from trade', presents the theory of comparative advantage. This theory explains why individuals trade with their neighbours, and why nations trade with other nations. Much of economics is about the coordination of economic activity through market forces. As a starting point for this analysis, students see in this chapter why economic interdependence can benefit everyone. This is done using a familiar example of trade in household chores among flatmates.

The next three chapters introduce the basic tools of supply and demand. Chapter 4, 'The market forces of supply and demand', develops the supply curve, the demand curve and the notion of market equilibrium. Chapter 5, 'Elasticity and its application', introduces the concept of elasticity and uses it in three applications to quite different markets. Chapter 6, 'Supply, demand and government policies', uses these tools to examine price controls, such as rent control and the award wage system, and tax incidence.

Attention then turns to welfare analysis using the tools of supply and demand. Chapter 7, 'Consumers, producers and the efficiency of markets', extends the analysis of supply and demand using the concepts of consumer surplus and producer surplus. It begins by developing the link between consumers' willingness to pay and the demand curve and the link between producers' costs of production and the supply curve. It then shows that the market equilibrium maximises the sum of the producer and consumer surplus. In this book, students learn about the efficiency of market allocations early in their studies.

The next two chapters apply the concepts of producer and consumer surplus to questions of policy. Chapter 8, 'Application: The costs of taxation', examines the deadweight loss of taxation. Chapter 9, 'Application: International trade', examines the winners and losers from international trade and the debate about protectionist trade policies.

Having examined why market allocations are often desirable, the book then considers how the government can sometimes improve on market allocations. Chapter 10, 'Externalities', examines why external effects such as pollution can render market outcomes inefficient. It also examines the possible public and private solutions to those inefficiencies. This has become highly relevant as policymakers attempt to deal with mitigating the causes of climate change. Chapter 11, 'Public goods and common resources', considers the inefficiencies that arise for goods that have no market price, such as national defence. Chapter 12, 'The design of the tax system', examines how the government raises the revenue necessary to pay for public goods. It presents some institutional background about the tax system and then discusses how the goals of efficiency and equity come into play in the design of a tax system.

The next five chapters examine firm behaviour and industrial organisation. Chapter 13, 'The costs of production', discusses what to include in a firm's costs and introduces cost curves. Chapter 14, 'Firms in competitive markets', analyses the behaviour of price-taking firms and derives the market supply curve. Chapter 15, 'Monopoly', discusses the behaviour of a firm that is the sole seller in its market. It discusses the inefficiency of monopoly pricing and the value of price discrimination. Chapter 16, 'Business strategy', examines markets when there are only a few sellers and so strategic interactions are important. It uses the prisoners' dilemma as the model for examining strategic interaction. Chapter 17, 'Competition policy' describes the policy instruments used by governments to control monopoly power and preserve competition in markets. Chapter 18, 'Monopolistic competition', examines behaviour in a market in which many sellers offer similar but differentiated products. It also discusses the debate about the effects of advertising.

Microeconomic reform is discussed throughout the chapters on firm behaviour and industrial organisation rather than as a separate topic. For instance, the role of privatisation is included in chapter 15, and competition and trade practices issues are discussed in chapter 17. Also, note that chapter 16 includes an appendix that can be used to teach students about the differences between price and quantity competition in oligopoly. This appendix makes the latest game-theoretic thinking on these issues accessible to introductory economics students.

The next three chapters examine issues related to labour markets. Chapter 19, 'The markets for the factors of production', emphasises the link between factor prices and marginal productivity. It includes an appendix on the firm demand for labour under imperfect competition and monopoly. Chapter 20, 'Earnings, unions and discrimination', discusses the determinants of equilibrium wages, including compensating differentials, human capital, unions, efficiency wages and discrimination. The union discussion goes beyond simplistic analyses of unions and monopolists, introducing union behaviour as part of a bargaining equilibrium in bilateral monopoly. The discussion of human capital and efficiency wages proves a convenient point to introduce students to the concepts of signalling and asymmetric information. Chapter 21, 'Income inequity and poverty,' examines the degree of inequality in Australian society, the alternative views about the government's role in changing the distribution of income, and the various policies aimed at helping society's poorest members.

Chapter 22, 'The theory of consumer choice', analyses individual decision making using budget constraints and indifference curves. Finally, Chapter 23 goes beyond standard microeconomics to examine cutting-edge issues such as the role of information, political economy and behavioural economics; all of which help explain more of what happens in the real world. These last two chapters cover material that is somewhat more advanced than the rest of the book. Some instructors may want to skip the last chapter, depending on the emphases of their courses and the interests of their students. Instructors who do cover this material may want to move it earlier, and we have written this chapter so that it can be covered any time after the basics of supply and demand have been introduced.

Joshua S. Gans
Stephen P. King

Preface to the original edition

During my twenty-year career as a student, the course that excited me most was the two-semester sequence on the principles of economics I took during my freshman year in college. It is no exaggeration to say that it changed my life.

I had grown up in a family that often discussed politics over the dinner table. The pros and cons of various solutions to society's problems generated fervent debate. But, in school, I had been drawn to the sciences. Whereas politics seemed vague, rambling and subjective, science was analytic, systematic and objective. While political debate continued without end, science made progress.

My freshman course on the principles of economics opened my eyes to a new way of thinking. Economics combines the virtues of politics and science. It is, truly, a social science. Its subject matter is society – how people choose to lead their lives and how they interact with one another. But it approaches its subject with the dispassion of a science. By bringing the methods of science to the questions of politics, economics tries to make progress on the fundamental challenges that all societies face.

I was drawn to write this book in the hope that I could convey some of the excitement about economics that I felt as a student in my first economics course. Economics is a subject in which a little knowledge goes a long way. (The same cannot be said, for instance, of the study of physics or the Japanese language.) Economists have a unique way of viewing the world, much of which can be taught in one or two semesters. My goal in this book is to transmit this way of thinking to the widest possible audience and to convince readers that it illuminates much about the world around them.

I am a firm believer that everyone should study the fundamental ideas that economics has to offer. One of the purposes of general education is to make people more informed about the world in order to make them better citizens. The study of economics, as much as any discipline, serves this goal. Writing an economics textbook is, therefore, a great honor and a great responsibility. It is one way that economists can help promote better government and a more prosperous future. As the great economist Paul Samuelson put it, 'I don't care who writes a nation's laws, or crafts its advanced treaties, if I can write its economics textbooks.'

N. Gregory Mankiw
July 2000

To the students

'Economics is a study of mankind in the ordinary business of life.' So wrote Alfred Marshall, the great nineteenth-century economist, in his textbook, *Principles of Economics*. Although we have learned much about the economy since Marshall's time, this definition of economics is as true today as it was in 1890, when the first edition of his text was published.

Why should you, as a student entering the twenty-first century, embark on the study of economics? There are three reasons.

The first reason to study economics is that it will help you understand the world in which you live. There are many questions about the economy that might spark your curiosity. Why are houses more expensive in Sydney than in Perth? Why do airlines charge less for a return ticket if the traveller stays over a Saturday night? Why are some people paid so much to play tennis? Why are living standards so meagre in many African countries? Why do some countries have high rates of inflation while others have stable prices? Why are jobs easy to find in some years and hard to find in others? These are just a few of the questions that a course in economics will help you answer.

The second reason to study economics is that it will make you a more astute participant in the economy. As you go about your life, you make many economic decisions. While you are a student, you decide how many years you will continue with your studies. Once you take a job, you decide how much of your income to spend, how much to save and how to invest your savings. Someday you may find yourself running a small business or a large corporation, and you will decide what prices to charge for your products. The insights developed in the coming chapters will give you a new perspective on how best to make these decisions. Studying economics will not by itself make you rich, but it will give you some tools that may help in that endeavour.

The third reason to study economics is that it will give you a better understanding of the potential and limits of economic policy. As a voter, you help choose the policies that guide the allocation of society's resources. When deciding which policies to support, you may find yourself asking various questions about economics. What are the burdens associated with alternative forms of taxation? What are the effects of free trade with other countries? What is the best way to protect the environment? How does a government budget deficit affect the economy? These and similar questions are always on the minds of policymakers whether they work for a local council or the prime minister's office.

Thus, the principles of economics can be applied in many of life's situations. Whether the future finds you reading the newspaper, running a business or running a country, you will be glad that you studied economics.

Joshua S. Gans
Stephen P. King
N. Gregory Mankiw

About the authors

Joshua Gans holds the Skoll Chair in Innovation and Entrepreneurship at the Rotman School of Management, University of Toronto. He studied economics at the University of Queensland and Stanford University. He currently teaches network and digital market strategy. Professor Gans's research ranges over many fields of economics including economic growth, game theory, regulation and the economics of technological change and innovation. His work has been published in academic journals including the *American Economic Review*, *Journal of Economic Perspectives*, *Journal of Political Economy* and the *Rand Journal of Economics*. Joshua also has written the popular book, *Parentonomics* (published by MIT Press) and founded the Core Economics blog (economics.com.au). Currently, he is an associate editor at *Management Science* and the *Journal of Industrial Economics*. He has also undertaken consulting activities (through his consulting firm, CoRE Research), advising governments and private firms on the impact of microeconomic reform and competition policy in Australia. In 2007, he was awarded the Economic Society of Australia's Young Economist Award for the Australian economist under 40 who has made the most significant contribution to economic knowledge. In 2008, he was elected as a Fellow of the Academy of Social Sciences Australia.

Professor Gans lives in Toronto with his spouse and three children.

Stephen King is Professor of Economics at Monash University and a Member of the Economic Regulation Authority of Western Australia. Prior to joining Monash, Stephen was a Commissioner at the Australian Competition and Consumer Commission. After starting (and stopping) studying forestry and botany, Stephen completed an economics degree at the Australian National University. He completed his PhD at Harvard University in 1991. Stephen has taught a variety of courses, including introductory courses at Harvard University and the University of Melbourne.

Professor King specialises in industrial economics, although his research has covered a wide range of areas, including game theory, corporate finance, privatisation and tax policy. His work has been published in academic journals such as the *Journal of Industrial Economics, European Economic Review* and *Journal of Political Economy*. Stephen regularly provides advice to both government and private firms on a range of issues relating to regulation and competition policy. He is a Lay Member of the High Court of New Zealand and a Fellow of the Academy of Social Sciences in Australia.

Professor King lives in Melbourne with his wife. Their two children have run away from home to study at university.

N. Gregory Mankiw is Professor of Economics at Harvard University. As a student, he studied economics at Princeton University and MIT. As a teacher, he has taught macroeconomics, microeconomics, statistics and principles of economics. He even spent one summer long ago as a sailing instructor on Long Beach Island.

Professor Mankiw is a prolific writer and a regular participant in academic and policy debates. His work has been published in scholarly journals, such as the *American Economic Review*, *Journal of Political Economy* and *Quarterly Journal of Economics*, and in more popular forums, such as the *New York Times*, *Boston Globe* and the *Wall Street Journal*. He is also the author of the best-selling intermediate-level textbook *Macroeconomics* (Worth Publishers). In addition to his teaching, research and writing, Professor Mankiw is a research associate of the National Bureau of Economic Research, an adviser to the Federal Reserve Bank of Boston and the Congressional Budget Office, and a member of the ETS test development committee for the advanced placement exam in economics.

Professor Mankiw lives in Wellesley, Massachusetts, with his wife and three children.

Acknowledgements

In updating this book, we have benefited from the input of a wide range of talented people. We would like to thank all those people who helped us with this task. We would also like to thank those economists who read and commented on portions of both this edition and the previous editions, including:

Ershard Ali, Auckland Institute
Jeff Borland, University of Melbourne
Michael Cameron, University of Waikato
Neil Campbell, Bond University
Vivek Chaudhri, University of Melbourne
Mark Crosby, University of Melbourne
Peter Dawkins, University of Melbourne
Laurel Dawson, Deakin University
Sarath Delpachitra, University of Southern Queensland
Robert Dixon, University of Melbourne
Paul Flatau, Murdoch University
Chris Fleming, Griffith University
Cathy Fletcher, Monash University
John Forster, Griffith University
Michael Francis, University of Canberra
John Freebairn, University of Melbourne
Chris Geller, Deakin University
Mary Graham, Deakin University
Bob Gregory, Australian National University
Ian Harper, University of Melbourne
Ian Harriss, Charles Sturt University
John Hicks, Charles Sturt University
Sarah Jennings, University of Tasmania
Chris Jones, Australian National University
Geoff Kelly, University of Wollongong
Steven Kemp, Curtin University
Monica Keneley, Deakin University
Parvinder Kler, University of Queensland
Micheal Kowalik, Australian Defence Force Academy
Radhika Lahiri, Queensland University of Technology
Boon Lee, Queensland Institute of Technology
Andrew Leigh, Australian National University
Shravan Luckraz, Bond University
Jakob Madsen, Monash University
Gary Magee, Latrobe University
Ian McDonald, University of Melbourne
Alan Morris, Victoria University of Technology
Mark Morrison, Charles Sturt University
Andrew Nadolny, University of Newcastle
Owen Nguyen, Australian Maritime College
Senada Nukic, University of South Australia
David Owens, Swinburne University of Technology
Greg Parry, Edith Cowan University
John Perkins, University of New South Wales
Clive Reynoldson, Edith Cowan University
John Rodgers, University of Western Australia
Amal Sanyal, Lincoln University
John Searle, University of Southern Queensland
Martin Shanahan, University of South Australia
Sharshi Sharma, Victoria University of Technology
Leanne Smith, Massey University
Lindsay Smyrk, Victoria University of Technology
Luz Stenberg, University of Notre Dame
Robin Stonecash, Macquarie University
Judy Taylor, Monash University
Di Thomson, Deakin University
John Tressler, University of Waikato
Nishi Verma, Monash University
Thea Vinnicombe, Bond University
Neil Warren, University of New South Wales
Philip Williams, University of Melbourne
Ed Wilson, University of Wollongong
John Wood, Edith Cowan University
Christabel Zhang, Victoria University
Steffen Ziss, Sydney University

Finally, we give special acknowledgement to our team of research assistants – Teresa Fels, Richard Hayes, Richard Scheelings, Anna Kim and Kimberly Jin – who have worked on this project.

Resources guide

FOR THE STUDENT

As you read this text you will find a wealth of features in every chapter to enhance your study of microeconomics and help you understand how it is applied in the real world.

Learning objectives are listed at the start of each chapter giving you a clear sense of what the chapter will cover.

The *Introduction* is a short story, focused on the chapter topic, about how microeconomics affects you on a daily basis without you even noticing.

Where you see this symbol, you should refer to the *Ten lessons from economics* found in chapter 1 of this text.

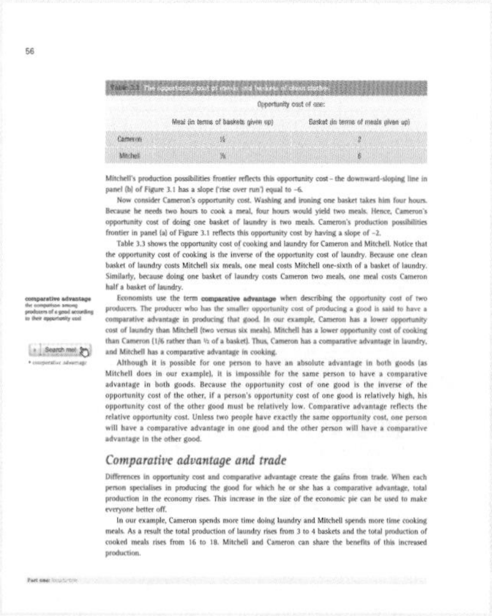

When *key terms* are used in the text for the first time, they are bolded, coloured and defined in the margins. This will help you identify key concepts throughout the text.

comparative advantage
the comparison among producers of a good according to their opportunity cost

Current economic news and events are presented as *In the news*. This selection of media and journal clippings will explore how microeconomic ideas shed light on current affairs.

IN THE NEWS . . .

Throughout the chapter there are quick quizzes to assess your knowledge and comprehension of key topics.

Useful microeconomic facts can be found in the *FYI* boxes. They will provide you with additional information and material to support key concepts within each chapter.

fyi

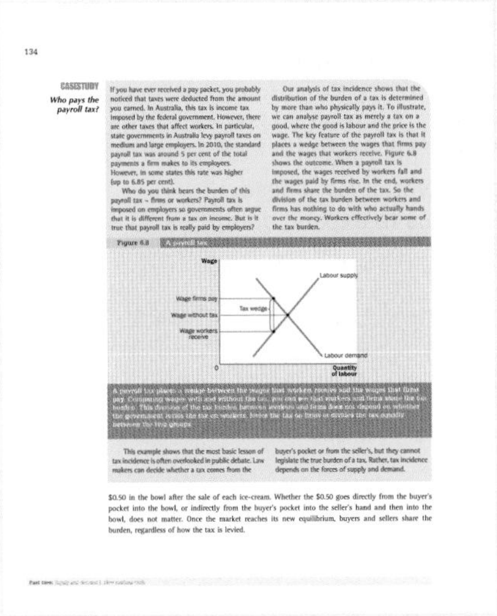

Case studies throughout the book will help you conceptualise key issues in the text, demonstrating how your knowledge can be applied to real-world situations.

CASESTUDY

At the end of each chapter there are several learning tools that will help you review the chapter and key concepts.

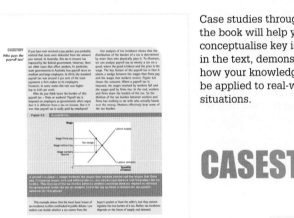

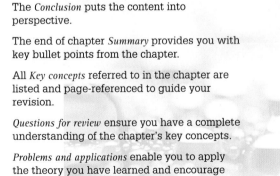

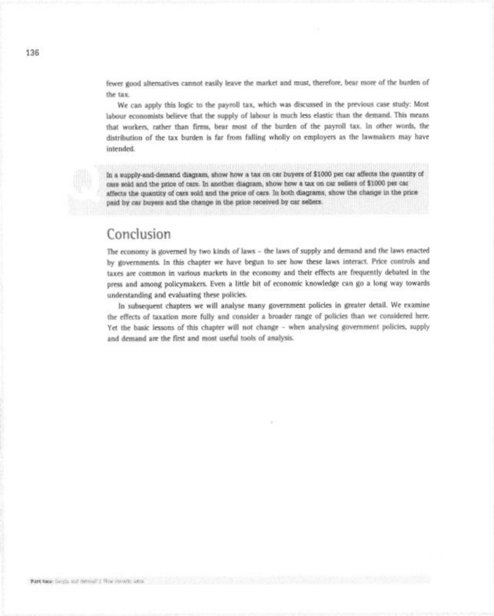

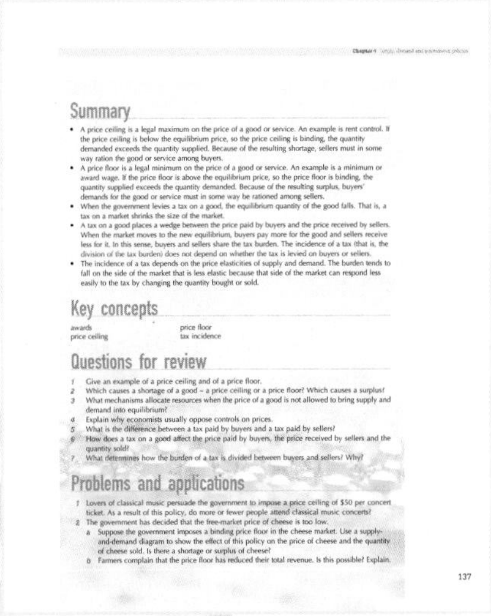

The *Conclusion* puts the content into perspective.

The end of chapter *Summary* provides you with key bullet points from the chapter.

All *Key concepts* referred to in the chapter are listed and page-referenced to guide your revision.

Questions for review ensure you have a complete understanding of the chapter's key concepts.

Problems and applications enable you to apply the theory you have learned and encourage group discussion.

Online resources

Visit **http://login.cengagebrain.com** and login using the code card at the front of this book for access to the ***Principles of Microeconomics Coursemate website***. You will find an ebook, quizzing, flashcards, crosswords, graphing workshops, videos and more tools to help you excel in your studies.

From **http://login.cengagebrain.com** you can also access *Search me! economics*. Fast and convenient, this resource is updated daily and provides you with 24-hour access to full-text articles from hundreds of scholarly and popular journals, ebooks and newspapers, including *The Australian* and *The New York Times*.

Use the *Search me! economics* keywords provided in the margins of each chapter to explore topics further and find current references. These terms will get you started, then try your own search terms to expand your knowledge.

For the instructor

Cengage Learning is pleased to provide you with a selection of resources that have been developed to supplement the fifth edition of ***Principles of Microeconomics***. These resources are available on the instructor's companion website accessible via **http://login.cengage.com**.

Instructor's manual

The ***Instructor's manual*** provides you with a wealth of content to help set up and administer an introductory microeconomics course. It includes learning objectives, chapter outlines, key points, figures from the text, adjunct teaching and warm-up activities as well as solutions to problems in the text.

PowerPoint presentations

Chapter-by-chapter ***PowerPoint presentations*** cover the main concepts addressed within the text and can be edited to suit your own requirements. Use these slides to enhance your lecture presentations and to reinforce the key principles of your subject, or for student handouts.

ExamView test bank

ExamView helps you to create, customise and deliver tests in minutes for both print and online applications. The Quick Test Wizard and Online Test Wizard guide you step by step through the test-creation process. With ExamView's complete word-processing abilities, you can add an unlimited number of new questions to the bank, edit existing questions and build tests of up to 250 questions using up to 12 question types. You can also export the files into Blackboard or WebCT.

Artwork

These digital files of graphs, tables and exhibits from the book can be used in a variety of media. Add them into your course management system, use them within student handouts or copy them into lecture presentations.

PART ONE
Introduction

1

Ten lessons from economics

Learning objectives

In this chapter you will:

- learn that economics is about the allocation of scarce resources
- examine some of the trade-offs that people face
- learn the meaning of opportunity cost
- see how to use marginal reasoning when making decisions
- discuss how incentives affect people's behaviour
- consider why trade among people or nations can be good for everyone
- discuss why markets are a good, but not perfect, way to allocate resources
- learn what determines some trends in the overall economy.

The word *economy* comes from the Greek word for 'one who manages a household'. At first, this origin might seem peculiar. But, in fact, households and economies have much in common.

A household faces many decisions. It must decide which members of the household do which tasks and what each member gets in return. Who cooks dinner? Who does the laundry? Who gets the extra dessert at dinner? Who chooses what TV show to watch? In short, the household must allocate its scarce resources among its various members, taking into account each member's abilities, efforts and desires.

Like a household, a society faces many decisions. A society must decide what jobs will be done and who will do them. It needs some people to grow food, other people to make clothing, and still others to design computer software. Once society has allocated people (as well as land, buildings and machines) to various jobs, it must also allocate the output of the goods and services that they produce. It must decide who will eat caviar and who will eat potatoes. It must decide who will drive a Porsche and who will take the bus.

The management of society's resources is important because resources are scarce. **Scarcity** means that society has limited resources and therefore cannot produce all the goods and services people wish to have. Just as each member of a household cannot get everything he or she wants, each individual in society cannot attain the highest standard of living to which he or she might aspire.

scarcity
the limited nature of society's resources

Economics is the study of how society manages its scarce resources. In most societies, resources are allocated not by an all-powerful dictator but through the combined actions of millions of households and firms. Economists, therefore, study how people make decisions – how much they work, what they buy, how much they save and how they invest their savings. Economists also study how people interact with one another. For instance, they examine how the buyers and sellers of a good interact to determine the price at which the good is sold and the quantity that is sold. Finally, economists analyse forces and trends that affect the economy as a whole, including the growth in average income, the fraction of the population that cannot find work and the rate at which prices are rising.

economics
the study of how society manages its scarce resources

The study of economics has many facets, but it is unified by several central ideas. In the rest of this chapter, we look at *Ten Lessons from Economics*. Don't worry if you don't understand them all at first or if you are not completely convinced. We will explore these ideas more fully in later chapters. The 10 lessons are introduced here to give you an overview of what economics is all about.

How people make decisions

There is no mystery about what an 'economy' is. Whether we are talking about the economy of Sydney, of Australia or of the whole world, an economy is just a group of people interacting with one another as they go about their lives. Because the behaviour of an economy reflects the behaviour of the individuals who make up the economy, we begin our study of economics with four lessons on individual decision making.

Lesson 1: People face trade-offs

You may have heard the saying: 'There is no such thing as a free lunch'. To get one thing that we like, we usually have to give up another thing that we like. Making decisions requires trading off one goal against another.

Consider a student who must decide how to allocate her most valuable resource – her time. She can spend all her time studying economics; she can spend all her time studying psychology; or she can divide her time between the two fields. For every hour she studies one subject, she gives up an hour she could have used studying the other. And for every hour she spends studying, she gives up an hour that she could have spent sleeping, bike riding, watching TV or working at her part-time job for some extra spending money.

Or consider parents deciding how to spend their family income. They can buy food or clothing, or have a holiday. Or they can save some of the family income for retirement or the children's education. When they choose to spend an extra dollar on one of these goods, they have one less dollar to spend on some other good.

When people are grouped into societies, they face different kinds of trade-offs. The classic trade-off is between 'guns and butter'. The more we spend on defence to protect our shores from foreign aggressors (guns), the less we can spend on personal goods to raise our standard of living at home (butter). Also important in modern society is the trade-off between a clean environment and a high level of income. Laws that require firms to reduce pollution usually raise the cost of producing goods and services. Because of the higher costs, these firms end up earning smaller profits, paying lower wages, charging higher prices or some combination of these three. Thus, while pollution regulations give us the benefit of a cleaner environment and the improved health that comes with it, they have the cost of reducing the incomes of the regulated firms' owners, workers and customers.

efficiency
the property of society getting the most it can from its scarce resources

equity
the property of distributing economic prosperity fairly among the members of society

Another trade-off society faces is between efficiency and equity. **Efficiency** means that society is getting the most it can from its scarce resources. **Equity** means that the benefits of those resources are distributed fairly among society's members. In other words, efficiency refers to the size of the economic pie, and equity refers to how the pie is divided. Often, when government policies are being designed, these two goals conflict.

Consider, for instance, policies aimed at achieving a more equitable distribution of economic wellbeing. Some of these policies, such as the age pension or unemployment benefits, try to help those members of society who are most in need. Others, such as the individual income tax, ask the financially successful to contribute more than others to support the government. Although these policies have the benefit of achieving greater equity, they have a cost in terms of reduced efficiency. When the government redistributes income from the rich to the poor, it can reduce the reward for working hard; as a result, people may work less and produce fewer goods and services. In other words, as the government tries to cut the economic pie into more equitable slices, the pie may get smaller.

Recognising that people face trade-offs does not by itself tell us what decisions they will or should make. A student should not abandon the study of psychology just because doing so would increase the time available for the study of economics. Society should not stop protecting the environment just because environmental regulations reduce our material standard of living. The poor should not be ignored just because helping them distorts work incentives. Nonetheless, acknowledging life's trade-offs is important because people are likely to make good decisions only if they understand the options that they have available. Our study of economics starts by acknowledging life's trade-offs.

Lesson 2: The cost of something is what you give up to get it

Because people face trade-offs, making decisions requires comparing the costs and benefits of alternative courses of action. In many cases, however, the cost of some action is not as obvious as it might first appear.

Consider, for example, the decision whether to go to university. The benefits include intellectual enrichment and a lifetime of better job opportunities. But what is the cost? To answer this question, you might be tempted to add up the money you or your parents spend on fees, books, rent and food. Yet this total does not truly represent what you give up to spend a year at university.

There are two problems with this calculation. First, it includes some things that are not really costs of university education. Even if you quit university, you would need a place to sleep and food to eat. Rent and food are costs of going to university only to the extent that they are more expensive because you are going to university. For instance, you might have to move cities to attend university and live away from home. Indeed, the cost of your room and food at your residential college or home might be less than the rent and food expenses that you would pay living on your own. In this case, the savings on the room and food are a benefit of going to university.

Second, this calculation ignores the largest cost of going to university - your time. When you spend a year listening to lectures, reading textbooks and writing assignments, you cannot spend that time working at a job. For most students, the wages given up to attend university are the largest single cost of their education.

The **opportunity cost** of an item is what you give up to get that item. When making any decision, such as whether to attend university, decision makers should be aware of the opportunity costs that accompany each possible action. In fact, they usually are. For example, some young athletes can earn millions if they forgo university and play professional sports. Their opportunity cost of university is very high. It is not surprising that they often decide that the benefit of a university education is not worth the opportunity cost.

opportunity cost
whatever must be given up to obtain some item

Lesson 3: Rational people think at the margin

Economists normally assume that people are rational. Rational people systematically and purposefully do the best they can do to achieve their objectives, given the opportunities they have. As you study economics, you will encounter firms that decide how many workers to hire and how much of their product to manufacture and sell to maximise profits. You will encounter individuals who decide how much time to spend working, and what goods and services to buy with the resulting income to achieve the highest possible level of satisfaction.

Search me!
▸ opportunity cost

Rational people know that decisions in life are rarely black and white but usually involve shades of grey. At dinnertime, the decision you face is not between fasting or eating like a pig but whether to take that extra spoonful of mashed potatoes. When exams roll around, your decision is not between blowing them off or studying 24 hours a day but whether to spend an extra hour reviewing your notes instead of watching TV. Economists use the term **marginal change** to describe a small incremental adjustment to an existing plan of action. Keep in mind that *margin* means 'edge', so marginal changes are adjustments around the edges of what you are doing. Rational people often make decisions by comparing *marginal benefits* and *marginal cost.*

marginal change
a small incremental adjustment to a plan of action

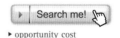

For example, consider an airline deciding how much to charge passengers who fly standby. Suppose that flying a 200-seat plane from Brisbane to Perth costs the airline $100 000. In this case, the average cost of each seat is $100 000/200, which is $500. One might be tempted to conclude that the airline should never sell a ticket for less than $500. Actually, the airline can often raise its profits by thinking at the margin. Imagine that a plane is about to take off with 10 empty seats and a standby passenger waiting at the gate will pay $300 for a seat. Should the airline sell the ticket? Of course it should. If the plane has empty seats, the cost of adding one more passenger is tiny. Although the *average* cost of flying a passenger is $500, the *marginal* cost is merely the cost of the sandwich and coffee that the extra passenger will consume. As long as the standby passenger pays more than the marginal cost, selling the ticket is profitable.

Marginal decision making can help explain some otherwise puzzling economic phenomena. Here is a classic question: Why is water so cheap, while diamonds are so expensive? Humans need water to survive, while diamonds are unnecessary; but for some reason, people are willing to pay much more for a diamond than for a cup of water. The reason is that a person's willingness to pay for a good is based on the marginal benefit that an extra unit of the good would yield. The marginal benefit, in turn, depends on how many units a person already has. Although water is essential, the marginal benefit of an extra cup is small because water is plentiful. By contrast, no one needs diamonds to survive, but because diamonds are so rare, people consider the marginal benefit of an extra diamond to be large.

A rational decision maker takes an action if and only if the marginal benefit of the action exceeds the marginal cost. This principle can explain why airlines are willing to sell a ticket below the average cost and why people are willing to pay more for diamonds than for water. It can take some time to get used to the logic of marginal thinking, but the study of economics will give you ample opportunity to practice.

Lesson 4: People respond to incentives

An incentive is something that induces a person to act., such as the prospect of a punishment or a reward. Because rational people make decisions by comparing costs and benefits, they respond to incentives. You will see that incentives play a central role in the study of economics. One economist went so far as to suggest that the entire field could be summarised simply: 'People respond to incentives. The rest is commentary'.

Incentives are crucial to analysing how markets work. For example, when the price of an apple rises, for instance, people decide to eat fewer apples. At the same time, apple orchards decide to hire more workers and harvest more apples. In other words, a higher price in a market provides an incentive for buyers to consume less and an incentive for sellers to produce more. As we will see, the influence of prices on the behaviour of consumers and producers is crucial for understanding how the economy allocates scarce resources.

Public policymakers should never forget about incentives. Many policies change the costs or benefits that people face and, therefore, alter their behaviour. A tax on petrol, for instance, encourages people to drive smaller, more fuel-efficient cars. That is one reason people drive smaller cars in Europe and Australia, where petrol taxes are higher, than in the United States, where petrol taxes are low. A petrol tax also encourages people to take public transportation rather than drive, and to live closer to where they work. If the tax were larger, more people would be driving hybrid cars, and if it were large enough, they would switch to electric cars.

When policymakers fail to consider how behaviour might change as a result, their policies can have effects that they did not intend. For example, consider public policy toward seat belts and car safety. In the 1950s, few cars had seat belts. Today all cars do, and in Australia it is compulsory to wear seat belts. The reason for the change is public policy. In the late 1960s, the rising death toll from motor vehicle accidents in Australia generated much public concern over car safety. State governments responded and in December 1970 the Victorian State Government passed legislation requiring car drivers and passengers to wear seat belts. Other states followed and by 1973 it was compulsory throughout Australia to wear seat belts.

How does a seat belt law affect car safety? The direct effect is obvious. When wearing seat belts is compulsory, more people wear seat belts, and the probability of surviving a major car accident rises. In this sense, seat belts save lives. This direct impact of seat belts on safety is what motivated Australian governments to change the law.

But that is not the end of the story because the law also affects behaviour by changing incentives. In this case, the relevant behaviour is the speed and care with which drivers operate their cars. Driving slowly and carefully is costly because it uses the driver's time and energy. When deciding how safely to drive, rational people compare the marginal benefit from safer driving with the marginal cost. They drive more slowly and carefully when the benefit of increased safety is high. This explains why people drive more slowly and carefully when roads are wet and slippery than when roads are clear.

Now consider how a seat belt law alters a driver's cost–benefit calculation. Seat belts make accidents less costly because they reduce the probability of injury or death. In other words, wearing a seat belt reduces the benefits of slow and careful driving. People respond to wearing seat belts as they would to an improvement in road conditions – by driving faster and less carefully. The result of a seat belt law, therefore, is a larger number of accidents. The decline in safe driving has a clear, adverse impact on pedestrians who are more likely to find themselves in an accident but, unlike the drivers, are not protected by a seat belt. Thus, a seat belt law tends to increase the number of pedestrian deaths.

At first, this discussion of incentives and seat belts might seem like idle speculation. Yet in a classic 1975 study, economist Sam Peltzman argued that car safety laws in the United States have, in fact, had many of these effects. According to Peltzman's evidence, US laws produced both fewer deaths per accident and more accidents. He concluded that the net result was little change in the number of driver deaths and an increase in the number of pedestrian deaths.

Peltzman's analysis of car safety is an offbeat and controversial example of the general principle that people respond to incentives. It implies that more recent changes to car safety laws, such as requiring air bags and advanced braking systems in new cars, may mean more deaths for pedestrians and cyclists. When analysing any policy, we must consider not only the direct effects but also the less obvious, indirect effects that work through incentives. If the policy changes incentives, it will cause people to alter their behaviour.

Q

List and briefly explain the four lessons of individual decision making.
Describe an important trade-off you recently faced.
Describe an incentive your parents offered you in an effort to influence your behaviour.

CASESTUDY

Choosing when the stork comes

The Australian government now pays $5000 for every baby born. It is an open issue whether this encourages more babies but the story of the 'baby bonus', as it is called, has lessons for how people might respond to incentives and why governments (and others) need to anticipate those responses.

In May 2004, the then Treasurer, Peter Costello, announced a $3000 payment (rising to $5000 in 2008) for every child born after 1 July 2004. This meant that the parents of someone whose birthday was 30 June 2004 or earlier would receive nothing. But hold off a day or so, and they would get $3000. This created an incentive for parents to delay births if they could. And by agreeing with their doctors to schedule planned caesareans and inducements a little later, births could be moved.

>>

The following graph shows what happened.

Figure 1.1 Births in Australia, June–July 2004

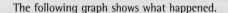

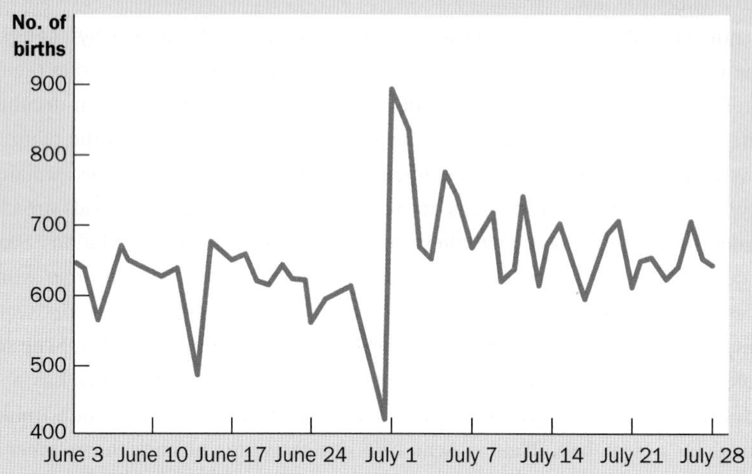

Notice that there was a dip in births in the last week of June followed by a sharp rise on 1 July 2004. Indeed, that day had the most number of recorded births on a single day in Australian history. And if you think this might just be 'fiddling the books', 2 July had the seventh-highest number of births.

In their paper, 'Born on the First of July', Joshua Gans and Andrew Leigh estimated that 1167 births were shifted from June to July that year, all as a result of the baby bonus. Medical organisations raised concerns about the health consequences of maternity hospital congestion caused by this, while economists argued that the policy should have been 'phased-in' so there were no big jumps in payments on any given day.

Nonetheless, the Howard government did not heed those warnings and raised the baby bonus by $834 on 1 July 2006. Gans and Leigh discovered that shifts in birth timing occurred again then but of a lower magnitude (around 700 births).

Joshua Gans and Andrew Leigh, 'Born on the First of July', *Journal of Public Economics*, Vol. 93, Nos 1–2, February 2009, pp. 246–63.

How people interact

The first four lessons discussed how individuals make decisions. As we go about our lives, many of our decisions affect not only ourselves but other people as well. The next three lessons present some key ideas about how people interact with one another.

Lesson 5: Trade can make everyone better off

You may have heard on the news how Australian workers compete with overseas workers for jobs and Australian businesses compete with overseas firms for sales. In some ways, this competition is real because Australian workers and firms produce many of the same goods that are produced overseas. Holden and Mazda compete for the same customers in the market for cars. Clothing firms in Victoria compete with those in Taiwan to sell shirts.

Yet it is easy to be misled when thinking about competition among countries. Trade between Australia and another country is not like a sports contest, where one side wins and the other side loses. In fact, the opposite is true – trade between two countries can make each country better off and, hence, workers (on average) better off.

To see why, consider how trade affects your family. When a member of your family looks for a job, he or she competes against members of other families who are looking for jobs. Families also compete against one another when they go shopping, because each family wants to buy the best goods at the lowest prices. So, in a sense, each family in the economy is competing with all other families.

Despite this competition, your family would not be better off isolating itself from all other families. If it did, your family would need to grow its own food, make its own clothes and build its own home. Clearly, your family gains much from its ability to trade with others. Trade allows each person to specialise in the activities he or she does best, whether it is farming, sewing or home building. By trading with others, people can buy a greater variety of goods and services at lower cost.

Countries as well as families benefit from the ability to trade with one another. Trade allows countries to specialise in what they do best and to enjoy a greater variety of goods and services. The Japanese, the French, the Saudi Arabians and the Vietnamese are as much our partners in the world economy as they are our competitors.

Lesson 6: Markets are usually a good way to organise economic activity

The collapse of communism in the Soviet Union and Eastern Europe in the 1980s may be the most important change in the world during the past 50 years. Communist countries worked on the premise that government workers were in the best position to guide economic activity. These workers, called central planners, decided what goods and services were produced, how much was produced and who produced and consumed these goods and services. The theory behind central planning was that only the government could organise economic activity in a way that promoted economic wellbeing for the country as a whole.

Most countries that once had centrally planned economies have abandoned this system and are instead developing market economies. In a **market economy**, the decisions of a central planner are replaced by the decisions of millions of firms and households. Firms decide whom to hire and what to make. Households decide which firms to work for and what to buy with their incomes. These firms and households interact in the marketplace, where prices and self-interest guide their decisions.

market economy
an economy that allocates resources through the decentralised decisions of many firms and households as they interact in markets for goods and services

At first glance, the success of market economies is puzzling. In a market economy, no one is looking out for the economic wellbeing of society as a whole. Decisions are made by millions of self-interested households and firms. It might sound like chaos. Yet this is not the case. Market economies have proven remarkably successful in organising economic activity to promote overall economic wellbeing.

In his 1776 book *An Inquiry into the Nature and Causes of the Wealth of Nations*, economist Adam Smith explained the success of market economies. He noted that households and firms interacting in markets act as if they are guided by an 'invisible hand' that leads them to desirable market outcomes. One of our goals in this book is to understand how this **invisible hand** works its magic.

invisible hand
The idea that buyers and sellers freely interacting in a market economy will create an outcome that allocates goods and services to those people who value them most highly and makes the best use of our scarce resources

As you study economics, you will learn that prices are the instrument with which the invisible hand directs economic activity. In any market, buyers look at the price when determining how much to demand, and sellers look at the price when deciding how much to supply. As a result of the decisions that buyers and sellers make, prices reflect both the value of a good to society and the cost to society of making the good. Smith's great insight was that prices adjust to guide these individual buyers and sellers to reach outcomes that, in many cases, maximise the wellbeing of society as a whole.

Smith's insight has an important corollary: When the government prevents prices from adjusting naturally to supply and demand, it impedes the invisible hand's ability to coordinate the millions of households and firms that make up the economy. This corollary explains why taxes adversely affect the allocation of resources. Taxes distort prices and thus the decisions of households and firms. It also explains the great harm caused by policies that directly control prices, such as rent control. And it explains the failure of communism. In communist countries, prices were not determined in the marketplace but were dictated by government central planners. These planners lacked the necessary information about consumers' tastes and producers' costs, which in a market economy is reflected in prices. Central planners failed because they tried to run the economy with one hand tied behind their backs – the invisible hand of the marketplace.

fyi

Adam Smith and the role of markets

Adam Smith

Adam Smith is often seen as the founder of modern economics. When his great book *An Inquiry into the Nature and Causes of the Wealth of Nations* was published in 1776, England and Europe were going through a period of major social, political and economic upheaval. The industrial revolution was changing the economic landscape just as the American and the French revolutions were to change the political and social landscape. Smith's book reflects a point of view that was gaining importance at the time – that individuals are usually best left to their own devices, without the heavy hand of government guiding their actions. This political philosophy provides the intellectual basis for the market economy, and for free society more generally.

To Smith, individuals interacting through the marketplace, guided only by their self-interest, promote general economic wellbeing. This view was based on three principles that contradicted the conventional wisdom of Smith's day. First, it involves a view that the individual is best able to determine the value of a product. This theory of value opposed the mercantilist view of the time that certain goods, such as gold, were intrinsically valuable and that successful commercial policy for a nation involved the hoarding of these intrinsically valuable goods. Second, Smith argued that individual specialisation is a key way to create value. This idea led to the theory of comparative advantage that we will discuss in chapter 3. Third, Smith argued that market-based interaction can not only replace centrally coordinated commercial interaction but is likely to be superior to centrally planned systems. While a monarch or a parliament could organise trade and commerce through laws that set prices and restricted certain types of market interactions, this is likely to result in less value creation and national wealth than the relatively unfettered interaction of individuals in the marketplace. We discuss the interaction between government policies and economic welfare throughout this book.

Considerable advances in economics have been made since 1776. But many of Smith's insights remain at the centre of modern economics. Our analysis in the coming chapters will allow us to express Smith's ideas and conclusions more precisely and to analyse fully the strengths and weaknesses of a market-based economy.

Lesson 7: Governments can sometimes improve market outcomes

If the invisible hand of the market is so great, why do we need government? One purpose of studying economics is to refine your view about the proper role and scope of government policy.

One reason we need government is that the invisible hand can work its magic only if government enforces the rules and maintains the institutions that are key to a market economy. Most important, markets work only if property rights are enforced so individuals can own and control scarce resources. A farmer won't grow food if he expects his crop to be stolen; a restaurant won't serve meals unless it is assured that customers will pay before they leave; and an entertainment company won't produce DVDs if too many potential customers avoid paying by making illegal copies. We all rely on government-provided police and courts to enforce our rights over the things we produce.

Yet there is another reason we need government. While markets are usually a good way to organise economic activity, this rule has some important exceptions. There are two broad reasons for a government to intervene in the economy and change the allocation of resources that people would choose on their own: to promote efficiency and to promote equity. That is, most policies aim either to enlarge the economic pie or to change how the pie is divided.

Consider first the goal of efficiency. Although the invisible hand usually leads markets to allocate resources to maximise the size of the economic pie, this is not always the case. Economists use the term **market failure** to refer to a situation in which the market on its own fails to allocate resources efficiently.

market failure
a situation in which a market left on its own fails to allocate resources efficiently

One possible cause of market failure is an externality. An **externality** is the impact of one person's actions on the wellbeing of a bystander. Pollution is a classic example. If a chemical factory does not bear the entire cost of the smoke it emits, it is likely to emit too much. In this case, the government can raise economic wellbeing through environmental regulation.

externality
the uncompensated impact of one person's actions on the wellbeing of a bystander. A positive externality makes the bystander better off. A negative externality makes the bystander worse off.

Another possible cause of market failure is **market power**, which refers to the ability of a single person (or small group of people) to unduly influence market prices. For example, suppose that everyone in town needs water but there is only one well. The owner of the well has market power over the sale of water. He is not subject to the rigorous competition with which the invisible hand normally keeps self-interest in check. In this case, regulating the price that the monopolist charges may improve economic efficiency.

market power
the ability of a single economic actor (or small group of actors) to have a substantial influence on market prices

Now consider the goal of equity. Even when the invisible hand is yielding efficient outcomes, it can nonetheless leave big differences in economic wellbeing. A market economy rewards people according to their ability to produce things that other people are willing to pay for. The world's best soccer player earns more than the world's best chess player simply because people are willing to pay more to see soccer than chess. The invisible hand does not ensure that everyone has sufficient food, decent clothing and adequate health care. Many public policies, such as the tax and social welfare systems, aim to achieve a more equitable distribution of economic wellbeing.

To say that the government can improve on market outcomes at times does not mean that it always *will*. Public policy is made by politicians operating in a political process that is far from perfect. Sometimes policies are designed simply to reward the politically powerful. Sometimes they are made by well-intentioned leaders who are not fully informed. As you study economics, you will become a better judge of when a government policy is justifiable because it promotes efficiency or equity and when it is not.

List and briefly explain the three lessons concerning economic interactions.
Why is a country better off not isolating itself from all other countries?
Why do we have markets and, according to economists, what roles should governments play in them?

fyi

Why markets make us better off

Australia's Productivity Commission is a government agency that investigates ways to improve Australia's economic prosperity. As this excerpt from a speech by Gary Banks, the head of the Productivity Commission, shows, the answer is simple: markets!

It's easy to lose sight of the simple function of markets. They are a means of connecting willing buyers and sellers to their mutual benefit. That's all they do. Of course, if they do it well, they achieve a lot. But, like the old saying about oils, 'markets ain't markets': some operate a lot better than others. History tells us that those societies with better functioning markets have been the most successful economically, and often the most successful socially as well.

Indeed, the economic progress of mankind is broadly coextensive with the evolution of markets: from localised barter, to monetised transactions encompassing large numbers of people over large distances. How rapidly and effectively markets have developed has depended in turn on the development of institutions and rules to facilitate them and to reduce the costs of transactions in particular. The key ones are how well property rights are defined; how effectively suppliers compete; how well informed are buyers; and the nature and reach of mechanisms for legal redress when things go wrong.

Through the medium of prices, competitive markets ensure that a country's resources get put to use where they can do the most good – taking account of what value people place on different goods and services, and how much those goods and services cost to produce. Competitive markets also ensure that the 'better mousetrap' gets appropriately rewarded, in turn providing incentives for innovation and lower cost production which underpin the growth process.

The logic of markets is that all this happens in a decentralised way, with the actions of many unrelated individuals coordinated spontaneously through the prices they face – Adam Smith's 'invisible hand'. Importantly, emerging shortages and surpluses, which are inherent to any economic system, can be signalled automatically in a competitive market through price movements, precipitating spontaneous actions by both buyers and sellers that eventually serve to eliminate them. If a queue persists, whether it be for taxis or hospital beds, you can be sure that a well-functioning market does not.

As noted, not all societies have been persuaded by the logic of markets. However, experiments around the world with alternative systems have only served to demonstrate their value. And indeed we've seen a progressive shift towards, or back to, markets across the globe in recent decades; a move which has generally paid off for the countries concerned. Since 1980, world GDP has risen by two and a half times, or an unprecedented 40 per cent per capita, with millions of people rising out of extreme poverty.

For example, China's performance since the end of the Cultural Revolution, when it tentatively began to open the door to markets, speaks for itself. Since the beginning of the reforms in China in 1978, we've seen real GDP in that country grow by more than 10 per cent a year. That in turn has seen dramatic reductions in poverty, rises in life expectancy and gains in other indicators of wellbeing and capability, like literacy and health. The OECD has described China's advance to a market economy as among the greatest economic success stories of modern times.

The power of markets to produce prosperity has also been reaffirmed within market economies themselves, wherever impediments to the functioning of particular markets have been reduced, or markets have been introduced to industries or activities where none had previously existed.

Australia itself illustrates how important it is to a country's economic performance to make use of markets in a way that achieves the right balance between freedom and intervention. For much of the previous century, that balance shifted decidedly in favour of intervention. Successive governments imposed policies that impeded competition, distorted prices, constrained business and raised its costs.

For many years, the costs of the inefficiencies that multiplied under that regime were masked by the performance of our broadacre agriculture and mining sectors. But by 1983, when the Hawke government came to power, Australia was falling off the sheep's back. Productivity and income growth were low, deficits had become relatively high, and our per capita GDP had slipped from fifth to fifteenth in the OECD. The 'banana republic' loomed, in Treasurer Keating's evocative phrase.

The fact that we were able to reverse our economic decline, unlike those Latin American countries that shared top billing with us on the global GDP ladder at the beginning of last century, was largely due to the structural reforms set in train by the Hawke/Keating government. Key strands of those reforms were directed at freeing up markets, exposing industry to international competition and allowing prices to perform their proper allocative role, while undertaking reforms to make government infrastructure services more efficient and labour markets more flexible.

The consequent transformation of Australia's economy, from one that was inward looking, high cost and inflexible, to an innovative, adaptable and competitive one, brought a resurgence in productivity and income growth. Australia climbed back to eighth in the OECD's per capita GDP rankings by the end of the century.

Source: *Markets: How free?*, A presentation to the Whitlam Institute by Gary Banks, Chairman, Productivity Commission, 30/11/2009. Copyright Commonwealth of Australia, Productivity Commission. Reproduced by permission.

How the economy as a whole works

We started by discussing how individuals make decisions and then looked at how people interact with one another. All these decisions and interactions together make up 'the economy'. The last three lessons concern the workings of the economy as a whole.

Lesson 8: A country's standard of living depends on its ability to produce goods and services

The differences in living standards around the world are staggering. In 2009, the average Australian had an income (in US dollars) of about $39 000. In the same year, the average South Korean earned $28 000, the average New Zealander earned $27 000 and the average Indian earned $3000. Not surprisingly, this large variation in average income is reflected in various measures of the quality of life. Citizens of high-income countries have more TV sets, more cars, better nutrition, better health care and longer life expectancy than citizens of low-income countries.

Changes in living standards over time are also large. In Australia, incomes have historically grown about 2 per cent per year (after adjusting for changes in the cost of living). At this rate, average real income doubles every 35 years. In some countries, economic growth has been even more rapid. In South Korea, for instance, average income has doubled in the past 15 years. In China, average income has been growing at around 8 per cent per year since 2000, a rate of growth that will see it double in just under 10 years.

What explains these large differences in living standards among countries and over time? The answer is surprisingly simple. Almost all variation in living standards is attributable to differences in countries' **productivity** – that is, the amount of goods and services produced from each hour of a worker's time. In nations where workers can produce a large quantity of goods and services per unit of time, most people enjoy a high standard of living; in nations where workers are less productive, most people must endure a more meagre existence. Similarly, the growth rate of a nation's productivity determines the growth rate of its average income.

productivity
the quantity of goods and services produced from each hour of a worker's time

The fundamental relationship between productivity and living standards is simple, but its implications are far-reaching. If productivity is the primary determinant of living standards, other explanations must be of secondary importance. For example, it might be tempting to credit labour unions or award wage laws for the rise in living standards of Australian workers over the past century. Yet the real hero of Australian workers is their rising productivity.

The relationship between productivity and living standards also has profound implications for public policy. When thinking about how any policy will affect living standards, the key question is how it will affect our ability to produce goods and services. To boost living standards, policymakers need to raise productivity by ensuring that workers are well educated, have the tools needed to produce goods and services and have access to the best available technology.

Over the past decade, for example, much debate in Australia has centred on the government's budget deficit – the excess of government spending over government revenue. The major parties in the 2010 federal election campaign both stated that they would reduce the government budget deficit. As we will see, concern over the budget deficit is based largely on its adverse impact on productivity. When the government needs to finance a budget deficit, it does so by borrowing in financial markets, much as a student might borrow to pay for postgraduate education or a firm might borrow to finance a new factory. As the government borrows to finance its deficit, it reduces the quantity of funds available for other borrowers. The budget deficit thereby reduces investment both in human capital (the student's education) and physical capital (the firm's factory). Because lower investment today means lower productivity in the future, budget deficits are generally thought to depress growth in living standards.

Lesson 9: Prices rise when the government prints too much money

In January 1921, a daily newspaper in Germany cost 0.30 of a mark. Less than two years later, in November 1922, the same newspaper cost 70 000 000 marks. All other prices in the economy rose by similar amounts. This episode is one of history's most spectacular examples of **inflation**, an increase in the overall level of prices in the economy.

inflation
an increase in the overall level of prices in the economy

Although Australia and New Zealand have never experienced inflation even close to that in Germany in the 1920s, inflation has at times been an economic problem. During the 1970s, for instance, the overall level of prices more than doubled, and political leaders lived under the catchcry 'Fight Inflation First!' In contrast, in the first decade of the 21st century, inflation has run at about 2.5 per cent per year; at this rate it would take almost 30 years for prices to double. Because high inflation imposes various costs on society, keeping inflation at a low level is a goal of economic policymakers around the world.

What causes inflation? While there is some disagreement among economists about inflation in the short term, the answer in the long term is clear. In most cases of large or persistent inflation, the culprit turns out to be the same – growth in the quantity of money. When a government creates large quantities of the nation's money, the value of the money falls. In Germany in the early 1920s, when prices were, on average, tripling every month, the quantity of money was also tripling every month. Although less dramatic, the economic history of Australia, New Zealand and the United States points to a similar conclusion – the high inflation of the 1970s was associated with rapid growth in the quantity of money, and the low inflation of the 1990s and 2000s has been associated with slow growth in the quantity of money.

Lesson 10: Society faces a short-term trade-off between inflation and unemployment

If long-term inflation is so easy to explain, why do policymakers sometimes have trouble ridding the economy of it? One reason is that reducing inflation is often thought to cause a temporary rise in unemployment. This trade-off between inflation and unemployment is called the **Phillips curve**, after the economist who first examined this relationship.

Phillips curve
the short-term trade-off between inflation and unemployment

The Phillips curve remains a controversial topic among economists, but most economists today accept the idea that there is a short-term trade-off between inflation and unemployment. According to a common explanation, this trade-off arises because some prices are slow to adjust. Suppose, for example, that the government reduces the quantity of money in the economy. In the long term, the only result of this policy change will be a fall in the overall level of prices. Yet not all prices will adjust immediately. It may take several years before all firms issue new catalogues, all unions make wage concessions, and all restaurants print new menus. That is, prices are said to be *sticky* in the short term.

"WELL IT MAY HAVE BEEN 68 CENTS WHEN YOU GOT IN LINE, BUT IT'S 74 CENTS NOW!"

Source: © Tribune Media Services, Inc. All Rights Reserved. Reprinted with permission.

Because prices are sticky, various types of government policy have short-term effects that differ from their long-term effects. When the government reduces the quantity of money, for instance, it reduces the amount that people spend. Lower spending, together with prices that are stuck too high, reduces the quantity of goods and services that firms sell. Lower sales, in turn, cause firms to lay off workers. Thus, the reduction in the quantity of money raises unemployment temporarily until prices have fully adjusted to the change.

The trade-off between inflation and unemployment is only temporary, but it can last for several years. The Phillips curve is, therefore, crucial for understanding many developments in the economy.

In particular, policymakers can exploit this trade-off using various policy instruments. By changing the amount that the government spends, the amount it taxes and the amount of money it prints, policymakers can, in the short term, influence the combination of inflation and unemployment that the economy experiences. Because these instruments of monetary and fiscal policy are potentially so powerful, how policymakers should use these instruments to control the economy, if at all, is a subject of continuing debate.

Q List and briefly explain the three lessons that describe how the economy as a whole works.

Conclusion

You now have a taste of what economics is all about. In the coming chapters we will develop many specific insights about people, markets and economies. Mastering these insights will take some effort, but it is not an overwhelming task. The field of economics is based on a few basic ideas that can be applied in many different situations.

Throughout this book we will refer to the *Ten Lessons from Economics* highlighted in this chapter and summarised in Table 1.1. Whenever we do so, a 'key' icon will show up in the margin, as it does now. But even when that icon is absent, you should keep these keys in mind. Often, even the most sophisticated economic analysis is built using the 10 key ideas introduced here.

Table 1.1 Ten lessons from economics

How people make decisions	1: People face trade-offs
	2: The cost of something is what you give up to get it
	3: Rational people think at the margin
	4: People respond to incentives
How people interact	5: Trade can make everyone better off
	6: Markets are usually a good way to organise economic activity
	7: Governments can sometimes improve market outcomes
How the economy as a whole works	8: A country's standard of living depends on its ability to produce goods and services
	9: Prices rise when the government prints too much money
	10: Society faces a short-term trade-off between inflation and unemployment

Summary

- The fundamental lessons about individual decision making are that people face trade-offs among alternative goals, that the cost of any action is measured in terms of forgone opportunities, that rational people make decisions by comparing marginal costs and marginal benefits, and that people change their behaviour in response to the incentives they face.
- The fundamental lessons about interactions among people are that trade can be mutually beneficial, that markets are usually a good way of coordinating trade among people, and that the government can potentially improve market outcomes if there is some market failure or if the market outcome is inequitable.
- The fundamental lessons about the economy as a whole are that productivity is the ultimate source of living standards, that money growth is the ultimate source of inflation, and that society faces a short-term trade-off between inflation and unemployment.

Key concepts

economics
efficiency
equity
externality
inflation
invisible hand
marginal change
market economy
market failure
market power
opportunity cost
Phillips curve
productivity
scarcity

Questions for review

1 Give three examples of important trade-offs that you face in your life.
2 What is the opportunity cost of seeing a movie?
3 Water is necessary for life. Is the marginal benefit of a glass of water large or small?
4 Why should policymakers think about incentives?
5 Why isn't trade among countries like a game with some winners and some losers?
6 What does the 'invisible hand' of the marketplace do?
7 What are 'efficiency' and 'equity', and what do they have to do with government policy?
8 Why is productivity important?
9 What is inflation, and what causes it?
10 How are inflation and unemployment related in the short term?

Problems and applications

1 Describe some of the trade-offs faced by each of the following:
   a a family deciding whether to buy a new car
   b a politician deciding whether to increase spending on national parks
   c a company director deciding whether to open a new factory
   d a professor deciding whether to prepare for a lecture.
2 You are trying to decide whether to take a holiday. Most of the costs of the holiday (airfare, hotel, forgone wages) are measured in dollars, but the benefits of the holiday are psychological. How can you compare the benefits with the costs?

3 You were planning to spend Saturday working at your part-time job, but a friend asks you to go swimming. What is the true cost of going swimming? Now suppose that you had been planning to spend the day studying at the library. What is the cost of going swimming in this case? Explain.

4 You win $100 in a lottery. You have a choice between spending the money now or putting it away for a year in a bank account that pays 5 per cent interest. What is the opportunity cost of spending the $100 now?

5 The company that you manage has invested $5 million in developing a new product, but the development is not quite finished. At a recent meeting, your salespeople report that the introduction of competing products has reduced the expected sales of your new product to $3 million. If it would cost $1 million to finish development, should you go ahead and do so? What is the most that you should pay to complete development?

6 The pension system provides income for people when they retire. Recipients with more income from other sources receive smaller pension benefits (after taxes) than recipients with less income from other sources.
   a How does the provision of pensions affect people's incentive to save while working?
   b How does the reduction in after-tax pension benefits associated with higher income affect people's incentive to work past retirement age?

7 There has been some discussion about changes to unemployment benefits that will result in payments being withdrawn after two years for those able to work.
   a How do these changes in the laws affect the incentives for working?
   b How might these changes represent a trade-off between equity and efficiency?

8 Your flatmate is a better cook than you are, but you can clean more quickly than your flatmate can. If your flatmate did all of the cooking and you did all of the cleaning, would your chores take you more or less time than if you divided each task evenly? Give a similar example of how specialisation and trade can make two countries both better off.

9 Suppose Australia adopted central planning for its economy and you became the chief planner. Among the millions of decisions that you need to make for next year are how many DVDs to produce, what videos to record and who should receive the discs.
   a To make these decisions intelligently, what information would you need about the DVD industry? What information would you need about each person in Australia?
   b How would your decisions about DVDs affect some of your other decisions, such as how many DVD players to make or television sets to produce? How might some of your other decisions about the economy change your views about DVDs?

10 Explain whether each of the following government activities is motivated by a concern about equity or a concern about efficiency. In the case of efficiency, discuss the type of market failure involved.
   a Regulating local telephone prices
   b Providing some poor people with vouchers that can be used to buy food
   c Prohibiting smoking in public places
   d Breaking up the electricity industry into smaller generating companies
   e Imposing higher personal income tax rates on people with higher incomes
   f Instituting laws against driving while intoxicated.

11 'Everyone in society should be guaranteed the best health care possible.' Discuss this point of view from the standpoints of equity and efficiency.

12 In what ways is your standard of living different from that of your parents or grandparents when they were your age? Why have these changes occurred?

13 Suppose Australians decided to save more of their incomes. If banks lend this money to businesses, which use the money to build new factories, how might higher saving lead to faster productivity growth? Who do you suppose benefits from higher productivity? Is society getting a free lunch?

14 Suppose that when people wake up tomorrow, they discover that the government has given them an additional amount of money equal to the amount they already had. Explain what effect this doubling of the money supply is likely to have on:

a the total amount spent on goods and services

b the quantity of goods and services purchased if prices are sticky

c the prices of goods and services if prices can adjust.

15 Imagine that you are a policymaker trying to decide whether to reduce the rate of inflation. To make an intelligent decision, what would you need to know about inflation, unemployment and the trade-off between them?

16 On 1 July 1979, Australia eliminated inheritance taxes. These taxes were a portion of the estate of the wealthiest deceased. What do you think this did to the pattern of deaths around June and July 1979?

Search me!

Search me!

When accessing information about microeconomics use the following keywords in any combinations you require:

- opportunity cost

CourseMate

CourseMate

For more multimedia resources and activities on economics, visit the Economics CourseMate website.

2

Thinking like an economist

Learning objectives

In this chapter you will:

- see how economists apply the methods of science
- consider how assumptions and models can shed light on the world
- learn two simple models – the circular-flow diagram and the production possibilities frontier
- distinguish between microeconomics and macroeconomics
- learn the difference between positive and normative statements
- examine the role of economists in making policy
- consider why economists sometimes disagree with one another.

Every field of study has its own language and its own way of thinking. Mathematicians talk about axioms, integrals and vector spaces. Psychologists talk about ego, id and cognitive dissonance. Lawyers talk about premeditation, torts and promissory estoppel.

Economics is no different. Supply, demand, elasticity, comparative advantage, consumer surplus, deadweight loss – these terms are part of the economist's language. In the coming chapters, you will encounter many new terms and some familiar words that economists use in specialised ways. At first, this new language may seem needlessly obscure. But, as you will see, its value lies in its ability to provide you with a new and useful way of thinking about the world in which you live.

The purpose of this book is to help you learn the economist's way of thinking. Just as you cannot become a mathematician, psychologist or lawyer overnight, learning to think like an economist will take some time. Yet with a combination of theory, case studies and examples of economics in the news, this book will give you ample opportunity to develop and practise this skill.

Before delving into the substance and details of economics, it is helpful to have an overview of how economists approach the world. This chapter, therefore, discusses the field's methodology. What is distinctive about how economists confront a question? What does it mean to think like an economist?

The economist as scientist

Economists try to tackle their subject with a scientist's objectivity. They approach the study of the economy in much the same way as a physicist approaches the study of matter and a biologist approaches the study of life – they devise theories, collect data and then analyse these data in an attempt to verify or refute their theories.

To beginners, it can seem odd to claim that economics is a science. After all, economists do not work with test tubes or telescopes. The essence of science, however, is the *scientific method* – the dispassionate development and testing of theories about how the world works. This method of inquiry is as applicable to studying a nation's economy as it is to studying the earth's gravity or a species' evolution. As Albert Einstein once put it: 'The whole of science is nothing more than the refinement of everyday thinking'.

Although Einstein's comment is as true for social sciences such as economics as it is for natural sciences such as physics, most people are not accustomed to looking at society through the eyes of a scientist. So let's discuss some of the ways in which economists apply the logic of science to examine how an economy works.

The scientific method: Observation, theory and more observation

Isaac Newton, the famous seventeenth-century scientist and mathematician, allegedly became intrigued one day when he saw an apple fall from an apple tree. This observation motivated Newton to develop a theory of gravity that applies not only to an apple falling to the earth but also to any two objects in the universe. Subsequent testing of Newton's theory has shown that it works well in many (but not all) circumstances. Because Newton's theory has been so successful at explaining observation, the theory is still taught today in undergraduate physics courses around the world.

Peanuts

This interplay between theory and observation also occurs in the field of economics. An economist might live in a country experiencing rapid increases in prices and be moved by this observation to develop a theory of inflation. The theory might assert that high inflation arises when the government prints too much money. (As you may recall, this was one of the *Ten Lessons from Economics* in chapter 1.) To test this theory, the economist could collect and analyse data on prices and money from many different countries. If growth in the quantity of money were not at all related to the rate at which prices are rising, the economist would start to doubt the validity of his theory of inflation. If money growth and inflation were strongly correlated in international data, as in fact they are, the economist would gain confidence in his theory.

Although economists use theory and observation like other scientists, they do face an obstacle that makes their task especially challenging – experiments are often difficult in economics. Physicists studying gravity can drop many objects in their laboratories to generate data to test their theories. By contrast, economists studying inflation are not allowed to control a nation's monetary policy simply to generate useful data. Economists, like astronomers and evolutionary biologists, usually have to make do with whatever data the world happens to give them.

To find a substitute for laboratory experiments, economists pay close attention to the natural experiments offered by history. When a war in the Middle East interrupts the flow of crude oil, for instance, oil prices around the world skyrocket. For consumers of oil and oil products, such an event depresses living standards. For economic policymakers, it poses a difficult choice about how best to respond. But for economic scientists, the event provides an opportunity to study the effects of a key natural resource on the world's economies and this opportunity persists long after the wartime increase in oil prices is over. Throughout this book, therefore, we consider many historical episodes. These episodes are valuable to study because they give us insight into the economy of the past and, more importantly, because they allow us to illustrate and evaluate economic theories of the present.

The role of assumptions

If you ask a physicist how long it would take for a marble to fall from the top of a 10-storey building, she will answer the question by assuming that the marble falls in a vacuum. Of course, this assumption is false. In fact, the building is surrounded by air, which exerts friction on the falling marble and slows it down. Yet the physicist will correctly point out that friction on the marble is so small that its effect is negligible. Assuming the marble falls in a vacuum greatly simplifies the problem without substantially affecting the answer.

Economists make assumptions for the same reason – assumptions can make the world easier to understand. To study the effects of international trade, for example, we may assume that the world consists of only two countries and that each country produces only two goods. Of course, the real world consists of dozens of countries, each of which produces thousands of different types of goods. But by assuming two countries and two goods, we can focus our thinking. Once we understand international trade in an imaginary world with two countries and two goods, we are in a better position to understand international trade in the more complex world in which we live.

The art in scientific thinking – whether in physics, biology or economics – is deciding which assumptions to make. Suppose, for instance, that we were dropping a beach ball rather than a marble from the top of the building. Our physicist would realise that the assumption of no friction is far less accurate in this case: Friction exerts a greater force on a beach ball than on a marble. The assumption that gravity works in a vacuum is reasonable for studying a falling marble but not for studying a falling beach ball.

Similarly, economists use different assumptions to answer different questions. Suppose that we want to study what happens to the economy when the government changes the number of dollars in circulation. An important piece of this analysis, it turns out, is how prices respond. Many prices in the economy change infrequently; the newsagency prices of magazines, for instance, change only every few years. Knowing this fact may lead us to make different assumptions when studying the effects of the policy change over different time horizons. For studying the short-term effects of the policy, we may assume that prices do not change much. We may even make the extreme and artificial assumption that all prices are completely fixed. For studying the long-term effects of the policy, however, we may assume that all prices are completely flexible. Just as a physicist uses different assumptions when studying falling marbles and falling beach balls, economists use different assumptions when studying the short-term and long-term effects of a change in the quantity of money.

Economic models

Secondary school biology teachers teach basic anatomy with plastic replicas of the human body. These models have all the major organs – the heart, the liver, the kidneys and so on. The models allow teachers to show their students in a simple way how the important parts of the body fit together. Of course, these plastic models are not actual human bodies, and no one would mistake the model for a real person. These models are stylised and they omit many details. Yet despite this lack of realism – indeed, because of this lack of realism – studying these models is useful for learning how the human body works.

Economists also use models to learn about the world, but instead of being made of plastic, they are most often composed of diagrams and equations. Like a biology teacher's plastic model, economic models omit many details to allow us to see what is truly important. Just as the biology teacher's model does not include all of the body's muscles and capillaries, an economist's model does not include every feature of the economy.

As we use models to examine various economic issues throughout this book, you will see that all the models are built on assumptions. Just as a physicist begins the analysis of a falling marble by assuming away the existence of friction, economists assume away many of the details of the economy that are irrelevant for studying the question at hand. All models – in physics, biology or economics – simplify reality in order to improve our understanding of it.

Our first model: The circular-flow diagram

The economy consists of millions of people engaged in many activities – buying, selling, working, hiring, manufacturing and so on. To understand how the economy works, we must find some way to simplify our thinking about all these activities. In other words, we need a model that explains, in general terms, how the economy is organised and how participants in the economy interact with one another.

circular-flow diagram
a visual model of the economy that shows how dollars flow through markets among households and firms

Figure 2.1 presents a visual model of the economy, called a **circular-flow diagram**. In this model, the economy has two types of decision makers – households and firms. Firms produce goods and services using various inputs, such as labour, land and capital (buildings and machines). These inputs are called the *factors of production*. Households own the factors of production and consume all the goods and services that the firms produce.

Figure 2.1 The circular flow

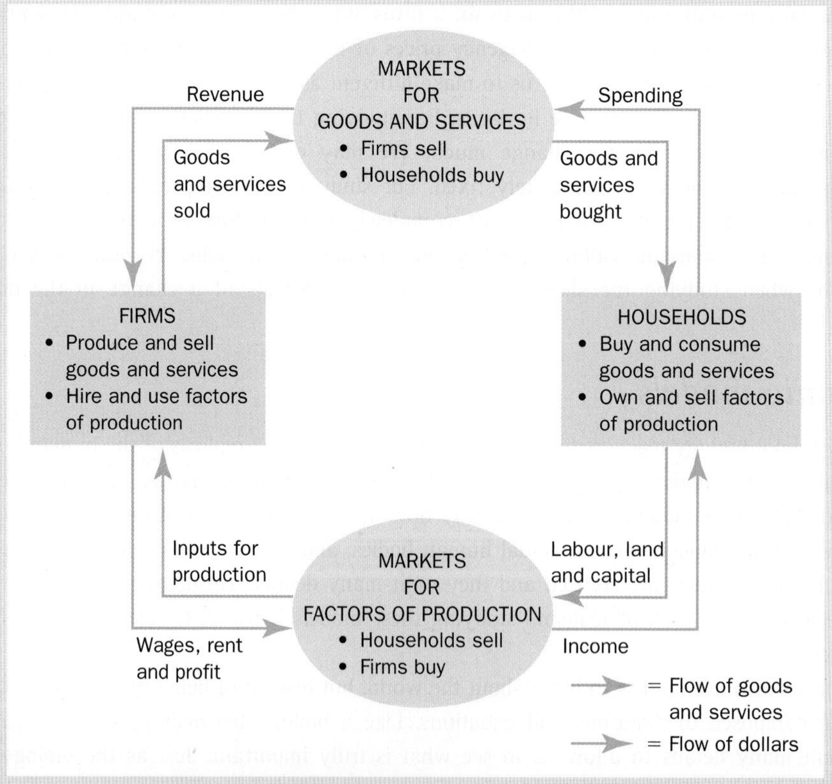

This diagram is a schematic representation of the organisation of the economy. Decisions are made by households and firms. Households and firms interact in the markets for goods and services (where households are buyers and firms are sellers) and in the markets for the factors of production (where firms are buyers and households are sellers). The outer set of arrows shows the flow of dollars and the inner set of arrows shows the corresponding flow of goods and services.

Households and firms interact in two types of markets. In the *markets for goods and services*, households are buyers and firms are sellers. In particular, households buy the output of goods and services that firms produce. In the *markets for the factors of production*, households are sellers and firms are buyers. In these markets, households provide firms with the inputs that the firms use to produce goods and services. The circular-flow diagram offers a simple way of organising all the economic transactions that occur between households and firms in the economy.

The two loops in the circular-flow diagram are distinct but related. The inner loop of the circular-flow diagram represents the flows of goods and services between households and firms. The households sell the use of their labour, land and capital to the firms in the markets for the factors of production. The firms then use these factors to produce goods and services, which in turn are sold to households in the markets for goods and services. Hence, the factors of production flow from households to firms, and goods and services flow from firms to households.

The outer loop of the circular-flow diagram represents the corresponding flow of dollars. The households spend money to buy goods and services from the firms. The firms use some of the revenue from these sales to pay for the factors of production, such as the wages of their workers. What is left is the profit of the firm owners, who themselves are members of households. Hence, spending on goods and services flows from households to firms, and income in the form of wages, rent and profit flows from firms to households.

Let's take a tour of the circular flow by following a dollar coin as it makes its way from person to person through the economy. Imagine that the dollar begins at a household, sitting in, say, your pocket. If you want to buy a cup of coffee, you take the dollar to one of the economy's markets for goods and services, such as your local café. There you spend it on your favourite drink. When the dollar moves into the café's cash register, it becomes revenue for the firm. The dollar doesn't stay at the café for long, however, because that firm uses it to buy inputs in the markets for factors of production. For instance, the café might use the dollar to pay rent to its landlord for the space it occupies or to pay the wages of its workers. In either case, the dollar enters the income of some household and, once again, is back in someone's pocket. At that point, the story of the economy's circular flow starts again.

The circular-flow diagram is a very simple model of the economy. It dispenses with various details that, for some purposes, are significant. A more complex and realistic circular-flow model would include, for instance, the roles of government and international trade. Yet these details are not crucial for a basic understanding of how the economy is organised. Because of its simplicity, this circular-flow diagram is useful to keep in mind when thinking about how the pieces of the economy fit together.

Our second model: The production possibilities frontier

Most economic models, unlike the circular-flow diagram, are built using the tools of mathematics. Here we consider one of the simplest models, called the production possibilities frontier, and see how this model illustrates some basic economic ideas.

production possibilities frontier
a graph that shows the various combinations of output that the economy can possibly produce given the available factors of production and the available production technology

Although real economies produce thousands of goods and services, let's imagine an economy that produces only two goods – cars and computers. Together the car industry and the computer industry use all of the economy's factors of production. The **production possibilities frontier** is a graph that shows the various combinations of output – in this case, cars and computers – that the economy can

Figure 2.2 The production possibilities frontier

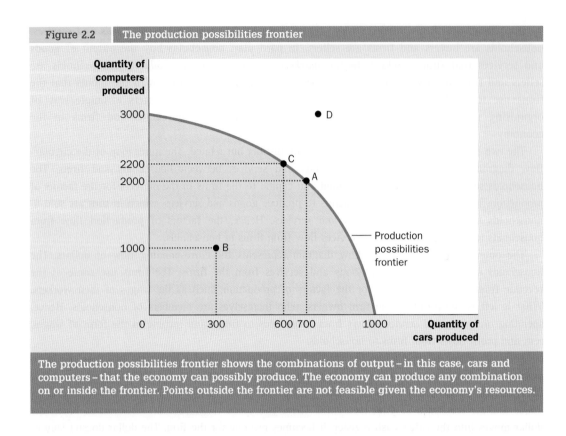

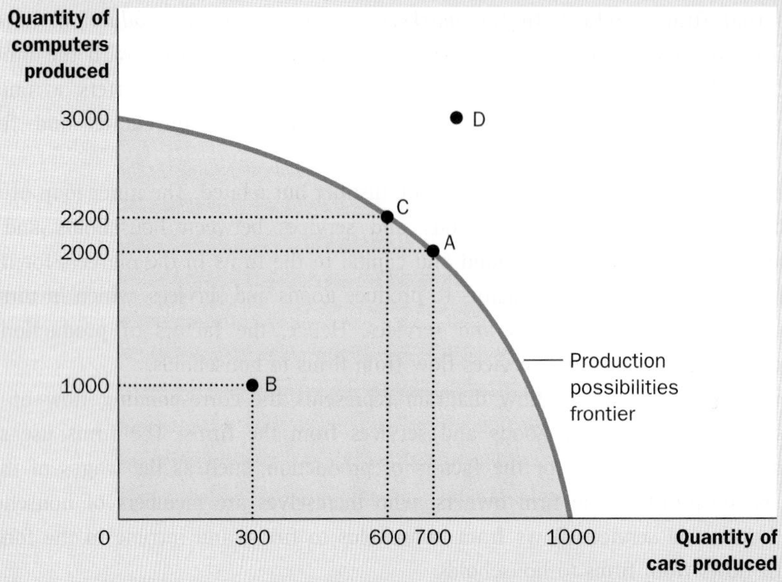

The production possibilities frontier shows the combinations of output – in this case, cars and computers – that the economy can possibly produce. The economy can produce any combination on or inside the frontier. Points outside the frontier are not feasible given the economy's resources.

possibly produce given the available factors of production and the available production technology that firms can use to turn these factors into output.

Search me!

▸ production possibilities frontier

Figure 2.2 is an example of a production possibilities frontier. In this economy, if all resources were used in the car industry, the economy would produce 1000 cars and no computers. If all resources were used in the computer industry, the economy would produce 3000 computers and no cars. The two end points of the production possibilities frontier represent these extreme possibilities.

More likely, the economy divides its resources between the two industries, producing some cars and some computers. For example, it could produce 700 cars and 2000 computers, shown in the figure by point A. Or, by moving some of the factors of production to the computer industry from the car industry, the economy can produce 600 cars and 2200 computers, represented by point C.

Because resources are scarce, not every conceivable outcome is feasible. For example, no matter how resources are allocated between the two industries, the economy cannot produce the amount of cars and computers represented by point D. Given the technology available for manufacturing cars and computers, the economy does not have the factors of production to support that level of output. With the resources it has, the economy can produce at any point on or inside the production possibilities frontier, but it cannot produce at points outside the frontier.

An outcome is said to be *efficient* if the economy is getting all it can from the scarce resources it has available. Points on (rather than inside) the production possibilities frontier represent efficient levels of production. When the economy is producing at such a point, say point A, there is no way of producing more of one good without producing less of the other. The same holds for point C. But, point B represents an *inefficient* outcome. For some reason, perhaps widespread unemployment, the economy is producing less than it could from the resources it has available – it is producing only 300 cars and 1000 computers. If the source of the inefficiency was eliminated, the economy could move from point B to either point A or point C, increasing production of both cars and computers.

One of the *Ten Lessons from Economics* discussed in chapter 1 is that people face trade-offs. The production possibilities frontier shows one trade-off that society faces. Once we have reached the efficient points on the frontier, the only way of producing more of one good is to produce less of the other. When the economy moves from point A to point C, for instance, society produces more computers but at the expense of producing fewer cars.

This trade-off helps us to understand another of the *Ten Lessons from Economics*: The cost of something is what you give up to get it. This is called the *opportunity cost.* The production possibilities frontier shows the opportunity cost of one good as measured in terms of the other good. When society reallocates some of the factors of production from the computer industry to the car industry, moving the economy from point C to point A, it gives up 200 computers to get 100 additional cars. In other words, when the economy is at point C, the opportunity cost of 100 cars is 200 computers.

Notice that the production possibilities frontier in Figure 2.2 is bowed outwards. This means that the opportunity cost of cars in terms of computers depends on how much of each good the economy is producing. When the economy is using most of its resources to make computers, the production possibilities frontier is relatively flat. Workers and machines best suited to making cars, like skilled autoworkers, are being used to make computers. If some of these skilled autoworkers are moved from computer production to the car industry, the economy will not have to lose much computer production to increase car production. Each computer the economy gives up yields a substantial increase in the number of cars. The opportunity cost of a car, in terms of computers forgone, is small. In contrast, when the economy is using most of its resources to make cars, the production possibilities frontier is quite steep. In this case, the resources best suited to making cars are already in the car industry. Producing an additional car means moving some of the best computer technicians out of the computer industry and making them autoworkers. As a result, producing an additional car will mean a substantial loss of computer output. The opportunity cost of a car is high, and the production possibilities frontier is steep.

The production possibilities frontier shows the trade-off between the production of different goods at a given time, but the trade-off can change over time. For example, suppose a technological advance in the computer industry raises the number of computers that a worker can produce each week. This advance expands society's set of opportunities. For any given number of cars, the economy can make more computers. If the economy does not make any computers, it can still only produce 1000 cars, so one endpoint of the frontier stays the same. But the rest of the production possibilities frontier shifts outwards, as in Figure 2.3.

This figure illustrates economic growth. Society can move production from a point on the old frontier to a point on the new frontier. Which point it chooses depends on its preferences for the two goods. In this example, society moves from point A to point E, enjoying more computers (2100 instead of 2000) and more cars (750 instead of 700).

Figure 2.3 A shift in the production possibilities frontier

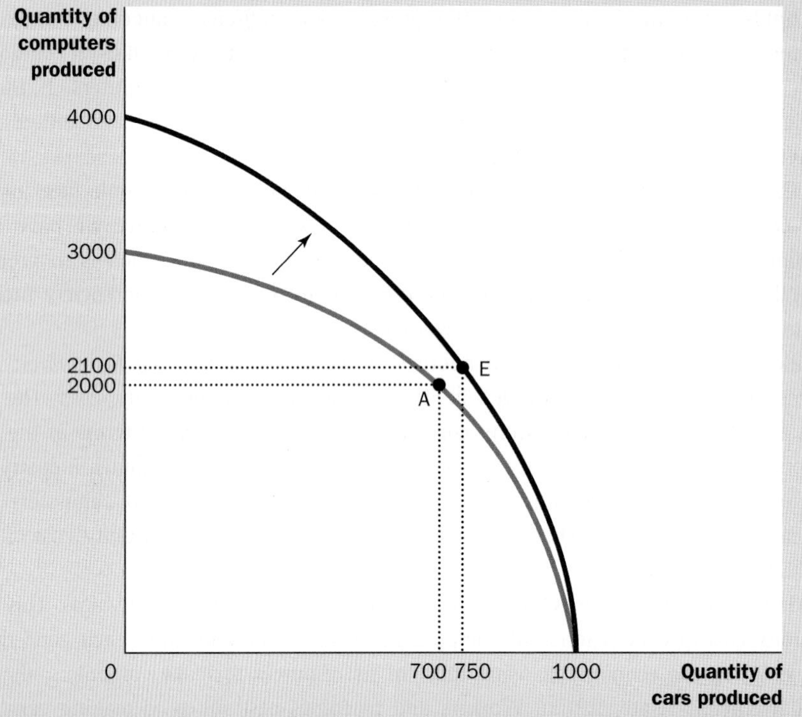

An economic advance in the computer industry shifts the production possibilities frontier outwards, increasing the number of cars and computers the economy can produce.

The production possibilities frontier simplifies a complex economy to highlight some basic but powerful ideas: scarcity, efficiency, trade-offs, opportunity cost and economic growth. As you study economics, these ideas will recur in various forms. The production possibilities frontier offers one simple way of thinking about them.

Microeconomics and macroeconomics

Many subjects are studied on various levels. Consider biology, for example. Molecular biologists study the chemical compounds that make up living things. Cellular biologists study cells, which are made up of many chemical compounds and, at the same time, are themselves the building blocks of living organisms. Evolutionary biologists study the many varieties of animals and plants and how species change gradually over the centuries.

Economics is also studied on various levels. We can study the decisions of individual households and firms. We can study the interaction of households and firms in markets for specific goods and services. Or we can study the operation of the economy as a whole, which is just the sum of the activities of all these decision makers in all these markets.

microeconomics
the study of how households and firms make decisions and how they interact in markets

The field of economics is traditionally divided into two broad subfields. **Microeconomics** is the study of how households and firms make decisions and how they interact in specific markets.

Macroeconomics is the study of economy-wide phenomena. A microeconomist might study the effects of the discovery of a new gas reserve in Queensland on energy production, the impact of foreign competition on the domestic car industry or the effects of compulsory school attendance on workers' earnings. A macroeconomist might study the effects of borrowing by the federal government, the changes over time in the economy's rate of unemployment or alternative policies to raise growth in national living standards.

macroeconomics
the study of economy-wide phenomena, including inflation, unemployment and economic growth

Microeconomics and macroeconomics are closely intertwined. Because changes in the overall economy arise from the decisions of millions of individuals, it is impossible to understand macroeconomic developments without considering the associated microeconomic decisions. For example, a macroeconomist might study the effect of a cut in income tax on the overall production of goods and services. To analyse this issue, the macroeconomist must consider how the tax cut affects the decisions of households about how much to spend on goods and services.

Despite the inherent link between microeconomics and macroeconomics, the two fields are distinct. Because microeconomics and macroeconomics tackle different questions, each field has its own set of models, which are often taught in separate courses.

Q

In what sense is economics like a science? Define *microeconomics* and *macroeconomics*.

The economist as policy adviser

Often, economists are asked to explain the causes of economic events. Why, for example, is unemployment higher for teenagers than for older workers? Sometimes economists are asked to recommend policies to improve economic outcomes. What, for instance, should the government do to improve the economic wellbeing of teenagers? When economists are trying to explain the world, they are scientists. When they are trying to improve it, they are policy advisers.

Positive versus normative analysis

To help clarify the two roles that economists play, let's examine the use of language. Because scientists and policymakers have different goals, they use language in different ways.

For example, suppose that two people are discussing minimum-wage laws. Here are two statements you might hear:

Polly: Minimum-wage laws cause unemployment.

Norma: The government should raise the minimum wage.

Ignoring for now whether you agree with these statements, notice that Polly and Norma differ in what they are trying to do. Polly is speaking like a scientist – she is making a claim about how the world works. Norma is speaking like a policymaker – she is making a claim about how she would like to change the world.

positive statements
claims that attempt to describe the world as it is

In general, statements about the world are of two types. One type, such as Polly's, is positive. **Positive statements** are descriptive. They make a claim about how the world *is*. A second type of statement, such as Norma's, is normative. **Normative statements** are prescriptive. They make a claim about how the world *ought to be*.

normative statements
claims that attempt to prescribe how the world should be

fyi Who studies economics?

As a university student, you might be asking yourself: How many economics classes should I take? How useful will this stuff be to me later in life? Economics can seem abstract at first, but the field is fundamentally very practical, and the study of economics is useful in many different career paths. Here is a small sampling of some well-known people who majored in economics when they were at university.

Donald Trump	Business and TV mogul
Meg Witman	Former Chief Executive Officer, eBay
Budiono	Vice President of Indonesia
Cate Blanchett	Actor
Arnold Schwarzenegger	Former actor and politician
Kofi Annan	Former Secretary General, United Nations
Gary Banks	Head of Australian Productivity Commission
Danny Glover	Actor
Warren Buffett	Financier
Manmohan Singh	Prime Minister of India
Lionel Richie	Singer
Sam Walton	Founder of WalMart
Mari Pangestu	Indonesian Minister of Trade
Tiger Woods	Golfer
Steve Ballmer	Chief Executive Officer, Microsoft
Lara Dutta	Miss Universe 2000 and actor
Duck-Woo Nam	Former Prime Minister of South Korea
Scott Adams	Cartoonist (creator of Dilbert)
Mick Jagger	Singer for the Rolling Stones

Having studied at the London School of Economics may not help Mick Jagger hit the high notes, but it has probably given him some insight about how to invest the substantial sums he has earned during his rock-'n'-roll career.

When asked in 2005 why the Rolling Stones were going on tour again, former economics major Mick Jagger replied, 'Supply and demand'. Keith Richards added, 'If the demand's there, we'll supply'.

Source: photos.com/Getty Images.

Source: AAP Image/AP Photo/Risto Bozovic.

A key difference between positive and normative statements is how we judge their validity. We can, in principle, confirm or refute positive statements by examining evidence. An economist might evaluate Polly's statement by analysing data on changes in minimum wages and changes in unemployment over time. In contrast, evaluating normative statements involves values as well as facts. Norma's statement cannot be judged using data alone. Deciding what is good or bad policy is not merely a matter of science. It also involves our views on ethics, religion and political philosophy.

Of course, positive and normative statements may be related. Our positive views about how the world works affect our normative views about what policies are desirable. Polly's claim that the minimum wage causes unemployment, if true, might lead us to reject Norma's conclusion that the government should raise the minimum wage. Yet our normative conclusions cannot come from positive analysis alone. Instead, they require both positive analysis and value judgements.

As you study economics, keep in mind the distinction between positive and normative statements. Much of economics just tries to explain how the economy works. Yet often the goal of economics is to improve how the economy works. When you hear economists making normative statements, you know they have crossed the line from scientist to policy adviser.

Economists in government

Former US President Harry Truman once said that he wanted to find a one-armed economist. When he asked his economists for advice, they always answered, 'On the one hand, ... On the other hand, ...'

Truman was right in realising that economists' advice is not always straightforward. This tendency is rooted in one of the *Ten Lessons from Economics* in chapter 1 – people face trade-offs. Economists are aware that trade-offs are involved in most policy decisions. A policy might increase efficiency at the cost of equity. It might help future generations but hurt current generations. An economist who says that all policy decisions are easy is an economist not to be trusted.

Nonetheless, economists play an important role in many areas of governmental decision making. In Australia, economists work in the Treasury and the Department of Finance to provide advice on taxation and fiscal policy. They give the government advice on microeconomic reform through research conducted at the Productivity Commission. Economists help construct statistical information at the Australian Bureau of Statistics (ABS) and assess competition policy issues at the Australian Competition and Consumer Commission (ACCC). Economists skilled in macroeconomic, monetary and financial issues are employed at all levels of the Reserve Bank. Table 2.1 lists the websites of some of these agencies.

Similar roles are undertaken by economists in many countries. The president of the United States appoints a Council of Economic Advisers, which has three members and a staff of several dozen economists. The council has no duty other than to advise the president and to write the annual *Economic Report of the President*. Perhaps the most influential economist in the world is the person who chairs the Federal Reserve – the central bank of the United States. Financial markets around the world hang on any word, or indeed thought, of the current chairperson who has direct control over monetary policy in the United States.

Table 2.1 Websites

Commonwealth Treasury	www.treasury.gov.au
Reserve Bank of Australia	www.rba.gov.au
Australian Competition and Consumer Commission	www.accc.gov.au
Australian Bureau of Statistics	www.abs.gov.au
Productivity Commission	www.pc.gov.au

Here are the websites for a few of the government agencies that are responsible for collecting economic data and making economic policy.

The influence of economists on policy goes beyond their role as advisers and policymakers; their research and writings often affect policy indirectly. Economist John Maynard Keynes offered this observation:

> The ideas of economists and political philosophers, both when they are right and when they are wrong, are more powerful than is commonly understood. Indeed, the world is ruled by little else. Practical men, who believe themselves to be quite exempt from intellectual influences, are usually the slaves of some defunct economist. Madmen in authority, who hear voices in the air, are distilling their frenzy from some academic scribbler of a few years back.

Although these words were written in 1935, they remain true today. Indeed, the 'academic scribbler' now influencing public policy is often Keynes himself.

Q

Give an example of a positive statement and an example of a normative statement. Name three parts of government that regularly rely on advice from economists.

Why economists disagree

'If all economists were laid end to end, they would not reach a conclusion.' This quip from George Bernard Shaw is revealing. Economists as a group are often criticised for giving conflicting advice to policymakers. Former US President Ronald Reagan once joked that if the game Trivial Pursuit were designed for economists, it would have 100 questions and 3000 answers.

Why do economists so often appear to give conflicting advice to policymakers? There are two basic reasons:

- Economists may disagree about the validity of alternative positive theories about how the world works.
- Economists may have different values and, therefore, different normative views about what policies should try to accomplish.

Let's discuss each of these reasons.

Differences in scientific judgements

Several centuries ago, astronomers debated whether the earth or the sun was at the centre of the heavens. More recently, meteorologists have debated whether the earth is experiencing 'global warming'. Science is a search for understanding about the world around us. It is not surprising that, as the search continues, scientists can disagree about the direction in which truth lies.

Economists often disagree for the same reason. Economics is a young science and there is still much to be learned. Economists sometimes disagree because they have different hunches about the validity of alternative theories or about the size of important parameters.

For example, economists disagree about whether the government should levy taxes based on a household's income or its consumption (spending). In Australia, advocates of a switch from the old income tax system to the goods and services tax (GST) introduced in 2000 believed that the change would encourage households to save more, because income that is saved would not be taxed. Higher saving, in turn, would lead to more rapid growth in productivity and living standards. Those against the GST believed that household saving would not respond much to a change in the tax laws. These two groups of economists held (and continue to hold) different views about the tax system because they have different positive views about the responsiveness of saving to tax incentives.

Differences in values

Suppose that Peter and Paula both take the same amount of water from the town well. To pay for maintaining the well, the town taxes its residents. Peter has income of $50 000 and is taxed $5000, or 10 per cent of his income. Paula has income of $10 000 and is taxed $2000, or 20 per cent of her income.

Is this policy fair? If not, who pays too much and who pays too little? Does it matter whether Paula's low income is due to a medical disability or to her decision to pursue a career in acting? Does it matter whether Peter's high income is due to a large inheritance or to his willingness to work long hours at a dreary job?

These are difficult questions on which people are likely to disagree. If the town hired two experts to study how the town should tax its residents to pay for the well, we would not be surprised if they offered conflicting advice.

This simple example shows why economists sometimes disagree about public policy. As we learned earlier in our discussion of normative and positive analysis, policies cannot be judged on scientific grounds alone. Economists give conflicting advice sometimes because they have different values. Perfecting the science of economics will not tell us whether Peter or Paula pays too much.

Perception versus reality

Because of differences in scientific judgements and differences in values, some disagreement among economists is inevitable. Yet one should not overstate the amount of disagreement. Economists agree with one another far more than is sometimes understood.

Table 2.2 contains 10 propositions about economic policy. In a survey of economics professors in Australia, these propositions were endorsed by an overwhelming majority of respondents. The views of these economists reflect those generated by similar surveys around the world. However, by contrast, most of these propositions would fail to command a similar consensus among the general public.

The first proposition in the table is about rent control, a policy that sets a legal maximum on the amount landlords can charge for their properties. For reasons we will discuss in chapter 6, almost all economists believe that rent control adversely affects the availability and quality of housing and is a very costly way of helping the most needy members of society. Nonetheless, governments in many countries choose to ignore the advice of economists and place ceilings on the rents that landlords may charge their tenants.

The second proposition in the table concerns tariffs and import quotas, two policies that restrict trade among nations. For reasons we will discuss in chapter 3 and more fully in chapter 9, almost all economists oppose such barriers to free trade. Nonetheless, over the years, governments in Australia and elsewhere have chosen to restrict the import of certain goods. Attempts to secure trade agreements, such as the North American Free Trade Agreement (between the United States, Canada and Mexico), the European Union, and APEC (Asia Pacific Economic Cooperation), faced considerable

Table 2.2 Ten propositions with which most economists agree

	Proposition	Percentage of economists who agree
1	A ceiling on rents reduces the quantity and quality of housing available.	96%
2	Tariffs and import quotas usually reduce general economic welfare.	92%
3	Flexible and floating exchange rates offer an effective international monetary arrangement.	77%
4	Fiscal policy (e.g., tax cut and/or government expenditure increase) has a significant stimulative impact on a less than fully employed economy.	81%
5	In the short term, unemployment can be reduced by increasing the rate of inflation.	60%
6	Cash payments increase the welfare of recipients to a greater degree than do transfers-in-kind of equal cash value.	75%
7	Trade practices laws should be used vigorously to reduce monopoly power in Australia.	81%
8	A minimum wage increases unemployment among young and unskilled workers.	85%
9	The government should restructure the social security system along the lines of a 'negative income tax'.	77%
10	Effluent taxes and marketable pollution permits represent a better approach to pollution control than imposition of pollution ceilings.	87%

Source: Adapted from Malcolm Anderson and Richard Blandy, 'What Australian economics professors think', *Australian Economic Review*, no. 100, 1992, pp. 17–40.

domestic opposition in the respective countries, despite overwhelming support from economists. In these cases, economists did offer united advice, but many politicians chose to ignore it.

Why do policies such as rent control and import quotas persist if the experts are united in their opposition? The reason may be that economists have not yet convinced the general public that these policies are undesirable. One of the purposes of this book is to help you understand the economist's view of these and other subjects and, perhaps, to persuade you that it is the right one.

Q

Give two reasons why two economic advisers to the federal government might disagree about a question of policy.

Let's get going

The first two chapters of this book have introduced you to the ideas and methods of economics. We are now ready to get to work. In the next chapter we start learning in more detail about the principles of economic behaviour and economic policy.

As you proceed through this book, you will be asked to draw on many of your intellectual skills. It may be helpful to keep in mind some advice from the great economist John Maynard Keynes:

> The study of economics does not seem to require any specialised gifts of an unusually high order. Is it not ... a very easy subject compared with the higher branches of philosophy or pure science? An easy subject, at which very few excel! The paradox finds its explanation, perhaps, in that the master-economist must possess a rare *combination* of gifts. He must be mathematician, historian, statesman, philosopher – in some degree. He must understand symbols and speak in words. He must contemplate the particular in terms of the general, and touch abstract and concrete in the same flight of thought. He must study the present in the light of the past for the purposes of the future. No part of man's nature or his institutions must lie entirely outside his regard. He must be purposeful and disinterested in a simultaneous mood; as aloof and incorruptible as an artist, yet sometimes as near the earth as a politician.

It is a tall order. But with practice, you will become more and more accustomed to thinking like an economist.

Summary

- Economists try to approach their subject with a scientist's objectivity. Like all scientists, they make appropriate assumptions and build simplified models in order to understand the world around them.
- The field of economics is divided into two subfields – microeconomics and macroeconomics. Microeconomists study decision making by households and firms and the interaction among households and firms in the marketplace. Macroeconomists study the forces and trends that affect the economy as a whole.
- A positive statement is an assertion about how the world *is*. A normative statement is an assertion about how the world *ought to be*. When economists make normative statements, they are acting more as policymakers than scientists.
- Economists who advise policymakers offer conflicting advice either because of differences in scientific judgements or because of differences in values. At other times, economists are united in the advice they offer, but policymakers may choose to ignore it.

Key concepts

circular-flow diagram
macroeconomics
microeconomics
normative statements
positive statements
production possibilities frontier

Questions for review

1. How is economics like a science?
2. Why do economists make assumptions?
3. Should an economic model describe reality exactly?
4. Draw and explain a production possibilities frontier for an economy that produces milk and biscuits. What happens to this frontier if a disease kills half of the economy's cow population?
5. What are the two subfields into which economics is divided? Explain what each subfield studies.
6. What is the difference between a positive and a normative statement? Give an example of each.
7. Why do economists sometimes offer conflicting advice to policymakers?

Problems and applications

1. Describe some unusual language used in one of the other fields that you are studying. Why are these special terms useful?
2. One common assumption in economics is that the products of different firms in the same industry are indistinguishable. For each of the following industries, discuss whether this is a reasonable assumption:
   a. steel
   b. novels
   c. wheat
   d. fast food.
3. Draw a circular-flow diagram. Identify the parts of the model that correspond to the flow of goods and services and the flow of dollars for each of the following activities:

  - *a* Sam pays a shopkeeper $1 for a litre of milk.
  - *b* Terry earns $4.50 per hour working at a fast-food restaurant.
  - *c* Uma spends $7 to see a film.
  - *d* Violet earns $10 000 from her 10 per cent ownership of Acme Industrial.

4 Imagine a society that produces military goods and consumer goods, which we'll call 'guns' and 'butter'.
  - *a* Draw a production possibilities frontier for guns and butter. Explain why it most likely has a bowed-out shape.
  - *b* Show a point that is impossible for the economy to achieve. Show a point that is feasible but inefficient.
  - *c* Imagine that the society has two political parties, call them the Hawks (who want a strong military) and the Doves (who want a smaller military). Show a point on your production possibilities frontier that the Hawks might choose and a point the Doves might choose.
  - *d* Imagine that an aggressive neighbouring country reduces the size of its military. As a result, both the Hawks and the Doves reduce their desired production of guns by the same amount. Which party would get the bigger 'peace dividend', measured by the increase in butter production? Explain.

5 The first lesson from economics discussed in chapter 1 is that people face trade-offs. Use a production possibilities frontier to illustrate society's trade-off between a clean environment and high incomes. What do you suppose determines the shape and position of the frontier? Show what happens to the frontier if engineers develop a car engine with almost no emissions.

6 An economy consists of three workers: Larry, Moe and Curly. Each works 10 hours a day and can produce two services: mowing lawns and washing cars. In an hour, Larry can either mow one lawn or wash one car; Moe can either mow one lawn or wash two cars; and Curly can either mow two lawns or wash one car.
  - *a* Calculate how much of each service is produced under the following circumstances, which we label A, B, C, and D:
    - *i* All three spend all their time mowing lawns. (A)
    - *ii* All three spend all their time washing cars. (B)
    - *iii* All three spend half their time on each activity. (C)
    - *iv* Larry spends half his time on each activity, while Moe only washes cars and Curly only mows lawns. (D)

    Graph the production possibilities frontier for this economy. Using your answers to part (a), identify points A, B, C and D on your graph.
  - *b* Explain why the production possibilities frontier has the shape it does.
  - *c* Are any of the allocations calculated in part (a) inefficient? Explain.

7 Classify the following topics as relating to microeconomics or macroeconomics:
  - *a* a family's decision about how much income to save
  - *b* the effect of government regulations on car emissions
  - *c* the impact of higher saving on economic growth
  - *d* a firm's decision about how many workers to hire
  - *e* the relationship between the inflation rate and changes in the quantity of money.

8 Classify each of the following statements as positive or normative. Explain.
  - *a* Society faces a short-term trade-off between inflation and unemployment.
  - *b* A reduction in the rate of growth of money will reduce the rate of inflation.
  - *c* The Reserve Bank should reduce the rate of growth of money.
  - *d* Society ought to require people on social security benefits to look for jobs.
  - *e* Lower tax rates encourage more work and more saving.

9 If you were prime minister, would you be more interested in your economic advisers' positive views or their normative views? Why?

10 Would you expect economists to disagree less about public policy as time goes on? Why or why not? Can their differences be completely eliminated? Why or why not?

Search me!

Search me!

When accessing information about microeconomics use the following keywords in any combinations you require:

- production possibilities frontier

CourseMate

CourseMate

For more multimedia resources and activities on economics, visit the Economics CourseMate website.

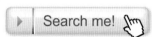

APPENDIX

Graphing – a brief review

Many of the concepts that economists study can be expressed with numbers – the price of bananas, the quantity of bananas sold, the cost of growing bananas and so on. Often these economic variables are related to one another. When the price of bananas rises, people buy fewer bananas. One way of expressing the relationships among variables is with graphs.

Graphs serve two purposes. First, when economists develop economic theories, graphs offer a way to express visually ideas that might be less clear if described with equations or words. Second, when economists analyse economic data, graphs provide a way of finding how variables are, in fact, related in the world. Whether we are working with theory or with data, graphs provide a lens through which a recognisable forest emerges from a multitude of trees.

Numerical information can be expressed graphically in many ways, just as a thought can be expressed in words in many ways. A good writer chooses words that will make an argument clear, a description pleasing or a scene dramatic. An effective economist chooses the type of graph that best suits the purpose at hand.

In this appendix we discuss how economists use graphs to study the mathematical relationships among variables. We also discuss some of the pitfalls that can arise in the use of graphical methods.

Graphs of a single variable

Three common graphs are shown in Figure 2A.1. The *pie chart* in panel (a) shows the sources of tax revenue for the federal government. A slice of the pie represents each source's share of the total. The *bar graph* in panel (b) compares how much various large corporations are worth. The height of each bar represents the dollar value of each firm. The *time-series graph* in panel (c) traces the Australian–US dollar exchange rate over time. The height of the line shows the number of US dollars that can be bought by one Australian dollar in each year. You have probably seen similar graphs presented in newspapers and magazines.

Graphs of two variables: The coordinate system

The three graphs in Figure 2A.1 are useful in showing how a variable changes over time or across individuals, but they are limited in how much they can tell us. These graphs display information only on a single variable. Economists are often concerned with the relationships between variables. Thus, they need to be able to display two variables on a single graph. The *coordinate system* makes this possible.

Figure 2A.1 Types of graphs

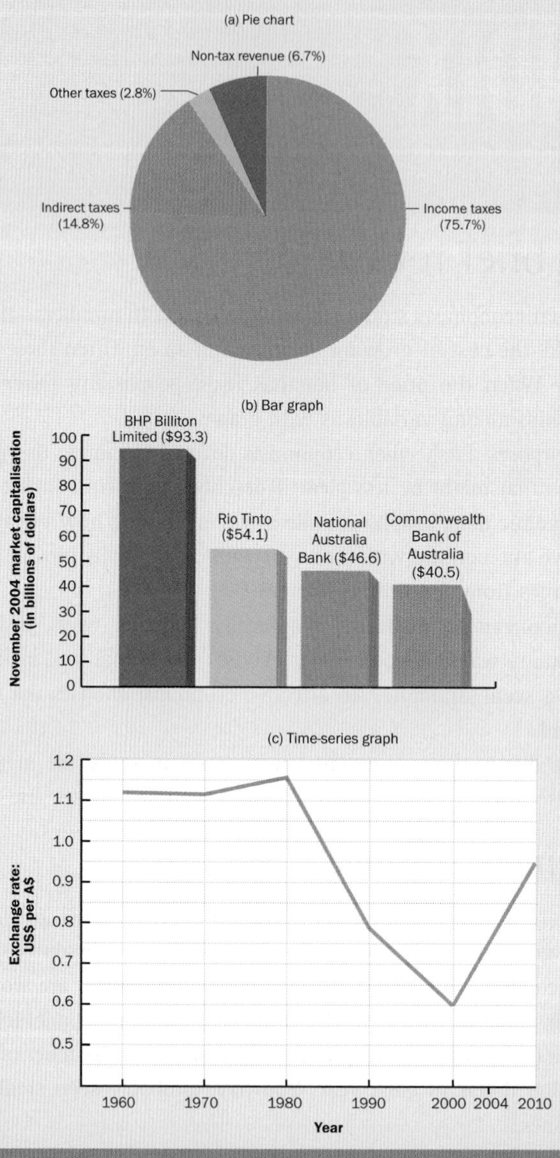

The pie chart in panel (a) shows the sources of revenue for the federal government. The bar graph in panel (b) compares how much various large corporations are worth. The time-series graph in panel (c) traces the Australian–US dollar exchange rate over time.

Source: (a) Department of the Treasury: www.budget.gov.au/2003-04/fbo/html/fbo-02.htm, 2003–04 Final Budget Outcome plus Appendix; (b) *Personal Investor*, January 2005, vol. 23, no. 1; (c) Reserve Bank of Australia Bulletin, June figures.

Suppose you want to examine the relationship between study time and average mark. For each student in your class, you could record a pair of numbers – hours per week spent studying and average mark. These numbers could then be placed in parentheses as an *ordered pair* and appear as a single point on the graph. Albert, for instance, is represented by the ordered pair (25 hours per week, 75 per cent average), and his 'what-me-worry?' classmate Alfred is represented by the ordered pair (five hours per week, 40 per cent average).

We can graph these ordered pairs on a two-dimensional grid. The first number in each ordered pair, called the *x-coordinate*, tells us the horizontal location of the point. The second number, called the *y-coordinate*, tells us the vertical location of the point. The point with both an *x*-coordinate and a *y*-coordinate of zero is known as the *origin*. The two coordinates in the ordered pair tell us where the point is located in relation to the origin – *x* units to the right of the origin and *y* units above it.

Figure 2A.2 graphs average marks against study time for Albert, Alfred and their classmates. This type of graph is called a *scatterplot* because it plots scattered points. Looking at this graph, we immediately notice that points further to the right also tend to be higher. Because higher study time

Figure 2A.2 Using the coordinate system

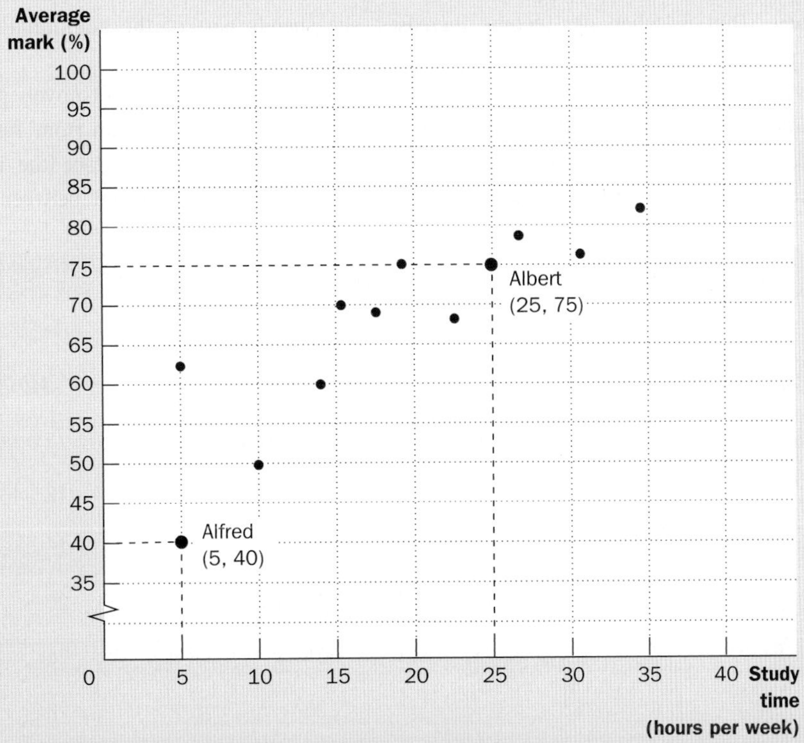

Average mark is measured on the vertical axis and study time on the horizontal axis. Albert, Alfred and their classmates are represented by various points. We can see from the graph that students who study more tend to get higher marks.

is associated with higher marks, we say that these two variables have a *positive correlation.* In contrast, if we were to graph party time and marks, it is likely that we would find that higher party time is associated with lower marks, and we would call this a *negative correlation.* In either case, the coordinate system makes the correlation between the two variables easy to see.

Curves in the coordinate system

Students who study more do tend to get higher marks, but other factors also influence a student's mark. Previous preparation is an important factor, for instance, as are talent, attention from teachers, even eating a good breakfast. A scatterplot like Figure 2A.2 does not attempt to isolate the effect that study has on marks from the effects of other variables. Often, however, economists prefer looking at how one variable affects another, holding everything else constant.

To see how this is done, let's consider one of the most important graphs in economics – the *demand curve.* The demand curve traces the effect of a good's price on the quantity of the good consumers want to buy. Table 2A.1 shows how the number of novels that Emma buys depends on her income and on the price of novels. When novels are cheap, Emma buys them in large quantities. As they become more expensive, she borrows books from the library instead of buying them or chooses to go to a film instead of reading. Similarly, at any given price, Emma buys more novels when she has a higher income. That is, when her income increases, she spends part of the additional income on novels and part on other goods.

We now have three variables – the price of novels, income and the number of novels purchased – which is more than we can represent in two dimensions. To put the information from Table 2A.1 in graphical form, we need to hold one of the three variables constant and trace the relationship between the other two. Because the demand curve represents the relationship between price and

Table 2A.1 Novels purchased by Emma

	Income		
Price	*$20 000*	*$30 000*	*$40 000*
$10	2 novels	5 novels	8 novels
9	6	9	12
8	10	13	16
7	14	17	20
6	18	21	24
5	22	25	28
	Demand curve, D_3	Demand curve, D_1	Demand curve, D_2

This table shows the number of novels Emma buys at various incomes and prices. For any given level of income, the data on price and quantity demanded can be graphed to produce Emma's demand curve for novels.

quantity demanded, we hold Emma's income constant and show how the number of novels she buys varies with the price of novels.

Suppose that Emma's income is $30 000 per year. If we place the number of novels Emma purchases on the *x*-axis and the price of novels on the *y*-axis, we can graphically represent the third column of Table 2A.1. When the points that represent these entries from the table – (five novels, $10), (nine novels, $9) and so on – are connected, they form a line. This line, shown in Figure 2A.3, is known as Emma's demand curve for novels; it tells us how many novels Emma purchases at any given price. The demand curve is downward-sloping, indicating that the quantity of novels demanded is negatively related to the price.

Now suppose that Emma's income rises to $40 000 per year. At any given price, Emma will purchase more novels than she did at her previous level of income. Just as earlier we drew Emma's demand curve for novels using the entries from the third column of Table 2A.1, we now draw a new demand curve using the entries from the fourth column of the table. This new demand curve (curve D_2) is shown alongside the old one (curve D_1) in Figure 2A.4; the new curve is a similar line drawn further to the right. We therefore say that Emma's demand curve for novels *shifts* to the right when her income increases. Likewise, if Emma's income were to fall to $20 000 per year, she would buy fewer novels at any given price and her demand curve would shift to the left (to curve D_3).

Figure 2A.3 Demand curve

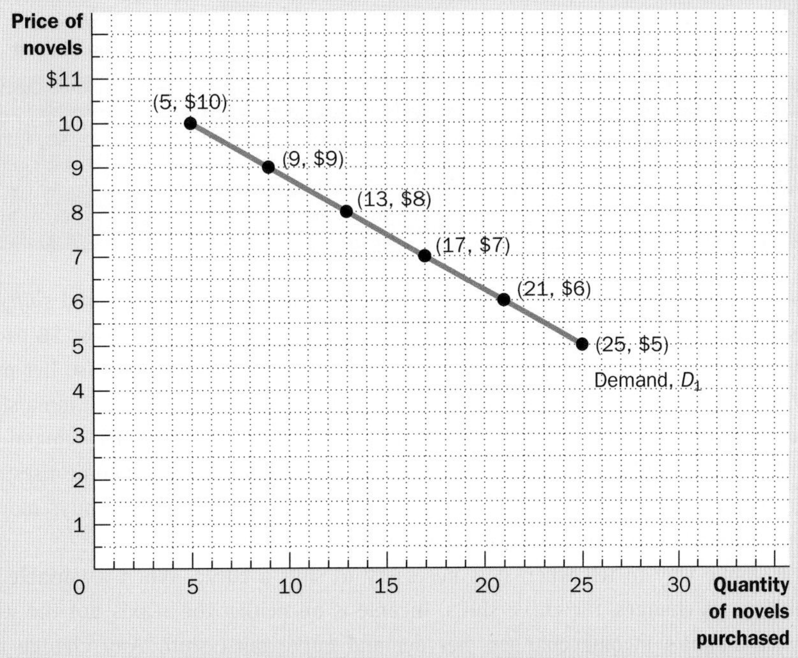

The line D_1 shows how Emma's purchases of novels depend on the price of novels when her income is held constant. Because the price and the quantity demanded are negatively related, the demand curve slopes downwards.

Figure 2A.4 Shifting demand curves

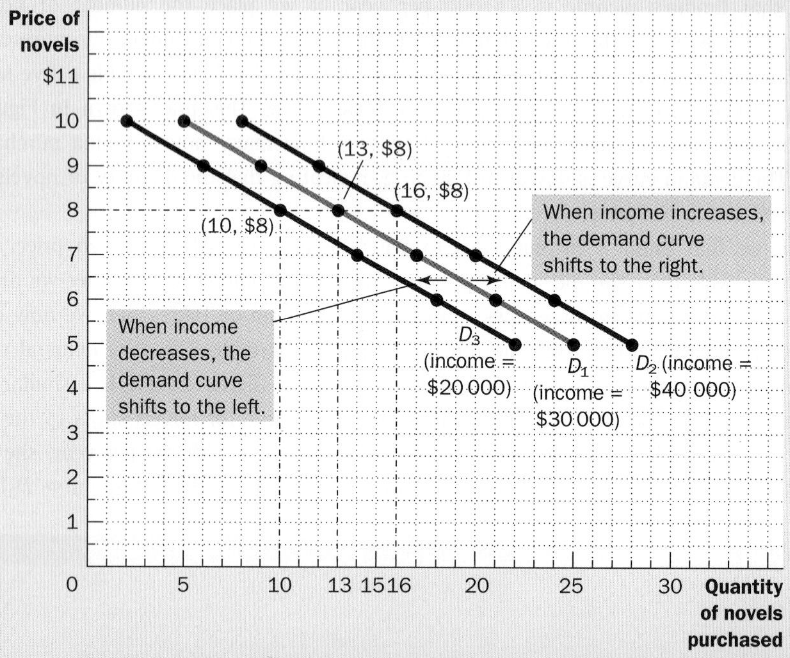

The location of Emma's demand curve for novels depends on how much income she earns. The more she earns, the more novels she will purchase at any given price, and the further to the right her demand curve will lie. Curve D_1 represents Emma's original demand curve when her income is $30 000 per year. If her income rises to $40 000 per year, her demand curve shifts to D_2. If her income falls to $20 000 per year, her demand curve shifts to D_3.

In economics, it is important to distinguish between *movements along a curve* and *shifts of a curve.* As we can see from Figure 2A.3, if Emma earns $30 000 per year and novels cost $8 each, she will purchase 13 novels per year. If the price of novels falls to $7, Emma will increase her purchases of novels to 17 per year. The demand curve, however, stays fixed in the same place. Emma still buys the same number of novels *at each price*, but as the price falls she moves along her demand curve from left to right. In contrast, if the price of novels remains fixed at $8 but her income rises to $40 000, Emma increases her purchases of novels from 13 to 16 per year. Because Emma buys more novels *at each price*, her demand curve shifts out, as shown in Figure 2A.4.

There is a simple way to tell when it is necessary to shift a curve. When a variable that is not named on either axis changes, the curve shifts. Income is on neither the x-axis nor the y-axis of the graph, so when Emma's income changes, her demand curve must shift. Any change that affects Emma's purchasing habits besides a change in the price of novels will result in a shift in her demand curve. If, for instance, the public library closes and Emma must buy all the books she wants to read, she will demand more novels at each price and her demand curve will shift to the right. Or if the price of films falls and Emma spends more time at the pictures and less time reading, she will demand fewer novels at each price, and her demand curve will shift to the left. In contrast, when a variable on an axis of the graph changes, the curve does not shift. We read the change as a movement along the curve.

Slope and elasticity

One question we might want to ask about Emma is how much her purchasing habits respond to price. Look at the demand curve shown in Figure 2A.5. If this curve is very steep, Emma purchases nearly the same number of novels regardless of whether they are cheap or expensive. If this curve is much flatter, the number of novels Emma purchases is more sensitive to changes in the price. To answer questions about how much one variable responds to changes in another variable, we can use the concept of *slope*.

The slope of a line is the ratio of the vertical distance covered to the horizontal distance covered as we move along the line. This definition is usually written out in mathematical symbols as follows:

$$\text{Slope} = \frac{\Delta y}{\Delta x}$$

Figure 2A.5 **Calculating the slope of a line**

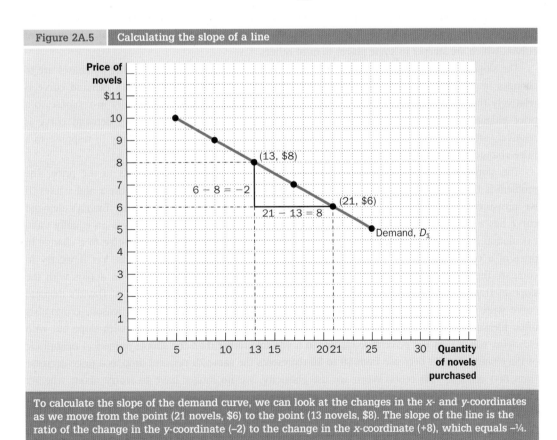

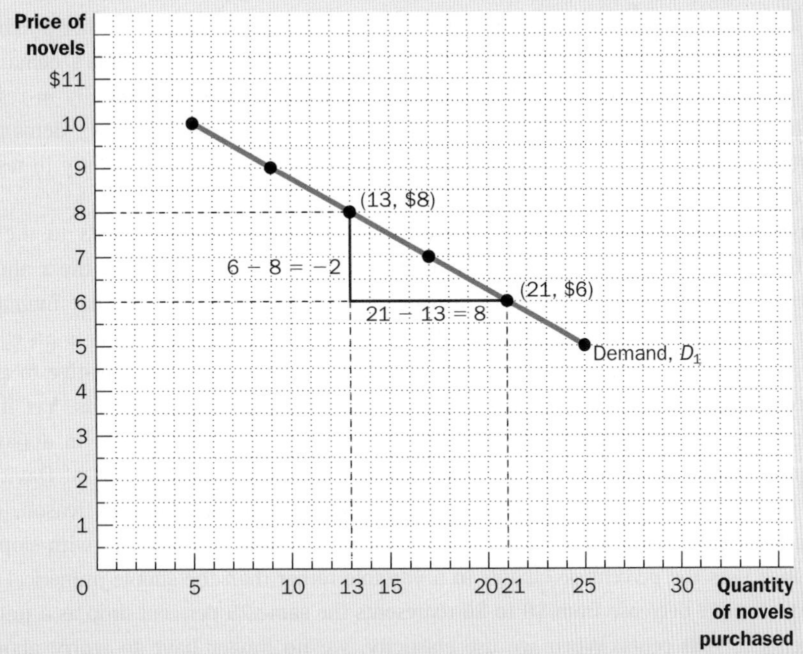

To calculate the slope of the demand curve, we can look at the changes in the *x*- and *y*-coordinates as we move from the point (21 novels, $6) to the point (13 novels, $8). The slope of the line is the ratio of the change in the *y*-coordinate (–2) to the change in the *x*-coordinate (+8), which equals –¼.

where the Greek letter Δ (delta) stands for the change in a variable. In other words, the slope of a line is equal to the 'rise' (change in y) divided by the 'run' (change in x). The slope will be a small positive number for a fairly flat upward-sloping line, a large positive number for a steep upward-sloping line, and a negative number for a downward-sloping line. A horizontal line has a slope of zero because in this case the y-variable never changes; a vertical line is defined to have an infinite slope because the y-variable can take any value without the x-variable changing at all.

What is the slope of Emma's demand curve for novels? First of all, because the curve slopes down, we know the slope will be negative. To calculate a numerical value for the slope, we must choose two points on the line. With Emma's income at $30 000, she will purchase 21 novels at a price of $6 or 13 novels at a price of $8. When we apply the slope formula, we are concerned with the change between these two points; in other words, we are concerned with the difference between them, which lets us know that we will have to subtract one set of values from the other, as follows:

$$\text{Slope} = \frac{\text{first y-coordinate} - \text{second y-coordinate}}{\text{first x-coordinate} - \text{second x-coordinate}} = \frac{6-8}{21-13} = \frac{-2}{8} = \frac{-1}{4}$$

Figure 2A.5 shows graphically how this calculation works. Try calculating the slope of Emma's demand curve using two different points. You should get exactly the same result, $-1/4$. One of the properties of a straight line is that it has the same slope everywhere. This is not true of other types of curves, which are steeper in some places than in others.

The slope of Emma's demand curve tells us something about how responsive her purchases are to changes in the price. A small slope (a number close to zero) means that Emma's demand curve is relatively flat; in this case, she adjusts the number of novels she buys substantially in response to a price change. A larger slope (a number further from zero) means that Emma's demand curve is relatively steep; in this case, she adjusts the number of novels she buys only slightly in response to a price change.

The slope, however, is not a perfect measure of how much Emma responds to the price. The problem is that the slope depends on the units used to measure the variables on the x and y axes. If we measured the price of novels in cents instead of dollars, we would find that Emma's demand curve has a slope of $-100/4$ or -25, rather than $-1/4$ as we found originally. This is an equally valid calculation and tells us a useful fact – that Emma's demand for novels is less sensitive to a change in price of a certain number of cents than a change of the same number of dollars. Yet if we try to compare the slope of Emma's demand curve for novels with the price measured in dollars with the slope of Don's demand curve with the price measured in pesos or with the slope of David's demand curve with the price measured in pounds, great confusion will ensue. For this reason, economists often measure the sensitivity of one variable to changes in another variable not with slope but with *elasticity*, which uses the *percentage* change in a variable rather than the simple numerical magnitude of the change. A price decrease from $8 to $6 represents the same 25 per cent drop as a price decrease from 800 cents to 600 cents. When we use elasticity, we no longer have to worry about whether variables are always expressed in the same units because percentage changes are the same no matter what units are used. We examine elasticities in more detail in chapter 5.

Cause and effect

Economists often use graphs to advance an argument about how the economy works. In other words, they use graphs to argue about how one set of events causes another set of events. With a graph like the demand curve, there is no doubt about cause and effect. Because we are varying price and holding all other variables constant, we know that changes in the price of novels cause changes in the quantity Emma demands. Remember, however, that our demand curve came from a hypothetical example. When graphing data from the real world, it is often more difficult to establish how one variable affects another.

The first problem is that it is difficult to hold everything else constant when measuring how one variable affects another. If we are not able to hold variables constant, we might decide that one variable on our graph is causing changes in the other variable when actually those changes are caused by a third *omitted variable* not pictured on the graph. Even if we have identified the correct two variables to look at, we might run into a second problem – *reverse causality*. In other words, we might decide that A causes B when in fact B causes A. The omitted-variable and reverse-causality traps require us to proceed with caution when using graphs to draw conclusions about causes and effects.

Omitted variables

To see how omitting a variable can lead to a deceptive graph, let's consider an example. Imagine that the government, spurred by public concern about the large number of deaths from cancer, commissions an exhaustive study from Big Brother Statistical Services. Big Brother examines many of the items found in people's homes to see which of them are associated with the risk of cancer. Big Brother reports a strong relationship between two variables – the number of cigarette lighters that a household owns and the probability that someone in the household will develop cancer. Figure 2A.6 shows this relationship.

Figure 2A.6 **Graph with an omitted variable**

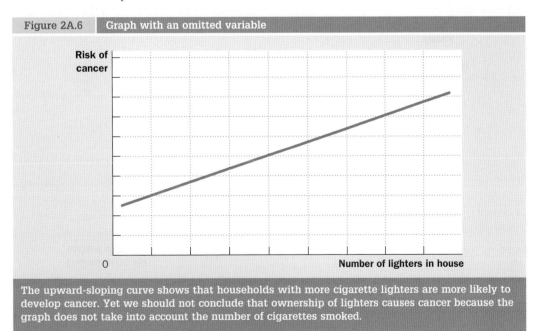

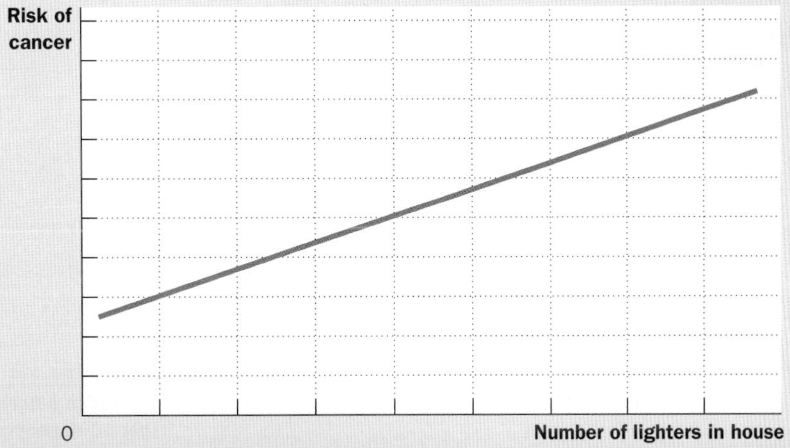

The upward-sloping curve shows that households with more cigarette lighters are more likely to develop cancer. Yet we should not conclude that ownership of lighters causes cancer because the graph does not take into account the number of cigarettes smoked.

What should we make of this result? Big Brother advises a quick policy response. It recommends that the government discourage the ownership of cigarette lighters by taxing their sale. It also recommends that the government require warning labels: 'Big Brother has determined that this lighter is dangerous to your health'.

In judging the validity of Big Brother's analysis, one question is paramount. Has Big Brother held constant every relevant variable except the one under consideration? If the answer is no, the results are suspect. An easy explanation for Figure 2A.6 is that people who own more cigarette lighters are more likely to smoke cigarettes and that cigarettes, not lighters, cause cancer. If Figure 2A.6 does not hold constant the amount of smoking, it does not tell us the true effect of owning a cigarette lighter.

This story illustrates an important principle – when you see a graph being used to support an argument about cause and effect, it is important to ask whether the movements of an omitted variable could explain the results you see.

Reverse causality

Economists can also make mistakes about causality by misreading its direction. To see how this is possible, suppose the Association of Australian Anarchists commissions a study of crime in Australia and arrives at Figure 2A.7, which plots the number of violent crimes per thousand people in major cities against the number of police officers per thousand people. The anarchists note the curve's upward slope and argue that since police increase rather than decrease the amount of urban violence, law enforcement should be abolished.

If we could run a controlled experiment, we would avoid the danger of reverse causality. To run an experiment, we would set the number of police officers in different cities randomly and then examine

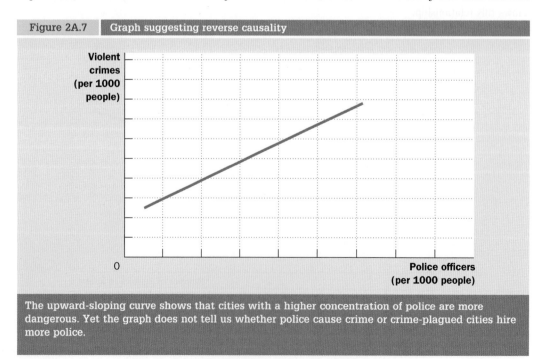

Figure 2A.7 Graph suggesting reverse causality

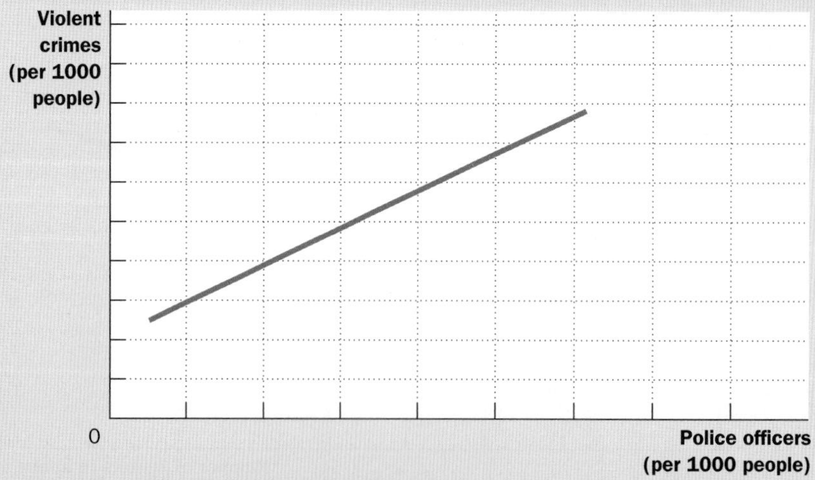

The upward-sloping curve shows that cities with a higher concentration of police are more dangerous. Yet the graph does not tell us whether police cause crime or crime-plagued cities hire more police.

the correlation between police and crime. Figure 2A.7, however, is not based on such an experiment. We simply observe that more dangerous cities have more police officers. The explanation for this may be that more dangerous cities hire more police. In other words, rather than police causing crime, crime may cause police. Nothing in the graph itself allows us to establish the direction of causality.

It might seem that an easy way to determine the direction of causality is to examine which variable moves first. If we see crime increase and then the police force expand, we reach one conclusion. If we see the police force expand and then crime increase, we reach the other. Yet there is also a flaw with this approach – often people change their behaviour not in response to a change in their present conditions but in response to a change in their *expectations* of future conditions. A city that expects a major crime wave in the future, for instance, might well hire more police now. This problem is even easier to see in the case of babies and station wagons. Couples often buy a station wagon in anticipation of the birth of a child. The station wagon comes before the baby, but we would not want to conclude that the sale of station wagons causes the population to grow!

There is no exhaustive set of rules that specifies when it is appropriate to draw causal conclusions from graphs. Yet just keeping in mind that cigarette lighters don't cause cancer (omitted variable) and station wagons don't cause babies (reverse causality) will keep you from falling for many faulty economic arguments.

3

Interdependence and the gains from trade

Learning objectives

In this chapter you will:

- consider how everyone can benefit when people trade with one another
- learn the meaning of absolute advantage and comparative advantage
- see how comparative advantage explains the gains from trade
- apply the theory of comparative advantage to everyday life and national policy.

Consider your typical day. You wake up in the morning and you pour yourself juice from oranges grown in the Riverina District of New South Wales and coffee from beans grown in Indonesia. Over breakfast, you watch a news program broadcast from Sydney on your television made in China. You get dressed in clothes made from cotton grown in the United States and sewn in factories in Thailand. You drive to university in a car made of parts manufactured in more than a dozen countries around the world. Then you open up your economics textbook written by one author living in Massachusetts and two others in Melbourne, published by a company located in Melbourne, and printed on paper made from trees grown in Tasmania.

Every day you rely on many people from around the world, most of whom you have never met, to provide you with the goods and services that you enjoy. Such interdependence is possible because people trade with one another. Those people who provide you with goods and services are not acting out of generosity. Nor is some government agency directing them to satisfy your desires. Instead, people provide you and other consumers with the goods and services they produce because they get something in return.

In subsequent chapters we will examine how our economy coordinates the activities of millions of people with varying tastes and abilities. As a starting point for this analysis, here we consider the reasons for economic interdependence. One of the *Ten Lessons from Economics* highlighted in chapter 1 is that trade can make everyone better off. This lesson explains why people trade with their neighbours and why nations trade with other nations. In this chapter we examine this idea more closely. What exactly do people gain when they trade with one another? Why do people choose to become interdependent?

A parable for the modern economy

To understand why people choose to depend on others for goods and services and how this choice improves their lives, let's look at a simple economy – the economy inside a household. Imagine that there are two tasks that need to be completed in the household – cooking and laundry. And there are two people living in the house – Mitchell and Cameron – each of whom like to eat and to wear clean and neatly ironed clothes.

The gains from trade are most obvious if Mitchell can only cook and Cameron can only do the laundry. In one scenario, Mitchell and Cameron could choose to have nothing to do with each other. Mitchell would cook for himself and Cameron would wash and iron his own clothes. Mitchell's clothes would never be cleaned. But after several months of eating cold meat and biscuits, Cameron might decide that self-sufficiency is not all it's cracked up to be. Mitchell, whose clothing could not have a worse odour, would be likely to agree. It is easy to see that trade would allow them to enjoy greater variety – each could eat well and wear clean clothes.

Although this scene illustrates very simply how everyone can benefit from trade, the gains would be similar if Mitchell and Cameron were each capable of doing the other task, but only at great cost. Suppose, for example, that Mitchell is able to wash and iron clothes, but that he is not very good at it. Similarly, suppose that Cameron is able to cook but has not had the experience and so can prepare only a few basic dishes. In this case, it is easy to see that Mitchell and Cameron can each benefit by specialising in what he does best and then trading with the other.

The gains from trade are less obvious, however, when one person is better at producing *every* good. For example, suppose that Mitchell is better at cooking *and* better at washing and ironing than Cameron. In this case, should Mitchell choose to remain self-sufficient? Or is there still reason for him to trade with Cameron? To answer this question, we need to look more closely at the factors that affect such a decision.

Production possibilities

Suppose that Mitchell and Cameron each have 12 spare hours a week to work on household tasks and can devote this time to cooking, laundry or a combination of the two. Table 3.1 shows the amount of time each person requires to produce one unit of each good – a decent meal and a basket of clean clothes. Cameron can wash and iron a basket of clothes in four hours and cook a meal in two hours. Mitchell, who is more productive in both activities, needs only half an hour to cook a meal and can wash and iron a basket of clothes in three hours.

Panel (a) of Figure 3.1 illustrates the amounts of laundry and cooking that Cameron can produce. If Cameron devotes all 12 hours of his time to laundry, he cleans three baskets of clothes but does not cook. If he devotes all his time to cooking, he produces six meals and washes no clothes. If Cameron spends four hours doing laundry and eight hours cooking, he cooks four meals and washes and irons one basket of clothes. The figure shows these three possible outcomes and all others in between.

Table 3.1 The production opportunities of Cameron and Mitchell

	Hours needed to make:		Maximum amount produced in 12 hours:	
	1 meal	1 basket	Meals	Baskets
Cameron	2	4	6	3
Mitchell	½	3	24	4

Figure 3.1 The production possibilities frontier

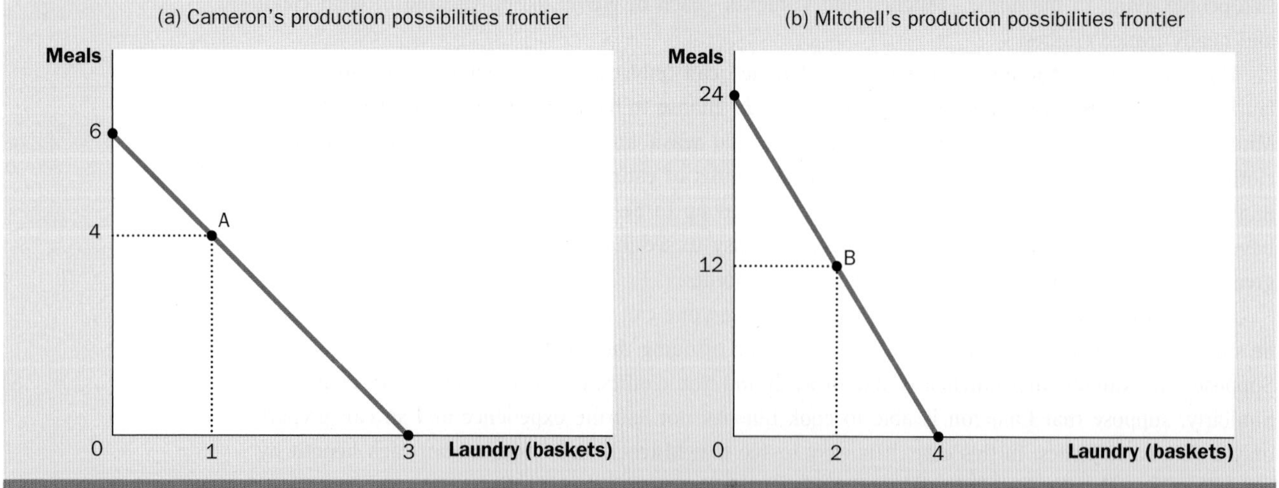

Panel (a) shows the combinations of meals and laundry that Cameron can produce. Panel (b) shows the combinations of meals and laundry that Mitchell can produce. Both production possibilities frontiers are derived from table 3.1 and the assumption that Cameron and Mitchell each work 12 hours per week on domestic chores.

The graph (a) is Cameron's production possibilities frontier. As we discussed in chapter 2, a production possibilities frontier shows the various mixes of output that an economy can produce. It illustrates one of the *Ten Lessons from Economics* in chapter 1 – people face trade-offs. Here Cameron faces a trade-off between time spent cooking and doing laundry. You may recall that the production possibilities frontier in chapter 2 was drawn bowed out; in this case, the trade-off between the two goods depends on the amounts being produced. Here, however, Cameron's 'technology' (as summarised in Table 3.1) allows him to switch between one task and the other at a constant rate. In this case, the production possibilities frontier is a straight line.

Panel (b) of Figure 3.1 shows the production possibilities frontier for Mitchell. If Mitchell devotes all 12 hours of his time to cooking, he produces 24 meals but does no laundry. If he devotes all his time to laundry, he washes four baskets but cooks no meals. If Mitchell divides his time equally, spending six hours on each activity, he cooks 12 meals and washes two baskets of clothes per week. Once again, the production possibilities frontier shows all the possible outcomes.

If Mitchell and Cameron choose to go it alone, rather than trade with each other, then each consumes exactly what he produces. In this case, the production possibilities frontier is also the consumption possibilities frontier. That is, without trade, Figure 3.1 shows the possible combinations of cooking and laundry that Mitchell and Cameron can each produce and then consume.

Although these production possibilities frontiers are useful in showing the trade-offs that Mitchell and Cameron face, they do not tell us what they will actually choose to do. To determine their choices, we need to know the tastes of Mitchell and Cameron. Let's suppose they choose the combinations identified by points A and B in Figure 3.1 – Cameron produces and consumes four meals and washes one basket while Mitchell produces and consumes 12 meals and washes two baskets of clothing.

Specialisation and trade

After several months of combination B, Mitchell gets an idea and talks to Cameron:

Mitchell: Cameron, have I got a deal for you! I know how to improve life for both of us. I think you should stop cooking altogether and devote all your time to laundry. According to my calculations, if you work 12 hours a week washing and ironing, you'll get three baskets done every week. If you do one basket of laundry for me each week and an extra one every second week, then I'll cook you five meals a week. In the end, you'll be able to eat cooked meals more often and you will get your clothes cleaner as well. Indeed, another half basket. If you go along with my plan, you'll eat well and look better! *[To illustrate his point, Mitchell shows Cameron panel (a) of* Figure 3.2.]

Cameron: *(sounding sceptical)* That seems like a good deal for me. But I don't understand why you are offering it. If the deal is so good for me, it can't be good for you too.

Mitchell: Oh, but it is! If I spend nine hours a week cooking and three hours doing laundry, I'll make 18 meals and also have time spare to wash another basket. After I give you five meals in exchange for the extra basket-and-a-half you wash and iron, I'll be able to eat 13 meals at home but I'll have more clean shirts, trousers and, most importantly, socks and underwear. In the end, I will be much happier than I am now. *[He points out panel (b) of* Figure 3.2.]

Cameron: I don't know ... This sounds too good to be true. I don't want you coming back to me next week and complaining about having to do all the cooking.

Mitchell: It's really not as complicated as it seems at first. Here – I've summarised my proposal for you in a simple table. *[Mitchell hands Cameron a copy of Table 3.2.]*

Cameron: (*after pausing to study the table*) These calculations seem correct, but I'm puzzled. How can this deal make us both better off?

Mitchell: We can both benefit because trade allows each of us to specialise in doing what we do best. You will spend more time doing laundry and less time cooking. I will spend more time cooking and less time washing and ironing. I like to iron my clothes but I am, you must admit, a much better cook. As a result of specialisation and trade, each of us can consume more of the great meals that I cook and wear cleaner clothes without taking more time out of our other activities. What could be better?

Figure 3.2 **How trade expands the set of consumption opportunities**

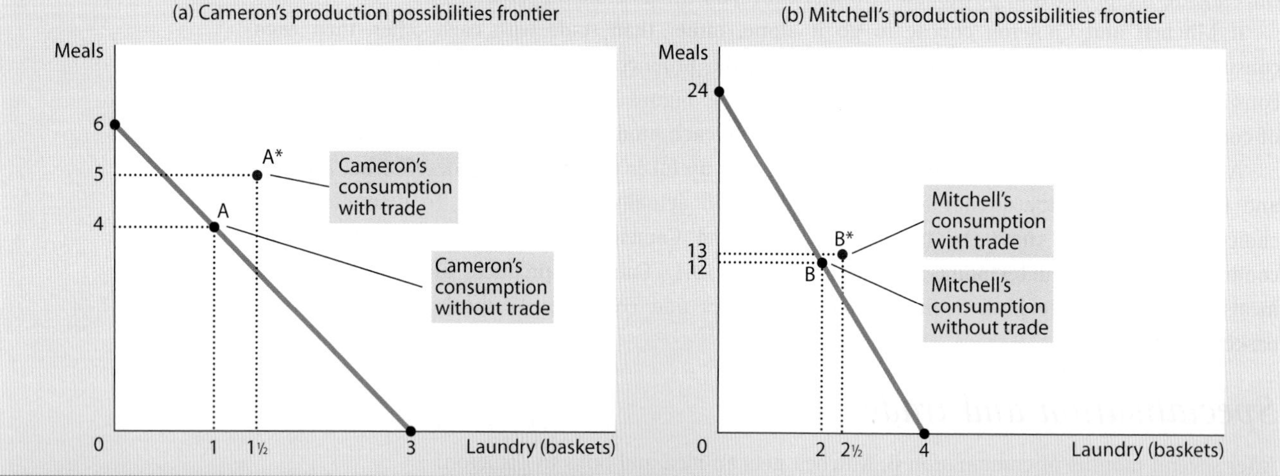

The proposed trade between Cameron and Mitchell offers each a combination of meals and baskets of clean clothes that would be impossible in the absence of trade. In panel (a), Cameron gets to consume at point A* rather than point A. In panel (b), Mitchell gets to consume at point B* rather than point B. Trade allows each to consume more meals and have more clean clothes.

Table 3.2 **The gains from trade: A summary**

	Without trade:	With trade:			
	Production and consumption	Production	Trade	Consumption	Gains from trade
Cameron	4 meals	0 meals	Gets 5 meals	5 meals	1 meal
	1 basket	3 baskets	for 1½ baskets	1½ baskets	½ basket
Mitchell	12 meals	18 meals	Gives 5 meals	13 meals	1 meal
	2 baskets	1 basket	for 1½ baskets	2½ baskets	½ basket

Q

Draw an example of a production possibilities frontier for Robinson Crusoe, a shipwrecked sailor who spends his time gathering coconuts and catching fish. Does this frontier limit Crusoe's consumption of coconuts and fish if he lives by himself? Does he face the same limits if he can trade with native residents on the island?

The principle of comparative advantage

Mitchell's explanation of the gains from trade, though correct, poses a puzzle – if Mitchell is better at both cooking and laundry, how can Cameron ever specialise in doing what he does best? Cameron doesn't seem to do anything best. To solve this puzzle, we need to look at the principle of *comparative advantage*.

As a first step in developing this principle, consider the following question. In our example, who does the laundry at lower cost – Cameron or Mitchell? There are two possible answers and in these two answers lie both the solution to our puzzle and the key to understanding the gains from trade.

Absolute advantage

One way to answer the question about the cost of doing the laundry is to compare the inputs required by the two housemates. Economists use the term **absolute advantage** when comparing the productivity of one person, firm or nation with that of another. The producer that requires a smaller quantity of inputs to produce a good is said to have an absolute advantage in producing that good.

absolute advantage
the comparison among producers of a good according to their productivity

In our example, time is the only input, so we can determine absolute advantage by looking at how much time each type of production takes. Mitchell has an absolute advantage both in laundry and cooking, because he requires less time than Cameron to produce a unit of either good. Mitchell needs only three hours to do a basket of laundry, whereas Cameron needs four hours. Similarly, Mitchell needs only half an hour to cook a meal whereas Cameron needs two hours. Based on this information, we can conclude that Mitchell has the lower cost of laundry and a lower cost of cooking, if we measure cost by the quantity of inputs.

Search me!
▸ absolute advantage

Opportunity cost and comparative advantage

There is another way to look at the cost of laundry. Rather than comparing inputs required, we can compare the opportunity costs. Recall from chapter 1 that the opportunity cost of some item is what we give up to get that item. In our example, we assumed that Cameron and Mitchell each spend 12 hours a week on household tasks. Time spent doing laundry, therefore, takes away from time available for cooking. When reallocating time between the two goods, Mitchell and Cameron give up units of one good to produce units of the other good, moving along their production possibility frontiers. The opportunity cost measures the trade-off between the two goods that each faces.

Let's first consider Mitchell's opportunity cost. According to Table 3.1, doing a basket of clothes takes Mitchell three hours of work. When Mitchell spends that three hours doing laundry, he spends three hours less cooking. Because Mitchell needs only half an hour to produce one meal, three hours of work would yield six meals. Hence, Mitchell's opportunity cost of one basket is six meals.

Table 3.3 The opportunity cost of meals and baskets of clean clothes

	Opportunity cost of one:	
	Meal (in terms of baskets given up)	Basket (in terms of meals given up)
Cameron	½	2
Mitchell	⅙	6

Mitchell's production possibilities frontier reflects this opportunity cost – the downward-sloping line in panel (b) of Figure 3.1 has a slope ('rise over run') equal to –6.

Now consider Cameron's opportunity cost. Washing and ironing one basket takes him four hours. Because he needs two hours to cook a meal, four hours would yield two meals. Hence, Cameron's opportunity cost of doing one basket of laundry is two meals. Cameron's production possibilities frontier in panel (a) of Figure 3.1 reflects this opportunity cost by having a slope of –2.

Table 3.3 shows the opportunity cost of cooking and laundry for Cameron and Mitchell. Notice that the opportunity cost of cooking is the inverse of the opportunity cost of laundry. Because one clean basket of laundry costs Mitchell six meals, one meal costs Mitchell one-sixth of a basket of laundry. Similarly, because doing one basket of laundry costs Cameron two meals, one meal costs Cameron half a basket of laundry.

comparative advantage
the comparison among producers of a good according to their opportunity cost

Economists use the term **comparative advantage** when describing the opportunity cost of two producers. The producer who has the smaller opportunity cost of producing a good is said to have a comparative advantage in producing that good. In our example, Cameron has a lower opportunity cost of laundry than Mitchell (two versus six meals). Mitchell has a lower opportunity cost of cooking than Cameron (1/6 rather than ½ of a basket). Thus, Cameron has a comparative advantage in laundry, and Mitchell has a comparative advantage in cooking.

Search me!
▸ comparative advantage

Although it is possible for one person to have an absolute advantage in both goods (as Mitchell does in our example), it is impossible for the same person to have a comparative advantage in both goods. Because the opportunity cost of one good is the inverse of the opportunity cost of the other, if a person's opportunity cost of one good is relatively high, his opportunity cost of the other good must be relatively low. Comparative advantage reflects the relative opportunity cost. Unless two people have exactly the same opportunity cost, one person will have a comparative advantage in one good and the other person will have a comparative advantage in the other good.

Comparative advantage and trade

Differences in opportunity cost and comparative advantage create the gains from trade. When each person specialises in producing the good for which he or she has a comparative advantage, total production in the economy rises. This increase in the size of the economic pie can be used to make everyone better off.

In our example, Cameron spends more time doing laundry and Mitchell spends more time cooking meals. As a result the total production of laundry rises from 3 to 4 baskets and the total production of cooked meals rises from 16 to 18. Mitchell and Cameron can share the benefits of this increased production.

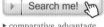

We can also look at the gains from trade in terms of the price that each person pays the other. Because Mitchell and Cameron have different opportunity costs, they can both get a 'bargain'. That is, each benefits from trade by obtaining a good at a price that is lower than his opportunity cost of that good.

Consider the proposed deal from Cameron's viewpoint. Cameron gets five meals in exchange for cleaning an extra one-and-a-half baskets of laundry. In other words, Cameron buys each meal for a price of 3/10 of a basket of laundry. This price of a meal is lower than his opportunity cost of cooking, which is 1/2 a basket. Thus, Cameron benefits from the deal because he gets to buy meals at a good price.

Now consider the deal from Mitchell's viewpoint. Mitchell buys a basket of laundry for a price of just over three meals. This price of laundry is lower than his opportunity cost of laundry, which is six meals. Thus, Mitchell benefits because he gets to buy a laundry service at a good price.

These benefits arise because each person concentrates on the activity for which he has the lower opportunity cost – Cameron spends more time doing laundry and Mitchell spends more time cooking. As a result, the total production of clean clothing and the total production of meals both rise, and Cameron and Mitchell share the benefits of this increased production.

The moral of the story of Mitchell and Cameron should now be clear – *trade can benefit everyone in society because it allows people to specialise in activities in which they have a comparative advantage.*

Q

Robinson Crusoe can gather 10 coconuts or catch one fish per hour. His friend Friday can gather 30 coconuts or catch two fish per hour. What is Crusoe's opportunity cost of catching one fish? What is Friday's? Who has an absolute advantage in catching fish? Who has a comparative advantage in catching fish?

Applications of comparative advantage

The principle of comparative advantage explains interdependence and the gains from trade. Because interdependence is so prevalent in the modern world, the principle of comparative advantage has many applications. Here are two examples, one fanciful and one of great practical importance.

Should Roger Federer mow his own lawn?

Roger Federer is a great athlete. He is one of the best tennis players in the world and has 16 grand slam titles – more than any other male tennis player. Very likely, he is better at other activities, too. For example, Roger can probably mow his lawn faster than anyone else. But just because he can mow his lawn fast, does this mean he *should*?

To answer this question, we can use the concepts of opportunity cost and comparative advantage. Let's say that Roger can mow his lawn in two hours. In that same two hours, he could film a television commercial for sports shoes and earn $1 000 000. In contrast, Becky, the girl next door, can mow Roger's lawn in four hours. In that same four hours, she could work at Coles supermarket and earn $40.

In this example, Roger's opportunity cost of mowing the lawn is $1 000 000, and Becky's opportunity cost is $40. Roger has an absolute advantage in mowing lawns because he can do the work in less time. Yet Becky has a comparative advantage in mowing lawns because she has the lower opportunity cost.

The gains from trade in this example are tremendous. Rather than mowing his own lawn, Roger should make the commercial and hire Becky to mow the lawn. As long as he pays her more than $40 and less than $1 000 000, both of them are better off.

Should a country trade with other countries?

imports
goods produced abroad and sold domestically

exports
goods produced domestically and sold abroad

Just as individuals can benefit from specialisation and trade with one another, as Mitchell and Cameron did, so can populations of people in different countries. Many of the goods that Australians enjoy are produced abroad and many of the goods produced in Australia are sold abroad. Goods produced abroad and sold domestically are called **imports**. Goods produced domestically and sold abroad are called **exports**.

To see how countries can benefit from trade, suppose there are two countries, Australia and Japan, and two goods, food and cars. Imagine that the two countries produce cars equally well – an Australian worker and a Japanese worker can each produce one car per month. In contrast, because Australia has more and better land, it is better at producing food – an Australian worker can produce two tonnes of food per month, whereas a Japanese worker can produce only one tonne of food per month.

The principle of comparative advantage states that each good should be produced by the country that has the smaller opportunity cost of producing that good. Because the opportunity cost of a car is two tonnes of food in Australia but only one tonne of food in Japan, Japan has a comparative advantage in producing cars. Japan should produce more cars than it wants for its own use and export some of them to Australia. Similarly, because the opportunity cost of a tonne of food is one car in Japan but only half a car in Australia, Australia has a comparative advantage in producing food. Australia should produce more food than it wants to consume and export some of it to Japan. Through specialisation and trade, both countries can have more food and more cars.

In reality, of course, the issues involved in trade among nations are more complex than this example suggests, as we will see in chapter 9. Most important among these issues is that each country has many citizens with different interests. International trade can make some individuals worse off, even as it makes the country as a whole better off. When Australia exports food and imports cars, the impact on an Australian farmer is not the same as the impact on an Australian car worker. Yet contrary to the opinions sometimes voiced by politicians and political commentators, international trade is not like war, in which some countries win and others lose. Trade allows all countries to achieve greater prosperity.

IN THE NEWS . . .

WHO HAS A COMPARATIVE ADVANTAGE IN SLAYING OGRES?

A decade ago, no one would have asked which nation has a comparative advantage in slaying ogres. But technology is changing the goods and services that are traded between countries.

Ogre to slay? Outsource it to Chinese

by David Barboza

Fuzhou, China – One of China's newest factories operates here in the basement of an old warehouse. Posters of World of Warcraft and Magic Land hang above a corps of young people glued to their computer screens, pounding away at their keyboards in the latest hustle for money.

The people working at this clandestine locale are 'gold farmers'. Every day, in 12-hour shifts, they 'play' computer games by killing onscreen monsters and winning battles, harvesting artificial gold coins and other virtual goods as rewards that, as it turns out, can be transformed into real cash.

That is because, from Seoul to San Francisco, affluent online gamers who lack the time and patience to work their way up to the higher levels of gamedom are willing to pay the young Chinese here to play the early rounds for them.

'For 12 hours a day, 7 days a week, my colleagues and I are killing monsters', said a 23-year-old gamer who works here in this makeshift factory and goes by the online code name Wandering. 'I make about $250 a month, which is pretty good compared with the other jobs I've had. And I can play games all day.'

He and his comrades have created yet another new business out of cheap Chinese labor. They are tapping into the fast-growing world of 'massively multiplayer online games', which involve role playing and often revolve around fantasy or warfare in medieval kingdoms or distant galaxies ...

For the Chinese in game-playing factories like these, though, it is not all fun and games. These workers have strict quotas and are supervised by bosses who equip them with computers, software and Internet connections to thrash online trolls, gnomes and ogres.

As they grind through the games, they accumulate virtual currency that is valuable to game players around the world. The games allow players to trade currency to other players, who can then use it to buy better armor, amulets, magic spells and other accoutrements to climb to higher levels or create more powerful characters.

The Internet is now filled with classified advertisements from small companies – many of them here in China – auctioning for real money their powerful figures, called avatars ...

'It's unimaginable how big this is', says Chen Yu, 27, who employs 20 full-time gamers here in Fuzhou. 'They say that in some of these popular games, 40 or 50 percent of the players are actually Chinese farmers.'

Source: From *The New York Times*, 9 December 2005, pp. 9-10

fyi The legacy of Adam Smith and David Ricardo

Economists have long understood the principle of comparative advantage. Here is how the great economist Adam Smith put the argument:

> It is a maxim of every prudent master of a family, never to attempt to make at home what it will cost him more to make than to buy. The tailor does not attempt to make his own shoes, but buys them off the shoemaker. The shoemaker does not attempt to make his own clothes but employs a tailor. The farmer attempts to make neither the one nor the other, but employs those different artificers. All of them find it for their interest to employ their whole industry in a way in which they have some advantage over their neighbours, and to purchase with a part of its produce, or what is the same thing, with the price of part of it, whatever else they have occasion for.

This quotation is from Smith's 1776 book *An Inquiry into the Nature and Causes of the Wealth of Nations.* This book was a landmark in the analysis of trade and economic interdependence. Many economists consider Smith to be the founder of modern economics.

Smith's book inspired David Ricardo, a millionaire stockbroker, to become an economist. In his 1817 book *Principles of Political Economy and Taxation*, Ricardo developed the principle of comparative advantage as we know it today. His defence of free trade was not a mere academic exercise. Ricardo put his economic beliefs to work as a member of the British Parliament, where he opposed the Corn Laws, which restricted the import of grain.

David Ricardo

The conclusions of Adam Smith and David Ricardo on the gains from trade have held up well

>>

over time. Although economists often disagree on questions of policy, they are united in their support of free trade. Moreover, the central argument for free trade has not changed much in the past two centuries. Even though the field of economics has broadened its scope and refined its theories since the time of Smith and Ricardo, economists' opposition to trade restrictions is still based largely on the principle of comparative advantage.

Q

Suppose that the world's fastest typist happens to be trained in brain surgery. Should that person type for herself or hire a secretary? Explain.

Conclusion

You should now understand more fully the benefits of living in an interdependent economy. When Chinese companies buy Australian iron ore, when residents of Tasmania buy a mango grown in the Northern Territory, and when you spend Friday night babysitting for neighbours rather than going out, the same economic forces are at work. The principle of comparative advantage shows that trade can make everyone better off.

Having seen why interdependence is desirable, you might naturally ask how it is possible. How do free societies coordinate the diverse activities of all the people involved in their economies? What ensures that goods and services will go from those who should be producing them to those who should be consuming them?

In a world with only two people, such as Mitchell and Cameron, the answer is simple – these two people can directly bargain and allocate resources between themselves. In the real world with millions of people, the answer is less obvious. We take up this issue in the next chapter, where we see that free societies allocate resources through the market forces of supply and demand.

Summary

- Each person consumes goods and services produced by many other people both in our country and around the world. Interdependence and trade are desirable because they allow everyone to enjoy a greater quantity and variety of goods and services.
- There are two ways to compare the ability of two people in producing a good. The person who can produce the good with the smaller quantity of inputs is said to have an *absolute advantage* in producing the good. The person who has the smaller opportunity cost of producing the good is said to have a *comparative advantage*. The gains from trade are based on comparative advantage, not absolute advantage.
- Trade makes everyone better off because it allows people to specialise in those activities in which they have a comparative advantage.
- The principle of comparative advantage applies to countries as well as to people. Economists use the principle of comparative advantage to advocate free trade among countries.

Key concepts

absolute advantage
comparative advantage
exports
imports

Questions for review

1 Explain how absolute advantage and comparative advantage differ.
2 Give an example in which one person has an absolute advantage in doing something but another person has a comparative advantage.
3 Is absolute advantage or comparative advantage more important for trade? Explain your answer using the example in your answer to question 2.
4 Will a nation tend to export or import goods for which it has a comparative advantage? Explain.
5 Why do economists oppose policies that restrict trade among nations?

Problems and applications

1 Consider Cameron and Mitchell from our example in this chapter. Explain why Cameron's opportunity cost of producing one basket of clean clothing is two meals. Explain why Mitchell's opportunity cost of producing one meal is 1/6 of a washed and ironed basket of clothing.
2 Maria can read 20 pages of economics in an hour. She can also read 50 pages of sociology in an hour. She spends five hours per day studying.
   a Draw Maria's production possibilities frontier for reading economics and sociology.
   b What is Maria's opportunity cost of reading 100 pages of sociology?
3 Australian and Japanese workers can each produce four cars a year. An Australian worker can produce 10 tonnes of grain a year, whereas a Japanese worker can produce five tonnes of grain a year. To keep things simple, assume that each country has 100 million workers.
   a For this situation, construct a table similar to Table 3.1.
   b Graph the production possibilities frontier of the Australian and Japanese economies.

- c For Australia, what is the opportunity cost of a car? Of grain? For Japan, what is the opportunity cost of a car? Of grain? Put this information in a table similar to Table 3.3.
- d Which country has an absolute advantage in producing cars? In producing grain?
- e Which country has a comparative advantage in producing cars? In producing grain?
- f Without trade, half of each country's workers produce cars and half produce grain. What quantities of cars and grain does each country produce?
- g Starting from a position without trade, give an example in which trade makes each country better off.

4 Monica and Rachel are flatmates. They spend most of their time working, but they leave some time for their favourite activities – making pizza and fine coffee. Monica takes five minutes to make a pot of coffee and half an hour to make a pizza. Rachel takes 15 minutes to make a pot of coffee and one hour to make a pizza.
- a What is each flatmate's opportunity cost of making a pizza? Who has the absolute advantage in making pizza? Who has the comparative advantage in making pizza?
- b If Rachel and Monica trade foods with each other, who will trade away pizza in exchange for coffee?
- c The price of pizza can be expressed in terms of pots of coffee. What is the highest price at which pizza can be traded that would make both flatmates better off? What is the lowest price? Explain.

5 Suppose that there are 10 million workers in South Korea and that each of these workers can produce either two cars or 30 bags of wheat in a year.
- a What is the opportunity cost of producing a car in South Korea? What is the opportunity cost of producing a bag of wheat in South Korea? Explain the relationship between the opportunity costs of the two goods.
- b Draw South Korea's production possibilities frontier. If South Korea chooses to consume 10 million cars, how much wheat can it consume without trade? Label this point on the production possibilities frontier.
- c Now suppose that Thailand offers to buy 10 million cars from South Korea in exchange for 20 bags of wheat per car. If South Korea continues to consume 10 million cars, how much wheat does this deal allow South Korea to consume? Label this point on your diagram. Should South Korea accept the deal?

6 Consider a professor who is writing a book. The professor can both write the chapters and gather the needed data faster than anyone else at her university. Still, she pays a student to collect data at the library. Is this sensible? Explain.

7 England and Scotland both produce scones and jumpers. Suppose that an English worker can produce 50 scones per hour or one jumper per hour. Suppose that a Scottish worker can produce 40 scones per hour or two jumpers per hour.
- a Which country has the absolute advantage in the production of each good? Which country has the comparative advantage?
- b If England and Scotland decide to trade, which commodity will Scotland trade to England? Explain.
- c If a Scottish worker could produce only one jumper per hour, would Scotland still gain from trade? Would England still gain from trade? Explain.

8 The following table describes the production possibilities of two cities in the country of Footballia:

	Maroon shirts per worker per hour	Blue shirts per worker per hour
Brisbane	3	3
Sydney	2	1

- *a* Without trade, what is the price of blue shirts (in terms of maroon shirts) in Brisbane? What is the price in Sydney?
- *b* Which city has an absolute advantage in the production of each colour shirt? Which city has a comparative advantage in the production of each colour shirt?
- *c* If the cities trade with each other, which colour shirt will each export?
- *d* What is the range of prices at which trade can occur?

9 Suppose that all goods can be produced with fewer worker hours in Germany than in France.

- *a* In what sense is the cost of all goods lower in Germany than in France?
- *b* In what sense is the cost of some goods lower in France?
- *c* If Germany and France traded with each other, would both countries be better off as a result? Explain in the context of your answers to parts (a) and (b).

10 Are the following statements true or false? Explain in each case.

- *a* 'Two countries can achieve gains from trade even if one of the countries has an absolute advantage in the production of all goods.'
- *b* 'Certain very talented people have a comparative advantage in everything they do.'
- *c* 'If a certain trade is good for one person, it can't be good for the other one.'

Search me!

Search me!

When accessing information about microeconomics use the following keywords in any combinations you require:

- absolute advantage
- comparative advantage

CourseMate

CourseMate

For more multimedia resources and activities on economics, visit the Economics CourseMate website.

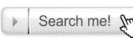

PART TWO

Supply and demand I: How markets work

4

The market forces of supply and demand

Learning objectives

In this chapter you will:

- learn what a competitive market is
- examine what determines the demand for a good in a competitive market
- examine what determines the supply of a good in a competitive market
- see how supply and demand together set the price of a good and the quantity sold
- consider the key role of prices in allocating scarce resources in market economies.

When a cyclone hits Queensland, the price of bananas rises in supermarkets throughout the country. On Tuesdays, movie theatres discount tickets. When a war breaks out in the Middle East, the price of petrol in Australia and elsewhere rises, and the price of a used Ford Falcon falls. What do these events have in common? They all show the workings of supply and demand.

Supply and *demand* are the two words that economists use most often – and for good reason. Supply and demand are the forces that make market economies work. They determine the quantity of each good produced and the price at which it is sold. If you want to know how any event or policy will affect the economy, you must think first about how it will affect supply and demand.

This chapter introduces the theory of supply and demand. It considers how buyers and sellers behave and how they interact with one another. It shows how supply and demand determine prices in a market economy and how prices, in turn, allocate the economy's scarce resources.

Markets and competition

The terms *supply* and *demand* refer to the behaviour of people as they interact with one another in competitive markets. Before discussing how buyers and sellers behave, let's first consider more fully what we mean by the terms *market* and *competition.*

What is a market?

A **market** is a group of buyers and sellers of a particular good or service. The buyers as a group determine the demand for the product and the sellers as a group determine the supply of the product. Before discussing how buyers and sellers behave, let's first consider more fully what we mean by the terms *market* and *competition.*

market
a group of buyers and sellers of a particular good or service

Markets take many forms. Sometimes markets are highly organised, such as the sharemarket or the market for some agricultural commodities, like the Sydney fish market. In these markets, buyers and sellers meet at a specific time and place, where an auctioneer helps set prices and arrange sales.

More often, markets are less organised. For example, consider the market for ice-cream in a particular town. Buyers of ice-cream do not meet together at any one time. The sellers of ice-cream are in different locations and offer somewhat different products. There is no auctioneer calling out the price of ice-cream. Each seller posts a price for an ice-cream and each buyer decides how much ice-cream to buy at each store. Nonetheless, these consumers and producers of ice-cream are closely connected. The ice-cream buyers are choosing from the various ice-cream sellers to satisfy their cravings and the ice-cream sellers are all trying to appeal to the same ice-cream buyers to make their businesses successful. Even though it is not as organised, the group of ice-cream buyers and ice-cream sellers forms a market.

What is competition?

The market for ice-cream, like most markets in the economy, is highly competitive. Each buyer knows that there are several sellers from which to choose. Each seller is aware that their product is similar to that offered by other sellers. As a result, the price of ice cream and the quantity of ice cream sold are not determined by any single buyer or seller. Rather, price and quantity are determined by all buyers and sellers as they interact in the marketplace.

Economists use the term **competitive market** to describe a market in which there are so many buyers and so many sellers that each has a negligible impact on the market price. Each seller has limited control over the price because other sellers are offering similar products. A seller has little

competitive market
a market in which there are many buyers and many sellers so that each has a negligible impact on the market price

reason to charge less than the going price and if more is charged then buyers will make their purchases elsewhere. Similarly, no single buyer of ice-cream can influence the price of ice-cream because each buyer purchases only a small amount.

In this chapter, we assume that markets are *perfectly competitive*. To reach this highest form of competition, a market must have two characteristics:

1 The goods offered for sale are all exactly the same.
2 The buyers and sellers are so numerous that no single buyer or seller has any influence over the market price.

Because buyers and sellers in a perfectly competitive market must accept the price the market determines, they are said to be *price takers*. At the market price, buyers can buy all they want and sellers can sell all they want.

There are some markets in which the assumption of perfect competition applies perfectly. In the international wheat market, for example, there are thousands of farmers who sell wheat and millions of consumers who use wheat and wheat products. Because no single buyer or seller can influence the price of wheat, each takes the price as given.

Not all goods and services, however, are sold in perfectly competitive markets. Some markets have only one seller and this seller sets the price. Such a seller is called a *monopoly*. Your local water company, for instance, may be a monopoly. Residents of your town probably have only one company from which to buy tap water. Still other markets fall between the extremes of perfect competition and monopoly.

Despite the diversity of market types we find in the world, assuming perfect competition is a useful simplification and, therefore, a natural place to start. Perfectly competitive markets are easier to analyse because everyone participating in the market takes the price as given by market conditions. Moreover, because some degree of competition is present in most markets, many of the lessons that we learn by studying supply and demand under perfect competition apply in more complicated markets as well.

Q

What is a market? What are the characteristics of a perfectly competitive market?

Demand

We begin our study of markets by examining the behaviour of buyers. To focus our thinking, let's keep in mind a particular good – ice-cream.

The demand curve: The relationship between price and quantity demanded

quantity demanded
the amount of a good that buyers are willing and able to purchase

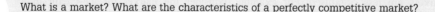

The **quantity demanded** of any good is the amount of the good that buyers are willing and able to purchase. As we will see, many things determine the quantity demanded of any good, but in our analysis of how markets work, one determinant plays a central role – the price of the good. If the price of ice-cream rose to \$20 per scoop, you would buy less ice-cream. You might buy frozen yoghurt instead. If the price of ice-cream fell to \$0.20 per scoop, you would buy more. Because the quantity demanded falls as the price rises and rises as the price falls, we say that the quantity demanded is *negatively related* to the price. This relationship between price and quantity demanded is true for most goods in the economy and, in fact, is so pervasive that economists call it the **law of demand.** Other things being equal, when the price of a good rises, the quantity demanded of the good falls and when the price falls, the quantity demanded rises.

law of demand
the claim that, other things being equal, the quantity demanded of a good falls when the price of the good rises

Table 4.1 shows how many ice-creams Catherine buys each month at different prices of ice-cream. If ice-creams are free, Catherine eats 12 ice-creams per month. At $0.50 each, Catherine buys

Table 4.1 Catherine's demand schedule

Price of an ice-cream	Quantity of ice-creams demanded
$0.00	12
0.50	10
1.00	8
1.50	6
2.00	4
2.50	2
3.00	0

Figure 4.1 Catherine's demand curve

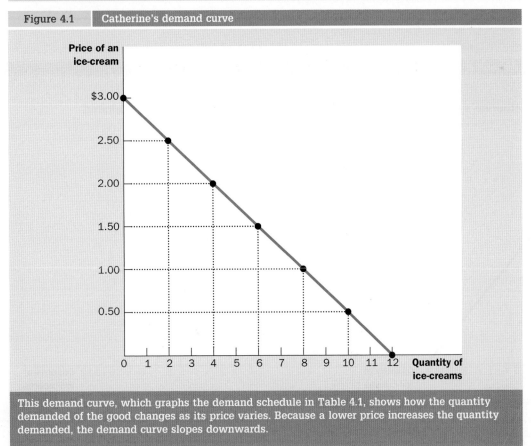

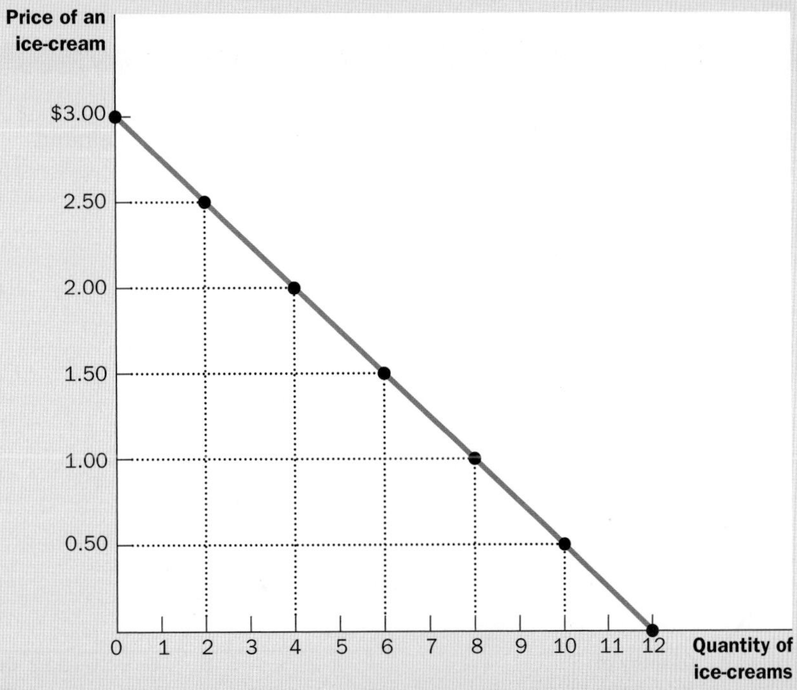

This demand curve, which graphs the demand schedule in Table 4.1, shows how the quantity demanded of the good changes as its price varies. Because a lower price increases the quantity demanded, the demand curve slopes downwards.

demand schedule
a table that shows the relationship between the price of a good and the quantity demanded

demand curve
a graph of the relationship between the price of a good and the quantity demanded

10 ice-creams per month. As the price rises further, she buys fewer and fewer ice-creams. When the price reaches $3.00, Catherine doesn't buy any ice-cream at all. Table 4.1 is a **demand schedule,** a table that shows the relationship between the price of a good and the quantity demanded, holding constant everything else that influences how much of the good consumers want to buy.

The graph in Figure 4.1 uses the numbers from the table to illustrate the law of demand. By convention, the price of ice-cream is on the vertical axis and the quantity of ice-cream demanded is on the horizontal axis. The downward-sloping line relating price and quantity demanded is called the **demand curve.**

Table 4.2 Individual and market demand schedules

Price of an ice-cream	Catherine		Nicholas		Market
$0.00	12	+	7	=	19
0.50	10		6		16
1.00	8		5		13
1.50	6		4		10
2.00	4		3		7
2.50	2		2		4
3.00	0		1		1

Figure 4.2 Market demand as the sum of individual demands

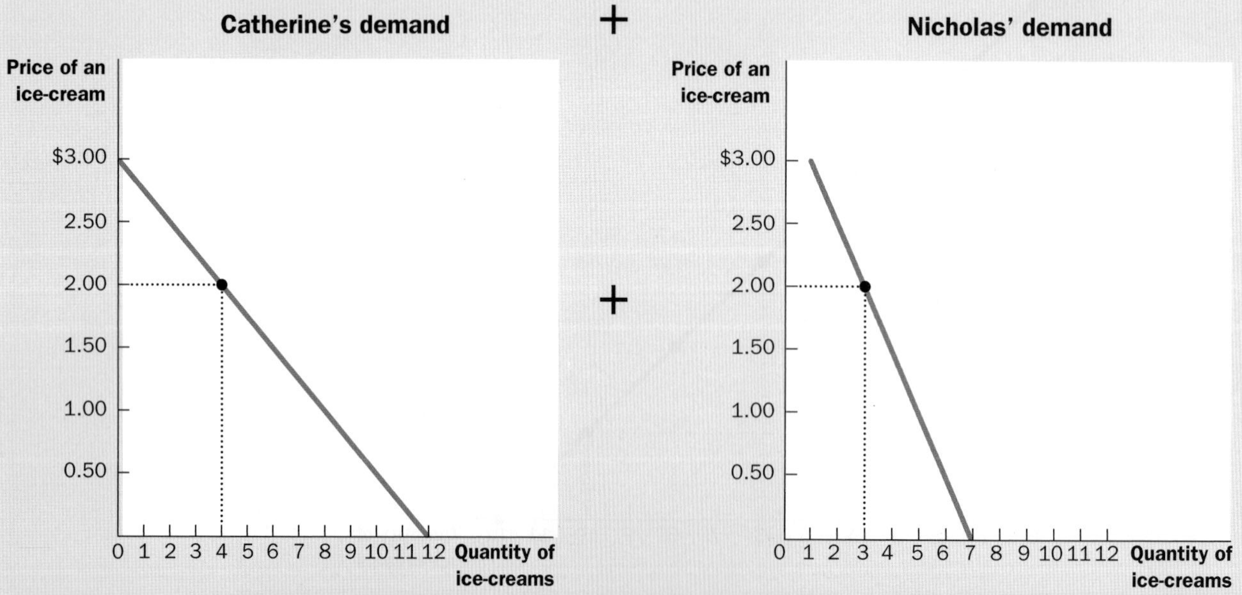

The market demand curve is found by adding horizontally the individual demand curves. At a price of $2, Catherine demands four ice-creams, and Nicholas demands three ice-creams. The quantity demanded in the market at this price is seven ice-creams.

Market demand versus individual demand

The demand curve in Figure 4.1 shows an individual's demand for a product. To analyse how markets work, we need to determine the *market demand*, which is the sum of all the individual demands for a particular good or service.

The table in Figure 4.2 shows the demand schedules for ice-cream of two people – Catherine and Nicholas. At any price, Catherine's demand schedule tells us how much ice-cream she buys, and Nicholas's demand schedule tells us how much ice-cream he buys. The market demand is the sum of the two individual demands.

The graph in Figure 4.2 shows the demand curves that correspond to these demand schedules. Notice that we add the individual demand curves *horizontally* to obtain the market demand curve. That is, to find the total quantity demanded at any price, we add the individual quantities found on the horizontal axis of the individual demand curves. Because we are interested in analysing how markets work, we will work most often with the market demand curve. The market demand curve shows how the total quantity demanded of a good varies as the price of the good varies, while all other factors that affect how much consumers want to buy are held constant.

Shifts in the demand curve

Because the market demand curve holds other things constant, it need not be stable over time. If something happens to alter the quantity demanded at any given price, the demand curve shifts. For example, suppose that medical researchers suddenly announce a new discovery – people who regularly

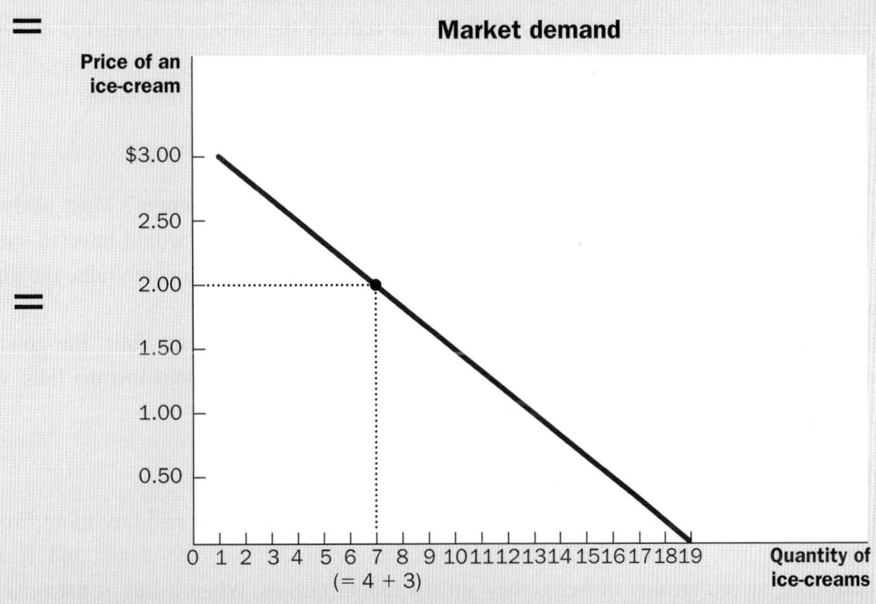

Figure 4.3 Shifts in the demand curve

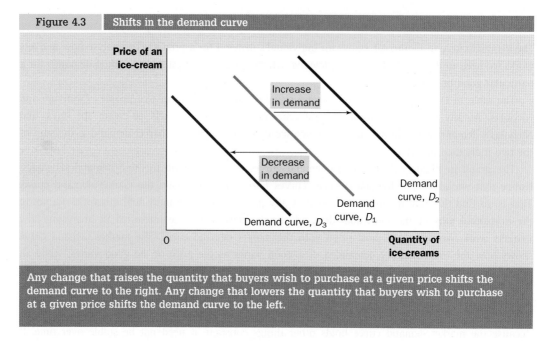

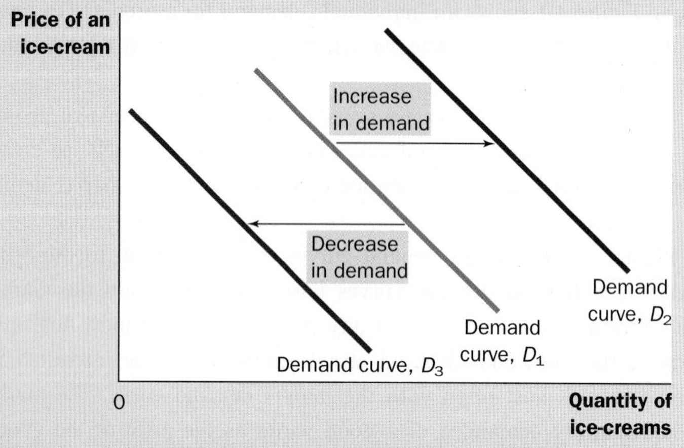

Any change that raises the quantity that buyers wish to purchase at a given price shifts the demand curve to the right. Any change that lowers the quantity that buyers wish to purchase at a given price shifts the demand curve to the left.

eat ice-cream live longer, healthier lives. The discovery would raise the demand for ice-cream. At any given price, buyers would now want to purchase a larger quantity of ice-cream and the demand curve for ice-cream would shift.

Figure 4.3 illustrates shifts in demand. Any change that increases the quantity demanded at any given price, such as our imaginary discovery by medical researchers, shifts the demand curve to the right and is called *an increase in demand.* Any change that reduces the quantity demanded at every price shifts the demand curve to the left and is called *a decrease in demand.*

There are many variables that can shift the demand curve. Here are the most important:

Income

What would happen to your demand for ice-cream if you lost your job one summer? Most likely, it would fall. A lower income means that you have less to spend in total, so you would have to spend less on some – and probably most – goods. If the demand for a good falls when income falls, the good is called a **normal good.**

normal good
a good for which, other things being equal, an increase in income leads to an increase in quantity demanded

Not all goods are normal goods. If the demand for a good rises when income falls, the good is called an **inferior good**. An example of an inferior good might be bus rides. As your income falls, you are less likely to buy a car or take a taxi and more likely to take the bus.

inferior good
a good for which, other things being equal, an increase in income leads to a decrease in quantity demanded

Prices of related goods

Suppose that the price of frozen yoghurt falls. The law of demand says that you will buy more frozen yoghurt. At the same time, you will probably buy less ice-cream. Because ice-cream and frozen yoghurt are both cold, sweet, creamy desserts, they satisfy similar desires. When a fall in the price of one good reduces the demand for another good, the two goods are called **substitutes**. Substitutes are often pairs of goods that are used in place of each other, like hot dogs and hamburgers, butter and margarine, and movie tickets and DVD rentals.

substitutes
two goods for which a decrease in the price of one good leads to a decrease in the demand for the other good

Now suppose that the price of chocolate topping falls. According to the law of demand, you will buy more chocolate topping. Yet, in this case, you will buy more ice-cream as well, since ice-cream and topping are often used together. When a fall in the price of one good raises the demand for another good, the two goods are called **complements**. Complements are often pairs of goods that are used together, such as petrol and cars, computers and software, and skis and ski-lift tickets.

complements
two goods for which a decrease in the price of one good leads to an increase in the demand for the other good

Tastes

The most obvious determinant of your demand is your tastes. If you like ice-cream, you buy more of it. Economists normally do not try to explain people's tastes because tastes are based on historical and psychological forces that are beyond the realm of economics. Economists do, however, examine what happens when tastes change.

Expectations

Your expectations about the future may affect your demand for a good or service today. If you expect to earn a higher income next month, you may choose to save less now and spend more of your current income buying ice-cream. If you expect the price of ice-cream to fall tomorrow, you may be less willing to buy an ice-cream at today's price.

Number of buyers

In addition to the preceding factors, which influence the behaviour of individual buyers, market demand depends on the number of these buyers. If Peter, another consumer of ice-cream, were to join Catherine and Nicholas, the quantity demanded in the market would be higher at every price and the demand curve would shift to the right.

Summary

The demand curve shows what happens to the quantity demanded of a good when its price varies, holding constant all the other variables that influence buyers. When one of these other variables changes, the demand curve shifts. Table 4.3 lists all the variables that influence how much consumers choose to buy of a good.

Table 4.3 Variables that influence buyers

Variables that affect quantity demanded	A change in this variable ...
Price	Represents a movement along the demand curve
Income	Shifts the demand curve
Prices of related goods	Shifts the demand curve
Tastes	Shifts the demand curve
Expectations	Shifts the demand curve
Number of buyers	Shifts the demand curve

fyi — *Ceteris paribus*

Whenever you see a demand curve, remember that it is drawn holding many things fixed. Catherine's demand curve in Figure 4.1 shows what happens to the quantity of ice-cream Catherine wants to buy when only the price of ice-cream varies. The curve is drawn assuming that Catherine's income, tastes, expectations and the prices of related products are not changing.

Economists use the term *ceteris paribus* to signify that all the relevant variables, except those being studied at that moment, are held constant. This Latin phrase means 'other things being equal'. The demand curve slopes downwards because, *ceteris paribus*, lower prices mean a greater quantity demanded.

Although the term *ceteris paribus* refers to a hypothetical situation in which some variables are assumed to be constant, in the real world many things change at the same time. For this reason, when we use the tools of supply and demand to analyse events or policies, it is important to keep in mind what is being held fixed and what is not.

ceteris paribus
a Latin phrase, translated as 'other things being equal', used as a reminder that all variables other than the ones being studied are assumed to be constant

CASESTUDY

Two ways to reduce the quantity of smoking demanded

Public policymakers often want to reduce the amount that people smoke because of smoking's adverse health effects. There are two ways that policy can attempt to achieve this goal.

One way to reduce smoking is to shift the demand curve for cigarettes and other tobacco products. Public service announcements, mandatory health warnings on cigarette packets and the prohibition of cigarette advertising on television are all policies aimed at reducing the quantity of cigarettes demanded at any given price. If successful, these policies shift the demand curve for cigarettes to the left, as in panel (a) of figure 4.4.

Alternatively, policymakers can try to raise the price of cigarettes. If the government taxes the manufacture of cigarettes, for example, cigarette companies pass much of this tax on to consumers in the form of higher prices. A higher price encourages smokers to reduce the amount of cigarettes they smoke. In this case, the reduced amount of smoking does not represent a shift in the demand curve. Instead, it represents a movement along the same demand curve to a point with a higher price and lower quantity, as in panel (b) of figure 4.4.

How much does the amount of smoking respond to changes in the price of cigarettes? Economists have attempted to answer this question by studying what happens when the tax on cigarettes changes. They have found that a 10 per cent increase in the price causes a 4 per cent reduction in the quantity demanded. Teenagers are found to be especially sensitive to the price of cigarettes – a 10 per cent increase in the price causes a 12 per cent drop in teenage smoking.

A related question is how the price of cigarettes affects the demand for illicit drugs, such as marijuana. Opponents of cigarette taxes often argue that tobacco and marijuana are substitutes, so that high cigarette prices encourage marijuana use. By contrast, many experts on substance abuse view tobacco as a 'gateway drug' leading the young to experiment with other harmful substances. Most studies of the data are consistent with this view – they find that higher cigarette prices are associated with reduced use of marijuana. In other words, tobacco and marijuana appear to be complements rather than substitutes.

What is the best way to stop this?

Source: photos.com/Getty Images.

Figure 4.4 **Shifts in the demand curve versus movements along the demand curve**

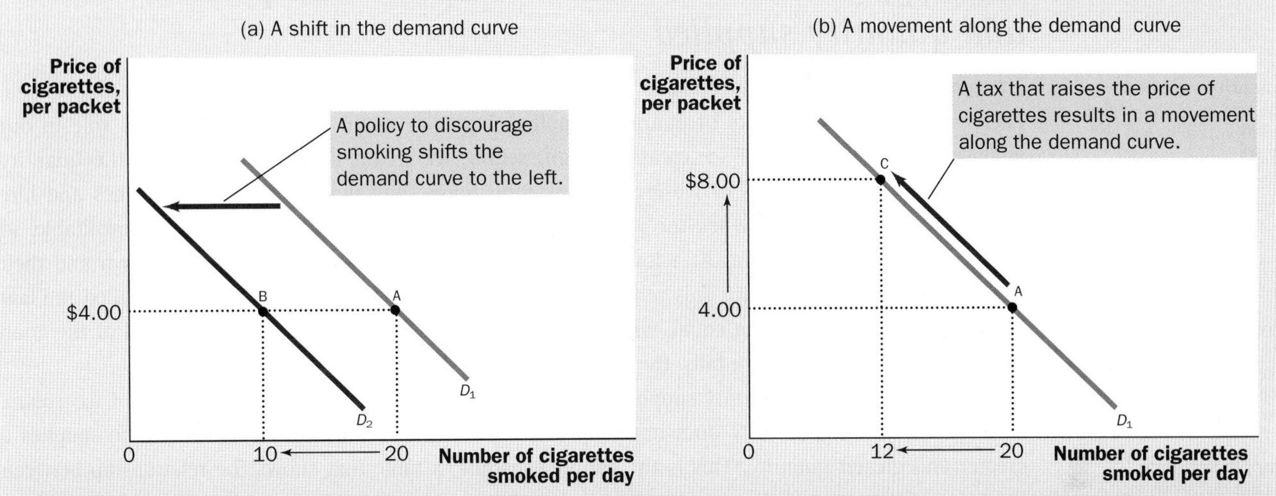

If warnings on cigarette packets convince smokers to smoke less, the demand curve for cigarettes shifts to the left. In panel (a), the demand curve shifts from D_1 to D_2. At a price of $4 per packet, the quantity demanded falls from 20 to 10 cigarettes per day, as reflected by the shift from point A to point B. In contrast, if a tax raises the price of cigarettes, the demand curve does not shift. Instead, we observe a movement to a different point on the demand curve. In panel (b), when the price rises from $4 to $8, the quantity demanded falls from 20 to 12 cigarettes per day, as reflected by the movement from point A to point C.

Q

List the determinants of the demand for pizza. Give an example of a demand schedule for pizza, and graph the implied demand curve. Give an example of something that would shift this demand curve. Would a change in the price of pizza shift this demand curve?

Notice the special role that the price of the good plays: A change in the good's price represents a movement along the demand curve, whereas a change in one of the other variables shifts the demand curve.

If you have trouble remembering whether you need to shift or move along the demand curve, it helps to recall a lesson from the appendix to chapter 2. A curve shifts when there is a change in a relevant variable that is not measured on either axis. Because the price is on the vertical axis, a change in price represents a movement along the demand curve. By contrast, income, the prices of related goods, tastes, expectations and the number of buyers are not measured on either axis, so a change in one of these variables shifts the demand curve.

Supply

We now turn to the other side of the market and examine the behaviour of sellers. Once again, to focus our thinking, let's consider the market for ice-cream.

The supply curve: The relationship between price and quantity supplied

quantity supplied
the amount of a good that sellers are willing and able to sell

law of supply
the claim that, other things being equal, the quantity supplied of a good rises when the price of the good rises

supply schedule
a table that shows the relationship between the price of a good and the quantity supplied

supply curve
a graph of the relationship between the price of a good and the quantity supplied

The **quantity supplied** of any good or service is the amount that sellers are willing and able to sell. There are many determinants of quantity supplied, but once again price plays a special role in our analysis. When the price of ice-cream is high, selling ice-cream is profitable and so the quantity supplied is large. The sellers of ice-cream work long hours, buy many ice-cream machines and hire many workers. In contrast, when the price of ice-cream is low, selling ice-cream is less profitable, so sellers produce less ice-cream. At a low price, some sellers may even choose to shut down and their quantity supplied falls to zero. This relationship between price and quantity supplied is called the **law of supply** – other things being equal, when the price of a good rises, the quantity supplied of the good also rises, and when the price falls, the quantity supplied falls as well.

Table 4.4 shows the quantity supplied by Tony, an ice-cream seller, at various prices of ice-cream. At a price below $1.00, Tony does not supply any ice-cream at all. As the price rises, he supplies a greater and greater quantity. This is the **supply schedule**, a table that shows the relationship between the price of a good and the quantity supplied, holding constant everything else that influences how much producers of the good want to sell.

The graph in Figure 4.5 uses the numbers from the table to illustrate the law of supply. The curve relating price and quantity supplied is called the **supply curve**. The supply curve slopes upwards because, other things being equal, a higher price means a greater quantity supplied.

Table 4.4 Tony's supply schedule

Price of an ice-cream ($)	Quantity of ice-creams supplied
0.00	0
0.50	0
1.00	1
1.50	2
2.00	3
2.50	4
3.00	5

Figure 4.5 Tony's supply curve

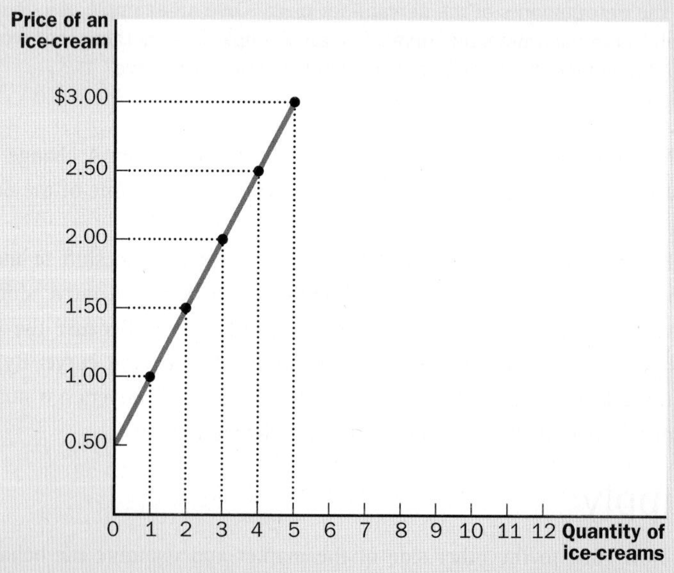

This supply curve, which graphs the supply schedule in Table 4.4, shows how the quantity supplied of the good changes as its price varies. Because a higher price increases the quantity supplied, the supply curve slopes upwards.

Market supply versus individual supply

Just as market demand is the sum of the demands of all buyers, market supply is the sum of the supplies of all sellers. Table 4.5 shows the supply schedules for two ice-cream producers – Tony and Sonia. At any price, Tony's supply schedule tells us how much ice-cream Tony supplies, and Sonia's supply schedule tells us how much ice-cream Sonia supplies. The market supply is the sum of the two individual supplies.

The graph in Figure 4.6 shows the supply curves that correspond to the supply schedules. As with demand curves, we add the individual supply curves *horizontally* to obtain the market supply curve. That is, to find the total quantity supplied at any price, we add the individual quantities found on the horizontal axis of the individual supply curves. The market supply curve shows how the total quantity supplied varies as the price of the good varies, holding constant all the other factors beyond price that influence producers' decisions about how much to sell.

Shifts in the supply curve

Because the market supply curve holds other things constant, the curve shifts when one of these other factors changes. For example, suppose that the price of sugar falls. Because sugar is an input into producing ice-cream, the fall in the price of sugar makes selling ice-cream more profitable. This raises the supply of ice-cream; at any given price sellers are now willing to produce a larger quantity. Thus, the supply curve for ice-cream shifts to the right.

Figure 4.7 illustrates shifts in supply. Any change that raises quantity supplied at every price, such as a fall in the price of sugar, shifts the supply curve to the right and is called *an increase in supply.* Similarly, any change that reduces the quantity supplied at every price shifts the supply curve to the left and is called *a decrease in supply.*

There are many variables that can shift the supply curve. Here are some of the most important:

Input prices

To produce their output of ice-cream, sellers use various inputs – cream, sugar, flavouring, ice-cream machines, the buildings in which the ice-cream is made, and the labour of workers to mix the ingredients and operate the machines. When the price of one or more of these inputs rises, producing ice-cream is less profitable and sellers supply less ice-cream. If input prices rise substantially, some sellers might shut down and supply no ice-cream at all. Thus, the quantity supplied of a good is negatively related to the price of the inputs used to make the good.

Technology

The technology for turning the inputs into ice-cream is yet another determinant of the quantity supplied. The invention of the mechanised ice-cream machine, for example, reduced the amount of labour necessary to make ice-cream. By reducing sellers' costs, the advance in technology raised the quantity of ice-cream supplied.

Expectations

The quantity of ice-cream a seller supplies today may depend on its expectations about the future. For example, if a seller expects the price of ice-cream to rise in the future, it may put some of its current production into storage and supply less to the market today.

Number of sellers

In addition to the preceding factors, which influence the behaviour of individual sellers, market supply depends on the number of sellers. If Tony or Sonia were to retire from the ice-cream business, the supply in the market would fall.

Table 4.5 Individual and market supply schedule

Price of an ice-cream	Tony		Sonia		Market
$0.00	0	+	0	=	0
0.50	0		0		0
1.00	1		0		1
1.50	2		2		4
2.00	3		4		7
2.50	4		6		10
3.00	5		8		13

Figure 4.6 Market supply as the sum of individual supplies

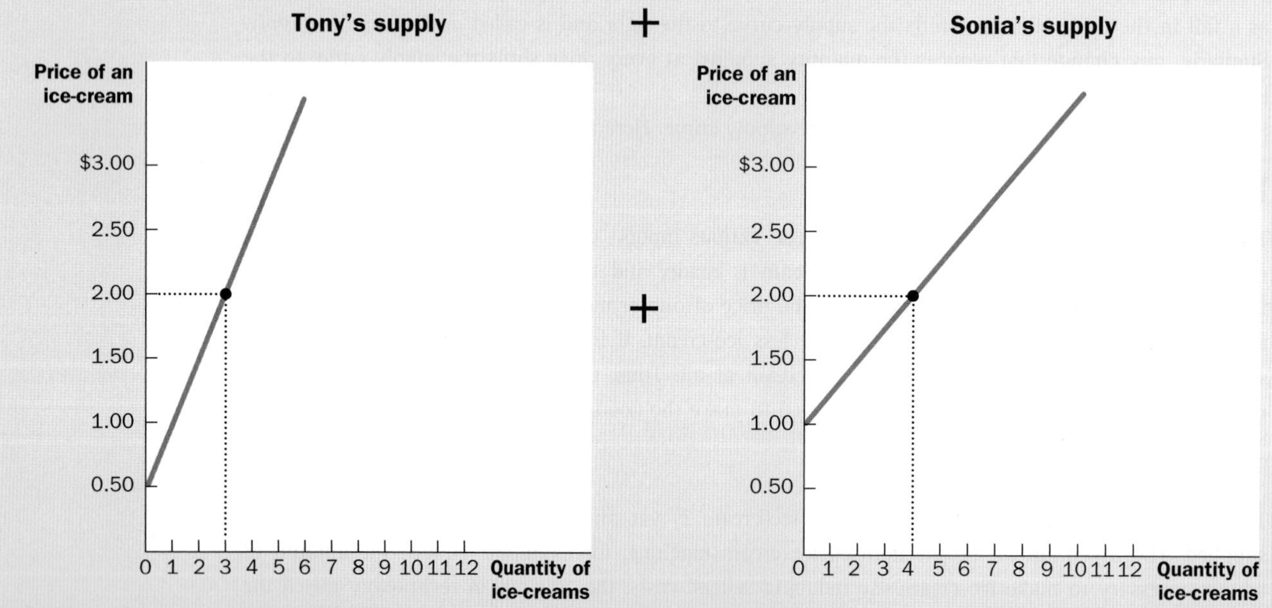

The market supply curve is found by adding horizontally the individual supply curves. At a price of $2, Tony supplies three ice-creams and Sonia supplies four ice-creams. The quantity supplied in the market at this price is seven ice-creams.

Summary

The supply curve shows what happens to the quantity supplied of a good when its price varies, holding constant all the other variables that influence sellers. When one of these other variables changes, the supply curve shifts.

Table 4.6 lists the variables that affect how much producers choose to sell of any good. Again, notice the special role that the price of the good plays – a change in the good's price represents a movement along the supply curve, whereas a change in one of the other variables shifts the supply curve.

Q

List the determinants of the supply of pizza. Give an example of a supply schedule for pizza, and graph the implied supply curve. Give an example of something that would shift this supply curve. Would a change in the price of pizza shift this supply curve?

Supply and demand together

Having analysed supply and demand separately, we now combine them to see how they determine the quantity of a good sold in a market and its price.

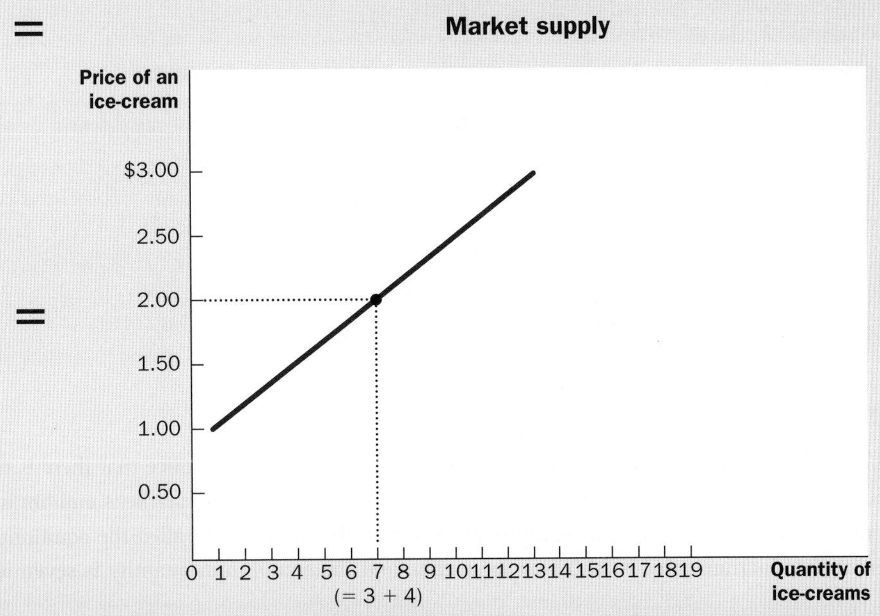

Figure 4.7 Shifts in the supply curve

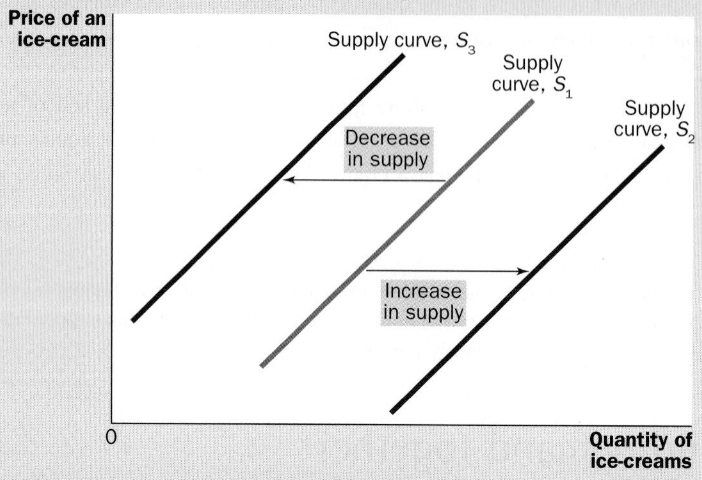

Any change that raises the quantity that sellers wish to produce at a given price shifts the supply curve to the right. Any change that lowers the quantity that sellers wish to produce at a given price shifts the supply curve to the left.

Table 4.6 Variables that influence sellers

Variables that affect quantity supplied	A change in this variable …
Price	Represents a movement along the supply curve
Input prices	Shifts the supply curve
Technology	Shifts the supply curve
Expectations	Shifts the supply curve
Number of sellers	Shifts the supply curve

Equilibrium

Figure 4.8 shows the market supply curve and market demand curve together. Notice that there is one point at which the supply and demand curves intersect. This point is called the market's **equilibrium**. The price at this intersection is called the **equilibrium price** and the quantity is called the **equilibrium quantity**. Here the equilibrium price is $2.00 per ice-cream, and the equilibrium quantity is seven ice-creams.

equilibrium a situation in which supply and demand have been brought into balance

equilibrium price the price that balances supply and demand

equilibrium quantity the quantity supplied and the quantity demanded when the price has adjusted to balance supply and demand

Equilibrium is defined by the dictionary as a situation in which various forces are in balance – and this also describes a market's equilibrium. *At the equilibrium price, the quantity of the good that buyers are willing and able to buy exactly balances the quantity that sellers are willing and able to sell.* The equilibrium price is sometimes called the market-clearing price because, at this price, everyone in the market has been satisfied – buyers have bought all they want to buy, and sellers have sold all they want to sell.

Figure 4.8 The equilibrium of supply and demand

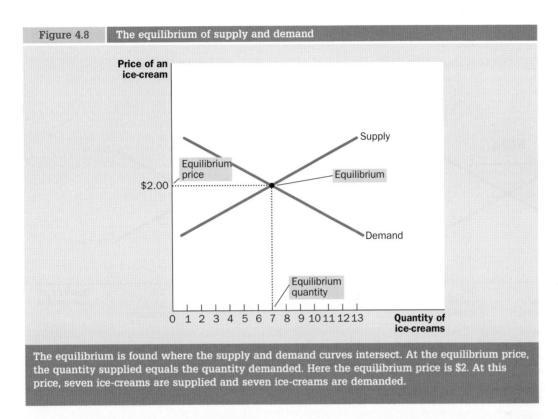

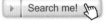

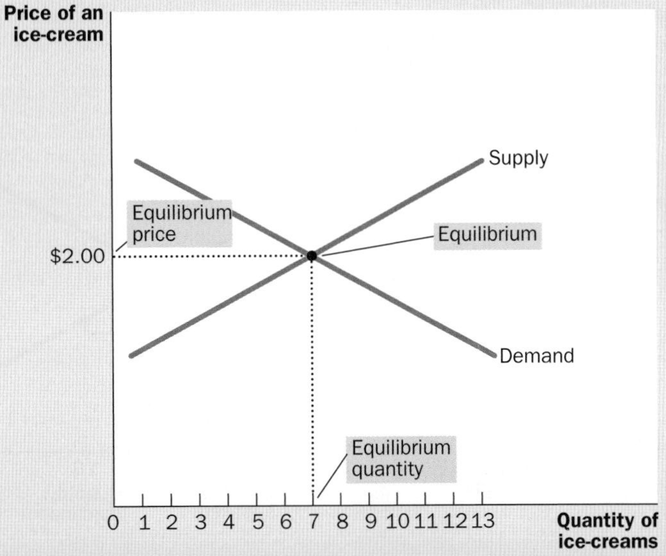

The equilibrium is found where the supply and demand curves intersect. At the equilibrium price, the quantity supplied equals the quantity demanded. Here the equilibrium price is $2. At this price, seven ice-creams are supplied and seven ice-creams are demanded.

The actions of buyers and sellers naturally move markets towards the equilibrium of supply and demand. To see why, consider what happens when the market price is not equal to the equilibrium price.

Suppose first that the market price is above the equilibrium price, as in panel (a) of Figure 4.9. At a price of $2.50 per ice-cream, the quantity of the good supplied (10 ice-creams) exceeds the quantity demanded (four ice-creams). There is a **surplus** of the good – suppliers are unable to sell all they want at the going price. A surplus is sometimes called a situation of *excess supply*. When there is a surplus in the ice-cream market, for instance, sellers of ice-cream find their freezers increasingly full of ice-cream they would like to sell but cannot. They respond to the excess supply by cutting their prices. Falling prices, in turn, increase the quantity demanded and decrease the quantity supplied. These changes represent movements *along* the supply and demand curves (not shifts in the curves). Prices continue to fall until the market reaches the equilibrium.

surplus
a situation in which quantity supplied is greater than quantity demanded

Suppose now that the market price is below the equilibrium price, as in panel (b) of Figure 4.9. In this case, the price is $1.50 per ice-cream and the quantity of the good demanded exceeds the quantity supplied. There is a **shortage** of the good – demanders are unable to buy all they want at the going price. A shortage is sometimes called a situation of *excess demand*. When a shortage occurs in the ice-cream market, buyers have to wait in long lines for a chance to buy the few ice-creams that are available. With too many buyers chasing too few goods, sellers can respond to excess demand by raising their prices without losing sales. These price increases cause the quantity demanded to fall and the quantity supplied to rise. Once again, these changes represent movements *along* the supply and demand curves and they move the market towards the equilibrium.

Search me!
▸ equilibrium price

shortage
a situation in which quantity demanded is greater than quantity supplied

Figure 4.9 **Markets not in equilibrium**

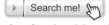

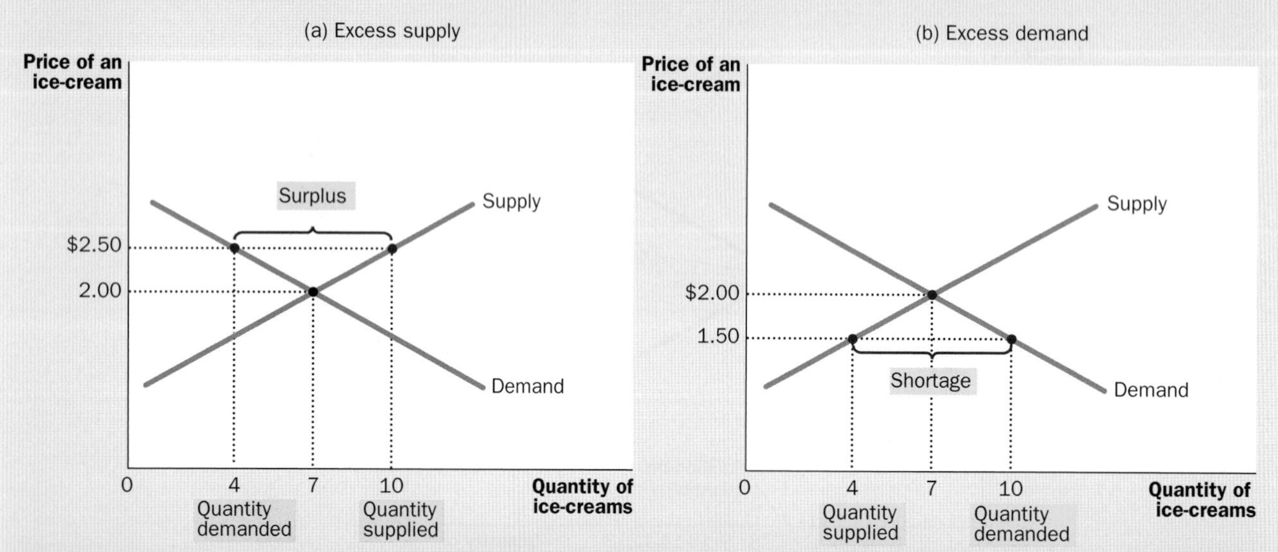

In panel (a), there is excess supply. Because the market price of $2.50 is above the equilibrium price, the quantity supplied (10 ice-creams) exceeds the quantity demanded (four ice-creams). Suppliers try to increase sales by cutting the price of an ice-cream and this moves the price towards its equilibrium level. In panel (b), there is excess demand. Because the market price of $1.50 is below the equilibrium price, the quantity demanded (10 ice-creams) exceeds the quantity supplied (four ice-creams). Because too many buyers are chasing too few goods, suppliers can take advantage of the shortage by raising the price. Hence, in both cases, the price adjustment moves the market towards the equilibrium of supply and demand.

Thus, regardless of whether the price starts off too high or too low, the activities of the many buyers and sellers automatically push the market price towards the equilibrium price. Once the market reaches its equilibrium, all buyers and sellers are satisfied and there is no upward or downward pressure on the price. How quickly equilibrium is reached varies from market to market, depending on how quickly prices adjust. In most free markets, however, surpluses and shortages are only temporary because prices eventually move towards their equilibrium levels. Indeed, this phenomenon is so pervasive that it is sometimes called the **law of supply and demand** – the price of any good adjusts to bring the supply and demand for that good into balance.

law of supply and demand
the claim that the price of any good adjusts to bring the supply and demand for that good into balance

Three steps for analysing changes in equilibrium

So far we have seen how supply and demand together determine a market's equilibrium, which in turn determines the price of the good and the amount of the good that buyers purchase and sellers produce. The equilibrium price and quantity depend on the position of the supply and demand curves. When some event shifts one of these curves, the equilibrium in the market changes, resulting in a new price and a new quantity exchanged between buyers and sellers. The analysis of such a change is called *comparative statics* because it involves comparing an old equilibrium and a new equilibrium.

Search me!
▸ law of supply and demand

When analysing how some event affects a market, we proceed in three steps. First, we decide whether the event shifts the supply curve, the demand curve or, in some cases, both curves. Second, we decide whether the curve shifts to the right or to the left. Third, we use the supply-and-demand

Table 4.7 A three-step program for doing comparative statics
1 Decide whether the event shifts the supply or demand curve (or perhaps both).
2 Decide in which direction the curve shifts.
3 Use the supply-and-demand diagram to see how the shift changes the equilibrium.

diagram to compare the initial and the new equilibrium, which shows how the shift affects the equilibrium price and quantity. Table 4.7 summarises these three steps. To see how this recipe is used, let's consider various events that might affect the market for ice-cream.

Example: A change in market equilibrium due to a shift in demand

Suppose that one summer the weather is very hot. How does this event affect the market for ice-cream? To answer this question, let's follow our three steps.

1 The hot weather affects the demand curve by changing people's taste for ice-cream. That is, the weather changes the amount of ice-cream that people want to buy at any given price. The supply curve is unchanged because the weather does not directly affect the firms that sell ice-cream.
2 Because hot weather makes people want to eat more ice-cream, the demand curve shifts to the right. Figure 4.10 shows this increase in demand as the shift in the demand curve from D_1 to D_2. This shift indicates that the quantity of ice-cream demanded is higher at every price.
3 At the old price of $2, there is now an excess demand for ice-cream and this shortage induces sellers to raise the price. As Figure 4.10 shows, the increase in demand raises the equilibrium price from $2.00 to $2.50 and the equilibrium quantity from seven to 10 ice-creams. In other words, the hot weather increases the price of ice-cream and the quantity of ice-cream sold.

Shifts in curves versus movements along curves

Notice that when hot weather drives up the price of ice-cream, the amount of ice-cream that firms supply rises, even though the supply curve remains the same. In this case, economists say there has been an increase in 'quantity supplied' but no change in 'supply'.

'Supply' refers to the position of the supply curve, whereas the 'quantity supplied' refers to the amount suppliers wish to sell. In this example, supply does not change because the weather does not alter firms' desire to sell at any given price. Instead, the hot weather alters consumers' desire to buy at any given price and thereby shifts the demand curve. The increase in demand causes the equilibrium price to rise. When the price rises, the quantity supplied rises. This increase in quantity supplied is represented by the movement along the supply curve.

To summarise, a shift *in* the supply curve is called a 'change in supply' and a shift *in* the demand curve is called a 'change in demand'. A movement *along* a fixed supply curve is called a 'change in the quantity supplied', and a movement *along* a fixed demand curve is called a 'change in the quantity demanded'.

Example: A change in supply

Suppose that, during another summer, a bushfire destroys several ice-cream factories. How does this event affect the market for ice-cream? Once again, to answer this question, we follow our three steps.

Figure 4.10 How an increase in demand affects the equilibrium

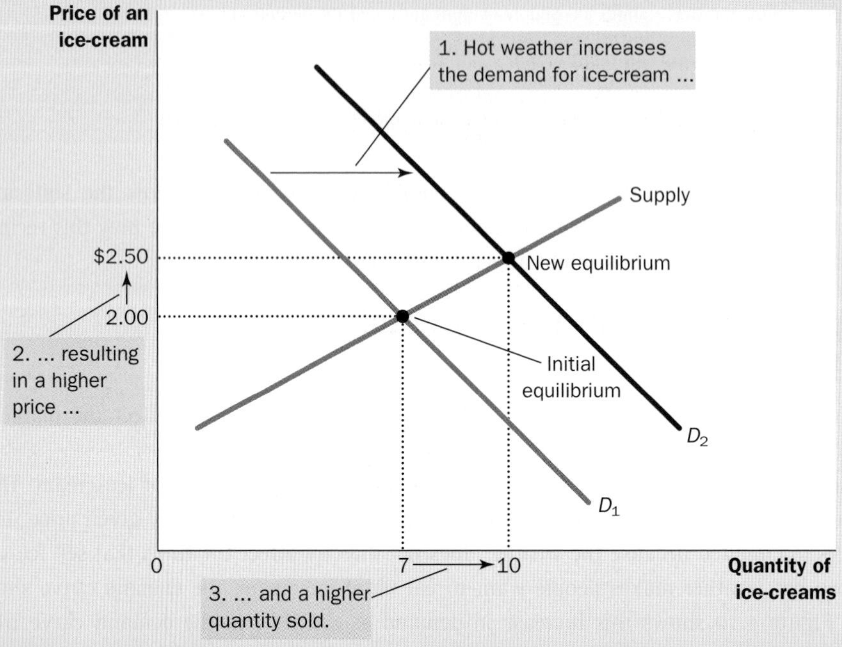

An event that raises quantity demanded at any given price shifts the demand curve to the right. The equilibrium price and the equilibrium quantity both rise. Here, an abnormally hot summer causes buyers to demand more ice-cream. The demand curve shifts from D_1 to D_2, which causes the equilibrium price to rise from $2.00 to $2.50 and the equilibrium quantity to rise from seven to 10 ice-creams.

1 The fire affects the supply curve. By reducing the number of sellers, the fire changes the amount of ice-cream that firms produce and sell at any given price. The demand curve is unchanged because the fire does not directly change the amount of ice-cream households wish to buy.
2 The supply curve shifts to the left because, at every price, the total amount that firms are willing and able to sell is reduced. Figure 4.11 illustrates this decrease in supply as a shift in the supply curve from S_1 to S_2.
3 At the old price of $2.00 there is now an excess demand for ice-cream. This shortage causes ice-cream sellers to raise the price. As Figure 4.11 shows, the shift in the supply curve raises the equilibrium price from $2.00 to $2.50 and lowers the equilibrium quantity from seven to four ice-creams. As a result of the fire, the price of ice-cream rises and the quantity of ice-cream sold falls.

Example: A change in both supply and demand

Now suppose that the hot weather and the fire occur at the same time. To analyse this combination of events, we again follow our three steps.

1 We determine that both curves must shift. The hot weather affects the demand curve because it alters the amount of ice-cream that households want to buy at any given price. At the same time, the fire alters the supply curve because it changes the amount of ice-cream that firms want to sell at any given price.

Figure 4.11 How a decrease in supply affects the equilibrium

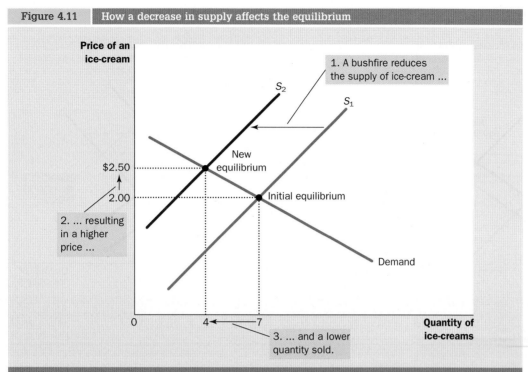

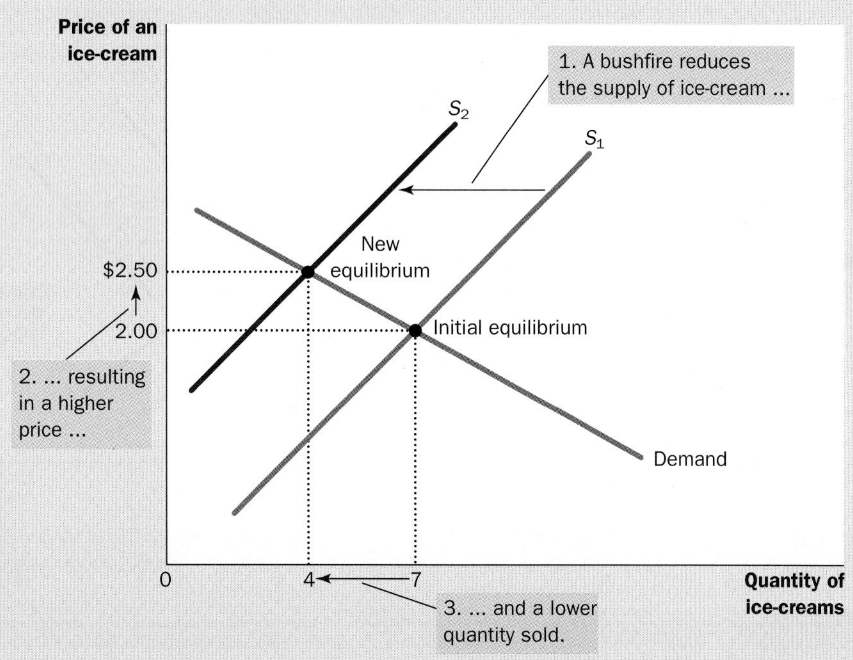

An event that reduces quantity supplied at a given price shifts the supply curve to the left. The equilibrium price rises, and the equilibrium quantity falls. Here, a bushfire causes sellers to supply less ice-cream. The supply curve shifts from S_1 to S_2, which causes the equilibrium price to rise from \$2.00 to \$2.50 and the equilibrium quantity to fall from seven to four ice-creams.

2 The curves shift in the same directions as they did in our previous analysis – the demand curve shifts to the right and the supply curve shifts to the left. Figure 4.12 illustrates these shifts.

3 As Figure 4.12 shows, there are two possible outcomes that might result, depending on the relative size of the demand and supply shifts. In both cases, the equilibrium price rises. In panel (a), where demand increases substantially and supply falls just a little, the equilibrium quantity also rises. In contrast, in panel (b), where supply falls substantially and demand rises just a little, the equilibrium quantity falls. Thus, these events certainly raise the price of ice-cream, but their impact on the amount of ice-cream sold is ambiguous.

Q

Analyse what happens to the market for pizza if the price of tomatoes rises. Analyse what happens to the market for pizza if the price of hamburgers falls.

Conclusion: How prices allocate resources

This chapter has analysed supply and demand in a single market. Although our discussion has centred around the market for ice-cream, the lessons learned here apply in most other markets as well. Whenever you go to a shop to buy something, you are contributing to the demand for that item.

Figure 4.12 **A shift in both supply and demand**

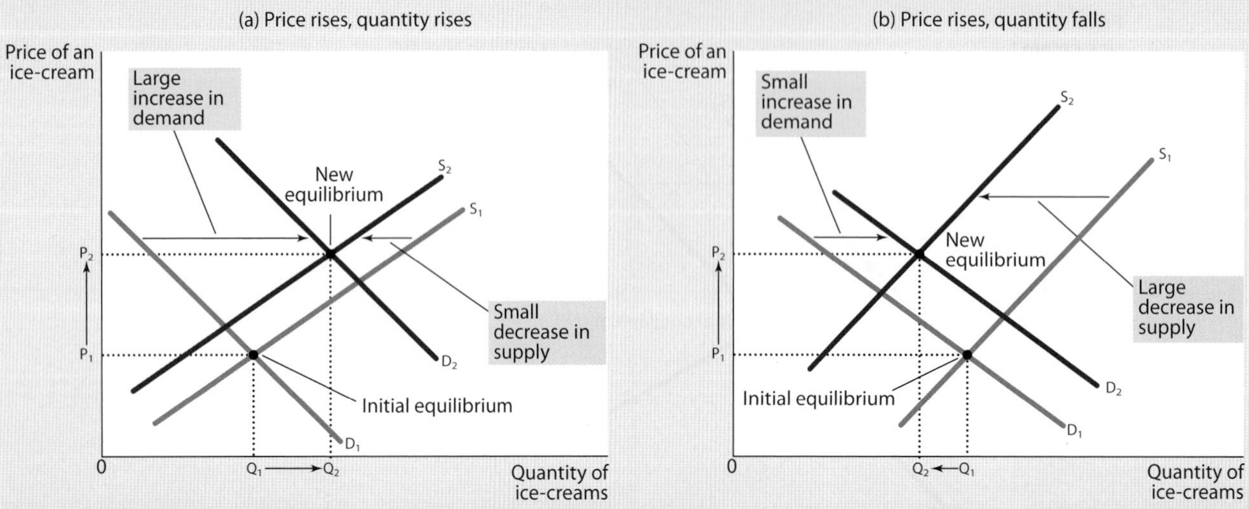

Here we observe a simultaneous increase in demand and decrease in supply. Two outcomes are possible. In panel (a), the equilibrium price rises from P_1 to P_2, and the equilibrium quantity rises from Q_1 to Q_2. In panel (b), the equilibrium price again rises from P_1 to P_2, but the equilibrium quantity falls from Q_1 to Q_2.

Whenever you look for a job, you are contributing to the supply of labour services. Because supply and demand are such pervasive economic phenomena, the model of supply and demand is a powerful tool for analysis. We will be using this model repeatedly in the following chapters.

One of the *Ten Lessons from Economics* discussed in chapter 1 is that markets are usually a good way to organise economic activity. Although it is still too early to judge whether market outcomes are good or bad, in this chapter we have begun to see how markets work. In any economic system, scarce resources have to be allocated among competing uses. Market economies harness the forces of supply and demand to serve that end. Supply and demand together determine the prices of the economy's many different goods and services; prices in turn are the signals that guide the allocation of resources.

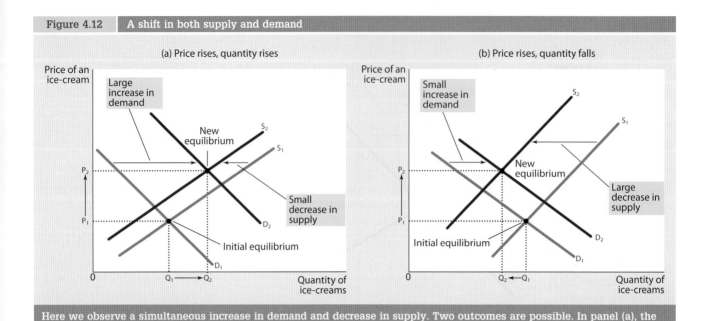

'Two dollars.' '– and seventy-five cents.'

Source: Day, J. Robert © Robert J. Day/The New Yorker Collection/www.cartoonbank.com.

For example, consider the allocation of beachfront land. Because the amount of this land is limited, not everyone can enjoy the luxury of living by the beach. Who gets this resource? The answer is: Whoever is willing to pay the price. The price of beachfront land adjusts until the quantity of land demanded exactly balances the quantity supplied. Thus, in market economies, prices are the mechanism for rationing scarce resources.

Similarly, prices determine who produces each good and how much is produced. For instance, consider farming. Because we need food to survive, it is crucial that some people work on farms. What determines who is a farmer and who is not? In a free society, there is no government planning agency making this decision and ensuring an adequate supply of food. Instead, the allocation of workers to farms is based on the job decisions of millions of workers. This decentralised system works well because these decisions depend on prices. The prices of food and the wages of farm workers (the price of their labour) adjust to ensure that enough people choose to be farmers.

If a person had never seen a market economy in action, the whole idea might seem preposterous. Economies are large groups of people engaged in many interdependent activities. What prevents decentralised decision making from degenerating into chaos? What coordinates the actions of the millions of people with their varying abilities and desires? What ensures that what needs to get done does, in fact, get done? The answer, in a word, is *prices*. If market economies are guided by an invisible hand, as Adam Smith famously suggested, then the price system is the baton that the invisible hand uses to conduct the economic orchestra.

IN THE NEWS . . .

MOTHER NATURE SHIFTS THE SUPPLY CURVE

In this chapter we have seen three examples of how to use supply and demand curves to analyse a change in equilibrium. Whenever an event shifts the supply curve, the demand curve, or perhaps both curves, you can use these tools to predict how the event will alter the price and quantity sold in equilibrium. This article provides another example of how a natural disaster that reduces supply reduces the quantity sold and raises the price.

Bananas to recover quickly

by Tony Koch

Banana prices, which have risen because of crop devastation caused by Cyclone Yasi, will not stay high for long because of lessons learned by progressive farmers when Cyclone Larry caused similar havoc in 2006.

The advance notice of Yasi to growers in the Tully and Innisfail areas allowed a frenzied few days of picking mature fruit and storing it in packing sheds, ensuring at least two weeks' supply.

As well, farmers deleafed young trees, leaving just the stems standing, and these were not knocked over by the cyclonic winds as were the mature trees.

Australian banana production is 286 000 tonnes a year, or about 25 million cartons, each with 13 kg of fruit.

Gross value of the produce is $500 million based on an average wholesale price of $20 a carton.

The industry is estimated to be worth more than $870m to the broader economy through the employment it provides and ancillary services. North Queensland has 12 000ha of plantations, producing about 85 per cent of Australia's crop.

More than 3000 people are employed directly in the banana industry in the cyclone-affected areas.

>>

The Australian Banana Growers Council reported last week that 95 per cent of the crop in Tully and Innisfail was lost, or about 10 200ha, as well as 10 per cent on the Atherton Tableland (1350ha) and 100 per cent at Cardwell (630ha). Council chief executive Jonathan Eccles said about 5 per cent of crops in the Innisfail-Tully area had been deleafed, which will mean those crops can be harvested four months or so earlier than crops that must be planted now.

'Banana supply from Innisfail and Tully will not be back to normal for at least six months, with full supply not expected before December 2011,' he said.

'As well as the deleafing helping some get back into production quicker, Cyclone Yasi affected crops differently from the way Larry did.

'This time the stems were broken off higher up, about a metre and a half, and that stem is being left to provide nourishment for the adjoining sucker.

'The third thing working for farmers is that Yasi has come at the end of January and Larry hit towards the end of March, so there is a difference of six or seven weeks of summer growing season available.

'If we get another warm winter like last year, the plants will also grow faster, so there are some positives to come from all this.'

Mr Eccles said there was a lot less damage to farm infrastructure this time.

The big winners in the supply and demand for bananas are the few growers with 308ha under production at Lakeland on the Atherton Tableland. They suffered no loss from Yasi.

Source: Tony Koch/*The Australian*, 21 Feb 2011.

Summary

- Economists use the model of supply and demand to analyse competitive markets. In a competitive market, there are many buyers and sellers, each of whom has little or no influence on the market price.
- The demand curve shows how the quantity of a good demanded depends on the price. According to the law of demand, as the price of a good falls, the quantity demanded rises. Therefore, the demand curve slopes downwards.
- In addition to price, other determinants of the quantity demanded include income, tastes, expectations, and the prices of substitutes and complements. If one of these other determinants changes, the demand curve shifts.
- The supply curve shows how the quantity of a good supplied depends on the price. According to the law of supply, as the price of a good rises, the quantity supplied rises. Therefore, the supply curve slopes upwards.
- In addition to price, other determinants of the quantity supplied include input prices, technology and expectations. If one of these other determinants changes, the supply curve shifts.
- The intersection of the supply and demand curves determines the market equilibrium. At the equilibrium price, the quantity demanded equals the quantity supplied.
- The behaviour of buyers and sellers naturally drives markets towards their equilibrium. When the market price is above the equilibrium price, there is excess supply, which causes the market price to fall. When the market price is below the equilibrium price, there is excess demand, which causes the market price to rise.
- To analyse how any event influences a market, we use the supply-and-demand diagram to examine how the event affects the equilibrium price and quantity. To do this we follow three steps. First, we decide whether the event shifts the supply curve or the demand curve. Second, we decide in which direction the curve shifts. Third, we compare the new equilibrium with the old equilibrium.
- In market economies, prices are the signals that guide economic decisions and thereby allocate scarce resources. For every good in the economy, the price ensures that supply and demand are in balance. The equilibrium price then determines how much of the good buyers choose to purchase and how much sellers choose to produce.

Key concepts

ceteris paribus
competitive market
complements
demand curve
demand schedule
equilibrium price
equilibrium quantity
equilibrium
inferior good
law of demand
law of supply and demand
law of supply
market
normal good
quantity demanded
quantity supplied
shortage
substitutes
supply curve
supply schedule
surplus

Questions for review

1 What is a competitive market?
2 What determines the quantity of a good that buyers demand?
3 What are the demand schedule and the demand curve, and how are they related?
4 Why does the demand curve slope downwards?
5 Does a change in consumers' tastes lead to a movement along the demand curve or a shift in the demand curve? Does a change in price lead to a movement along the demand curve or a shift in the demand curve?
6 What determines the quantity of a good that sellers supply?
7 What are the supply schedule and the supply curve, and how are they related?
8 Why does the supply curve slope upwards?
9 Does a change in producers' technology lead to a movement along the supply curve or a shift in the supply curve? Does a change in price lead to a movement along the supply curve or a shift in the supply curve?
10 Define the equilibrium of a market. Describe the forces that move a market towards its equilibrium.
11 Beer and pies are complements because they are often enjoyed together. When the price of beer rises, what happens to the supply, demand, quantity supplied, quantity demanded and the price in the market for pies?
12 Describe the role of prices in market economies.

Problems and applications

1 Explain each of the following statements using supply-and-demand diagrams.
   a When a cyclone hits Queensland, the price of bananas rises in supermarkets throughout the country.
   b On Tuesdays, picture theatres discount tickets.
   c When a war breaks out in the Middle East, the price of petrol rises and the price of a used Ford Falcon falls.
2 'An increase in the demand for notebooks raises the quantity of notebooks demanded, but not the quantity supplied.' Is this statement true or false? Explain.
3 Consider the market for station wagons. For each of the events listed here, identify which of the determinants of demand or supply are affected. Also indicate whether demand or supply is increased or decreased.
   a People decide to have more children.
   b A strike by steelworkers raises steel prices.
   c Engineers develop new automated machinery for the production of station wagons.
   d The price of mini-vans rises.
   e A stock market crash lowers people's wealth.
4 During the 1990s, technological advance reduced the cost of computer chips. How do you think this affected the market for computers? For computer software? For typewriters?
5 Using supply-and-demand diagrams, show the effect of the following events on the market for woollen jumpers:
   a an outbreak of 'foot-and-mouth' disease hits sheep farms in New Zealand
   b the price of leather jackets falls

c Lily Allen appears in a woollen jumper in her latest video
d new knitting machines are invented.

6 Suppose that in the year 2005 the number of births is temporarily high. How does this baby boom affect the price of baby-sitting services in 2010 and 2020? (*Hint:* five-year-olds need baby-sitters, whereas 15-year-olds can be baby-sitters.)

7 Tomato sauce is a complement (as well as a condiment) for hot dogs. If the price of hot dogs rises, what happens to the market for tomato sauce? For tomatoes? For tomato juice? For orange juice?

8 The case study presented in the chapter discussed cigarette taxes as a way to reduce smoking. Now think about the markets for other tobacco products such as cigars and pipe tobacco.
a Are these goods substitutes or complements for cigarettes?
b Using a supply-and-demand diagram, show what happens in the markets for cigars and pipe tobacco if the tax on cigarettes is increased.
c If policymakers wanted to reduce total tobacco consumption, what policies could they combine with the cigarette tax?

9 The market for pizza has the following demand and supply schedules:

Price ($)	Quantity demanded	Quantity supplied
4	135	26
5	104	53
6	81	81
7	68	98
8	53	110
9	39	121

Graph the demand and supply curves. What is the equilibrium price and quantity in this market? If the actual price in this market were above the equilibrium price, what would drive the market towards the equilibrium? If the actual price in this market were below the equilibrium price, what would drive the market towards the equilibrium?

10 In July 2010, vandals in North Queensland poisoned four million tomato seedlings by putting herbicide into the irrigation water. The seedlings were killed. These seedlings would have produced many of the tomatoes that were planned to be sold in Australia in October 2010.
a Using the tools of supply and demand, consider the effect of the poisoning of the tomato seedlings on the market for tomatoes in Australia in October 2010.
b Tomatoes are a major ingredient in salads. News reports suggested that the poisoning would lead to a 'salad surcharge' with restaurants raising the price of salads. Do you agree with this prediction? Why or why not?
c Lettuce is also an ingredient in salads. How will the poisoning of the tomato seedlings affect the price of lettuce and the quantity of lettuce sold? Does your answer depend on whether or not chefs can change the mix of lettuce and tomatoes in a salad?
d News reports suggested that the price of tomatoes would only rise in October. There would not be an effect in August. Do you think this is correct? Does your answer depend on whether or not tomatoes can be stored?

11 Suppose that the price of tickets at your local picture theatre is determined by market forces. Currently, the demand and supply schedules are as follows:

Price ($)	Quantity demanded	Quantity supplied
4	1000	800
8	800	800
12	600	800
16	400	800
20	200	800

a Draw the demand and supply curves. What is unusual about this supply curve? Why might this be true?

b What are the equilibrium price and quantity of tickets?

c Demographers tell you that next year there will be more film goers in the area.The additional people will have the following demand schedule:

Price ($)	Quantity demanded
4	400
8	300
12	200
16	100

Now add the old demand schedule and the demand schedule for the new people to calculate the new demand schedule for the entire area. What will be the new equilibrium price and quantity?

12 An article in *The New York Times* (18 October 1990) described a successful marketing campaign by the French champagne industry. The article also noted: 'Many executives felt giddy about the stratospheric champagne prices. But they also feared that such sharp price increases would cause demand to decline, which would then cause prices to plunge.' What mistake are the executives making in their analysis of the situation? Illustrate your answer with a graph.

13 (This question requires the use of secondary school algebra.) Market research has revealed the following information about the market for bars of chocolate – the demand schedule can be represented by the equation $Q_D = 1600 - 300P$, where Q_D is the quantity demanded and P is the price. The supply schedule can be represented by the equation $Q_S = 1400 + 700P$, where Q_S is the quantity supplied. Calculate the equilibrium price and quantity in the market for bars of chocolate.

Search me!

Search me!

When accessing information about microeconomics use the following keywords in any combinations you require:

- equilibrium price
- law of supply and demand

CourseMate

CourseMate

For more multimedia resources and activities on economics, visit the Economics CourseMate website.

5

Elasticity and its application

Learning objectives

In this chapter you will:

- learn the meaning of the elasticity of demand
- examine what determines the elasticity of demand
- learn the meaning of the elasticity of supply
- examine what determines the elasticity of supply
- apply the concept of elasticity in three very different markets.

Imagine that some event drives up the price of petrol in Australia. It could be a war in the Middle East that disrupts the world supply of oil, a booming Chinese economy that boosts the world demand for oil, or a new tax on petrol passed by parliament. How would Australian consumers respond to the higher price?

It is easy to answer this question in broad fashion: Consumers would buy less. That is simply the law of demand we learned in the previous chapter But you might want a precise answer. By how much would consumption of petrol fall? This question can be answered using a concept called *elasticity,* which we develop in this chapter.

Elasticity is a measure of how much buyers and sellers respond to changes in market conditions. When studying how some event or policy affects a market, we can discuss not only the direction of the effects but their magnitude as well. Elasticity is useful in many applications, as we see later in this chapter.

Before proceeding, however, you might be curious about the answer to the petrol question. Many studies have examined consumers' response to petrol prices in developed countries like Australia. They typically find that the quantity demanded responds more in the long run than it does in the short run. A 10 per cent increase in petrol prices reduces petrol consumption by about 2.5 per cent after a year and about 6 per cent after five years. About half of the long-run reduction in quantity demanded arises because people drive less and half arises because they switch to more fuel-efficient cars. Both responses are reflected in the demand curve for petrol and its elasticity.

The elasticity of demand

When we introduced demand in chapter 4, we noted that buyers usually demand more of a good when its price is lower, when their incomes are higher, when the prices of substitutes for the good are higher or when the prices of complements of the good are lower. Our discussion of demand was qualitative, not quantitative. That is, we discussed the direction in which quantity demanded moves, but not the size of the change. To measure how much demand responds to changes in its determinants, economists use the concept of **elasticity.**

elasticity
a measure of the responsiveness of quantity demanded or quantity supplied to one of its determinants

The price elasticity of demand and its determinants

The law of demand states that a fall in the price of a good raises the quantity demanded. The **price elasticity of demand** measures how much the quantity demanded responds to a change in price. Demand for a good is said to be elastic if the quantity demanded responds substantially to changes in the price. Demand is said to be inelastic if the quantity demanded responds only slightly to changes in the price.

price elasticity of demand
a measure of how much the quantity demanded of a good responds to a change in the price of that good, calculated as the percentage change in quantity demanded divided by the percentage change in price

The price elasticity of demand for any good measures how willing consumers are to buy less of the good as its price rises. Because the demand curve reflects the many economic, social and psychological forces that shape consumers' preferences, there is no simple, universal rule for what determines the demand curve's elasticity. Based on experience, however, we can state some general rules about what influences the price elasticity of demand.

Availability of close substitutes

Goods with close substitutes tend to have more elastic demand because it is easier for consumers to switch from that good to others. For example, butter and margarine are easily substitutable. A small increase in the price of butter, assuming the price of margarine is held fixed, causes the quantity of butter sold to fall by a large amount. In contrast, because eggs are a food without a close substitute, the demand for eggs is probably less elastic than the demand for butter.

Search me!
▸ price elasticity of demand

Necessities versus luxuries

Necessities tend to have inelastic demands, whereas goods that are luxuries have elastic demands. When the price of a visit to the doctor rises, people will not dramatically alter the number of times they go to the doctor, although they might go a little less often. In contrast, when the price of yachts rises, the quantity demanded falls substantially. The reason is that most people view visits to the doctor as a necessity and yachts as a luxury. Whether a good is a necessity or a luxury depends not on the intrinsic properties of the good but on the preferences of the buyer. For an avid sailor with few health concerns, a yacht might be a necessity with inelastic demand and visits to the doctor a luxury with elastic demand.

Definition of the market

The elasticity of demand in any market depends on how we draw the boundaries of the market. Narrowly defined markets tend to have more elastic demand than broadly defined markets, since it is easier to find close substitutes for narrowly defined goods. For example, food, a broad category, has a fairly inelastic demand because there are no good substitutes for food. Ice-cream, a more narrow category, has a more elastic demand because it is easy to substitute other desserts for ice-cream. Vanilla ice-cream, a very narrow category, has a very elastic demand because other flavours of ice-cream are almost perfect substitutes for vanilla.

Time horizon

Goods tend to have more elastic demand over longer time horizons. When the price of petrol rises, the quantity of petrol demanded falls only slightly in the first few months. Over time, however, people buy more fuel-efficient cars, switch to public transport or move closer to where they work. Within several years, the quantity of petrol demanded falls more substantially.

Computing the price elasticity of demand

Now that we have discussed the price elasticity of demand in general terms, let's be more precise about how it is measured. Economists calculate the price elasticity of demand as the percentage change in the quantity demanded divided by the percentage change in the price. That is:

$$\text{Price elasticity of demand} = \frac{\text{Percentage change in quantity demanded}}{\text{Percentage change in price}}$$

For example, suppose that a 10 per cent increase in the price of an ice-cream causes the amount of ice-cream you buy to fall by 20 per cent. We calculate your elasticity of demand as:

$$\text{Price elasticity of demand} = \frac{20\%}{10\%} = 2$$

In this example, the elasticity is 2, reflecting that the change in the quantity demanded is proportionately twice as large as the change in the price.

Because the quantity demanded of a good is negatively related to its price, the percentage change in quantity will always have the opposite sign to the percentage change in price. In this example, the percentage change in price is a *positive* 10 per cent (reflecting an increase), and the percentage change in quantity demanded is a *negative* 20 per cent (reflecting a decrease). For this reason, price elasticities of demand are sometimes reported as negative numbers. In this book we follow the common practice of dropping the minus sign and reporting all price elasticities as positive numbers. (Mathematicians call this the *absolute value.*) With this convention, a larger price elasticity implies a greater responsiveness of quantity demanded to a change in price.

The variety of demand curves

Economists classify demand curves according to their elasticity. Demand is *elastic* when the elasticity is greater than 1, so that quantity moves proportionately more than the price. Demand is *inelastic* when the elasticity is less than 1, so that quantity moves proportionately less than the price. If the elasticity is exactly 1, so that quantity moves the same amount proportionately as price, demand is said to have *unit elasticity.*

Because the price elasticity of demand measures how much quantity demanded responds to the price, it is closely related to the slope of the demand curve. (For a discussion of slope and elasticity, see the appendix to chapter 2.) The following rule of thumb is a useful guide: The flatter the demand curve that passes through a given point, the greater the price elasticity of demand; the steeper the demand curve that passes through a given point, the smaller the price elasticity of demand.

Figure 5.1 shows five cases. In the extreme case of a zero elasticity, demand is *perfectly inelastic,* and the demand curve is vertical. In this case, regardless of the price, the quantity demanded stays

fyi

The midpoint method: A better way to calculate percentage changes and elasticities

If you try calculating the price elasticity of demand between two points on a demand curve, you will quickly notice an annoying problem: The elasticity from point A to point B seems different from the elasticity from point B to point A. For example, consider these numbers:

Point A: Price = \$4   Quantity = 120
Point B: Price = \$6   Quantity = 80

Going from point A to point B, the price rises by 50 per cent, and the quantity falls by 33 per cent, indicating that the price elasticity of demand is 33/50, or 0.66. By contrast, going from point B to point A, the price falls by 33 per cent, and the quantity rises by 50 per cent, indicating that the price elasticity of demand is 50/30, or 1.5.

One way to avoid this problem is to use the *midpoint method* for calculating elasticities. Rather than computing a percentage change using the standard way (by dividing the change by the initial level), the midpoint method computes a percentage by dividing the change by the midpoint of the initial and final levels. For instance, \$5 is the midpoint of \$4 and \$6. Therefore, according to the midpoint method, a change from \$4 to \$6 is considered a 40 per cent rise, because (6 – 4)/5 × 100 = 40. Similarly, a change from \$6 to \$4 is considered a 40 per cent fall.

Because the midpoint method gives the same answer regardless of the direction of change, it is often used when calculating the price elasticity of demand between two points. In our example, the midpoint between point A and point B is:

Midpoint: Price = \$5   Quantity = 100

According to the midpoint method, when going from point A to point B, the price rises by 40 per cent and the quantity falls by 40 per cent. Similarly, when going from point B to point A, the price falls by 40 per cent and the quantity rises by 40 per cent. In both directions, the price elasticity of demand equals 1.

We can express the midpoint method with the following formula for the price elasticity of demand between two points, denoted (Q_1, P_1) and (Q_2, P_2):

$$\text{Price elasticity of demand} = \frac{[Q_2 - Q_1]/[[Q_2 + Q_1]/2]}{[P_2 - P_1]/[[P_2 + P_1]/2]}$$

The numerator is the percentage change in quantity computed using the midpoint method, and the denominator is the percentage change in price computed using the midpoint method. If you ever need to calculate elasticities, you should use this formula.

Throughout this book, however, we only rarely need to perform such calculations. For our purposes, what elasticity represents – the responsiveness of quantity demanded to price – is more important than how it is calculated.

Figure 5.1 The price elasticity of demand

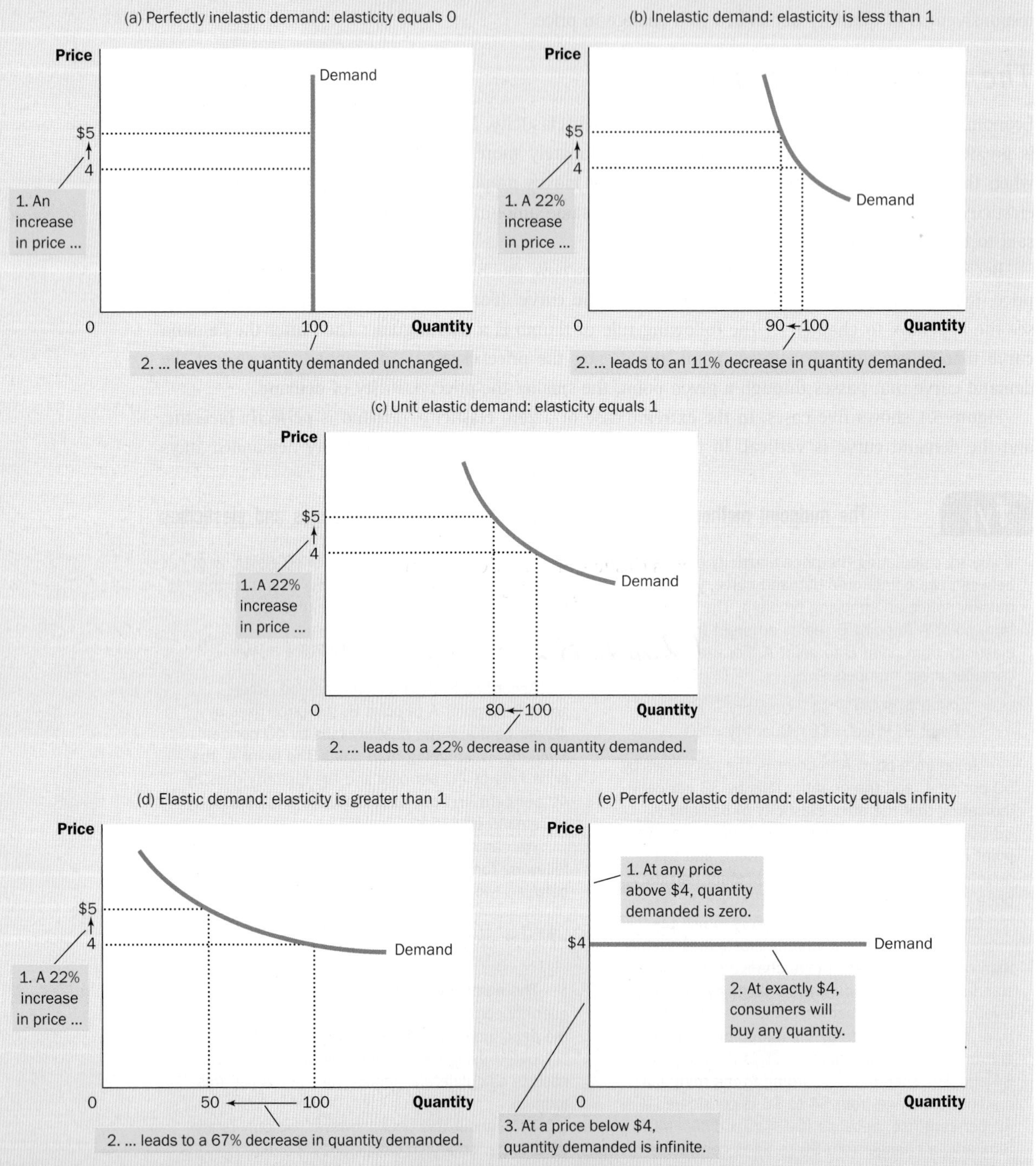
(a) Perfectly inelastic demand: elasticity equals 0
Price
Demand
$5
4
1. An increase in price ...
0
100
Quantity
2. ... leaves the quantity demanded unchanged.
(b) Inelastic demand: elasticity is less than 1
Price
$5
4
Demand
1. A 22% increase in price ...
0
90
100
Quantity
2. ... leads to an 11% decrease in quantity demanded.
(c) Unit elastic demand: elasticity equals 1
Price
$5
4
Demand
1. A 22% increase in price ...
0
80
100
Quantity
2. ... leads to a 22% decrease in quantity demanded.
(d) Elastic demand: elasticity is greater than 1
Price
$5
4
Demand
1. A 22% increase in price ...
0
50
100
Quantity
2. ... leads to a 67% decrease in quantity demanded.
(e) Perfectly elastic demand: elasticity equals infinity
Price
1. At any price above $4, quantity demanded is zero.
$4
Demand
2. At exactly $4, consumers will buy any quantity.
0
Quantity
3. At a price below $4, quantity demanded is infinite.

The price elasticity of demand determines whether the demand curve is steep or flat. Note that all percentage changes are calculated using the midpoint method.

the same. As the elasticity rises, the demand curve gets flatter and flatter. At the opposite extreme, demand is *perfectly elastic*. This occurs as the price elasticity of demand approaches infinity and the demand curve becomes horizontal, reflecting the fact that very small changes in the price lead to huge changes in the quantity demanded.

Finally, if you have trouble keeping straight the terms *elastic* and *inelastic*, here's a memory trick for you: *I*nelastic curves, such as in panel (a) of Figure 5.1, look like the letter I. *E*lastic curves, as in panel (e), look like the letter E. This may not be a deep insight, but it might help on your next exam.

Total revenue and the price elasticity of demand

When studying changes in supply or demand in a market, one variable we often want to study is **total revenue (in a market)**, the amount paid by buyers and received by sellers of the good. In any market, total revenue is $P \times Q$, the price of the good times the quantity of the good sold. We can show total revenue graphically, as in Figure 5.2. The height of the box under the demand curve is P, and the width is Q. The area of this box, $P \times Q$, equals the total revenue in this market. In Figure 5.2, where $P = \$4$ and $Q = 100$, total revenue is $\$4 \times 100$, or \$400.

total revenue (in a market)
the amount paid by buyers and received by sellers of a good, calculated as the price of the good times the quantity sold

How does total revenue change as one moves along the demand curve? The answer depends on the price elasticity of demand. If demand is inelastic, as in Figure 5.3, then an increase in the price causes an increase in total revenue. Here an increase in price from \$1 to \$3 causes the quantity demanded to fall only from 100 to 80, and so total revenue rises from \$100 to \$240. An increase in price raises $P \times Q$ because the fall in Q is proportionately smaller than the rise in P.

We obtain the opposite result if demand is elastic – an increase in the price causes a decrease in total revenue. In Figure 5.4, for instance, when the price rises from \$4 to \$5, the quantity demanded falls from

Figure 5.2 **Total revenue**

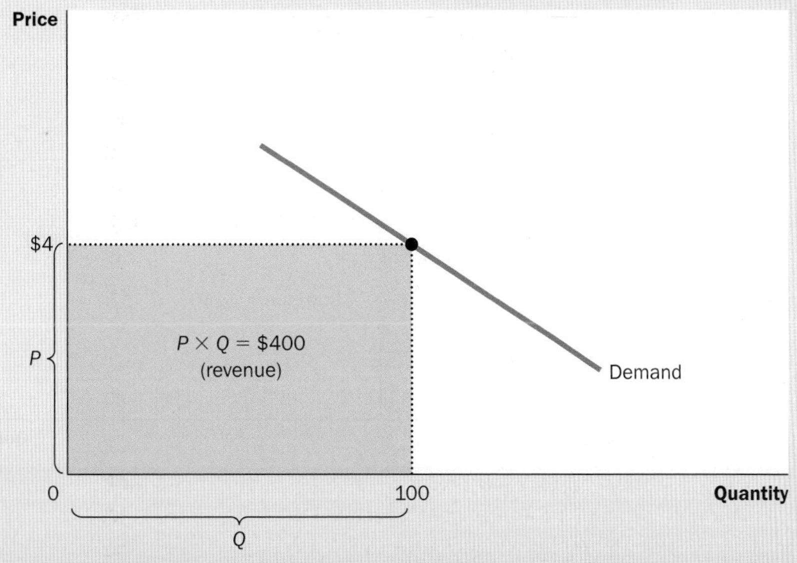

The total amount paid by buyers, and received as revenue by sellers, equals the area of the box under the demand curve, $P \times Q$. Here, at a price of \$4, the quantity demanded is 100, and total revenue is \$400.

Figure 5.3 How total revenue changes when price changes: inelastic demand

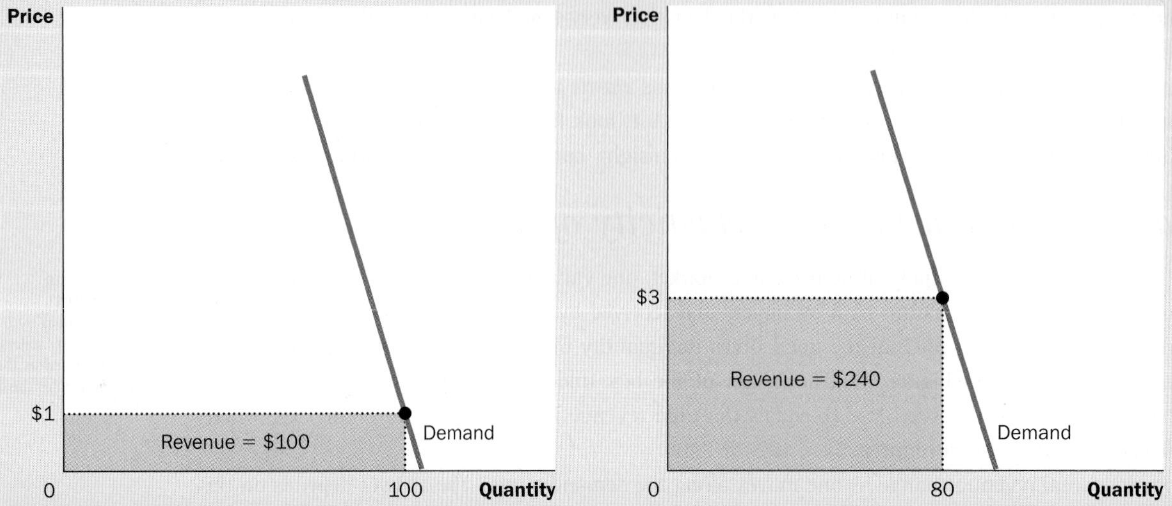

With an inelastic demand curve, an increase in the price leads to a decrease in quantity demanded that is proportionately smaller. Therefore, total revenue (the product of price and quantity) increases. Here, an increase in the price from $1 to $3 causes the quantity demanded to fall from 100 to 80, and total revenue rises from $100 to $240.

Figure 5.4 How total revenue changes when price changes: elastic demand

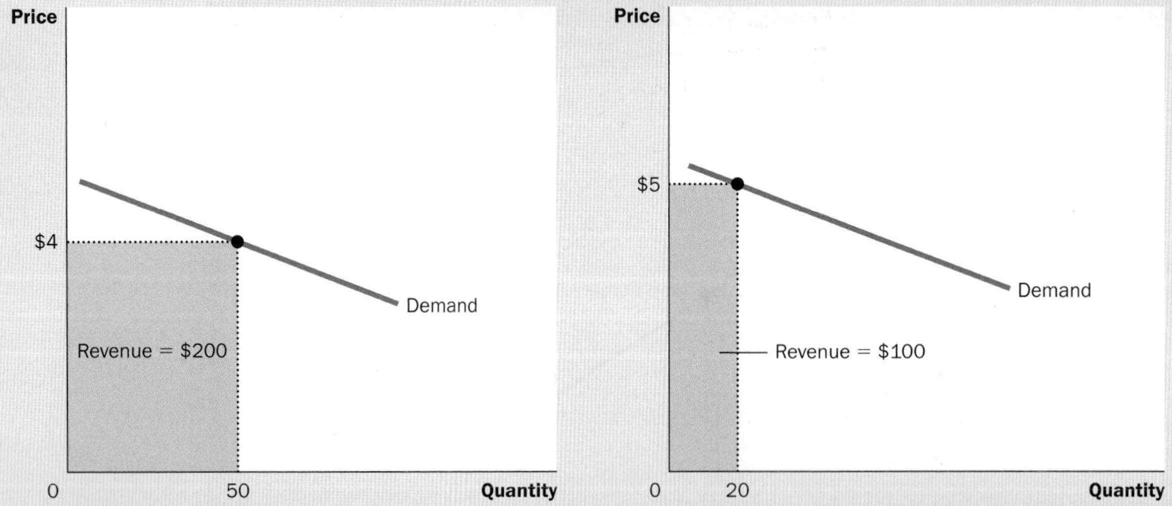

With an elastic demand curve, an increase in the price leads to a decrease in quantity demanded that is proportionately larger. Therefore, total revenue (the product of price and quantity) decreases. Here, an increase in the price from $4 to $5 causes the quantity demanded to fall from 50 to 20, so total revenue falls from $200 to $100.

50 to 20, and so total revenue falls from \$200 to \$100. Because demand is elastic, the reduction in the quantity demanded is so great that it more than offsets the increase in the price. That is, an increase in price reduces $P \times Q$ because the fall in Q is proportionately greater than the rise in P.

Although the examples in these two figures are extreme, they illustrate some general rules:

- When a demand curve is inelastic (a price elasticity less than 1), a price increase raises total revenue and a price decrease reduces total revenue.
- When a demand curve is elastic (a price elasticity greater than 1), a price increase reduces total revenue and a price decrease raises total revenue.
- In the special case of unit elastic demand (a price elasticity exactly equal to 1), a change in the price does not affect total revenue.

CASESTUDY

Pricing admission to an art gallery

You are curator of a major art gallery. Your financial controller tells you that the gallery is running short of funds and suggests that you consider altering the price of admission to increase total revenue. What do you do? Do you raise the price of admission, or do you lower it?

The answer depends on the elasticity of demand. If the demand for visits to the gallery is inelastic, then an increase in the price of admission would increase total revenue. But if the demand is elastic, then an increase in price would cause the number of visitors to fall by so much that total revenue would decrease. In this case, you should cut the price. The number of visitors would rise by so much that total revenue would increase.

If the price of admission were higher, how much smaller would this crowd be?

Source: iStockphoto.

To estimate the price elasticity of demand, you would need to turn to your statisticians. They might use historical data to study how gallery attendance varied from year to year as the admission price changed. Or they might use data on attendance at various galleries around the country to see how the admission price affects attendance. In studying either of these sets of data, the statisticians would need to take account of other factors that affect attendance – weather, population, size of collection and so on – in order to isolate the effect of price. In the end, such data analysis would provide an estimate of the price elasticity of demand, which you could use in deciding how to respond to your financial problem.

Other demand elasticities

In addition to the price elasticity of demand, economists also use other elasticities to describe the behaviour of buyers in a market.

The income elasticity of demand

Economists use the **income elasticity of demand** to measure how the quantity demanded changes as consumer income changes. The income elasticity is the percentage change in quantity demanded divided by the percentage change in income. That is:

income elasticity of demand
a measure of how much the quantity demanded of a good responds to a change in consumers' income, calculated as the percentage change in quantity demanded divided by the percentage change in income

$$\text{Income elasticity of demand} = \frac{\text{Percentage change in quantity demanded}}{\text{Percentage change in income}}$$

Search me!

▸ income elasticity of demand

As we discussed in chapter 4, most goods are normal goods – higher income raises quantity demanded. Because quantity demanded and income move in the same direction, normal goods have positive income elasticities. A few goods, such as second-hand clothes, are inferior goods – higher income lowers the quantity demanded. Because quantity demanded and income move in opposite directions, inferior goods have negative income elasticities.

Even among normal goods, income elasticities vary substantially in size. Necessities, such as food and clothing, tend to have small income elasticities because consumers, regardless of how low their incomes, choose to buy some of these goods. Luxuries, such as caviar and furs, tend to have large income elasticities because consumers feel that they can do without these goods altogether if their income is too low.

The cross-price elasticity of demand

cross-price elasticity of demand
a measure of how much the quantity demanded of one good responds to a change in the price of another good, computed as the percentage change in quantity demanded of the first good divided by the percentage change in the price of the second good.

Economists use the **cross-price elasticity of demand** to measure how the quantity demanded of one good changes as the price of another good changes. It is calculated as the percentage change in quantity demanded of good 1 divided by the percentage change in the price of good 2. That is:

$$\text{Cross-price elasticity of demand} = \frac{\text{Percentage change in quantity of good 1}}{\text{Percentage change in price of good 2}}$$

fyi

Elasticity and total revenue along a linear demand curve

Although some demand curves have an elasticity that is the same along the entire curve, that is not always the case. An example of a demand curve along which elasticity changes is a straight line, as shown in Figure 5.5. A linear demand curve has a constant slope. Recall that slope is defined as 'rise over run', which here is the ratio of the change in price ('rise') to the change in quantity ('run'). In this case, the demand curve's slope is constant because each $1 increase in price causes the same 2-unit decrease in the quantity demanded.

Figure 5.5 **A linear demand curve**

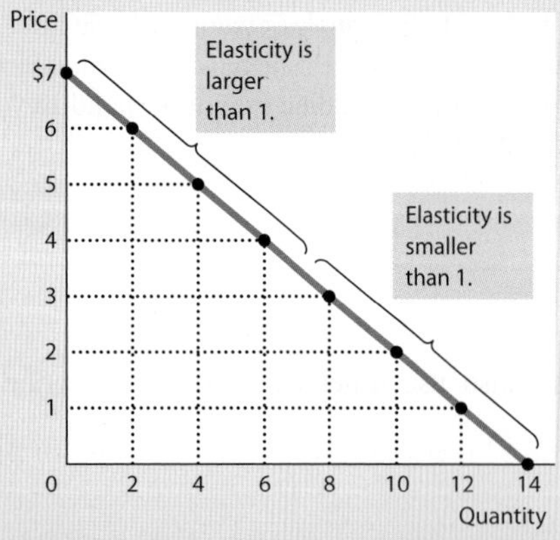

The slope of a linear demand curve is constant, but its elasticity is not.

Even though the slope of a linear demand curve is constant, the elasticity is not. The reason is that the slope is the ratio of *changes* in the two variables, whereas the elasticity is the ratio of *percentage changes* in the two variables. You can see this most easily by looking at Table 5.1. This table shows the demand schedule for the linear demand curve in Figure 5.5 and calculates the price elasticity of demand using the midpoint method discussed earlier. At points with low price and high quantity, the demand curve is inelastic. At points with a high price and low quantity, the demand curve is elastic.

Table 5.1 also presents total revenue at each point on the demand curve. These numbers illustrate the relationship between total revenue and elasticity. When the price is $1, for instance, demand is inelastic and a price increase to $2 raises total revenue. When the price is $5, demand is elastic and a price increase to $6 reduces total revenue. Between $3 and $4, demand is exactly unit elastic and total revenue is the same at these two prices.

Table 5.1 Calculating the elasticity of a linear demand curve

Price($)	Quantity	Total revenue (price × quantity)	% change in price	% change in quantity	Elasticity	Description
0	14	$0				
1	12	12	200	15	0.1	Inelastic
2	10	20	67	18	0.3	Inelastic
3	8	24	40	22	0.6	Inelastic
4	6	24	29	29	1.0	Unit elastic
5	4	20	22	40	1.8	Elastic
6	2	12	18	67	3.7	Elastic
7	0	0	15	200	13.0	Elastic

Whether the cross-price elasticity is a positive or negative number depends on whether the two goods are substitutes or complements. As we discussed in chapter 4, substitutes are goods that are typically used in place of one another, such as hamburgers and hot dogs. Because the price of hot dogs and the quantity of hamburgers demanded move in the same direction, the cross-price elasticity is positive. Conversely, complements are goods that are typically used together, such as computers and software. In this case, the cross-price elasticity is negative, indicating that an increase in the price of computers reduces the quantity of software demanded.

IN THE NEWS . . .

ON THE ROAD WITH ELASTICITY

How should a firm that operates a private toll road set a price for its service? This article considers the problem of pricing for the City Link toll road in Melbourne. Answering the question of pricing requires an understanding of the demand curve and its elasticity.

City Link to lift tolls 11%

by Sushi Das

City Link tolls will jump a staggering 11 per cent after July 1 – a move the road's owner conceded yesterday was likely to lead to motorists avoiding the tollway and putting further pressure on local roads.

The increase takes into account the Federal Government's GST and a regular quarterly toll increase of more than 1 per cent.

Transurban managing director Kim Edwards said motorists were likely to divert off the link in the short-term to avoid the GST, but would return once they factored in income tax cuts.

'I suspect that like all businesses there will be some impact for a short term but I don't think it will be sustained,' Mr Edwards said.

The Victorian Government and the RACV believe tolls are too high and cheaper packages are needed to attract more motorists.

>>

Under Transurban's contract with the state, it may increase tolls every three months to a maximum of 4.5 per cent annually or the CPI rate – whichever is higher.

Transport Minister Peter Batchelor said the GST would mean that some people would find it hard to pay for City Link tolls, and might turn to residential streets.

'It (the GST) is going to make the tolls more expensive, it's going to make it more difficult for people to use the tollway. It stands to reason,' Mr Batchelor said.

RACV spokesman David Cumming said he was concerned motorists had been slugged with such a large increase in tolls so early in City Link's operation.

'It's bad news because next time Transurban has the right to take in whatever inflation is … we all know that on projections the GST will lead to about an 8 per cent increase in CPI,' he said. 'There is no doubt that Transurban intends to take the maximum allowed increase every time it occurs. They are doing that to keep faith with their shareholders.'

While Transurban is pleased with strong growth in the use of the southern link, the numbers of vehicles using the western link are below expectations.

VicRoads figures show there has been a significant traffic increase on roads in Melbourne's north west, especially on Mount Alexander and Pascoe Vale roads.

Mr Cumming said motorists would decide if their tax cuts were enough to pay for additional costs in petrol and tolls.

Source: Sushi Das/*The Age*, 17 June 2000.

Q

Define *price elasticity of demand*. Explain the relationship between total revenue and the price elasticity of demand.

IN THE NEWS …

CAN YOU MEASURE PRICE ELASTICITY WITHOUT UPSETTING YOUR CUSTOMERS?

In order to determine your customer's price elasticity, you need to see what they will choose to buy at different prices. As this story shows, trying that experiment can have unintended consequences.

On the web, price tags blur; what you pay could depend on who you are

by David Streitfeld

Few things stir up a consumer revolt quicker than the notion that someone else is getting a better deal. That's a lesson Amazon.com has just learned.

Amazon, the largest and most potent force in e-commerce, was recently revealed to be selling the same DVD movies for different prices to different customers. It was the first major Web test of a strategy called 'dynamic pricing', which gauges a shopper's desire, measures his means and then charges accordingly.

The Internet was supposed to empower consumers, letting them compare deals with the click of a mouse. But it is also supplying retailers with information about their customers that they never had before, along with the technology to use all this accumulated data. While prices have always varied by geography, local competition and whim, retailers were never able to effectively target individuals until the Web.

'Dynamic pricing is the new reality, and it's going to be used by more and more retailers,' said Vernon Keenan, a San Francisco Internet consultant. 'In the future, what you pay will be determined by where you live and who you are. It's unfair, but that doesn't mean it's not going to happen.'

With its detailed records on the buying habits of 23 million consumers, Amazon is perfectly situated to employ dynamic pricing on a massive scale. But its trial ran into a snag early this month when the regulars discussing DVDs at the Web site DVDTalk.com noticed something odd.

One man recounted how he ordered the DVD of Julie Taymor's 'Titus', paying $24.49. The next week he went back to Amazon and saw that the price had jumped to $26.24. As an experiment, he stripped his computer of the electronic tags that identified him to Amazon as a regular customer. Then the price fell to $22.74.

'Amazon was trying to figure out how much their loyal customers would pay', said Barrett Ladd, a retail analyst with Gomez Advisors. 'And the customers found out.'

A number of DVDTalk.com visitors were particularly distressed to find that prices seemed to be higher for regular customers. 'They must figure that with repeat Amazon customers they have "won" them over and they can charge them slightly higher prices since they are loyal and "don't mind and/or don't notice" that they are being charged three to five per cent more for some items,' wrote a user whose online handle is Deep Sleep.

Amazon says the pricing variations, which it stopped as soon as the complaints began coming in from DVDTalk members, were completely random.

'It was done to determine consumer responses to different discount levels,' said spokesman Bill Curry. 'This was a pure and simple price test. This was not dynamic pricing. We don't do that and have no plans ever to do that.'

But an Amazon customer service representative called it exactly that in an e-mail to a DVDTalk member.

'I would first like to send along my most sincere apology for any confusion or frustration caused by our dynamic price test,' wrote the company's Galen Sather. 'Dynamic testing of a customer base is a common practice among both brick & mortar and internet companies.'

Indeed, physical stores have always had varied pricing. Prices might be higher in an affluent neighborhood or lower, depending on the goods being sold. A stereo system or camera purchased in certain neighborhoods of Manhattan would almost always be cheaper than in a small town with only one electronics store. Industries as basic as airlines and automobiles routinely adjust their prices because of the consumer's negotiating skills and general savvy.

Still, these traditional methods used to calculate prices are sledgehammers compared with the Internet's scalpel. For one thing, the Web provides a continuous feedback loop: The more the consumer buys from a Web site, the more the site knows about him and the weaker his bargaining position is. It's as if the corner drugstore could see you coming down the sidewalk, clutching your fevered brow, and then double the price of aspirin.

'Any retailer would love to do dynamic pricing if they could,' said analyst Ladd. 'If you could make the optimum amount of money from a consumer who's willing to pay more, that's a beautiful thing.'...

Amazon swears it won't happen there again. 'Dynamic pricing is stupid, because people will find out,' said spokesman Curry. 'Fortunately, it only took us two instances to see this.'

The retailer has worked very hard, and largely successfully, to build an image of itself as the most consumer-centric business ever. Technology writers have penned love songs to the site, while analysts routinely commend it for excellent customer relations.

No wonder Amazon hasn't exactly been issuing news releases about its tests of dynamic pricing.

'It's not the kind of communication you can offer to your customers and expect them to accept,' said Jupiter analyst May. 'This is an initiative that can only be undertaken in a clandestine manner. No customer, no matter what their net worth, is going to be willing to pay more than anyone else.'

>>

May argues that this was 'a major moment' in e-commerce – not only because it was the first widespread test of a powerful pricing tool but also because Amazon backed off so quickly and so definitively.

'This is an admission that, online even more than off-line, the consumer is always right,' May said. 'Word of mouth spreads quicker online. Amazon can't afford to alienate its most important asset, its customer base.'

The elasticity of supply

When we introduced supply in chapter 4, we noted that sellers of a good increase the quantity supplied when the price of the good rises, when their input prices fall or when their technology improves. To turn from qualitative to quantitative statements about supply, we once again use the concept of elasticity.

The price elasticity of supply and its determinants

price elasticity of supply a measure of how much the quantity supplied of a good responds to a change in the price of that good, calculated as the percentage change in quantity supplied divided by the percentage change in price

The law of supply states that higher prices raise the quantity supplied. The **price elasticity of supply** measures how much the quantity supplied responds to changes in the price. Supply of a good is said to be *elastic* if the quantity supplied responds substantially to changes in the price. Supply is said to be *inelastic* if the quantity supplied responds only slightly to changes in the price.

The price elasticity of supply depends on the flexibility of sellers to change the amount of the good they produce. For example, beachfront land has an inelastic supply because it is almost impossible to produce more of it. In contrast, manufactured goods, such as books, cars and televisions, have elastic supplies because the firms that produce them can run their factories longer in response to a higher price.

In most markets, a key determinant of the price elasticity of supply is the time period being considered. Supply is usually more elastic in the long run than in the short run. Over short periods of time, firms cannot easily change the size of their factories to make more or less of a good. Thus, in the short run, the quantity supplied is not very responsive to the price. In contrast, over longer periods, firms can build new factories or close old ones. In addition, new firms can enter a market and old firms can shut down. Thus, in the long run, the quantity supplied can respond substantially to the price.

Computing the price elasticity of supply

Now that we have some idea about what the price elasticity of supply is, let's be more precise. Economists calculate the price elasticity of supply as the percentage change in the quantity supplied divided by the percentage change in the price. That is:

$$\text{Price elasticity of supply} = \frac{\text{Percentage change in quantity supplied}}{\text{Percentage change in price}}$$

For example, suppose that an increase in the price of milk from \$1.00 to \$1.10 a litre raises the amount that dairy farmers produce from 10 000 to 11 500 litres per month. We calculate the percentage change in price as:

$$\text{Percentage change in price} = (1.10 - 1.00)/1.00 \times 100 = 10\%$$

Similarly, we calculate the percentage change in quantity supplied as:

Percentage change in quantity supplied = (11 500 − 10 000)/10 000 × 100 = 15%

In this case, the price elasticity of supply is:

$$\text{Price elasticity of supply} = \frac{15\%}{10\%} = 1.5$$

In this example, the elasticity of 1.5 is greater than 1, which reflects the fact that the quantity supplied moves proportionately more than the price.

The variety of supply curves

Because the price elasticity of supply measures the responsiveness of quantity supplied to the price, it is reflected in the appearance of the supply curve. Figure 5.6 shows five cases. In the extreme case of a zero elasticity, supply is *perfectly inelastic,* and the supply curve is vertical. In this case, the quantity supplied is the same regardless of the price. As the elasticity rises, the supply curve gets flatter, which shows that the quantity supplied responds more to changes in the price. At the opposite extreme, supply is *perfectly elastic.* This occurs as the price elasticity of supply approaches infinity and the supply curve is horizontal, meaning that very small changes in the price lead to very large changes in the quantity supplied.

In some markets, the elasticity of supply is not constant but varies over the supply curve. Figure 5.7 shows a typical case for an industry in which firms have factories with a limited capacity for production. For low levels of quantity supplied, the elasticity of supply is high, indicating that firms respond substantially to changes in the price. In this region, firms have capacity for production that is not being used, such as plant and equipment sitting idle for all or part of the day. Small increases in price make it profitable for firms to begin using this idle capacity. As the quantity supplied rises, firms begin to reach capacity. Once capacity is fully used, increasing production further requires the construction of new factories. To induce firms to incur this extra expense, the price must rise substantially, so supply becomes less elastic.

Figure 5.7 presents a numerical example of this phenomenon. When the price rises from $3 to $4 (a 29 per cent increase according to the midpoint method), the quantity supplied rises from 100 to 200 (a 67 per cent increase). Because quantity supplied moves proportionately more than the price, the supply curve has elasticity greater than 1. In contrast, when the price rises from $12 to $15 (a 22 per cent increase), the quantity supplied rises from 500 to 525 (a 5 per cent increase). In this case, quantity supplied moves proportionately less than the price, so the elasticity is less than 1.

Q

Define *price elasticity of supply.* Explain why the price elasticity of supply might be different in the long run than in the short run.

Three applications of supply, demand and elasticity

Can good news for farming be bad news for farmers? Why would the Organization of Petroleum Exporting Countries (OPEC) fail to keep the price of oil high? Does greater enforcement of drug laws

Figure 5.6 **The price elasticity of supply**

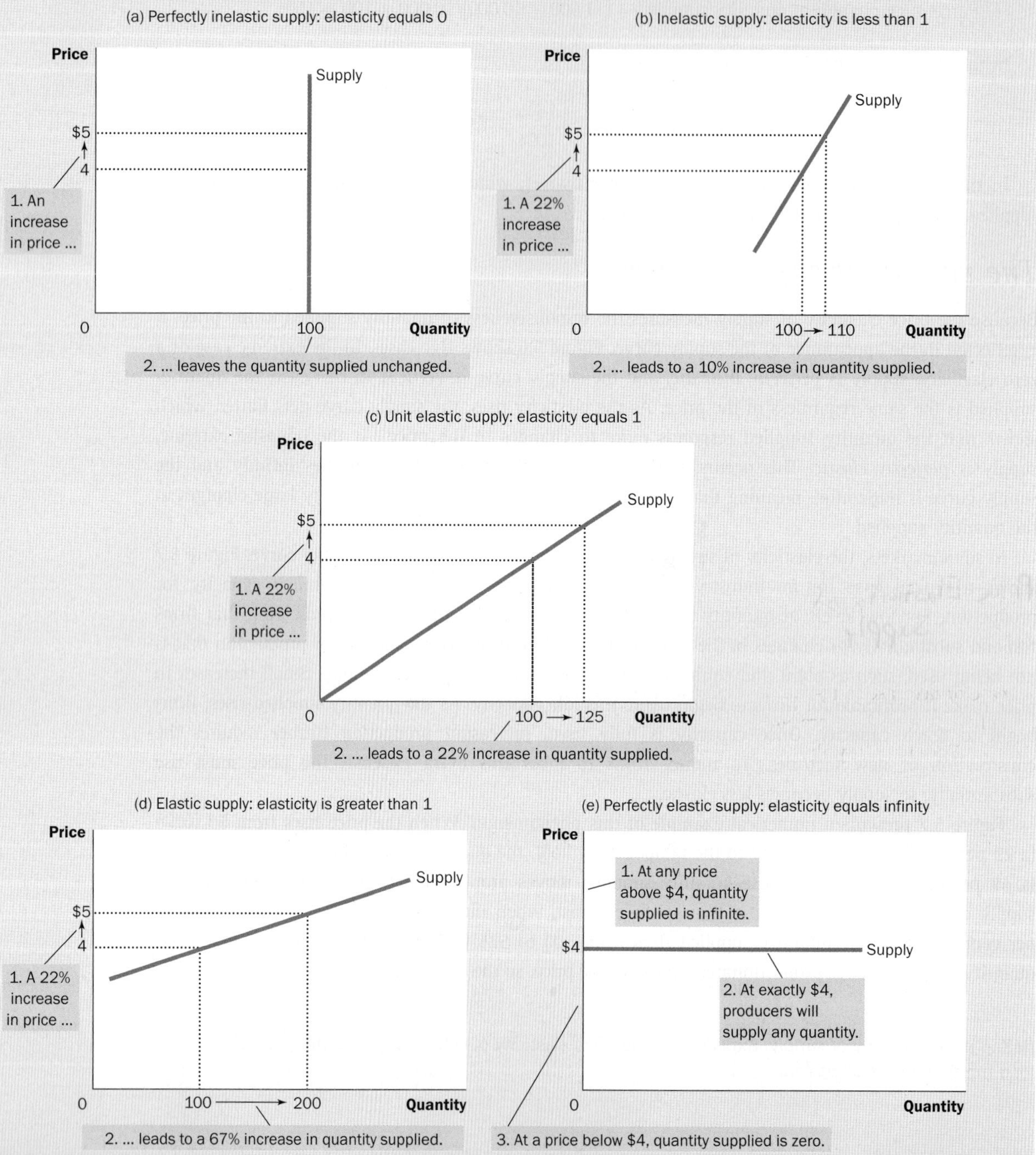
(a) Perfectly inelastic supply: elasticity equals 0
Price
Supply
$5
4
1. An increase in price ...
0
100
Quantity
2. ... leaves the quantity supplied unchanged.
(b) Inelastic supply: elasticity is less than 1
Price
Supply
$5
4
1. A 22% increase in price ...
0
100→ 110
Quantity
2. ... leads to a 10% increase in quantity supplied.
(c) Unit elastic supply: elasticity equals 1
Price
Supply
$5
4
1. A 22% increase in price ...
0
100 → 125
Quantity
2. ... leads to a 22% increase in quantity supplied.
(d) Elastic supply: elasticity is greater than 1
Price
Supply
$5
4
1. A 22% increase in price ...
0
100 → 200
Quantity
2. ... leads to a 67% increase in quantity supplied.
(e) Perfectly elastic supply: elasticity equals infinity
Price
1. At any price above $4, quantity supplied is infinite.
$4
Supply
2. At exactly $4, producers will supply any quantity.
0
Quantity
3. At a price below $4, quantity supplied is zero.

The price elasticity of supply determines whether the supply curve is steep or flat. Note that all percentage changes are calculated using the midpoint method.

Figure 5.7 How the price elasticity of supply can vary

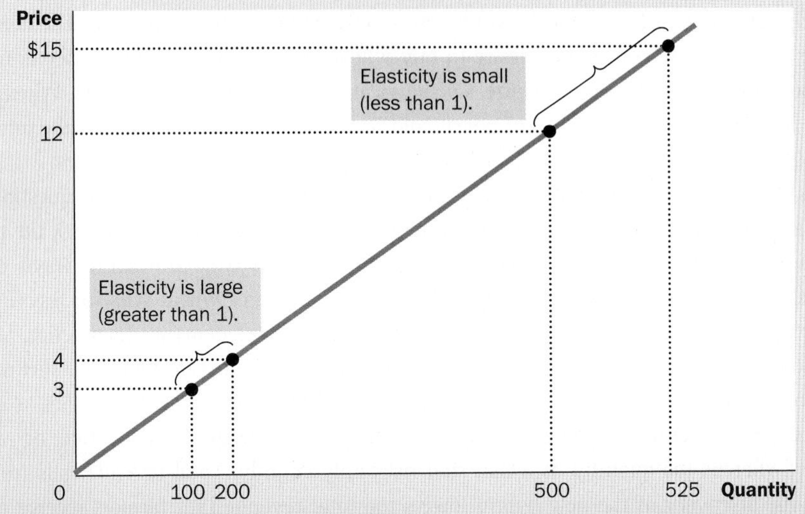

Because firms often have a maximum capacity for production, the elasticity of supply may be very high at low levels of quantity supplied and very low at high levels of quantity supplied. Here, an increase in price from $3 to $4 increases the quantity supplied from 100 to 200. Because the increase in quantity supplied of 100 per cent is larger than the increase in price of 33 per cent, the supply curve is elastic in this range. In contrast, when the price rises from $12 to $15, the quantity supplied rises from 500 to only 525. Because the increase in quantity supplied of 5 per cent is smaller than the increase in price of 25 per cent, the supply curve is inelastic in this range.

increase or decrease drug-related crime? At first, these questions might seem to have little in common. Yet all three questions are about markets and all markets are subject to the forces of supply and demand. Here we apply the versatile tools of supply, demand and elasticity to answer these seemingly complex questions.

Can good news for farming be bad news for farmers?

Imagine yourself as a West Australian wheat farmer. Because you earn all your income from selling wheat, you devote much effort to making your land as productive as possible. You monitor weather and soil conditions, check your fields for pests and disease and study the latest advances in farm technology. You know that the more wheat you grow, the more you will have to sell after the harvest and the higher will be your income and your standard of living.

One day, the University of Western Australia announces a major discovery. Researchers in its agronomy department have devised a new hybrid of wheat that raises the amount farmers can produce from each acre of land by 20 per cent. How should you react to this news? Does this discovery make you better off or worse off than you were before?

Recall from chapter 4 that we answer such questions in three steps. First, we examine whether the supply or demand curve shifts. Second, we consider in which direction the curve shifts. Third, we use the supply-and-demand diagram to see how the market equilibrium changes.

In this case, the discovery of the new hybrid affects the supply curve. Because the hybrid increases the amount of wheat that can be produced on each hectare of land, farmers are now willing to supply more wheat at any given price. In other words, the supply curve shifts to the right. The demand curve remains the same because consumers' desire to buy wheat products at any given price is not affected by the introduction of a new hybrid. Figure 5.8 shows an example of such a change. When the supply curve shifts from S_1 to S_2, the quantity of wheat sold increases from 100 to 110 and the price of wheat falls from \$3 to \$2.

But does this discovery make farmers better off? As a first cut to answering this question, consider what happens to the total revenue received by farmers. Farmers' total revenue is $P \times Q$, the price of the wheat times the quantity sold. The discovery affects farmers in two conflicting ways. The hybrid allows farmers to produce more wheat (Q rises), but now each bag of wheat sells for less (P falls).

Whether total revenue rises or falls depends on the elasticity of demand. In practice, the demand for basic foodstuffs such as wheat is usually inelastic, for these items are relatively inexpensive and have few good substitutes. When the demand curve is inelastic, as it is in Figure 5.8, a decrease in price causes total revenue to fall. You can see this in the figure – the price of wheat falls substantially, whereas the quantity of wheat sold rises only slightly. Total revenue falls from \$300 to \$220. Thus, the discovery of the new hybrid lowers the total revenue that farmers receive for the sale of their crops.

If farmers are made worse off by the discovery of this new hybrid, why do they adopt it? The answer to this question goes to the heart of how competitive markets work. Because each farmer is a

Figure 5.8 **An increase in supply in the market for wheat**

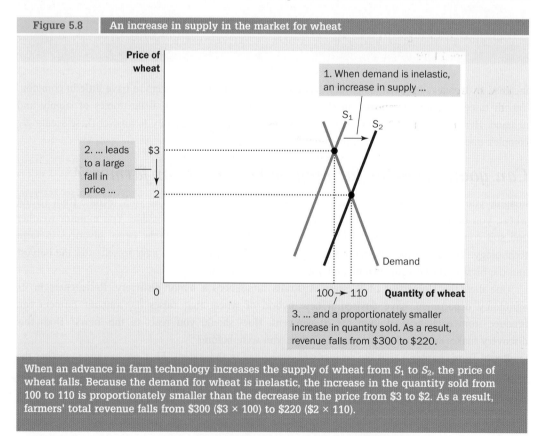

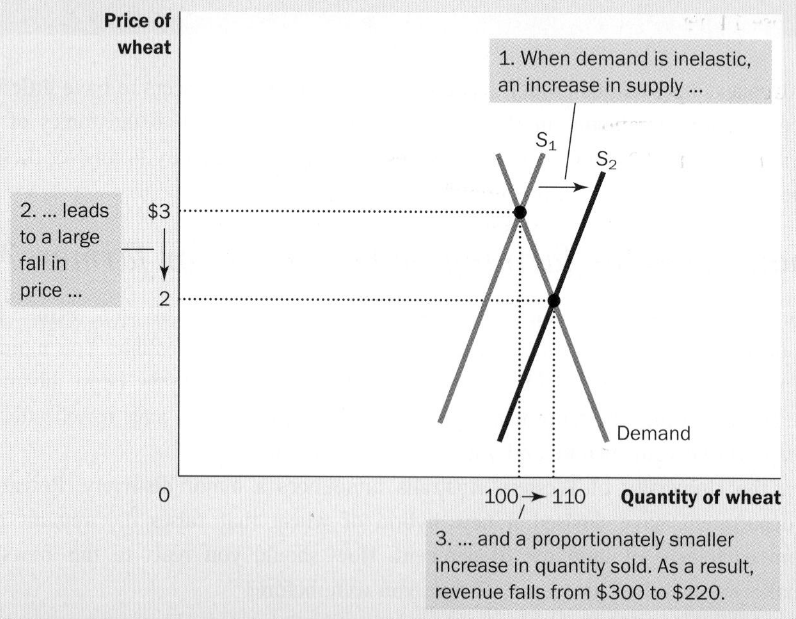

When an advance in farm technology increases the supply of wheat from S_1 to S_2, the price of wheat falls. Because the demand for wheat is inelastic, the increase in the quantity sold from 100 to 110 is proportionately smaller than the decrease in the price from \$3 to \$2. As a result, farmers' total revenue falls from \$300 (\$3 × 100) to \$220 (\$2 × 110).

small part of the market for wheat, he or she takes the price of wheat as given. For any given price of wheat, it is better to use the new hybrid in order to produce and sell more wheat. Yet when all farmers do this, the supply of wheat rises, the price falls and farmers are worse off.

This analysis of the market for farm products also helps to explain a seeming paradox of public policy – certain farm policies try to help farmers by getting farmers to destroy some of their crops. For example, in the 1980s the Australian government paid winemakers to pull up their grape vines. The purpose of these programs is to reduce the supply of farm products and thereby raise prices. Because demand is inelastic, farmers as a group receive greater total revenue if they supply a smaller crop to the market. No single farmer would choose to destroy crops alone, since each takes the market price as given. But if all farmers do so together, each can be better off.

When analysing the effects of farm technology or farm policy, it is important to keep in mind that what is good for farmers is not necessarily good for society as a whole. Improvement in farm technology can be bad for farmers who become increasingly unnecessary, but it is surely good for consumers who pay less for food. Similarly, a policy aimed at reducing the supply of farm products may raise the incomes of farmers, but it does so at the expense of consumers.

Why did OPEC fail to keep the price of oil high?

Many of the most disruptive events for the world's economies over the past several decades have originated in the world market for oil. In the 1970s, members of OPEC decided to raise the world price of oil in order to increase their incomes. These countries accomplished this goal by jointly reducing the amount of oil they supplied. From 1973 to 1974, the price of oil (adjusted for overall inflation) rose more than 50 per cent. Then, a few years later, OPEC did the same thing again. The price of oil rose 14 per cent in 1979, followed by 34 per cent in 1980 and 34 per cent in 1981.

Yet OPEC found it difficult to maintain a high price. From 1982 to 1985, the price of oil steadily declined by about 10 per cent per year. Dissatisfaction and disarray soon prevailed among the OPEC countries. In 1986, cooperation among OPEC members completely broke down and the price of oil plunged 45 per cent. In 1990, the price of oil (adjusted for overall inflation) was back to where it was in 1970, and stayed at that low level throughout most of the 1990s. (In the first decade of the 21st century, the price of oil fluctuated substantially once again, but the main driving force was changes in world demand rather than OPEC supply restrictions. Early in the decade, oil demand and prices spiked up, in part because of a large and rapidly growing Chinese economy. They plunged in 2008–09 as the world economy fell into a deep recession and then started rising once again as the world economy started to recover.)

The OPEC episodes of the 1970s and 1980s show how supply and demand can behave differently in the short run and in the long run. In the short run, both the supply and demand for oil are relatively inelastic. Supply is inelastic because the quantity of known oil reserves and the capacity for oil extraction cannot be changed quickly. Demand is inelastic because buying habits do not respond immediately to changes in price. Many drivers with old cars that 'guzzle' petrol and oil, for instance, will just pay the higher price. Thus, as panel (a) of Figure 5.9 shows, the short-run supply and demand curves are steep. When the supply of oil shifts from S_1 to S_2, the price increase from P_1 to P_2 is large.

The situation is very different in the long run. Over long periods of time, producers of oil outside of OPEC respond to high prices by increasing oil exploration and by erecting new drilling rigs. Consumers respond with greater conservation, for instance by replacing old inefficient cars with newer efficient

Figure 5.9 A reduction in supply in the world market for oil

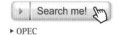

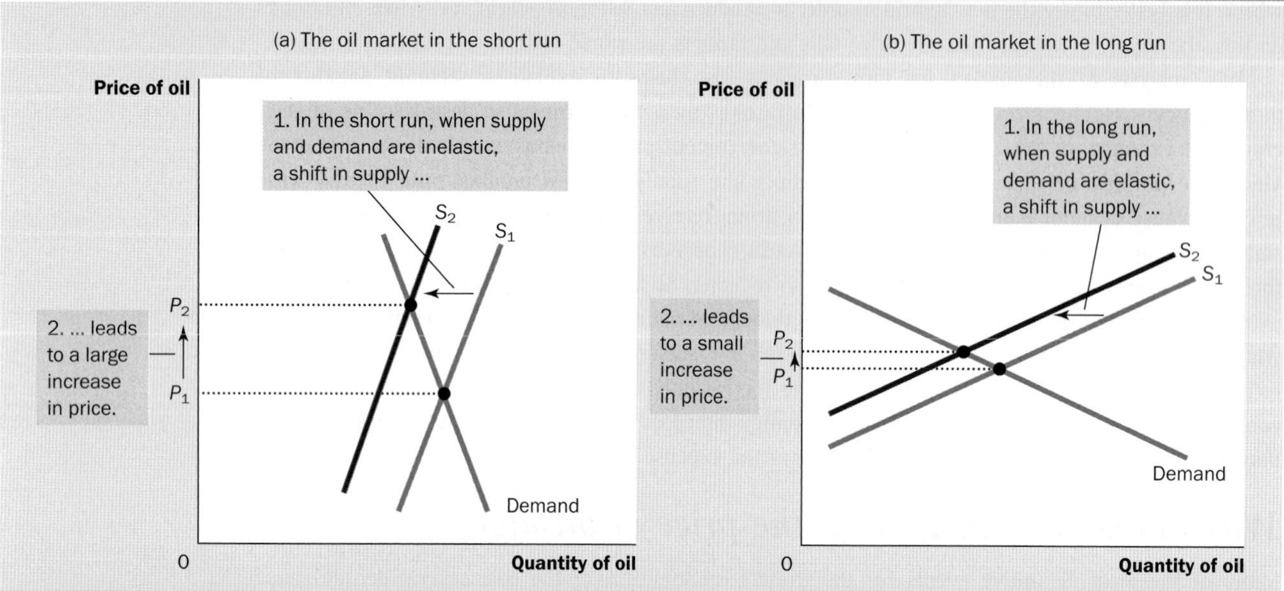

When the supply of oil falls, the response depends on the time horizon. In the short run, supply and demand are relatively inelastic, as in panel (a). Thus, when the supply curve shifts from S_1 to S_2, the price rises substantially. In contrast, in the long run, supply and demand are relatively elastic, as in panel (b). In this case, the same size shift in the supply curve (S_1 to S_2) causes a smaller increase in the price.

ones. Thus, as panel (b) of Figure 5.9 shows, the long-run supply and demand curves are more elastic. In the long run, the shift in the supply curve from S_1 to S_2 causes a much smaller increase in the price.

This analysis shows why OPEC succeeded in maintaining a high price of oil only in the short run. When OPEC countries agreed to reduce their production of oil, they shifted the supply curve to the left. Even though each OPEC member sold less oil, the price rose by so much in the short run that OPEC's incomes rose. In contrast, in the long run when supply and demand are more elastic, the same reduction in supply, measured by the horizontal shift in the supply curve, caused a smaller increase in the price. Thus, OPEC's coordinated reduction in supply proved less profitable in the long run.

Search me!
▸ OPEC

OPEC still exists today and it has from time to time succeeded at reducing supply and raising prices. The cartel now seems to understand that raising prices is easier in the short run than in the long run.

Do drug bans increase or decrease drug-related crime?

A persistent problem facing our society is the use of illegal drugs, such as heroin, cocaine and crack. Drug use has several adverse effects. One is that drug dependency can ruin the lives of drug users and their families. Another is that drug addicts often turn to robbery and other violent crimes to obtain the money needed to support their habit. To discourage the use of illegal drugs, many governments devote billions of dollars each year to reduce the flow of drugs into their countries. Let's use the tools of supply and demand to examine this policy of drug prohibition.

Suppose the Australian government increases the number of customs inspectors and police officers devoted to preventing imports of drugs. What happens in the market for illegal drugs? As is usual, we answer this question in three steps. First, we consider whether the supply or demand curve shifts. Second, we consider the direction of the shift. Third, we see how the shift affects the equilibrium price and quantity.

Although the purpose of drug prohibition is to reduce drug use, its direct impact is on the sellers of drugs rather than the buyers. When the government stops some drugs from entering the country and arrests more smugglers, it raises the cost of selling drugs and, therefore, reduces the quantity of drugs supplied at any given price. The demand for drugs – the amount buyers want at any given price – is not changed. As panel (a) of Figure 5.10 shows, prohibition shifts the supply curve to the left from S_1 to S_2 and leaves the demand curve the same. The equilibrium price of drugs rises from P_1 to P_2, and the equilibrium quantity falls from Q_1 to Q_2. The fall in the equilibrium quantity shows that drug prohibition does reduce drug use.

But what about the amount of drug-related crime? To answer this question, consider the total amount that drug users pay for the drugs they buy. Because few drug addicts are likely to break their destructive habits in response to a higher price, it is likely that the demand for drugs is inelastic, as it is drawn in the figure. If demand is inelastic, then an increase in price raises total revenue in the drug market. That is, because drug prohibition raises the price of drugs proportionately more than it reduces drug use, it raises the total amount of money that drug users pay for drugs. Addicts who already had

Figure 5.10 **Policies to reduce the use of illegal drugs**

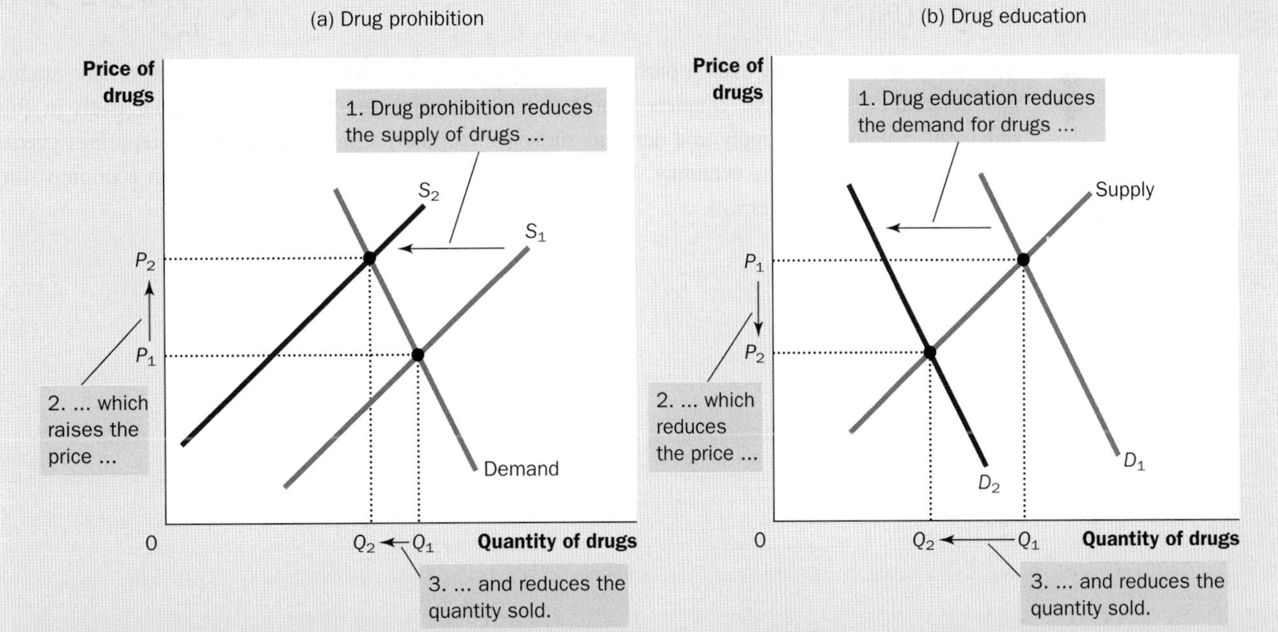
(a) Drug prohibition
Price of drugs
1. Drug prohibition reduces the supply of drugs ...
S2
S1
P2
P1
2. ... which raises the price ...
Demand
0
Q2
Q1
Quantity of drugs
3. ... and reduces the quantity sold.
(b) Drug education
Price of drugs
1. Drug education reduces the demand for drugs ...
Supply
P1
P2
2. ... which reduces the price ...
D1
D2
0
Q2
Q1
Quantity of drugs
3. ... and reduces the quantity sold.

Drug prohibition reduces the supply of drugs from S_1 to S_2, as in panel (a). If the demand for drugs is inelastic, then the total amount paid by drug users rises, even as the amount of drug use falls. In contrast, drug education reduces the demand for drugs from D_1 to D_2, as in panel (b). Because both price and quantity fall, the amount paid by drug users falls.

to steal to support their habits would have an even greater need for quick cash. Thus, drug bans could increase drug-related crime.

Because of this adverse effect of drug prohibition, some analysts argue for alternative approaches to the drug problem. Rather than trying to reduce the supply of drugs, policymakers might try to reduce the demand by pursuing a policy of drug education. Successful drug education has the effects shown in panel (b) of Figure 5.10. The demand curve shifts to the left from D_1 to D_2. As a result, the equilibrium quantity falls from Q_1 to Q_2, and the equilibrium price falls from P_1 to P_2. Total revenue, which is price times quantity, also falls. Thus, in contrast to drug prohibition, drug education can reduce both drug use and drug-related crime.

Advocates of drug prohibition might argue that the effects of this policy are different in the long run than in the short run, because the elasticity of demand may depend on the time horizon. The demand for drugs is probably inelastic over short periods of time because higher prices do not substantially affect drug use by established addicts. But demand may be more elastic over longer periods of time because higher prices would discourage experimentation with drugs among the young and, over time, lead to fewer drug addicts. In this case, drug prohibition would increase drug-related crime in the short run but decrease it in the long run.

Q

How might a drought that destroys half of all farm crops be good for farmers? If such a drought is good for farmers, why don't farmers destroy their own crops in the absence of a drought?

Conclusion

According to an old quip, even a parrot can become an economist simply by learning to say 'supply and demand'. The last two chapters should have convinced you that there is much truth in this statement. The tools of supply and demand allow you to analyse many of the most important events and policies that shape the economy. You are now well on your way to becoming an economist (or, at least, a well-educated parrot).

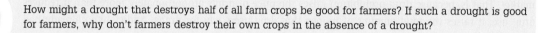

Summary

- The price elasticity of demand measures how much the quantity demanded responds to changes in the price. Demand tends to be more elastic if the good is a luxury rather than a necessity, if close substitutes are available, if the market is narrowly defined, or if buyers have substantial time to react to a price change.
- The price elasticity of demand is calculated as the percentage change in quantity demanded divided by the percentage change in price. If the elasticity is less than 1, so that quantity demanded moves proportionately less than the price, demand is said to be inelastic. If the elasticity is greater than 1, so that quantity demanded moves proportionately more than the price, demand is said to be elastic.
- Total revenue, the total amount paid for a good, equals the price of the good times the quantity sold. For inelastic demand curves, total revenue rises as price rises. For elastic demand curves, total revenue falls as price rises.
- The income elasticity of demand measures how much the quantity demanded responds to changes in consumers' income. The cross-price elasticity of demand measure how much the quantity demanded of one good responds to the price of another good.
- The price elasticity of supply measures how much the quantity supplied responds to changes in the price. This elasticity often depends on the time horizon under consideration. In most markets, supply is more elastic in the long run than in the short run.
- The price elasticity of supply is calculated as the percentage change in quantity supplied divided by the percentage change in price. If the elasticity is less than 1, so that quantity supplied moves proportionately less than the price, supply is said to be inelastic. If the elasticity is greater than 1, so that quantity supplied moves proportionately more than the price, supply is said to be elastic.
- The tools of supply and demand can be applied in many different kinds of markets. This chapter uses them to analyse the market for wheat, the market for oil and the market for illegal drugs.

Key concepts

cross-price elasticity of demand
elasticity
income elasticity of demand
price elasticity of demand
price elasticity of supply
total revenue

Questions for review

1. Define the price elasticity of demand and the income elasticity of demand.
2. List and explain some of the determinants of the price elasticity of demand.
3. If the elasticity is greater than 1, is demand elastic or inelastic? If the elasticity equals 0, is demand perfectly elastic or perfectly inelastic?
4. On a supply-and-demand diagram, show total spending by consumers. How does this compare with total revenue received by producers?
5. If demand is elastic, how will an increase in price change total revenue? Explain.
6. What do we call a good whose income elasticity is less than 0?
7. What is the formula for the price elasticity of supply? Explain what this measures.
8. What is the price elasticity of supply of Picasso paintings?

9 Is the price elasticity of supply usually larger in the short run or in the long run? Why?

10 In the 1970s, OPEC caused a dramatic increase in the price of oil. What prevented the organisation from maintaining this high price through the 1980s?

Problems and applications

1 For each of the following pairs of goods, which good would you expect to have more elastic demand and why?

a required textbooks or mystery novels

b beethoven recordings or classical music recordings in general

c bus trips during the next six months or bus trips during the next five years

d lemonade or water.

2 Suppose that business travellers and holiday-makers have the following demand for airline tickets from Sydney to Melbourne:

Price ($)	Quantity demanded (business travellers)	Quantity demanded (holiday-makers)
150	2100	1000
200	2000	800
250	1900	600
300	1800	400

a As the price of tickets rises from $200 to $250, what is the price elasticity of demand for (i) business travellers and (ii) holiday-makers?

b Why might holiday-makers have a different elasticity than business travellers?

3 Suppose that your demand schedule for compact discs is as follows:

Price ($)	Quantity demanded (income = $10 000)	Quantity demanded (income = $12 000)
8	40	50
10	32	45
12	24	30
14	16	20

a Calculate your price elasticity of demand as the price of compact discs increases from $8 to $10 if (i) your income is $10 000, and (ii) your income is $12 000.

b Calculate your income elasticity of demand as your income increases from $10 000 to $12 000 if (i) the price is $12, and (ii) the price is $16.

4 Emily has decided always to spend one-third of her income on clothing.
   a What is her income elasticity of clothing demand?
   b What is her price elasticity of clothing demand?
   c If Emily's tastes change and she decides to spend only a quarter of her income on clothing, how does her demand curve change? What is her income elasticity and price elasticity now?

5 *The New York Times* (17 February 1996) reported that subway use declined after a fare increase: 'There were nearly four million fewer riders in December 1995, the first full month after the price of a token increased 25 cents to $1.50, than in the previous December, a 4.3 per cent decline.'
   a Use these data to estimate the price elasticity of demand for subway rides.
   b According to your estimate, what happens to the revenue when the fare rises?
   c Why might your estimate of the elasticity be unreliable?

6 Two drivers – Tom and Jerry – each drive up to a petrol station. Before looking at the price and starting to pump petrol, Tom says: 'I will buy 10 litres of petrol'. Jerry says: 'I will buy $10 of petrol'. What is each driver's price elasticity of demand?

7 Economists have observed that spending on restaurant meals declines more during economic downturns than does spending on food to be eaten at home. How might the concept of elasticity help to explain this phenomenon?

8 Consider public policy aimed at smoking.
   a Studies indicate that the price elasticity of demand for cigarettes is about 0.4. If a packet of cigarettes currently costs $8 and the government wants to reduce smoking by 20 per cent, by how much should it increase the price?
   b If the government permanently increases the price of cigarettes, will the policy have a larger effect on smoking one year from now or five years from now?
   c Studies also find that teenagers have a higher price elasticity than do adults. Why might this be true?

9 Would you expect the price elasticity of *demand* to be larger in the market for all ice-cream or the market for vanilla ice-cream? Would you expect the price elasticity of *supply* to be larger in the market for all ice-cream or the market for vanilla ice-cream? Be sure to explain your answers.

10 Pharmaceutical drugs have an inelastic demand, and computers have an elastic demand. Suppose that technological advance doubles the supply of both products (that is, the quantity supplied at each price is twice what it was).
   a What happens to the equilibrium price and quantity in each market?
   b Which product experiences a larger change in price?
   c Which product experiences a larger change in quantity?
   d What happens to total consumer spending on each product?

11 Beachfront resorts have an inelastic supply and cars have an elastic supply. Suppose that a rise in population doubles the demand for both products (that is, the quantity demanded at each price is twice what it was).
   a What happens to the equilibrium price and quantity in each market?
   b Which product experiences a larger change in price?
   c Which product experiences a larger change in quantity?
   d What happens to total consumer spending on each product?

12 Flooding in the Queensland Granite Belt destroyed thousands of hectares of grapevines.
   a Vineyard owners whose vines were destroyed by the floods were much worse off, but those whose vines were not destroyed benefited from the floods. Why?
   b What information would you need about the market for wine in order to assess whether vineyard owners as a group were hurt or helped by the floods?

13 Explain why the following might be true. A drought around the world raises the total revenue that farmers receive from the sale of grain, but a drought only in Queensland reduces the total revenue that Queensland farmers receive.

14 Because better weather makes farmland more productive, farmland in regions with good weather conditions is more expensive than farmland in regions with bad weather conditions. Over time, however, as advances in technology have made all farmland more productive, the price of farmland (adjusted for overall inflation) has fallen. Use the concept of elasticity to explain why productivity and farmland prices are positively related across space but negatively related over time.

15 In the 1980s, the government imposed a sales tax on the purchase of luxury cars. The revenue collected from the tax equals the tax rate multiplied by total spending on such cars. There have been suggestions that the government could earn more tax revenue by increasing the tax rate on luxury cars. Would such an increase necessarily raise tax revenue? Explain.

Search me!

Search me!

When accessing information about microeconomics use the following keywords in any combinations you require:

- price elasticity of demand
- income elasticity of demand
- OPEC

CourseMate

CourseMate

For more multimedia resources and activities on economics, visit the Economics CourseMate website.

6

Supply, demand and government policies

Learning objectives

In this chapter you will:

- examine the effects of government policies that place a ceiling on prices
- examine the effects of government policies that put a floor under prices
- consider how a tax on a good affects the price of the good and the quantity sold
- learn that taxes levied on buyers and taxes levied on sellers are equivalent
- see how the burden of a tax is split between buyers and sellers.

Economists have two roles. As scientists, they develop and test theories to explain the world around them. As policy advisors, they use their theories to try to change the world for the better. The focus of the past two chapters has been scientific. We have seen how supply and demand determine the price of a good and the quantity of the good sold. We have also seen how various events shift supply and demand and thereby change the equilibrium price and quantity.

This chapter offers our first look at policy. Here we analyse various types of government policies using only the tools of supply and demand. As you will see, the analysis yields some surprising results. Policies often have effects that their architects did not intend or anticipate.

We begin by considering policies that directly control prices. For example, rent-control laws dictate a maximum rent that landlords may charge tenants. Minimum-wage laws dictate the lowest wage that firms may pay workers. Price controls are usually imposed when policymakers believe that the market price of a good or service is unfair to buyers or sellers. Yet, as we will see, these policies can generate inequities of their own.

After our discussion of price controls, we next consider the impact of taxes. Policymakers use taxes both to influence market outcomes and to raise revenue for public purposes. Although the prevalence of taxes in our economy is obvious, their effects are not. For example, when the government levies a tax on the amount that firms pay their workers, do the firms or the workers bear the burden of the tax? The answer is not at all clear – until we apply the powerful tools of supply and demand.

Controls on prices

To see how price controls affect market outcomes, let's look once again at the market for ice-cream. As we saw in chapter 4, if ice-cream is sold in a competitive market free of government regulation, the price of ice-cream adjusts to balance supply and demand – at the equilibrium price, the quantity of ice-cream that buyers want to buy exactly equals the quantity that sellers want to sell. To be concrete, suppose the equilibrium price is $3 per ice-cream.

Not everyone may be happy with the outcome of this free-market process. Let's say the Australian Association of Ice-cream Eaters complains that the $3 price is too high for everyone to enjoy an ice-cream a day (their recommended daily allowance). Meanwhile, the National Organisation of Ice-cream Makers complains that the $3 price – the result of 'cutthroat competition' – is depressing the incomes of its members. Each of these groups lobbies the government to pass laws that alter the market outcome by directly controlling prices.

Because buyers of any good always want a lower price and sellers want a higher price, the interests of the two groups conflict. If the Ice-cream Eaters are successful in their lobbying, the government imposes a legal maximum on the price at which ice-cream can be sold, called a **price ceiling**. If the Ice-cream Makers are successful, the government imposes a legal minimum on the price, called a **price floor**. Let us consider the effects of these policies in turn.

price ceiling
a legal maximum on the price at which a good can be sold

price floor
a legal minimum on the price at which a good can be sold

Search me!
- price ceiling
- price floor

How price ceilings affect market outcomes

When the government, moved by the complaints of the Ice-cream Eaters, imposes a price ceiling on the market for ice-cream, two outcomes are possible. In panel (a) of Figure 6.1, the

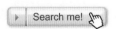

Figure 6.1 A market with a price ceiling

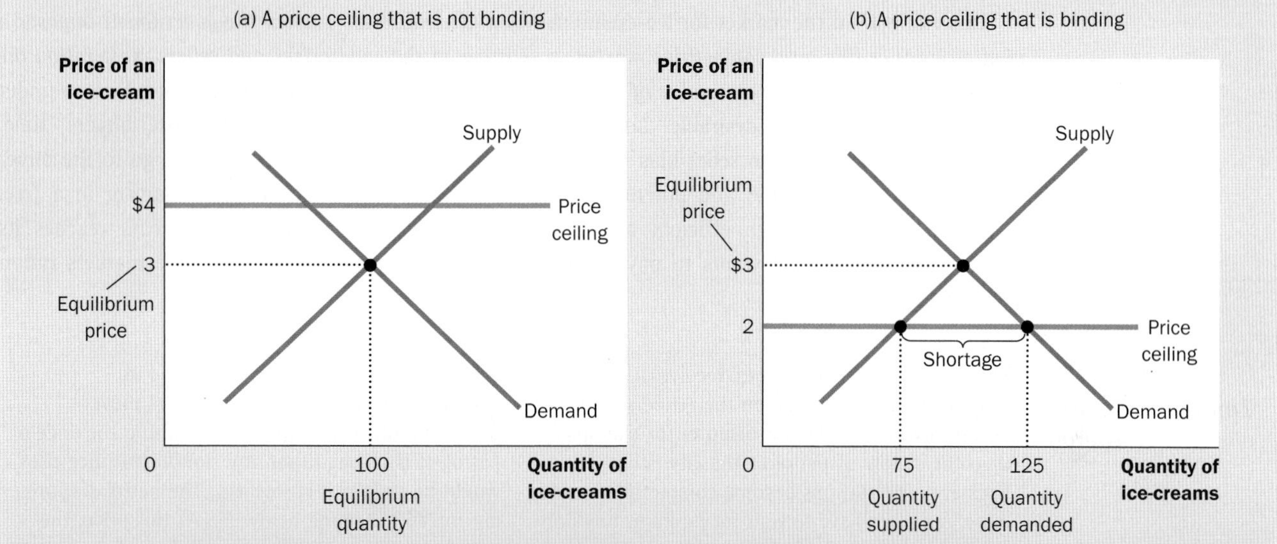

In panel (a), the government imposes a price ceiling of $4. Because the price ceiling is above the equilibrium price of $3, the price ceiling has no effect and the market can reach the equilibrium of supply and demand. In this equilibrium, quantity supplied and quantity demanded both equal 100 ice-creams. In panel (b), the government imposes a price ceiling of $2. Because the price ceiling is below the equilibrium price of $3, the market price equals $2. At this price, 125 ice-creams are demanded and only 75 are supplied, so there is a shortage of 50 ice-creams.

government imposes a price ceiling of $4 per ice-cream. In this case, because the price that balances supply and demand ($3) is below the ceiling, the price ceiling is *not binding.* Market forces naturally move the economy to the equilibrium and the price ceiling has no effect on the price or the quantity sold.

Panel (b) of figure 6.1 shows the other, more interesting, possibility. In this case, the government imposes a price ceiling of $2 per ice-cream. Because the equilibrium price of $3 is above the price ceiling, the ceiling is a *binding constraint* on the market. The forces of supply and demand tend to move the price towards the equilibrium price, but when the market price hits the ceiling, it can, by law, rise no further. Thus, the market price equals the price ceiling. At this price, the quantity of ice-cream demanded (125 ice-creams in the figure) exceeds the quantity supplied (75 ice-creams). There is a shortage of ice-cream, so some people who want to buy ice-cream at the going price are unable to do so.

When a shortage of ice-cream develops because of this price ceiling, some mechanism for rationing ice-cream will naturally develop. The mechanism could be long lines – buyers who are willing to arrive early and wait in line get an ice-cream, whereas those unwilling to wait do not. Alternatively, sellers could ration ice-cream according to their own personal biases, selling it only to friends, relatives or members of their own racial or ethnic group. Notice that even though the price ceiling was motivated by a desire to help buyers of ice-cream, not all buyers benefit from the policy. Some buyers do get to pay a lower price, although they may have to wait in line to do so, but other buyers cannot get any ice-cream at all.

This example in the market for ice-cream shows a general result – *when the government imposes a binding price ceiling on a competitive market, a shortage of the good arises and sellers must ration the scarce goods among the large number of potential buyers.* The rationing mechanisms that develop under price ceilings are rarely desirable. Long lines are inefficient, because they waste buyers' time. Discrimination according to seller bias is both inefficient (because the good does not go to the buyer who values it most highly) and potentially unfair. In contrast, the rationing mechanism in a free, competitive market is both efficient and impersonal. When the market for ice-cream reaches its equilibrium, anyone who wants to pay the market price can get an ice-cream. Free markets ration goods with prices.

CASESTUDY

Lines at the petrol station

Most major Australian cities receive their petrol from a single refinery. When the refinery reduces output, owing to a labour dispute, for example, then the supply of petrol to the city is cut. Long lines at petrol stations become commonplace, and motorists often have to wait for hours to buy only a few litres of petrol. A similar phenomenon occurred in the United States in 1973. Then, as we discussed in the last chapter, the Organization of Petroleum Exporting Countries (OPEC) raised the price of crude oil in world oil markets. Because crude oil is the major component used in making petrol, the higher oil prices reduced the supply of petrol. This also led to long lines for petrol in the United States.

Who is responsible for such long lines at petrol stations? If the supply of petrol has been cut because of a strike, most people blame either the oil companies or the unions. But the industrial dispute explains the cut in the supply of petrol, not the long lines. Similarly, the OPEC action also explains the reduction in the supply of petrol, but not the queues. These, most economists would argue, are due to government regulations that prevent petrol stations from raising the price they can charge for petrol.

Figure 6.2 shows what happens. As panel (a) shows, before the labour dispute, the supply of petrol is given by S_1 and the equilibrium price is P_1. But panel (b) shows that the dispute at the refinery cuts the supply of petrol back to S_2. If the petrol market were unregulated, the price of petrol would rise to P_2 and there would be no shortage. Instead, state governments prevent petrol stations from significantly raising the price of petrol. It is claimed that any significant price rises would be unfair to customers. The petrol stations are forced to charge below P_2. At this price, the petrol stations are willing to sell Q_S and consumers are willing to buy Q_D. Thus, the shift in the supply curve causes a severe shortage.

The ban on price rises not only creates long lines at petrol stations, it also reduces the incentive for producers to ship petrol in from other states. If the price of petrol increased to P_2, it would pay enterprising petrol station owners to buy petrol in an area unaffected by the dispute and have it delivered to their stations. By not allowing the price to rise, the government eliminates this incentive to bring in petrol supplies.

When the government prevents the price of petrol from rising during an industrial dispute, it says that it is protecting customers from 'price gouging' (increases in prices after strikes or disasters). Governments also prevent price gouging after natural disasters, when the supply of food and water is cut and the equilibrium price of these goods rises sharply. While governments prevent prices from rising for equity reasons – so that poorer people trapped by the disaster are not forced to pay higher prices – the laws against price gouging create shortages and reduce the incentives to ship more food and water into the affected regions.

Figure 6.2 **The market for petrol with a price ceiling**

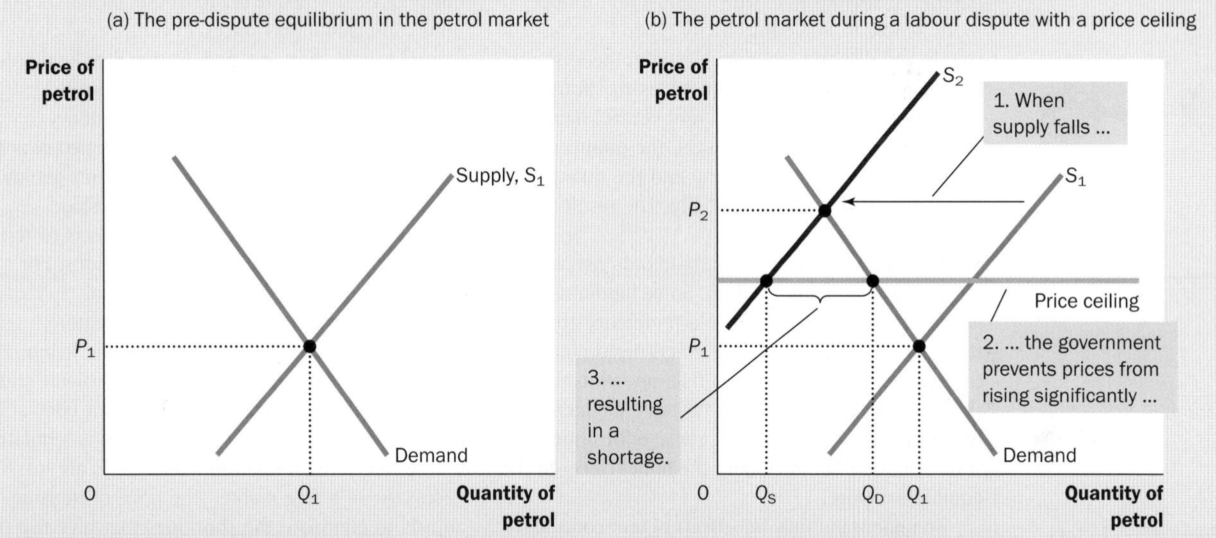

Panel (a) shows the petrol market when there is no price ceiling. The equilibrium price is P_1 and petrol sales are Q_1. Panel (b) shows the petrol market during an industrial dispute. The supply curve shifts to the left from S_1 to S_2. In the absence of government intervention, the price would have risen from P_1 to P_2. If the government imposes a price ceiling, this cannot happen. At the binding price ceiling, consumers are willing to buy Q_D, but producers of petrol are willing to sell only Q_S. The difference between quantity demanded and quantity supplied, $Q_D - Q_S$, measures the petrol shortage.

CASESTUDY

Rent control in the short run and long run

One common example of a price ceiling is rent control. In many cities around the world, local governments place a ceiling on rents that landlords may charge their tenants. The goal of this policy is to help the poor by making housing more affordable. Economists often criticise rent control, arguing that it is a highly inefficient way to help the poor raise their standard of living. One economist called rent control 'the best way to destroy a city, other than bombing'.

The adverse effects of rent control are less apparent to the general population because these effects occur over many years. In the short run, landlords have a fixed number of flats to rent and they cannot adjust this number quickly as market conditions change. Moreover, the number of people searching for housing in a city may not be highly responsive to rents in the short run because people take time to adjust their housing arrangements. Therefore, the short run supply of and demand for housing are relatively inelastic.

Panel (a) of Figure 6.3 shows the effects in the short run of rent control on the housing market. As with any price ceiling, rent control causes a shortage. Yet because supply and demand are inelastic in the short run, the initial shortage caused by rent control is small. The main effect in the short run is to reduce rents.

In the long run, the story is very different because the buyers and sellers of rental housing respond more to market conditions as time passes. On the supply side, landlords respond to low rents by not building new flats and by failing to maintain existing ones. On the demand side, low rents encourage people to find their own

>>

accommodation (rather than living with their parents or sharing flats with friends) and induce more people to move into a city. Therefore, both supply and demand are more elastic in the long run.

Panel (b) of Figure 6.3 illustrates the housing market in the long run. When rent control depresses rents below the equilibrium level, the quantity of flats supplied falls substantially and the quantity of flats demanded rises substantially. The result is a large shortage of housing.

In cities with rent control, landlords use various mechanisms to ration housing. Some landlords keep long waiting lists. Others give a preference to tenants without children. Still others discriminate on the basis of race. Sometimes, flats are allocated to those willing to offer under-the-table payments to real estate agents. In essence, these bribes bring the total price of a flat (including the bribe) closer to the equilibrium price.

To understand fully the effects of rent control, we have to remember one of the *Ten Lessons from Economics* from chapter 1 –people respond to incentives. In free markets, landlords try to keep their buildings clean and safe because desirable flats or home units command higher prices. In contrast, when rent control creates shortages and waiting lists, landlords lose their incentive to be responsive to tenants' concerns. Why should a landlord spend money to maintain and improve the property when people are waiting to get in as it is? In the end, tenants get lower rents, but they also get lower quality housing.

Policymakers often react to the effects of rent control by imposing additional regulations. For example, there are laws that make racial discrimination in housing illegal and require landlords to provide minimally adequate living conditions. These laws, however, are difficult and costly to enforce. In contrast, when rent control is eliminated and the market for housing is regulated by the forces of competition, such laws are less necessary. In a free market, the price of housing adjusts to eliminate the shortages that give rise to undesirable landlord behaviour.

Figure 6.3 **Rent control in the short run and in the long run**

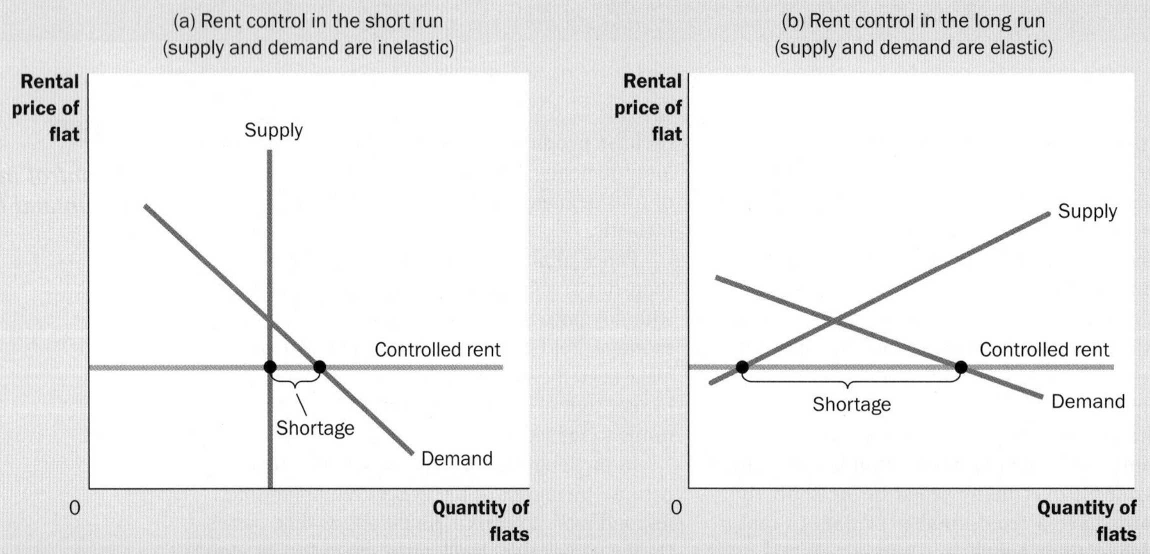

Panel (a) shows the effects in the short run of rent control – because the supply of and demand for flats are relatively inelastic, the price ceiling imposed by a rent-control law causes only a small shortage of housing. Panel (b) shows the effects in the long run of rent control – because the supply of and demand for flats are more elastic, rent control causes a large shortage.

IN THE NEWS . . .

RENT CONTROL IN MUMBAI, INDIA

Rent control plays a large role in many countries around the world. These laws are often justified as protecting tenants. However, the consequences can be extreme! As this article outlines, rent control in Mumbai (Bombay) India, one of the world's largest cities, has led to buildings being neglected and collapsing, killing the residents.

Nobody touches the Act

by Dilip D'Souza

Strolling through downtown Bombay one day during the recent monsoon, I passed a sign nailed high on an entrance to a building. It said: 'This building is dangerous. It may collapse at any time. Enter at your own risk'.

An unsettling sign any time. But at the time, it carried a special meaning, because the city was in the midst of what at least two papers called an 'epidemic' of building collapses: four in a week. The most recent had been the previous Monday. An 80-year-old edifice near the old Metro cinema crumbled, killing six people.

One more tragedy, in a monsoon season laced with tragedy.

So laced, that even the words took on special meanings. Take 'collapse'. On that terrible July 26, an entire Saki Naka hillside collapsed, destroying over a hundred huts and 75 or 80 lives. Take 'epidemic'. Two weeks after the July deluge, people began dying of diseases contracted that day, likely by walking through chest-deep water contaminated with urine and faeces and other random bits of Bombay filth.

Over two hundred people died like that.

And then, the building collapse epidemic.

Yet the truth is that buildings that crumble are an old Bombay tradition. Every monsoon, a few more give up the battle to stay erect. Weakened by years of neglect and disrepair, they come down, invariably taking lives. And behind all this are, as is another Bombay tradition, some intricate and often seedy goings-on.

In 1996, the Tavadia building in Bora Bazaar collapsed, taking 18 lives with it. About six weeks earlier, a man was found dead in a cinema theatre in Pune. One Ramesh Kini, he was a tenant in a building in Dadar owned by one Laxmichand Shah.

Why have I mentioned both these probably forgotten episodes, and in the same paragraph?

Because they have something in common: the foolish law that governs rental property in Bombay. Whatever benefits the Rent Control Act may have had at one time, today it is little but a threat to property and lives. If it is not repealed we must expect what happened at the Tavadia building, as well as what happened to Ramesh Kini, to keep happening.

The Act is simple: it freezes rent at a certain level. During World War II, floods of people, especially soldiers, came into the city. To prevent greedy landlords charging extortionate rent from them, the British put rent control in place. A limited number of buildings were brought under the Act when it first came into force. The Act allowed thousands of people to find affordable housing at rents that were kept frozen at 1940 levels as long as the tenants stayed. (Rents could be raised if a new tenant came in.)

Of course, by now many of those wartime tenants have died. Their children and grandchildren stay on in the same flats, paying the same rents. I know a couple who lived in a gorgeous flat in an old building near Churchgate. For years, they paid the rent for the flat that the man's father had signed up for half a century earlier: twenty rupees a month. (Yes.) The amount they extracted from their landlord, just for giving him his flat back eventually, allowed them to buy themselves a home in a small town in another state. That's where they are today.

By no means is this a unique or even unusual story.

Naturally, the amount a landlord earns from rent cannot begin to pay the costs of maintenance on his aging building. So he stops maintaining it and will not carry out repairs. The

>>

building becomes steadily weaker. In the end, it falls down, killing several of its tenants.

By no means is that a unique or unusual story either.

The strange thing about this state of affairs is not just that tenants pay absurdly low rents. They also want their landlords to carry out repairs and keep their buildings in shape. They also are unwilling to pay for the repairs themselves.

For example, one of the tenants of the Tavadia building told the press that she was paying a rent of Rs 100. But, as the *Times of India* reported, 'she felt that the tragedy could have been averted had the landlord ... not ignored their repeated pleas to repair the building'. It was in such bad shape, she went on, that 'anyone walking with heavy steps would set off a tremor'.

The lady lost her father in the collapse. I wish she and her fellow tenants had offered to pay to maintain the building. Her father might still be alive. I hope she understands that now.

But there is a more sinister side to the Act too. Real estate prices are so inflated in this city that many tenants can never hope to move from their rent-controlled flats. (Unless they move, like my Churchgate friends did, to a small town). So they have no option but to stay. Landlords, meanwhile, know how lucrative it would be to sell their property, particularly to a builder. But what's to be done with tenants who won't leave?

Landlords try persuasion. They try pleading. They try the courts, but that takes years. Eventually, some landlords turn to threats and force. That's what Ramesh Kini had to face. Eventually, he may have killed himself. Or he may have been done in by thugs. His death really remains a mystery, but in a profound way, Rent Control had a lot to do with it.

Everyone knows the damage the Rent Control Act does. But why isn't something done about it?

The simple answer: numbers. Tenants outnumber landlords. The low rent the Act has them paying outweighs all other considerations – they want to keep paying it. Politicians know all about numbers. They are aware that the first of their breed who makes a move on the Rent Control Act will promptly lose the votes of millions of tenants. He will probably gain the votes of landlords, but that's poor compensation.

Which means: nobody touches the Act.

But there's a more complex answer as well. The Act can't be seen in isolation. The high price of real estate; the well known corrupt, violent but mutually beneficial connection between politicians and builders; the steps we have deliberately ignored that would have served to keep land prices down – all of these have played roles in the persistence of this pernicious law. All have also flourished because of the Act. All will have to be taken into account in any review of the Act.

Which also means: nobody touches the Act.

Source: Dilip d'Souza/*India Together* Magazine, 24 November 2005.

How price floors affect market outcomes

To examine the effects of another kind of government price control, let's return to the market for ice-cream. Imagine now that the government is persuaded by the pleas of the National Organisation of Ice-cream Makers whose members feel that the $3 equilibrium price is too low. In this case, the government might institute a price floor. Price floors, like price ceilings, are an attempt by the government to maintain prices at other than equilibrium levels. Whereas a price ceiling places a legal maximum on prices, a price floor places a legal minimum.

When the government imposes a price floor on the ice-cream market, two outcomes are possible. If the government imposes a price floor of $2 per ice-cream when the equilibrium price is $3, we obtain the outcome in panel (a) of Figure 6.4. In this case, because the equilibrium price is above the floor, the price floor is not binding. Market forces naturally move the economy to the equilibrium and the price floor has no effect.

Figure 6.4 A market with a price floor

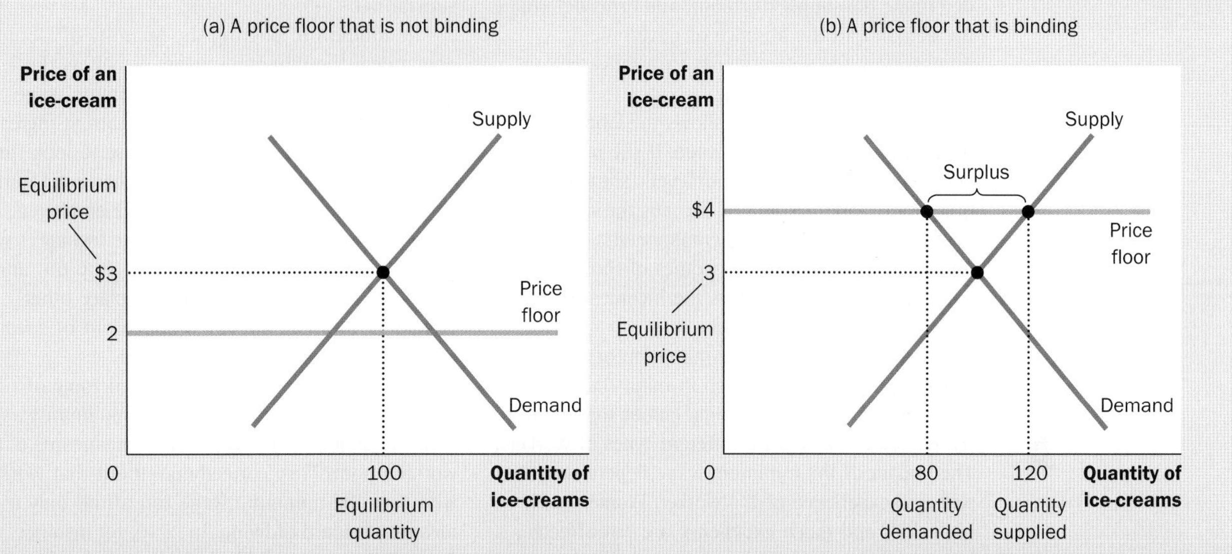

In panel (a), the government imposes a price floor of $2. Because this is below the equilibrium price of $3, the price floor has no effect. The market price adjusts to balance supply and demand. At the equilibrium, quantity supplied and quantity demanded both equal 100 ice-creams. In panel (b), the government imposes a price floor of $4, which is above the equilibrium price of $3. Therefore, the market price equals $4. Because 120 ice-creams are supplied at this price and only 80 are demanded, there is a surplus of 40 ice-creams.

Panel (b) of Figure 6.4 shows what happens when the government imposes a price floor of $4 per ice-cream. In this case, because the equilibrium price of $3 is below the floor, the price floor is a binding constraint on the market. The forces of supply and demand tend to move the price towards the equilibrium price, but when the market price hits the floor, it can fall no further. The market price equals the price floor. At this floor, the quantity of ice-cream supplied (120 ice-creams) exceeds the quantity demanded (80). Some people who want to sell ice-cream at the going price are unable to. Thus, *a binding price floor causes a surplus.*

Just as the shortages resulting from price ceilings can lead to undesirable rationing mechanisms, so can the surpluses resulting from price floors. In the case of a price floor, some sellers are unable to sell all they want at the market price. The sellers who appeal to the personal biases of the buyers, perhaps because of racial or familial ties, are better able to sell their goods than those who do not. In contrast, in a free market, the price serves as the rationing mechanism and sellers can sell all they want at the equilibrium price.

CASESTUDY

Minimum wage rates

An important example of a price floor is a minimum wage. Minimum-wage laws dictate the lowest price for labour that any employer may pay. In Australia, a federal government body, Fair Work Australia, sets **awards** which include the minimum wage rates that can be paid to particular workers in particular industries. (Until 2009, this role was fulfilled by the Fair Pay Commission.) Unlike other countries, such as the United States, Australia does not have a single minimum wage but a system of awards.

To examine the effects of a minimum wage or award rate, we must consider the market for labour in a particular industry. Panel (a) of Figure 6.5 shows the labour market which, like all markets, is

awards
the minimum wage rates that can be paid to particular workers in particular industries

>>

subject to the forces of supply and demand. Workers determine the supply of labour, and firms determine the demand. In the absence of government intervention, the wage adjusts to balance labour supply and labour demand.

Panel (b) of Figure 6.5 shows the labour market with a minimum or award wage. If the minimum wage is above the equilibrium level, as it is here, the quantity of labour supplied exceeds the quantity demanded. The result is unemployment. Thus, the minimum wage raises the incomes of those workers who have jobs, but it lowers the incomes of those workers who cannot find jobs.

To fully understand the minimum or award wage, it is important to keep in mind that the economy contains not a single labour market, but many labour markets for different types of workers. The impact of the minimum wage depends on the skill and experience of the worker. Workers with high skills and much experience are not affected, because their equilibrium wages are well above the minimum. For these workers, award wage rates are not binding.

Minimum wages have their greatest impact on the market for teenage labour. The equilibrium wages of teenagers tend to be low because teenagers are among the least skilled and least experienced members of the labour force. In addition, teenagers are often willing to accept a lower wage in exchange for on-the-job training. This effect is recognised in Australia where there is a separate minimum wage for teenagers – the 'junior' award. Even so, teenagers are more likely to be paid at this minimum rate, whereas other members of the labour force may be paid above-award wages.

Many economists have examined how minimum-wage laws affect the teenage labour market. These researchers compare the changes in the minimum wage over time with the changes in teenage employment. Although there is some debate about how much the minimum wage affects employment, the typical study finds that a 10 per cent increase in the minimum wage depresses teenage employment between 1 per cent and 3 per cent. In interpreting this estimate, note that a 10 per cent increase in the minimum wage does not raise the average wage of teenagers by 10 per cent. A change in the law does not directly affect those teenagers who are already paid well above the minimum. Moreover, enforcement of minimum-wage laws is not perfect. Thus, the estimated drop in employment of 1 per cent to 3 per cent is substantial.

In addition to altering the quantity of labour demanded, the minimum wage also alters the quantity supplied. Because the minimum wage raises the wage that teenagers can earn, it increases the number of teenagers who choose to look for jobs. Studies have found that a higher minimum wage influences which teenagers are employed. When the minimum wage rises, some teenagers who are still attending school choose to drop out and take jobs. These new drop-outs displace other teenagers who had already dropped out of school and who now become unemployed.

The minimum wage is a frequent topic of political debate. Advocates of the minimum wage view the policy as one way to raise the income of the working poor. They correctly point out that workers who earn the minimum wage can afford only a meagre standard of living. In 2010, for instance, the Australian Council of Trade Unions – representing employees – argued to Fair Work Australia that the minimum wage applying to all workers should be increased by $27 per week. Their argument was based on the idea that there should be community standards for minimum wages and that low wage workers need sufficient income to meet their needs. Many advocates of the minimum wage admit that it potentially has some adverse effects, including unemployment, but they believe that these effects are small and that, all things considered, a higher minimum wage makes the poor better off.

Opponents of the minimum wage contend that it is not the best way to combat poverty. They note that high minimum wages and junior wages cause unemployment, encourage teenagers to drop out of school and prevent some unskilled workers from getting the on-the-job training they need. Moreover, opponents of the minimum wage point out that the minimum wage is a poorly targeted policy. Not all award-wage workers are heads of households trying to help their families escape poverty. Many award-wage earners are teenagers from middle-class homes working at part-time jobs for extra spending money.

In June 2010, Fair Work Australia concluded its first annual wage review. It accepted the argument that minimum wages provide a fair safety net for workers and raised the award minimum wages by $26 per week, resulting in a national minimum wage of $15 per hour.

Figure 6.5 How the minimum wage affects the labour market

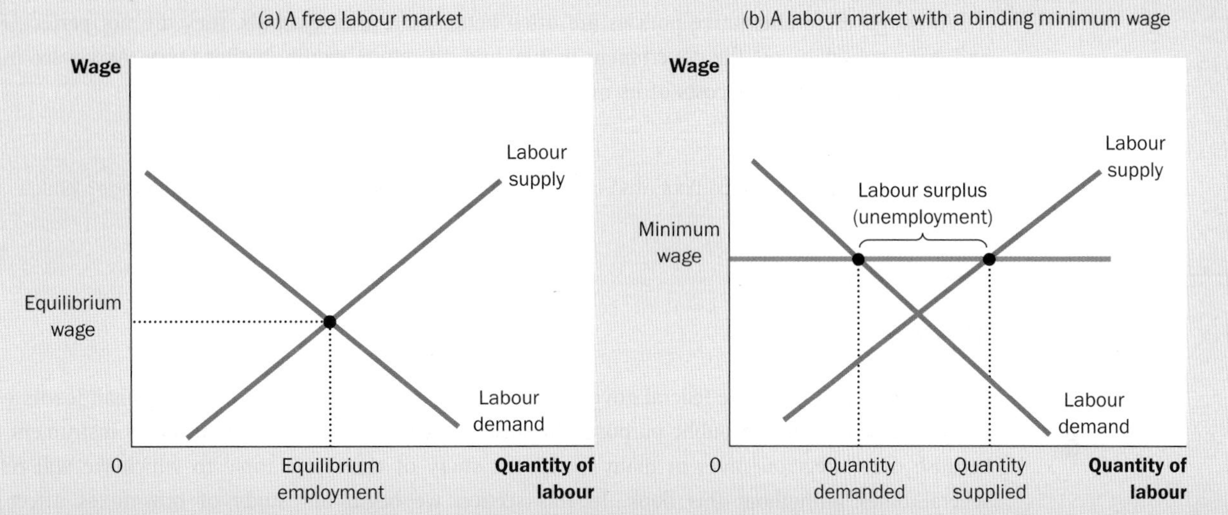

Panel (a) shows a labour market in which the wage adjusts to balance labour supply and labour demand. Panel (b) shows the impact of a binding minimum or award wage. Because the minimum wage is a price floor, it causes a surplus – the quantity of labour supplied exceeds the quantity demanded. The result is unemployment.

Evaluating price controls

One of the *Ten Lessons from Economics* discussed in chapter 1 is that markets are usually a good way to organise economic activity. That lesson explains why economists almost always oppose price ceilings and price floors. To economists, prices are not the outcome of some haphazard process. Prices, they contend, are the result of the millions of business and consumer decisions that lie behind the supply and demand curves. Prices have the crucial job of balancing supply and demand and, thereby, coordinating economic activity. When policymakers set prices by legal decree, they obscure the signals that normally guide the allocation of society's resources.

Another one of the *Ten Lessons from Economics* is that governments can sometimes improve market outcomes. Indeed, policymakers are led to control prices because they view the market's outcome as unfair. Price controls are often aimed at helping the poor. For instance, rent-control laws try to make housing affordable for everyone and minimum-wage laws try to help people escape poverty.

Yet price controls often hurt those they are trying to help. Rent control may keep rents low, but it also discourages landlords from maintaining their buildings and makes housing hard to find. Minimum-wage laws may raise the incomes of some workers, but they also cause other workers to be unemployed.

Helping those in need can be accomplished in ways other than controlling prices. For instance, the government can make housing more affordable by paying a fraction of the rent for poor families. In Australia, low-income families are eligible for rent assistance of up to around $75 per week. Unlike rent control, such rent subsidies do not reduce the quantity of housing supplied and, therefore, do not lead to housing shortages. Similarly, wage subsidies raise the living standards of the working poor without discouraging firms from hiring them.

Although these alternative policies are often better than price controls, they are not perfect. Rent and wage subsidies cost the government money and, therefore, require higher taxes. As we see in the next section, taxation has costs of its own.

Q

Define price ceiling and price floor, and give an example of each. Which leads to a shortage? Which leads to a surplus? Why?

Taxes

All governments – from the federal government in Canberra to local governments in small towns – use taxes to raise revenue for public purposes. Because taxes are such an important policy instrument and because they affect our lives in many ways, the study of taxes is a topic to which we will return several times throughout this book. In this section we begin our study of how taxes affect the economy.

To set the stage for our analysis, imagine that a local government decides to hold an annual ice-cream celebration – with a parade, fireworks and speeches by town officials. To raise revenue to pay for the event, it decides to place a $0.50 tax on the sale of ice-creams. When the plan is announced, our two lobbying groups swing into action. The National Organisation of Ice-cream Makers claims that its members are struggling to survive in a competitive market and it argues that *buyers* of ice-cream should have to pay the tax. The Australian Association of Ice-cream Eaters claims that consumers of ice-cream are having trouble making ends meet and it argues that *sellers* of ice-cream should pay the tax. The mayor, hoping to reach a compromise, suggests that half the tax be paid by the buyers and half be paid by the sellers.

To analyse these proposals, we need to consider a simple but subtle question. When the government levies a tax on a good, who bears the burden of the tax – the people buying the good or the people selling the good? Or, if buyers and sellers share the tax burden, what determines how the burden is divided? Can the government simply legislate the division of the burden, as the mayor is suggesting, or is the division determined by more fundamental forces in the economy? Economists use the term **tax incidence** to refer to these questions about the distribution of a tax burden. As we will see, we can learn some surprising lessons about tax incidence just by applying the tools of supply and demand.

tax incidence
the study of who bears the burden of taxation

Search me!
▸ tax incidence

How taxes on buyers affect market outcomes

We begin by considering a tax levied on buyers of a good. Suppose, for instance, that our local government passes a law requiring buyers of ice-creams to send $0.50 to the government for each ice-cream they buy. How does this law affect the buyers and sellers of ice-cream? To answer this question, we can follow the three steps in chapter 4 for analysing supply and demand:

1 we decide whether the law affects the supply or demand curve
2 we decide which way the curve shifts
3 we examine how the shift affects the equilibrium.

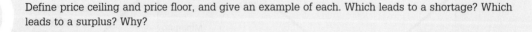

Step one

The initial impact of the tax is on the demand for ice-cream. The supply curve is not affected because, for any given price of ice-cream, sellers have the same incentive to provide ice-cream to the market. In contrast, buyers now have to pay a tax to the government (as well as the price to the sellers) whenever they buy ice-cream. Thus, the tax shifts the demand curve for ice-cream.

Step two

We next determine the direction of the shift. Because the tax on buyers makes buying ice-cream less attractive, buyers demand a smaller quantity of ice-cream at every price. As a result, the demand curve shifts to the left (or, equivalently, downwards), as shown in Figure 6.6.

In addition to determining the direction in which the demand curve shifts, we can also be precise about the size of the shift. Because of the $0.50 tax levied on buyers, the effective price to buyers is now $0.50 higher than the market price (whatever the market price happens to be). For example, if the market price of an ice-cream happened to be $2.00, the effective price to buyers would be $2.50. Because buyers look at their total cost including the tax, they demand a quantity of ice-cream as if the market price were $0.50 higher than it actually is. In other words, to induce buyers to demand any given quantity, the market price must now be $0.50 lower to make up for the effect of the tax. Thus, the tax shifts the demand curve *downward* from D_1 to D_2 by exactly the size of the tax ($0.50).

Figure 6.6 **A tax on buyers**

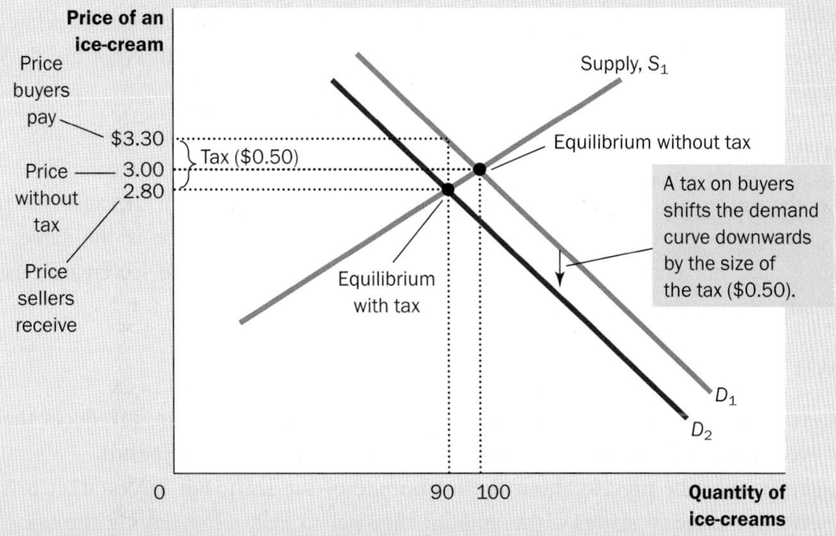

When a tax of $0.50 is levied on buyers, the demand curve shifts down by $0.50 from D_1 to D_2. The equilibrium quantity falls from 100 to 90 ice-creams. The price that sellers receive falls from $3.00 to $2.80. The price that buyers pay (including the tax) rises from $3.00 to $3.30. Even though the tax is levied on buyers, buyers and sellers share the burden of the tax.

Step three

Having determined how the demand curve shifts, we can now see the effect of the tax by comparing the initial equilibrium and the new equilibrium. You can see in the figure that the equilibrium price of ice-cream falls from \$3.00 to \$2.80 and the equilibrium quantity falls from 100 to 90 ice-creams. Because sellers sell less and buyers buy less in the new equilibrium, the tax on ice-cream reduces the size of the ice-cream market.

Implications

We can now turn to the question of tax incidence: Who pays the tax? Although buyers send the entire tax to the government, buyers and sellers share the burden. Because the market price falls from \$3.00 to \$2.80 when the tax is introduced, sellers receive \$0.20 less for each ice-cream than they did without the tax. Thus, the tax makes sellers worse off. Buyers pay sellers a lower price (\$2.80), but the effective price including the tax rises from \$3.00 before the tax to \$3.30 with the tax (\$2.80 + \$0.50 = \$3.30). Thus, the tax also makes buyers worse off.

To sum up, this analysis yields two lessons:

- Taxes discourage market activity. When a good is taxed, the quantity of the good sold is smaller in the new equilibrium.
- Buyers and sellers share the burden of taxes. In the new equilibrium, buyers pay more for the good and sellers receive less.

How taxes on sellers affect market outcomes

Now consider a tax levied on sellers of a good. Suppose the local government passes a law requiring sellers of ice-creams to send \$0.50 to the government for each one they sell. What are the effects of this law? Again, we apply our three steps.

Step one

In this case, the immediate impact of the tax is on the sellers of ice-cream. Because the tax is not levied on buyers, the quantity of ice-cream demanded at any given price is the same; thus, the demand curve does not change. By contrast, the tax on sellers makes the ice-cream business less profitable at any given price, so it shifts the supply curve.

Step two

Because the tax on sellers raises the cost of producing and selling ice-cream, it reduces the quantity supplied at every price. The supply curve shifts to the left (or equivalently, upward).

Once again, we can be precise about the magnitude of the shift. For any market price of ice-cream, the effective price to sellers – the amount they get to keep after paying the tax – is \$0.50 lower. For example, if the market price of an ice-cream happened to be \$2.00, the effective price received by sellers would be \$1.50. Whatever the market price, sellers will supply a quantity of ice-cream as if the price were \$0.50 lower than it is. Put differently, to induce sellers to supply any given quantity, the market price must now be \$0.50 higher to compensate for the effect of the tax. Thus, as shown in Figure 6.7, the supply curve shifts *upward* from S_1 to S_2 by exactly the size of the tax (\$0.50).

Figure 6.7 A tax on sellers

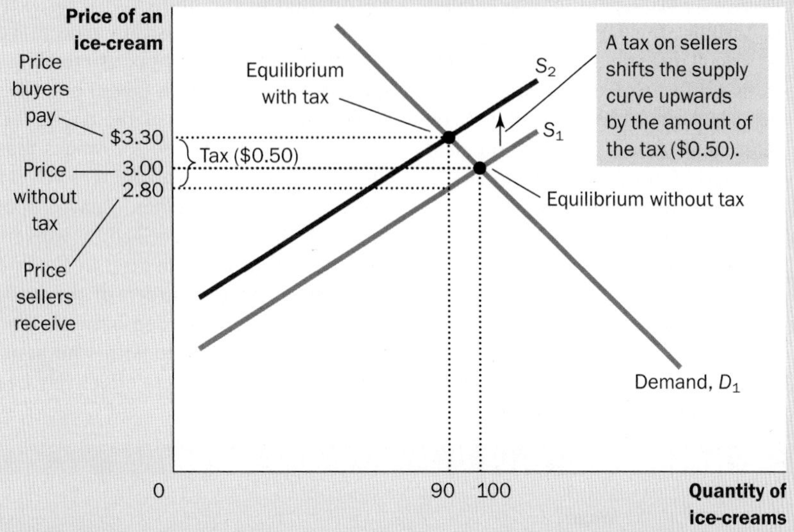

When a tax of $0.50 is levied on sellers, the supply curve shifts up by $0.50 from S_1 to S_2. The equilibrium quantity falls from 100 to 90 ice-creams. The price that buyers pay rises from $3.00 to $3.30. The price that sellers receive (after paying the tax) falls from $3.00 to $2.80. Even though the tax is levied on sellers, buyers and sellers share the burden of the tax.

Step three

Having determined how the supply curve shifts, we can now compare the initial and the new equilibrium. The figure shows that the equilibrium price of ice-cream rises from $3.00 to $3.30, and the equilibrium quantity falls from 100 to 90 ice-creams. Once again, the tax reduces the size of the ice-cream market. And once again, buyers and sellers share the burden of the tax. Because the market price rises, buyers pay $0.30 more for each ice-cream than they did before the tax was enacted. Sellers receive a higher price than they did without the tax, but the effective price (after paying the tax) falls from $3.00 to $2.80.

Implications

If you compare Figures 6.6 and 6.7, you will notice a surprising conclusion – *taxes on buyers and taxes on sellers are equivalent.* In both cases, the tax places a wedge between the price that buyers pay and the price that sellers receive. The wedge between the buyers' price and the sellers' price is the same, regardless of whether the tax is levied on buyers or sellers. In either case, the wedge shifts the relative position of the supply and demand curves. In the new equilibrium, buyers and sellers share the burden of the tax. The only difference between taxes on buyers and taxes on sellers is who sends the money to the government.

The equivalence of these two taxes is perhaps easier to understand if we imagine that the government collects the $0.50 ice-cream tax in a bowl on the counter of each ice-cream shop. When the government levies the tax on buyers, the buyer is required to place $0.50 in the bowl every time an ice-cream is bought. When the government levies the tax on sellers, the seller is required to place

CASESTUDY

Who pays the payroll tax?

If you have ever received a pay packet, you probably noticed that taxes were deducted from the amount you earned. In Australia, this tax is income tax imposed by the federal government. However, there are other taxes that affect workers. In particular, state governments in Australia levy payroll taxes on medium and large employers. In 2010, the standard payroll tax was around 5 per cent of the total payments a firm makes to its employees. However, in some states this rate was higher (up to 6.85 per cent).

Who do you think bears the burden of this payroll tax – firms or workers? Payroll tax is imposed on employers so governments often argue that it is different from a tax on income. But is it true that payroll tax is really paid by employers?

Our analysis of tax incidence shows that the distribution of the burden of a tax is determined by more than who physically pays it. To illustrate, we can analyse payroll tax as merely a tax on a good, where the good is labour and the price is the wage. The key feature of the payroll tax is that it places a wedge between the wages that firms pay and the wages that workers receive. Figure 6.8 shows the outcome. When a payroll tax is imposed, the wages received by workers fall and the wages paid by firms rise. In the end, workers and firms share the burden of the tax. So the division of the tax burden between workers and firms has nothing to do with who actually hands over the money. Workers effectively bear some of the tax burden.

Figure 6.8 **A payroll tax**

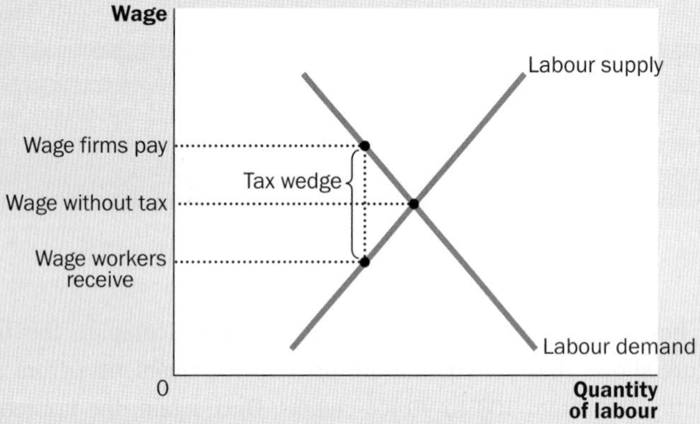

A payroll tax places a wedge between the wages that workers receive and the wages that firms pay. Comparing wages with and without the tax, you can see that workers and firms share the tax burden. This division of the tax burden between workers and firms does not depend on whether the government levies the tax on workers, levies the tax on firms or divides the tax equally between the two groups.

This example shows that the most basic lesson of tax incidence is often overlooked in public debate. Law makers can decide whether a tax comes from the buyer's pocket or from the seller's, but they cannot legislate the true burden of a tax. Rather, tax incidence depends on the forces of supply and demand.

$0.50 in the bowl after the sale of each ice-cream. Whether the $0.50 goes directly from the buyer's pocket into the bowl, or indirectly from the buyer's pocket into the seller's hand and then into the bowl, does not matter. Once the market reaches its new equilibrium, buyers and sellers share the burden, regardless of how the tax is levied.

Elasticity and tax incidence

When a good is taxed, buyers and sellers of the good share the burden of the tax. But how exactly is the tax burden divided? Only rarely will it be shared equally. To see how the burden is divided, consider the impact of taxation in the two markets in Figure 6.9. In both cases, the figure shows the initial demand curve, the initial supply curve and a tax that drives a wedge between the amount paid by buyers and the amount received by sellers. (Not drawn in either panel of the figure is the new supply or demand curve. Which curve shifts depends on whether the tax is levied on buyers or sellers. As we have seen, this is irrelevant for the incidence of the tax.) The difference in the two panels is the relative elasticity of supply and demand.

Panel (a) of Figure 6.9 shows a tax in a market with very elastic supply and relatively inelastic demand – that is, sellers are very responsive to the price of the good, whereas buyers are not very responsive. When a tax is imposed on a market with these elasticities, the price received by sellers does not fall much, so sellers bear only a small burden. In contrast, the price paid by buyers rises substantially, indicating that buyers bear most of the burden of the tax.

Panel (b) of Figure 6.9 shows a tax in a market with relatively inelastic supply and very elastic demand. In this case, sellers are not very responsive to the price, whereas buyers are very responsive. The figure shows that when a tax is imposed, the price paid by buyers does not rise much and the price received by sellers falls substantially. Thus, sellers bear most of the burden of the tax.

The two panels of Figure 6.9 show a general lesson about how the burden of a tax is divided – *a tax burden falls more heavily on the side of the market that is less elastic.* Why is this true? In essence, the elasticity measures the willingness of buyers or sellers to leave the market when conditions become unfavourable. A small elasticity of demand means that buyers do not have good alternatives to consuming this particular good. A small elasticity of supply means that sellers do not have good alternatives to producing this particular good. When the good is taxed, the side of the market with

Figure 6.9 **How the burden of a tax is divided**

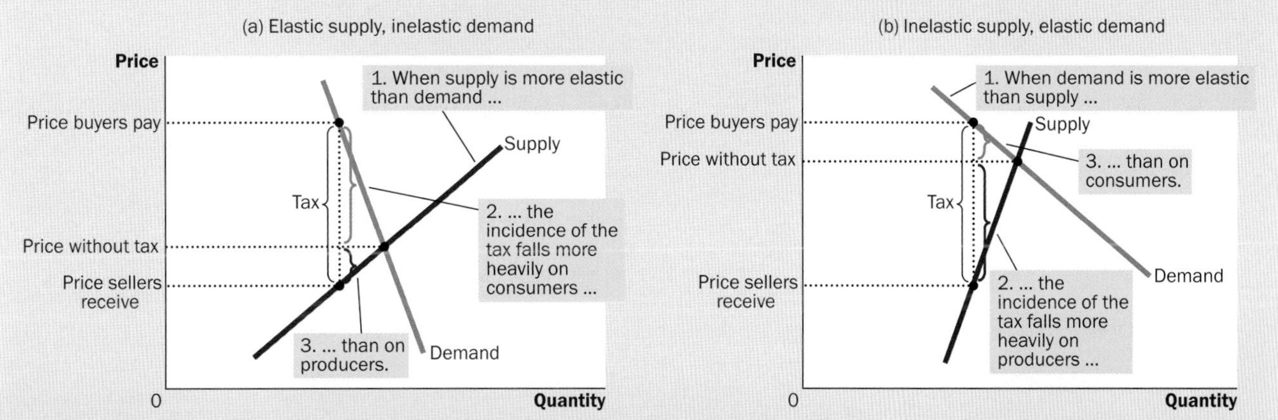

In panel (a), the supply curve is elastic and the demand curve is inelastic. In this case, the price received by sellers falls only slightly and the price paid by buyers rises substantially. Thus, buyers bear most of the burden of the tax. In panel (b), the supply curve is inelastic and the demand curve is elastic. In this case, the price received by sellers falls substantially and the price paid by buyers rises only slightly. Thus, sellers bear most of the burden of the tax.

fewer good alternatives cannot easily leave the market and must, therefore, bear more of the burden of the tax.

We can apply this logic to the payroll tax, which was discussed in the previous case study: Most labour economists believe that the supply of labour is much less elastic than the demand. This means that workers, rather than firms, bear most of the burden of the payroll tax. In other words, the distribution of the tax burden is far from falling wholly on employers as the lawmakers may have intended.

Q

In a supply-and-demand diagram, show how a tax on car buyers of $1000 per car affects the quantity of cars sold and the price of cars. In another diagram, show how a tax on car sellers of $1000 per car affects the quantity of cars sold and the price of cars. In both diagrams, show the change in the price paid by car buyers and the change in the price received by car sellers.

Conclusion

The economy is governed by two kinds of laws – the laws of supply and demand and the laws enacted by governments. In this chapter we have begun to see how these laws interact. Price controls and taxes are common in various markets in the economy and their effects are frequently debated in the press and among policymakers. Even a little bit of economic knowledge can go a long way towards understanding and evaluating these policies.

In subsequent chapters we will analyse many government policies in greater detail. We examine the effects of taxation more fully and consider a broader range of policies than we considered here. Yet the basic lessons of this chapter will not change – when analysing government policies, supply and demand are the first and most useful tools of analysis.

Summary

- A price ceiling is a legal maximum on the price of a good or service. An example is rent control. If the price ceiling is below the equilibrium price, so the price ceiling is binding, the quantity demanded exceeds the quantity supplied. Because of the resulting shortage, sellers must in some way ration the good or service among buyers.
- A price floor is a legal minimum on the price of a good or service. An example is a minimum or award wage. If the price floor is above the equilibrium price, so the price floor is binding, the quantity supplied exceeds the quantity demanded. Because of the resulting surplus, buyers' demands for the good or service must in some way be rationed among sellers.
- When the government levies a tax on a good, the equilibrium quantity of the good falls. That is, a tax on a market shrinks the size of the market.
- A tax on a good places a wedge between the price paid by buyers and the price received by sellers. When the market moves to the new equilibrium, buyers pay more for the good and sellers receive less for it. In this sense, buyers and sellers share the tax burden. The incidence of a tax (that is, the division of the tax burden) does not depend on whether the tax is levied on buyers or sellers.
- The incidence of a tax depends on the price elasticities of supply and demand. The burden tends to fall on the side of the market that is less elastic because that side of the market can respond less easily to the tax by changing the quantity bought or sold.

Key concepts

awards	price floor
price ceiling	tax incidence

Questions for review

1 Give an example of a price ceiling and of a price floor.
2 Which causes a shortage of a good – a price ceiling or a price floor? Which causes a surplus?
3 What mechanisms allocate resources when the price of a good is not allowed to bring supply and demand into equilibrium?
4 Explain why economists usually oppose controls on prices.
5 What is the difference between a tax paid by buyers and a tax paid by sellers?
6 How does a tax on a good affect the price paid by buyers, the price received by sellers and the quantity sold?
7 What determines how the burden of a tax is divided between buyers and sellers? Why?

Problems and applications

1 Lovers of classical music persuade the government to impose a price ceiling of $50 per concert ticket. As a result of this policy, do more or fewer people attend classical music concerts?
2 The government has decided that the free-market price of cheese is too low.
   a Suppose the government imposes a binding price floor in the cheese market. Use a supply-and-demand diagram to show the effect of this policy on the price of cheese and the quantity of cheese sold. Is there a shortage or surplus of cheese?
   b Farmers complain that the price floor has reduced their total revenue. Is this possible? Explain.

c In response to farmers' complaints, the government agrees to purchase all of the surplus cheese at the price floor. Compared with the basic price floor, who benefits from this new policy? Who loses?

3 A recent study found that the demand and supply schedules for frisbees are as follows:

Price per frisbee	Quantity demanded	Quantity supplied
$11	1 million	15 million
10	2	12
9	4	9
8	6	6
7	8	3
6	10	1

a What are the equilibrium price and quantity of frisbees?

b Frisbee manufacturers persuade the government that frisbee production improves scientists' understanding of aerodynamics and thus is important for national security. A concerned government votes to impose a price floor $2 above the equilibrium price. What is the new market price? How many frisbees are sold?

c Irate university students march on Canberra and demand a reduction in the price of frisbees. An even more concerned parliament votes to repeal the price floor and impose a price ceiling $1 below the former price floor. What is the new market price? How many frisbees are sold?

4 Suppose the federal government requires beer drinkers to pay a $2 tax on each carton of beer purchased. (In fact, both the federal and state governments impose beer taxes of some sort.)

a Draw a supply-and-demand diagram of the market for beer without the tax. Show the price paid by consumers, the price received by producers and the quantity of beer sold. What is the difference between the price paid by consumers and the price received by producers?

b Now draw a supply-and-demand diagram for the beer market with the tax. Show the price paid by consumers, the price received by producers and the quantity of beer sold. What is the difference between the price paid by consumers and the price received by producers? Has the quantity of beer sold increased or decreased?

5 If the government places a $500 tax on luxury cars, will the price paid by consumers rise by more than $500, less than $500 or exactly $500? Explain.

6 The federal government decides that Australia should reduce air pollution by reducing its use of petrol. The government imposes a $0.50 tax for each litre of petrol sold.

a Should this tax be imposed on producers or consumers? Explain carefully using a supply-and-demand diagram.

b If the demand for petrol were more elastic, would this tax be more effective or less effective in reducing the quantity of petrol consumed? Explain using both words and a diagram.

c Are consumers of petrol helped or hurt by this tax? Why?

d Are workers in the oil industry helped or hurt by this tax? Why?

7 A case study in this chapter discusses minimum or award wages.

a Suppose the award wage in a particular industry is above the equilibrium wage in the market for unskilled labour. Using a supply-and-demand diagram of the market for unskilled labour, show the market wage, the number of workers who are employed and the number of workers who are unemployed. Also show the total wage payments to unskilled workers.

b Now suppose that Fair Work Australia proposes an increase in the award wage. What effect would this increase have on employment? Does the change in employment depend on the elasticity of demand, the elasticity of supply, both elasticities or neither?

c What effect would this increase in the award wage have on unemployment? Does the change in unemployment depend on the elasticity of demand, the elasticity of supply, both elasticities or neither?

d If the demand for unskilled labour were inelastic, would the proposed increase in the award wage raise or lower total wage payments to unskilled workers? Would your answer change if the demand for unskilled labour were elastic?

8 An alcopop is a sweet pre-mixed alcoholic drink. Consider the following policies, each of which is aimed at reducing the amount of alcopops consumed by people in Australia. Illustrate each of these proposed policies in a supply-and-demand diagram of the alcopop market.

a a tax on alcopop buyers

b a tax on alcopop sellers

c a price floor on alcopops.

9 The Australian government administers two programs that affect the market for cigarettes. Media campaigns and labelling requirements are aimed at making the public aware of the dangers of cigarette smoking. At the same time, there is a tax on cigarettes.

a How do these two programs affect cigarette consumption? Use a graph of the cigarette market in your answer.

b What is the combined effect of these two programs on the price of cigarettes?

10 In 2001, the Australian government, in response to political pressure, cut the excise (or wholesale) tax on petrol by 1.5 cents per litre.

a In the absence of other policies (for example, price controls), do you think that the price of petrol that consumers pay (that is, the price at the pump) will fall by 1.5 cents?

b Who, apart from consumers, is likely to benefit from this tax cut?

c To ensure that the price consumers paid for petrol fell by the full 1.5 cents, the government attempted to enforce this through its competition regulator, the ACCC. Will producer profits rise, fall or stay the same if this price control is effective?

11 (This question requires the use of secondary school algebra.) Suppose the demand curve for pizza can be represented by the equation $Q^D = 20 - 2P$, where Q^D is the quantity demanded and P is the price. The supply curve for pizza can be represented by the equation $Q^S = P - 1$, where Q^S is the quantity supplied. Suppose the government imposes a $3 tax per pizza. How much more will consumers now pay for a pizza? (*Hint:* The prices in the demand and supply equations are no longer equal. The price that determines quantity demanded now equals the price that determines quantity supplied plus $3.)

12 A subsidy is the opposite of a tax. With a $0.50 tax on the buyers of ice-creams, the government collects $0.50 for each ice-cream purchased; with a $0.50 subsidy for the buyers of ice-creams, the government pays buyers $0.50 for each ice-cream purchased.

a Show the effect of a $0.50 subsidy per ice-cream on the demand curve for ice-creams, the effective price paid by consumers, the effective price received by sellers and the quantity of ice-creams sold.

b Do consumers gain or lose from this policy? Do producers gain or lose? Does the government gain or lose?

Search me!

When accessing information about microeconomics use the following keywords in any combinations you require:

- price ceiling
- price floor
- tax incidence

CourseMate

CourseMate

For more multimedia resources and activities on economics, visit the Economics CourseMate website.

PART THREE

Supply and demand II: Markets and welfare

7

Consumers, producers and the efficiency of markets

Learning objectives

In this chapter you will:

- examine the link between buyers' willingness to pay for a good and the demand curve
- learn how to define and measure consumer surplus
- examine the link between sellers' costs of producing a good and the supply curve
- learn how to define and measure producer surplus
- see that the equilibrium of supply and demand maximises total surplus in a market.

When consumers go to florists to buy roses and other types of flowers for Valentine's Day or Mother's Day, they may be disappointed that the price of a bunch is as high as it is. At the same time, when flower growers bring to market the flowers they have grown, they wish that the price of flowers were even higher. These views are not surprising; buyers always want to pay less and sellers always want to get paid more. But is there a 'right price' for flowers from the standpoint of society as a whole?

In previous chapters we saw how, in market economies, the forces of supply and demand determine the prices of goods and services and the quantities sold. So far, however, we have described the way markets allocate scarce resources without directly considering the question of whether these market allocations are desirable. In other words, our analysis has been positive (what is) rather than normative (what should be). We know that the price of a bunch of roses adjusts to ensure that the quantity of roses supplied equals the quantity of roses demanded. But, at this equilibrium, is the quantity of roses produced and consumed too small, too large or just right?

In this chapter we take up the topic of **welfare economics**, the study of how the allocation of resources affects economic wellbeing. We begin by examining the benefits that buyers and sellers receive from taking part in a market. We then examine how society can make these benefits as large as possible. This analysis leads to a profound conclusion – the equilibrium of supply and demand in a market maximises the total benefits received by buyers and sellers.

welfare economics
the study of how the allocation of resources affects economic wellbeing

As you may recall from chapter 1, one of the *Ten Lessons from Economics* discussed how markets are usually a good way to organise economic activity. The study of welfare economics explains this idea more fully. It also answers our question about the right price of flowers; the price that balances the supply and demand for flowers is, in a particular sense, the best one because it maximises the total welfare of flower consumers and flower producers. No consumer or producer of flowers aims to achieve this goal, but their joint actions, directed by market prices, moves them towards a welfare-maximising outcome – as if led by an invisible hand.

Consumer surplus

We begin our study of welfare economics by looking at the benefits buyers receive from participating in a market.

Willingness to pay

Imagine that you own a mint-condition recording of Michael Jackson's first solo album. Because you are not a Michael Jackson fan, you decide to sell it. One way to do so is to hold an auction.

Four Jackson fans show up for your auction: John, Paul, George and Ringo. Each of them would like to own the album, but there is a limit to the amount that each is willing to pay for it. Table 7.1

Table 7.1 Four possible buyers' willingness to pay

Buyer	Willingness to pay
John	$100
Paul	80
George	70
Ringo	50

willingness to pay
the maximum amount that a buyer will pay for a good

Search me!

▸ willingness to pay

shows the maximum price that each of the four possible buyers would pay. Each buyer's maximum is called his **willingness to pay** and it measures how much that buyer values the good. Each buyer would be eager to buy the album at a price less than his willingness to pay, would refuse to buy the album at a price more than his willingness to pay and would be indifferent about buying the album at a price exactly equal to his willingness to pay.

To sell your album, you begin the bidding at a low price, say $10. Because all four buyers are willing to pay much more, the price rises quickly. The bidding stops when John bids $80 (or slightly more). At this point, Paul, George and Ringo have dropped out of the bidding, because they are unwilling to bid any more than $80. John pays you $80 and gets the album. Note that the album has gone to the buyer who values the album most highly.

What benefit does John receive from buying the Michael Jackson album? In a sense, John has found a real bargain – he is willing to pay $100 for the album but pays only $80 for it. We say that John receives consumer surplus of $20. **Consumer surplus** is the amount a buyer is willing to pay for a good minus the amount the buyer actually pays for it.

consumer surplus
a buyer's willingness to pay minus the amount the buyer actually pays

Search me!

▸ consumer surplus

Consumer surplus measures the benefit to buyers of participating in a market. In this example, John receives a $20 benefit from participating in the auction because he pays only $80 for a good he values at $100. Paul, George and Ringo get no consumer surplus from participating in the auction, because they left without the album and without paying anything.

Now consider a somewhat different example. Suppose that you had two identical Michael Jackson albums to sell. Again, you auction them off to the four possible buyers. To keep things simple, we assume that both albums are to be sold for the same price and that no buyer is interested in buying more than one album. Therefore, the price rises until two buyers are left.

In this case, the bidding stops when John and Paul bid $70 (or slightly higher). At this price, John and Paul are each happy to buy an album, and George and Ringo are not willing to bid any higher. John and Paul each receive consumer surplus equal to his willingness to pay minus the price. John's consumer surplus is $30 and Paul's is $10. John's consumer surplus is higher now than it was previously, because he gets the same album but pays less for it. The total consumer surplus in the market is $40.

Using the demand curve to measure consumer surplus

Consumer surplus is closely related to the demand curve for a product. To see how they are related, let's continue our example and consider the demand curve for this rare Michael Jackson album.

We begin by using the willingness to pay of the four possible buyers to find the demand schedule for the album. Table 7.2 shows the demand schedule that corresponds to Table 7.1. If the price is above

Table 7.2 The demand schedule for the buyers in Table 7.1

Price	Buyers	Quantity demanded
More than $100	None	0
$80 to $100	John	1
$70 to $80	John, Paul	2
$50 to $70	John, Paul, George	3
$50 or less	John, Paul, George, Ringo	4

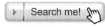

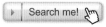

Figure 7.1 The demand curve

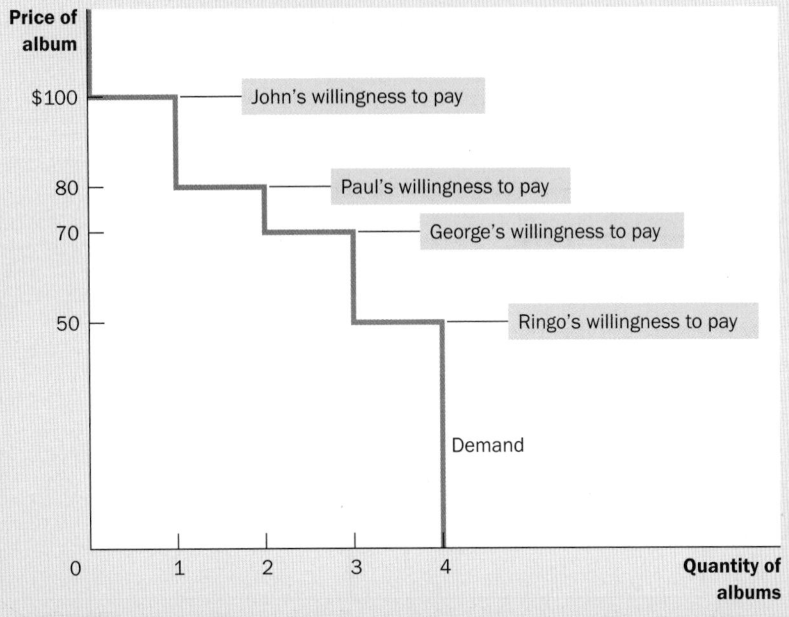

This figure graphs the demand curve from the demand schedule in Table 7.2. Note that the height of the demand curve reflects buyers' willingness to pay.

$100, the quantity demanded in the market is 0, because no buyer is willing to pay that much. If the price is between $80 and $100, the quantity demanded is one, because only John is willing to pay such a high price. If the price is between $70 and $80, the quantity demanded is two, because both John and Paul are willing to pay the price. We can continue this analysis for other prices as well. In this way, the demand schedule is derived from the willingness to pay of the four possible buyers.

Figure 7.1 graphs the demand curve that corresponds to this demand schedule. Note the relationship between the height of the demand curve and the buyers' willingness to pay. At any quantity, the price given by the demand curve shows the willingness to pay of the marginal buyer, the buyer who would leave the market first if the price were any higher. At a quantity of four albums, for instance, the demand curve has a height of $50, the price that Ringo (the marginal buyer) is willing to pay for an album. At a quantity of three albums, the demand curve has a height of $70, the price that George (who is now the marginal buyer) is willing to pay.

Because the demand curve reflects buyers' willingness to pay, we can also use it to measure consumer surplus. Figure 7.2 uses the demand curve to calculate consumer surplus in our example. In panel (a), the price is $80 (or slightly above), and the quantity demanded is one. Note that the area above the price and below the demand curve equals $20. This amount is exactly the consumer surplus we calculated earlier when only one album is sold.

Panel (b) of Figure 7.2 shows consumer surplus when the price is $70 (or slightly above). In this case, the area above the price and below the demand curve equals the total area of the two rectangles; John's consumer surplus at this price is $30 and Paul's is $10. This area equals a total of $40. Once again, this amount is the consumer surplus we calculated earlier.

Figure 7.2 Measuring consumer surplus with the demand curve

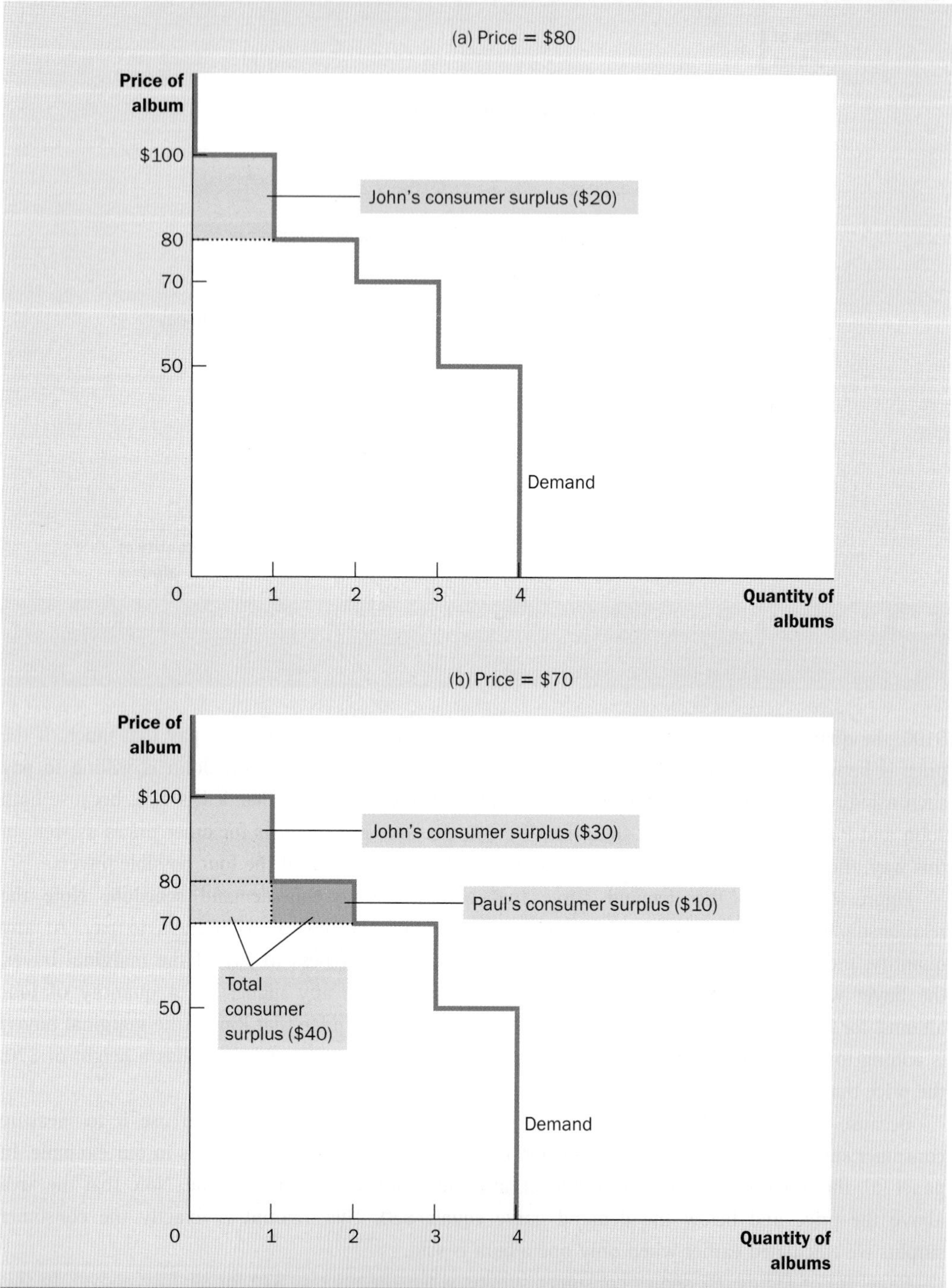

In panel (a), the price of the good is $80 and the consumer surplus is $20. In panel (b), the price of the good is $70 and the consumer surplus is $40.

The lesson from this example holds for all demand curves – the area below the demand curve and above the price measures the consumer surplus in a market. The reason is that the height of the demand curve measures the value buyers place on the good, as measured by their willingness to pay for it. The difference between this willingness to pay and the market price is each buyer's consumer surplus. Thus, the total area below the demand curve and above the price is the sum of the consumer surplus of all buyers in the market for a good or service.

How a lower price raises consumer surplus

Because buyers always want to pay less for the goods they buy, a lower price makes buyers of a good better off. But how much does buyers' wellbeing rise in response to a lower price? We can use the concept of consumer surplus to answer this question precisely.

Figure 7.3 shows a typical downward-sloping demand curve. Although this demand curve appears somewhat different in shape from the steplike demand curves in our previous two figures, the ideas we have just developed apply nonetheless – consumer surplus is the area above the price and below the demand curve. In panel (a), consumer surplus at a price of P_1 is the area of triangle ABC.

Now suppose that the price falls from P_1 to P_2, as shown in panel (b). The consumer surplus now equals area ADF. The increase in consumer surplus attributable to the lower price is the area BCFD.

This increase in consumer surplus is composed of two parts. First, those buyers who were already buying Q_1 of the good at the higher price P_1 are better off because they now pay less. The increase in consumer surplus of existing buyers is the reduction in the amount they pay; it equals the area of the rectangle BCED. Second, some new buyers enter the market because they are now willing to buy the good at the lower price and some existing buyers may decide to buy more of the good at the lower price. As a result, the quantity demanded in the market increases from Q_1 to Q_2. The consumer surplus from these new sales of the good is the area of the triangle CEF.

What does consumer surplus measure?

Our goal in developing the concept of consumer surplus is to make normative judgements about the desirability of market outcomes. Now that you have seen what consumer surplus is, let's consider whether it is a good measure of economic wellbeing.

Imagine that you are a policymaker trying to design a good economic system. Would you care about the amount of consumer surplus? Consumer surplus, the amount that buyers are willing to pay for a good minus the amount they actually pay for it, measures the benefit that buyers receive from a good *as the buyers themselves perceive it*. Thus, consumer surplus is a good measure of economic wellbeing if policymakers want to respect the preferences of buyers.

In some circumstances, policymakers might choose not to care about consumer surplus because they do not respect the preferences that drive buyer behaviour. For example, drug addicts are willing to pay a high price for heroin. Yet we would not say that addicts get a large benefit from being able to buy heroin at a low price (even though addicts might say they do). From the standpoint of society, willingness to pay in this instance is not a good measure of the buyers' benefit, and consumer surplus is not a good measure of economic wellbeing, because addicts are not looking after their own best interests.

In most markets, however, consumer surplus does reflect economic wellbeing. Economists normally presume that buyers are rational when they make decisions and that their preferences should be

Figure 7.3 How the price affects consumer surplus

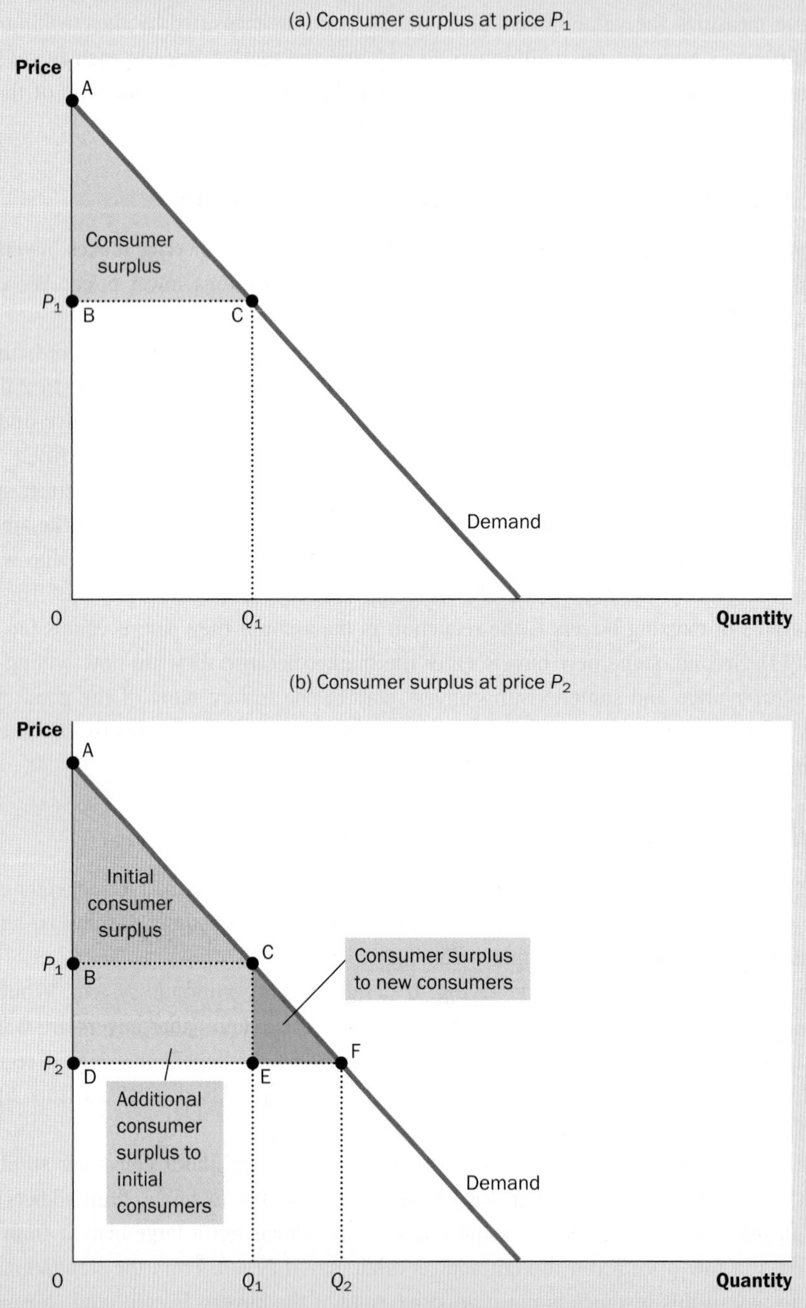

In panel (a), the price is P_1, the quantity demanded is Q_1, and consumer surplus equals the area of the triangle ABC. When the price falls from P_1 to P_2, as in panel (b), the quantity demanded rises from Q_1 to Q_2, and the consumer surplus rises to the area of the triangle ADF. The increase in consumer surplus (area BCFD) occurs in part because existing consumers now pay less (area BCED) and in part because new consumers enter the market at the lower price (area CEF).

respected. In this case, consumers are the best judges of how much benefit they receive from the goods they buy.

Draw a demand curve for a bunch of roses. In your diagram, show a price for a bunch and the consumer surplus that results from this price. Explain in words what this consumer surplus measures.

Producer surplus

We now turn to the other side of the market and consider the benefits sellers receive from participating in a market. As you will see, our analysis of sellers' welfare is similar to our analysis of buyers' welfare.

Cost and the willingness to sell

Imagine now that you are a homeowner and you need to get your house painted. You turn to four sellers of painting services: Alice, Emmett, Rosalie and Jasper. Each painter is willing to do the work for you if the price is right. You decide to take bids from the four painters and auction off the job to the painter who will do the work for the lowest price.

Each painter is willing to take the job if the price they receive exceeds their cost of doing the work. Here the term **cost** should be interpreted as the painters' opportunity cost; it includes both the painters' out-of-pocket expenses (for paint, brushes and so on) and the value that the painters place on their own time. Table 7.3 shows each painter's cost. Because a painter's cost is the lowest price they would accept for their work, cost is a measure of their willingness to sell their services. Each painter would be eager to sell their services at a price greater than their cost and each would refuse to sell their services at a price that is less than their cost. At a price exactly equal to their cost, each painter would be indifferent about selling their services: each would be equally happy getting the job or using their time and energy for another purpose.

cost
the value of everything a seller must give up to produce a good

When you take bids from the painters, the price might start off high, but it quickly falls as the painters compete for the job. Once Jasper has bid $600 (or slightly less), he is the sole remaining bidder. Jasper is happy to do the job for this price, because his cost is only $500. Alice, Emmett and Rosalie are unwilling to do the job for less than $600. Note that the job goes to the painter who can do the work at the lowest cost.

Table 7.3 The costs of four possible sellers

Seller	Cost ($)
Alice	900
Emmett	800
Rosalie	600
Jasper	500

producer surplus
the amount a seller is paid for a good minus the seller's cost

Search me!

▸ producer surplus

What benefit does Jasper receive from getting the job? Because he is willing to do the work for $500 but gets $600 for doing it, we say that he receives producer surplus of $100. **Producer surplus** is the amount a seller is paid minus the cost of production. Producer surplus measures the benefit to sellers of participating in a market.

Now consider a somewhat different example. Suppose that you have two houses that need painting. Again, you auction off the jobs to the four painters. Let's assume that no painter is able to paint both houses and that you will pay the same amount to paint each house. Therefore, the price falls until two painters are left.

In this case, the bidding stops when Rosalie and Jasper each offer to do the job for a price of $800 (or slightly less). At this price, Rosalie and Jasper are willing to do the work and Alice and Emmett are not willing to bid a lower price. At a price of $800, Jasper receives producer surplus of $300 and Rosalie receives producer surplus of $200. The total producer surplus in the market is $500.

Using the supply curve to measure producer surplus

Just as consumer surplus is closely related to the demand curve, producer surplus is closely related to the supply curve. To see how, let's continue our example.

We begin by using the costs of the four painters to find the supply schedule for painting services. Table 7.4 shows the supply schedule that corresponds to the costs in Table 7.3. If the price is below $500, none of the four painters is willing to do the job, so the quantity supplied is 0. If the price is between $500 and $600, only Jasper is willing to do the job, so the quantity supplied is one. If the price is between $600 and $800, Rosalie and Jasper are willing to do the job, so the quantity supplied is two, and so on. Thus, the supply schedule is derived from the costs of the four painters.

Figure 7.4 graphs the supply curve that corresponds to this supply schedule. Note that the height of the supply curve is related to the sellers' costs. At any quantity, the price given by the supply curve shows the cost of the marginal seller, the seller who would leave the market first if the price were any lower. At a quantity of four houses, for instance, the supply curve has a height of $900, the cost that Alice (the marginal seller) incurs to provide her painting services. At a quantity of three houses, the supply curve has a height of $800, the cost that Emmett (who is now the marginal seller) incurs.

Because the supply curve reflects sellers' costs, we can use it to measure producer surplus. Figure 7.5 uses the supply curve to calculate producer surplus in our example. In panel (a), we assume that the price is $600. In this case, the quantity supplied is one. Note that the area below the price and above the supply curve equals $100. This amount is exactly the producer surplus we calculated earlier for Jasper.

Table 7.4 The supply schedule for the sellers in Table 7.3

Price	Sellers	Quantity supplied
$900 or more	Alice, Emmett, Rosalie, Jasper	4
$800 to $900	Emmett, Rosalie, Jasper	3
$600 to $800	Rosalie, Jasper	2
$500 to $600	Jasper	1
Less than $500	None	0

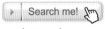

Figure 7.4 The supply curve

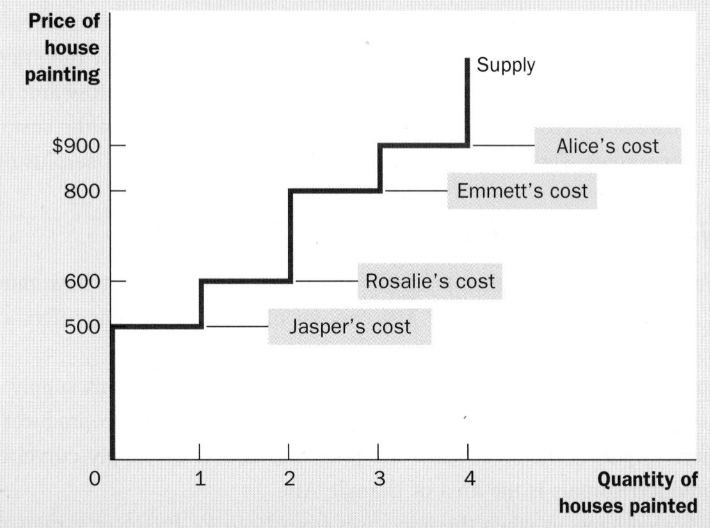

This figure graphs the supply curve from the supply schedule in Table 7.4. Note that the height of the supply curve reflects sellers' costs.

Figure 7.5 Measuring producer surplus with the supply curve

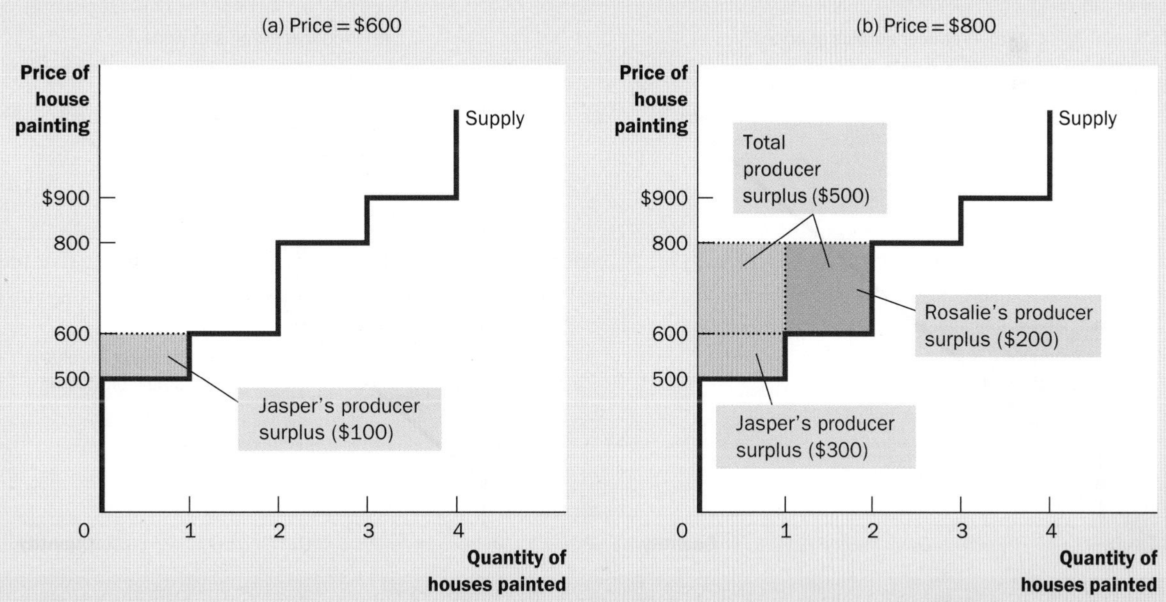

In panel (a), the price of the good is $600 and the producer surplus is $100. In panel (b), the price of the good is $800 and the producer surplus is $500.

Panel (b) of Figure 7.5 shows producer surplus at a price of $800. In this case, the area below the price and above the supply curve equals the total area of the two rectangles. This area equals $500, the producer surplus we calculated earlier for Rosalie and Jasper when two houses needed painting.

The lesson from this example applies to all supply curves – the area below the price and above the supply curve measures the producer surplus in a market. The logic is straightforward; the height of the supply curve measures sellers' costs, and the difference between the price and the cost of production is each seller's producer surplus. Thus, the total area is the sum of the producer surplus of all sellers.

How a higher price raises producer surplus

Sellers always want to receive a higher price for the goods they sell. But how much does sellers' wellbeing rise in response to a higher price? The concept of producer surplus offers a precise answer to this question.

Figure 7.6 shows a typical upward-sloping supply curve. Even though this supply curve differs in shape from the steplike supply curves in the previous figure, we measure producer surplus in the same way; producer surplus is the area below the price and above the supply curve. In panel (a), the price is P_1, and producer surplus is the area of triangle ABC.

Panel (b) shows what happens when the price rises from P_1 to P_2. Producer surplus now equals area ADF. This increase in producer surplus has two parts. First, those sellers who were already selling Q_1 of the good at the lower price P_1 are better off because they now get more for what they sell. The increase in producer surplus for existing sellers equals the area of the rectangle BCED. Second, some existing

Figure 7.6 How the price affects producer surplus

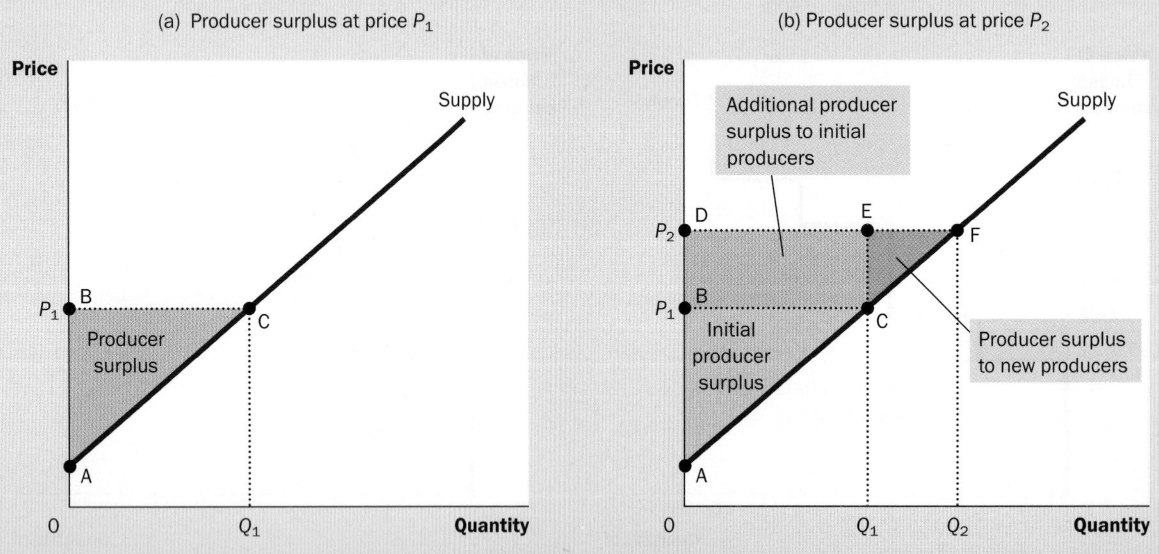

In panel (a), the price is P_1, the quantity demanded is Q_1, and producer surplus equals the area of the triangle ABC. When the price rises from P_1 to P_2, as in panel (b), the quantity supplied rises from Q_1 to Q_2, and the producer surplus rises to the area of the triangle ADF. The increase in producer surplus (area BCFD) occurs in part because existing producers now receive more (area BCED) and in part because new producers enter the market at the higher price (area CEF).

sellers choose to sell more and some new sellers enter the market because they are now willing to produce the good at the higher price, resulting in an increase in the quantity supplied from Q_1 to Q_2. The producer surplus from this increase in production and sales is the area of the triangle CEF.

As this analysis shows, we use producer surplus to measure the wellbeing of sellers in much the same way as we use consumer surplus to measure the wellbeing of buyers. Because these two measures of economic welfare are so similar, it is natural to use them together. And, indeed, that is exactly what we do in the next section.

Q

Draw a supply curve for a bunch of roses. In your diagram, show a price for a bunch of roses and the producer surplus that results from this price. Explain in words what this producer surplus measures.

Market efficiency

Consumer surplus and producer surplus are the basic tools that economists use to study the welfare of buyers and sellers in a market. These tools can help us consider a fundamental economic question: Is the allocation of resources determined by free markets in any way desirable?

The benevolent social planner

To evaluate market outcomes, we introduce into our analysis a new, hypothetical character, called the benevolent social planner. The benevolent social planner is an all-knowing, all-powerful, well-intentioned dictator. The planner wants to maximise the economic wellbeing of everyone in society. What do you suppose this planner should do? Should he just leave buyers and sellers at the equilibrium that they reach naturally on their own? Or can he increase economic wellbeing by altering the market outcome in some way?

To answer this question, the planner must first decide how to measure the economic wellbeing of a society. One possible measure is the sum of consumer and producer surplus, which we call *total surplus*. Consumer surplus is the benefit that buyers receive from participating in a market and producer surplus is the benefit that sellers receive. It is therefore natural to use total surplus as a measure of society's economic wellbeing.

To better understand this measure of economic wellbeing, recall how we measure consumer and producer surplus. We define consumer surplus as:

$$\text{consumer surplus} = \text{Value to buyers} - \text{Amount paid by buyers}$$

Similarly, we define producer surplus as:

$$\text{Producer surplus} = \text{Amount received by sellers} - \text{Costs of sellers}$$

When we add consumer and producer surplus together, we obtain:

$$\text{Total surplus} = \text{Value to buyers} - \text{Amount paid by buyers} + \text{Amount received by sellers} - \text{Costs of sellers}$$

The amount paid by buyers equals the amount received by sellers, so the middle two terms in this expression cancel each other. As a result, we can write total surplus as:

$$\text{Total surplus} = \text{Value to buyers} - \text{Costs of sellers}$$

Total surplus in a market is the total value to buyers of the goods, as measured by their willingness to pay, minus the costs to sellers of providing those goods.

If an allocation of resources maximises total surplus, we say that the allocation exhibits *efficiency*. If an allocation is not efficient, then some of the gains from trade among buyers and sellers are not being realised. For example, an allocation is inefficient if a good is not being produced by the sellers with lowest cost. In this case, moving production from a high-cost producer to a low-cost producer will lower the total costs of sellers and raise total surplus. Similarly, an allocation is inefficient if a good is not being consumed by the buyers who value it most highly. In this case, moving consumption of the good from a buyer with a low valuation to a buyer with a high valuation will raise total surplus.

In addition to efficiency, the social planner might also care about *equity* – the fairness of the distribution of wellbeing among the various buyers and sellers. In essence, the gains from trade in a market are like a pie to be distributed among the market participants. The question of efficiency is whether the pie is as big as possible. The question of equity is whether the pie is divided fairly. Evaluating the equity of a market outcome is more difficult than evaluating the efficiency. Whereas efficiency is an objective goal that can be judged on strictly positive grounds, equity involves normative judgements that go beyond economics and enter into the realm of political philosophy.

In this chapter we concentrate on efficiency as the social planner's goal. Keep in mind, however, that real policymakers often care about equity as well. That is, they care about both the size of the economic pie and how the pie gets sliced and distributed among members of society.

fyi

The invisible hand of the marketplace

The efficiency of free markets is, at first, a surprising idea. After all, no one is looking out for the general economic welfare. Free markets contain many buyers and sellers, and all of them are interested primarily in their own wellbeing. Yet despite decentralised decision making and self-interested decision makers, the result is not chaos but efficiency.

The virtue of free markets was well understood by the great economist Adam Smith. Here is what he wrote in his 1776 classic, *An Inquiry into the Nature and Causes of the Wealth of Nations:*

> Man has almost constant occasion for the help of his brethren, and it is vain for him to expect it from their benevolence only. He will be more likely to prevail if he can interest their self-love in his favour, and show them that it is for their own advantage to do for him what he requires of them ... It is not from the benevolence of the butcher, the brewer, or the baker that we expect our dinner, but from their regard to their own interest ...
>
> Every individual ... neither intends to promote the public interest, nor knows how much he is promoting it ... He intends only his own gain, and he is in this, as in many other cases, led by an invisible hand to promote an end which was no part of his intention. Nor is it always the worse for the society that it was no part of it. By pursuing his own interest he frequently promotes that of the society more effectually than when he really intends to promote it.

Smith is saying that participants in the economy are motivated by self-interest and that the 'invisible hand' of the marketplace guides this self-interest into promoting general economic wellbeing.

Smith's insights remain true today. Indeed, our analysis in this chapter allows us to express Smith's view more precisely by showing that the equilibrium of supply and demand maximises the sum of consumer and producer surplus.

Evaluating the market equilibrium

Figure 7.7 shows consumer and producer surplus when a market reaches the equilibrium of supply and demand. Recall that consumer surplus equals the area above the price and under the demand curve

Figure 7.7 Consumer and producer surplus in the market equilibrium

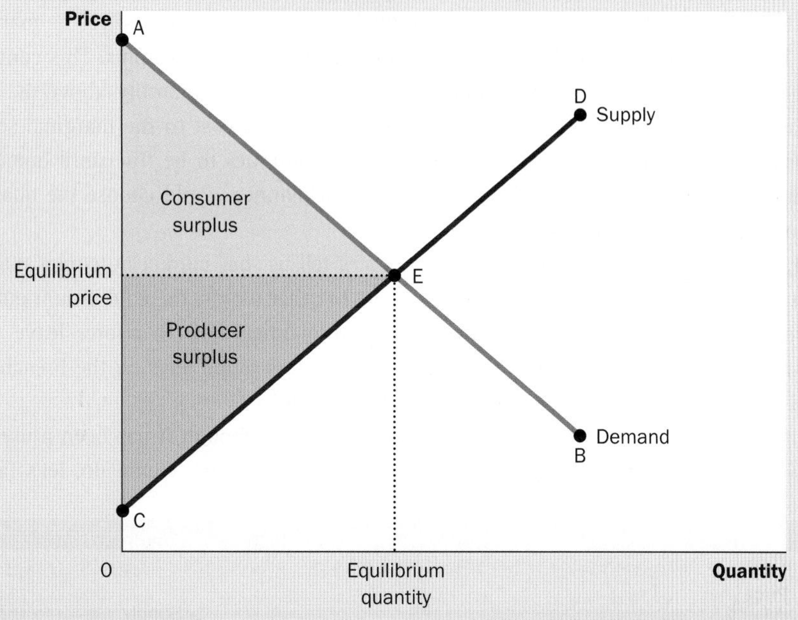

Total surplus – the sum of consumer and producer surplus – is the area between the supply and demand curves up to the equilibrium quantity.

and producer surplus equals the area below the price and above the supply curve. Thus, the total area between the supply and demand curves up to the point of equilibrium represents the total surplus from this market.

Is this equilibrium allocation of resources efficient? Does it maximise total surplus? To answer these questions, keep in mind that when a market is in equilibrium the price determines which buyers and sellers participate in the market. Those buyers who value the good more than the price (represented by the segment AE on the demand curve) choose to buy the good; those buyers who value it less than the price (represented by the segment EB) do not. Similarly, those sellers whose costs are less than the price (represented by the segment CE on the supply curve) choose to produce and sell the good; those sellers whose costs are greater than the price (represented by the segment ED) do not.

These observations lead to two insights about market outcomes:

1 Free markets allocate the supply of goods to the buyers who value them most highly, as measured by their willingness to pay.
2 Free markets allocate the demand for goods to the sellers who can produce them at lowest cost.

Thus, given the quantity produced and sold in a market equilibrium, the social planner cannot increase economic wellbeing by changing the allocation of consumption among buyers or the allocation of production among sellers.

But can the social planner raise total economic wellbeing by increasing or decreasing the quantity of the good? The answer is no, as stated in this third insight about market outcomes:

3 Free markets produce the quantity of goods that maximises the sum of consumer and producer surplus.

Figure 7.8 illustrates why this is true. To interpret this figure, keep in mind that the demand curve reflects the value to buyers and the supply curve reflects the cost to sellers. At any quantity below the equilibrium level, such as Q_1, the value to the marginal buyer exceeds the cost to the marginal seller. As a result, increasing the quantity produced and consumed raises total surplus. This continues to be true until the quantity reaches the equilibrium level. Similarly, at any quantity above the equilibrium level, such as Q_2, the value to the marginal buyer is less than the cost to the marginal seller. In this case, decreasing the quantity raises total surplus and this continues to be true until quantity falls to the equilibrium level. To maximise total surplus, the social planner would choose the quantity where the supply and demand curves intersect.

Together, these three insights about market outcomes tell us that market outcomes make the sum of consumer and producer surplus as large as it can be. In other words, the equilibrium outcome is an efficient allocation of resources. The benevolent social planner can, therefore, leave the market outcome just as one finds it. This policy of leaving well enough alone goes by the French expression *laissez-faire*, which literally translated means 'allow them to do'.

Society is lucky that the planner doesn't need to intervene. Although it has been a useful exercise imagining what an all-knowing, all-powerful, well-intentioned dictator would do, let's face it: Such

Figure 7.8 **The efficiency of the equilibrium quantity**

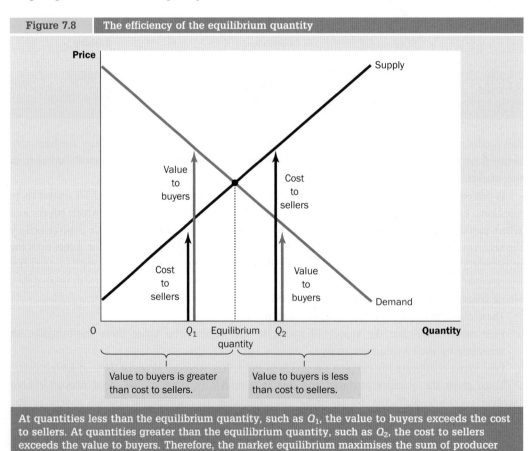

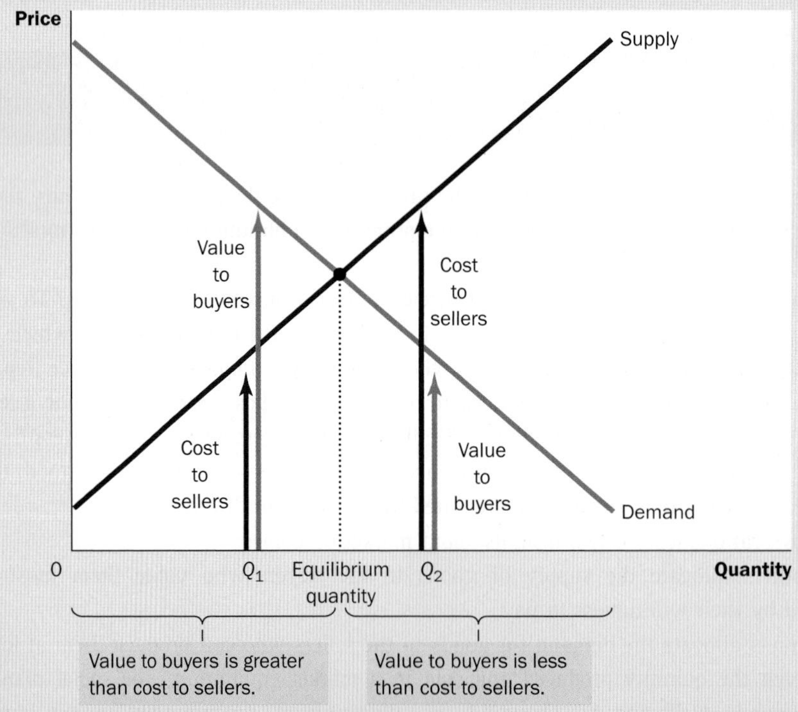

At quantities less than the equilibrium quantity, such as Q_1, the value to buyers exceeds the cost to sellers. At quantities greater than the equilibrium quantity, such as Q_2, the cost to sellers exceeds the value to buyers. Therefore, the market equilibrium maximises the sum of producer and consumer surplus.

characters are hard to come by. Dictators are rarely benevolent and even if we found someone so virtuous he would lack crucial information.

Suppose our social planner tried to choose an efficient allocation of resources on his own, instead of relying on market forces. To do so, he would need to know the value of a particular good to every potential consumer in the market and the cost of every potential producer. And he would need this information not only for this market but for every one of the many thousands of markets in the economy. The task is practically impossible, which explains why centrally planned economies never work very well.

The planner's job becomes easy, however, once he takes on a partner: Adam Smith's invisible hand of the marketplace. The invisible hand takes all the information about buyers and sellers into account and guides everyone in the market to the best outcome as judged by the standard of economic efficiency. It is, truly, a remarkable feat. That is why economists so often advocate free markets as the best way to organise economic activity.

CASESTUDY

Should there be a market in organs?

Some years ago, a Boston newspaper reported the story of Susan Stephens, a woman whose son needed a kidney transplant. When the doctor learned that the mother's kidney was not compatible, he proposed a novel solution: If Stephens donated one of her kidneys to a stranger, her son would move to the top of the kidney waiting list. The mother accepted the deal and soon two patients had the transplant they were waiting for.

The ingenuity of the doctor's proposal and the nobility of the mother's act cannot be doubted. But the story raises many intriguing questions. If the mother could trade a kidney for a kidney, would the hospital allow her to trade a kidney for an expensive, experimental cancer treatment that she could not afford otherwise? Should she be allowed to exchange her kidney for free tuition for her son at the hospital's medical school? Should she be able to sell her kidney so she can use the cash to trade in her old Toyota for a new Lexus?

In many countries, including Australia, it is illegal for a person to sell their organs. In essence, in the market for organs, the government has imposed a price ceiling of zero. The result, as with any binding price ceiling, is a shortage of the good. The deal in the Stephens case did not fall under this prohibition because no cash exchanged hands.

Some countries, however, have illicit markets in organs. The World Health Organization estimates that 10 per cent of all organ transplants, including around 15 000 kidneys each year, involve a patient from a rich country buying an illegal organ from a citizen of a poorer nation. The temptation to the world's poorest people to sell their 'spare' organs is high. A kidney can sell for around $1500 or more in the illegal trade. This may not sound like much to you or me. But it can be many years income to a person living in dire poverty.

Some economists believe that there would be large benefits to allowing a free market in organs. People are born with two kidneys, but they usually need only one. Meanwhile, a few people suffer from illnesses that leave them without any working kidneys. Despite the obvious gains from trade, the current situation is dire. In Australia, the average wait for a kidney transplant is 3.8 years and there are up to 50 deaths a year from people on the waiting list because a kidney cannot be found. In Europe, on average 12 people die each day waiting for an organ transplant. If those needing a kidney were allowed to buy one from those who have two, the price would rise to balance supply and demand. Sellers would be better off with the extra cash in their pockets. Buyers would be better off with the organ they need to save their lives. The shortage of kidneys would disappear.

Such a market would lead to an efficient allocation of resources, but critics of this plan worry about fairness. A market for organs, they argue, would benefit the rich at the expense of the poor, because organs would then be allocated to those most willing and able to pay. But you can also question the fairness of the current system. Now, most of us walk around with an extra organ that we don't really need, while some of our fellow citizens are dying to get one. Is that fair?

Q

Draw the supply and demand for roses. In the equilibrium, show producer and consumer surplus. Explain why producing more roses would lower total surplus.

Conclusion: Market efficiency and market failure

This chapter introduced the basic tools of welfare economics – consumer and producer surplus – and used them to evaluate the efficiency of free markets. We showed that the forces of supply and demand allocate resources efficiently. That is, even though buyers and sellers in a market are concerned only about their own welfare, they are together led by an invisible hand to an equilibrium that maximises the total benefits to buyers and sellers.

A word of warning is in order. To conclude that markets are efficient, we made several assumptions about how markets work. When these assumptions do not hold, our conclusion that the market equilibrium is efficient may no longer be true. As we close this chapter, let's consider briefly two of the most important of these assumptions.

First, our analysis assumed that markets are perfectly competitive. In the world, however, competition is sometimes far from perfect. In some markets, a single buyer or seller (or a small group of them) may be able to control market prices. This ability to influence prices is called *market power*. Market power can cause markets to be inefficient because it keeps the price and quantity away from the equilibrium of supply and demand.

Second, our analysis assumed that the outcome in a market matters only to the buyers and sellers in that market. Yet, in the real world, the decisions of buyers and sellers sometimes affect people who are not participants in the market at all. Pollution is the classic example of a market outcome that affects people not in the market. Such side effects, called *externalities*, cause welfare in a market to depend on more than just the value to the buyers and the costs of the sellers. Because buyers and sellers do not take these side effects into account when deciding how much to consume and produce, the equilibrium in a market can be inefficient from the standpoint of society as a whole.

Market power and externalities are examples of a general phenomenon called *market failure* – the inability of some unregulated markets to allocate resources efficiently. When markets fail, public policy can potentially remedy the problem and increase economic efficiency. Microeconomists devote much effort to studying when market failure is likely and what sorts of policies are best at correcting market failures. As you continue your study of economics, you will see that the tools of welfare economics developed here are readily adapted to that endeavour.

Despite the possibility of market failure, the invisible hand of the marketplace is extraordinarily important. In many markets, the assumptions we made in this chapter work well and the conclusion of market efficiency applies directly. Moreover, our analysis of welfare economics and market efficiency can be used to shed light on the effects of various government policies. In the next two chapters we apply the tools we have just developed to study two important policy issues – the welfare effects of taxation and of international trade.

IN THE NEWS . . .

TICKET SCALPING

If an economy is to allocate its scarce resources efficiently, goods must get to those consumers who value them most highly. Ticket scalping is one example of how markets reach efficient outcomes. Scalpers buy tickets to plays, concerts and sports events and then sell the tickets at a price above their original cost. By charging the highest price the market will bear, scalpers help ensure that consumers with the greatest willingness to pay for the tickets actually do get them. But scalping is usually illegal in Australia, unlike the United States. This article looks at the incentives behind this ban on scalping and how it hurts Australian sports fans.

Search me!

▸ ticket scalping

The ticket-scalping myth

by Gareth Parker

Tonight I'm going to a baseball game at Citi Field – the home of my beloved New York Mets – a brand new ballpark that opened this year in the car park of adjacent old Shea Stadium.

We've got great seats behind home plate, and we paid less than half of the face value on the ticket to obtain them. How? Ticket scalpers.

In Australia, scalping is a dirty word that inspires revulsion in 'real fans' and is outlawed by State Governments. In the United States, the practice is, with a few minor exceptions, completely legal and, thanks to the internet, a quick, safe and convenient way to obtain tickets to any sporting, concert or theatre event you could wish to see.

Online ticket brokers, like StubHub.com, have created an efficient and transparent market for tickets of every stripe. Sellers are usually individual ticket holders (but also professional speculators) and prices are driven by supply and demand.

For a game like tonight's, between the Mets and the Atlanta Braves, prices are cheap because it's late in the season and both teams are out of playoff contention. Good news for buyers like us, because we can get great seats at a discount. Some seats for tonight's game, in the Upper Deck of the stadium, are literally being offered for sale for a dollar, substantially below their face value of $15.

A series this coming weekend however, between fierce rivals the New York Yankees and Boston Red Sox, is a different story. The teams, whose fans despise each other, are locked in a deathly serious fight for the American League East title and the three game series to be played on Friday, Saturday and Sunday will be crucial in deciding the race.

As such, tickets on StubHub.com are being offered for substantially higher than face value, in most cases, because the demand from fans supports the premium.

Either way, it's fans – both buyers and sellers – who decide how much each seat is worth through an efficient mechanism made possible by a willingness on the part of American lawmakers to let markets do what they do.

StubHub.com and the other ticket brokers make their money by charging a service fee on each transaction, a practice that would be familiar to anyone who has bought or sold shares on the Australian Stock Exchange.

Which brings us to the AFL grand final, and the annual outrageous fraud that is perpetuated on the average football fan.

The face value price for tickets to Saturday's clash between Geelong and St Kilda ranges from $142.50 to $245. But only a fraction of the 100 000 people who pack the MCG will have been fortunate enough to obtain a ticket at those prices.

As was reported on thewest.com.au this week, just one quarter of the tickets available were allocated for sale to the members of the competing clubs.

Twenty-one thousand tickets will go to AFL Members, 23 000 to members of the MCC, 7500 to AFL sponsors, invitees and corporates, 5000 to members of Etihad Stadium's pricey Medallion Club and 1000 each to the 14 non-competing AFL clubs.

The allocations to MCC and AFL members are eminently defensible given the game and

>>

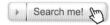

where it is played, but it's what happens to all those other tickets controlled by the AFL and the non-competing clubs where things get outrageous.

Thanks to a handy bit of law passed by the Victorian Labor Government a few years ago (when former Carlton ruckman Justin Madden was Sports Minister) the grand final is a so-called 'declared event' under Victoria's anti-scalping legislation.

This means that no-one may re-sell grand final tickets at a premium without written approval from the league. And conveniently, the league only gives that approval to itself, its clubs and a select band of corporate resellers, who package up the $142.50 – $250 tickets with a lunch and/or accommodation and sell them for up to $2000 a pop.

In effect, Victoria's anti-scalping law, which in theory is meant to protect fans from being ripped off, in fact enables and authorises the AFL and its clubs to perpetrate the annual bald-faced fleecing of football fans desperate to see the biggest game of the year.

Yet somehow, every year, we read stories like this one in the Melbourne *Herald Sun* under the headline:

> SCALP AT YOUR PERIL
>
> Grand Final ticket scalpers outside the MCG will find themselves up against a crack team on Saturday.
>
> Police, Melbourne City Council bylaws officers and State Government officials will all be looking to apprehend unscrupulous sellers.

How good of the State to protect the real scalpers from competition. The inspectors should start right at AFL House in the Docklands.

Enjoy the weekend's game. In the local parlance, I'll be rooting for the Saints!

Source: Gareth Parker/*The West Australian*, 23 September 2009.

Summary

- Consumer surplus equals buyers' willingness to pay for a good minus the amount they actually pay for it and it measures the benefit buyers get from participating in a market. Consumer surplus can be calculated by finding the area below the demand curve and above the price.
- Producer surplus equals the amount sellers receive for their goods minus their costs of production and it measures the benefit sellers get from participating in a market. Producer surplus can be calculated by finding the area below the price and above the supply curve.
- An allocation of resources that maximises the sum of consumer and producer surplus is said to be efficient. Policymakers are often concerned with the efficiency, as well as the equity, of economic outcomes.
- The equilibrium of supply and demand maximises the sum of consumer and producer surplus. That is, the invisible hand of the marketplace leads buyers and sellers to allocate resources efficiently.
- Markets do not allocate resources efficiently in the presence of market failures such as market power or externalities.

Key concepts

consumer surplus
cost
producer surplus
welfare economics
willingness to pay

Questions for review

1 Explain how buyers' willingness to pay, consumer surplus and the demand curve are related.
2 Explain how sellers' costs, producer surplus and the supply curve are related.
3 In a supply-and-demand diagram, show producer and consumer surplus in the market equilibrium.
4 What is efficiency? Is it the only goal of economic policymakers?
5 What does the invisible hand do?
6 Name two types of market failure. Explain why each may cause market outcomes to be inefficient.

Problems and applications

1 Lanlan buys an iPod for $120 and gets consumer surplus of $80.
   a What is her willingness to pay?
   b If she had bought the iPod on sale for $90, what would her consumer surplus have been?
   c If the price of an iPod were $250, what would her consumer surplus have been?
2 A plant disease in South Australia damages the grape crop. What happens to consumer surplus in the market for grapes? What happens to consumer surplus in the market for wine? Illustrate your answers with diagrams.
3 Suppose the demand for French bread rises. What happens to producer surplus in the market for French bread? What happens to producer surplus in the market for flour? Illustrate your answer with diagrams.

4 It is a hot day, and Bert is very thirsty. Here is the value he places on a bottle of water:

Value of first bottle	$7
Value of second bottle	5
Value of third bottle	3
Value of fourth bottle	1

a From this information, derive Bert's demand schedule. Graph his demand curve for bottled water.

b If the price of a bottle of water is $4, how many bottles does Bert buy? How much consumer surplus does Bert get from his purchases? Show Bert's consumer surplus in your graph.

c If the price falls to $2, how does quantity demanded change? How does Bert's consumer surplus change? Show these changes in your graph.

5 Ernie owns a water pump. Because pumping large amounts of water is harder than pumping small amounts, the cost of producing a bottle of water rises as he pumps more. Here is the cost he incurs to produce each bottle of water:

Cost of first bottle	$1
Cost of second bottle	3
Cost of third bottle	5
Cost of fourth bottle	7

a From this information, derive Ernie's supply schedule. Graph his supply curve for bottled water.

b If the price of a bottle of water is $4, how many bottles does Ernie produce and sell? How much producer surplus does Ernie get from these sales? Show Ernie's producer surplus in your graph.

c If the price rises to $6, how does quantity supplied change? How does Ernie's producer surplus change? Show these changes in your graph.

6 Consider a market in which Bert from problem 4 is the buyer and Ernie from problem 5 is the seller.

a Use Ernie's supply schedule and Bert's demand schedule to find the quantity supplied and quantity demanded at prices of $2, $4 and $6. Which of these prices brings supply and demand into equilibrium?

b What are consumer surplus, producer surplus and total surplus in this equilibrium?

c If Ernie produced and Bert consumed one less bottle of water, what would happen to total surplus?

d If Ernie produced and Bert consumed one additional bottle of water, what would happen to total surplus?

7 The cost of producing flat screen TVs has fallen substantially over the past decade. Let's consider some implications of this fact.

a Use a supply-and-demand diagram to show the effect of falling production costs on the price and quantity of flat screen TVs sold.

b In your diagram, show what happens to consumer surplus and producer surplus.

c Suppose the supply of flat screen TVs is very elastic. Who benefits most from falling production costs – consumers or producers of these TVs?

8 There are four consumers willing to pay the following amounts for haircuts:

Dave: \$14; Charlie: \$4; Alice: \$16; Kitty: \$10

There are four hairdressing salons with the following costs:

Firm A: \$6; Firm B: \$12; Firm C: \$8; Firm D: \$4

Each firm has the capacity to produce only one haircut. For efficiency, how many haircuts should be given? Which businesses should cut hair and which consumers should have their hair cut? How large is the maximum possible total surplus?

9 A friend of yours is considering two providers of mobile phone services. Provider A charges \$120 per month for the service regardless of the number of phone calls made. Provider B does not have a fixed service fee but instead charges \$1 per minute for calls. Your friend's monthly demand for minutes of calling is given by the equation $Q^D = 150 - 50P$, where P is the price of a minute.

a With each provider, what is the cost to your friend of an extra minute on the phone?

b In light of your answer to (a), how many minutes would your friend spend on the phone with each provider?

c How much would he end up paying each provider every month?

d How much consumer surplus would he obtain with each provider? (*Hint*: Graph the demand curve and recall the formula for the area of a triangle.)

e Which provider would you recommend that your friend choose? Why?

10 Consider how private health insurance affects the quantity of health care services performed. Suppose that the typical medical procedure has a cost of \$100, yet a person with private health insurance pays only \$20 out-of-pocket when she chooses to have an additional procedure performed. Her health fund pays the remaining \$80. (The health fund will recoup the \$80 through higher premiums for everybody, but the share paid by this individual is small.)

a Draw the demand curve in the market for private medical care. (In your diagram, the horizontal axis should represent the number of medical procedures.) Show the quantity of procedures demanded if each procedure has a price of \$100.

b On your diagram, show the quantity of procedures demanded if consumers pay only \$20 per procedure. If the cost of each procedure to society is truly \$100, and if individuals have private health insurance as just described, will the number of procedures performed maximise total surplus? Explain.

c Economists often blame the health insurance system for excessive use of medical care. Given your analysis, why might the use of care be viewed as 'excessive'?

d What sort of policies might prevent this excessive use?

11 Many parts of eastern Australia experienced a severe drought in recent years.

a Use a diagram of the water market to show the effects of the drought on the equilibrium price and quantity of water.

b Many communities did not allow the price of water to change, however. What is the effect of this policy on the water market? Show on your diagram any surplus or shortage that arises.

c Suppose, instead, that the price of water was allowed to increase until the quantity demanded equalled the quantity supplied. Would the resulting allocation of water be more efficient? In your view, would it be more or less fair than the proportionate reductions in water use? What could be done to make the market solution more fair?

Search me!

Search me!

When accessing information microeconomics use the following keywords in any combinations you require:

- consumer surplus
- producer surplus
- ticket scalping
- willingness to pay

CourseMate

CourseMate

For more multimedia resources and activities on economics, visit the Economics CourseMate website.

8

Application: The costs of taxation

Learning objectives

In this chapter you will:

- examine how taxes reduce consumer and producer surplus
- learn the meaning and causes of the deadweight loss of a tax
- consider why some taxes have larger deadweight losses than others
- examine how tax revenue and deadweight loss vary with the size of a tax.

Taxes are often a source of heated political debate. In 1808, William Bligh, Governor of colonial Australia, was thrown out of office over taxation concerns in the infamous Rum Rebellion. Two hundred years later, in 2010, Kevin Rudd, Prime Minister of Australia, was thrown out of office, in large part due to his handling of a government proposal for a super-profit tax on the mining industry. Yet few people would deny that some level of taxation is necessary to help fund government expenditure.

Because taxation has such a major impact on the modern economy, we return to the topic several times throughout this book as we expand the set of tools we have at your disposal. We began our study of taxes in chapter 6. There we saw how a tax on a good affects its price and the quantity sold and how the forces of supply and demand divide the burden of a tax between buyers and sellers. In this chapter we extend this analysis and look at how taxes affect welfare, the economic wellbeing of participants in a market.

The effects of taxes on welfare might at first seem obvious. The government imposes taxes to raise revenue and that revenue must come out of someone's pocket. As we saw in chapter 6, both buyers and sellers are worse off when a good is taxed; a tax raises the price buyers pay and lowers the price sellers receive. Yet to understand fully how taxes affect economic wellbeing, we must compare the reduced welfare of buyers and sellers with the amount of revenue the government raises. The tools of consumer and producer surplus allow us to make this comparison. The analysis will show that the costs of taxes to buyers and sellers exceed the revenue raised by the government.

The deadweight loss of taxation

We begin by recalling one of the surprising lessons from chapter 6 – it does not matter whether a tax on a good is levied on buyers or on sellers of the good. When a tax is levied on buyers, the demand curve shifts downwards by the size of the tax; when it is levied on sellers, the supply curve shifts upwards by that amount. In either case, when the tax is imposed, the price paid by buyers rises and the price received by sellers falls. In the end, the elasticities of supply and demand determine how the tax burden is distributed between producers and consumers. This distribution is the same, regardless of how the tax is levied.

Figure 8.1 shows these effects. To simplify our discussion, this figure does not show a shift in either the supply or demand curve, although one curve must shift. Which curve shifts depends on whether the tax is levied on sellers (the supply curve shifts) or buyers (the demand curve shifts). In this chapter, we can keep the analysis general and simplify the graphs by not bothering to show the shift. The key result is that the tax places a wedge between the price buyers pay and the price sellers receive. Because of this tax wedge, the quantity sold falls below the level that would be sold without a tax. In other words, a tax on a good causes the size of the market for the good to shrink. These results should be familiar from chapter 6.

How a tax affects market participants

Let's use the tools of welfare economics to measure the gains and losses from a tax on a good. To do this, we must take into account how the tax affects buyers, sellers and the government. The benefit received by buyers in a market is measured by consumer surplus – the amount buyers are willing to pay for the good minus the amount they actually pay for it. The benefit received by sellers in a market is measured by producer surplus – the amount sellers receive for the good minus their costs. These are precisely the measures of economic welfare we used in chapter 7.

Figure 8.1 The effects of a tax

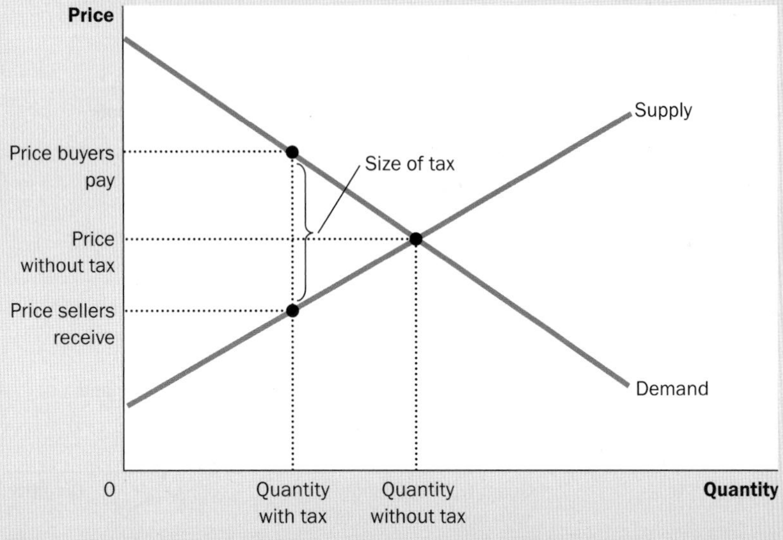

A tax on a good places a wedge between the price that buyers pay and the price that sellers receive. The quantity of the good sold falls.

What about the third interested party, the government? If T is the size of the tax and Q is the quantity of the good sold, then the government gets total tax revenue of $T \times Q$. It can use this tax revenue to provide services, such as roads, police and education, or to help the needy. Therefore, to analyse how taxes affect economic wellbeing, we use tax revenue to measure the government's benefit from the tax. Keep in mind, however, that this benefit actually accrues not to the government but to those on whom the revenue is spent.

Figure 8.2 shows that the government's tax revenue is represented by the rectangle between the supply and demand curves. The height of this rectangle is the size of the tax, T, and the width of the rectangle is the quantity of the good sold, Q. Because a rectangle's area is its height times its width, this rectangle's area is $T \times Q$, which equals the tax revenue.

Welfare without a tax

To see how a tax affects welfare, we begin by considering welfare before the government has imposed a tax. Figure 8.3 shows the supply-and-demand diagram and marks the key areas with the letters A to F.

Without a tax, the price and quantity are found at the intersection of the supply and demand curves. The price is P_1, and the quantity sold is Q_1. Because the demand curve reflects buyers' willingness to pay, consumer surplus is the area between the demand curve and the price, A + B + C. Similarly, because the supply curve reflects sellers' costs, producer surplus is the area between the supply curve and the price, D + E + F. In this case, because there is no tax, tax revenue equals zero.

Total surplus, the sum of consumer and producer surplus, equals the area A + B + C + D + E + F. In other words, as we saw in chapter 7, total surplus is the area between the supply and demand curves up to the equilibrium quantity. The 'Without tax' column of Table 8.1 summarises these conclusions.

Figure 8.2 **Tax revenue**

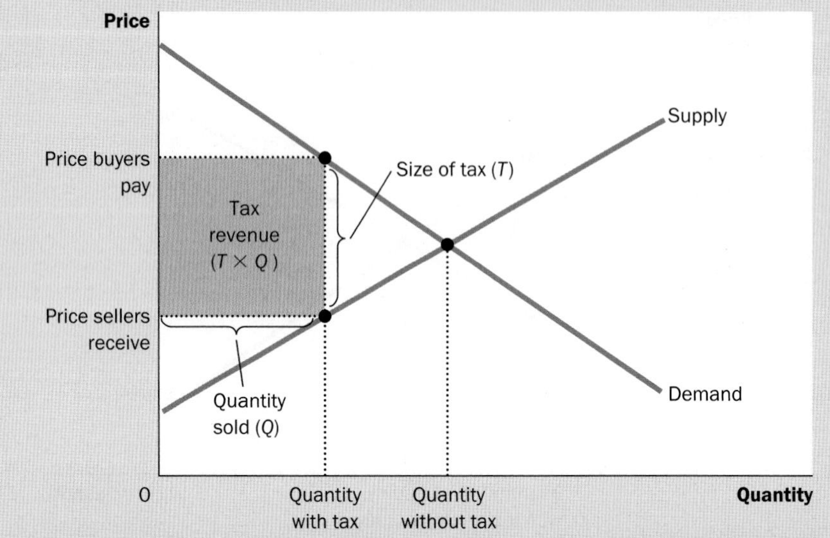

The tax revenue that the government collects equals $T \times Q$, the size of the tax T times the quantity sold Q. Thus, tax revenue equals the area of the rectangle between the supply and demand curves.

Figure 8.3 **How a tax affects welfare**

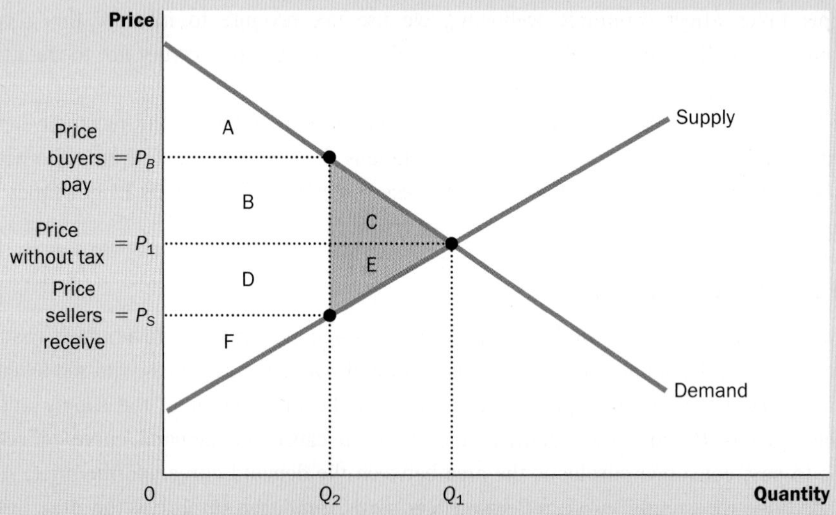

A tax on a good reduces consumer surplus (by the area B + C) and producer surplus (by the area D + E). Because the fall in producer and consumer surplus exceeds tax revenue (area B + D), the tax is said to impose a deadweight loss (area C + E).

Table 8.1 Changes in welfare from a tax

	Without tax	With tax	Change
Consumer surplus	A+B+C	A	–(B+C)
Producer surplus	D+E+F	F	–(D+E)
Tax revenue	None	B+D	+(B+D)
Total surplus	A+B+C+D+E+F	A+B+D+F	–(C+E)

This table refers to the areas marked in Figure 8.3 to show how a tax affects the welfare of buyers and sellers in a market.

Welfare with a tax

Now consider welfare after the tax is imposed. The price paid by buyers rises from P_1 to P_B, so consumer surplus now equals only area A (the area below the demand curve and above the buyers' price). The price received by sellers falls from P_1 to P_S, so producer surplus now equals only area F (the area above the supply curve and below the sellers' price). The quantity sold falls from Q_1 to Q_2, and the government collects tax revenue equal to the area B + D.

To calculate total surplus with the tax, we add consumer surplus, producer surplus and tax revenue. Thus, we find that total surplus is area A + B + D + F. The 'With tax' column of Table 8.1 provides a summary.

Changes in welfare

We can now see the effects of the tax by comparing welfare before and after the tax is imposed. The last column in Table 8.1 shows the changes. The tax causes consumer surplus to fall by the area B + C and producer surplus to fall by the area D + E. Tax revenue rises by the area B + D. Not surprisingly, the tax makes buyers and sellers worse off and the government better off.

The change in total welfare includes the change in consumer surplus (which is negative), the change in producer surplus (which is also negative) and the change in tax revenue (which is positive). When we add these three pieces together, we find that total surplus in the market falls by the area C + E. *Thus, the losses to buyers and sellers from a tax exceed the revenue raised by the government.* The reduction in total surplus that results when a tax (or some other policy) distorts a market is called the **deadweight loss.** The area C + E measures the size of the deadweight loss.

deadweight loss
the reduction in total surplus that results from a market distortion such as a tax or a monopoly price

To understand why taxes impose deadweight losses, recall one of the *Ten Lessons from Economics* in chapter 1 – people respond to incentives. In chapter 7 we saw that markets normally allocate scarce resources efficiently. That is, the equilibrium of supply and demand maximises the total surplus of buyers and sellers in a market. When a tax raises the price to buyers and lowers the price to sellers, however, it gives buyers an incentive to consume less and sellers an incentive to produce less than they would in the absence of the tax. As buyers and sellers respond to these incentives, the size of the market shrinks below its optimum (as shown in Figure 8.3 by the movement from Q_1 to Q_2). Thus, because taxes distort incentives, they cause markets to allocate resources inefficiently.

Search me!
▸ deadweight loss

Deadweight losses and the gains from trade

To gain some insight into why taxes result in deadweight losses, consider an example. Imagine that Joe cleans Jane's house each week for \$100. The opportunity cost of Joe's time is \$80 and the value of a clean house to Jane is \$120. Thus, Joe and Jane each receive a \$20 benefit from their deal. The total surplus of \$40 measures the gains from trade in this particular transaction.

Now suppose that the government levies a \$50 tax on the providers of cleaning services. There is now no price that Jane can pay Joe that will leave both of them better off after paying the tax. The most Jane would be willing to pay is \$120, but then Joe would be left with only \$70 after paying the tax, which is less than his \$80 cost. Conversely, for Joe to receive his opportunity cost of \$80, Jane would need to pay \$130, which is above the \$120 value she places on a clean house. As a result, Jane and Joe cancel their arrangement. Joe goes without the income and Jane lives in a dirtier house.

The tax has made Joe and Jane worse off by a total of \$40, because they have each lost \$20 of surplus. At the same time, the government collects no revenue from Joe and Jane because they decide to cancel their arrangement. The \$40 is pure deadweight loss; it is a loss to buyers and sellers in a market not offset by an increase in government revenue. From this example, we can see the ultimate source of deadweight losses – *taxes cause deadweight losses because they prevent buyers and sellers from realising some of the gains from trade.*

The area of the triangle between the supply and demand curves (area C + E in Figure 8.3) measures these losses. This loss can be seen more easily in Figure 8.4 by recalling that the demand curve reflects the value of the good to consumers and that the supply curve reflects the costs of producers. When the

Figure 8.4 **The deadweight loss**

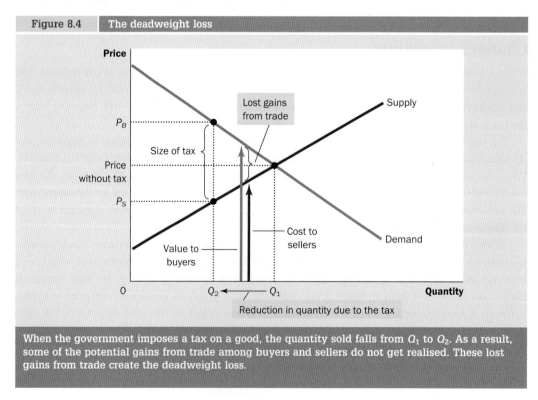

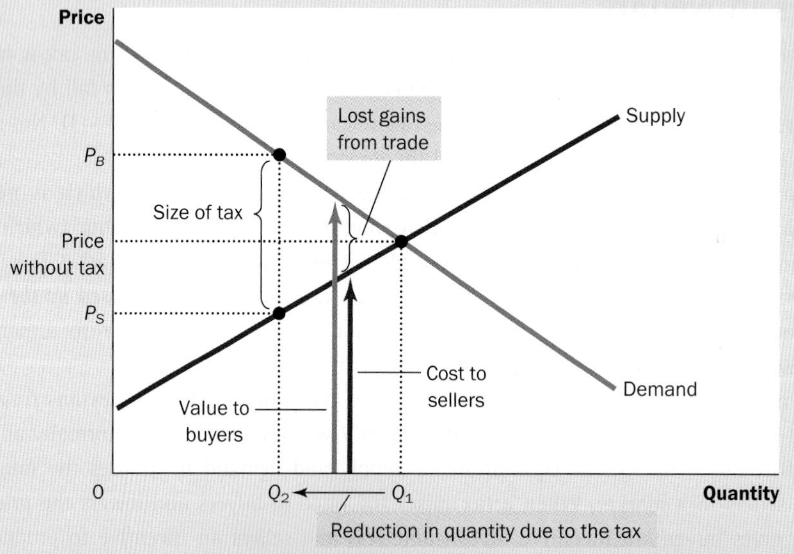

When the government imposes a tax on a good, the quantity sold falls from Q_1 to Q_2. As a result, some of the potential gains from trade among buyers and sellers do not get realised. These lost gains from trade create the deadweight loss.

tax raises the price to buyers to P_B and lowers the price to sellers to P_S, the marginal buyers and sellers leave the market, so the quantity sold falls from Q_1 to Q_2. Yet, as the figure shows, the value of the good to these buyers still exceeds the cost to these sellers. At every quantity between Q_1 to Q_2 the situation is the same as in our example with Joe and Jane. The gains from trade - the difference between buyers' value and sellers' cost - are less than the tax. As a result, these trades do not get made once the tax is imposed. The deadweight loss is the surplus lost because the tax discourages these mutually advantageous trades.

Q

Draw the supply and demand curve for ice-cream. If the government imposes a tax on ice-cream, show what happens to the quantity sold, the price paid by buyers and the price paid by sellers. In your diagram, show the deadweight loss from the tax. Explain the meaning of the deadweight loss.

The determinants of the deadweight loss

What determines whether the deadweight loss from a tax is large or small? The answer is the price elasticities of supply and demand, which measure how much the quantity supplied and quantity demanded respond to changes in the price.

Let's consider first how the elasticity of supply affects the size of the deadweight loss. In the top two panels of Figure 8.5, the demand curve and the size of the tax are the same. The only difference in these figures is the elasticity of the supply curve. In panel (a), the supply curve is relatively inelastic - quantity supplied responds only slightly to changes in the price. In panel (b), the supply curve is relatively elastic - quantity supplied responds substantially to changes in the price. Notice that the deadweight loss, the area of the triangle between the supply and demand curves, is larger when the supply curve is more elastic.

Similarly, the bottom two panels of Figure 8.5 show how the elasticity of demand affects the size of the deadweight loss. Here the supply curve and the size of the tax are held constant. In panel (c), the demand curve is relatively inelastic and the deadweight loss is small. In panel (d), the demand curve is more elastic and the deadweight loss from the tax is larger.

The lesson from this figure is easy to explain. A tax has a deadweight loss because it induces buyers and sellers to change their behaviour. The tax raises the price paid by buyers, so they consume less. At the same time, the tax lowers the price received by sellers, so they produce less. Because of these changes in behaviour, the size of the market shrinks below the optimum. The elasticities of supply and demand measure how much sellers and buyers respond to the changes in the price and, therefore, determine how much the tax distorts the market outcome. *Hence, the greater the elasticities of supply and demand, the greater the deadweight loss of a tax.*

Figure 8.5 Tax distortions and elasticities

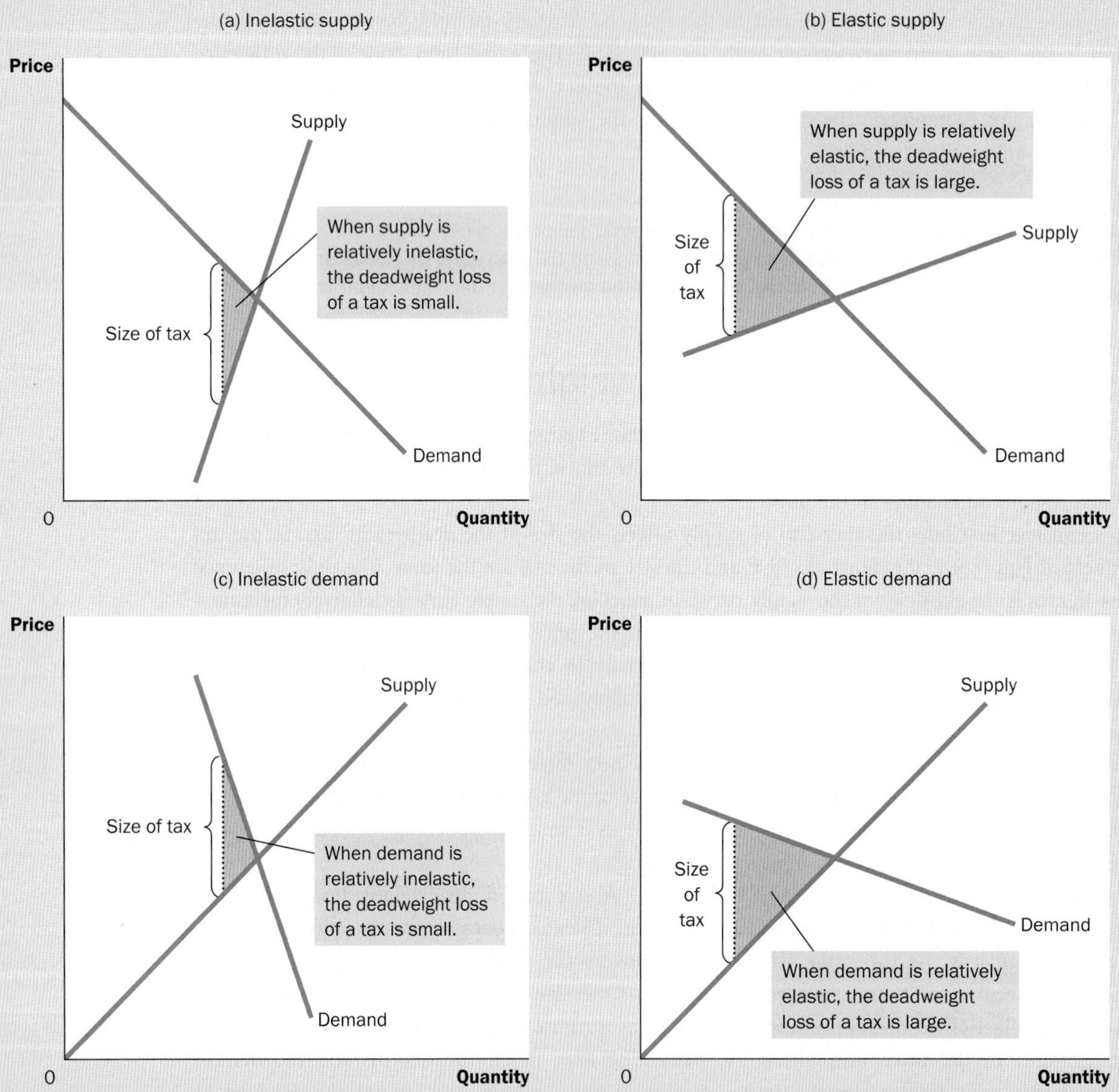
(a) Inelastic supply
Price
Supply
When supply is relatively inelastic, the deadweight loss of a tax is small.
Size of tax
Demand
0
Quantity
(b) Elastic supply
Price
When supply is relatively elastic, the deadweight loss of a tax is large.
Size of tax
Supply
Demand
0
Quantity
(c) Inelastic demand
Price
Supply
Size of tax
When demand is relatively inelastic, the deadweight loss of a tax is small.
Demand
0
Quantity
(d) Elastic demand
Price
Supply
Size of tax
Demand
When demand is relatively elastic, the deadweight loss of a tax is large.
0
Quantity

In panels (a) and (b), the demand curve and the size of the tax are the same, but the price elasticity of supply is different. Notice that the more elastic the supply curve, the larger the deadweight loss of the tax. In panels (c) and (d), the supply curve and the size of the tax are the same, but the price elasticity of demand is different. Notice that the more elastic the demand curve, the larger the deadweight loss of the tax.

CASESTUDY

The deadweight loss debate

Supply, demand, elasticity, deadweight loss – all this economic theory is enough to make your head spin. But believe it or not, these ideas go to the heart of a profound political question: How big should the government be? The reason the debate hinges on these concepts is that the larger the deadweight loss of taxation, the larger the cost of any government program. If taxation entails very large deadweight losses, then these losses are a strong argument for a leaner government that does less and taxes less. By contrast, if taxes impose only small deadweight losses, then government programs are less costly than they otherwise might be.

So how big are the deadweight losses of taxation? This is a question about which economists disagree. To see the nature of this disagreement, consider the most important tax in the Australian economy – the tax on labour. The most important example of this is income taxes. Many state governments also tax the payrolls of firms. Even a goods and services tax (nominally a tax on consumption) taxes labour because so much income is consumed. A labour tax places a wedge between the wages that firms pay and the wages that workers receive. If we add all forms of labour taxes together, the *marginal tax rate* on labour income – the tax on the last dollar of earnings – is almost 50 per cent for many workers.

Although the size of the labour tax is easy to determine, the deadweight loss of this tax is less straightforward. Economists disagree on whether labour taxes have a large or small deadweight loss. The disagreement arises from different views about the elasticity of labour supply.

Economists who argue that labour taxes are not very distorting believe that labour supply is fairly inelastic. Most people, they claim, would work full time regardless of the wage. If so, the labour supply curve is almost vertical and a tax on labour has a small deadweight loss.

Economists who argue that labour taxes are highly distorting believe that labour supply is more elastic. They admit that some groups of workers may supply their labour inelastically but claim that many other groups respond more to incentives. Here are some examples:

- Many workers can adjust the number of hours they work – for instance, by working overtime. The higher the wage, the more hours they choose to work.
- Some families have second wage earners – often married women with children – with some discretion over whether to do unpaid work at home or paid work in the marketplace. When deciding whether to take a job, these second wage earners compare the benefits of being at home (including savings on the cost of child care) with the wages they could earn.
- Many of the elderly can choose when to retire, and their decisions are partly based on the wage. Once they are retired, the wage determines their incentive to work part time.

In each of these cases, the quantity of labour supplied responds to the wage (the price of labour). Thus, the decisions of these workers are distorted when their labour earnings are taxed. Labour taxes encourage workers to work fewer hours, second wage earners to stay at home and the elderly to retire early.

These two views on labour taxation persist to this day. Indeed, whenever you see two political candidates debating whether the government should provide more services or reduce the tax burden, keep in mind that part of the disagreement may rest on different views about the elasticity of labour supply and the deadweight loss of taxation.

Q

The demand for beer is more elastic than the demand for milk. Would a tax on beer or a tax on milk have a larger deadweight loss? Why?

Deadweight loss and tax revenue as taxes vary

Taxes rarely stay the same for long periods of time. Policymakers in local, state and federal governments are always considering raising one tax or lowering another. Here we consider what happens to the deadweight loss and tax revenue when the size of a tax changes.

Figure 8.6 shows the effects of a small, medium and large tax, holding constant the market's supply and demand curves. The deadweight loss – the reduction in total surplus that results when the tax reduces the size of a market below the optimum – equals the area of the triangle between the supply and demand curves. For the small tax in panel (a), the area of the deadweight loss triangle is quite small. But as the size of a tax rises in panels (b) and (c), the deadweight loss grows larger and larger.

Figure 8.6 **Deadweight loss and tax revenue from three taxes of different size**

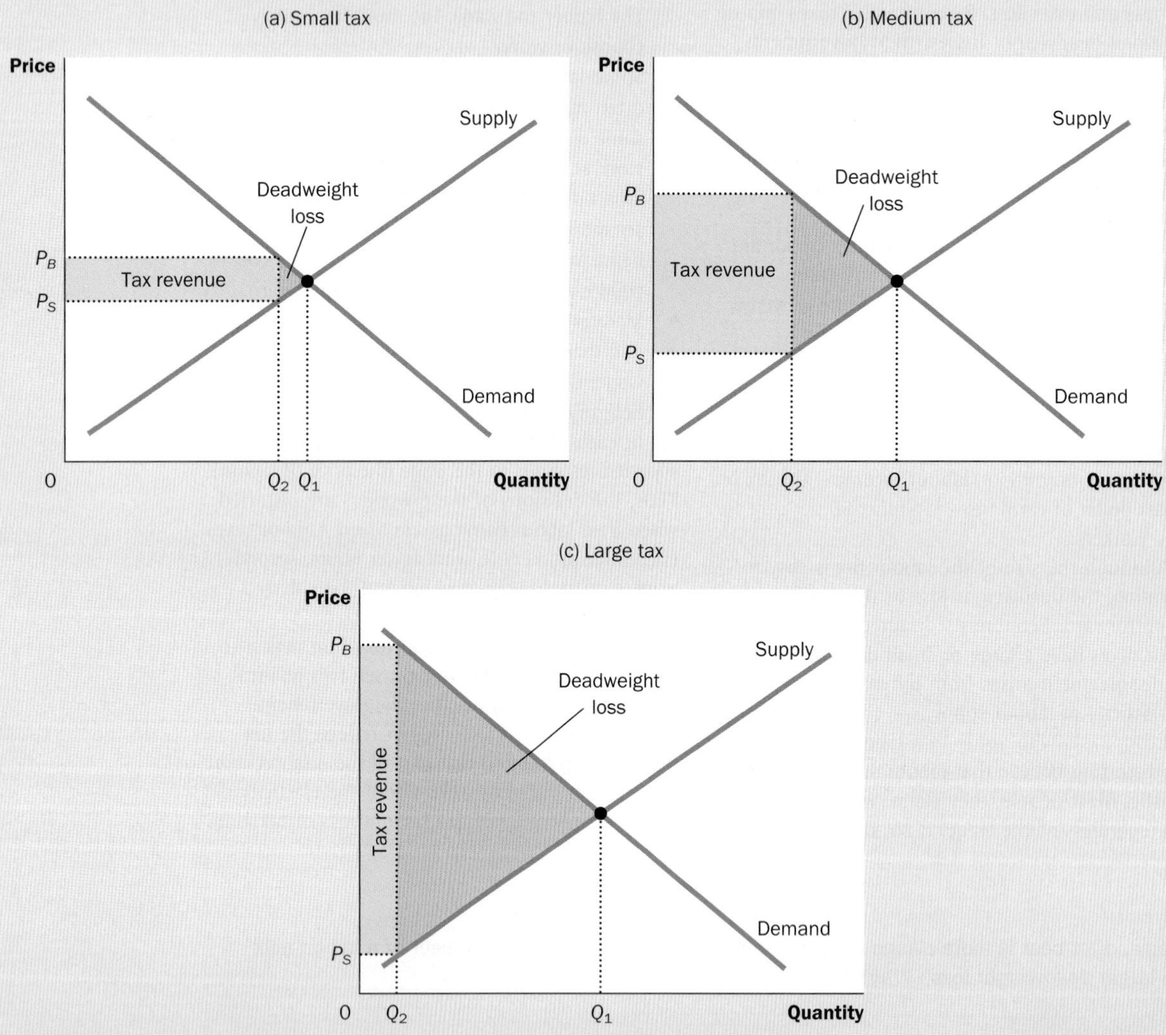

The deadweight loss is the reduction in total surplus due to the tax. Tax revenue is the amount of the tax times the amount of the good sold. In panel (a), a small tax has a small deadweight loss and raises a small amount of revenue. In panel (b), a somewhat larger tax has a larger deadweight loss and raises a larger amount of revenue. In panel (c), a very large tax has a very large deadweight loss, but because it has reduced the size of the market so much, the tax raises only a small amount of revenue.

Indeed, the deadweight loss of a tax rises even more rapidly than the size of the tax. The reason is that the deadweight loss is an area of a triangle, and an area of a triangle depends on the *square* of the size of the tax. If we double the size of a tax, for instance, the base and height of the triangle double, so the deadweight loss rises by a factor of 4. If we triple the size of a tax, the base and height triple, so the deadweight loss rises by a factor of 9.

The government's tax revenue is the size of the tax times the amount of the good sold. As Figure 8.6 shows, tax revenue equals the area of the rectangle between the supply and demand curves. For the small tax in panel (a), tax revenue is small. As the size of a tax rises from panel (a) to panel (b), tax revenue grows. But as the size of the tax rises further from panel (b) to panel (c), tax revenue falls because the higher tax drastically reduces the size of the market. For a very large tax, no revenue would be raised, because people would stop buying and selling the good altogether.

Figure 8.7 summarises these results. In panel (a) we see that, as the size of a tax increases, its deadweight loss quickly gets larger. In contrast, panel (b) shows that tax revenue first rises with the size of the tax; but then, as the tax gets larger, the market shrinks so much that tax revenue starts to fall.

Figure 8.7 **How deadweight loss and tax revenue vary with the size of a tax**

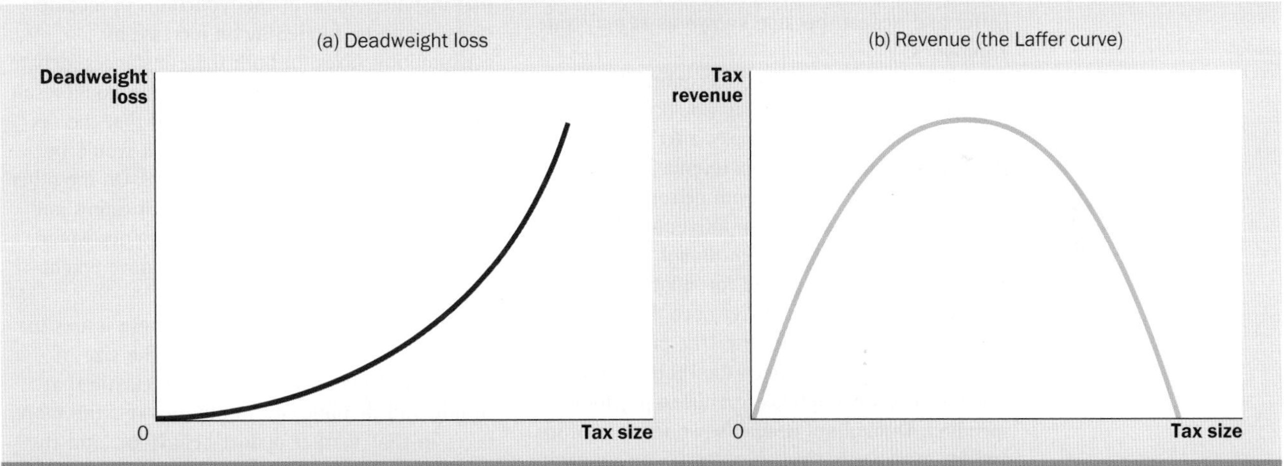

Panel (a) shows that as the size of a tax grows larger, the deadweight loss grows larger. Panel (b) shows that tax revenue first rises, then falls. This relationship is sometimes called the Laffer curve.

CASESTUDY

The Laffer curve and supply-side economics

One day in 1974, economist Arthur Laffer sat in a Washington restaurant with some prominent journalists and politicians. He took out a serviette and drew a figure on it to show how tax rates affect tax revenue. It looked much like panel (b) of our Figure 8.7. Laffer then suggested that the United States was on the downward-sloping side of this curve. Tax rates were so high, he argued, that reducing them would actually raise tax revenue.

Few economists took Laffer's suggestion seriously. The idea that a cut in tax rates could raise tax revenue was correct as a matter of economic theory, but there was more doubt about whether it would do so in practice. There was no evidence for Laffer's view that US tax rates had in fact reached such extreme levels.

Nonetheless, the *Laffer curve* (as it became known) captured the imagination of Ronald

>>

Reagan, who became US President in the 1980s. David Stockman, budget director in the first Reagan administration, offers the following story:

> [Reagan] had once been on the Laffer curve himself. 'I came into the Big Money making pictures during World War II,' he would always say. At that time the wartime income surtax hit 90 per cent. 'You could only make four pictures and then you were in the top bracket,' he would continue. 'So we all quit working after four pictures and went off to the country.' High tax rates caused less work. Low tax rates caused more. His experience proved it.

When Reagan ran for president in 1980, he made cutting taxes part of his platform. Reagan argued that taxes were so high that they were discouraging hard work. He argued that lower taxes would give people the proper incentive to work, which would raise economic wellbeing and perhaps even tax revenue. Because the cut in tax rates was intended to encourage people to increase the quantity of labour they supplied, the views of Laffer and Reagan became known as *supply-side economics*.

Subsequent history failed to confirm Laffer's conjecture that lower tax rates would raise tax revenue. When Reagan cut taxes after he was elected, the result was less tax revenue, not more. In the United States, revenue from personal income taxes (per person, adjusted for inflation) fell by 9 per cent from 1980 to 1984, even though average income (per person, adjusted for inflation) grew by 4 per cent over this period. Yet once the policy was in place, it was hard to reverse. The tax cut helped begin a long period in which the US government failed to collect enough tax revenue to pay for all its spending. Throughout Reagan's two terms in office, and for many years thereafter, the US government ran large budget deficits.

Yet Laffer's argument is not completely without merit. Although an overall cut in tax rates does reduce revenue, there is evidence that some taxpayers may be on the wrong side of the Laffer curve. In the 1980s, tax revenue collected from the richest Americans, who face the highest tax rates, did rise when their taxes were cut. The idea that cutting taxes can raise revenue may be correct if applied to those taxpayers facing the highest tax rates. In addition, Laffer's argument may be more plausible when applied to other countries, where tax rates are much higher than in the United States. In Sweden in the early 1980s, for instance, the typical worker faced a marginal tax rate of about 80 per cent. Such a high tax rate provides a substantial disincentive to work. Studies have suggested that Sweden would indeed have raised more tax revenue if it had lowered its tax rates.

These ideas have also played a role in political debate in Australia. In 1990, the Liberal Party, under Andrew Peacock, had as a key part of its platform a simplification and reduction of marginal tax rates. Similarly, such reductions and simplifications were part of the Liberal Party's 'Fightback' policy in the 1993 election although, in that instance, some of the reductions in income taxes would be funded by an increase in consumption taxes. In both these instances, debate raged as to what change in tax revenue would result from the policy. The Liberals argued that the tax revenue change would be minor as it would be offset by Laffer-style incentive effects. On the other hand, Labor was sceptical about such claims and argued, successfully, that the tax changes would have to be accompanied by cuts to government spending.

Policymakers disagree about these issues in part because they disagree about the size of the relevant elasticities. The more elastic that supply and demand are in any market, the more taxes in that market distort behaviour, and the more likely it is that a tax cut will raise tax revenue. There is no debate, however, about the general lesson – how much revenue the government gains or loses from a tax change cannot be calculated just by looking at tax rates; it also depends on how the tax change affects people's behaviour.

IN THE NEWS . . .

TAX REFORM AND THE HENRY REPORT

On 2 May 2010, the federal government released the final report of an inquiry called *Australia's Future Tax System* – the so-called 'Henry report'. This report led to significant debate about tax reform in the lead up to the 2010 federal election. Despite the wide-ranging reforms proposed in the report, debate focused on one particular aspect, a recommended super-profit tax on the mining industry. This tax was controversial and was one of the reasons why, on 24 June 2010, Prime Minister Kevin Rudd resigned and was replaced by Australia's first female Prime Minister, Julia Gillard.

The really hard work on tax reform starts now

In September last year, Kevin Rudd publicly put himself in the shoes of the reformist Labor prime ministers Bob Hawke and Paul Keating. At the Canberra launch of Paul Kelly's book *The March of Patriots*, the Prime Minister declared Labor the true party of reform. Now, with the release of the Henry tax report, Mr Rudd has the opportunity to get with the program and make good his claim of being a reforming leader. Of course, Labor faces challenges in an election year, but it must not drop the ball on tax. There is room for real vision in responding to the Henry review. Just imagine, for example, what Mr Hawke would have done, given access to the $9 billion in annual revenue that will flow from the super-profits tax on miners? Mr Rudd is applying the revenue to useful projects such as superannuation but he has missed the opportunity to use it to manage the boom-and-bust cycle in resources by pouring it into a sovereign fund.

The Henry report is rich in ideas on how to deliver a fairer, simpler approach to tax that would also drive economic activity. The report sets out a 'tax and transfer system that would position Australia to deal with the demographic, economic and environmental challenges of the 21st century and would enhance community wellbeing'. Led by Treasury Secretary Ken Henry, the review group has taken a long-term perspective, up to 2050, recommending an overhaul of the architecture to create a system that 'would be robust, capable of supporting large structural change, dealing with unforeseeable external shocks and encouraging patterns of economic activity that prove fiscally and environmentally sustainable'. That represents a big national project and, as George Megalogenis writes today, implementing Henry lock, stock and barrel would leave us with a very different nation.

There are two areas in particular, personal tax rates and state taxes, that should continue to be debated. The recommendation for a flatter personal tax system is radical but would deliver a more transparent and efficient system. All income under $25 000 would be tax-free; all other income up to $180 000 would attract tax of 35 per cent (in effect, a flat tax for the great bulk of taxpayers); income beyond $180 000 would be taxed at 45 per cent. Pensions, allowances and other transfer payments would be tax free, thus removing the inefficient transfers that create wasteful tax-welfare churn. The report argues that while personal income is the most important means of raising revenue in developed countries, contributing 37 per cent of Australian tax revenue, it discourages workforce participation and savings. The flatter system would go some way to address this problem. A $25 000 threshold would help remove disincentives to move from welfare to work by ensuring that recipients are not punitively taxed as benefits are withdrawn.

Streamlining the messy and inefficient patchwork of state taxes ought to be a prominent goal of tax reform. Under the Henry vision, stamp duty on property could be replaced with consumption taxes or a land tax on the family home (the latter ruled out by Wayne Swan); and other inefficient taxes such as payroll tax would give way to a low-rate destination cash flow tax, in effect a state consumption tax (still on the table but not picked up by the Treasurer). While the politics of one-off stamp duty paid by the purchaser versus an annual land tax paid by the

>>

owner might appear to make this reform difficult to sell, the aim of property taxes should be to avoid distorting price signals, while favouring home ownership. Affordable housing and worker mobility are important economic goals, yet there is evidence that stamp duty can act as a deterrent to house purchase. The idea of a cash flow tax to replace payroll tax is evidence of the Dr Henry's shrewdness. The government ruled out any changes to the rate or the base of GST but the cash flow tax has slipped under the radar, giving the states the opportunity to impose a consumption tax of their own and create a more flexible revenue stream for themselves.

For the moment, the resource super-profits tax on mining dominates debate. This newspaper is broadly supportive of the tax, believing minerals belong to the nation, not the companies that extract them. The estimated $9 billion will cut company tax, give superannuation assistance to low-income earners and fund infrastructure. There are good arguments for these, but the government has missed the chance to pay down debt or create some form of sovereign fund for smoothing the economy in a resources downturn. It justified its tax on miners by arguing Australia has a two-speed economy: mining and the rest. It opted to address that imbalance by immediate spending. It should take a leaf out of the Henry report and recognise real tax reform sometimes requires a much longer time perspective.

Source: Opinion, *The Australian*, 4 May 2010.

Q

If the government doubles the tax on petrol, can you be sure that revenue from the petrol tax will rise? Can you be sure that the deadweight loss from the petrol tax will rise? Explain.

Conclusion

It has been said that taxes are the price we pay for a civilised society. Indeed, our society cannot exist without some form of taxes. We all expect the government to provide us with certain services, such as roads, parks, police and defence. These public services require tax revenue.

This chapter has shed some light on how high the price of civilised society can be. One of the *Ten Lessons from Economics* discussed in chapter 1 is that markets are usually a good way to organise economic activity. Here we have seen that when the government imposes taxes on buyers or sellers of a good, however, society loses some of the benefits of market efficiency. Taxes are costly to market participants not only because taxes transfer resources from those participants to the government, but also because they alter incentives and distort market outcomes.

The analysis presented here and in chapter 6 should give you a good basis for understanding the economic impact of taxes, but this is not the end of the story. Microeconomists study how best to design a tax system, including how to strike the right balance between equity and efficiency. Macroeconomists study how taxes influence the overall economy and how policymakers can use the tax system to stablise economic activity and to achieve more rapid economic growth. So don't be surprised that, as you continue your study of economics, the subject of taxation comes up yet again.

Summary

- A tax on a good reduces the welfare of buyers and sellers of the good, and the reduction in consumer and producer surplus usually exceeds the revenue raised by the government. The fall in total surplus – the sum of consumer surplus, producer surplus and tax revenue – is called the deadweight loss of the tax.
- Taxes have deadweight losses because they cause buyers to consume less and sellers to produce less, and this change in behaviour shrinks the size of the market below the level that maximises total surplus. Because the elasticities of supply and demand measure how much market participants respond to market conditions, larger elasticities imply larger deadweight losses.
- As a tax grows larger it distorts incentives more and its deadweight loss grows larger. Because a tax reduces the size of the market, however, tax revenue does not continually increase. It first rises with the size of a tax, but if a tax gets large enough, tax revenue starts to fall.

Key concept

deadweight loss

Questions for review

1 What happens to consumer and producer surplus when the sale of a good is taxed? How does the change in consumer and producer surplus compare with the tax revenue? Explain.

2 Draw a supply-and-demand diagram with a tax on the sale of the good. Show the deadweight loss. Show the tax revenue.

3 How do the elasticities of supply and demand affect the deadweight loss of a tax? Why do they have this effect?

4 Why do experts disagree about whether labour taxes have small or large deadweight losses?

5 What happens to the deadweight loss and tax revenue when a tax is increased?

Problems and applications

1 The market for meat pies is characterised by a downward-sloping demand curve and an upward-sloping supply curve.
   a Draw the competitive market equilibrium. Label the price, quantity, consumer surplus and producer surplus. Is there any deadweight loss? Explain.
   b Suppose that the government forces each pie shop to pay a $1 tax on each pie sold. Illustrate the effect of this tax on the pie market, being sure to label the consumer surplus, producer surplus, government revenue and deadweight loss. How does each area compare with the pre-tax case?
   c If the tax were removed, pie-eaters and sellers would be better off, but the government would lose tax revenue. Suppose that consumers and producers voluntarily transferred some of their gains to the government. Could all parties (including the government) be better off than they were with a tax? Explain using the labelled areas in your graph.

2 Evaluate the following two statements. Do you agree? Why or why not?
   a 'A tax that has no deadweight loss cannot raise any revenue for the government.'
   b 'A tax that raises no revenue for the government cannot have any deadweight loss.'

3 Consider the market for rubber bands.
   a If this market has very elastic supply and very inelastic demand, how would the burden of a tax on rubber bands be shared between consumers and producers? Use the tools of consumer surplus and producer surplus in your answer.
   b If this market has very inelastic supply and very elastic demand, how would the burden of a tax on rubber bands be shared between consumers and producers? Contrast your answer with your answer to part (a).
4 Suppose that the government imposes a tax on natural gas.
   a Is the deadweight loss from this tax likely to be greater in the first year after it is imposed or in the fifth year? Explain.
   b Is the revenue collected from this tax likely to be greater in the first year after it is imposed or in the fifth year? Explain.
5 After an economics lecture one day, your friend suggests that taxing food would be a good way to raise revenue because the demand for food is quite inelastic. In what sense is taxing food a 'good' way to raise revenue? In what sense is it not a 'good' way to raise revenue?
6 The government places a tax on the purchase of socks.
   a Illustrate the effect of this tax on equilibrium price and quantity in the sock market. Identify the following areas both before and after the imposition of the tax: total spending by consumers, total revenue for producers and government tax revenue.
   b Does the price received by producers rise or fall? Can you tell whether total receipts for producers rise or fall? Explain.
   c Does the price paid by consumers rise or fall? Can you tell whether total spending by consumers rises or falls? Explain carefully. (*Hint:* Think about elasticity.) If total consumer spending falls, does consumer surplus rise? Explain.
7 Suppose the government currently raises $100 million through a $0.01 tax on widgets and another $100 million through a $0.10 tax on gadgets. If the tax rate on widgets was doubled and the tax on gadgets was eliminated, would the government raise more money than today, less money or the same amount of money? Explain.
8 Most states tax the purchase of new cars. Suppose that Victoria currently requires car dealers to pay the state $100 for each car sold and plans to increase the tax to $150 per car next year.
   a Illustrate the effect of this tax increase on the quantity of cars sold in Victoria, the price paid by consumers and the price received by producers.
   b Create a table that shows the levels of consumer surplus, producer surplus, government revenue and total surplus both before and after the tax increase.
   c What is the change in government revenue? Is it positive or negative?
   d What is the change in deadweight loss? Is it positive or negative?
   e Give one reason that the demand for cars in Victoria might be fairly elastic. Does this make the additional tax more or less likely to increase government revenue? How might states try to reduce the elasticity of demand?
9 About 30 years ago the British government imposed a 'poll tax' that required each person to pay a flat amount to the government independent of his or her income or wealth. What is the effect of such a tax on economic efficiency? What is the effect on economic equity? Do you think this was a popular tax?
10 This chapter analysed the welfare effects of a tax on a good. Consider now the opposite policy. Suppose that the government subsidises a good – for each unit of the good sold, the government pays $2 to the buyer. How does the subsidy affect consumer surplus, producer surplus, tax revenue and total surplus? Does a subsidy lead to a deadweight loss? Explain.

11 Suppose that a market is described by the following supply and demand equations:

$$Q^S = 2P$$

$$Q^D = 300 - P$$

a Solve for the equilibrium price and the equilibrium quantity.

b Suppose that a tax of T is placed on buyers, so the new demand equation is:

$$Q^D = 300 - (P + T)$$

Solve for the new equilibrium. What happens to the price received by sellers, the price paid by buyers and the quantity sold?

c Tax revenue is $T \times Q$. Use your answer to part (b) to solve for tax revenue as a function of T. Graph this relationship for T between 0 and 300.

d The deadweight loss of a tax is the area of the triangle between the supply and demand curves. Recalling that the area of a triangle is ½ × base × height, solve for deadweight loss as a function of T.

Graph this relationship for T between 0 and 300. (*Hint:* Looking sideways, the base of the deadweight loss triangle is T, and the height is the difference between the quantity sold with the tax and the quantity sold without the tax.)

e The government now levies a tax on this good of $200 per unit. Is this a good policy? Why or why not? Can you propose a better policy?

Search me!

Search me!

When accessing information about microeconomics use the following keywords in any combinations you require:

- deadweight loss

CourseMate

CourseMate

For more multimedia resources and activities on economics, visit the Economics CourseMate website.

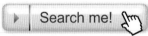

9

Application: International trade

Learning objectives

In this chapter you will:

- consider what determines whether a country imports or exports a good
- examine who wins and who loses from international trade
- learn that the gains to winners from international trade exceed the losses to losers
- analyse the welfare effects of tariffs and import quotas
- examine the arguments people use to advocate trade restrictions.

If you check the labels on the clothes you are now wearing, you will probably find that some of your clothes were made in another country. A century ago, textiles and clothing in Australia were mostly produced locally, but that is no longer the case. Faced with foreign competitors that could produce quality goods at low cost, many Australian firms found it increasingly difficult to produce and sell textiles and clothing at a profit. As a result, they laid off their workers and shut down their factories. Today, much of the textiles and clothing that Australians consume are imported from abroad.

The story of the textiles industry raises important questions for economic policy. How does international trade affect economic wellbeing? Who gains and who loses from free trade among countries, and how do the gains compare with the losses?

Chapter 3 introduced the study of international trade by applying the principle of comparative advantage. According to this principle, all countries can benefit from trading with one another because trade allows each country to specialise in doing what it does relatively best. But the analysis in chapter 3 was incomplete. It did not explain how the international marketplace achieves these gains from trade or how the gains are distributed among various economic participants.

We now return to the study of international trade and take up these questions. Over the past several chapters, we have developed many tools for analysing how markets work – supply, demand, equilibrium, consumer surplus, producer surplus and so on. With these tools we can learn more about the effects of international trade on economic wellbeing.

The determinants of trade

Consider the market for steel. The steel market is well suited to examining the gains and losses from international trade – steel is made in many countries around the world and there is much world trade in steel. Moreover, the steel market is one in which policymakers often consider (and sometimes implement) trade restrictions in order to protect domestic steel producers from foreign competitors. We examine here the steel market in the imaginary country of Isoland.

The equilibrium without trade

As our story begins, the Isolandian steel market is isolated from the rest of the world. By government decree, no one in Isoland is allowed to import or export steel and the penalty for violating the decree is so large that no one dares try.

Because there is no international trade, the market for steel in Isoland consists of Isolandian buyers and sellers. As Figure 9.1 shows, the domestic price adjusts to balance the quantity supplied by domestic sellers and the quantity demanded by domestic buyers. The figure shows the consumer and producer surplus in the equilibrium without trade. The sum of consumer and producer surplus measures the total benefits that buyers and sellers receive from the steel market.

Now suppose that, in an election upset, Isoland elects a new prime minister. The prime minister campaigned on a platform of 'change' and promised the voters bold new ideas. Her first act is to assemble a team of economists to evaluate Isolandian trade policy. She asks them to report back on three questions:

- If the government allowed Isolandians to import and export steel, what would happen to the price of steel and the quantity of steel sold in the domestic steel market?

Figure 9.1 The equilibrium without international trade

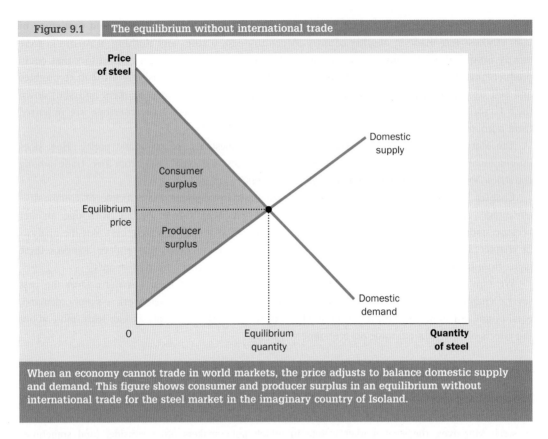

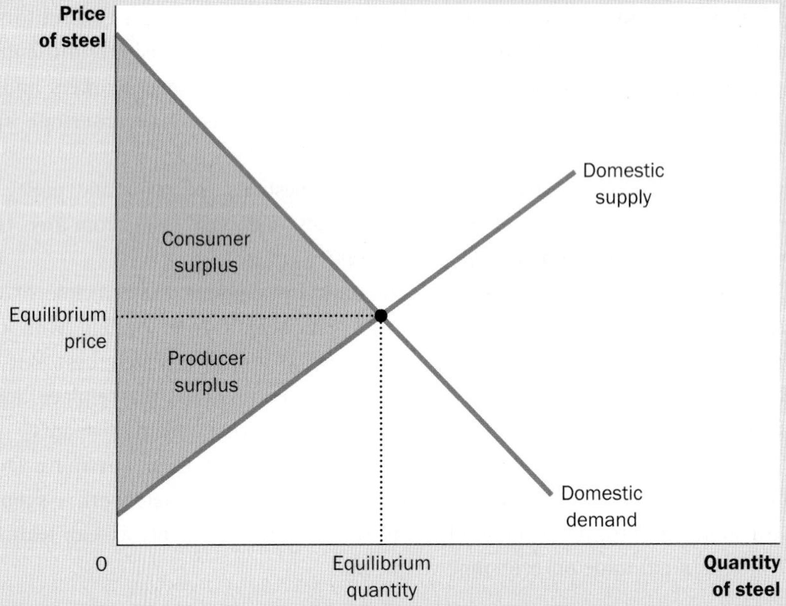

When an economy cannot trade in world markets, the price adjusts to balance domestic supply and demand. This figure shows consumer and producer surplus in an equilibrium without international trade for the steel market in the imaginary country of Isoland.

- Who would gain from free trade in steel and who would lose, and would the gains exceed the losses?
- Should a tariff (a tax on steel imports) or an import quota (a limit on steel imports) be part of the new trade policy?

After reviewing supply and demand in their favourite textbook (this one, of course), the Isolandian economics team begins its analysis.

The world price and comparative advantage

The first issue our economists take up is whether Isoland is likely to become a steel importer or a steel exporter. In other words, if free trade were allowed, would Isolandians end up buying or selling steel in world markets?

world price
the price of a good that prevails in the world market for that good

To answer this question, the economists compare the current Isolandian price of steel with the price of steel in other countries. We call the price prevailing in world markets the **world price**. If the world price of steel is higher than the domestic price, then Isoland would become an exporter of steel once trade is permitted. Isolandian steel producers would be eager to receive the higher prices available abroad and would start selling their steel to buyers in other countries. Conversely, if the world price of steel is lower than the domestic price, then Isoland would become an importer of steel. Because foreign sellers offer a better price, Isolandian steel consumers would quickly start buying steel from other countries.

In essence, comparing the world price and the domestic price before trade indicates whether Isoland has a comparative advantage in producing steel. The domestic price reflects the opportunity cost of steel – it tells us how much an Isolandian must give up to get one unit of steel. If the domestic price is low, the cost of producing steel in Isoland is low, suggesting that Isoland has a comparative advantage in producing steel relative to the rest of the world. If the domestic price is high, then the cost of producing steel in Isoland is high, suggesting that foreign countries have a comparative advantage in producing steel.

As we saw in chapter 3, trade among nations is ultimately based on comparative advantage. That is, trade is beneficial because it allows each nation to specialise in doing what it does relatively best. By comparing the world price and the domestic price before trade, we can determine whether Isoland is better or worse at producing steel than the rest of the world.

Q

The country of Autarka does not allow international trade. In Autarka, you can buy a pure wool suit for 3 ounces of gold. Meanwhile, in neighbouring countries, you can buy the same suit for 2 ounces of gold. If Autarka were to allow free trade, would it import or export wool suits? Why?

The winners and losers from trade

To analyse the welfare effects of free trade, the Isolandian economists begin with the assumption that Isoland is a small economy compared with the rest of the world, so its actions have a negligible effect on world markets. The small-economy assumption has a specific implication for analysing the steel market – if Isoland is a small economy, then the change in Isoland's trade policy will not affect the world price of steel. The Isolandians are said to be *price takers* in the world economy. That is, they take the world price of steel as given. They can sell steel at this price and be exporters or buy steel at this price and be importers.

The small-economy assumption is not necessary to analyse the gains and losses from international trade. But the Isolandian economists know from experience that this assumption greatly simplifies the analysis. They also know that the basic lessons do not change in the more complicated case of a large economy.

fyi

Comparing prices and comparative advantages

When comparing prices of goods in different countries, it is important to pay attention to the units in which prices are quoted. One country may quote prices in dollars, whereas another quotes them in pesos. To compare prices, we need to measure them in terms of some item valued in both countries – ounces of gold, barrels of crude oil or bags of wheat. The price of a good measured in terms of another good is called a *relative price*. Because relative prices measure opportunity costs, they determine comparative advantage and patterns of trade.

Here is an example. In Isoland, the price of steel is $1000 a tonne and the price of wheat is $200 a bag. In Neighbourland, the price of steel is 10 000 pesos a tonne and the price of wheat is 1000 pesos a bag. Now consider these questions: Which country has cheaper steel? Which country has cheaper wheat?

To answer these questions, we can express the price of steel in terms of wheat. This relative price gives us the amount of wheat that a person must give up to obtain 1 tonne of steel. In Isoland, the price of a tonne of steel is five bags of wheat. In Neighbourland, the price of a tonne of steel is 10 bags of wheat. Thus, the price of steel (measured in bags of wheat) is lower in Isoland than in Neighbourland, indicating that Isoland has a comparative advantage in producing steel.

We can similarly compare the price of wheat in the two countries. In Isoland, the price of a bag of wheat is 1/5 tonne of steel. In Neighbourland, the

>>

price of a bag of wheat is 1/10 tonne of steel. The price of wheat (measured in tonnes of steel) is lower in Neighbourland, indicating that Neighbourland has a comparative advantage in producing wheat.

Notice that the price of wheat in terms of steel is the inverse of the price of steel in terms of wheat. If the price of steel (in terms of wheat) is lower in one country, the price of wheat (in terms of steel) must be lower in the other. Thus, unless the prices are exactly the same, one country must have a comparative advantage in one good and the other country must have a comparative advantage in the other good.

The gains and losses of an exporting country

Figure 9.2 shows the Isolandian steel market when the domestic equilibrium price before trade is below the world price. Once free trade is allowed, the domestic price rises to equal the world price. No seller of steel would accept less than the world price and no buyer would pay more than the world price.

With the domestic price now equal to the world price, the domestic quantity supplied differs from the domestic quantity demanded. The supply curve shows the quantity of steel supplied by Isolandian sellers. The demand curve shows the quantity of steel demanded by Isolandian buyers. Because the domestic quantity supplied is greater than the domestic quantity demanded, Isoland sells steel to other countries. Thus, Isoland becomes a steel exporter.

Although domestic quantity supplied and domestic quantity demanded differ, the steel market is still in equilibrium because there is now another participant in the market – the rest of the world. One

Figure 9.2 **International trade in an exporting country**

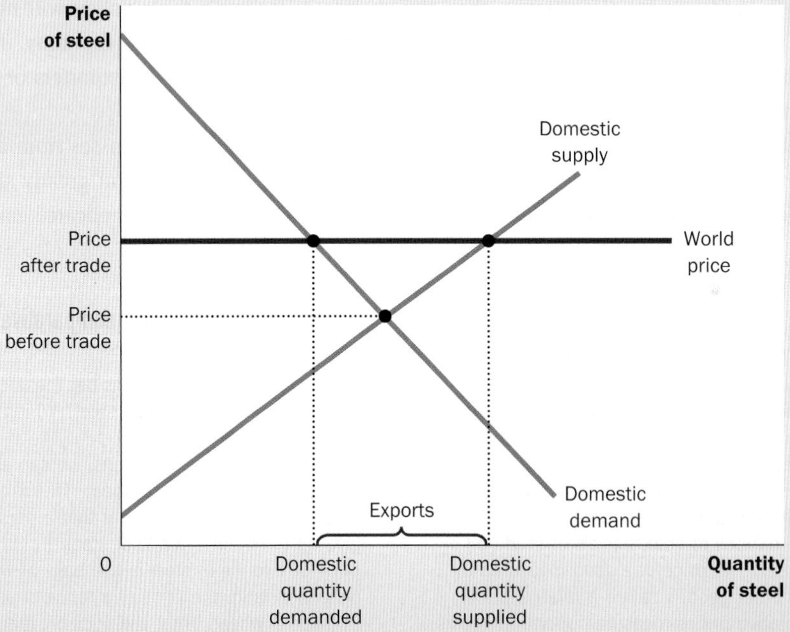

Once trade is allowed, the domestic price rises to equal the world price. The supply curve shows the quantity of steel produced domestically and the demand curve shows the quantity consumed domestically. Exports from Isoland equal the difference between the domestic quantity supplied and the domestic quantity demanded at the world price.

can view the horizontal line at the world price as representing the demand for steel from the rest of the world. This demand curve is perfectly elastic because Isoland, as a small economy, can sell as much steel as it wants at the world price.

Now consider the gains and losses from opening up trade. Clearly, not everyone benefits. Trade forces the domestic price to rise to the world price. Domestic producers of steel are better off because they can now sell steel at a higher price, but domestic consumers of steel are worse off because they have to buy steel at a higher price.

To measure these gains and losses, we look at the changes in consumer and producer surplus, which are shown in Figure 9.3 and summarised in Table 9.1. Before trade is allowed, the price of steel

Figure 9.3 How free trade affects welfare in an exporting country

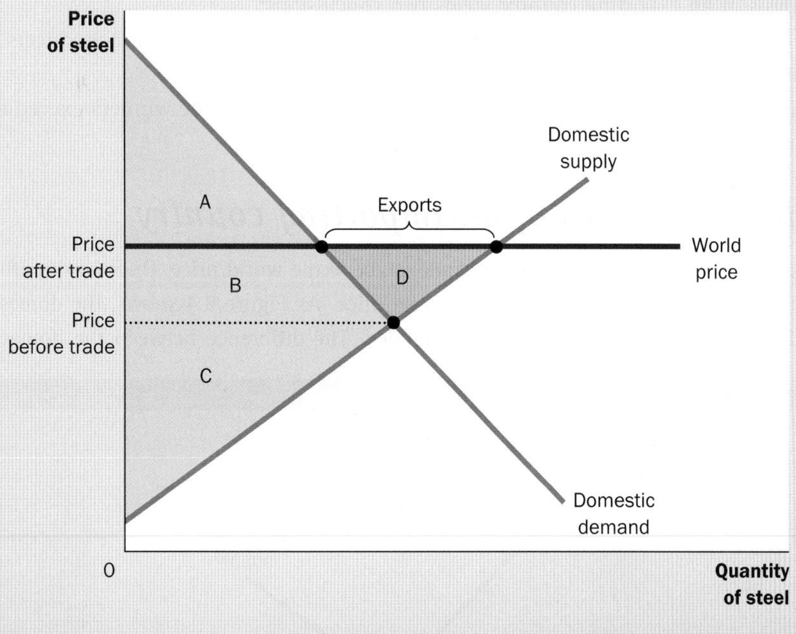

When the domestic price rises to equal the world price, sellers are better off (producer surplus rises from C to B + C + D), and buyers are worse off (consumer surplus falls from A + B to A). Total surplus rises by an amount equal to area D, indicating that trade raises the economic wellbeing of the country as a whole.

Table 9.1 Changes in welfare from free trade: The case of an exporting country

	Before trade	After trade	Change
Consumer surplus	A + B	A	− B
Producer surplus	C	B + C + D	+ (B + D)
Total surplus	A + B + C	A + B + C + D	+ D

The area D shows the increase in total surplus and represents the gains from trade.

This table examines changes in economic welfare resulting from opening up a market to international trade. Letters refer to the regions marked in figure 9.3.

adjusts to balance domestic supply and domestic demand. Consumer surplus, the area between the demand curve and the before-trade price, is area A + B. Producer surplus, the area between the supply curve and the before-trade price, is area C. Total surplus before trade, the sum of consumer and producer surplus, is area A + B + C.

After trade is allowed, the domestic price rises to the world price. Consumer surplus is area A (the area between the demand curve and the world price). Producer surplus is area B + C + D (the area between the supply curve and the world price). Thus, total surplus with trade is area A + B + C + D.

These welfare calculations show who wins and who loses from trade in an exporting country. Sellers benefit, since producer surplus increases by the area B + D. Buyers are worse off, since consumer surplus decreases by the area B. Because the gains of sellers exceed the losses of buyers by the area D, total surplus in Isoland increases.

This analysis of an exporting country yields two conclusions:

- When a country allows trade and becomes an exporter of a good, domestic producers of the good are better off and domestic consumers of the good are worse off.
- Trade raises the economic wellbeing of a nation, for the gains of the winners exceed the losses of the losers.

The gains and losses of an importing country

Now suppose that the domestic price before trade is above the world price. Once again, after free trade is allowed, the domestic price must equal the world price. As Figure 9.4 shows, the domestic quantity supplied is less than the domestic quantity demanded. The difference between the domestic quantity

Figure 9.4 International trade in an importing country

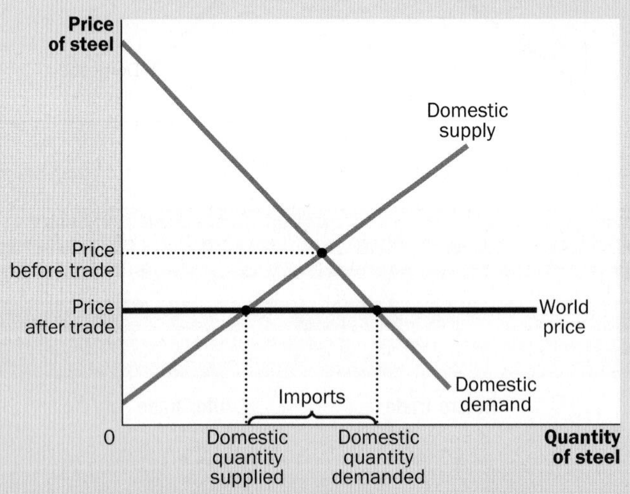

Once trade is allowed, the domestic price falls to equal the world price. The supply curve shows the amount produced domestically and the demand curve shows the amount consumed domestically. Imports equal the difference between the domestic quantity demanded and the domestic quantity supplied at the world price.

demanded and the domestic quantity supplied is bought from other countries, and Isoland becomes a steel importer.

In this case, the horizontal line at the world price represents the supply of the rest of the world. This supply curve is perfectly elastic because Isoland is a small economy and, therefore, can buy as much steel as it wants at the world price.

Now consider the gains and losses from trade. Once again, not everyone benefits. When trade forces the domestic price to fall, domestic consumers are better off (they can now buy steel at a lower price), and domestic producers are worse off (they now have to sell steel at a lower price). Changes in consumer and producer surplus measure the size of the gains and losses, as shown in Table 9.2 and Figure 9.5. Before trade, consumer surplus is area A, producer surplus is area B + C, and total surplus is area A + B + C. After trade is allowed, consumer surplus is area A + B + D, producer surplus is area C, and total surplus is area A + B + C + D.

Figure 9.5 How free trade affects welfare in an importing country

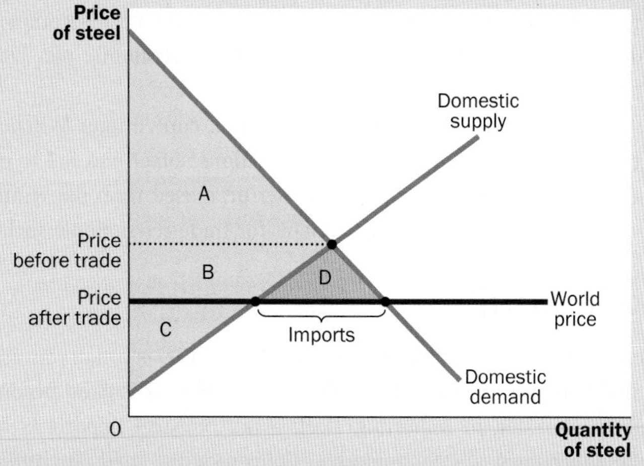

When the domestic price falls to equal the world price, buyers are better off (consumer surplus rises from A to A + B + D), and sellers are worse off (producer surplus falls from B + C to C). Total surplus rises by an amount equal to area D, indicating that trade raises the economic wellbeing of the country as a whole.

Table 9.2 Changes in welfare from free trade: The case of an importing country

	Before trade	After trade	Change
Consumer surplus	A	A + B + D	+ (B + D)
Producer surplus	B + C	C	− B
Total surplus	A + B + C	A + B + C + D	+ D

The area D shows the increase in total surplus and represents the gains from trade.

The table examines changes in economic welfare resulting from opening up a market to international trade. Letters refer to the regions marked in figure 9.5.

These welfare calculations show who wins and who loses from trade in an importing country. Buyers benefit because consumer surplus increases by the area B + D. Sellers are worse off because producer surplus falls by the area B. The gains of buyers exceed the losses of sellers and total surplus increases by the area D.

This analysis of an importing country yields two conclusions parallel to those for an exporting country:

- When a country allows trade and becomes an importer of a good, domestic consumers of the good are better off and domestic producers of the good are worse off.
- Trade raises the economic wellbeing of a nation, for the gains of the winners exceed the losses of the losers.

Now that we have completed our analysis of trade, we can better understand one of the *Ten Lessons from Economics* in chapter 1 – trade can make everyone better off. If Isoland opens up its steel market to international trade, that change will create winners and losers, regardless of whether Isoland ends up exporting or importing steel. In either case, however, the gains of the winners exceed the losses of the losers, so the winners could compensate the losers and still be better off. In this sense, trade can make everyone better off. But will trade make everyone better off? Probably not. In practice, compensation for the losers from international trade is rare. Without such compensation, opening up to international trade is a policy that expands the size of the economic pie, while perhaps leaving some participants in the economy with a smaller slice.

We can now see why the debate over trade policy is often contentious. Whenever a policy creates winners and losers, the stage is set for a political battle. Nations sometimes fail to enjoy the gains from trade simply because the losers from free trade are better organised than the winners. The losers may convert their cohesiveness into political clout and lobby for trade restrictions, such as tariffs.

The effects of a tariff

tariff
a tax on goods produced abroad and sold domestically

Search me!

▸ tariff

The Isolandian economists next consider the effects of a **tariff** – a tax on imported goods. The economists quickly realise that a tariff on steel will have no effect if Isoland becomes a steel exporter. If no one in Isoland is interested in importing steel, a tax on steel imports is irrelevant. The tariff matters only if Isoland becomes a steel importer. Concentrating their attention on this case, the economists compare welfare with and without the tariff.

The graph in Figure 9.6 shows the Isolandian market for steel. Under free trade, the domestic price equals the world price. A tariff raises the price of imported steel above the world price by the amount of the tariff. Domestic suppliers of steel, who compete with suppliers of imported steel, can now sell their steel for the world price plus the amount of the tariff. Thus, the price of steel – both imported and domestic – rises by the amount of the tariff and is, therefore, closer to the price that would prevail without trade.

The change in price affects the behaviour of domestic buyers and sellers. Because the tariff raises the price of steel, it reduces the domestic quantity demanded from Q_1^D to Q_2^D and raises the domestic quantity supplied from Q_1^S to Q_2^S *Thus, the tariff reduces the quantity of imports and moves the domestic market closer to its equilibrium without trade.*

Now consider the gains and losses from the tariff. Because the tariff raises the domestic price, domestic sellers are better off and domestic buyers are worse off. In addition, the government raises revenue. To measure these gains and losses, we look at the changes in consumer surplus, producer surplus and government revenue. These changes are summarised in Table 9.3.

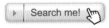

Before the tariff, the domestic price equals the world price. Consumer surplus, the area between the demand curve and the world price, is area A + B + C + D + E + F. Producer surplus, the area between the supply curve and the world price, is area G. Government revenue equals zero. Total surplus, the sum of consumer surplus, producer surplus and government revenue, is area A + B + C + D + E + F + G.

Once the government imposes a tariff, the domestic price exceeds the world price by the amount of the tariff. Consumer surplus is now area A + B. Producer surplus is area C + G. Government revenue,

Figure 9.6 **The effects of a tariff**

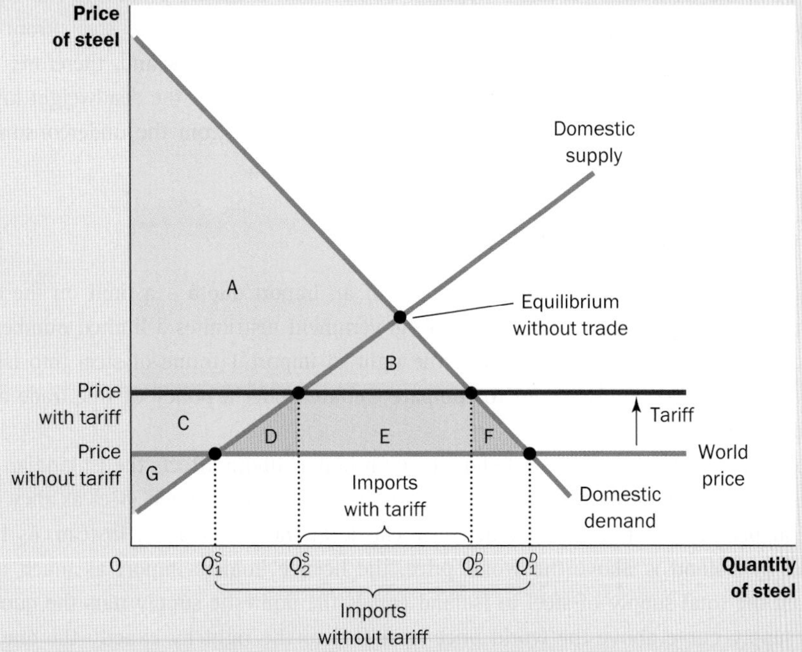

A tariff reduces the quantity of imports and moves a market closer to the equilibrium that would exist without trade. Total surplus falls by an amount equal to area D + F. These two triangles represent the deadweight loss from the tariff.

Table 9.3 Changes in welfare from a tariff

	Before tariff	After tariff	Change
Consumer surplus	A + B + C + D + E + F	A + B	−(C + D + E + F)
Producer surplus	G	C + G	+ C
Government revenue	None	E	+ E
Total surplus	A + B + C + D + E + F + G	A + B + C + E + G	−(D + F)

The area D + F shows the fall in total surplus and represents the deadweight loss of the tariff.

This table compares economic welfare when trade is unrestricted and when trade is restricted with a tariff. Letters refer to the regions marked in figure 9.6.

which is the quantity of after-tariff imports times the size of the tariff, is area E. Thus, total surplus with the tariff is area A + B +C + E + G.

To determine the total welfare effects of the tariff, we add the change in consumer surplus (which is negative), the change in producer surplus (positive) and the change in government revenue (positive). We find that total surplus in the market decreases by the area D + F. This fall in total surplus is called the *deadweight loss* of the tariff.

A tariff causes a deadweight loss because it is a type of tax. Like most taxes, it distorts incentives and pushes the allocation of scarce resources away from the optimum. In this case, we can identify two effects. First, the tariff on steel raises the price of steel that domestic producers can charge above the world price and, as a result, encourages them to increase production of steel (from Q_1^S to Q_2^S). Second, the tariff raises the price that domestic steel buyers have to pay and, therefore, encourages them to reduce consumption of steel (from Q_1^D to Q_2^D). Area D represents the deadweight loss from the overproduction of steel, and area F represents the deadweight loss from the underconsumption. The total deadweight loss of the tariff is the sum of these two triangles.

The effects of an import quota

import quota
a limit on the quantity of a good produced abroad that can be sold domestically

The Isolandian economists next consider the effects of an **import quota** – a limit on the quantity of imports. In particular, imagine that the Isolandian government distributes a limited number of import licences. Each licence gives the licence holder the right to import 1 tonne of steel into Isoland from abroad. The Isolandian economists want to compare welfare under a policy of free trade and welfare with the addition of this import quota.

The graph in Figure 9.7 and Table 9.4 show how an import quota affects the Isolandian market for steel. Because the import quota prevents Isolandians from buying as much steel as they want from abroad, the supply of steel is no longer perfectly elastic at the world price. Instead, as long as the price of steel in Isoland is above the world price, the licence holders import as much as they are permitted, and the total supply of steel in Isoland equals the domestic supply plus the quota amount. That is, the supply curve above the world price is shifted to the right by exactly the amount of the quota. (The supply curve below the world price does not shift because, in this case, importing is not profitable for the licence holders.)

The price of steel in Isoland adjusts to balance supply (domestic plus imported) and demand. As the figure shows, the quota causes the price of steel to rise above the world price. The domestic quantity demanded falls from Q_1^D to Q_2^D, and the domestic quantity supplied rises from Q_1^S to Q_2^S. Not surprisingly, the import quota reduces steel imports.

Now consider the gains and losses from the quota. Because the quota raises the domestic price above the world price, domestic sellers are better off and domestic buyers are worse off. In addition, the licence holders are better off because they make a profit from buying at the world price and selling at the higher domestic price. To measure these gains and losses, we look at the changes in consumer surplus, producer surplus and licence-holder surplus.

Before the government imposes the quota, the domestic price equals the world price. Consumer surplus, the area between the demand curve and the world price, is area A + B + C + D + E' + E" + F. Producer surplus, the area between the supply curve and the world price, is area G. The surplus of licence holders equals zero because there are no licences. Total surplus, the sum of consumer, producer and licence-holder surplus, is area A + B + C + D + E' + E" + F + G.

Figure 9.7 The effects of an import quota

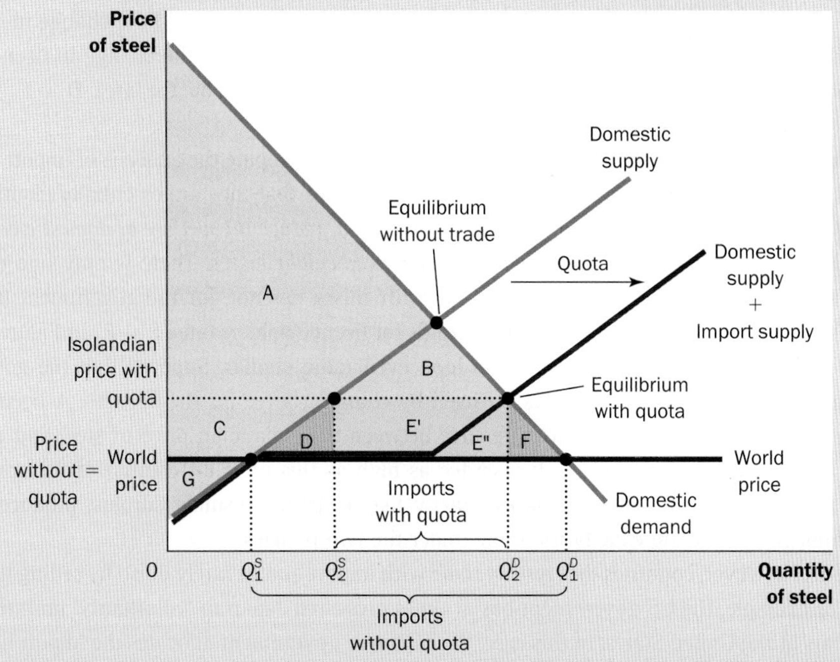

An import quota, like a tariff, reduces the quantity of imports and moves a market closer to the equilibrium that would exist without trade. Total surplus falls by an amount equal to area D + F. These two triangles represent the deadweight loss from the quota. In addition, the import quota transfers E' + E" to whoever holds the import licences.

Table 9.4 Changes in welfare from an import quota

	Before quota	After quota	Change
Consumer surplus	A + B + C + D + E'+ E"+ F	A + B	−(C + D + E'+ E"+ F)
Producer surplus	G	C + G	+ C
Licence-holder surplus	None	E' + E"	+ (E' + E")
Total surplus	A + B + C + D + E' + E" F + G	A + B + C + E' + E" + G	− (D + F)

The area D + F shows the fall in total surplus and represents the deadweight loss of the quota.

The table compares economic welfare when trade is unrestricted and when trade is restricted with an import quota. Letters refer to the regions marked in figure 9.7.

After the government imposes the import quota and issues the licences, the domestic price exceeds the world price. Domestic consumers get surplus equal to area A + B and domestic producers get surplus equal to area C + G. The licence holders make a profit on each unit imported equal to the difference between the Isolandian price of steel and the world price. Their surplus equals this price differential times the quantity of imports. Thus, it equals the area of the rectangle E' + E". Total surplus with the quota is the area A + B + C + E' + E" + G.

To see how total welfare changes with the imposition of the quota, we add the change in consumer surplus (which is negative), the change in producer surplus (positive) and the change in licence-holder surplus (positive). We find that total surplus in the market decreases by the area D + F. This area represents the deadweight loss of the import quota.

This analysis should seem somewhat familiar. Indeed, if you compare the analysis of import quotas in Figure 9.7 with the analysis of tariffs in Figure 9.6, you will see that they are essentially identical. *Both tariffs and import quotas raise the domestic price of the good, reduce the welfare of domestic consumers, increase the welfare of domestic producers and cause deadweight losses.* There is only one difference between these two types of trade restrictions – a tariff raises revenue for the government (area E in Figure 9.6), whereas an import quota creates a surplus for licence holders (area E' + E" in Figure 9.7).

Tariffs and import quotas can be made to look even more similar. Suppose that the government tries to capture the licence-holder surplus for itself by charging a fee for the licences. A licence to sell one tonne of steel is worth exactly the difference between the Isolandian price of steel and the world price, and the government can set the licence fee as high as this price differential. If the government does this, the licence fee for imports works exactly like a tariff; consumer surplus, producer surplus and government revenue are exactly the same under the two policies.

In practice, however, countries that restrict trade with import quotas rarely do so by selling the import licences. For example, the US government has at times pressured Japan to 'voluntarily' limit the sale of Japanese cars in the United States. In this case, the Japanese government allocates the import licences to Japanese firms and the surplus from these licences (area E' + E") accrues to those firms. This kind of import quota is, from the standpoint of US welfare, strictly worse than a US tariff on imported cars. Both a tariff and an import quota raise prices, restrict trade and cause deadweight losses, but at least the tariff produces revenue for the US government rather than for Japanese car companies.

Although in our analysis so far import quotas and tariffs appear to cause similar deadweight losses, a quota can potentially cause an even larger deadweight loss, depending on the mechanism used to allocate the import licences. Suppose that when Isoland imposes a quota, everyone understands that the licences will go to those who spend the most resources lobbying the Isolandian government. In this case, there is an implicit licence fee – the cost of lobbying. The revenues from this fee, however, rather than being collected by the government, are spent on lobbying expenses. The deadweight losses from this type of quota include not only the losses from overproduction (area D) and underconsumption (area F) but also whatever part of the licence-holder surplus (area E' + E") is wasted on the cost of lobbying.

The lessons for trade policy

The team of Isolandian economists can now write to the new prime minister:

> Dear Prime Minister,
>
> You asked us three questions about opening up trade. After much hard work, we have the answers.
>
> *Question:* If the government allowed Isolandians to import and export steel, what would happen to the price of steel and the quantity of steel sold in the domestic steel market?
>
> *Answer:* Once trade is allowed, the Isolandian price of steel would be driven to equal the price prevailing around the world.
>
> If the world price is now higher than the Isolandian price, our price would rise. The higher price would reduce the amount of steel Isolandians

consume and raise the amount of steel that Isolandians produce. Isoland would, therefore, become a steel exporter. This occurs because, in this case, Isoland would have a comparative advantage in producing steel.

Conversely, if the world price is now lower than the Isolandian price, our price would fall. The lower price would raise the amount of steel that Isolandians consume and lower the amount of steel that Isolandians produce. Isoland would, therefore, become a steel importer. This occurs because, in this case, other countries would have a comparative advantage in producing steel.

Question: Who would gain from free trade in steel and who would lose, and would the gains exceed the losses?

Answer: The answer depends on whether the price rises or falls when trade is allowed. If the price rises, producers of steel gain and consumers of steel lose.

If the price falls, consumers gain, and producers lose. In both cases, the gains are larger than the losses. Thus, free trade raises the total welfare of Isolandians.

Question: Should a tariff or an import quota be part of the new trade policy?

Answer: A tariff, like most taxes, has deadweight losses – the revenue raised would be smaller than the losses to the buyers and sellers. In this case, the deadweight losses occur because the tariff would move the economy closer to our current no-trade equilibrium. An import quota works much like a tariff and would cause similar deadweight losses. The best policy, from the standpoint of economic efficiency, would be to allow trade without a tariff or an import quota.

We hope you find these answers helpful as you decide on your new policy.

Your faithful servants,

Isolandian economics team

fyi

Other benefits of international trade

Our conclusions so far have been based on the standard analysis of international trade. As we have seen, there are winners and losers when a nation opens itself up to trade, but the gains to the winners exceed the losses to the losers. Yet the case for free trade can be made even stronger. There are several other economic benefits of trade beyond those emphasised in the standard analysis.

Here, in a nutshell, are some of these other benefits:

- *Increased variety of goods:* Goods produced in different countries are not exactly the same. German beer, for instance, is not the same as Australian beer. Free trade gives consumers in all countries greater variety from which to choose.
- *Lower costs through economies of scale:* Some goods can be produced at low cost only if they are produced in large quantities – a phenomenon called *economies of scale.* A firm in a small country cannot take full advantage of economies of scale if it can sell only in the domestic market. Free trade gives firms access to larger world markets and allows them to realise economies of scale more fully.
- *Increased competition:* A company shielded from foreign competitors is more likely to have market power, which in turn gives it the ability to raise prices above competitive levels. This is a type of market failure. Opening up trade fosters competition and gives the invisible hand a better chance to work its magic.
- *Enhanced flow of ideas:* The transfer of technological advances around the world is often thought to be linked to international trade in the goods that embody those advances. The best way for a poor, agricultural nation to learn about the computer revolution, for instance, is to buy some computers from abroad, rather than trying to make them domestically.

Thus, free international trade increases variety for consumers, allows firms to take advantage of economies of scale, makes markets more competitive and facilitates the spread of technology. If the Isolandian economists thought these effects were important, their advice to their prime minister would be even more forceful.

Q

Draw the supply and demand curve for pure wool suits in the country of Autarka. When trade is allowed, the price of a suit falls from 3 to 2 ounces of gold. In your diagram, what is the change in consumer surplus, the change in producer surplus and the change in total surplus? How would a tariff on suit imports alter these effects?

The arguments for restricting trade

The letter from the economics team persuades the new prime minister of Isoland to consider opening up trade in steel. She notes that the domestic price is now high compared with the world price. Free trade would, therefore, cause the price of steel to fall and hurt domestic steel producers. Before implementing the new policy, she asks Isolandian steel companies to comment on the economists' advice.

Not surprisingly, the steel companies are opposed to free trade in steel. They believe that the government should protect the domestic steel industry from foreign competition. Let's consider some of the arguments they might give to support their position and how the economics team would respond.

The jobs argument

Opponents of free trade often argue that trade with other countries destroys domestic jobs. In our example, free trade in steel would cause the price of steel to fall, reducing the quantity of steel produced in Isoland and thus reducing employment in the Isolandian steel industry. Some Isolandian steel workers would lose their jobs.

Yet free trade creates jobs at the same time that it destroys them. When Isolandians buy steel from other countries, other countries obtain the resources to buy other goods from Isoland. Isolandian workers would move from the steel industry to those industries in which Isoland has a comparative advantage. Although the transition may impose hardship on some workers initially, it allows Isolandians as a whole to enjoy a higher standard of living.

Opponents of trade are often sceptical that trade creates jobs. They might respond that *everything* can be produced more cheaply abroad. Under free trade, they might argue, Isolandians could not be profitably employed in any industry. As chapter 3 explains, however, the gains from trade are based on comparative advantage, not absolute advantage. Even if one country is better than another country at producing everything, each country can still gain from trading with the other. Workers in each country will eventually find jobs in the industry in which that country has a comparative advantage.

The national security argument

When an industry is threatened with competition from other countries, opponents of free trade often argue that the industry is vital for national security. In our example, Isolandian steel companies might point out that steel is used to make guns and tanks. With free trade, Isoland could become dependent on foreign countries to supply steel. If a war later broke out, Isoland might be unable to produce enough steel and weapons to defend itself.

Economists acknowledge that protecting key industries may be appropriate when there are legitimate concerns over national security. Yet they fear that this argument may be used too quickly by producers eager to gain at consumers' expense. The US watchmaking industry, for instance, long argued that it was vital for national security, claiming that its skilled workers would be necessary in wartime. Certainly, it is tempting for those in an industry to exaggerate their role in national defence in order to obtain protection from foreign competition.

IN THE NEWS ...

SHOULD THE WINNERS FROM FREE TRADE COMPENSATE THE LOSERS?

Politicians and pundits often say that the government should help workers made worse off by international trade by, for example, paying for their retraining. In this opinion piece, an economist makes the opposite case.

What to expect when you're free trading

by Steven E. Landsburg

All economists know that when American jobs are outsourced, Americans as a group are net winners. What we lose through lower wages is more than offset by what we gain through lower prices. In other words, the winners can more than afford to compensate the losers. Does that mean they ought to? Does it create a moral mandate for taxpayer-subsidized retraining programs? ...

Um, no. Even if you've just lost your job, there's something fundamentally churlish about blaming the very phenomenon that's elevated you above the subsistence level since the day you were born. If the world owes you compensation for enduring the downside of trade, what do you owe the world for enjoying the upside?

I doubt there's a human being on earth who hasn't benefited from the opportunity to trade freely with his neighbors. Imagine what your life would be like if you had to grow your own food, make your own clothes and rely on your grandmother's home remedies for health care. Access to a trained physician might reduce the demand for grandma's home remedies, but – especially at her age – she's still got plenty of reason to be thankful for having a doctor.

Some people suggest, however, that it makes sense to isolate the moral effects of a single new trading opportunity or free trade agreement. Surely we have fellow citizens who are hurt by those agreements, at least in the limited sense that they'd be better off in a world where trade flourishes, except in this one instance. What do we owe those fellow citizens?

One way to think about that is to ask what your moral instincts tell you in analogous situations. Suppose, after years of buying shampoo at your local pharmacy, you discover you can order the same shampoo for less money on the Web. Do you have an obligation to compensate your pharmacist? If you move to a cheaper apartment, should you compensate your landlord? When you eat at McDonald's, should you compensate the owners of the diner next door? Public policy should not be designed to advance moral instincts that we all reject every day of our lives.

In what morally relevant way, then, might displaced workers differ from displaced pharmacists or displaced landlords? You might argue that pharmacists and landlords have always faced cutthroat competition and therefore knew what they were getting into, while decades of tariffs and quotas have led manufacturing workers to expect a modicum of protection. That expectation led them to develop certain skills, and now it's unfair to pull the rug out from under them.

Once again, that argument does not mesh with our everyday instincts. For many decades, schoolyard bullying has been a profitable occupation. All across America, bullies have built up skills so they can take advantage of that opportunity. If we toughen the rules to make bullying unprofitable, must we compensate the bullies?

Bullying and protectionism have a lot in common. They both use force (either directly or through the power of the law) to enrich someone else at your involuntary expense. If you're forced to pay $20 an hour to an American for goods you could have bought from a Mexican for $5 an hour, you're being extorted. When a free trade agreement allows you to buy from the Mexican after all, rejoice in your liberation.

Source: From *The New York Times*, 16 January 2008

National security concerns in Australia led to the introduction of tariffs to protect manufacturing industries after the Second World War. This policy was tied to immigration – it was argued that protecting manufacturing industries would create jobs for immigrant workers. Raising Australia's population through immigration would help protect the country from future invasion. As a result, between the 1950s and 1970s, Australia had some of the highest manufacturing tariffs among industrial countries.

The infant industry argument

New industries sometimes argue for temporary trade restrictions in order to help them get started. After a period of protection, the argument goes, these industries will mature and be able to compete with foreign competitors.

Similarly, older industries sometimes argue that they need temporary protection in order to help them adjust to new conditions. For example, Australia introduced quotas on imported motor vehicles, clothing, footwear and textiles in 1975 to give the local industries time to 'adjust' to increasing foreign competition. These restrictions lasted until the late 1980s and early 1990s.

Economists are often sceptical about such claims. The main reason is that the infant industry argument is difficult to implement in practice. To apply protection successfully, the government would need to decide which industries will eventually be profitable and decide whether the benefits of establishing these industries exceed the costs to consumers of protection. Yet 'picking winners' is extraordinarily difficult. It is made even more difficult by the political process, which often awards protection to those industries that are politically powerful. And once a powerful industry is protected from foreign competition, the 'temporary' policy is hard to remove.

In addition, many economists are sceptical about the infant industry argument even in principle. Suppose, for instance, that the Isolandian steel industry is young and unable to compete profitably against foreign rivals. Yet there is reason to believe that the industry can be profitable in the long run. In this case, the owners of the firms should be willing to incur temporary losses in order to obtain the eventual profits. Protection is not necessary for an industry to grow. Firms in various industries – such as many biotechnology firms today – incur temporary losses in the hope of growing and becoming profitable in the future. And many of them succeed, even without protection from foreign competition.

The unfair competition argument

A common argument is that free trade is desirable only if all countries play by the same rules. If firms in different countries are subject to different laws and regulations, then it is unfair (the argument goes) to expect the firms to compete in the international marketplace. For instance, in 2010, independent senator Bob Katter was reported by the *Cairns Post* as supporting protection for Australian farmers due to 'unfair' foreign competition:

> The government is closing down agriculture in this country. Four years ago Australia became the net importer of fruit and vegetables. This nation will be a net importer of food ... we will be the begging bowl of Australia, not the fruit bowl of Asia. If you are a poor damn Australian farmer you have no subsidy at all. We can't compete giving our competitor a 30m start over a 100m race.

Source: Kylie Regenzani, 'Katter opens up on agriculture', *Cairns Post*, 15 October 2010.

Suppose that the government of Neighbourland subsidises wheat production by giving wheat farmers large tax breaks. Isolandian wheat farmers might argue that they should be protected from this foreign competition because Neighbourland is not competing fairly.

Would it, in fact, hurt Isoland to buy wheat from another country at a subsidised price? Certainly, Isolandian wheat producers would suffer, but Isolandian wheat consumers would benefit from the low price. Moreover, the case for free trade is no different; the gains of the consumers from buying at the low price would exceed the losses of the producers. Neighbourland's subsidy to its wheat farmers may be a bad policy, but it is the taxpayers of Neighbourland who bear the burden. Isoland can benefit from the opportunity to buy wheat at a subsidised price.

The protection-as-a-bargaining-chip argument

Another argument for trade restrictions concerns the strategy of bargaining. Many policymakers claim to support free trade but, at the same time, argue that trade restrictions can be useful when we bargain with our trading partners. They claim that the threat of a trade restriction can help remove a trade restriction already imposed by a foreign government. For example, Isoland might threaten to impose a tariff on steel unless Neighbourland removes its tariff on wheat. If Neighbourland responds to this threat by removing its tariff, the result can be freer trade.

The problem with this bargaining strategy is that the threat may not work. If it doesn't work, the country has a difficult choice. It can carry out its threat and implement the trade restriction, which would reduce its own economic welfare. Or it can back down from its threat, which would cause it to lose prestige in international affairs. Faced with this choice, the country would probably wish that it had never made the threat in the first place.

Search me!

▸ free trade agreement

CASESTUDY

Trade agreements and the World Trade Organization

A country can take one of two approaches to achieving free trade. It can take a unilateral approach and remove its trade restrictions on its own. This is the approach that Great Britain took in the nineteenth century and that Chile and South Korea have taken in recent years. Alternatively, a country can take a *multilateral* approach and reduce its trade restrictions while other countries do the same. In other words, it can bargain with its trading partners in an attempt to reduce trade restrictions around the world. In recent times, the Australian government has favoured this approach.

One important example of a multilateral approach is the free trade agreement negotiated between Australia and the US. That agreement removed 97 per cent of US tariffs on non-agricultural goods (excluding textiles and clothing, which will be duty free from 2015). The agreement will result in consumer benefits in cars, metals, paper and chemicals. Two-thirds of agricultural tariffs will be removed, including those on lamb but not the important crop of sugar. It would also harmonise intellectual property laws, something that caused political tension, especially with regard to pharmaceuticals and copyright.

Another example of a multilateral deal is the General Agreement on Tariffs and Trade (GATT), which is a continuing series of negotiations among many of the world's countries with the goal of promoting free trade. GATT was founded after the Second World War as a response to the high tariffs imposed during the Great Depression of the 1930s. Many economists believe these tariffs contributed to the economic hardship during that period. GATT has successfully reduced the average tariff among member countries from about 40 per cent after the Second World War to about 5 per cent today.

The rules established under GATT are now enforced by an international institution called the World Trade Organization (WTO). The WTO was established in 1995 and has its headquarters in Geneva, Switzerland. As of January 2009, 153 countries have joined the organisation, accounting for more than 97 per cent of world trade. The functions of the WTO are to administer trade agreements, provide a forum for negotiations and handle disputes that arise among member countries.

>>

What are the pros and cons of the multilateral approach to free trade? One advantage is that the multilateral approach has the potential to result in freer trade than a unilateral approach because it can reduce trade restrictions abroad as well as at home. At the same time, however, if international negotiations fail, the result could be more restricted trade than under a unilateral approach.

In addition, the multilateral approach may have a political advantage. In most markets, producers are fewer and better organised than consumers – and thus wield greater political influence. Reducing the Isolandian tariff on steel, for example, may be politically difficult if considered by itself. The steel companies would oppose free trade and the users of steel who would benefit are so numerous that organising their support would be difficult. Yet suppose that Neighbourland promises to reduce its tariff on wheat at the same time that Isoland reduces its tariff on steel. In this case, the Isolandian wheat farmers, who are also politically powerful, would back the agreement. Thus, the multilateral approach to free trade can sometimes win political support when a unilateral reduction cannot.

The textile industry of Autarka advocates a ban on the import of pure wool suits. Give five arguments its lobbyists might make. Respond to each of these arguments.

Conclusion

Economists and the general public often disagree about free trade. In 1997, the Industry Commission released a report recommending the reduction and removal of Australian tariffs on textiles and clothing. The federal government decided not to implement the recommendations. Opponents viewed the freer trade as a threat to job security and the living standards of Australians currently employed in the textile industry. In contrast, economists overwhelmingly supported the report's recommendations. They viewed the tariff reductions as a way of reducing the relative prices paid for clothing and, hence, improving the consumption possibilities of Australians. Recently, similar debates have raged over cars, CDs and books, with varying outcomes. However, in each debate there was widespread agreement among economists that such tariff reductions were desirable.

IN THE NEWS . . .

EU SAUCE POLICY

Enforcing tariff protection can be a difficult task. The following article documents how vegetable producers became concerned that vegies were slipping under trade barriers by dosing themselves in sauce.

One lump or two? A saucy tale from Europe

Brussels: How many lumps are allowed in a sauce before it can be considered a vegetable? This question – to be considered by a European Union committee on January 10th – may sound absurd. But trade worth hundreds of millions of euros rests on the answer.

The reason: whereas the EU tariff on imported sauce is only 20%, the tariff on an imported vegetable is 288%. Protectionists in the EU – mainly vegetable producers from the south – fear that vegetables may sneak into Europe disguised as tinned sauces. They have argued that, if a sauce is more than 20% made up of lumps of fruit or vegetable, it should be considered a vegetable. That hits such culinary delights as Unilever's

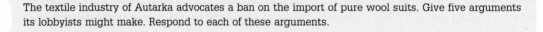

Chicken Tonight, Heinz's Teletubbies pasta in sauce and Dolmio's Pasta Gusto.

Of course any multinational food producer worth its sauce has already shifted production to within the EU so as to get round the tariffs. The €200m of sauce that EU countries still import is thus mainly lump-free. But other sauce markets now apply the lump test too, and their tariffs hit about half of the EU's annual sauce exports of around €244m.

Big food producers such as Mars, Unilever and Nestlé were so irritated by these rules that they took a case against the EU to the World Customs Organisation. But, although the ruling went against the EU, there is no provision for sanctions. The EU has, however, graciously agreed to reconsider its rules. The European Commission is proposing raising the lump threshold to 30%. Still too low, scream the food companies, arguing – reasonably enough – that consumer perception should be the test; and that most people can tell the difference between a turnip and a tin of Teletubbies pasta in sauce. But the EU seems unlikely to change its mind. So the food companies may just have to lump it.

Source: *The Economist*, 3 January 2002. © The Economist Newspaper Limited, London 2002.

In many ways, Australia itself is an ongoing experiment that confirms the virtues of free trade. At the turn of the century, Australia made an important commitment to unrestricted trade among the states, and the country as a whole has benefited from the specialisation that trade allows. Bananas are grown in Queensland, oil is pumped from Bass Strait, wine is made in the Hunter and Barossa valleys, and so on. Australians would not enjoy the high standard of living they do today if people could consume only those goods and services produced in their own states. The world could similarly benefit from free trade among countries.

IN THE NEWS . . .

AUSTRALIA AND FREE TRADE

Over the past 40 years, Australia has significantly reduced its self-imposed impediments to international trade. Tariffs on imports have been reduced and quotas have been removed in a variety of areas. This article reviews some of these reforms and considers the pressure on the government to restrict imports.

Free trade push should boost economic activity

It is reassuring then that the new Trade minister, Craig Emerson, is confidently putting free trade at the top of the agenda, even though it is unlikely to yield many photo opportunities in the current political climate. Sandwiched between the regulatory policies of the Greens and independents like Bob Katter, who wants to block foreign bananas and manipulate exchange rates, it is an encouraging sign that the Gillard government might not throw up the white flag and surrender to the pre-modern tendencies of those who hold the balance of power. It is no coincidence that Dr Emerson's political career began as a senior adviser to the Hawke administration. Alongside Resources Minister Martin Ferguson and Regional Australia Minister Simon Crean, Dr Emerson's elevation to Cabinet has strengthened the government's ability to foster investment and jobs by making Australia more competitive.

The free trade challenge should not be underestimated. The international trade liberalisation process that began in Doha, Qatar, in 2001 ground to a halt in mid-2008 as the global financial crisis unfolded. But after a tentative recovery in Europe and the US, the time is right for nations to re-engage with this vexed yet vital reform. Major opportunities to

>>

kick-start the process will arise at the G20 summit in Seoul and at APEC in November.

It augurs well that faced with high unemployment and unpopularity, the Obama administration has recognised that the US will rebuild prosperity faster by boosting economic activity through trade than by raising the protectionist shutters. In particular, the US needs to rebalance its one-sided trading relationship with China, in which the US is incurring monthly deficits of $US25 billion, driven by the low value of the Chinese currency.

Australia also has a great deal to gain from the process. Re-building tariff walls would be a bad mistake. The experience of the past 20 years shows Australians benefit from reduced protection even when other countries maintain their own barriers, as imported equipment becomes cheaper. Since the Doha collapse, our trade officials have concentrated on pursuing bilateral agreements with China, Japan, Korea and Malaysia. But such initiatives do not preclude Australia from being proactive in wider trade liberalisation. This nation has vast opportunities to increase the export of services, which account for three-quarters of GDP but little more than 20 per cent of exports.

Dr Emerson is following a well-trodden path for Labor, the party responsible for much of the reform that opened up the Australian economy to the world, beginning with Gough Whitlam's tariff cuts in 1973. The process picked up pace in the Hawke/Keating years with more cuts in 1988 and 1991 and Australia leading the way in forming the Cairns group of 19 free trading agricultural export nations in response to spiralling EU agricultural trade barriers. We would urge Dr Emerson to stand firm against any push from the EU and the US to include more environmental and labour standards in bilateral or multilateral trade deals which amount to back-door protection.

As Australia's average industry assistance fell from more than 30 per cent in 1970 to less than five per cent, *The Australian* supported the transformation consistently for the prosperity it brought. For at least two centuries, economic theory has recognised the power of 'comparative advantage', or the dividend that flows from each country focusing on what it produces best and trading for the rest. In practice, real-world experience has confirmed the truth of the theory repeatedly.

Source: *The Australian*, 24 September 2010.

To better understand economists' view of trade, let's continue our parable. Suppose that the country of Isoland ignores the advice of its economics team and decides not to allow free trade in steel. The country remains in the equilibrium without international trade.

Then, one day, some Isolandian inventor discovers a new way to make steel at very low cost. The process is quite mysterious, however, and the inventor insists on keeping it a secret. What is odd is that the inventor doesn't need any workers or iron ore to make steel. The only input required by this process is wheat.

The inventor is hailed as a genius. Because steel is used in so many products, the invention lowers the cost of many goods and allows all Isolandians to enjoy a higher standard of living. Workers who had previously produced steel do suffer when their factories close, but eventually they find work in other industries. Some become farmers and grow the wheat that the inventor turns into steel. Others enter new industries that emerge as a result of higher Isolandian living standards. Everyone understands that the displacement of these workers is an inevitable part of progress.

After several years, a newspaper reporter decides to investigate this mysterious new steel process. She sneaks into the inventor's factory and learns that the inventor is a fraud. The inventor has not been making steel at all. Instead, he has been illegally shipping wheat abroad and importing steel from other countries. The only thing that the inventor had discovered was the gains from international trade.

When the truth is finally revealed, the government shuts down the inventor's operation. The price of steel rises and workers return to jobs in steel factories. Living standards in Isoland fall back to their former levels. The inventor is jailed and held up to public ridicule. After all, he was no inventor. He was just an economist.

Source: DOONESBURY © 2004 G.B. Trudeau. Reprinted with permission of UNIVERSAL UCLICK. All rights reserved.

Summary

- The effects of free trade can be determined by comparing the domestic price without trade with the world price. A low domestic price indicates that the country has a comparative advantage in producing the good and that the country will become an exporter. A high domestic price indicates that the rest of the world has a comparative advantage in producing the good and that the country will become an importer.
- When a country allows trade and becomes an exporter of a good, producers of the good are better off and consumers of the good are worse off. When a country allows trade and becomes an importer of a good, consumers are better off and producers are worse off. In both cases, the gains from trade exceed the losses.
- A tariff – a tax on imports – moves a market closer to the equilibrium that would exist without trade and, therefore, reduces the gains from trade. Although domestic producers are better off and the government raises revenue, the losses to consumers exceed these gains.
- An import quota has effects that are similar to those of a tariff. Under a quota, however, the holders of the import licences receive the revenue that the government would collect with a tariff.
- There are various arguments for restricting trade – protecting jobs, defending national security, helping infant industries, preventing unfair competition and responding to foreign trade restrictions. Although some of these arguments have some merit in some cases, economists believe that free trade is usually the better policy.

Key concepts

import quota | tariff | world price

Questions for review

1 What does the domestic price that prevails without international trade tell us about a nation's comparative advantage?
2 When does a country become an exporter of a good? An importer?
3 Draw the supply-and-demand diagram for an importing country. What is consumer surplus and producer surplus before trade is allowed? What is consumer surplus and producer surplus with free trade? What is the change in total surplus?
4 Describe what a tariff is, and describe its economic effects.
5 What is an import quota? Compare its economic effects with those of a tariff.
6 List five arguments often given to support trade restrictions. How do economists respond to these arguments?
7 What is the difference between the unilateral and multilateral approaches to achieving free trade? Give an example of each.

Problems and applications

1 Australia represents a small part of the world banana market.
   a Draw a diagram depicting the equilibrium in the Australian banana market without international trade. Identify the equilibrium price, equilibrium quantity, consumer surplus and producer surplus.

b Suppose that the world banana price is below the Australian price before trade and that the Australian banana market is now opened to trade. Identify the new equilibrium price, quantity consumed, quantity produced domestically and quantity imported. Also show the change in the surplus of domestic consumers and producers. Has domestic total surplus increased or decreased?

c In 2011, Cyclone Yasi devastated the banana crop in Queensland. Prices rose but the government resisted pressure to allow banana imports from the Philippines. What impact did that have on consumers in Australia?

2 The world price of wine is below the price that would prevail in India in the absence of trade.

a Assuming that Indian imports of wine are a small part of total world wine production, draw a graph for the Indian market for wine under free trade. Identify consumer surplus, producer surplus and total surplus in an appropriate table.

b Australia is a major wine exporter. Suppose that a virulent disease destroys much of the grape harvest in Australia. What effect does this shock have on the world price of wine? Using your graph and table from part (a), show the effect on consumer surplus, producer surplus and total surplus in India. Who are the winners and losers? Is India as a whole better or worse off?

3 The world price of cotton is below the no-trade price in Country A and above the no-trade price in Country B. Using supply-and-demand diagrams and welfare tables such as those in the chapter, show the gains from trade in each country. Compare your results for the two countries.

4 If the world price of a good is above the no-trade price in a country, what is the effect of a tariff on that good? If the world price is below the no-trade price, what is the effect of a tariff that exceeds the difference between those prices?

5 Suppose that the federal government imposes a tariff on imported cars to protect the Australian car industry from foreign competition. Assuming that Australia is a price taker in the world car market, show on a diagram the change in the quantity of imports, the loss to Australian consumers, the gain to Australian manufacturers, government revenue and the deadweight loss associated with the tariff. The loss to consumers can be separated into three parts: a transfer to domestic producers, a transfer to the government and a deadweight loss. Use your diagram to identify these three parts.

6 The following table presents the demand and supply schedules for watches in Australia and Switzerland (which we assume are the only two countries in the world).

Price per watch	Q^D in Australia (thousands)	Q^S in Australia (thousands)	Q^D in Switzerland (thousands)	Q^S in Switzerland (thousands)
$10	110	0	80	30
20	90	20	50	50
30	70	40	35	65
40	60	60	20	80
50	50	80	5	95
60	40	95	0	105
70	30	105	0	110
80	20	110	0	115

a With no international trade, what are the equilibrium price and quantity in the Australian watch market and in the Swiss watch market?

b Now suppose that trade is opened between Australia and Switzerland only. What is the new equilibrium price in the world market for watches? How does it compare with the no-trade prices of watches in the two countries?

c What is the total quantity of watch production at the new equilibrium in the two countries? Which country exports watches? How many?

d When trade opens, what happens to the quantity of watches produced, and thus employment, in the Australian watch industry? In the Swiss watch industry? Who benefits and who loses from the opening of trade?

7 Imagine that winemakers in New South Wales petitioned the state government to tax wines imported from South Australia. They argue that this tax would raise both tax revenue for the state government and employment in the New South Wales wine industry. Do you agree with these claims? Is it a good policy?

8 Many developing countries have less restrictive labour laws than Australia. For example, child labour is common in parts of Asia. Some commentators argue that trade with these countries is undesirable. It encourages exploitation of workers and provides unfair competition to Australian producers. Other commentators argue that this trade helps the poor. Without trade, the poor in developing countries would not even have their current jobs and would be worse off.
List three arguments for and against Australia trading with developing countries that have weak labour laws. Which arguments do you think are stronger? Why?

9 When the government of Tradeland decides to impose an import quota on foreign cars, three proposals are suggested: (1) sell the import licences in an auction; (2) distribute the licences randomly in a lottery; (3) let people wait in line and distribute the licences on a first-come, first-served basis. Compare the effects of these policies. Which policy do you think has the largest deadweight losses? Which policy has the smallest deadweight losses? Why? (*Hint:* The government's other ways of raising tax revenue all cause deadweight losses themselves.)

10 In a press release on 17 April 1997, the Australian Democrats announced their support for a tariff on sugar imports into Australia. The tariff on sugar at the time was $55 per tonne.

a Illustrate the effect of this tariff on the Australian sugar market. Label the relevant prices and quantities under free trade and under the tariff.

b Analyse the effects of the sugar tariff using the tools of welfare analysis.

c The Cairns Council claimed that the removal of the sugar tariff would lead to a loss of $2 million in revenue to five local sugar mills and the loss of many jobs. Do you think that these claims justify maintaining the tariff?

d Many overseas countries also protect their local sugar industries. The *Wall Street Journal* (26 June 1990) stated that the protection of the US sugar industry 'has helped make possible the spectacular rise of the high-fructose corn syrup industry'. Why would protecting the sugar industry have this effect? (*Hint:* Do you think sugar and corn syrup are substitutes or complements?)

11 (This question is challenging.) Consider a small country that exports steel. Suppose that a 'pro-trade' government decides to subsidise the export of steel by paying a certain amount for each tonne sold abroad. How does this export subsidy affect the domestic price of steel, the quantity of steel produced, the quantity of steel consumed and the quantity of steel exported? How does it affect consumer surplus, producer surplus, government revenue and total surplus? (*Hint:* The analysis of an export subsidy is similar to the analysis of a tariff.)

Search me!

When accessing information about microeconomics use the following keywords in any combinations you require:

- free trade agreement
- tariff

CourseMate

For more multimedia resources and activities on economics, visit the Economics CourseMate website.

PART FOUR

The economics of the public sector

10

Externalities

Learning objectives

In this chapter you will:

- learn what an externality is
- see why externalities can make market outcomes inefficient
- examine how people can sometimes solve the problem of externalities on their own
- consider why private solutions to externalities sometimes do not work
- examine the various government policies aimed at solving the problem of externalities.

Firms that make and sell paper also create, as a by-product of the manufacturing process, a chemical called dioxin. Scientists believe that once dioxin enters the environment, it raises the population's risk of cancer, birth defects and other health problems.

Is the production and release of dioxin a problem for society? In chapters 4 to 9 we examined how markets allocate scarce resources with the forces of supply and demand, and we saw that the equilibrium of supply and demand is typically an efficient allocation of resources. To use Adam Smith's famous metaphor, the 'invisible hand' of the marketplace leads self-interested buyers and sellers in a market to maximise the total benefit that society derives from that market. This insight is the basis for one of the *Ten Lessons from Economics* in chapter 1 – markets are usually a good way to organise economic activity. Should we conclude, therefore, that the invisible hand prevents firms in the paper market from emitting too much dioxin?

Markets do many things well, but they do not do everything well. In this chapter we begin our study of another one of the *Ten Lessons from Economics* – governments can sometimes improve market outcomes. We examine why markets sometimes fail to allocate resources efficiently, how government policies can potentially improve the market's allocation and what kinds of policies are likely to work best.

The market failures examined in this chapter fall under a general category called *externalities*. An **externality** arises when a person engages in an activity that influences the wellbeing of a bystander but the person neither pays nor receives any compensation for that effect. If the effect on the bystander is adverse, it is called a *negative externality*; if it is beneficial, it is called a *positive externality*. In the presence of externalities, society's interest in a market outcome extends beyond the wellbeing of buyers and sellers in the market; it also includes the wellbeing of bystanders who are affected. Because buyers and sellers neglect the external effects of their actions when deciding how much to demand or supply, the market equilibrium is not efficient in the presence of externalities. That is, the equilibrium fails to maximise the total benefit to society as a whole. The release of dioxin into the environment, for instance, is a negative externality. Self-interested paper firms will not consider the full cost of the pollution they create and, therefore, will emit too much unless the government prevents or discourages them from doing so.

externality
the uncompensated impact of one person's actions on the wellbeing of a bystander

Externalities come in many varieties, as do the policy responses that try to deal with the market failure. Here are some examples:

- The exhaust from cars is a negative externality because it creates smog that other people have to breathe. As a result of this externality, drivers tend to pollute too much. Governments attempt to solve this problem by setting emission standards for cars. They also tax petrol in order to reduce the amount that people drive.
- Restored historic buildings convey a positive externality because people who walk or drive by them enjoy their beauty and the sense of history that these buildings provide. Building owners do not get the full benefit of restoration and, therefore, tend to discard older buildings too quickly. In Australia, state governments can declare designated buildings as historic buildings. Private owners of these buildings generally cannot demolish them and must maintain them, at least to a minimum standard.
- Lawn-mowers create a negative externality when neighbours are disturbed by the noise. The person using the lawn-mower does not bear the full cost of the noise and, therefore, does not fully consider the noise created when choosing a time to mow the lawn. Local governments overcome this problem by limiting the times people can use lawn-mowers and other noisy equipment.

- Research into new technologies provides a positive externality because it creates knowledge that other people can use. Because inventors cannot capture the full benefits of their inventions, they tend to devote too few resources to research. The federal government tackles this problem partially through the patent system, which gives inventors an exclusive use of their inventions for a period of time, and also by providing tax breaks for research.

In each case, decision makers are failing to take account of the external effects of their behaviour. The government responds by trying to influence this behaviour to protect the interests of bystanders.

Externalities and market inefficiency

In this section we use the tools from chapter 7 to examine how externalities affect economic wellbeing. The analysis shows precisely why externalities cause markets to allocate resources inefficiently. Later in the chapter we examine various ways in which private actors and public policymakers may remedy this type of market failure.

Welfare economics: A recap

We begin by recalling the key lessons of welfare economics from chapter 7. To make our analysis concrete, we will consider a specific market – the market for aluminium. Figure 10.1 shows the supply and demand curves in the market for aluminium.

As you should recall from chapter 7, the supply and demand curves contain important information about costs and benefits. The demand curve for aluminium reflects the value of aluminium to consumers, as measured by the prices they are willing to pay. At any given quantity, the height of the demand curve shows the willingness to pay of the marginal buyer. In other words, it shows the value of the last unit of aluminium bought. Similarly, the supply curve reflects the costs of

Figure 10.1 The market for aluminium

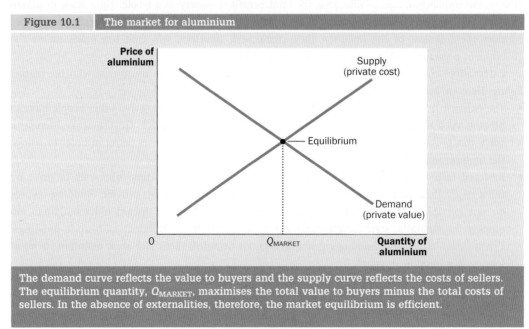

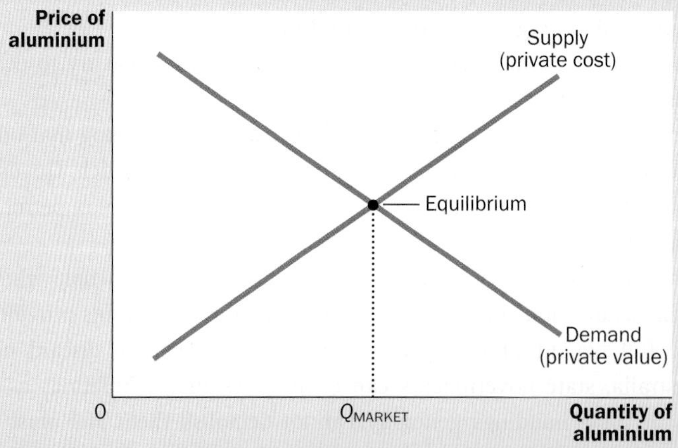

The demand curve reflects the value to buyers and the supply curve reflects the costs of sellers. The equilibrium quantity, Q_{MARKET}, maximises the total value to buyers minus the total costs of sellers. In the absence of externalities, therefore, the market equilibrium is efficient.

aluminium producers. At any given quantity, the height of the supply curve shows the cost to the marginal seller. In other words, it shows the cost of the last unit of aluminium sold.

In the absence of government intervention, the price adjusts to balance the supply and demand for aluminium. The quantity produced and consumed in the market equilibrium, shown as Q_{MARKET} in Figure 10.1, is efficient in the sense that it maximises the sum of producer and consumer surplus. That is, the market allocates resources in a way that maximises the total value to the consumers who buy and use aluminium minus the total costs to the producers who make and sell aluminium.

Negative externalities in production

Now let's suppose that aluminium factories emit pollution. For each unit of aluminium produced, a certain amount of smoke enters the atmosphere. Because this smoke creates a health risk for those who breathe the air, it is a negative externality. How does this externality affect the efficiency of the market outcome?

Because of the externality, the cost to society of producing aluminium is larger than the cost to the aluminium producers. For each unit of aluminium produced, the social cost includes the private costs of the aluminium producers plus the costs to those bystanders adversely affected by the pollution. Figure 10.2 shows the social cost of producing aluminium. The social-cost curve is above the supply curve because it takes into account the external costs imposed on society by aluminium production. At any given quantity, the height of the social-cost curve shows the private cost of the marginal seller and the extra social cost of the pollution created when the marginal unit of aluminium is produced. The difference between these two curves reflects the cost of the pollution emitted.

Figure 10.2 Pollution and the social optimum

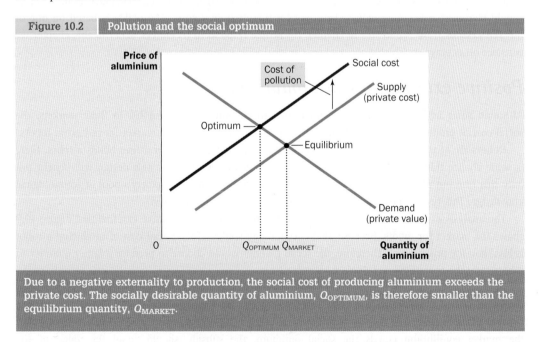

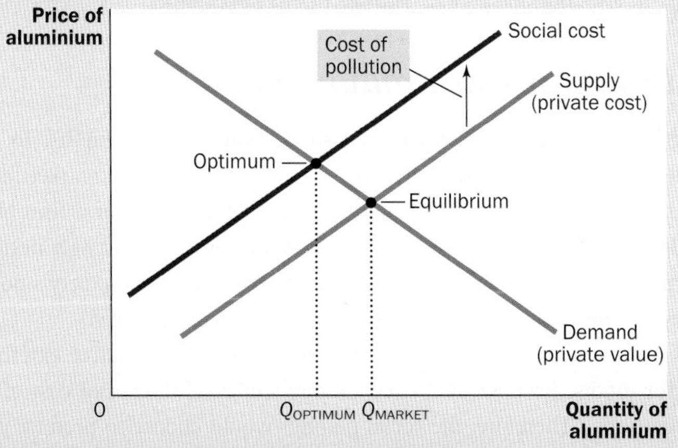

Due to a negative externality to production, the social cost of producing aluminium exceeds the private cost. The socially desirable quantity of aluminium, $Q_{OPTIMUM}$, is therefore smaller than the equilibrium quantity, Q_{MARKET}.

What quantity of aluminium should be produced? To answer this question, we once again consider what a benevolent social planner would do. The planner wants to maximise the total surplus derived from the market – the value to consumers of aluminium minus the cost of producing aluminium. The planner understands, however, that the cost of producing aluminium includes the external costs of the pollution.

The planner would choose the level of aluminium production at which the demand curve crosses the social-cost curve. This intersection determines the optimal amount of aluminium from the standpoint of society as a whole. Below this level of production, the value of the aluminium to consumers (as measured by the height of the demand curve) exceeds the social cost of producing it (as measured by the height of the social-cost curve). The planner does not produce more than this level because the social cost of producing additional aluminium exceeds the value to consumers.

Note that the equilibrium quantity of aluminium, Q_{MARKET}, is larger than the socially desirable quantity, $Q_{OPTIMUM}$. The reason for this inefficiency is that the market equilibrium reflects only the private costs of production. In the market equilibrium, the marginal consumer values aluminium at less than the social cost of producing it. That is, at Q_{MARKET} the demand curve lies below the social-cost curve. Thus, reducing aluminium production and consumption below the equilibrium level raises total economic wellbeing.

How can the social planner achieve the optimal outcome? One way would be to tax aluminium producers for each tonne of aluminium sold. The tax would shift the supply curve for aluminium upwards by the size of the tax. If the tax accurately reflected the social cost of pollutants released into the atmosphere, the new supply curve would coincide with the social-cost curve. In the new market equilibrium, aluminium producers would produce the socially desirable quantity of aluminium.

internalising an externality
altering incentives so that people take into account the external effects of their actions

The use of such a tax is said to be **internalising an externality** because it gives buyers and sellers in the market an incentive to take into account the external effects of their actions. Aluminium producers would, in essence, take the costs of pollution into account when deciding how much aluminium to supply because the tax now makes them pay for these external costs. The policy is based on one of the *Ten Lessons from Economics in* chapter 1 – people respond to incentives. Later in this chapter we consider other ways in which policymakers can deal with externalities.

Positive externalities in production

Although some activities impose costs on third parties, others yield benefits. In these markets, the social cost of production is less than the private cost. One example is the market for industrial robots.

Robots are at the frontier of a rapidly changing technology. Whenever a firm builds a robot, there is some chance that the firm will discover a new and better design. This new design will benefit not only this firm but also society as a whole because the design will enter society's pool of technological knowledge. This type of positive externality is called a *technology spillover.*

The analysis of positive externalities is similar to the analysis of negative externalities. Figure 10.3 shows the market for robots. Because of the technology spillover, the social cost of producing a robot is less than the private cost. Therefore, the social planner would choose to produce a larger quantity of robots than the private market does.

In this case, the government can internalise the externality by subsidising the production of robots. If the government paid firms for each robot produced, the supply curve would shift down by the amount of the subsidy and this shift would increase the equilibrium quantity of robots. To ensure that the market equilibrium equals the social optimum, the subsidy should equal the value of the technology spillover.

Figure 10.3 Technology spillover and the social optimum

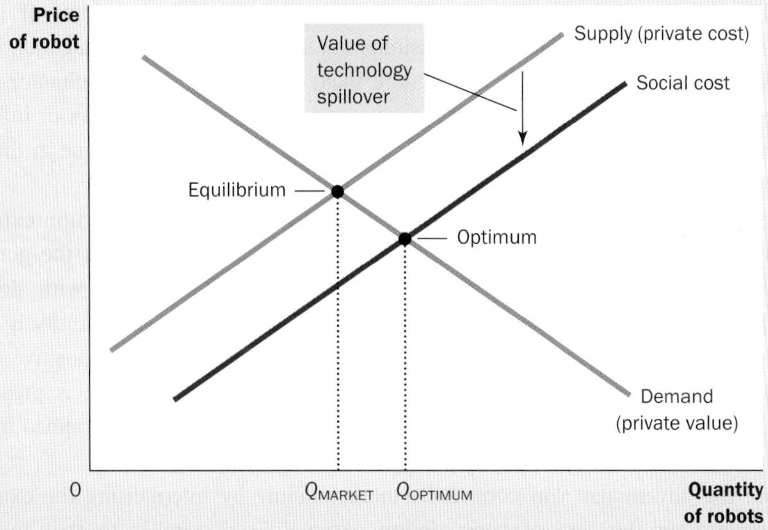

In the presence of a positive externality to production, the social cost of producing robots is less than the private cost. The socially desirable quantity of robots, $Q_{OPTIMUM}$, is therefore larger than the equilibrium quantity, Q_{MARKET}.

CASESTUDY

The debate about technology policy

On 31 October 2010, ASIMO, a humanoid robot created in Japan by Honda, celebrated its 10th anniversary. While ASIMO probably is the best-known humanoid robot – its birthday was even celebrated with a new smartphone app – other companies have developed similar robots. For example, GM has developed Robonaut 2, a humanoid robot that could be used on the International Space Station.

How large are technology spillovers from inventions like ASIMO and what do they imply for public policy? This is an important question because technological progress is the key to why living standards rise from generation to generation. Yet it is also a difficult question on which economists often disagree.

Some economists believe that technology spillovers are pervasive and that the government should encourage those industries that yield the largest spillovers. For instance, these economists argue that if making computer chips yields greater spillovers than making potato chips, then the government should use the tax laws to encourage the production of computer chips relative to the production of potato chips. Government intervention in the economy that aims to promote technology-enhancing industries is called *technology policy*.

Other economists are sceptical about technology policy. Even if technology spillovers are common, the success of a technology policy requires that the government be able to measure the size of the spillovers from different markets. This measurement problem is difficult at best. Moreover, without precise measurements, the political system may end up subsidising those industries with the most political clout, rather than those that yield the largest positive externalities.

Another way to deal with technology spillovers is patent protection. The patent laws protect the rights of inventors by giving them exclusive use of their inventions for a period of time. When a firm makes a technological breakthrough, it can patent the idea and capture much of the economic benefit for itself. The patent is said to internalise the externality by giving the firm a property right over its invention. If other firms want to use the new technology, they have to obtain permission from the inventing firm and pay it a royalty. Thus, the patent system gives firms a greater incentive to engage in research and other activities that advance technology.

Externalities in consumption

The externalities we have discussed so far are associated with the production of goods. Some externalities, however, are associated with consumption. The consumption of alcohol, for instance, yields negative externalities if consumers are more likely to drive under its influence and risk the lives of others. Similarly, vaccination against a contagious disease such as measles or influenza yields positive externalities because it lowers the risk of catching the disease for everyone in the population, even those who are not vaccinated.

The analysis of consumption externalities is similar to the analysis of production externalities. As Figure 10.4 shows, the demand curve no longer reflects the social value from the good. Panel (a) shows the case of a negative consumption externality, such as that associated with alcohol. In this case, the social value is less than the private value, and the socially optimal quantity is smaller than the quantity determined by the private market. Panel (b) shows the case of a positive consumption externality, like that associated with a vaccine. In this case, the social value is greater than the private value, and the socially optimal quantity is greater than the quantity determined by the private market.

Once again, the government can correct the market failure by internalising the externality. The appropriate response in the case of consumption externalities is similar to that in the case of production externalities. To move the market equilibrium closer to the social optimum, a negative externality requires a tax and a positive externality requires a subsidy. In fact, that is exactly the policy the government follows; alcoholic beverages are among the most highly taxed goods in our economy and vaccination is heavily subsidised through preschool programs and the medical system.

As you may have noticed by now, these examples of externalities lead to some general lessons: *Negative externalities in production or consumption lead markets to produce a larger quantity than is*

Figure 10.4 **Consumption externalities**

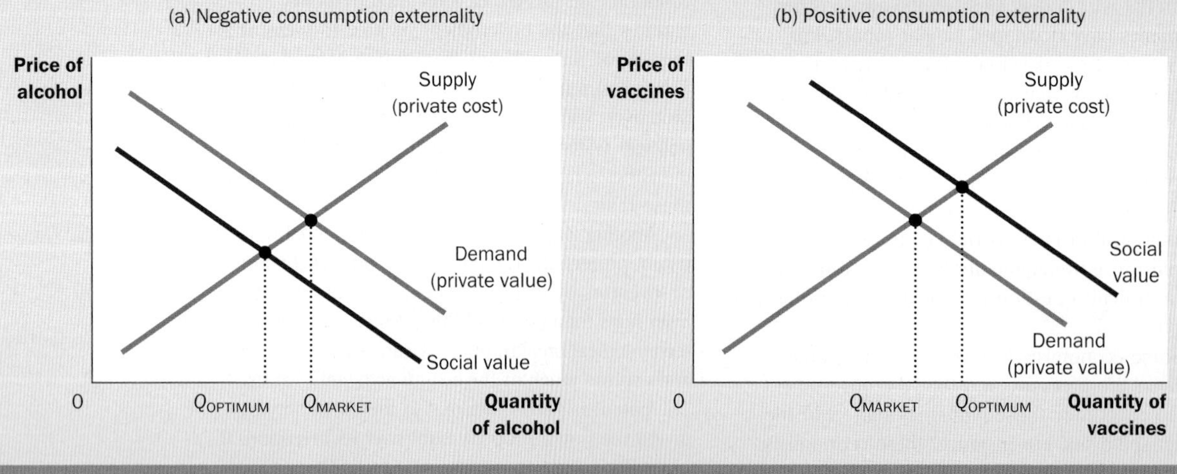

Panel (a) shows a market with a negative consumption externality, such as the market for alcoholic beverages. The curve representing social value is lower than the demand curve, and the socially desirable quantity, $Q_{OPTIMUM}$, is less than the equilibrium quantity, Q_{MARKET}. Panel (b) shows a market with a positive consumption externality, such as the market for vaccines. The curve representing social value is above the demand curve, and the socially desirable quantity, $Q_{OPTIMUM}$, is greater than the equilibrium quantity, Q_{MARKET}.

socially desirable. Positive externalities in production or consumption lead markets to produce a smaller quantity than is socially desirable. To remedy the problem, the government can internalise the externality by taxing goods that have negative externalities and subsidising goods that have positive externalities.

Q

Give an example of a negative externality and a positive externality. Explain why market outcomes are inefficient in the presence of externalities.

CASESTUDY

Externalities and global warming

In 1936, a Swedish chemist suggested that carbon dioxide released from burning coal could create a 'greenhouse effect' in the atmosphere, leading to global warming. In October 2006, a report for the British government on global warming (the Stern report) concluded that there is now overwhelming scientific evidence that climate change is a serious global threat. The report urged immediate action to reduce emissions of greenhouse gases such as carbon dioxide.

The Stern report was authored, not by a climate scientist, but by an economist, Nicholas Stern. While science can tell us the source and extent of the problem, greenhouse gas pollution is a classic case of a negative externality in production. Greenhouse gases are produced whenever fossil fuels are burnt to provide energy, whether it is to light our houses, make paper to write on or take us to the shopping mall. As the Stern report noted, the producers of greenhouse gases face little or no economic incentive to reduce emissions and do not have to compensate those who lose out because of climate change. Because producers do not face the external cost of burning fossil fuels, too much of this fuel is burnt from society's perspective.

To solve the problems of climate change, we need to understand the best ways to deal with negative externalities. We discuss these solutions in the remainder of this chapter.

Private solutions to externalities

We have discussed why externalities lead markets to allocate resources inefficiently, but have mentioned only briefly how this inefficiency can be remedied. In practice, both private individuals and public policymakers respond to externalities in various ways. All of the remedies share the goal of moving the allocation of resources closer to the social optimum. In this section we examine private solutions.

The types of private solutions

Although externalities tend to cause markets to be inefficient, government action is not always needed to solve the problem. In some circumstances, people can develop private solutions.

Sometimes, the problem of externalities is solved by moral codes and social sanctions. Consider, for instance, why most people do not litter. Although there are laws against littering, these laws are not vigorously enforced. Most people do not litter simply because it is the wrong thing to do. The Golden Rule taught to most children says: 'Do unto others as you would have them do unto you'. This moral injunction tells us to take account of how our actions affect other people. In economic terms, it tells us to internalise externalities.

Another private solution to externalities is charities, many of which are established to deal with externalities. For example, Greenpeace, whose goal is to protect the environment, is a non-profit organisation funded by private donations. As another example, private individuals and corporations sometimes sponsor scholarships and prizes for university students, in part because education has positive externalities for society.

The private market can often solve the problem of externalities by relying on the self-interest of the relevant parties. Sometimes the solution takes the form of integrating different types of business. For example, consider an apple grower and a beekeeper located next to each other. Each business confers a positive externality on the other – by pollinating the flowers on the trees, the bees help the orchard produce apples. At the same time, the bees use the nectar they get from the apple trees to produce honey. Nonetheless, when the apple grower is deciding how many trees to plant and the beekeeper is deciding how many bees to keep, they neglect the positive externality. As a result, the apple grower plants too few trees and the beekeeper keeps too few bees. These externalities could be internalised if the beekeeper bought the apple orchard or if the apple grower bought the beehive; both activities would then take place within the same firm and this single firm could choose the right number of trees and bees. Internalising externalities is one reason that some firms are involved in different types of business.

Another way for the private market to deal with external effects is for the interested parties to enter into a contract. In the example above, a contract between the apple grower and the beekeeper can solve the problem of too few trees and too few bees. The contract can specify the number of trees, the number of bees and perhaps a payment from one party to the other. By setting the right number of trees and bees, the contract can solve the inefficiency that normally arises from these externalities and make both parties better off.

The Coase theorem

How effective is the private market in dealing with externalities? A famous result, called the **Coase theorem** after economist Ronald Coase, suggests that it can be very effective in some circumstances. According to the Coase theorem, if private parties can bargain without cost over the allocation of resources, then the private market will always solve the problem of externalities and allocate resources efficiently.

Coase theorem
the proposition that if private parties can bargain without cost over the allocation of resources, they can solve the problem of externalities on their own

To see how the Coase theorem works, consider an example. Suppose that Fred owns a dog that barks and disturbs Barney, Fred's neighbour. Fred gets a benefit from owning the dog, but his dog confers a negative externality on Barney. Should Fred be forced to send his dog to the pound, or should Barney have to suffer sleepless nights because of the dog's barking?

Search me!
▸ Coase theorem

Consider first what outcome is socially efficient. A social planner, considering the two alternatives, would compare the benefit that Fred gets from the dog with the cost that Barney bears from the barking. If the benefit exceeds the cost, it is efficient for Fred to keep the dog and for Barney to live with the barking. Yet if the cost exceeds the benefit, then Fred should get rid of the dog.

According to the Coase theorem, the private market will reach the efficient outcome on its own. How? Barney can simply offer to pay Fred to get rid of the dog. Fred will accept the deal if the amount of money Barney offers is greater than the benefit of keeping the dog.

By bargaining over the price, Fred and Barney can always reach the efficient outcome. For instance, suppose that Fred gets a $500 benefit from the dog and Barney bears an $800 cost from the barking. In this case, Barney can offer Fred $600 to get rid of the dog and Fred will gladly accept. Both parties are better off than they were before and the efficient outcome is reached.

It is possible, of course, that Barney would not be willing to offer any price that Fred would accept. For instance, suppose that Fred gets a $1000 benefit from the dog and Barney bears an $800 cost from the barking. In this case, Fred would turn down any offer below $1000 and Barney would not offer any amount above $800. Therefore, Fred ends up keeping the dog. Given these costs and benefits, however, this outcome is efficient.

So far, we have assumed that Fred has the legal right to keep a barking dog. In other words, we have assumed that Fred can keep his dog unless Barney pays him enough to induce him to give up the dog voluntarily. How different would the outcome be, on the other hand, if Barney had the legal right to peace and quiet?

According to the Coase theorem, the initial distribution of rights does not matter for the market's ability to reach the efficient outcome. For instance, suppose that Barney can legally compel Fred to get rid of the dog. Although having this right works to Barney's advantage, it probably will not change the outcome. In this case, Fred can offer to pay Barney to allow him to keep the dog. If the benefit of the dog to Fred exceeds the cost of the barking to Barney, then Fred and Barney will strike a bargain in which Fred keeps the dog.

Although Fred and Barney can reach the efficient outcome regardless of how rights are initially distributed, the distribution of rights is not irrelevant; it determines the distribution of economic wellbeing. Whether Fred has the right to a barking dog or Barney has the right to peace and quiet determines who pays whom in the final bargain. But, in either case, the two parties can bargain with each other and solve the externality problem. Fred will end up keeping the dog only if the benefit exceeds the cost.

To sum up: *The Coase theorem says that private economic actors can potentially solve the problem of externalities among themselves. Whatever the initial distribution of rights, the interested parties can reach a bargain in which everyone is better off and the outcome is efficient.*

Why private solutions do not always work

Despite the appealing logic of the Coase theorem, private individuals on their own often fail to resolve the problems caused by externalities. The Coase theorem applies only when the interested parties have no trouble reaching and enforcing an agreement. In the real world, however, bargaining does not always work, even when a mutually beneficial agreement is possible.

Sometimes the interested parties fail to solve an externality problem because of **transaction costs**, the costs that parties incur in the process of agreeing and following through on a bargain. In our example, imagine that Fred and Barney speak different languages so that, to reach an agreement, they will need to hire a translator. If the benefit of solving the barking problem is less than the cost of the translator, Fred and Barney might choose to leave the problem unsolved. In more realistic examples, the transaction costs are the expenses not of translators but of the lawyers required to draft and enforce contracts.

transaction costs
the costs that parties incur in the process of agreeing and following through on a bargain

At other times, bargaining simply breaks down. The recurrence of wars and strikes shows that reaching agreement can be difficult and that failing to reach agreement can be costly. The problem is often that each party tries to hold out for a better deal. For example, suppose that Fred gets a $500 benefit from the dog and Barney bears an $800 cost from the barking. Although it is efficient for Barney to pay Fred to get rid of the dog, there are many prices that could lead to this outcome. Fred might demand $750 and Barney might offer only $550. As they haggle over the price, the inefficient outcome with the barking dog persists.

Reaching an efficient bargain is especially difficult when the number of interested parties is large because coordinating everyone is costly. For example, consider a factory that pollutes the water of a nearby river. The pollution confers a negative externality on the local fishermen. According to the Coase theorem, if the pollution is inefficient, then the factory and the fishermen could reach a bargain in which the fishermen pay the factory not to pollute. If there are many fishermen, however, trying to coordinate all of them in order to bargain with the factory may be almost impossible.

When private bargaining does not work, the government can sometimes play a role. The government is an institution designed for collective action. In this example, the government can act on behalf of the fishermen, even when it is impractical for the fishermen to act for themselves. In the next section, we examine how the government can try to remedy the problem of externalities.

Q

Give an example of a private solution to an externality. What is the Coase theorem? Why are private economic actors sometimes unable to solve the problems caused by an externality?

Public policies on externalities

When an externality causes a market to reach an inefficient allocation of resources, the government can respond in one of two ways. Command-and-control policies regulate behaviour directly. Market-based policies provide incentives so that private decision makers will choose to solve the problem on their own.

Command-and-control policies: Regulation

The government can remedy an externality by making certain activities either required or forbidden. For example, it is a crime to dump poisonous chemicals into the water supply. In this case, the external costs to society far exceed the benefits to the polluter. The government therefore institutes a command-and-control policy that prohibits this act altogether.

In most cases of pollution, however, the situation is not this simple. Despite the stated goals of some environmentalists, it would be impossible to prohibit all polluting activity. For example, virtually all forms of transport – even the horse – produce some undesirable polluting by-products. But it would not be sensible for the government to ban all transport. Thus, instead of trying to eradicate pollution altogether, society has to weigh the costs and benefits in order to decide the kinds and quantities of pollution it will allow. The environment protection agencies in each state are the government agencies with the task of regulating, auditing and monitoring activities that might damage the environment.

Environmental regulations can take many forms. Sometimes a government regulator, like an environment protection agency, dictates a maximum level of pollution that factories may emit. At other times the government regulator requires that firms adopt a particular technology to reduce emissions. In all cases, to design good rules, the regulators need to know the details about specific industries and about the alternative technologies that those industries could adopt. This information is often difficult for government regulators to obtain.

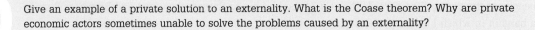

IN THE NEWS . . .

EXTERNALITY HAPPENS ...

The following article shows how local governments in Australia are trying to stamp out one externality.

From the people who put the P into parks and gardens

by Claire Hunter

At this Brighton park, dog excrement litters the grass, marked by flags placed by *The Age*.

Source: FairfaxPhotos.com/Bruce Postle.

Despite $500 fines, dog toilets and 'pooch patches', some people are still flouting council laws aimed at reducing the amount of dog poo in Melbourne's parks and reserves.

Ms Anne Burch, the manager of local laws and administration at Boroondara Council, said even with $500 fines for people who did not clean up their dog's droppings on council land or public places, and the trial of 'pooch patches', which resemble a sandpit for dogs, 'there is still a lot of dog poo out there'.

This week, *The Age* conducted a poo-in-a-park experiment to see how successful local laws were in combating the problem. Six of the seven parks visited were clean of dog droppings, but as the picture with its marker flags shows, the park at the North Road boat ramp in Brighton was not. Several dogs had clearly missed the dog toilet provided, and their owners had failed to clean up after them.

Mr Russell McMurray, regulator of the Bayside City Council, said the park showed that although council efforts to rid parks and reserves of dog poo were working, there was still room for improvement. Dog owners in the area will soon be legally required to carry a 'pooper scooper', defined as a paper or plastic bag or a device for picking up dog poo.

A local woman who walks her two dogs along the Brighton foreshore regularly says visitors cause the problem. 'It's annoying, the regulars do the right thing, it's the idiots who come down and you never see them again,' she said.

To help people clean up after their pooches, the council provides plastic bags in 10 of its 60 reserves and parks, as well as two dog toilets where people can deposit the waste into a hole in the ground, which contains a chemical to break down the dog poo.

Ms Burch said fines were difficult to enforce. A council officer or ranger has to witness the event and be able to say the offending dog poo definitely came from a certain dog. 'Dogs don't leave a piece of paper with their owners' name and address in their poo,' she said. Ms Burch said that although there were many responsible pet owners who did the right thing, there were still a lot who did not care: 'It's not the poor dog that's the problem, it's the owner,' she said.

Source: Claire Hunter/*The Age*.

Market-based policy 1: Corrective taxes and subsidies

Instead of regulating behaviour in response to an externality, the government can use market-based policies to align private incentives with social efficiency. For instance, as we saw earlier, the government can internalise the externality by taxing activities that have negative externalities and subsidising activities that have positive externalities. Taxes enacted to correct the effects of negative externalities are called **corrective taxes**. They are also called *Pigovian taxes* after economist Arthur Pigou (1877–1959), an early advocate of their use.

corrective tax
a tax enacted to correct the effects of a negative externality

An ideal corrective tax would equal the external cost from an activity with externalities and an ideal corrective subsidy would equal the external benefit from an activity with positive externalities.

Economists usually prefer corrective taxes over regulations as a way to deal with pollution because they can reduce pollution at a lower cost to society. To see why, let us consider an example.

Search me!
▸ corrective tax

Suppose that two factories – a paper mill and a steel mill – are each emitting 5000 tonnes of carbon dioxide into the atmosphere every year. The government decides that it wants to reduce the amount of these greenhouse gases. It considers two solutions:

- Regulation – the government could tell each factory to reduce its pollution to 3000 tonnes of carbon dioxide per year.
- Corrective tax – the government could levy a tax on each factory of $50 for each tonne of carbon dioxide it emits.

The regulation would dictate a level of pollution, whereas the tax would give factory owners an economic incentive to reduce pollution. Which solution do you think is better?

Most economists would prefer the tax. They would first point out that a tax is just as effective as a regulation in reducing the overall level of pollution. The government can achieve whatever level of pollution it wants by setting the tax at the appropriate level. The higher the tax, the larger the reduction in pollution. Indeed, if the tax is high enough, the factories will close down altogether, reducing pollution to zero.

Although regulation and corrective taxes are both capable of reducing pollution, the tax accomplishes this goal more efficiently. The regulation requires each factory to reduce pollution by the same amount, but an equal reduction is not necessarily the least expensive way to reduce greenhouse gases. It is possible that the paper mill can reduce pollution at a lower cost than the steel mill. If so, the paper mill would respond to the tax by reducing pollution substantially in order to avoid the tax, whereas the steel mill would respond by reducing pollution less and paying the tax.

In essence, the corrective tax places a price on the right to pollute. Just as markets allocate goods to those buyers who value them most highly, a corrective tax allocates pollution to those factories that face the highest cost of reducing it. Whatever the level of pollution the government chooses, it can achieve this goal at the lowest total cost using a tax.

Economists also argue that corrective taxes are better for the environment. Under the command-and-control policy of regulation, the factories have no reason to reduce emissions further once they have reached the target of 3000 tonnes of carbon dioxide. In contrast, the tax gives the factories an incentive to develop cleaner technologies, since a cleaner technology would reduce the amount of tax the factory has to pay.

Corrective taxes are unlike most other taxes. As we discussed in chapter 8, most taxes distort incentives and move the allocation of resources away from the social optimum. The reduction in economic wellbeing – that is, in consumer and producer surplus – exceeds the amount of revenue the government raises, resulting in a deadweight loss. In contrast, when externalities are present, society also cares about the wellbeing of the bystanders who are affected. Corrective taxes alter incentives to account for the presence of externalities and thereby move the allocation of resources closer to the social optimum. Thus, while corrective taxes raise revenue for the government, they enhance economic efficiency.

CASESTUDY

Taking out the garbage

In many places in the world, the collection of household garbage is a free service. Although it is funded from local rates or taxes, you do not pay any extra when you put out more garbage. To an economist, this means that you face a zero price for your use of the garbage service. As a result, it is likely you will produce too much garbage. By recycling and donating old clothing and the like to charity, you could reduce the amount of garbage. But while the price of garbage collection is zero and recycling or donating takes more time, there will be a tendency for residents as a whole to produce too much rubbish.

The discussion in this chapter suggests a solution to this problem – put a price on the amount of garbage collected and give residents an incentive to reduce the amount of garbage they put out by encouraging them towards alternatives such as recycling and donation. However, as two US economists, Don Fullerton and Thomas Kinnaman, show in a 1996 article in the *American Economic Review*, this simple solution is not so easy to implement in practice.

In the United States, many towns have established prices for each bin of garbage collected. They have done this by requiring residents to purchase stickers that they must place on their garbage bin if they want it to be collected when they put it out. However, when this scheme was implemented in the town of Charlottesville in 1992, Fullerton and Kinnaman found that the scheme had some undesirable consequences.

By putting a price on garbage bins, the number of bins put out for collection dropped substantially (by 37 per cent). However, in each bin, there was much more garbage (about 40 per cent more on average). Why? Because residents would cram more into each bin. If you have ever tried stomping your foot on the garbage in the bin to fit more in, this should not come as a surprise. You would also realise that such compacting is probably better done by garbage trucks than by individuals.

The actual drop in garbage collected was very little, but the bins bulged. What's more, there was far more garbage dumped on roadsides. There was an increase in recycling although there had been a general trend in this direction anyway.

The conclusion is that using Pigovian methods to reduce some activities can be difficult. In the case of garbage collection, it might simply be that the supply of garbage is relatively inelastic. So even high prices and fines might not do the job. And if recycling is the goal, perhaps making it easier for residents to recycle is a better policy. For instance, by providing a recycling collection service, the government can lower the relative cost of recycling compared with throwing stuff out.

Market-based policy 2: Tradeable pollution permits

Returning to our example of the paper mill and the steel mill, let us suppose that, despite the advice of its economists, the government adopts the regulation and requires each factory to reduce carbon dioxide emissions to 3000 tonnes per year. Then one day, after the regulation is in place and both mills have complied, the two firms go to the government with a proposal. The steel mill wants to increase its emissions by 1000 tonnes. The paper mill has agreed to reduce its emissions by the same amount if the steel mill pays it $5 million. Should the government allow the two factories to make this deal?

From the standpoint of economic efficiency, allowing the deal is good policy. The deal must make the owners of the two factories better off, because they are voluntarily agreeing to it. Moreover, the deal does not have any external effects because the total amount of pollution remains the same. Thus, social welfare is enhanced by allowing the paper mill to sell its right to pollute to the steel mill.

The same logic applies to any voluntary transfer of the right to pollute from one firm to another. If the government allows firms to make these deals, it will, in essence, have created a new scarce resource – pollution permits. A market to trade these permits will eventually develop and that market will be governed by the forces of supply and demand. The invisible hand will ensure that this new market efficiently allocates the right to pollute. That is, the permits will end up in the hands of those firms that value them most highly, as judged by their willingness to pay. A firm's willingness to pay for the right to pollute, in turn, will depend on its cost of reducing pollution: The more costly it is for a firm to cut back on pollution, the more it will be willing to pay for a permit.

One advantage of allowing a market for pollution permits is that the initial allocation of pollution permits among firms does not matter from the standpoint of economic efficiency. The logic behind this conclusion is similar to that behind the Coase theorem. Those firms that can reduce pollution most easily would be willing to sell whatever permits they get and those firms that can reduce pollution only at high cost would be willing to buy whatever permits they need. As long as there is a free market for the pollution rights, the final allocation will be efficient whatever the initial allocation.

Reducing pollution using pollution permits may seem quite different from using corrective taxes, but the two policies have much in common. In both cases, firms pay for their pollution. With corrective taxes, polluting firms must pay a tax to the government. With pollution permits, polluting firms must pay to buy the permit. (Even firms that already own permits must pay to pollute; the opportunity cost of polluting is what they could have received by selling their permits on the open market.) Both corrective taxes and pollution permits internalise the externality of pollution by making it costly for firms to pollute.

The similarity of the two policies can be seen by considering the market for pollution. Both panels in Figure 10.5 show the demand curve for the right to pollute. This curve shows that the lower the price of polluting, the more firms will choose to pollute. In panel (a), the government uses a corrective tax to set a price for pollution. In this case, the supply curve for pollution rights is perfectly elastic (because firms can pollute as much as they want by paying the tax), and the position of the demand curve determines the quantity of pollution. In panel (b), the government sets a quantity of pollution by issuing pollution permits. In this case, the supply curve for pollution rights is perfectly inelastic (because the quantity of pollution is fixed by the number of permits), and the position of the

Figure 10.5 **The equivalence of corrective taxes and pollution permits**

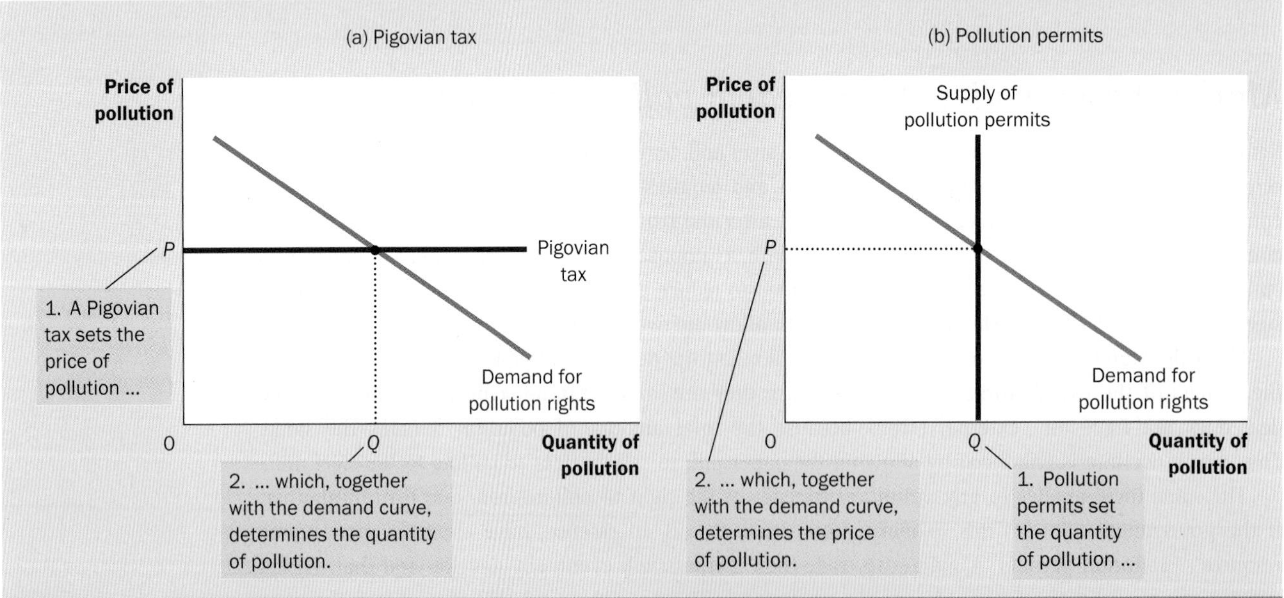

In panel (a), the government sets a price on pollution by levying a corrective tax and the demand curve determines the quantity of pollution. In panel (b), the government limits the quantity of pollution by limiting the number of pollution permits and the demand curve determines the price of pollution. The price and quantity of pollution are the same in the two cases.

demand curve determines the price of pollution. Hence, for any given demand curve for pollution, the government can achieve any point on the demand curve either by setting a price with a corrective tax or by setting a quantity with pollution permits.

In some circumstances, however, selling pollution permits may be better than levying a corrective tax. Suppose the government wants no more than 6000 tonnes of carbon dioxide to be emitted by the steel and paper mills. But because the government does not know the demand curve for pollution, it is not sure what size tax would achieve that goal. In this case, it can simply auction off 6000 pollution permits. The auction price would yield the appropriate size of the corrective tax.

The idea of the government auctioning off the right to pollute may at first sound like the creature of some economist's imagination. And, in fact, that is how the idea began. But tradeable pollution permits are used in the United States for sulphur dioxide and in Europe for greenhouse gases.

In Australia in 2008, the Garnaut report – a 600-page report commissioned by the federal government – recommended the use of tradeable pollution permits to cut greenhouse gas emissions. The report called the permits an emission trading scheme, or ETS. Pollution permits, like corrective taxes, are widely viewed as a cost-effective way to keep the environment clean. Indeed, as this book goes to press, Australia is in the process of introducing a carbon tax as a first step to establishing an ETS.

IN THE NEWS . . .

TAXES OR TRADING TO DEAL WITH GLOBAL WARMING?

In this chapter we noted how a market for pollution permits may be better than corrective taxes. In the following article Tim Harford notes that corrective taxes and pollution permits have both similarities and differences. But he argues that the differences mean that corrective taxes are a better way to deal with the threat of global warming.

Undercover economist: Emission impossible?

byTim Harford

A lot of people think it a good idea to reduce the amount of carbon dioxide we pump into the atmosphere. But not many have sensible ideas about the correct way to do that.

One contributor to the FT recently asserted that, 'An individual carbon trading scheme is more equitable and effective than carbon taxation as it reduces consumption quickly and dramatically.' All that carbon dioxide has clearly addled his thinking. It isn't possible to work out whether rationing would reduce emissions more than a tax until you know what the tax might be, or how generous the ration.

When it comes to reducing carbon emissions, the question 'How much?' is separate from the equally important question 'How?' The sensible choice is between a carbon tax and some kind of scheme to trade pollution permits. (Politicians prefer to bung cash at favoured initiatives; it's in their nature, but makes environmental gains harder to come by.) And for any level of environmental tax you can get the same carbon price and emissions reduction by using a permit quota instead.

That doesn't mean the two systems are equivalent. One difference is the cost of administering the system. Matt Prescott, the director of a Royal Society for the encouragement of Arts (RSA) research project into personal carbon allowances, paints an exciting picture of cheaply loading your carbon permits onto a credit card. I think it would be simpler just to administer a tax.

A second difference is where the revenue goes. A tax directs cash to the government levying it. A lot then depends on how the revenue is used: If it's distributed more heavily towards the poor, taxes are more progressive than a personal carbon allowance.

Permits enrich whoever starts with the permit: The government again, if the permits are auctioned off; or each person in society, if

>>

everybody gets an equal ration. The current vogue is to give permits to highly polluting corporations, which is handy for buying off the energy lobby but otherwise not much use.

A third difference is perhaps the most important but rarely discussed. A carbon tax gives us certainty about the price of carbon but not the quantity of emissions. A tradable permit scheme gives us certainty about the quantity of emissions, but not the price.

The question, then, is where the uncertainty is most damaging. Say we impose a tax, hoping for a 15 per cent reduction in emissions but getting only a 5 per cent fall. Is that less serious than a tradable permit scheme where we expected a carbon price of £25 a tonne but got a price of £75 a tonne?

It is indeed. The uncertainty about next year's emissions is not very worrying, because climate change is caused not by what happens next year, but by the accumulation of emissions since the industrial revolution. If we get the tax wrong and emit too much one year, it will be easy to fix. The economy, on the other hand, is more vulnerable to short-term shocks: Get the permit quota wrong, even for one year, and you could cause lasting damage.

Those environmentalists currently yelling that I am an idiot and am not committed to saving the planet have missed the point. The more you fear climate change, the more stringent the tax or quota should be. What I am saying is that whatever you decide about that, it is less risky to use a tax. The government expends so much effort taxing good things, such as saving and spending money. It would be a shame if it lacked the courage to tax something bad for a change.

Source: Tim Harford/*The Age*, 13 April 2007.

CASESTUDY

Using markets to solve climate change

While a market in tradeable pollution permits might sound fanciful, it exists in Europe, and is helping to limit global warming. The European Emissions Trading Scheme (ETS) was launched on 1 January 2005. Pollution permits are traded between companies in Europe. If a company wants to pollute then it needs to buy a permit. The permits are denominated in terms of tonnes of carbon dioxide, but apply to all greenhouse gases according to their contribution to global warming.

The ETS means that there is now a market price for pollution – between about $10 and $40 per tonne of carbon dioxide. The Scheme applies to over 10 000 large emitters of greenhouse gases.

Climate change is a global problem and the ETS shows how a market can be used to help solve this problem. A European firm that wants to emit carbon dioxide has two choices. It can buy a permit. Alternatively it can participate in a United Nations scheme to reduce greenhouse gases in developing countries. As a result, European firms have sponsored the disposal of the gas HFC-23 in China. This gas is cheap to dispose of and, tonne for tonne, has a global warming effect almost 12 000 times greater than carbon dioxide. As economics predicts, the ETS has given European polluters the incentive to reduce global emissions of greenhouse gases in the cheapest possible way.

The ETS has also provided incentives for companies to invent new ways to limit carbon dioxide pollution. For example, in Holland, carbon dioxide from an oil refinery is being used to help farmers grow fruit and vegetables in greenhouses, reducing emissions by 170 000 tonnes per year.

The ETS has had some problems. The price has been volatile, particularly as companies learn about the permit system and how they might be able to reduce emissions. It is widely agreed that too many permits were issued in 2005 and these permits were initially given away to companies rather than being auctioned. There have been high costs of setting up systems to monitor levels of greenhouse gas emissions. Also, some industries, such as airlines, have been exempt from the Scheme. Many of these problems will be addressed when the third phase of the ETS is launched in 2013.

Some economists, such as one of the authors of this textbook (Greg Mankiw) and Tim Harford in his *In the News* article in this chapter, argue that a system of corrective taxes would work better than a permit market. Others believe that a modified market that uses floors and ceilings to reduce price volatility would be better. Many economists, however, argue that some form of tradeable permit market is the best way to address the problem of global warming.

Objections to the economic analysis of pollution

Some environmentalists argue that clean air and clean water are fundamental human rights that should not be debased by considering them in economic terms. How can you put a price on clean air and clean water? The environment is so important, they say, that we should protect it as much as possible, regardless of the cost.

Economists have little sympathy with this type of argument. To economists, good environmental policy begins by acknowledging the first of the *Ten Lessons from Economics* in chapter 1 – people face trade-offs. Certainly, clean air and clean water have value. But their value must be compared with their opportunity cost – that is, with what one must give up to obtain them. Eliminating all pollution is impossible. Trying to eliminate all pollution would reverse many of the technological advances that allow us to enjoy a high standard of living. Few people would be willing to accept poor nutrition, inadequate medical care or shoddy housing in order to make the environment as clean as possible.

Economists argue that some environmental activists hurt their own cause by not thinking in economic terms. A clean environment can be viewed as simply another good. Like all normal goods it has a positive income elasticity: Rich countries can afford a cleaner environment than poor ones and, therefore, usually have more rigorous environmental protection. Further, like most other goods, clean air and clean water obey the law of demand: The lower the price of environmental protection, the more the public will want. The economic approach of using pollution permits and corrective taxes reduces the cost of environmental protection. It should, therefore, increase the public's demand for a clean environment.

Q

A glue factory and a steel mill emit smoke containing a chemical that is harmful if inhaled in large amounts. Describe three ways a government might respond to this externality. What are the pros and cons of each of your solutions?

Conclusion

The invisible hand is powerful but not omnipotent. A market's equilibrium maximises the sum of producer and consumer surplus. When the buyers and sellers in the market are the only interested parties, this outcome is efficient from the standpoint of society as a whole. But when there are external effects, such as pollution, evaluating a market outcome requires taking into account the wellbeing of third parties as well. In this case, the invisible hand of the marketplace may fail to allocate resources efficiently.

In some cases, people can solve the problem of externalities on their own. The Coase theorem suggests that the interested parties can bargain among themselves and agree on an efficient solution. Sometimes, however, an efficient outcome cannot be reached, perhaps because the large number of interested parties makes bargaining difficult.

When people cannot solve the problem of externalities privately, the government often steps in. Yet, even now, society should not abandon market forces entirely. Rather, the government can confront the problem by requiring decision makers to bear the full costs of their actions. Corrective taxes on emissions and pollution permits, for instance, are designed to internalise the externality of pollution. More and more, they are the policy of choice for those interested in protecting the environment. Market forces, properly redirected, are often the best remedy for market failure.

IN THE NEWS . . .

CHILDREN AS EXTERNALITIES

This tongue-in-cheek editorial from the *Economist*, an international news-magazine, calls attention to a common externality that is not fully appreciated.

Mum's the word: When children should be screened and not heard

A negative externality

Source: iStockphoto/Katrina Brown.

We live in increasingly intolerant times. Signs proliferate demanding no smoking, no spitting, no parking, even no walking … Posh clubs and restaurants have long had 'no jeans' rules, but these days you can be too smart. Some London hostelries have 'no suits' policies, for fear that boisterous city traders in suits might spoil the atmosphere. Environmentalists have long demanded all sorts of bans on cars. Mobile telephones are the latest target: Some trains, airline lounges, restaurants, and even golf courses are being designated 'no phone' areas.

If intolerance really has to be the spirit of this age, the *Economist* would like to suggest restrictions on another source of noise pollution: Children. Lest you dismiss this as mere prejudice, we can even produce a good economic argument for it. Smoking, driving, and mobile phones all cause what economists call 'negative externalities'. That is, the costs of these activities to other people tend to exceed the costs to the individuals of their proclivities. The invisible hand of the market fumbles, leading resources astray. Thus, because a driver's private motoring costs do not reflect the costs he imposes on others in the form of pollution and congestion, he uses the car more than is socially desirable. Likewise, it is argued, smokers take too little care to ensure that their acrid fumes do not damage other people around them.

Governments typically respond to such market failures in two ways. One is higher taxes, to make polluters pay the full cost of their anti-social behaviour. The other is regulation, such as emission standards or bans on smoking in public places. Both approaches might work for children.

For children, just like cigarettes or mobile phones, clearly impose a negative externality on people who are near them. Anybody who has suffered a 12-hour flight with a bawling baby in the row immediately ahead, or a bored youngster viciously kicking their seat from behind, will grasp this as quickly as they would love to grasp the youngster's neck. Here is a clear case of market failure: Parents do not bear the full costs (indeed young babies travel free), so they are too ready to take their noisy brats with them. Where is the invisible hand when it is needed to administer a good smack?

The solution is obvious. All airlines, trains, and restaurants should create child-free zones. Put all those children at the back of the plane and parents might make more effort to minimize their noise pollution. And instead of letting children pay less and babies go free, they should be charged (or taxed) more than adults, with the revenues used to subsidize seats immediately in front of the war-zone.

Passengers could then request a no-children seat, just as they now ask for a no-smoking one. As more women choose not to have children and the number of older people without young children increases, the demand for childfree travel will expand. Well, yes, it is a bit intolerant – but why shouldn't parents be treated as badly as smokers? And at least there is an obvious airline to pioneer the scheme: Virgin.

Source: *The Economist*, 5 December 1998.

Summary

- When a transaction between a buyer and a seller directly affects a third party, that effect is called an externality. Negative externalities, such as pollution, cause the socially desirable quantity in a market to be less than the equilibrium quantity. Positive externalities, such as technology spillovers, cause the socially desirable quantity to be greater than the equilibrium quantity.
- Those affected by externalities can sometimes solve the problem privately. For instance, when one business confers an externality on another business, the two businesses can internalise the externality by merging. Alternatively, the interested parties can solve the problem by signing a contract. According to the Coase theorem, if people can bargain without cost, then they can always reach an agreement in which resources are allocated efficiently. In many cases, however, reaching a bargain among the many interested parties is difficult, so the Coase theorem does not apply.
- When private parties cannot adequately deal with external effects, such as pollution, the government often steps in. Sometimes the government prevents socially inefficient activity by regulating behaviour. Other times it internalises an externality using corrective taxes. Another way to protect the environment is for the government to issue a limited number of pollution permits. The end result of this policy is largely the same as imposing corrective taxes on polluters.

Key concepts

Coase theorem
corrective tax
externality
internalising an externality
transaction costs

Questions for review

1 Give an example of a negative externality and of a positive externality.
2 Use a supply-and-demand diagram to explain the effect of a negative externality in production.
3 List some of the ways that the problems caused by externalities can be solved without government intervention.
4 Imagine that you are a non-smoker sharing a room with a smoker. According to the Coase theorem, what determines whether your room-mate smokes in the room? Is this outcome efficient? How do you and your room-mate reach this solution?
5 Why do economists prefer corrective taxes to regulations as a way of protecting the environment from pollution?

Problems and applications

1 Do you agree with the following statements? Why or why not?
  a 'The benefits of corrective taxes as a way of reducing pollution have to be weighed against the deadweight losses that these taxes cause.'
  b 'A negative production externality calls for a corrective tax on producers, whereas a negative consumption externality calls for a corrective tax on consumers.'

2 Consider the market for fire extinguishers.
   a Why might fire extinguishers exhibit positive externalities in consumption?
   b Draw a graph of the market for fire extinguishers, labelling the demand curve, the social-value curve, the supply curve and the social-cost curve.
   c Indicate the market equilibrium level of output and the efficient level of output. Give an explanation for why these quantities differ.
   d If the external benefit is $10 per extinguisher, describe a government policy that would result in the efficient outcome.
3 Contributions to charitable organisations are tax-deductible. In what way does this government policy encourage private solutions to externalities?
4 Kylie loves to play loud dance music. Paul loves opera and hates dance music. Unfortunately, they are next-door neighbours in an apartment building with paper-thin walls.
   a What is the externality here?
   b What command-and-control policy might the landlord impose? Could such a policy lead to an inefficient outcome?
   c Suppose the landlord lets the tenants do whatever they want. According to the Coase theorem, how might Kylie and Paul reach an efficient outcome on their own? What might prevent them from reaching an efficient outcome?
5 Smoke from wood fires is a major source of air pollution in southern Canberra. Suppose the ACT government is considering banning the use of wood fires because of the pollution they create. In making this decision, the government cares only about efficiency. Use a graph to illustrate the situation in which wood fires should be banned entirely. Now use a graph to illustrate the situation in which the use of wood fires should be reduced from the free-market level but not banned.
6 Greater consumption of alcohol leads to more motor vehicle accidents and, thus, imposes costs on people who do not drink and drive.
   a Illustrate the market for alcohol, labelling the demand curve, the social-value curve, the supply curve, the social-cost curve, the market equilibrium level of output and the efficient level of output.
   b On your graph, shade the area corresponding to the deadweight loss of the market equilibrium. (*Hint:* The deadweight loss occurs because some units of alcohol are consumed for which the social cost exceeds the social value.) Explain.
7 The former premier of Victoria, Sir Henry Bolte, is reported to have stated: 'We care about pollution, but it isn't as important as a $100 million factory'. Do you agree with this statement? If our aim is to maximise economic efficiency, discuss when we would prefer to build the factory and when we would prefer not to build the factory.
8 Many observers believe that the levels of pollution in our economy are too high.
   a If society wishes to reduce overall pollution by a certain amount, why is it efficient to have different amounts of reduction at different firms?
   b Command-and-control approaches often rely on uniform reductions among firms. Why are these approaches generally unable to target the firms that should undertake bigger reductions?
   c Economists argue that appropriate corrective taxes or tradeable pollution rights will result in efficient pollution reduction. How do these approaches target the firms that should undertake bigger reductions?
9 The Pristine River has two polluting firms on its banks. Acme Industrial and Creative Chemicals each dump 100 tonnes of glop into the river each year. The cost of reducing glop emissions per

tonne equals $10 for Acme and $100 for Creative. The local government wants to reduce overall pollution from 200 tonnes to 50 tonnes.

a If the government knew the cost of reduction for each firm, what reductions would it impose in order to reach its overall goal? What would be the cost to each firm and the total cost to the firms together?

b In a more typical situation, the government would not know the cost of pollution reduction at each firm. If the government decided to reach its overall goal by imposing uniform reductions on the firms, calculate the reduction made by each firm, the cost to each firm and the total cost to the firms together.

c Compare the total cost of pollution reduction in parts (a) and (b). If the government does not know the cost of reduction for each firm, is there still some way for it to reduce pollution to 50 tonnes at the total cost you calculated in part (a)? Explain.

10 Figure 10.5 shows that for any given demand curve for the right to pollute, the government can achieve the same outcome either by setting a price with a corrective tax or by setting a quantity with pollution permits. Suppose there is a sharp improvement in the technology for controlling pollution.

a Using graphs similar to those in Figure 10.5, illustrate the effect of this development on the demand for pollution rights.

b What is the effect on the price and quantity of pollution under each regulatory system? Explain.

11 Suppose that the government decides to issue tradeable permits for a certain form of pollution.

a Does it matter for economic efficiency whether the government distributes or auctions the permits? Does it matter in any other ways?

b If the government chooses to distribute the permits, does the allocation of permits among firms matter for efficiency? Does it matter in any other ways?

12 The main cause of global warming is carbon dioxide, which enters the atmosphere in varying amounts from different countries but is distributed equally around the globe within a year. Economists Martin and Kathleen Feldstein argue that the correct approach to global warming is not to ask individual countries to stabilise their emissions of carbon dioxide at current levels, as some have suggested. Instead, they argue that carbon dioxide emissions should be reduced in countries where the costs are least and the countries that bear that burden should be compensated by the rest of the world.

a Why is international cooperation necessary to reach an efficient outcome?

b Is it possible to devise a compensation scheme such that all countries would be better off than under a system of uniform emission reductions? Explain.

13 Some people object to market-based policies to reduce pollution, claiming that they place a dollar value on cleaning our air and water. Economists reply that society implicitly places a dollar value on environmental clean-up even under command-and-control policies. Discuss why this is true.

14 (This problem is challenging.) There are three industrial firms in Happy Valley.
The government wants to reduce pollution to 120 units, so it gives each firm 40 tradeable pollution permits.

Firm	Initial pollution level	Cost of reducing pollution by 1 unit
A	70 units	$20
B	80	25
C	50	10

a Who sells permits and how many do they sell? Who buys permits and how many do they buy? Briefly explain why the sellers and buyers are each willing to do so. What is the total cost of pollution reduction in this situation?

b How much higher would the costs of pollution reduction be if the permits could not be traded?

Search me!

Search me!

When accessing information about microeconomics use the following keywords in any combinations you require:

- conference presentation
- corrective tax
- Coase theorem

CourseMate

CourseMate

For more multimedia resources and activities on economics, visit the Economics CourseMate website.

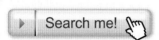

11

Public goods and common resources

Learning objectives

In this chapter you will:

- learn the defining characteristics of public goods and common resources
- examine why private markets fail to provide public goods
- consider some of the important public goods in our economy
- see why the cost–benefit analysis of public goods is both necessary and difficult
- examine why people tend to use common resources too much
- consider some of the important common resources in our economy.

An old song lyric maintains that 'the best things in life are free'. A moment's thought reveals a long list of goods that the songwriter could have had in mind. Nature provides some of them, such as rivers, mountains, beaches, lakes and oceans. The government provides others, such as playgrounds, libraries and bikepaths. In each case, people do not pay a fee when they choose to enjoy the benefit of the good.

Goods without prices provide a special challenge for economic analysis. Most goods in our economy are allocated in markets, where buyers pay for what they receive and sellers are paid for what they provide. For these goods, prices are the signals that guide the decisions of buyers and sellers. When goods are available free of charge, however, the market forces that normally allocate resources in our economy are absent.

In this chapter we examine the problems that arise for goods without market prices. Our analysis will shed light on one of the *Ten Lessons from Economics* in chapter 1 – governments can sometimes improve market outcomes. When a good does not have a price attached to it, private markets cannot ensure that the good is produced and consumed in the proper amounts. In such cases, government policy can potentially remedy the market failure and raise economic wellbeing.

The different kinds of goods

How well do markets work in providing the goods that people want? The answer to this question depends on the good being considered. As we discussed in chapter 7, we can rely on the market to provide the efficient number of ice-creams; the price of ice-creams adjusts to balance supply and demand, and this equilibrium maximises the sum of producer and consumer surplus. Yet, as we discussed in chapter 10, we cannot rely on the market to prevent aluminium manufacturers from polluting the air we breathe; buyers and sellers in a market typically do not take account of the external effects of their decisions. Thus, markets work well when the good is ice-cream, but they work badly when the good is clean air.

In thinking about the various goods in the economy, it is useful to group them according to two characteristics:

- Is the good **excludable**? That is, can people be prevented from using the good?
- Is the good **rival in consumption**? That is, does one person's use of the good diminish another person's ability to use it?

excludable
the property of a good whereby a person can be prevented from using it

rival in consumption
the property of a good whereby one person's use diminishes other people's use

Using these two characteristics, Figure 11.1 divides goods into four categories:

1 **Private goods** are both excludable and rival in consumption. Consider an ice-cream, for example. An ice-cream is excludable because it is possible to prevent someone from eating an ice-cream – you just don't give it to him. An ice-cream is rival in consumption because if one person eats an ice-cream, another person cannot eat the same ice-cream. Most goods in the economy are private goods like ice-creams: You don't get one unless you pay for it and once you get it you are the only person who benefits. When we analysed supply and demand in chapters 4, 5 and 6 and the efficiency of markets in chapters 7, 8 and 9, we implicitly assumed that goods were both excludable and rival in consumption.

private goods
goods that are both excludable and rival in consumption

2 **Public goods** are neither excludable nor rival in consumption. That is, people cannot be prevented from using a public good and one person's enjoyment of a public good does not reduce another person's enjoyment of it. For example, national defence is a public good. Once the country is defended from foreign aggressors, it is impossible to prevent any single person from enjoying the benefit of this defence (so it is not excludable). Moreover, when one person enjoys the benefit of defence, he does not reduce the benefit to anyone else (so it is not rival in consumption).

public goods
goods that are neither excludable nor rival in consumption

Figure 11.1 **Four types of goods**

		Rival in consumption: Yes	Rival in consumption: No
Excludable?	Yes	Private goods • Ice-creams • Clothing • Congested toll roads	Club goods • Fire protection • Cable TV • Uncongested toll roads
	No	Common resources • Fish in the ocean • The environment • Congested non-toll roads	Public goods • National defence • Knowledge • Uncongested non-toll roads

Goods can be grouped into four categories according to two questions: (1) Is the good excludable? That is, can people be prevented from using it? (2) Is the good rival? That is, does one person's use of the good diminish other people's use of it? This figure gives examples of goods in each of the four categories.

3 **Common resources** are rival in consumption but not excludable. For example, fish in the ocean are rival in consumption: When one person catches fish, there are fewer fish for the next person to catch. Yet these fish are not an excludable good because, given the vast size of the ocean, it is difficult to stop fishermen taking fish out of it.

common resources goods that are rival in consumption but not excludable

4 **Club goods** are excludable but not rival in consumption. For example, consider fire protection in a small town. It is easy to exclude people from enjoying this good; the fire brigade can just let their houses burn down. Yet fire protection is not rival in consumption. Firefighters spend much of their time waiting for a fire, so protecting an additional household is unlikely to reduce the protection available to others. In other words, once a town has set up a fire brigade, the extra cost of protecting one more household is small. We discuss club goods again in chapter 15, where we see that they are one type of a *natural monopoly.*

club goods goods that are excludable but not rival in consumption

Although Figure 11.1 offers a clean separation of goods into four categories, the boundaries between the categories are sometimes fuzzy. Whether goods are excludable or rival in consumption is often a matter of degree. Fish in an ocean may not be excludable because monitoring fishing is so difficult, but a large enough coast guard could make fish at least partly excludable. Similarly, although fish are generally rival in consumption, this would be less true if the population of fishermen were small relative to the population of fish. For purposes of our analysis, however, it will be helpful to group goods into these four categories.

In this chapter, we examine goods that are not excludable and, therefore, are available to everyone free of charge – public goods and common resources.

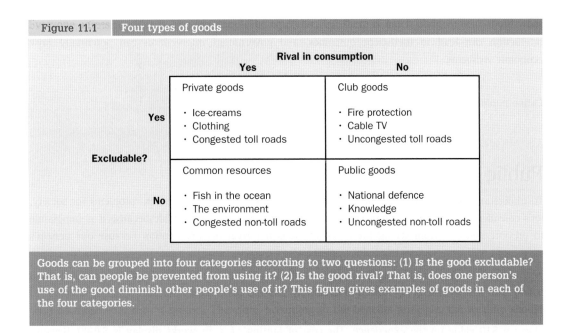

The study of public goods and common resources is closely related to the study of externalities. For both public goods and common resources, externalities arise because something of value has no price attached to it. If one person were to provide a public good, such as defence, other people would be better off and yet they could not be charged for this benefit. Similarly, when one person uses a common resource, such as the fish in the ocean, other people are worse off and yet they are not compensated for this loss. Because of these external effects, private decisions about consumption and production can lead to inefficient outcomes, and government intervention can potentially raise economic wellbeing.

Define *public goods* and *common resources* and give an example of each.

Public goods

To understand how public goods differ from other goods and why they present problems for society, let's consider an example – a fireworks display. This good is not excludable because it is impossible to prevent someone from seeing fireworks and it is not rival in consumption because one person's enjoyment of fireworks does not reduce anyone else's enjoyment of them.

The free-rider problem

The citizens of Smalltown like seeing fireworks on New Year's Eve. Each of the town's 500 residents places a \$10 value on the experience. The cost of putting on a fireworks display is \$1000. Because the \$5000 of benefits exceeds the \$1000 of costs, it is efficient for Smalltown residents to see fireworks on New Year's Eve.

Would the private market produce the efficient outcome? Probably not. Imagine that Ellen, a Smalltown entrepreneur, decided to put on a fireworks display. Ellen would have trouble selling tickets to the event because her potential customers would quickly figure out that they could see the fireworks even without a ticket. Fireworks are not excludable, so people have an incentive to be free riders. A **free rider** is a person who receives the benefit of a good but avoids paying for it. Because people would have an incentive to be free riders rather than ticket buyers, the market would fail to provide the efficient outcome.

free rider
a person who receives the benefit of a good but avoids paying for it

Search me!

▸ free-rider problem

One way to view this market failure is that it arises because of an externality. If Ellen did put on the fireworks display, she would confer an external benefit on those who saw the display without paying for it. When deciding whether to put on the display, Ellen ignores these external benefits. Even though a fireworks display is socially desirable, it is not privately profitable. As a result, Ellen makes the socially inefficient decision not to put on the display.

Although the private market fails to supply the fireworks display demanded by Smalltown residents, the solution to Smalltown's problem is obvious – the local government can sponsor a New Year's Eve celebration. The town council can raise everyone's taxes by \$2 and use the revenue to hire Ellen to produce the fireworks. Everyone in Smalltown is better off by \$8 – the \$10 at which residents value the fireworks minus the \$2 tax bill. Ellen can help Smalltown reach the efficient outcome as a public employee even though she could not do so as a private entrepreneur.

The story of Smalltown is stylised, but it is also realistic. In fact, many local governments in Australia and throughout the world do pay for New Year fireworks. Moreover, the story shows a general lesson about public goods; because public goods are not excludable, the free-rider problem prevents the private market from supplying them. The government, however, can potentially remedy the problem. If the government decides that the total benefits exceed the costs, it can provide the public good and pay for it with tax revenue, making everyone better off.

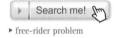

IN THE NEWS . . .

FREE RIDING ON THE INTERNET

An uncongested home wireless Internet connection is not rival in consumption. And if the homeowner doesn't secure the network with a password, it is also not excludable. As the following article shows, the growth of unprotected wireless Internet networks has resulted in a free-rider problem.

Hey neighbour, stop piggybacking on my wireless

by Michel Marriott

For a while, the wireless Internet connection Christine and Randy Brodeur installed last year seemed perfect. They were able to sit in their sunny Los Angeles backyard working on their laptop computers.

But they soon began noticing that their high-speed Internet access had become as slow as rush-hour traffic on the 405 freeway.

'I didn't know whether to blame it on the Santa Ana winds or what,' recalled Mrs. Brodeur, the chief executive of Socket Media, a marketing and public relations agency.

The 'what' turned out to be neighbors who had tapped into their system. The additional online traffic nearly choked out the Brodeurs, who pay a $40 monthly fee for their Internet service, slowing their access until it was practically unusable.

Piggybacking, the usually unauthorized tapping into someone else's wireless Internet connection, is no longer the exclusive domain of pilfering computer geeks or shady hackers cruising for unguarded networks. Ordinarily upstanding people are tapping in. As they do, new sets of Internet behaviors are creeping into America's popular culture.

'I don't think it's stealing,' said Edwin Caroso, a 21-year-old student at Miami Dade College, echoing an often-heard sentiment.

'I always find people out there who aren't protecting their connection, so I just feel free to go ahead and use it,' Mr. Caroso said. He added that he tapped into a stranger's network mainly for Web surfing, keeping up with e-mail, text chatting with friends in foreign countries and doing homework.

Many who piggyback say the practice does not feel like theft because it does not seem to take anything away from anyone. One occasional piggybacker recently compared it to 'reading the newspaper over someone's shoulder'.

Piggybacking, makers of wireless routers say, is increasingly an issue for people who live in densely populated areas like New York City or Chicago, or for anyone clustered in apartment buildings in which Wi-Fi radio waves, with an average range of about 200 feet, can easily bleed through walls, floors and ceilings. Large hotels that offer the service have become bubbling brooks of free access that spill out into nearby homes and restaurants.

'Wi-Fi is in the air, and it is a very low curb, if you will, to step up and use it,' said Mike Wolf of ABI Research, a high-technology market research company in Oyster Bay, N.Y.

This is especially true, Mr. Wolf said, because so many users do not bother to secure their networks with passwords or encryption programs. The programs are usually shipped with customers' wireless routers, devices that plug into an Internet connection and make access to it wireless. Many home network owners admit that they are oblivious to piggybackers …

David Cole, director of product management for Symantec Security Response, a unit of Symantec, a maker of computer security software, said consumers should understand that an open wireless network invites greater vulnerabilities than just a stampede of 'freeloading neighbors'.

He said savvy users could piggyback into unprotected computers to peer into files containing sensitive financial and personal information, release malicious viruses and worms that could do irreparable damage, or use the computer as a launching pad for identity theft or the uploading and downloading of child pornography.

>>

'The best case is that you end up giving a neighbor a free ride,' Mr. Cole said. 'The worst case is that someone can destroy your computer, take your files and do some really nefarious things with your network that gets you dragged into court.'

Mr. Cole said Symantec and other companies had created software that could not only lock out most network intruders but also protect computers and their content if an intruder managed to gain access.

Some users say they have protected their computers but have decided to keep their networks open as a passive protest of what they consider the exorbitant cost of Internet access.

'I'm sticking it to the man,' said Elaine Ball, an Internet subscriber who lives in Chicago. She complained that she paid $65 a month for Internet access until she recently switched to a $20-a-month promotion plan that would go up to $45 a month after the first three months.

'I open up my network, leave it wide open for anyone to jump on,' Ms. Ball said.

For the Brodeurs in Los Angeles, a close reading of their network's manual helped them to finally encrypt their network. The Brodeurs told their neighbors that the network belonged to them and not to the neighborhood. While apologetic, some neighbors still wanted access to it.

'Some of them asked me, "Could we pay?" But we didn't want to go into the Internet service provider business,' Mrs. Brodeur said. 'We gave some weird story about the network imposing some sort of lockdown protocol.'

Source: From *The New York Times*, 5 March 2006.

Some important public goods

There are many examples of public goods. Here we consider three of the most important.

National defence

The defence of a country is a classic example of a public good. It is also one of the most expensive. In 2010–11 the Australian government spent almost $21 billion on defence, or about $930 per person. People disagree about whether this amount is too small or too large, but almost no one doubts that some government spending for defence is necessary. Even those economists who advocate small government agree that defence is a public good the government should provide.

Basic research

Knowledge is created through research. In evaluating, the appropriate public policy towards knowledge creation, it is important to distinguish general knowledge from specific technological knowledge. Specific technological knowledge, such as the invention of a longer-lasting battery, a smaller microchip or a better digital music player, can be patented. The patent gives the inventor the exclusive right to the knowledge she has created for a period of time. Anyone else who wants to use the patented information has to pay the inventor for the right to do so. In other words, the patent makes the knowledge created by the inventor excludable.

By contrast, general knowledge is a public good. For example, a mathematician cannot patent a theorem. Once a theorem is proved, the knowledge is not excludable: The theorem enters society's general pool of knowledge that anyone can use without charge. The theorem is also not rival in consumption: One person's use of the theorem does not prevent any other person from using the theorem.

Profit-seeking firms spend a lot of research trying to develop new products that they can patent and sell, but they do not spend much on basic research. Their incentive, instead, is to free ride on the general knowledge created by others. As a result, in the absence of any public policy, society would devote too few resources to creating new knowledge.

The government tries to provide the public good of general knowledge in various ways. Government agencies, such as the Australian Research Council and the National Health and Medical Research Council, subsidise basic research in medicine, mathematics, physics, chemistry, biology and even economics. Some people justify government funding of space programs on the grounds that it adds to society's pool of knowledge. Certainly, many private goods, including bullet-proof vests and satellite communications systems, use materials that were first developed by scientists and engineers trying to land a person on the moon. Determining the appropriate level of governmental support for basic research is difficult because the benefits are hard to measure. Moreover, the politicians who allocate funds for research usually have little expertise in science and, therefore, are not in the best position to judge what lines of research will produce the largest benefits.

Fighting poverty

Many government programs are aimed at helping the poor. Unemployment benefits provide a basic income for individuals and families who do not have adequate alternative income. The old-age pension and disability support pension benefit specific low-income groups. Those with low incomes may also receive subsidised medical services. These benefit programs are financed by taxes on people who are financially more successful.

Economists disagree among themselves about what role the government should play in fighting poverty. Although we will discuss this debate more fully in chapter 21, here we note one important argument – advocates of anti-poverty programs claim that fighting poverty is a public good. Even if everyone prefers living in a society without poverty, fighting poverty is not a 'good' that private actions will adequately provide.

To see why, suppose someone tried to organise a group of wealthy individuals to try to eliminate poverty. They would be providing a public good. This good would not be rival in consumption: One person's enjoyment of living in a society without poverty would not reduce anyone else's enjoyment of it. The good would not be excludable: Once poverty is eliminated, no one can be prevented from taking pleasure in this fact. As a result, there would be a tendency for people to free ride on the generosity of others, enjoying the benefits of poverty elimination without contributing to the cause.

Because of the free-rider problem, eliminating poverty through private charity will probably not work. Yet government action can solve this problem. Taxing the wealthy to raise the living standards of the poor can potentially make everyone better off. The poor are better off because they now enjoy a

CASESTUDY

Are lighthouses public goods?

Some goods can switch between being public goods and being private goods depending on the circumstances. For example, a fireworks display is a public good if performed in a town with many residents. Yet if performed at a private amusement park, such as Luna Park or Disneyland, a fireworks display is more like a private good because visitors to the park pay for admission.

Another example is a lighthouse. Economists have long used lighthouses as an example of a public good. Lighthouses are used to mark specific locations along the coast so that passing ships can avoid treacherous waters. The benefit that the lighthouse provides to ships' captains is neither excludable nor rival, so each captain has an incentive to free ride by using the lighthouse to

>>

Use of the lighthouse is free to boat owners. Does this make the lighthouse a public good?

Source: iStockphoto/Neta Degany.

navigate without paying for the service. Because of this free-rider problem, private markets usually fail to provide the lighthouses that ships' captains need. As a result, most lighthouses today are operated by the government.

In some cases, however, lighthouses may be closer to private goods. On the coast of England in the nineteenth century, some lighthouses were privately owned and operated. The owner of the local lighthouse did not try to charge ships' captains for the service but did charge the owner of the nearby port. If the port owner did not pay, the lighthouse owner turned off the light and ships avoided that port.

In deciding whether something is a public good, one must determine the number of beneficiaries and whether these beneficiaries can be excluded from enjoying the good. A free-rider problem arises when the number of beneficiaries is large and exclusion of any one of them is impossible. If a lighthouse benefits many ships' captains, it is a public good. Yet if it primarily benefits a single port owner, it is more like a private good.

higher standard of living, and those paying the taxes are better off because they enjoy living in a society with less poverty.

The difficult job of cost–benefit analysis

So far we have seen that the government provides public goods because the private market on its own will not produce an efficient quantity. Yet deciding that the government must play a role is only the first step. The government must then determine what kinds of public goods to provide and in what quantities.

Suppose that the government is considering a public project, such as building a new highway. To judge whether to build the highway, it must compare the total benefits of all those who would use it with the costs of building and maintaining it. To make this decision, the government might hire a team of economists and engineers to conduct a study, called a **cost–benefit analysis**, the goal of which is to estimate the total costs and benefits of the project to society as a whole.

cost–benefit analysis
a study that compares the costs and benefits to society of providing a public good

Cost–benefit analysts have a tough job. Because the highway will be available to everyone free of charge, there is no price with which to judge the value of the highway. Simply asking people how much they would value the highway is not reliable. First, quantifying benefits is difficult using the results from a questionnaire. Second, respondents have little incentive to tell the truth. Those who would use the highway have an incentive to exaggerate the benefit they would receive in order to get the highway built. Those who would be harmed by the highway have an incentive to exaggerate the costs to them in order to prevent the highway from being built.

The efficient provision of public goods is, therefore, intrinsically more difficult than the efficient provision of private goods. Private goods are provided in the market. Buyers of a private good reveal the value they place on it by the prices they are willing to pay. Sellers reveal their costs by the prices they are willing to accept. In contrast, cost–benefit analysts do not observe any price signals when evaluating whether the government should provide a public good. Their findings on the costs and benefits of public projects are, therefore, rough approximations at best.

CASESTUDY

How much is a life worth?

Imagine that you have been elected to serve as a member of your local council. The town engineer comes to you with a proposal – the council can spend $10 000 to build and operate a traffic light at an intersection that now has only a stop sign. The benefit of the traffic light is increased safety. The engineer estimates, based on data from similar intersections, that the traffic light would reduce the risk of a fatal traffic accident over the lifetime of the traffic light from 1.6 per cent to 1.1 per cent. Should you spend the money for the new light?

Everyone would like to avoid the risk of this, but at what cost?

Source: FairfaxPhotos.com/Patrick Cummins.

To answer this question, you turn to cost–benefit analysis. But you quickly run into an obstacle – the costs and benefits must be measured in the same units if you are to compare them meaningfully. The cost is measured in dollars, but the benefit – the possibility of saving a person's life – is not directly monetary. In order to make your decision, you have to put a dollar value on a human life.

At first, you may be tempted to conclude that a human life is priceless. After all, there is probably no amount of money that you could be paid to voluntarily give up your life or that of a loved one. This suggests that a human life has an infinite dollar value.

For the purposes of cost–benefit analysis, however, this answer leads to nonsensical results. If we truly placed an infinite value on human life, we should be placing traffic lights on every street corner. Similarly, we should all be driving large cars with all the latest safety features, instead of smaller ones with fewer safety features. Yet traffic lights are not at every corner and people sometimes choose to buy small cars without air bags or anti-lock braking systems. In both our public and private decisions, we are at times willing to risk our lives in order to save some money.

Once we have accepted the idea that a person's life does have an implicit dollar value, how can we determine what that value is? One approach, sometimes used by courts to award compensation for injury or death, is to look at the total amount of money a person would have earned if that person had lived. Economists are often critical of this approach. It has the bizarre implication that the life of a retired person has no value.

A better way to value human life is to look at the risks that people are voluntarily willing to take and how much they must be paid for taking them. Mortality risk varies across jobs, for example, construction workers in high-rise buildings face greater risk of death than office workers. By comparing wages in risky and less risky occupations, controlling for education, experience and other determinants of wages, economists can get some sense about what value people put on their own lives. North American studies using this approach conclude that the value of a human life is about $10 million.

We can now return to our original example and respond to the town engineer. The traffic light reduces the risk of fatality by 0.5 per cent. Thus, the expected benefit from having the traffic light is 0.005 x $10 million, or $50 000. This estimate of the benefit well exceeds the cost of $10 000, so you should approve the project.

Q What is the *free-rider problem*? Why does the free-rider problem induce the government to provide public goods? How should the government decide whether to provide a public good?

Common resources

Common resources, like public goods, are not excludable; they are available free of charge to anyone who wants to use them. Common resources are, however, rival; one person's use of the common resource reduces other people's enjoyment of it. Thus, common resources give rise to a new problem. Once the good is provided, policymakers need to be concerned about how much it is used. This problem is best understood from the classic parable called the **Tragedy of the Commons**.

Tragedy of the Commons
a parable that illustrates why common resources get used more than is desirable from the standpoint of society as a whole

Search me!

▸ Tragedy of the Commons

The Tragedy of the Commons

Consider life in a small medieval English town. Of the many economic activities that take place in the town, one of the most important is raising sheep. Many of the town's families own flocks of sheep and support themselves by selling the sheep's wool, which is used to make clothing.

As our story begins, the sheep spend much of their time grazing on the land surrounding the town, called the Town Common. No family owns the land. Instead, the town residents own the land collectively and all the residents are allowed to graze their sheep on it. Collective ownership works well because land is plentiful. As long as everyone can get all the good grazing land they want, the Town Common is not a rival good, and allowing residents' sheep to graze for free causes no problems. Everyone in the town is happy.

As the years pass, the population of the town grows and so does the number of sheep grazing on the Town Common. With a growing number of sheep and a fixed amount of land, the land starts to lose its ability to replenish itself. Eventually, the land is grazed so heavily that it becomes barren. With no grass left on the Common, raising sheep is impossible and the town's once prosperous wool industry disappears. Many families lose their source of livelihood.

What causes the tragedy? Why do the shepherds allow the sheep population to grow so large that it destroys the Town Common? The reason is that social and private incentives differ. Avoiding the destruction of the grazing land depends on the collective action of the shepherds. If the shepherds could act together, they would reduce the sheep population to a size that the Common can support. Yet no single family has an incentive to reduce the size of its own flock because each flock represents only a small part of the problem.

In essence, the Tragedy of the Commons arises because of an externality. When one family's flock grazes on the common land, it reduces the quality of the land available for other families. Because people neglect this negative externality when deciding how many sheep to own, the result is an excessive number of sheep.

If the tragedy had been foreseen, the town could have solved the problem in various ways. It could have regulated the number of sheep in each family's flock, internalised the externality by taxing sheep or auctioned off a limited number of sheep-grazing permits. That is, the medieval town could have dealt with the problem of overgrazing in the way that modern society deals with the problem of pollution.

In the case of land, however, there is a simpler solution. The town can divide up the land among town families. Each family can enclose its parcel of land with a fence and then protect it from excessive grazing. In this way, the land becomes a private good rather than a common resource. This outcome in fact occurred during the enclosure movement in England in the seventeenth century.

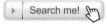

The Tragedy of the Commons is a story with a general lesson – when one person uses a common resource, other people's enjoyment of it is diminished. Because of this negative externality, common resources tend to be used excessively. The government can solve the problem by reducing use of the common resource through regulation or taxes. Alternatively, the government can sometimes turn the common resource into a private good.

IN THE NEWS . . .

THE TRAGEDY OF THE COD FISH

The Tragedy of the Commons still occurs with fishing today. Although individual countries own the rights to fish in their coastal waters, in the open ocean there is competition between fishing fleets to catch the available fish stocks. As this article shows, disputes over fishing have led to conflict between countries and almost the eradication of a fish which was once abundant in the Atlantic Ocean. Despite a ban on fishing off Newfoundland since 2003, fish stocks have not recovered.

Fished out

by Margaret Visser

'A species of fish too well known to require any description' reads the entry for cod in the *Cyclopedia of Commerce and Commercial Navigation* (1858). 'It is amazingly prolific' the article continues …

People have long enjoyed marvelling at the sheer amount, the endlessness of cod. The vast cod-grazing grounds off the American Atlantic coast may well have drawn the first Europeans to the continent … Reports … came back from America during the 16th century, of so many cod that there was scarcely room enough for the sea to hold them, so many that they could be fished by scooping with baskets … Today, cod at the once teeming Grand Banks off Newfoundland is considered an endangered species. Disaster struck very recently, and within a terrifyingly short time. In South Bay, for example, there were over a million cod in 1986; in 1996 it could be excitedly reported that the numbers had increased to fifteen thousand. What fish are left are small …

Cod, once they reach adulthood, have almost no enemies, except for humankind … We, as cod predators, have almost wiped out one of the richest resources of fish ever known …

Icelanders discovered earlier than anybody that, despite human determination to perceive cod as everlasting, cod-stocks were in fact diminishing as the 20th century progressed. This led to three Cod Wars (1958–61, 1971–72 and 1975–76), in which Britain, with the help of Germany, refused to accept Iceland's declaration of ownership of the seas 19 km around its coast. Iceland felt that it needed to control its waters in order to conserve the cod; Britain had overfished the North Sea, and sought fresh pastures …

All the practices of global merchandising are exemplified by the strategies of modern cod fishing. Desirable fish are kept; the rest are tossed back overboard, dead. Radio keeps the ships up to date as to what fish are wanted and not wanted.

If a fishing ground yields no more, the ships simply leave for somewhere not yet exhausted … The warnings of fishermen that the cod stocks were reducing went unheard, as factory ships continued hauling in their catch …

Fish farming can help us undo some of the damage we have done, but farmed fish need to be fed from resources of mackerel, herring and capelin which are expensive and themselves not in endless supply …

The great cod catastrophe may teach the required lessons – or it may not … Dare we hope that, as New Foundlanders put it, the cod 'come back'? – that, having learned something, we may yet be let off this particular hook?

Source: Copyright © 1997 by Mark Kurlansky.
From: *COD: A biography of the Fish That Changed the World* by Mark Kurlansky.
Reprinted by permission of Bloomsbury USA.

This lesson has been known for thousands of years. The ancient Greek philosopher Aristotle pointed out the problem: 'What is common to many is taken least care of, for all men have greater regard for what is their own than for what they possess in common with others'.

Some important common resources

There are many examples of common resources. In almost all cases, the same problem arises as in the Tragedy of the Commons – private decision makers use the common resource too much. Governments often regulate behaviour or impose fees in order to lessen the problem of overuse.

Clean air and global warming

As we discussed in chapter 10, markets do not adequately protect the environment. Pollution, such as greenhouse gas emissions, is a negative externality that can be remedied with regulations, corrective taxes or an emissions trading scheme. One can view this market failure as an example of a common-resource problem. The atmosphere is a common resource like open grazing land and excessive pollution is like excessive grazing. Environmental degradation and global warming are like a modern Tragedy of the Commons.

Oil deposits

Consider an oilfield so large that it lies under many properties with different owners. Any of the owners can drill and extract the oil, but when one owner extracts oil, less is available for the others. The oil is a common resource.

Just as the number of sheep grazing on the Town Common was inefficiently large, the number of wells drawing from the oilfield will be inefficiently large. Because each owner who drills a well imposes a negative externality on the other owners, the benefit to society of drilling a well is less than the benefit to the owner who drills it. That is, drilling a well can be privately profitable even when it is socially undesirable. If owners of the properties decide individually how many oil wells to drill, they will drill too many.

To ensure that the oil is extracted at lowest cost, some type of joint action among the owners is necessary to solve the common-resource problem. The Coase theorem, which we discussed in chapter 10, suggests that a private solution might be possible. The owners could reach an agreement among themselves about how to extract the oil and divide the profits. In essence, the owners would then act as if they were in a single business. Companies that own the right to drill for oil or gas from a single field often form production joint ventures. The companies jointly determine the total amount of oil or gas that is extracted and internalise the negative externality.

Congested roads

Roads can be either public goods or common resources. If a road is not congested, then one person's use does not affect anyone else. In this case, use is not rival in consumption, and the road is a public good. Yet if a road is congested, then use of that road yields a negative externality. When one person drives on the road, it becomes more crowded, and other people must drive more slowly. In this case, the road is a common resource.

One way for the government to overcome the problem of road congestion is to charge drivers a toll. A toll is, in essence, a corrective tax on the externality of congestion. Sometimes, as in the case of suburban roads, tolls are not a practical solution because the cost of collecting them is too high.

But several major cities, including London and Singapore, have found increasing tolls to be a very effective way to reduce congestion.

Sometimes congestion is a problem only at certain times of day. If a bridge is heavily travelled only during rush hour, for instance, the congestion externality is larger during this time than during other times of day. The efficient way to deal with these externalities is to charge higher tolls during rush hour. This toll would provide an incentive for drivers to alter their schedules in order to reduce traffic when congestion is greatest.

Another policy that responds to the problem of road congestion is the tax on petrol. Petrol is a complementary good to driving; an increase in the price of petrol tends to reduce the quantity of driving demanded. Therefore, a petrol tax reduces road congestion.

A petrol tax, however, is an imperfect solution to road congestion. The problem is that the petrol tax affects other decisions besides the amount of driving on congested roads. For example, the petrol tax discourages driving on uncongested roads, even though there is no congestion externality for these roads.

IN THE NEWS . . .

THE CASE FOR TOLL ROADS

Many economists think that drivers should be charged for the congestion that they create on our roads. This article explains why.

Why you'll love paying for roads that used to be free

by Eric A. Morris

To end the scourge of traffic congestion, Julius Caesar banned most carts from the streets of Rome during daylight hours. It didn't work – traffic jams just shifted to dusk. Two thousand years later, we have put a man on the moon and developed garments infinitely more practical than the toga, but we seem little nearer to solving the congestion problem.

If you live in a city, particularly a large one, you probably need little convincing that traffic congestion is frustrating and wasteful. According to the Texas Transportation Institute, the average American urban traveler lost 38 hours, nearly one full work week, to congestion in 2005. And congestion is getting worse, not better; urban travelers in 1982 were delayed only 14 hours that year.

Americans want action, but unfortunately there aren't too many great ideas about what that action might be. As Anthony Downs's excellent book *Still Stuck in Traffic: Coping With Peak-Hour Traffic Congestion* chronicles, most of the proposed solutions are too difficult to implement, won't work, or both.

Source: Shutterstock/Zhu Difeng.

Fortunately, there is one remedy which is both doable and largely guaranteed to succeed. In the space of a year or two we could have you zipping along the 405 or the LIE at the height of rush hour at a comfortable 55 miles per hour.

There's just one small problem with this silver bullet for congestion: many people seem to prefer the werewolf. Despite its merits, this policy, which is known as 'congestion pricing',

>>

'value pricing', or 'variable tolling', is not an easy political sell.

For decades, economists and other transportation thinkers have advocated imposing tolls that vary with congestion levels on roadways. Simply put, the more congestion, the higher the toll, until the congestion goes away.

To many people, this sounds like a scheme by mustache-twirling bureaucrats and their academic apologists to fleece drivers out of their hard-earned cash. Why should drivers have to pay to use roads their tax dollars have already paid for? Won't the remaining free roads be swamped as drivers are forced off the tolled roads? Won't the working-class and poor be the victims here, as the tolled routes turn into 'Lexus lanes'?

And besides, adopting this policy would mean listening to economists, and who wants to do that?

There's a real problem with this logic, which is that, on its own terms, it makes perfect sense (except for the listening to economists part). Opponents of tolls are certainly not stupid, and their arguments deserve serious consideration. But in the end, their concerns are largely overblown, and the benefits of tolling swamp the potential costs.

Unfortunately, it can be hard to convey this because the theory behind tolling is somewhat complex and counterintuitive. This is too bad, because variable tolling is an excellent public policy. Here's why: the basic economic theory is that when you give out something valuable – in this case, road space – for less than its true value, shortages result.

Ultimately, there's no free lunch; instead of paying with money, you pay with the effort and time needed to acquire the good. Think of Soviet shoppers spending their lives in endless queues to purchase artificially low-priced but exceedingly scarce goods. Then think of Americans who can fulfill nearly any consumerist fantasy quickly but at a monetary cost. Free but congested roads have left us shivering on the streets of Moscow.

To consider it another way, delay is an externality imposed by drivers on their peers. By driving onto a busy road and contributing to congestion, drivers slow the speeds of others – but they never have to pay for it, at least not directly. In the end, of course, everybody pays, because as we impose congestion on others, others impose it on us. This degenerates into a game that nobody can win.

Markets work best when externalities are internalized: i.e., you pay for the hassle you inflict on others ... Using tolls to help internalize the congestion externality would somewhat reduce the number of trips made on the most congested roads at the peak usage periods; some trips would be moved to less congested times and routes, and others would be foregone entirely. This way we would cut down on the congestion costs we impose on each other.

Granted, tolls cannot fully cope with accidents and other incidents, which are major causes of delay. But pricing can largely eliminate chronic, recurring congestion. No matter how high the demand for a road, there is a level of toll that will keep it flowing freely.

To make tolling truly effective, the price must be right. Too high a price drives away too many cars and the road does not function at its capacity. Too low a price and congestion isn't licked.

The best solution is to vary the tolls in real time based on an analysis of current traffic conditions. Pilot toll projects on roads (like the I-394 in Minnesota and the I-15 in Southern California) use sensors embedded in the pavement to monitor the number and speeds of vehicles on the facility.

A simple computer program then determines the number of cars that should be allowed in. The computer then calculates the level of toll that will attract that number of cars – and no more. Prices are then updated every few minutes on electronic message signs. Hi-tech transponders and antenna arrays make waiting at toll booths a thing of the past.

The bottom line is that speeds are kept high (over 45 m.p.h.) so that throughput is higher than when vehicles are allowed to crowd all at once onto roadways at rush hour, slowing traffic to a crawl.

To maximize efficiency, economists would like to price all travel, starting with the freeways. But given that elected officials have no burning desire to lose their jobs, a more realistic option, for now, is to toll just some freeway lanes that are either new capacity or underused carpool lanes. The other lanes would be left free – and congested. Drivers will then have a choice: wait or pay. Granted, neither is ideal. But right now drivers have no choice at all.

What's the bottom line here? The state of Washington recently opened congestion-priced lanes on its State Route 167. The peak toll in the first month of operation (reached on the evening of Wednesday, May 21) was $5.75. I know, I know, you would never pay such an exorbitant amount when America has taught you that free roads are your birthright. But that money bought Washington drivers a 27-minute time savings. Is a half hour of your time worth $6?

I think I already know the answer, and it is 'it depends'. Most people's value of time varies widely depending on their activities on any given day. Late for picking the kids up from daycare? Paying $6 to save a half hour is an incredible bargain. Have to clean the house? The longer your trip home takes, the better. Tolling will introduce a new level of flexibility and freedom into your life, giving you the power to tailor your travel costs to fit your schedule.

Source: Eric A. Morris/Freakonomics blog, 6 January 2009.

Fish, whales and other wildlife

Many species of animals are common resources. As discussed above, fish, for instance, have commercial value, and anyone can go to the ocean and catch whatever is available. Each person has little incentive to maintain the species for the next year. Just as excessive grazing can destroy the Town Common, excessive fishing can destroy commercially valuable marine populations.

Oceans remain one of the least regulated common resources. Two problems prevent an easy solution. First, many countries have access to the oceans, so any solution would require international cooperation among countries that hold different values. Second, because the oceans are so vast, enforcing any agreement is difficult. As a result, fishing rights have been a frequent source of international tension among normally friendly countries.

Within Australia, various laws aim to protect wildlife. For example, the government restricts duck hunting to a limited season each year. It also restricts the types of duck that may be hunted. These laws regulate the use of a common resource and help maintain the duck population.

CASESTUDY

Why the cow is not extinct

Throughout history, many species of animals have been threatened with extinction. When Europeans first arrived in North America, more than 60 million buffalo roamed the continent. Yet hunting the buffalo was so popular during the nineteenth century that by 1900 the animal's population fell to about 400 before the government stepped in to protect the species. In some African countries today, the elephant faces a similar challenge, as poachers kill the animals for the ivory in their tusks.

Yet not all animals with commercial value face this threat. The cow, for example, is a valuable source of food, but no one worries that the cow will soon be extinct. Indeed, the great demand for beef seems to ensure that the species will continue to thrive.

Why is the commercial value of ivory a threat to the elephant, and the commercial value of beef a guardian of the cow? The reason is that elephants are a common resource, whereas cows are a private good. Elephants roam freely without any owners. Each poacher has a strong incentive to kill as many elephants as he can find. Because poachers are numerous, each poacher has only a slight incentive to preserve the elephant population. In contrast, cows live on cattle stations that are privately owned. Station owners take great care to maintain the cow population on their stations because they reap the benefit of their efforts.

>>

Will the market protect me?

Source: photos.com/Getty Images.

Governments have tried to solve the elephant's problem in two ways. Some countries, such as Kenya, Tanzania and Uganda, have made it illegal to kill elephants and sell their ivory. Yet these laws have been hard to enforce, and elephant populations have continued to dwindle. In contrast, other countries, such as Botswana, Malawi, Namibia and Zimbabwe, have made elephants a private good by allowing people to kill elephants, but only those on their own property. Landowners now have an incentive to preserve the species on their own land and, as a result, elephant populations have started to rise. With private ownership and the profit motive now on its side, the African elephant might someday be as safe from extinction as the cow.

Q

Why do governments try to limit the use of common resources?

Conclusion: The importance of property rights

In this chapter and the previous one, we have seen there are some 'goods' that the market does not provide adequately. Markets do not ensure that the air we breathe is clean or that our country is defended from foreign aggressors. Instead, societies rely on the government to protect the environment and to provide defence.

Although the problems we considered in these chapters arise in many different markets, they share a common theme. In all cases, the market fails to allocate resources efficiently because property rights are not well established. That is, some item of value does not have an owner with the legal authority to control it. For example, although no one doubts that the 'good' of clean air or defence is valuable, no one has the right to attach a price to it and profit from its use. A factory pollutes too much because no one charges the factory for the pollution it emits. The market does not provide for defence because no one can charge those who are defended for the benefit they receive.

When the absence of property rights causes a market failure, the government can potentially solve the problem. Sometimes, as in the sale of pollution permits, the solution is for the government to help define property rights and thereby unleash market forces. At other times, as in the restriction on hunting seasons, the solution is for the government to regulate private behaviour. At still other times, as in the provision of defence, the solution is for the government to supply a good that the market fails to supply. In all cases, if the policy is well planned and well run, it can make the allocation of resources more efficient and thus raise economic wellbeing.

Summary

- Goods differ in whether they are excludable and whether they are rival in consumption. A good is excludable if it is possible to prevent someone from using it. A good is rival in consumption if one person's enjoyment of the good prevents other people from enjoying the same good. Markets work best for private goods, which are both excludable and rival. Markets do not work as well for other types of goods.
- Public goods are neither rival nor excludable. Examples of public goods include fireworks displays, defence and the creation of fundamental knowledge. Because people are not charged for their use of the public good, they have an incentive to free ride when the good is provided privately. Therefore, governments provide public goods, making their decision about the quantity based on cost–benefit analysis.
- Common resources are rival but not excludable. Some examples are common grazing land, clean air and congested roads. Because people are not charged for their use of common resources, they tend to use them excessively. Therefore, governments try to limit the use of common resources.

Key concepts

club goods	excludable	public goods
common resources	free rider	rival in consumption
cost–benefit analysis	private goods	Tragedy of the Commons

Questions for review

1. Explain what is meant by a good being 'excludable'. Explain what is meant by a good being 'rival in consumption'. Is a pizza excludable? Is it rival in consumption?
2. Define and give an example of a public good. Can the private market provide this good on its own? Explain.
3. What is cost–benefit analysis of public goods? Why is it important? Why is it hard?
4. Define and give an example of a common resource. Without government intervention, will people use this good too much or too little? Why?

Problems and applications

1. The text says that both public goods and common resources involve externalities.
   a. Are the externalities associated with public goods generally positive or negative? Use examples in your answer. Is the free-market quantity of public goods generally greater or less than the efficient quantity?
   b. Are the externalities associated with common resources generally positive or negative? Use examples in your answer. Is the free-market use of common resources generally greater or less than the efficient use?
2. Think about the goods and services provided by your local government.

a Using the classification in Figure 11.1, explain what category each of the following goods falls into:
i police protection
ii garbage collection
iii education
iv rural roads
v city streets.

b Why do you think the government provides items that are not public goods?

3 The text states that private firms will not undertake the efficient amount of basic scientific research.
a Explain why this is so. In your answer, classify basic research into one of the categories shown in Figure 11.1.
b What sort of policy has Australia adopted in response to this problem?
c It is often argued that this policy increases the technological capability of Australian producers relative to that of foreign firms. Is this argument consistent with your classification of basic research in part (a)? (*Hint:* Can excludability apply to some potential beneficiaries of a public good and not others?)

4 Why is there litter along most highways but rarely in people's yards?

5 The public transport systems in some cities charge higher fares during rush hour than during the rest of the day. Why might they do this?

6 Timber companies in Australia cut down many trees on publicly owned land and on privately owned land. Discuss the likely efficiency of logging on each type of land in the absence of government regulation. How do you think the government should regulate logging on publicly owned lands? Should similar regulations apply to privately owned land?

7 An *Economist* article (19 March 1994) states: 'In the past decade, most of the rich world's fisheries have been exploited to the point of near-exhaustion'. The article continues with an analysis of the problem and a discussion of possible private and government solutions:
a 'Do not blame fishermen for overfishing. They are behaving rationally, as they have always done.' In what sense is 'overfishing' rational for fishermen?
b 'A community, held together by ties of obligation and mutual self-interest, can manage a common resource on its own.' Explain how such management can work in principle, and what obstacles it faces in the real world.
c 'Until 1976 most world fish stocks were open to all comers, making conservation almost impossible. Then an international agreement extended some aspects of [national] jurisdiction from 12 to 200 miles offshore.' Using the concept of property rights, discuss how this agreement reduces the scope of the problem.
d The article notes that many governments come to the aid of suffering fishermen in ways that encourage increased fishing. How do such policies encourage a vicious cycle of overfishing?
e 'Only when fishermen believe they are assured a long-term and exclusive right to a fishery are they likely to manage it in the same far-sighted way as good farmers manage their land.' Defend this statement.
f What other policies to reduce overfishing might be considered?

8 In a market economy, information about the quality or function of goods and services is a valuable good in its own right. How does the private market provide this information? Can you think of any way in which the government plays a role in providing this information?

9 Do you think that the Internet is a public good? Why or why not?

10 High-income people are willing to pay more than low-income people to avoid the risk of death. For example, they are more likely to pay for safety features on cars. Do you think cost–benefit analysts should take this fact into account when evaluating public projects? Consider, for instance, a rich town and a poor town, both of which are considering the installation of a traffic light. Should the rich town use a higher dollar value for a human life in making this decision? Why or why not?

Search me!

Search me!

When accessing information about microeconomics use the following keywords in any combinations you require:

- free rider problem
- Tragedy of the Commons

CourseMate

CourseMate

For more multimedia resources and activities on economics, visit the Economics CourseMate website.

12

The design of the tax system

Learning objectives

In this chapter you will:

- get an overview of how the Australian government raises and spends money
- examine the efficiency costs of taxes
- learn alternative ways to judge the equity of a tax system
- see why studying tax incidence is crucial for evaluating tax equity
- consider the trade-off between efficiency and equity in the design of a tax system.

Benjamin Franklin, the great eighteenth-century American statesman, once noted that 'in this world nothing is certain but death and taxes'. But perhaps *Time* magazine better summarised popular opinion: 'There is one difference between a tax collector and a taxidermist – the taxidermist leaves the hide'.

Taxes are inevitable because we, as citizens, expect our government to provide us with various goods and services. The last two chapters have started to shed light on one of the *Ten Lessons from Economics* in chapter 1 – the government can sometimes improve market outcomes. When the government remedies an externality (such as air pollution), provides a public good (such as defence) or regulates the use of a common resource (such as fish in our rivers and streams), it can raise economic wellbeing. Yet the benefits of government come with costs. For the government to perform these and its many other functions, it needs to raise revenue through taxation.

We began our study of taxation in previous chapters, where we saw how a tax on a good affects supply and demand for that good. In chapter 6 we saw that a tax reduces the quantity sold in a market, and we examined how the burden of a tax is shared by buyers and sellers, depending on the elasticities of supply and demand. In chapter 8 we examined how taxes affect economic wellbeing. We learned that taxes cause deadweight losses; the reduction in consumer and producer surplus resulting from a tax exceeds the revenue raised by the government.

In this chapter we build on these lessons to discuss the design of a tax system. We begin with a financial overview of Australian government. When we think about the tax system, it is useful to know some basic facts about how Australian governments raise and spend money. We then consider the fundamental principles of taxation. Most people agree that taxes should impose as small a cost on society as possible and that the burden of taxes should be distributed fairly. That is, the tax system should be both *efficient* and *equitable*. As we will see, however, stating these goals is easier than achieving them.

A financial overview of Australian government

How much of the nation's income does the government take as taxes? Aggregate tax revenue for 2008–09 was approximately $339 billion, or around 28 per cent of the total Australian income. This was divided between the three levels of government. The federal government collected 82 per cent of all taxes, and state governments collected 15 per cent of taxes. Local governments directly collected only 3 per cent of tax revenue.

Tax revenue, as a percentage of total Australian income, has remained relatively constant over the last 20 years. In other words, government tax income has grown at about the same rate as the income of the rest of the economy. Australians pay relatively low tax overall when compared with most other developed nations. Although taxation revenues as a percentage of total income are lower in the United States, Japan and Korea than in Australia, they are higher in Canada, New Zealand and most Western European countries. Traditionally, Australia has relied more heavily on income taxes than other developed countries. This reliance increased steadily between 1950 and 2000. Income tax made up just over half of federal government tax revenue in the late 1950s. By the late 1990s, income tax accounted for almost 75 per cent of federal tax revenue. In July 2000, the federal government introduced a goods and services tax (GST). This tax on consumption reduced the federal government's dependence on income tax revenue and in 2008–09 income tax made up about 72 per cent of total federal government tax revenue.

The overall size of government tells only part of the story. Behind the total lie thousands of individual decisions about taxes and spending. To understand the government's finances more fully, let's look at the breakdown of the total into some broad categories.

The federal government

The federal government collects about four-fifths of the taxes in our economy. It raises this money in a number of ways and it finds even more ways to spend it.

Receipts

Figure 12.1 shows federal government receipts as a percentage of total Australian income since 1970. Revenue grew in the early 1970s but has since remained relatively stable at between 22 per cent and 27 per cent of income. Table 12.1 shows the expected tax receipts of the federal government in the 2010–11 financial year. Total tax receipts in this year were $302.5 billion, a number so large that it is hard to comprehend. To bring this astronomical number down to earth, we can divide it by the size of the Australian population, which was approximately 22.5 million at the end of 2010. We then find that the average Australian paid $13 444 to the federal government.

The largest source of revenue for the federal government is the individual income tax. By 31 October each year, Australian residents who earned more than $6000 over the previous 12 months must fill out a tax form to determine how much income tax they owe the government. People are

Figure 12.1 **Federal government receipts as a percentage of GDP**

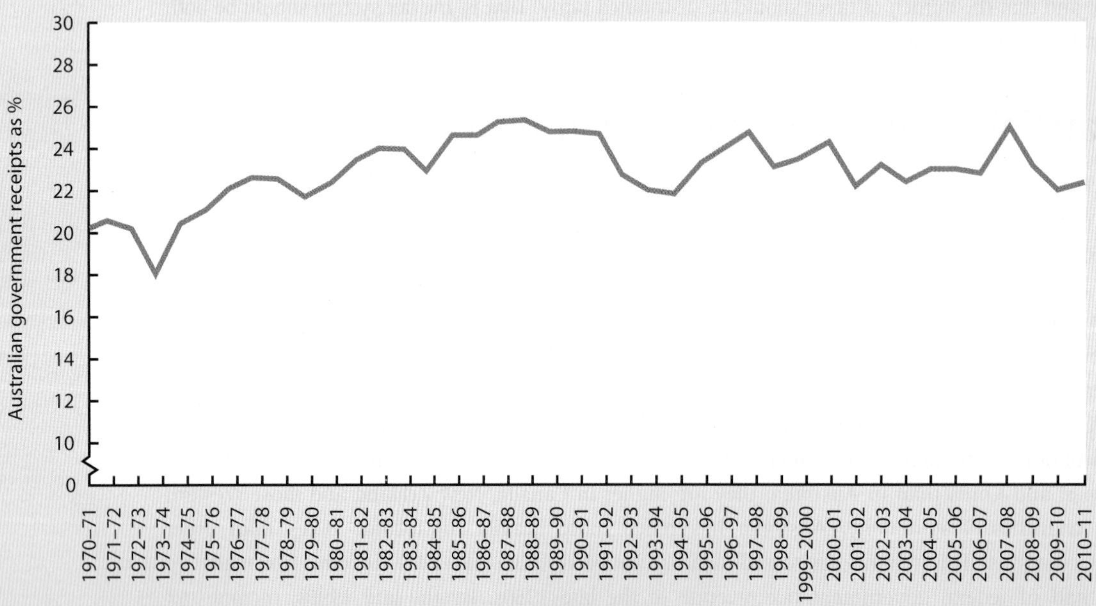

This figure shows the total receipts of the federal government as a percentage of gross domestic product (GDP), which measures total income in the economy. The figure shows that the federal government plays a large role in the Australian economy and that its role has remained fairly stable over the past 40 years.

Source: 2010–11 *Budget Paper No. 1*, statement 10, table 2 and equivalent table from previous years.

Table 12.1 Estimated tax receipts of the federal government, 2010–11

Tax	Amount ($ billions)	Amount per person ($)	% of tax receipts
Individual income taxes	137	6088	45
Company income taxes	66.5	2956	22
Goods and services tax	50	2222	17
Excise on petroleum products	13.1	582	4
Other excises	18.9	840	6
Other taxes	17	756	6
Total	302.5	13 444	100

Source: 2010–11 *Budget Paper No. 1*, statement 5, various tables.

required to report their income from all sources: wages from working, interest on savings, dividends from companies in which they own shares, profits from any small businesses they operate and so on. People's *tax liability* (how much they owe) is then based on their total income.

A person's income tax liability is not simply proportional to that person's income. Instead, the law requires a more complicated calculation. Taxable income is calculated by subtracting deductible expenses from total income. These expenses are usually related to earning income. For example, some travel expenses related to work are deductible. Some other expenses, such as donations of more than $2 to charitable organisations, are also deductible. An individual's tax liability may also be reduced, for example, if that person is a sole parent.

Once a person has calculated taxable income, the person's tax liability is calculated using the schedule shown in Table 12.2. This table presents the marginal tax rate – the tax rate applied to each additional dollar of income. Because the marginal tax rate rises as income rises, people with higher income pay a larger percentage of their income in taxes. (We discuss the concept of marginal tax rate more fully later in this chapter.)

Table 12.2 shows the marginal income tax rates from 2010–11. These rates have slowly declined over time, particularly for 'middle income' earners. For example, in 2007, the 30 per cent marginal

Table 12.2 Federal income tax rates: 2010–11

On taxable income ...	The tax rate is ...
Up to $6000	0%
From $6001 to $37 000	15
From $37 001 to $80 000	30
From $80 001 to $180 000	37
Over $180 001	45

tax rate began at an income of $34 000 rather than $37 000, while the marginal tax rate for people earning $80 000 to $180 000 per year has fallen from 40 per cent to 37 per cent.

In addition to the tax rates shown in Table 12.2, the federal government also charges people a levy of 1.5 per cent of their income. This levy partially offsets the cost of the government's universal health care program, Medicare. In the 1997–98 financial year, the federal government also introduced an extra surcharge of 1 per cent on high-income individuals and families. This surcharge is waived if the individual or family has private medical insurance and is intended to encourage high-income earners to take out this insurance.

Individual income tax made up almost half of all federal government tax revenue in 2006–07. In contrast, company income tax only makes up about 22 per cent of federal government tax revenue. The government taxes each company based on its profit – the amount the company receives for the goods or services it sells minus the costs of producing those goods or services. The company tax rate is set at 30 per cent.

Note that the federal government risks taxing company profits twice – once by company income tax when the business earns the profits and a second time by individual income tax when the company uses its profits to pay dividends to its shareholders. To limit this double taxation, the federal government allows people who receive dividend income to claim a credit for the amount of taxation already paid by the company.

In 2010–11, the GST raised about three-quarters as much revenue as company income tax. The GST applies to most of the things we buy or sell every day. The GST tax rate is set at 10 per cent and sellers must send the tax they collect to the federal government either every month or every three months, depending on the size of their business. The federal government, however, does not get to spend this revenue – the federal government passes it through to the state governments.

The federal government also receives revenue from other taxes on what we buy or sell. These taxes are called excises. The most important excise is on petroleum products, but the federal government also charges excise tax on alcoholic drinks, such as beer, and on tobacco. The government also taxes some international trade (approximately $6.7 billion). Together, excise taxes make up about one-tenth of federal government tax revenue. The 'other taxes' category in Table 12.1 is made up of a variety of taxes, including the fringe benefits tax (approximately $4 billion) and taxes on superannuation funds (approximately $7 billion). The fringe benefits tax applies when employees are given a non-monetary benefit by their employer. Superannuation funds help individuals save for retirement. While the federal government receives some revenue from taxes on these funds, the government also provides tax benefits to people if they save their income in a superannuation fund.

In addition to tax revenue, the federal government receives revenue from interest payments and from sales of products such as government publications. In 2010–11 the federal government received $19.4 billion in non-tax revenue.

Spending

Table 12.3 shows the spending of the federal government in 2010–11. Total spending was $285.8 billion, or $12 702 per person. This table also shows how the federal government's spending was divided among major categories.

The largest category in Table 12.3 is 'social security and welfare'. This involves a variety of programs including age pensions, disability support pensions and family allowances. Almost 40 per

Table 12.3 Budgeted spending of the federal government 2010–11

Category	Amount ($ billions)	Amount per person ($)	% of spending
Social security and welfare	115	5111	40.2
Health	56.9	2529	20.0
Defence	21	933	7.3
Education	32.9	1462	11.5
General public services	20.1	893	7.0
Other economic affairs	9	401	3.2
Other spending	30.9	1373	10.8
Total	$285.8	$12 702	100.0

Source: 2010–11 *Budget Paper No. 1*, statement 6.

cent of social security and welfare payments involve assistance to the aged. Another quarter of payments involve assistance to families with children.

The second largest category of spending is 'health'. The two main federal government health costs are medical benefits paid under the Medicare program and the cost of public hospitals, which the state governments operate with the help of money provided by the federal government. The federal government, using a 'stick and carrot' approach, has been trying to reduce Medicare costs by encouraging people to take out private health insurance. Middle-income earners receive the carrot – some of their private health insurance costs are reimbursed by the government. High-income earners receive the stick – if they do not take out private health insurance, they pay more income tax to the federal government.

Education makes up the next largest category of federal government expenditure. The main recipients of education funds are universities and schools. Most Australian universities are owned by government and the federal government pays over $8.1 billion to these institutions. But the process of funding higher education has changed since the late 1980s; we discuss these changes below.

Defence and 'General public services' each account for about $20 billion of federal government spending. Defence spending includes both the salaries of military personnel and the purchases of military equipment such as guns, planes and ships. Spending on defence fluctuates over time as international tensions and the political climate change. Not surprisingly, spending on defence rises substantially during wars.

'General public services' includes a variety of expenditures. The costs of operating parliament and some government departments are included in this category, as is foreign economic aid and Commonwealth-sponsored research, such as funding by the Australian Research Council.

'Other economic affairs', the sixth category in Table 12.3, includes tourist promotion, some employment training schemes and payments to economic regulators. As we will see later in this book, the federal government has passed laws to allow fair competition between firms. The organisations that enforce these laws are funded under this category of spending.

The federal government spends money in many other areas – on roads, communications, land management, national parks and so on. Rather than list all these areas, they are bundled under the final category in Table 12.3.

The federal government shares some of its tax revenue with the states. The revenue from the GST is passed on to the states. The states also receive money from the federal government that is tied to specific projects. These 'specific purpose payments' are included in Table 12.3. For example, the federal government helps pay for state-owned primary and secondary schools, and this is part of 'education' in the table. In 2010–11, the federal government paid approximately $16.3 billion to state and local governments.

In total, including GST payments to the states, the estimated spending of the federal government in 2010–11 was $354.6 billion. Total tax and non-tax receipts were lower, at $321.9 billion. This shortfall of receipts compared to spending is called a **budget deficit**. When receipts exceed spending, the government is said to run a **budget surplus**. The government finances a budget deficit by borrowing from the public. That is, it sells government debt to the private sector, including both investors in Australia and those abroad. When the government runs a budget surplus, it uses the excess receipts to reduce its outstanding debts.

budget deficit
an excess of government spending over government receipts

budget surplus
an excess of government receipts over government spending

State and local governments

State and local governments collect about 18 per cent of all taxes paid. Let's look at how they obtain tax revenue and how they spend it.

Receipts

The biggest source of revenue for state and local governments is transfers from the federal government, in particular the revenue from the GST. For example, federal government payments accounted for 46.4 per cent of Queensland state government revenue and about 50 per cent of Victorian state government revenue in 2010–11.

State governments also have their own taxes. The two most important taxes for state governments are payroll taxes and stamp duties. A payroll tax is a tax on the wages that a firm pays its workers. State governments have levied payroll taxes since 1971. Firms are usually liable for payroll tax only if their total wage bill is above a minimum threshold. For example, in New South Wales a firm pays payroll tax only if its monthly wages bill is above $50 000. Since July 2002, the payroll tax rate in New South Wales has been 6 per cent. In 2008–09, state governments raised $17 billion in payroll taxes.

Stamp duty was originally introduced in England in 1694 as a tax on certain legal documents. It is now a tax charged by the state governments on some transactions, most notably when someone buys or sells land. It raised $17 billion in total for state governments in 2008–09.

State governments also receive revenue from a variety of other taxes, such as taxes on insurance and motor vehicles. Gambling taxes are important to state governments. In 2010–11, gambling taxes raised about $1.7 billion for the Victorian state government, around 12.6 per cent of total tax revenue. In Queensland, gambling taxes raised about $0.96 billion in 2010–11, or just over 9 per cent of total tax revenue.

The main local government tax is municipal rates, which is a tax on property in the local government's area. In 2008–09 this tax totalled almost $11 billion. Local governments also receive small amounts of revenue from fees such as dog licences.

Spending

The largest expenditures for state and local governments are health and education. State governments pay much of the cost of public schools and hospitals. In total, state and local governments spend almost as much as the federal government on health and substantially more than the federal government on education.

State governments provide most of the funds to operate the public transport systems in our cities. Many of these systems operate at a loss – the amount we pay in fares does not cover the operating expense of the public transport system. State governments also fund most of our roads and the state police forces are paid for by the state governments. In addition, both state and local governments provide a variety of welfare services as well as many of our local amenities: libraries, garbage removal and park maintenance.

Q

What are the two most important sources of tax revenue for the federal government?
What are the two most important sources of tax revenue for state and local governments?

Taxes and efficiency

Now that we have seen how Australian governments at various levels raise and spend money, let's consider how one might evaluate tax policy. Obviously, the aim of a tax system is to raise revenue for the government. But there are many ways to raise any given amount of money. In designing a tax system, policymakers have two objectives: efficiency and equity.

One tax system is more efficient than another if it raises the same amount of revenue at a smaller cost to taxpayers. What are the costs of taxes to taxpayers? The most obvious cost is the tax payment itself. This transfer of money from the taxpayer to the government is an inevitable feature of any tax system. Yet taxes also impose two other costs, which well-designed tax policy tries to avoid or, at least, minimise:

- the deadweight losses that result when taxes distort the decisions that people make
- the administrative burdens that taxpayers bear as they comply with the tax laws.

An efficient tax system is one that imposes small deadweight losses and small administrative burdens.

Deadweight losses

Taxes affect the decisions that people make. If the government taxes ice-cream, people eat less ice-cream and more frozen yoghurt. If the government taxes housing, people live in smaller houses and spend more of their income on other things. If the government taxes labour earnings, people work less and enjoy more leisure.

Because taxes distort incentives, they entail deadweight losses. As we first discussed in chapter 8, the deadweight loss of a tax is the reduction in economic wellbeing of taxpayers in excess of the amount of revenue raised by the government. The deadweight loss is the inefficiency that a tax creates as people allocate resources according to the tax incentive rather than according to the true costs and benefits of the goods and services that they buy and sell.

To recall how taxes cause deadweight losses, consider an example. Suppose that Joe places an $8 value on a pizza and Jane places a $6 value on it. If there is no tax on pizza, the price of pizza will reflect the cost of making it. Let's suppose that the price of pizza is $5, so both Joe and Jane choose to buy one. Both consumers get some surplus of value over the amount paid. Joe gets consumer surplus of $3 and Jane gets consumer surplus of $1. Total surplus is $4.

Now suppose that the government levies a $2 tax on pizza and the price of pizza rises to $7. (This occurs if supply is perfectly elastic.) Joe still buys a pizza, but now he has consumer surplus of only $1. Jane now decides not to buy a pizza because its price is higher than its value to her. The government collects tax revenue of $2 on Joe's pizza. Total consumer surplus has fallen by $3 (from $4 to $1). Because total surplus has fallen by more than the tax revenue, the tax has a deadweight loss. In this case, the deadweight loss is $1.

Notice that the deadweight loss comes not from Joe, the person who pays the tax, but from Jane, the person who doesn't. The reduction in Joe's surplus of $2 exactly offsets the amount of revenue the government collects. The deadweight loss arises because the tax causes Jane to alter her behaviour. When the tax raises the price of pizza, Jane is worse off, and yet there is no offsetting revenue to the government. This reduction in Jane's welfare is the deadweight loss of the tax.

CASESTUDY

The goods and services tax

On 1 July 2001, the Australian government introduced a new goods and services tax (GST). The GST was accompanied by a change in individual income taxes and the reduction or elimination of some other taxes, such as wholesale sales tax. These were the biggest changes in the design of Australia's tax system for at least 30 years.

The GST is a type of consumption tax. Rather than taxing the amount of income that people earn, with a consumption tax the government taxes the amount that people spend. A consumption tax can be applied just to retail sales (called a retail sales tax) or can be levied at each stage of the production process. This multistage tax is known as a value-added tax (VAT) or, as in Australia, a goods and services tax (GST).

Most developed countries have a VAT or GST. New Zealand and Canada both introduced a GST in the 1990s, before Australia. The GST in Australia is set at 10 per cent, so when you buy a pizza or hire a video, the seller has to add 10 per cent onto the price as government tax. This tax level is low by international standards. The GST in New Zealand is set at 15 per cent, while European countries such as Germany and the United Kingdom have a GST of 17.5 per cent or higher. In Denmark, the GST is 25 per cent.

The debate in Australia leading up to the introduction of the GST focused on the costs of the tax system. As we noted earlier in this chapter, in the 1990s the Australian government relied heavily on revenue from individual income tax. One of the inefficiencies caused by this tax is that it can discourage saving. A GST avoids this distortion.

Spend?

Or save?

Source: © photos.com/Getty Images.

Suppose that 25-year-old Anne is considering saving $100. If she put this money in a savings account that earns 8 per cent and leaves it there, she would have $2172 when she reaches the age of 65. Yet if the government taxes a quarter of the interest income each year, the effective interest rate is only

6 per cent. After 40 years of earning 6 per cent, the $100 grows to only $1029, less than half of what it would have been without taxation. Thus, because interest income is taxed, saving is much less attractive.

In contrast, suppose that rather than taxing income, the government taxes a quarter of consumption expenditure. Then at the age of 65, Anne has $2172 and when she spends this money one-quarter goes to the government. This leaves Anne with $1629 to spend on anything she likes, compared with $1029 under the income tax. The shift from an income tax to a consumption tax has made saving more attractive to Anne.

It was also argued that the GST would help reduce tax evasion. With a multistage tax, like the GST, it is easier for tax officials to track transactions and to check that everyone is paying the correct level of tax. But a multistage tax also requires a lot of paperwork, and some economists argued that the increase in paperwork under the GST would increase business costs and help tax evasion. Overall, the evidence on tax evasion and a GST is mixed. In India, some states have a GST while others do not. A 2010 Indian government report found that tax evasion was higher following the introduction of a GST. However, some of the state taxes were poorly designed, making evasion relatively easy.

The introduction of the GST in Australia was strongly opposed by welfare groups who believe that a consumption tax will benefit the rich and harm the poor. If the marginal income tax rate is rising, like in Table 12.2, then those who have more income will on average pay more tax per dollar than those who have less income. But under a 10 per cent GST, rich and poor alike pay the same amount of tax when they buy a particular good or service. To reduce potential harm to the poor, the government lowered the income tax rates for people earning less than $60 000 per year. It also allowed some products to be exempt from the GST. The GST does not apply to all goods and services. Some goods and services, such as fresh food, medicine, education and child care, do not have GST included in their price. These products are exempt from GST because they are often important for the poorest people in society. The range of exemptions from a GST differs between countries. For example, in New Zealand, the GST applies to all goods and services except rental of residential property and some financial services.

Administrative burden

If you ask the typical person on 31 October for an opinion about the tax system, you might hear about the headache of filling out tax forms. The administrative burden of any tax system is part of the inefficiency it creates. This burden includes not only the time spent filling out tax return forms but also the time spent throughout the year keeping records for tax purposes and the resources the government has to use to enforce the tax laws.

More than three-quarters of individual taxpayers hire tax consultants and accountants to help them with their taxes and complete their tax return forms. This number has doubled since the late 1980s. Tax agents also help their clients arrange their affairs in a way that reduces the amount of taxes owed. This behaviour is legal tax avoidance, which is different from illegal tax evasion.

Critics of our tax system say that these advisers help their clients avoid taxes by abusing some of the detailed provisions of the tax code, often dubbed 'loopholes'. In some cases, loopholes are legislative mistakes; they arise from ambiguities or omissions in the tax laws. More often, they arise because the government has chosen to give special treatment to specific types of behaviour.

The resources devoted to complying with the tax laws are a type of deadweight loss. The government gets only the amount of taxes paid. In contrast, the taxpayer loses not only this amount but also the time and money spent documenting, calculating and avoiding taxes.

The compliance costs of the tax system involve companies as well as individuals. Companies must hire extra staff to calculate and pay income, GST and payroll taxes. Because of the complexity of the Australian tax system, the total administrative burden is likely to be very high compared with some other countries. In a 1997 article in the *Economic Record*, John Freebairn showed that the total administrative burden of the Australian tax system might be two or three times larger than that in the United Kingdom and the Netherlands, when measured as a percentage of tax revenue.

Marginal tax rates versus average tax rates

average tax rate
total taxes paid divided by total income

marginal tax rate
the extra taxes paid on an additional dollar of income

When discussing the efficiency and equity of income taxes, economists distinguish between two notions of the tax rate: the average and the marginal. The **average tax rate** is total taxes paid divided by total income. The **marginal tax rate** is the extra taxes paid on an additional dollar of income.

For example, suppose that the government taxes 20 per cent of the first $50 000 of income and 50 per cent of all income above $50 000. Under this system, a person who makes $60 000 pays a tax of $15 000 (the tax equals 0.20 × $50 000 plus 0.50 × $10 000). For this person, the average tax rate is $15 000/$60 000, or 25 per cent. But the marginal tax rate is 50 per cent because the amount of the tax would rise by $0.50 if the taxpayer earned an additional dollar.

The marginal and average tax rates each contain a useful piece of information. If we are trying to gauge the sacrifice made by a taxpayer, the average tax rate is more appropriate because it measures the fraction of income paid in taxes. In contrast, if we are trying to gauge how much the tax system distorts incentives, the marginal tax rate is more meaningful. One of the *Ten Lessons from Economics* in chapter 1 is that rational people think at the margin. A corollary to this lesson is that the marginal tax rate measures how much the tax system discourages people from working hard. If you are thinking of working an extra few hours, the marginal tax rate determines how much the government takes of your additional earnings. It is the marginal tax rate, therefore, that determines the deadweight loss of an income tax.

Source: DILBERT © 1996 Scott Adams. Used by permission of UNIVERSAL UCLICK. All rights reserved.

fyi **Tax avoidance and tax evasion**

It is understandable that people will want to minimise their tax payments. Like the free-rider problem we encountered in chapter 11, if people can reduce their personal tax bill then this will make them better off without significantly reducing the benefits they receive from government spending.

Tax minimisation falls into two broad categories – avoidance and evasion. Tax avoidance involves taxpayers using legal loopholes in the tax system to reduce their tax payments. Tax evasion is illegal and involves taxpayers deliberately misreporting their income or expenditures.

Sometimes the line between avoidance and evasion is unclear. In seventeenth-century England, taxes were levied on the number of windows in a dwelling. The idea was that this tax would better target the wealthy who could afford better housing with more windows. To avoid paying the tax, people would block up their windows when they knew the tax collector was coming. After the tax collector left, they would then unblock the windows. Whether this practice could be classified as avoidance or evasion is debatable. Either way, it created a deadweight loss as people spent time and energy blocking and unblocking windows.

IN THE NEWS . . .

USING THE INTERNET TO AVOID TAXES

Australia has a 10 per cent Goods and Services Tax (GST). When you buy something in Australia, the price includes the GST. But when you buy the same thing from overseas, you do not pay this tax to the Australian government. So the GST raises the incentive for individuals to buy overseas and transport their purchases to Australia. When the GST was introduced in 2001, such purchases were difficult for most consumers. But the Internet has now made them easy. We can buy music, books, clothing – pretty much anything that can be transported – from overseas via the Internet. This has started to affect the sales of local retailers. As the article below shows, some of those retailers are threatening to also set up overseas Internet outlets to avoid the GST.

Myer floats tax-free website

by Eli Greenblat and Clancy Yates

The boss of Australia's biggest department store, Myer, is investigating the merits of a China-based retail website to allow customers to shop GST-free.

Bernie Brookes told a business lunch in Melbourne yesterday other leading Australian businesses such as Woolworths and Bunnings could follow Myer's plan to operate a website from China that takes orders from Australian consumers as the sector grows increasingly angry over the leakage of sales to online stores. There has been frustration with the federal government's failure to act on an estimated $20 billion in sales on overseas sites that is not taxed.

'If we can't beat them we will join them,' Mr Brookes warned. 'We just want a level playing field. We will take jobs offshore and we will ship product out of China through our internet site, it's a bloody shame.'

Mr Brookes joins other retailers demanding government action, including Harvey Norman executive chairman Gerry Harvey who last week called for the current $1000 GST-free threshold to be lowered to curb shoppers buying online from overseas suppliers.

Online shopping's popularity has increased this year as the Australian dollar hit parity with the US dollar, making millions of items on American websites significantly cheaper than here.

Mr Brookes said a motivation to look at a China-based model for Myer's department store operations was the inaction and seeming lack of interest from federal Treasurer Wayne Swan. Assistant Treasurer Bill Shorten said the government was looking at the issue, but had no plans to put the GST on online shopping.

Mr Brookes said Myer's China-based website could be up and running by February, attracting a significant portion of the company's estimated $5 million a year in existing internet sales. Goods ordered from the site, such as dresses, jeans or coats, would be packed and shipped from its hub in Shenzhen, southern China, and avoid GST charges.

A spokeswoman for David Jones said it had no plans to create an offshore website.

Source: Eli Greenblat and Clancy Yates/*The Age*, 4 December 2010.

CASESTUDY

Marginal tax rates and the poverty trap

As Table 12.2 shows, the top marginal income tax rate in Australia at present is 45 per cent and only people who earn over $180 000 per year pay this rate. But these figures are misleading. In fact some poor people pay much higher marginal tax rates, as high as 80 per cent or more. These people are effectively taxed at a very high marginal rate because when they earn an extra dollar they lose some of the benefits that the government provides to people on low incomes. Earning more money may mean lower unemployment benefits, family allowance or rent assistance.

To see how effective marginal tax rates might be very high, suppose that Tom is receiving unemployment benefits. Tom has found a small amount of work – 5 hours per week at $10 per hour.

>>

Tom's total income is the $50 per week he earns plus unemployment benefits and rent assistance worth $150 per week. His total income per week is $200 and he pays no income tax. What if Tom is offered additional work for one hour per week? If he accepts the additional work, he is paid an extra $10. Tom's income is still too low for income tax so he receives the entire $10. However, because his income has increased, Tom's unemployment benefits are reduced. For example, unemployment benefits may fall by $1 for every extra $2 that a person earns. In this case, if Tom accepts the additional work he loses $5 in unemployment benefits. Rent assistance also depends on income, so that if Tom earns an extra $10 per week he may lose $3 in rent assistance. Overall, if Tom works for an extra hour he earns $10 but loses $8 – $5 in unemployment benefits and $3 in rent assistance. Working an extra hour raises his weekly income from $200 to only $202. His effective marginal tax rate is 80 per cent.

Although the figures given in the above example are only illustrative, they reflect a general problem for the poor – the more they earn the more their government benefits are reduced. Overall, the extra work may not be worthwhile. For example, research at the University of New South Wales shows how a family with one working parent and four children, whose private income rises by $200 per week, from $500 to $700, may receive a net gain of only $20 per week because of the loss of benefits. In such circumstances, the poor are trapped by the high effective marginal tax rates.

CASESTUDY

Iceland's natural experiment

In the 1980s, Iceland changed its tax system in a way that, as a side effect, provided a natural experiment to show how taxes affect an economy. Before the reform, people paid taxes based on their *previous* year's income. After the reform, people paid taxes based on their *current* income. Thus, taxes in 1987 were based on 1986 income, but taxes in 1988 were based on 1988 income. Income earned in 1987 was never taxed. For this one year of transition, the marginal income tax rate fell to zero.

As reported in a December 2001 article in the *American Economic Review*, the citizens of Iceland took advantage of this tax holiday. Total hours worked rose by about 3 per cent in 1987 and then fell back to the normal level in 1988. The production of goods and services in 1987 (as measured by real GDP) was 4 per cent higher than the average of the years before and the years after. This episode confirms one of the *Ten Lessons from Economics* – that people respond to incentives.

The fall in the Icelandic marginal tax rate was for one year only and this fact surely influenced the response. On the one hand, some people may have put off vacations and worked overtime to take advantage of the temporary incentive. On the other hand, no one would alter career plans, and no business would restructure its work environment, in response to an incentive that would soon disappear. A permanent change in the marginal tax rate could have either a larger or a smaller incentive effect than a temporary change.

Lump-sum taxes

lump-sum tax
a tax that is the same amount for every person

Suppose the government imposes a tax of $4000 on everyone; that is, everyone owes the same amount, regardless of earnings or any actions that a person might take. Such a tax is called a **lump-sum tax.**

A lump-sum tax shows clearly the difference between average and marginal tax rates. For a taxpayer with income of $20 000, the average tax rate of a $4000 lump-sum tax is 20 per cent; for a taxpayer with income of $40 000, the average tax rate is 10 per cent. For both taxpayers, the marginal tax rate is zero because an additional dollar of income would not change the amount of tax owed.

A lump-sum tax is the most efficient tax possible. Because a person's decisions do not alter the amount owed, the tax does not distort incentives and, therefore, does not cause deadweight losses.

IN THE NEWS . . .

REFORMING THE TAX SCHEME TO ALLEVIATE POVERTY

In the text we saw how poor people could face very high effective marginal tax rates due to the loss of benefits as their income rises. This is unfair. It also increases unemployment. For people caught in a poverty trap, it is better not to work or to work less hours. In this article, ANU economist Andrew Leigh argues that this could be avoided with some good old-fashioned targeted policies.

Help the poor, and cut taxes

by Andrew Leigh

This week's Treasury tussle featured an unusual moment, in which the debate turned to past reforms, and Peter Costello acknowledged the benefits of the macroeconomic reforms undertaken by previous Labor governments. But missed in the discussion was a chance to also consider another major shift of that era – from universal welfare to a carefully-targeted social safety net.

During the 1980s and early-1990s, means-tested public pensions, childcare benefits, and housing benefits meant that we could be proud of the way we looked after our poorest, while maintaining one of the lowest tax burdens in the developed world.

Unfortunately, the past decade has seen a steady slide away from that philosophy. With a few exceptions (such as the improved targeting of private school funding), much of the increased social spending in Australia has been devoted to universal benefits. The First Home Owner Grant, Private Healthcare Rebate, and Family Tax Benefit Part B are just three examples of policies that have enormous budgetary costs, but minimal social impact. By international standards, Australia's welfare system is still reasonably well targeted, but we're headed in the wrong direction.

Peter Saunders, from the Centre for Independent Studies, calls middle-class benefits the 'tax/welfare churn'. But this implies that the problem is simply one of moving money around. In fact, because taxes have an efficiency cost, each dollar raised in taxes reduces economic output. Estimates of the efficiency cost varies, but the best recent estimate for the 'deadweight burden' in Australia is around 20 cents in the dollar. Perhaps 'tax, burn and churn' would be a better description.

Since most middle-class welfare benefits would probably fail an economic cost-benefit test, why does a government that touts its economic credentials support it? Because middle-class welfare always passes the political cost–benefit test. The well-hewn median voter theorem has a simple prediction: Two parties competing for office will focus most of their energies on winning the support of the voter in the middle of the distribution. Targeted welfare may be good economics, but middle-class welfare is good politics. (As John Howard said last year, 'People like getting a cheque from the government.')

For its part, the Labor Party have raised questions in parliament about the wisdom of universal benefits, but have resisted calls to scrap such programs. Part of the explanation lies in the belief that universal programs are likely to be more politically robust than targeted ones: If we can put in place a program that will endure, why not accept a little waste? Yet the evidence for this argument is mixed. When the next recession hits, and the 'razor gang' comes to scrutinise at government spending, will they really preserve all those low-impact universal programs?

Moreover, there is a strong progressive argument in favour of targeted spending over universal benefits: It is more likely to reduce inequality. Rather than giving a flat education credit for two-thirds of families, why not pour more resources into improving the life chances of the neediest children?

Perhaps what we need is a new campaign advertisement, paid for by 'Australians for Helping the Poor *and* Lowering Taxes'. The commercial could start with a simple visual depiction of how middle class welfare works. A taxpayer hands over five $20 notes. The government representative calmly burns one of them, and hands back the remaining four.

>>

The voiceover could then point out that people enjoy getting the Baby Bonus, but there's little evidence that scrapping it would affect fertility rates or the wellbeing of new parents (camera shows new parents installing a plasma television). By contrast, an Indigenous child born today can expect to live as long as a non-Indigenous child born at the time of Federation (camera shows scenes from one of a dozen disadvantaged communities). If we scrapped the $1.1 billion Baby Bonus, we could put half the proceeds into tax cuts, and the other half into a series of randomised policy trials of programs designed to improve Indigenous health. Fade to black.

What is striking about middle-class welfare is that it offends values that both right and left should hold dear. Since our first major tax uprising at Eureka, Australians have resisted oppressive levels of taxation, and demanded that governments take no more from us than they need. At the same time, we have supported the underdog, reaching out a generous helping hand to those who need it most. A targeted welfare state fulfils both these principles. Middle-class welfare offends them both.

Commentators have long derided politicians who 'spin' the truth. But maybe the ones we need to watch for are those who spin our tax dollars out of our wallets and back in again – wasting 20 cents in the dollar along the way.

Source: Andrew Leigh/*Australian Financial Review*, 1 November 2007.

Because everyone can easily calculate the amount owed and because there is no benefit in hiring tax agents and accountants, the lump-sum tax imposes a minimal administrative burden on taxpayers.

If lump-sum taxes are so efficient, why do we rarely observe them in the real world? The reason is that efficiency is only one goal of the tax system. A lump-sum tax would take the same amount from the poor and the rich, an outcome most people would view as unfair. To understand the tax systems that we observe, we must therefore consider the other major goal of tax policy – equity.

Q

What is meant by the efficiency of a tax system? What can make a tax system inefficient?

Taxes and equity

Taxes have often been at the centre of heated (and sometimes violent) debate. Taxes contributed to the outbreak of the English civil wars in the 1640s. The Boston Tea Party in 1773, when American colonists dumped imported tea into Boston harbour, was a protest against high British taxes. The Eureka Stockade rebellion at Ballarat in 1854 was sparked by discontent over miners' licence fees.

Debate over tax policy is rarely fuelled by questions of efficiency. Instead, debate arises from disagreements over how the tax burden should be distributed. A US senator once mimicked the public debate with this rhyme:

Don't tax you.
Don't tax me.
Tax that fella behind the tree.

Of course, if we are to rely on the government to provide some of the goods and services we want, taxes must fall on someone. In this section we consider the equity of a tax system. How should the burden of taxes be divided among the population? How do we evaluate whether a tax system is fair?

Everyone agrees that the tax system should be equitable, but there is much disagreement about what equity means and how the equity of a tax system can be judged.

The benefits principle

One principle of taxation, called the **benefits principle**, states that people should pay taxes based on the benefits they receive from government services. This principle tries to make public goods similar to private goods. It seems fair that a person who often goes to the pictures pays more in total for picture tickets than a person who rarely goes. Similarly, a person who gets great benefit from a public good should pay more for it than a person who gets little benefit.

benefits principle
the idea that people should pay taxes based on the benefits they receive from government services

Petrol tax, for instance, is sometimes justified using the benefits principle. Road construction and maintenance are expensive and it seems only fair that those who use the roads should pay these costs. Because those who buy petrol are the same people who use the roads, a petrol tax might be viewed as a fair way to pay for this government service.

The benefits principle can also be used to argue that wealthy citizens should pay higher taxes than poorer ones. Why? Simply because the wealthy benefit more from public services. Consider, for example, the benefits of police protection from theft. Citizens with much to protect get greater benefit from police than do those with less to protect. Therefore, according to the benefits principle, the wealthy should contribute more than the poor to the cost of maintaining the police force. The same argument can be used for many other public services, such as fire protection, national defence and the court system.

It is even possible to use the benefits principle to argue for anti-poverty programs funded by taxes on the wealthy. As we discussed in chapter 11, people may prefer living in a society without poverty, suggesting that anti-poverty programs are a public good. If the wealthy place a greater dollar value on this public good than the middle class do, perhaps just because they have more to spend, then, according to the benefits principle, they should be taxed more heavily to pay for these programs.

The benefits principle is sometimes called 'user pays'. For government-provided services such as water, sewerage and, in some states, electricity, it seems fair that those who use relatively more of the service pay relatively more for the service.

The ability-to-pay principle

Another way to evaluate the equity of a tax system is called the **ability-to-pay principle**, which states that taxes should be levied on a person according to how well that person can shoulder the burden. This principle is sometimes justified by the claim that all citizens should make an 'equal sacrifice' to support the government. The magnitude of a person's sacrifice, however, depends not only on the size of the individual's tax payment but also on that person's income and other circumstances. A $1000 tax paid by a poor person may require a larger sacrifice than a $10 000 tax paid by a rich person.

ability-to-pay principle
the idea that taxes should be levied on a person according to how well that person can shoulder the burden

The ability-to-pay principle leads to two corollary notions of equity: **vertical equity** and **horizontal equity**. Vertical equity states that taxpayers with a greater ability to pay taxes should contribute a larger amount. Horizontal equity states that taxpayers with similar abilities to pay should contribute the same amount. Although these notions of equity are widely accepted, applying them to evaluate a tax system is rarely straightforward.

vertical equity
the idea that taxpayers with a greater ability to pay taxes should pay larger amounts

horizontal equity
the idea that taxpayers with similar abilities to pay taxes should pay the same amount

Vertical equity

If taxes are based on ability to pay, then richer taxpayers should pay more than poorer taxpayers. But how much more should the rich pay? Much of the debate over tax policy concerns this question.

Table 12.4 Three tax systems

	Proportional tax		Regressive tax		Progressive tax	
Income	*Amount of tax*	*Percentage of income*	*Amount of tax*	*Percentage of income*	*Amount of tax*	*Percentage of income*
$50 000	$12 500	25	$15 000	30	$10 000	20
100 000	25 000	25	25 000	25	25 000	25
200 000	50 000	25	40 000	20	60 000	30

proportional tax
a tax for which high-income and low-income taxpayers pay the same fraction of income

regressive tax
a tax for which high-income taxpayers pay a smaller fraction of their income than do low-income taxpayers

progressive tax
a tax for which high-income taxpayers pay a larger fraction of their income than do low-income taxpayers

Search me!
▸ regressive tax

Search me!
▸ progressive tax

Consider the three tax systems in Table 12.4. In each case, taxpayers with higher incomes pay more. Yet the systems differ in how quickly taxes rise with income. The first system is called **proportional** because all taxpayers pay the same fraction of income. The second system is called **regressive** because high-income taxpayers pay a smaller fraction of their income, even though they pay a larger amount. The third system is called **progressive** because high-income taxpayers pay a larger fraction of their income.

Which of these three tax systems is most fair? There is no obvious answer and economic theory does not offer any help in trying to find one. Equity, like beauty, is in the eye of the beholder.

Horizontal equity

If taxes are based on ability to pay, then similar taxpayers should pay similar amounts of taxes. But what determines if two taxpayers are similar? People differ in many ways. To evaluate whether a tax code is horizontally equitable, one must determine which differences are relevant to a taxpayer's ability to pay and which differences are not.

Suppose the Smith and Jones families each have an income of $100 000. The Smiths have no children, but Mr Smith has an illness that causes medical expenses of $10 000. The Joneses are in good health, but they have four children. Two of the Jones children are in private secondary schools, generating school fees of $20 000. Would it be fair for these two families to pay the same tax because they have the same income? Would it be fairer to give the Smiths a tax break to help them offset their high medical expenses? Would it be fairer to give the Joneses a tax break to help them with their education expenses?

CASESTUDY

How the burden of taxes is distributed

Much of the debate over tax policy concerns whether the wealthy pay their fair share of taxes. There is no purely objective way to make this judgement. In evaluating this issue for yourself, however, it is useful to know how much families with different incomes pay under the current tax system.

Table 12.5 shows how some selected taxes are distributed among income classes. To construct this table, people were ranked according to their household's income and placed into five groups of equal size, called quintiles. The first row of the table shows the average weekly income of each person's household, which includes private income and direct social security payments. The poorest one-fifth had an average income of $295.00 per week; the richest one-fifth had an average income of $2063.60 per week.

The other rows compare the distribution of personal income taxes and selected indirect taxes among these five groups. The poorest group paid 1.4 per cent of their income as personal income tax

Table 12.5 The burden of selected Australian taxes, 2001–02

	Persons by quintile of equivalent household disposable income				
	Lowest 20%	Second	Third	Fourth	Highest 20%
Gross household income ($ per week)	295.0	609.1	929.6	1288.9	2063.6
Taxes paid as share of gross income (%):					
Personal income tax	1.4	8.5	15.8	19.9	26.0
Selected indirect taxes	20.5	14.1	12.3	10.3	8.9

Calculated from: National Centre for Social and Economic Modelling, *The Distribution of Taxes and Government Benefits in Australia.* Ann Harding, Rachel Lloyd and Neil Warren. 2004. www.natsem.canberra.edu.au/publications/papers/cps/cp04/2004_008/cp2004_008.pdf

on average, but paid 20.5 per cent of their income on indirect taxes. The richest group paid 26.0 per cent of their income as personal income tax on average, but only 8.9 per cent of their income went to pay indirect taxes.

The table shows that personal income tax payments are progressive. Richer households tend to pay more of their income as personal income tax. But the degree of progressivity is less than we would expect simply by looking at the personal income tax rates. This suggests that higher income earners are able to use various loopholes in the tax system to reduce income tax payments.

Although income tax payments are progressive, the table shows that indirect taxes are regressive when expressed as a share of income. Poor households tend to spend most of their income and save little and indirect taxes apply to consumption. As a result, the poor pay a relatively larger share of their income on indirect taxes than do the rich.

There are no easy answers to these questions. In practice, the Australian income tax system is filled with special provisions that alter an individual's tax based on specific circumstances.

CASESTUDY

Who should pay for higher education?

When Gough Whitlam's Labor government was elected in 1972, one of its main policies was to remove university fees. Instead of students or their families paying for university education, the state would pay through tax revenue.

Supporters of state-paid university education argued that it would help the poor and disadvantaged. If they had to pay fees, students from poor families might be excluded from university even if they had achieved excellent results at secondary school. In addition, they argued that education was like a public good. Society gains from having more doctors, architects and engineers, so it is only fair that society pays.

Opponents of state-paid university education argued that most students going to university are from relatively well-off families. Having the government pay university fees would be inequitable because poor families would be paying through their taxes to educate well-off students. They also disputed the public good argument. Society may gain from having trained professionals, but this is a private benefit that we pay for when we visit the doctor or employ an engineer. As university graduates tend to earn high wages, it seems unfair that taxpayers should pay twice for this private benefit.

>>

In 1989, the Hawke Labor government introduced an innovative program to share the costs of university education between the student and the taxpayer. To avoid disadvantaging poor students, no student would have to pay fees before beginning university. Instead, the government would 'lend' the student the money. Further, to make sure that those students who received mainly private benefits from university education paid more of the costs of this education, loan repayments would be based on income that students earn after completing their studies.

This higher education contribution scheme, or HECS, was a world first. It has been modified since its introduction. For example, under the original HECS, students' future payments per course did not depend on which courses they enrolled in each year. The Howard Coalition government altered this in 1997 so that students in Law and Medicine paid more HECS than students in Computing and Economics, who themselves paid more than Arts and Nursing students. Under the original HECS scheme, students repaid their HECS loan only when their annual income exceeded the Australian average – approximately $32 000. This threshold has been changed a number of times and in 2004 students had to begin to repay their HECS debt even if their income was only $25 348 per year. From 2005, each university had the discretion to set higher HECS charges, subject to government limitations, but the HECS income repayment threshold was raised to $35 000 per year. The repayment threshold rises over time. In 2011–12 it is $44 912.

The success of the HECS scheme has led to its imitation in other countries. England introduced a similar scheme for university funding in 1998. The HECS scheme has also been extended in Australia, and is now part of the broader higher education loan program (HELP). The original scheme only applied to undergraduate degrees, but in 2002 the government introduced a similar scheme for postgraduate students. Although there is argument over the policy details of the HECS/HELP scheme, most economists would agree that it has created a more equitable split of the burden of higher education between the student and the taxpayer.

Tax incidence and tax equity

Tax incidence – the study of who bears the burden of taxes – is central to evaluating tax equity. As we first saw in chapter 6, the person who bears the burden of a tax is not always the person who gets the tax bill from the government. Because taxes alter supply and demand, they alter equilibrium prices. As a result, they affect people beyond those who, according to statute, actually pay the tax. When evaluating the vertical and horizontal equity of any tax, it is important to take account of these indirect effects.

Many discussions of tax equity ignore the indirect effects of taxes and are based on what economists derisively call the *flypaper theory* of tax incidence. According to this theory, the burden of a tax, like a fly on flypaper, sticks wherever it first lands. That assumption, however, is rarely valid.

For example, a person not trained in economics might argue that a tax on sports cars is vertically equitable because most buyers of sports cars are wealthy. Yet if these buyers can easily substitute other luxuries for sports cars, then a tax on sports cars might reduce only the sale of these cars. In the end, the burden of the tax will fall more on those who make and sell sports cars than on those who buy them. Because most workers who make and sell cars are not wealthy, the equity of a tax on sports cars could be quite different from what the flypaper theory indicates.

IN THE NEWS . . .

THE HECS EXPERIENCE

Australia was a world leader in using government income-contingent loans to pay for higher education. In this article, Ross Gittins looks at plans by Bruce Chapman, one of the designers of the HECS scheme and a Professor at the Australian National University, to extend it beyond higher education.

One HECS of a broader solution

by Ross Gittins

Has it ever occurred to you that one of the main roles of government is to help you manage some of the many risks you face in living your life? It probably hasn't. But when you think about it, it's obvious. That's what the welfare state is for.

There's a risk, for instance, of you being suddenly struck down by a major illness or accident. In a developing country, such an eventuality could reduce you and your family to penury. For us, however, a public ambulance whips you off to hospital, where Medicare ensures you get fixed up without charge.

Were the accident to have happened at work, of course, your expenses – including living expenses – are covered by the workers' compensation insurance the government obliges your employer to take out. Were some other accident to leave you physically or mentally incapacitated, the welfare state ensures you don't starve by providing you with a disability support pension.

Say you can't find a job to support yourself and your family. The welfare state keeps you off the breadline by giving you the dole. At least until WorkChoices, permanent employees who found their services no longer needed could expect a redundancy payment to help tide them over.

Or, say you just become too old to keep working. The government manages the problem by giving you the age pension to live on. Too frugal for your taste? That's why, of late, the government has made it compulsory for 9 per cent of your salary to be put away for you in superannuation savings.

All these things – and many more – are examples of the way governments are ready to manage the risks we run in everyday life. You could also say governments have road rules and speed limits to minimise the risk in crossing the road.

In his book *Government Managing Risk*, published by Routledge, Professor Bruce Chapman, of the Australian National University, expounds on a relatively new instrument governments can use to manage risk, 'income-contingent loans'. These are particularly useful for providing default insurance and consumption smoothing.

Never heard of it? Of course you have. You know it as HECS – the higher education contribution scheme. If you've always thought of HECS as just an impost on our young people you haven't understood its subtleties. The impost is the government's requirement that uni students make a contribution towards the cost of their tuition.

In some other countries, most would have to take out a commercial loan to pay their tuition fees. But not here – here they're able to pay with HECS. One advantage of HECS is that the interest rate charged is no higher than the inflation rate – usually only 2 or 3 per cent a year.

But the other great attraction of HECS is that repayments are income-contingent. That is, they vary with your income. You don't have to make any repayments until your income exceeds about $38 000 a year and thereafter the size of your repayments rises with your income according to a sliding scale.

With an ordinary commercial loan, you're required to make fixed, predetermined repayments come hell or high water. With HECS, if your income falls for any reason, the size of your repayments falls, too. If you lost your job and couldn't find another, so that your income fell back below $38 000, your repayments would cease for as long as you remained below the threshold.

This is why income-contingent loans are said to involve default insurance. Being unable to make repayments doesn't put you in default of the loan contract. And you can see how

>>

repayments that vary with your income help to smooth your consumption spending.

In these ways HECS, being a form of income-contingent loan, turns out to be an instrument government uses to help students manage the risks they run in incurring debts to pay their tuition fees.

One of the great practical advantages of HECS from the Government's perspective is that repayments are collected compulsorily through the tax system, thus reducing collection costs and bad debts.

HECS is an Australian invention. Since we introduced it in 1989 it has been copied in six other countries, including New Zealand, South Africa, Chile, Thailand and Britain.

With help from various contributors, Chapman makes the point that income-contingent loans could be used for many purposes beside tuition fees.

One possible use is for drought assistance. Rather than being given grants, farmers could receive income-contingent loans. The speed with which their incomes recovered after the drought would determine the speed with which the loan was repaid.

Shifting from grants to loans would be fairer. Why? Because the average owner of a drought-stricken property is a lot wealthier than the average taxpayer is. The farmers' problem isn't poverty, it is lack of ready capital to tide them over. Income-contingent loans would give help when it was needed while allowing repayment when it could be afforded.

Income-contingent loans would reduce the risk of farmers defaulting on their commercial loans and allow them to smooth their consumption between the good years and the bad.

Income-contingent loans could also be used to help people pay fines imposed on them by criminal courts. Courts can be reluctant to impose fines – or reluctant to impose fines as high as they should be – because they know the offenders don't have the money to pay.

So the court knows it will probably end up having to jail the offender for non-payment. But not if an income-contingent loan were available.

Another, highly pertinent application would be to use income-contingent loans to help low-income households facing eviction or mortgage default because of a temporary shortage of income due to job loss. As they found employment and their income recovered they could begin repaying the loan.

You see how these various applications involve tiding people over when they're hit by sudden but temporary shocks. You see, too, how much of what governments do involves helping people manage and minimise the risks attendant on daily life.

It would help for all of us – politicians and bureaucrats, voters and taxpayers – to see more clearly that this is what governments do. It then becomes easier to see how much use we could be making of assistance by means of income-contingent loans.

Source: Ross Gittins/*Sydney Morning Herald*, 28 March 2007.

CASESTUDY

Who pays company income tax?

Company income tax provides a good example of the importance of tax incidence for tax policy. Company taxes are popular among voters. After all, a company is not a person. Voters are always eager to have their taxes reduced and have some impersonal corporation pick up the tab.

But before deciding that the company tax is a good way for the government to raise revenue, we should consider who bears the burden of the tax. This is a difficult question on which economists disagree, but one thing is certain – *people pay all taxes*. When the government levies a tax on a company, the company is more like a tax collector than a taxpayer. The burden of the tax ultimately falls on people – the owners, customers or workers of the firm.

Many economists believe that workers and customers bear much of the burden of company tax. To see why, consider an example. Suppose that the Australian government decides to raise the tax on the income earned by car companies. At first, this tax hurts the owners of the car companies, who receive less profit. But, over time, these owners will respond to the tax. Because producing cars is less profitable, they invest less in building new car factories.

Instead, they invest their wealth in other ways – for example, by buying larger houses or by building factories in other industries or other countries. With fewer car factories, the supply of cars declines, as does the demand for car workers. Thus, a tax on companies making cars causes the price of cars to rise and the wages of car workers to fall.

The company tax shows how dangerous the flypaper theory of tax incidence can be. Company tax is popular in part because it appears to be paid by rich corporations. Yet those who bear the ultimate burden of the tax – the customers and workers of firms – are often not rich. If the true incidence of the company tax were more widely known, this tax might be less popular among voters.

Q

Explain the benefits principle and the ability-to-pay principle. What are vertical equity and horizontal equity? Why is studying tax incidence important for determining the equity of a tax system?

Conclusion: The trade-off between equity and efficiency

Almost everyone agrees that equity and efficiency are the two most important goals of a tax system. But these two goals often conflict. Many proposed changes to the tax laws increase efficiency while reducing equity, or increase equity while reducing efficiency. People disagree about tax policy often because they attach different weights to these two goals.

Over the past decade, Australia has experienced a major change in its tax system. The introduction of the GST has changed the way tax is collected in Australia. It has also changed the relationship between state and federal governments. While the federal government collects the GST revenue, it passes it on to the state governments. The old Australian tax system had many problems. It relied too heavily on income taxation, it was complex and had high compliance costs, and it was unfair and inequitable. At the same time, it has also been claimed that the new tax system is too complex, has even higher compliance costs and is even more inequitable.

Economics alone cannot determine the best way to balance the goals of efficiency and equity. This issue involves political philosophy as well as economics. But economists do have an important role in the political debate over tax policy; they can shed light on the trade-offs that society faces and can help us avoid policies that sacrifice efficiency without any benefit in terms of equity.

Summary

- Australian governments raise revenue using various taxes. The most important taxes for the federal government are individual and company income taxes. The federal government also collects the goods and services tax (GST), and passes the revenue from this tax to the state governments. The most important taxes for state and local governments are payroll taxes and municipal rates.
- The efficiency of a tax system refers to the costs it imposes on taxpayers. There are two costs of taxes beyond the transfer of resources from the taxpayer to the government. The first is the distortion in the allocation of resources that arises as taxes alter incentives and behaviour. The second is the administrative burden of complying with the tax laws.
- The equity of a tax system concerns whether the tax burden is distributed fairly among the population. According to the benefits principle, it is fair for people to pay taxes based on the benefits they receive from the government. According to the ability-to-pay principle, it is fair for people to pay taxes based on their capacity to handle the financial burden. When evaluating the equity of a tax system, it is important to remember a lesson from the study of tax incidence – the distribution of tax burdens is not the same as the distribution of tax bills.
- When considering changes in the tax laws, policymakers often face a trade-off between efficiency and equity. Much of the debate over tax policy arises because people give different weights to these two goals.

Key concepts

ability-to-pay principle
average tax rate
benefits principle
budget deficit
budget surplus
horizontal equity
lump-sum tax
marginal tax rate
progressive tax
proportional tax
regressive tax
vertical equity

Questions for review

1. Over the past several decades, has the federal government grown more or less slowly than the rest of the economy?
2. What are the two most important sources of revenue for the federal government?
3. Explain how the federal government avoids taxing company profits twice.
4. Why is the burden of a tax to taxpayers greater than the revenue received by the government?
5. Why might a GST lead to less distortion than an income tax? Could it lead to more distortion? How?
6. Give two arguments why wealthy taxpayers should pay more taxes than poor taxpayers.
7. What is the concept of horizontal equity and why is it hard to apply?

Problems and applications

1. When debating the merits of the GST, welfare groups like ACOSS argued that necessities, such as food and clothing, should be excluded from the new tax. When the tax was introduced, fresh food was excluded. Discuss the merits of this exclusion. Consider both efficiency and equity.

2 Federal government spending in Australia grew in the years between the 1950s and the 1980s, but has remained relatively constant as a share of GDP since the early 1980s. What changes in our economy and our society might explain this trend?

3 Each year the Federal Treasurer and the Minister for Finance circulate the budget papers. Using a recent issue of the budget papers at your library, answer the following questions and provide some numbers to support your answers.

   a Table 12.3 is based on the federal government's budget for 2010–11. It shows the budgeted spending for the 2010–11 financial year. Some types of spending are a larger part of total budget spending today than in the past. One example is social security and welfare. What other types of spending have been increasing as a percentage of total federal government spending? What types of spending have fallen as a percentage of total spending?

   b We noted that governments operate either a budget surplus or a budget deficit. How has the federal government deficit/surplus changed over recent years? How does this compare with the state governments?

   c The budget papers present figures on a wide range of social security programs. Look at three programs and analyse how spending on these programs has changed over recent years. Why might spending on individual programs change?

4 Explain how people's behaviour is affected by the following features of the tax laws.

   a Contributions to charity are tax-deductible.

   b Sales of beer are taxed.

   c Realised capital gains are taxed, but accrued gains are not (when people own shares that rise in value, they have an 'accrued' capital gain – if they sell the shares, they have a 'realised' gain).

   d State governments charge stamp duty on the sale and purchase of houses – the tax increases with the sale price of the house.

5 In 1997, the federal government changed the HECS charge for university courses. Before 1997, Arts courses were the same price as Economics courses. Since 1997, Arts courses have been cheaper than Economics courses. Explain how this change might affect enrolments in Arts and Economics courses.

6 We noted in the chapter how low-income earners could face effective marginal tax rates of 80 per cent or more. Consider people on unemployment benefits. If they accept an extra hour's work, they lose some of their benefits. What do you think is the effect of this feature of the unemployment benefit scheme on the labour supply of people on unemployment benefits? Explain.

7 Under Australian tax laws, interest payments on home mortgages are not tax-deductible. Under US tax laws, these interest payments are tax-deductible. How would this difference in tax laws alter consumer behaviour between the United States and Australia? Explain.

8 Categorise each of the following funding schemes as examples of the benefits principle or the ability-to-pay principle.

   a Visitors to some national parks pay an entrance fee.

   b Local property taxes support the maintenance of local roads.

   c The Victorian government charged a lump-sum tax on each household in the early 1990s to help reduce state debt.

9 Goods that are necessities often have highly inelastic demands. However, poor people spend relatively more of their income on necessities. What are the efficiency implications of introducing a tax on necessities? What are the equity implications? Would such a tax be progressive or regressive?

10 Any income tax schedule embodies two types of tax rates – average tax rates and marginal tax rates.

a The average tax rate is defined as total taxes paid divided by income. For the proportional tax system presented in Table 12.4, what are the average tax rates for people earning $50 000, $100 000 and $200 000? What are the corresponding average tax rates in the regressive and progressive tax systems?

b The marginal tax rate is defined as the extra taxes paid on additional income divided by the increase in income. Calculate the marginal tax rate for the proportional tax system as income rises from $50 000 to $100 000. Calculate the marginal tax rate as income rises from $100 000 to $200 000. Calculate the corresponding marginal tax rates for the regressive and progressive tax systems.

c Describe the relationship between average tax rates and marginal tax rates for each of the three tax systems. In general, which rate is relevant for someone deciding whether to accept a job that pays slightly more than her current job? Which rate is relevant for judging the vertical equity of a tax system?

11 What is the efficiency justification for taxing consumption rather than income? Is a consumption tax likely to be more or less progressive than an income tax? Explain your answer.

12 Under Australian tax law, the employer pays a payroll tax on employee wages. Does this legal obligation for payment indicate the true incidence of these taxes? Explain.

13 In the 1980s the government introduced a 'fringe benefits tax'. If employees received personal benefits from their employer, such as restaurant meals, then the company had to pay tax on this benefit. Advocates of the fringe benefits tax argued that it would stop relatively wealthy people avoiding tax by receiving benefits rather than money income. But the tax was strongly opposed by restaurant owners and employees. Explain.

Search me!

Search me!

When accessing information about microeconomics use the following keywords in any combinations you require:

- progressive tax
- regressive tax

CourseMate

CourseMate

For more multimedia resources and activities on economics, visit the Economics CourseMate website.

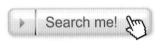

PART FIVE
Firm behaviour and the organisation of industry

13

The costs of production

Learning objectives

In this chapter you will:

- examine what items are included in a firm's costs of production
- analyse the link between a firm's production process and its total costs
- learn the meaning of average total cost and marginal cost and how they are related
- consider the shape of a typical firm's cost curves
- examine the relationship between short-run and long-run costs.

The goods and services you enjoy every day are produced by firms. You might drive a car produced by Toyota with tyres produced by Bridgestone, while listening to a radio produced by Sony. The economy is made up of thousands of firms. Some firms, such as these three companies, are large; they employ thousands of workers and have thousands of shareholders who share in the firms' profits. Other firms, such as the local hairdresser or newsagent, are small; they employ only a few workers and are owned by a single person or family.

In previous chapters we used the supply curve to summarise firms' production decisions. According to the law of supply, firms are willing to produce and sell a greater quantity of a good when the price of the good is high and this response leads to a supply curve that slopes upwards. For analysing many questions, the law of supply is all you need to know about firm behaviour.

In this chapter and the ones that follow, we examine firm behaviour in more detail. This topic will give you a better understanding of what decisions lie behind the supply curve in a market. In addition, it will introduce you to a part of economics called *industrial organisation* – the study of how firms' decisions regarding prices and quantities depend on the market conditions they face. The suburb in which you live, for instance, may have several fish and chip shops but only one electricity retailer. How does this difference in the number of firms affect the prices in these markets and the efficiency of the market outcomes? The field of industrial organisation considers exactly this question.

Before we turn to these issues, however, we need to discuss the costs of production. All firms, from Virgin Blue airlines to your local café, incur costs as they make the goods and services they sell. As we will see in the coming chapters, a firm's costs are a key determinant of its production and pricing decisions. In this chapter, we define some of the variables that economists use to measure a firm's costs and we consider the relationships among them.

What are costs?

We begin our discussion of costs at Poh's Cake Factory. Poh, the owner of the firm, buys flour, sugar and other cake ingredients. She also buys the mixers and ovens, and she hires workers to run this equipment. She then sells the resulting cakes to consumers. By examining some of the issues that Poh faces in her business, we can learn some lessons about costs that apply to all firms in the economy.

Total revenue, total cost and profit

We begin with the firm's objective. To understand what decisions a firm makes, we must understand what it is trying to do. It is conceivable that Poh started her firm because of an altruistic desire to provide the world with cakes or, perhaps, out of love for the cake business. More likely, however, Poh started her business to make money. Economists normally assume that the goal of a firm is to maximise profit and they find that this assumption works well in most cases.

What is a firm's profit? The amount that the firm receives for the sale of its output (cakes) is called its **total revenue (for a firm)**. The amount that the firm pays to buy inputs (flour, sugar, workers, ovens etc.) is called its **total cost**. Poh gets to keep any revenue that is not needed to cover costs. **Profit** is a firm's total revenue minus its total cost. That is:

$$\text{Profit} = \text{Total revenue} - \text{Total cost}$$

Poh's objective is to make her firm's profit as large as possible.

To see how a firm goes about maximising profit, we must consider fully how to measure its total revenue and its total cost. Total revenue is the easy part – it equals the quantity of output the firm

total revenue (for a firm)
the amount a firm receives for the sale of its output

total cost
the amount a firm pays to buy the inputs into production

profit
total revenue minus total cost

produces times the price at which it sells its output. If Poh produces 10 000 cakes and sells them at $2 a cake, her total revenue is $20 000. In contrast, the measurement of a firm's total costs is more subtle.

Costs as opportunity costs

When measuring costs at Poh's Cake Factory or any other firm, it is important to keep in mind one of the *Ten Lessons from Economics in* chapter 1 – the cost of something is what you give up to get it. Recall that the *opportunity cost* of an item refers to all those things that must be forgone to acquire that item. When economists speak of a firm's cost of production, they include all the opportunity costs of making its output of goods and services.

A firm's opportunity costs of production are sometimes obvious and sometimes less so. When Poh pays $1000 for flour, that $1000 is an opportunity cost because Poh can no longer use that $1000 to buy something else. Similarly, when Poh hires workers to make the cakes, the wages she pays are part of the firm's costs. These costs are *explicit.* In contrast, some of a firm's opportunity costs are *implicit.* Imagine that Poh is a skilled painter and could earn $100 per hour from her artwork. For every hour that Poh works at her cake factory she gives up $100 in income and this forgone income is also part of her costs. The total cost of Poh's business is the sum of the explicit costs and the implicit costs.

This distinction between explicit and implicit costs highlights an important difference between how economists and accountants analyse a business. Economists are interested in studying how firms make production and pricing decisions, so they include all opportunity costs when measuring costs. In contrast, accountants have the job of keeping track of the money that flows into and out of firms. As a result, they measure the explicit costs but often ignore the implicit costs.

The difference between economists and accountants is easy to see in the case of Poh's Cake Factory. When Poh gives up the opportunity to earn money by painting, her accountant will not count this as a cost of her cake business. Because no money flows out of the business to pay for this cost, it never shows up on the accountant's financial statements. An economist, however, will count the forgone income as a cost because it will affect the decisions that Poh makes in her cake business. For example, if Poh's earnings from her artwork rose from $100 to $500 per hour, she might decide that running her cake business is too costly and choose to shut down the factory in order to become a full-time artist.

The cost of capital as an opportunity cost

An important implicit cost of almost every business is the opportunity cost of the financial capital that has been invested in the business. Suppose, for instance, that Poh used $300 000 of her savings to buy her cake factory from the previous owner. If Poh had instead left this money deposited in a savings account that pays an interest rate of 5 per cent, she would have earned $15 000 per year. To own her cake factory, therefore, Poh has given up $15 000 a year in interest income. This $15 000 is one of the opportunity costs of Poh's business.

As we have already noted, economists and accountants treat costs differently and this is especially true in their treatment of the cost of capital. An economist views the $15 000 in interest income that Poh gives up every year as a cost of her business, even though it is an implicit cost. Poh's accountant, however, will not show this $15 000 as a cost because no money flows out of the business to pay for it.

To explore further the difference between economists and accountants, let's change the example slightly. Suppose now that Poh did not have the entire $300 000 to buy the factory but, instead, used

$100 000 of her own savings and borrowed $200 000 from a bank at an interest rate of 5 per cent. Poh's accountant, who measures only explicit costs, will now count the $10 000 interest paid on the bank loan every year as a cost because this amount of money now flows out of the firm. In contrast, according to an economist, the opportunity cost of owning the business is still $15 000. The opportunity cost equals the interest on the bank loan (an explicit cost of $10 000) plus the forgone interest on savings (an implicit cost of $5000).

Economic profit versus accounting profit

Now let's return to the firm's objective – profit. Because economists and accountants measure costs differently, they also measure profit differently. An economist measures a firm's *economic profit* as the firm's total revenue minus all the opportunity costs of producing the goods and services sold. An accountant measures the firm's *accounting profit* as the firm's total revenue minus only the firm's explicit costs.

Figure 13.1 summarises this difference. Notice that, because the accountant ignores the implicit costs, accounting profit is larger than economic profit. For a business to be profitable from an economist's standpoint, total revenue must cover all the opportunity costs, both explicit and implicit.

Economic profit is an important concept because it is what motivates the firms that supply goods and services. As we will see, a firm making positive economic profit will stay in business. It is covering all its opportunity costs and has some revenue left to reward the firm owners. When a firm is making economics losses (that is, when economic profits are negative), the business owners are failing to make enough to cover all the costs of production. Unless conditions change, the firm owners will eventually close the business down and exit the industry. To understand how industries evolve, we need to keep an eye on economic profit.

Figure 13.1 **Economists versus accountants**

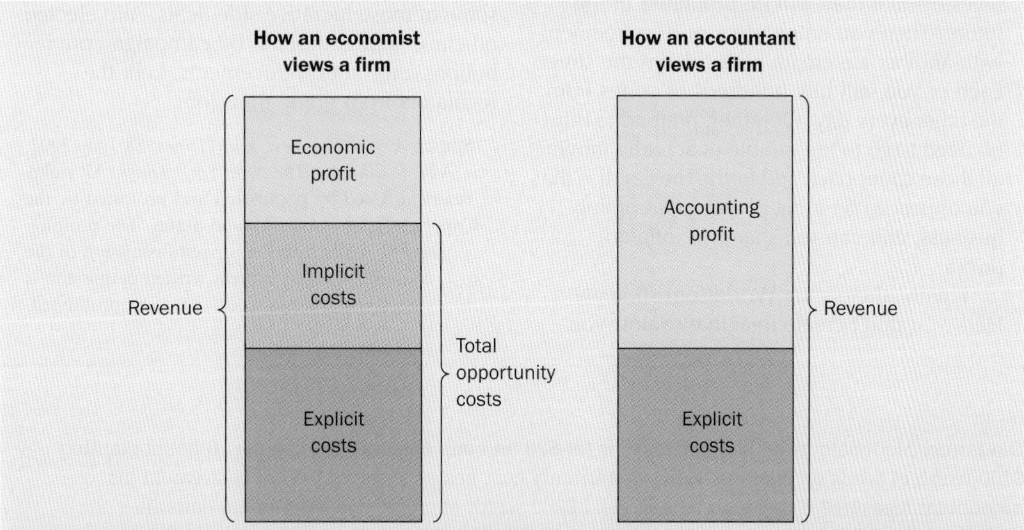

Economists include all opportunity costs when analysing a firm, whereas accountants measure only explicit costs. Therefore, economic profit is smaller than accounting profit.

IN THE NEWS . . .

TRUE PROFIT VERSUS FICTITIOUS PROFIT

The analysis of firm behaviour begins with the measurement of revenue, costs and profits. In the early 2000s, this topic made the news when several major companies were revealed to have lied about these key measures of performance. This article outlines how accounting measures can be manipulated by an unscrupulous business.

Flavors of fraud

by Paul Krugman

So you're the manager of an ice cream parlor. It's not very profitable, so how can you get rich? Each of the big business scandals uncovered so far suggests a different strategy for executive self-dealing.

First there's the Enron strategy. You sign contracts to provide customers with an ice cream cone a day for the next 30 years. You deliberately underestimate the cost of providing each cone; then you book all the projected profits on those future ice cream sales as part of this year's bottom line. Suddenly you appear to have a highly profitable business, and you can sell shares in your store at inflated prices.

Then there's the Dynegy strategy. Ice cream sales aren't profitable, but you convince investors that they will be profitable in the future. Then you enter into a quiet agreement with another ice cream parlor down the street: Each of you will buy hundreds of cones from the other every day. Or rather, pretend to buy – no need to go to the trouble of actually moving all those cones back and forth. The result is that you appear to be a big player in a coming business, and can sell shares at inflated prices ...

Finally, there's the WorldCom strategy. Here you don't create imaginary sales; you make real costs disappear, by pretending that operating expenses – cream, sugar, chocolate syrup – are part of the purchase price of a new refrigerator. So your unprofitable business seems, on paper, to be a highly profitable business that borrows money only to finance its purchases of new equipment. And you can sell shares at inflated prices.

Oh, I almost forgot: How do you enrich yourself personally? The easiest way is to give yourself lots of stock options, so that you benefit from those inflated prices ... I'm not saying that all U.S. corporations are corrupt. But it's clear that executives who want to be corrupt have faced few obstacles. Auditors weren't interested in giving a hard time to companies that gave them lots of consulting income; bank executives weren't interested [in] giving a hard time to companies that, as we learned in the Enron case, let them in on some of those lucrative side deals. And elected officials, kept compliant by campaign contributions and other inducements, kept the regulators from doing their job.

Source: From *The New York Times*, 28 June 2002, p. A27.

Q Old farmer McDonald gives bagpipe lessons for $20 an hour. One day, he spends 10 hours planting $100 worth of seeds on his farm. What opportunity cost has he incurred? What cost would his accountant measure? If these seeds will yield $200 worth of crops, does McDonald earn an accounting profit? Does he earn an economic profit?

Production and costs

Firms incur costs when they buy inputs to produce the goods and services that they plan to sell. In this section we examine this link between the firm's production process and its total cost. Once again, we consider Poh's Cake Factory.

In the analysis that follows, we make an important simplifying assumption: We assume that the size of Poh's factory is fixed and that Poh can vary the quantity of cake produced only by changing the number of workers. This assumption is realistic in the short run, but not in the long run. That is, Poh cannot build a larger factory overnight, but she can do so within a year or so. This analysis, therefore, should be viewed as describing the production decisions that Poh faces in the short run. We examine the relationship between costs and time horizon more fully later in the chapter.

The production function

Table 13.1 shows how the quantity of cakes Poh's factory produces per hour depends on the number of workers. If there are no workers in the factory, Poh produces no cakes. When there is one worker, she produces 50 cakes. When there are two workers, she produces 90 cakes, and so on. Figure 13.2 presents a graph of these two columns of numbers. The number of workers is on the horizontal axis, and the number of cakes produced is on the vertical axis. This relationship between the quantity of inputs (workers) and quantity of output (cakes) is called the **production function**.

production function
the relationship between quantity of inputs used to make a good and the quantity of output of that good

One of the *Ten Lessons from Economics* introduced in chapter 1 is that rational people think at the margin. As we will see in future chapters, this idea is the key to understanding how firms decide how many workers to hire and how much output to produce. To take a step towards these decisions, the third column in Table 13.1 gives the marginal product of a worker. The **marginal product** of any input into production is the increase in the quantity of output obtained from an additional unit of that input. When the number of workers goes from one to two, cake production increases from 50 to 90, so the marginal product of the second worker is 40 cakes. And when the number of workers goes from two to three, cake production increases from 90 to 120, so the marginal product of the third worker is 30 cakes.

marginal product
the increase in output that arises from an additional unit of input

Notice that, as the number of workers increases, the marginal product declines. The second worker has a marginal product of 40 cakes, the third worker has a marginal product of 30 cakes, and the

Table 13.1 A production function and total cost: Poh's Cake Factory

Number of workers	Output (quantity of cakes produced per hour)	Marginal product of labour	Cost of factory ($)	Cost of workers ($)	Total cost of inputs (cost of factory + cost of workers) ($)
0	0	—	30	$0	30
1	50	50	30	10	40
2	90	40	30	20	50
3	120	30	30	30	60
4	140	20	30	40	70
5	150	10	30	50	80

Figure 13.2 Poh's production function

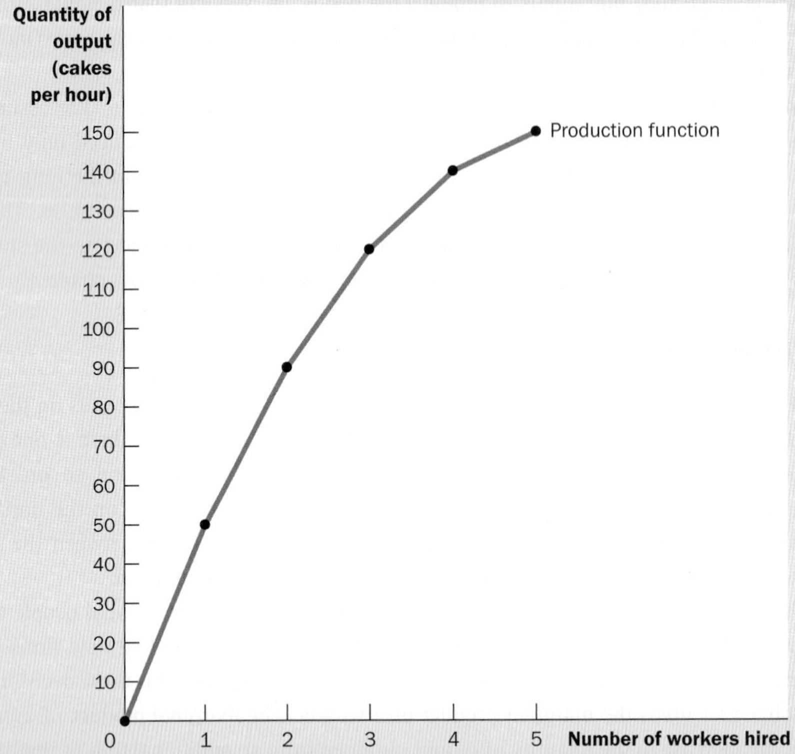

A production function shows the relationship between the number of workers hired and the quantity of output produced. Here the number of workers hired (on the horizontal axis) is from the first column in Table 13.1, and the quantity of output produced (on the vertical axis) is from the second column. The production function gets flatter as the number of workers increases, which reflects diminishing marginal product.

diminishing marginal product
the property whereby the marginal product of an input declines as the quantity of the input increases

fourth worker has a marginal product of 20 cakes. This property is called **diminishing marginal product.** At first, when only a few workers are hired, they have easy access to Poh's kitchen equipment. As the number of workers increases, additional workers have to share equipment and work in more crowded conditions. Hence, as more and more workers are hired, each additional worker contributes less to the production of cakes.

Diminishing marginal product is also apparent in Figure 13.2. The production function's slope ('rise over run') tells us the change in Poh's output of cakes ('rise') for each additional input of labour ('run'). That is, the slope of the production function measures the marginal product of a worker. As the number of workers increases, the marginal product declines, and the production function becomes flatter.

From the production function to the total-cost curve

The last three columns of Table 13.1 show Poh's cost of producing cakes. In this example, the cost of Poh's factory is $30 per hour and the cost of a worker is $10 per hour. If she hires one worker, her total cost is $40. If she hires two workers, her total cost is $50, and so on. The information in this table shows how the number of workers Poh hires is related to the quantity of cakes she produces and to her total cost of production.

Our goal in the next several chapters is to study firms' production and pricing decisions. For this purpose, the most important relationship in Table 13.1 is between quantity produced (in the second column) and total costs (in the sixth column). Figure 13.3 graphs these two columns of data with the quantity produced on the horizontal axis and total cost on the vertical axis. This graph is called the *total-cost curve.*

Now compare the total-cost curve in Figure 13.3 with the production function in Figure 13.2. These two curves are opposite sides of the same coin. The total-cost curve gets steeper as the amount produced rises, whereas the production function gets flatter as production rises. These changes in slope occur for the same reason. High production of cakes means that Poh's kitchen is crowded with many workers. Because the kitchen is crowded, each additional worker adds less to production, reflecting diminishing marginal product. Therefore, the production function is relatively flat. But now turn this logic around: When the kitchen is crowded, producing an additional cake requires a lot of additional labour and is thus very costly. Therefore, when the quantity produced is large, the total-cost curve is relatively steep.

Figure 13.3 **Poh's total-cost curve**

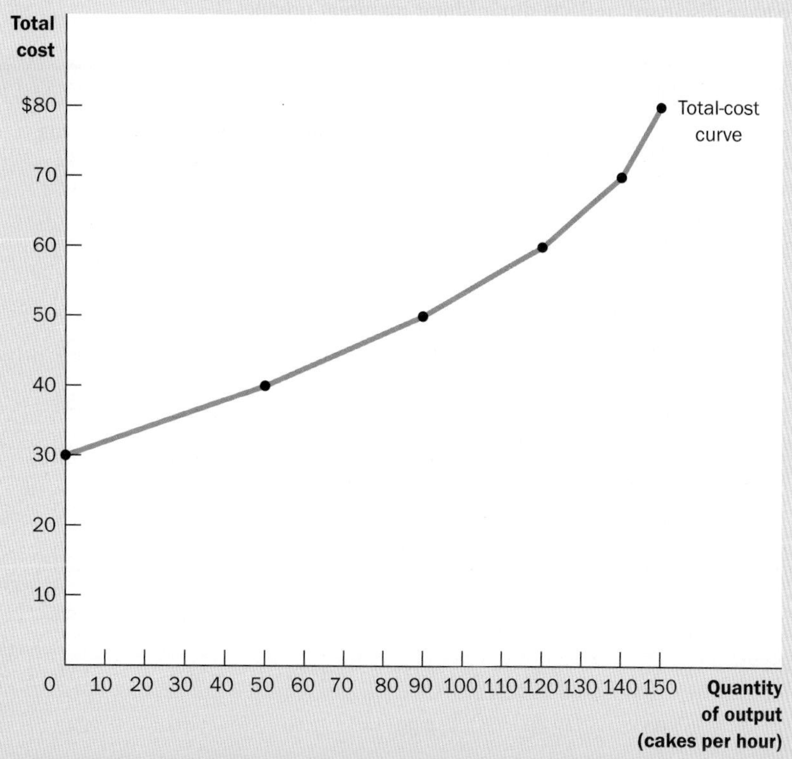

A total-cost curve shows the relationship between the quantity of output produced and total cost of production. Here the quantity of output produced (on the horizontal axis) is from the second column in Table 13.1, and the total cost (on the vertical axis) is from the sixth column. The total-cost curve gets steeper as the quantity of output increases because of diminishing marginal product.

Q If Farmer Jones plants no seeds on his farm, he gets no crop. If he plants one bag of seeds, he gets 5 kg of wheat. If he plants two bags, he gets 8 kg. If he plants three bags, he gets 10 kg. A bag of seeds costs $10 and seeds are his only cost. Use these data to graph the farmer's production function and total-cost curve. Explain their shapes.

The various measures of cost

Our analysis of Poh's Cake Factory demonstrated how a firm's total cost reflects its production function. From data on a firm's total cost, we can derive several related measures of cost, which will turn out to be useful when we analyse production and pricing decisions in future chapters. To see how these related measures are derived, we consider the example in Table 13.2. This table presents cost data on Poh's neighbour – George's Coffee Shop.

The first column of the table shows the number of cups of coffee that George might produce, ranging from 0 to 10 cups per hour. The second column shows George's total cost of producing coffee. Figure 13.4 plots George's total-cost curve. The quantity of coffee (from the first column) is on the horizontal axis, and total cost (from the second column) is on the vertical axis. George's total-cost curve has a shape similar to Poh's. In particular, it becomes steeper as the quantity produced rises, which (as we have discussed) reflects diminishing marginal product.

Table 13.2 The various measures of cost: George's Coffee Shop

Quantity of coffee (cups per hour)	Total cost ($)	Fixed cost ($)	Variable cost ($)	Average fixed cost ($)	Average variable cost ($)	Average total cost ($)	Marginal cost ($)
0	3.00	3.00	0.00	—	—	—	—
1	3.30	3.00	0.30	3.00	0.30	3.30	0.30
2	3.80	3.00	0.80	1.50	0.40	1.90	0.50
3	4.50	3.00	1.50	1.00	0.50	1.50	0.70
4	5.40	3.00	2.40	0.75	0.60	1.35	0.90
5	6.50	3.00	3.50	0.60	0.70	1.30	1.10
6	7.80	3.00	4.80	0.50	0.80	1.30	1.30
7	9.30	3.00	6.30	0.43	0.90	1.33	1.50
8	11.00	3.00	8.00	0.38	1.00	1.38	1.70
9	12.90	3.00	9.90	0.33	1.10	1.43	1.90
10	15.00	3.00	12.00	0.30	1.20	1.50	2.10

Figure 13.4 George's total-cost curve

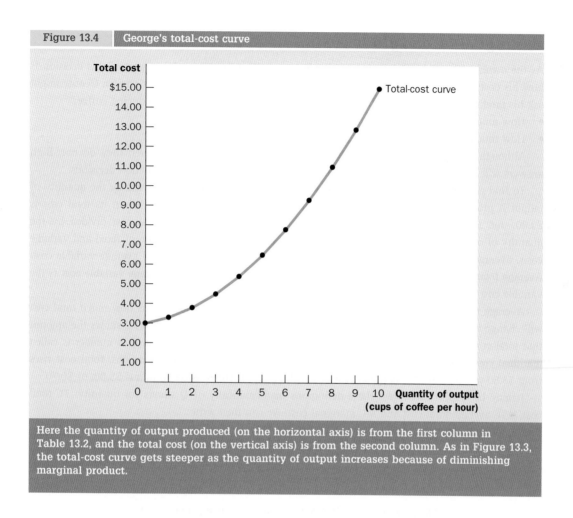

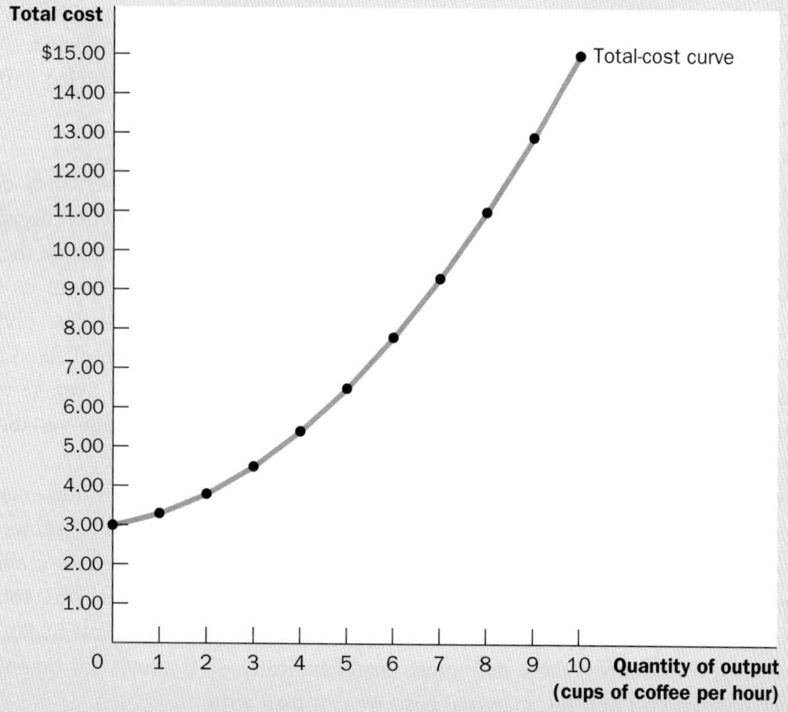

Here the quantity of output produced (on the horizontal axis) is from the first column in Table 13.2, and the total cost (on the vertical axis) is from the second column. As in Figure 13.3, the total-cost curve gets steeper as the quantity of output increases because of diminishing marginal product.

Fixed and variable costs

George's total cost can be divided into two types. Some costs, called **fixed costs**, do not vary with the quantity of output produced. They are incurred even if the firm produces nothing at all. George's fixed costs include the rent he pays because this cost is the same regardless of how much coffee he produces. Similarly, if George needs to hire a full-time bookkeeper to pay bills, regardless of the quantity of coffee produced, the bookkeeper's salary is a fixed cost. The third column in Table 13.2 shows George's fixed cost, which in this example is $3.00 per hour.

fixed costs
costs that do not vary with the quantity of output produced

Some of the firm's costs, called **variable costs**, change as the firm alters the quantity of output produced. George's variable costs include the cost of coffee beans, milk and sugar. The more coffee George makes, the more of these items he needs to buy. Similarly, if George has to hire more workers to make more coffee, the salaries of these workers are variable costs. The fourth column of the table shows George's variable cost. The variable cost is 0 if he produces nothing, $0.30 if he produces one cup of coffee, $0.80 if he produces two cups of coffee, and so on.

variable costs
costs that vary with the quantity of output produced

A firm's total cost is the sum of fixed and variable costs. In Table 13.2, total cost in the second column equals fixed cost in the third column plus variable cost in the fourth column.

Average and marginal cost

As the owner of his firm, George has to decide how much to produce. A key part of this decision is how his costs will vary as he changes the level of production. In making this decision, George might ask his production supervisor the following two questions about the cost of producing coffee:

- How much does it cost to make the typical cup of coffee?
- How much does it cost to increase production of coffee by one cup?

Although at first these two questions might seem to have the same answer, they do not. Both answers will turn out to be important for understanding how firms make production decisions.

average total cost
total cost divided by the quantity of output

average fixed cost
fixed costs divided by the quantity of output

average variable cost
variable costs divided by the quantity of output

marginal cost
the increase in total cost that arises from an extra unit of production

To find the cost of the typical unit produced, we would divide the firm's costs by the quantity of output it produces. For example, if the firm produces two cups of coffee per hour, its total cost is \$3.80, and the cost of the typical cup of coffee is \$3.80/2, or \$1.90. Total cost divided by the quantity of output is called **average total cost**. Because total cost is just the sum of fixed and variable costs, average total cost can be expressed as the sum of average fixed cost and average variable cost. **Average fixed cost** is the fixed cost divided by the quantity of output and **average variable cost** is the variable cost divided by the quantity of output.

Average total cost tells us the cost of the typical unit, but it does not tell us how much total cost will change as the firm alters its level of production. The last column in Table 13.2 shows the amount that total cost rises when the firm increases production by one unit of output. This number is called **marginal cost**. For example, if George increases production from two to three cups, total cost rises from \$3.80 to \$4.50, so the marginal cost of the third cup of coffee is \$4.50 minus \$3.80, or \$0.70.

It may be helpful to express these definitions mathematically. If Q stands for quantity, TC total cost, ATC average total cost and MC marginal cost, we can then write:

$$\text{Average Total Cost} = \text{Total cost/Quantity}$$
$$ATC = TC \,/\, Q$$

and

$$\text{Marginal Cost} = \text{(Change in total cost)/(Change in quantity)}$$
$$MC = \Delta TC/\Delta Q$$

Here Δ, the Greek letter delta, represents the change in a variable. These equations show how average total cost and marginal cost are derived from total cost. *Average total cost tells us the cost of a typical unit of output if total cost is divided evenly over all the units produced. Marginal cost tells us the increase in total cost that arises from producing an additional unit of output.* As we will see more fully in the next chapter, business managers like George need to keep in mind the concepts of average total cost and marginal cost when deciding how much of their product to supply to the market.

Cost curves and their shapes

Just as in previous chapters we found graphs of supply and demand useful when analysing the behaviour of markets, we will find graphs of average and marginal cost useful when analysing the behaviour of firms. Figure 13.5 graphs George's costs using the data from Table 13.2. The horizontal axis measures the quantity the firm produces, and the vertical axis measures marginal and average costs. The graph shows four curves: average total cost (ATC), average fixed cost (AFC), average variable cost (AVC) and marginal cost (MC).

Figure 13.5 George's average-cost and marginal-cost curves

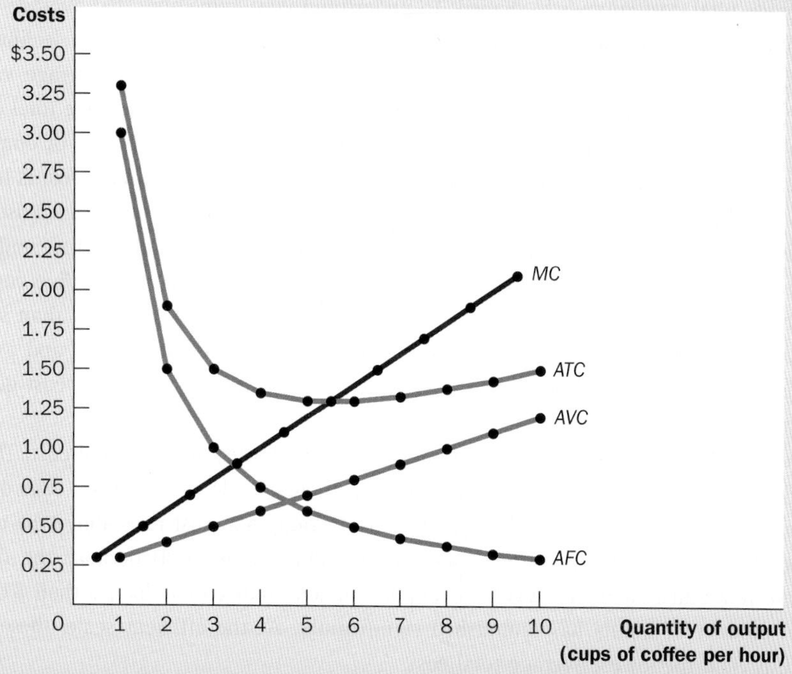

This figure shows the average total cost (*ATC*), average fixed cost (*AFC*), average variable cost (*AVC*) and marginal cost (*MC*) for George's Coffee Shop. All of these curves are obtained by graphing the data in Table 13.2. These cost curves show three features that are considered common: (1) marginal cost rises with the quantity of output; (2) the average-total-cost curve is U-shaped; (3) the marginal-cost curve crosses the average-total-cost curve at the minimum of average total cost.

The cost curves shown here for George's Coffee Shop have shapes that are common to the cost curves of many firms in the economy. Let's examine three features of these curves in particular: the shape of marginal cost, the shape of average total cost and the relationship between marginal and average total cost.

Rising marginal cost

George's marginal cost rises with the quantity of output produced. This reflects the property of diminishing marginal product. When George produces a small quantity of coffee he has few workers and much of his equipment is not being used. Because he can easily put these idle resources to use, the marginal product of an extra worker is high and the marginal cost of an extra cup of coffee is small. In contrast, when George is producing large quantities of coffee, his shop is crowded with workers and most of his equipment is fully utilised. George can produce more coffee by adding workers, but these new workers have to work in crowded conditions and may have to wait to use the equipment. Therefore, when the quantity of coffee produced is already high, the marginal product of an extra worker is low and the marginal cost of an extra cup of coffee is large.

U-shaped average total cost

George's average-total-cost curve is U-shaped. To understand why, remember that average total cost is the sum of average fixed cost and average variable cost. Average fixed cost always declines as output rises because the fixed cost is getting spread over a larger number of units. Average variable cost typically rises as output increases because of diminishing marginal product. Average total cost reflects the shapes of both average fixed cost and average variable cost. At very low levels of output, such as one or two cups per hour, average total cost is high. Even though average variable cost is low, average fixed cost is high because the fixed cost is spread over only a few units. As output increases, the fixed cost is spread over more units of output. Average fixed cost declines, rapidly at first and then more slowly. As a result, average total cost also declines until the firm's output reaches five cups of coffee per hour, when average total cost is $1.30 per cup. When the firm produces more than six cups per hour, however, the increase in average variable cost becomes the dominant force and average total cost starts rising. The tug of war between average fixed cost and average variable cost generates the U-shape in average total cost.

The bottom of the U-shape occurs at the quantity that minimises average total cost. This quantity is called the **efficient scale** of the firm. For George, the efficient scale is five or six cups of coffee per hour. If he produces more or less than this amount, his average total cost rises above the minimum of $1.30. At lower levels of output, average total cost is higher than $1.30 because the fixed cost is spread over so few units. At higher levels of output, average total cost is higher than $1.30 because the marginal product of inputs has diminished significantly. At the efficient scale, these two forces are balanced to yield the lowest average total cost.

efficient scale
the quantity of output that minimises average total cost

Search me!

▸ efficient scale

The relationship between marginal cost and average total cost

If you look at Figure 13.5 (or back at Table 13.2), you will see something that may be surprising at first. *Whenever marginal cost is less than average total cost, average total cost is falling. Whenever marginal cost is greater than average total cost, average total cost is rising.* This feature of George's cost curves is not a coincidence from the particular numbers used in the example – it is true for all firms.

To see why, consider an analogy to the game of cricket. Average total cost is like a batting average. Marginal cost is like the score that a player makes in the next game. If a player scores below his average in the next game, then his batting average will fall. If a player scores above his average in the next game, this high marginal score will raise his batting average. If a player scores exactly his average in the next game, his batting average will not change. The mathematics of average and marginal costs is exactly the same as the mathematics of average and marginal scores in cricket or any other sport.

This relationship between average total cost and marginal cost has an important corollary – *the marginal-cost curve crosses the average-total-cost curve at its minimum.* Why? At low levels of output, marginal cost is below average total cost, so average total cost is falling. But after the two curves cross, marginal cost rises above average total cost. For the reason we have just discussed, average total cost must start to rise at this level of output. Hence, this point of intersection is the minimum of average total cost. As you will see in the next chapter, this point of minimum average total cost plays a key role in the analysis of competitive firms.

Typical cost curves

In the examples we have examined so far, the firms exhibit diminishing marginal product and, therefore, rising marginal cost at all levels of output. In many firms, however, diminishing marginal product does

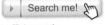

Table 13.3 The various measures of cost: Big Bob's Bagel Bin

Quantity of bagels (per hour)	Total cost ($)	Fixed cost ($)	Variable cost ($)	Average fixed cost ($)	Average variable cost ($)	Average total cost ($)	Marginal cost ($)
0	2.00	2.00	0.00	—	—	—	—
1	3.00	2.00	1.00	2.00	1.00	3.00	1.00
2	3.80	2.00	1.80	1.00	0.90	1.90	0.80
3	4.40	2.00	2.40	0.67	0.80	1.47	0.60
4	4.80	2.00	2.80	0.50	0.70	1.20	0.40
5	5.20	2.00	3.20	0.40	0.64	1.04	0.40
6	5.80	2.00	3.80	0.33	0.63	0.96	0.60
7	6.60	2.00	4.60	0.29	0.66	0.95	0.80
8	7.60	2.00	5.60	0.25	0.70	0.95	1.00
9	8.80	2.00	6.80	0.22	0.76	0.98	1.20
10	10.20	2.00	8.20	0.20	0.82	1.02	1.40
11	11.80	2.00	9.80	0.18	0.89	1.07	1.60
12	13.60	2.00	11.60	0.17	0.97	1.14	1.80
13	15.60	2.00	13.60	0.15	1.05	1.20	2.00
14	17.80	2.00	15.80	0.14	1.13	1.27	2.20

Figure 13.6 Big Bob's cost curves

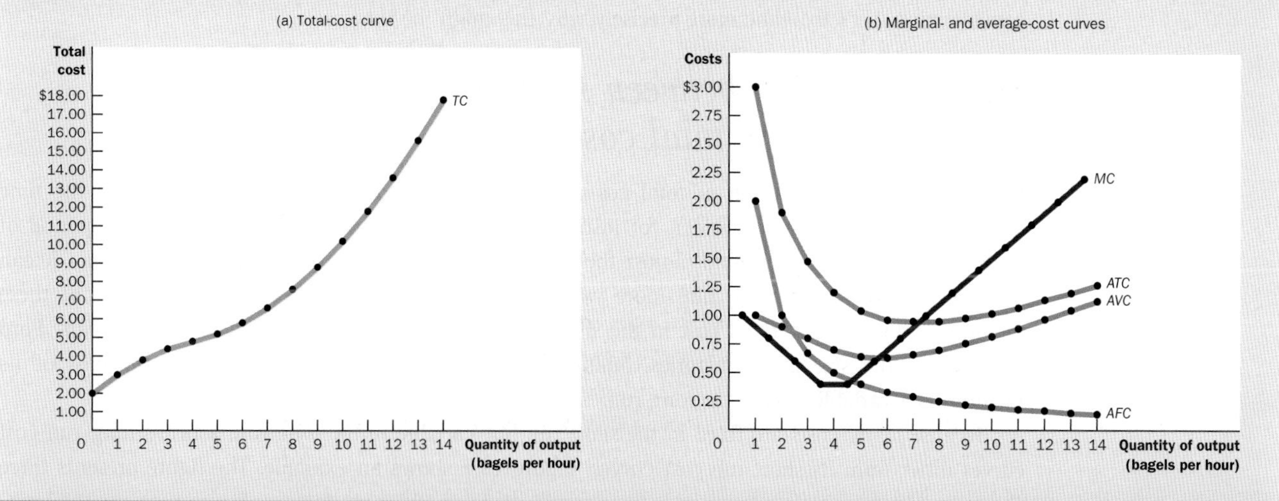

Many firms, like Big Bob's Bagel Bin, experience increasing marginal product before diminishing marginal product and, therefore, have cost curves like those in this figure. Panel (a) shows how total cost (*TC*) depends on the quantity produced. Panel (b) shows how average total cost (*ATC*), average fixed cost (*AFC*), average variable cost (*AVC*) and marginal cost (*MC*) depend on the quantity produced. These curves are derived by graphing the data from Table 13.3. Note that marginal cost and average variable cost fall for a while before starting to rise.

not start to occur immediately after the first worker is hired. Depending on the production process, the second or third worker might have higher marginal product than the first because a team of workers can divide tasks and work more productively than a single worker. Such firms would first experience increasing marginal product for a while before diminishing marginal product sets in.

Table 13.3 shows the cost data for such a firm, called Big Bob's Bagel Bin. These data are graphed in Figure 13.6. Panel (a) shows how total cost (*TC*) depends on the quantity produced, and panel (b) shows average total cost (*ATC*), average fixed cost (*AFC*), average variable cost (*AVC*) and marginal cost (*MC*). In the range of output from zero to four bagels per hour, the firm experiences increasing marginal product and the marginal-cost curve falls. After five bagels per hour, the firm starts to experience diminishing marginal product and the marginal-cost curve starts to rise. This combination of increasing and diminishing marginal product also makes the average-variable-cost curve U-shaped.

Despite these differences from our previous example, the cost curves shown here share the three properties that are most important to remember:

- Marginal cost eventually rises with the quantity of output.
- The average-total-cost curve is U-shaped.
- The marginal-cost curve crosses the average-total-cost curve at the minimum of average total cost.

Q

Suppose Honda's total cost of producing four cars is $225 000 and its total cost of producing five cars is $250 000. What is the average total cost of producing five cars? What is the marginal cost of the fifth car?

Draw the marginal-cost curve and the average-total-cost curve for a typical firm and explain why these curves cross where they do.

Costs in the short run and in the long run

We noted at the beginning of this chapter that a firm's costs might depend on the time horizon under consideration. Let's examine more precisely why this might be the case.

The relationship between short-run and long-run average total cost

For many firms, the division of total costs between fixed and variable costs depends on the time horizon being considered. Consider, for instance, a car manufacturer, such as Ford. Over a period of only a few months, Ford cannot adjust the number or size of its car factories. The only way it can produce additional cars is to hire more workers at the factories it already has. The cost of these factories is, therefore, a fixed cost in the short run. In contrast, over a period of several years, Ford can expand the size of its factories, build new factories or close old ones. Thus, the cost of its factories is a variable cost in the long run.

Because many costs are fixed in the short run but variable in the long run, a firm's long-run cost curves differ from its short-run cost curves. Figure 13.7 shows an example. The figure presents three short-run average-total-cost curves – for a small, medium and large factory. It also presents the long-run average-total-cost curve. As the firm moves along the long-run curve, it is adjusting the size of the factory to the quantity of production.

This graph shows how short-run and long-run costs are related. The long-run average-total-cost curve is a much flatter U-shape than the short-run average-total-cost curve. In addition, the

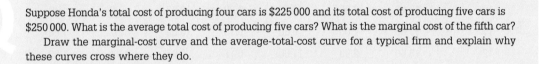

Figure 13.7 Average total cost in the short and long run

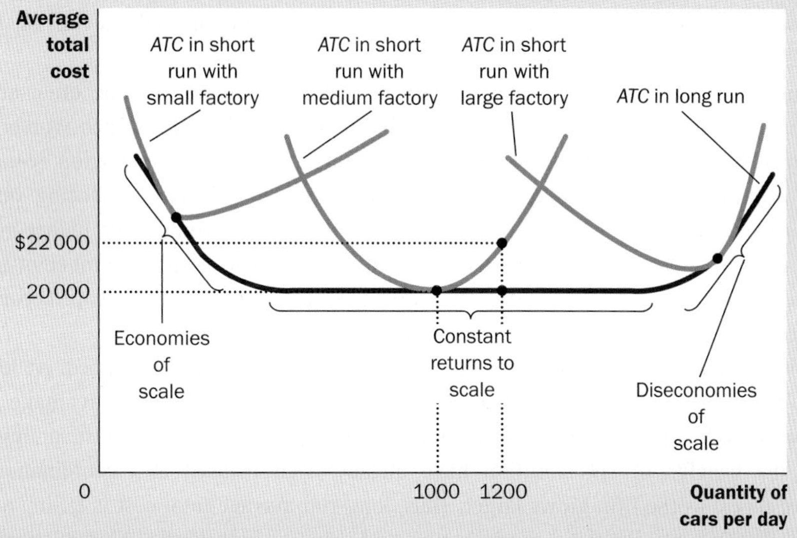

Because fixed costs are variable in the long run, the average-total-cost curve in the short run differs from the average-total-cost curve in the long run.

long-run curve lies below all of the short-run curves. These properties arise because of the greater flexibility firms have in the long run. In essence, in the long run, the firm gets to choose which short-run curve it wants to use. But in the short-run, it has to use whatever short-run curve it chose in the past.

The figure shows an example of how a change in production alters costs over different time horizons. Suppose that Ford currently uses a medium-sized factory and produces 1000 cars per day. If Ford wants to increase production from 1000 to 1200 cars per day, it has no choice in the short run but to hire more workers at its existing medium-sized factory. Because of diminishing marginal product, average total cost rises from $20 000 to $22 000 per car. In the long run, however, Ford can expand both the size of the factory and its workforce, and average total cost remains at $20 000.

How long does it take for a firm to get to the long run? The answer depends on the firm. It can take a year or longer for a major manufacturing firm, such as a car company, to expand its existing factory or to build a larger factory. By contrast, a person operating a stall at the local Trash and Treasure market can increase or decrease the size of their stall on a week-by-week basis. There is no single answer for how long it takes a firm to adjust its production facilities.

Economies and diseconomies of scale

The shape of the long-run average-total-cost curve conveys important information about the technology for producing a good. When long-run average total cost declines as output increases, there are said to be **economies of scale**. When long-run average total cost rises as output increases,

economies of scale
the property whereby long-run average total cost falls as the quantity of output increases

diseconomies of scale the property whereby long-run average total cost rises as the quantity of output increases

constant returns to scale the property whereby long-run average total cost stays the same as the quantity of output changes

Search me!

▸ economies of scale

there are said to be **diseconomies of scale** . When long-run average total cost does not vary with the level of output, there are said to be **constant returns to scale**. In this example, Ford has economies of scale at low levels of output, constant returns to scale at intermediate levels of output and diseconomies of scale at high levels of output.

What might cause economies or diseconomies of scale? Economies of scale often arise because higher production levels allow specialisation among workers, which permits each worker to become better at his or her assigned tasks. For instance, modern assembly-line production requires a large number of workers, each specialising in a particular task. If Ford were producing only a small quantity of cars, it could not take advantage of this approach and would have higher average total cost. Diseconomies of scale can arise because of coordination problems that are inherent in any large organisation. The more cars Ford produces the more stretched its management team becomes and the less effective the managers become at keeping costs down.

The analysis shows why long-run average-total-cost curves are often U-shaped. At low levels of production, the firm benefits from increased size because it can take advantage of greater specialisation. Coordination problems, meanwhile, are not yet acute. By contrast, at high levels of production, the benefits of specialisation have already been realised and coordination problems become more severe as the firm grows larger. Thus, long-run average total cost is falling at low levels of production because of increasing specialisation and rising at high levels of production because of increasing coordination problems.

Q

If Boeing produces nine jets per month, its long-run total cost is $9.0 million per month. If it produces 10 jets per month, its long-run total cost is $9.5 million per month. Does Boeing exhibit economies or diseconomies of scale?

Conclusion

The purpose of this chapter has been to develop some tools that we can use to study how firms make production and pricing decisions. You should now understand what economists mean by the term costs and how costs vary with the quantity of output a firm produces. To refresh your memory, Table 13.4 summarises some of the definitions we have encountered.

By themselves, a firm's cost curves do not tell us what decisions the firm will make. But, as you will begin to see in the next chapter, they are an important component of that decision.

Table 13.4 The many types of cost: A summary

Term	Definition	Mathematical description
Explicit costs	Costs that require an outlay of money by the firm	—
Implicit costs	Costs that do not require an outlay of money by the firm	—
Fixed costs	Costs that do not vary with the quantity of output produced	FC
Variable costs	Costs that do vary with the quantity of output produced	VC
Total cost	The market value of all the inputs that a firm uses in production	$TC = FC + VC$
Average fixed cost	Fixed costs divided by the quantity of output	$AFC = FC/Q$
Average variable cost	Variable costs divided by the quantity of output	$AVC = VC/Q$
Average total cost	Total cost divided by the quantity of output	$ATC = TC/Q$
Marginal cost	The increase in total cost that arises from an extra unit of production	$MC = \Delta TC/\Delta Q$

fyi

Lessons from a pin factory

'Jack of all trades, master of none.' This well-known saying helps explain why firms sometimes experience economies of scale. A person who tries to do everything usually ends up doing nothing very well. If a firm wants its workers to be as productive as they can be, it is often best to give them a limited task that they can master. But this is possible only if a firm employs a large number of workers and produces a large quantity of output.

In his celebrated book, *An Inquiry into the Nature and Causes of the Wealth of Nations*, Adam Smith described an example of this based on a visit he made to a pin factory. Smith was impressed by the specialisation among the workers that he observed and the resulting economies of scale. He wrote:

> One man draws out the wire, another straightens it, a third cuts it, a fourth points it, a fifth grinds it at the top for receiving the head; to make the head requires two or three distinct operations; to put it on is a peculiar business; to whiten it is another; it is even a trade by itself to put them into paper.

Smith reported that because of this specialisation, the pin factory produced thousands of pins per worker every day. He conjectured that if the workers had chosen to work separately, rather than as a team of specialists, 'they certainly could not each of them make twenty, perhaps not one pin a day'. In other words, because of specialisation, a large pin factory could achieve higher output per worker and lower average cost per pin than a small pin factory.

The specialisation that Smith observed in the pin factory is prevalent in the modern economy. If you want to build a house, for instance, you could try to do all the work yourself. But most people turn to a builder, who in turn hires carpenters, plumbers, electricians, painters and many other types of worker. These workers specialise in particular jobs, and this allows them to become better at their jobs than if they were generalists. Indeed, the use of specialisation to achieve economies of scale is one reason modern societies are as prosperous as they are.

Summary

- The goal of firms is to maximise profit, which equals total revenue minus total cost.
- When analysing a firm's behaviour, it is important to include all the opportunity costs of production. Some of the opportunity costs, such as the wages a firm pays its workers, are explicit. Other opportunity costs, such as the wages the firm owner gives up by working in the firm rather than taking another job, are implicit. Economic profit takes both explicit and implicit costs into account, whereas accounting profit considers only explicit costs.
- A firm's costs reflect its production process. A typical firm's production function gets flatter as the quantity of an input increases, displaying the property of diminishing marginal product. As a result, a firm's total-cost curve gets steeper as the quantity produced rises.
- A firm's total costs can be divided between fixed costs and variable costs. Fixed costs are costs that do not change when the firm alters the quantity of output produced. Variable costs are costs that do change when the firm alters the quantity of output produced.
- From a firm's total cost, two related measures of cost are derived. Average total cost is total cost divided by the quantity of output. Marginal cost is the amount by which total cost would rise if output were increased by one unit.
- When analysing firm behaviour, it is often useful to graph average total cost and marginal cost. For a typical firm, marginal cost rises with the quantity of output. Average total cost first falls as output increases and then rises as output increases further. The marginal-cost curve always crosses the average-total-cost curve at the minimum of average total cost.
- A firm's costs often depend on the time horizon being considered. In particular, many costs are fixed in the short run but variable in the long run. As a result, when the firm changes its level of production, average total cost may rise more in the short run than in the long run.

Key concepts

average fixed cost
average total cost
average variable cost
constant returns to scale
diminishing marginal product
diseconomies of scale
economies of scale
efficient scale
fixed costs
marginal cost
marginal product
production function
profit
total cost
total revenue (for a firm)
variable costs

Questions for review

1. What is the relationship between a firm's total revenue, profit and total cost?
2. Give an example of an opportunity cost that an accountant might not count as a cost. Why would the accountant ignore this cost?
3. Define total cost, average total cost and marginal cost. How are they related?
4. Draw the marginal-cost and average-total-cost curves for a typical firm. Explain why the curves have the shapes that they do and why they cross where they do.
5. How and why does a firm's average-total-cost curve differ in the short run and in the long run?
6. Define *economies of scale* and explain why they might arise. Define *diseconomies of scale* and explain why they might arise.

Problems and applications

1 This chapter discusses many types of costs: opportunity cost, total cost, fixed cost, variable cost, average total cost and marginal cost. Fill in the type of cost that best completes the phrases below:

a The true cost of taking some action is its ______________ .

b ______________ is falling when marginal cost is below it, and rising when marginal cost is above it.

c A cost that does not depend on the quantity produced is a ______________ .

d In the ice-cream industry in the short run, ______________ includes the cost of cream and sugar, but not the cost of the factory.

e Profits equal total revenue less ______________ .

f The cost of producing an extra unit of output is ______________ .

2 Your aunt is thinking about opening a hardware store. She estimates that it would cost $500 000 per year to rent the store and buy the stock. In addition, she would have to quit her $50 000 per year job as an accountant.

a Define opportunity cost.

b What is your aunt's opportunity cost of running a hardware store for a year? If your aunt thought she could sell $510 000 worth of merchandise in a year, should she open the store? Explain.

3 Suppose you go to university and live in a residential college on campus. You pay the college for your room and board.

a What is a cost of going to university that is not an opportunity cost?

b What is an explicit opportunity cost of attending university?

c What is an implicit opportunity cost of attending university?

4 A commercial fisherman notices the following relationship between hours spent fishing and the quantity of fish caught:

Hours	Quantity of fish (kg)
0	0
1	10
2	18
3	24
4	28
5	30

a What is the marginal product of each hour spent fishing?

b Use these data to graph the fisherman's production function. Explain its shape.

c The fisherman has a fixed cost of $10 (his rod). The opportunity cost of his time is $5 per hour. Graph the fisherman's total-cost curve. Explain its shape.

5 Nimbus Ltd, makes brooms and then sells them door-to-door. Here is the relationship between the number of workers and Nimbus's output in a given day.

Workers	Output	Marginal product	Total cost ($)	Average total cost ($)	Marginal cost ($)
0	0				
1	20				
2	50				
3	90				
4	120				
5	140				
6	150				
7	155				

a Fill in the column of marginal products. What pattern do you see? How might you explain it?

b A worker costs $100 a day and the firm has fixed costs of $200. Use this information to fill in the column for total cost.

c Fill in the column for average total cost. (Recall that $ATC = TC/Q$.) What pattern do you see?

d Now fill in the column for marginal cost. (Recall that $MC = DTC/DQ$.) What pattern do you see?

e Compare the column for marginal product and the column for marginal cost. Explain the relationship.

f Compare the column for average total cost and the column for marginal cost. Explain the relationship.

6 Suppose that you and your room-mate have started a hot dog delivery service on campus. List some of your fixed costs and describe why they are fixed. List some of your variable costs and describe why they are variable.

7 Consider the following cost information for a pie shop.

Q (dozens)	Total cost ($)	Variable cost ($)
0	300	0
1	350	50
2	390	90
3	420	120
4	450	150
5	490	190
6	540	240

a What is the pie shop's fixed cost?

b Construct a table in which you calculate the marginal cost per dozen pies using the information on total cost. Also calculate the marginal cost per dozen pies using the information on variable cost. What is the relationship between these sets of numbers? Comment.

8 You are thinking about setting up a doughnut van. The van itself costs $200. The ingredients for each doughnut cost $0.50.

a What is your fixed cost of doing business? What is your variable cost per doughnut?

b Construct a table showing your total cost, average total cost and marginal cost for output levels varying from 0 to 10 doughnuts. Draw the three cost curves.

9 Your cousin Vinnie owns a painting company with a total fixed cost of $200 and the following schedule for total variable cost:

Total variable cost ($)	Quantity of houses painted per month
10	1
20	2
40	3
80	4
160	5
320	6
640	7

Calculate average fixed cost, average variable cost and average total cost for each quantity. What is the efficient scale of the painting company?

10 Healthy Harry's Juice Bar has the following cost schedules:

Q (vats)	Variable cost ($)	Total cost ($)
0	0	30
1	10	40
2	25	55
3	45	75
4	70	100
5	100	130
6	135	165

a Calculate average variable cost, average total cost and marginal cost for each quantity.

b Graph all three curves. What is the relationship between the marginal-cost curve and the average-total-cost curve? Between the marginal-cost curve and the average-variable-cost curve? Explain.

11 Consider the following table of long-run total cost for three different firms:

Quantity	Firm A	Firm B	Firm C
1	$60	$11	$21
2	70	24	34
3	80	39	49
4	90	56	66
5	100	75	85
6	110	96	106
7	120	119	129

Does each of these firms experience economies of scale or diseconomies of scale?

Search me!

Search me!

When accessing information about microeconomics use the following keywords in any combinations you require:

- economies of scale
- efficient scale

CourseMate

CourseMate

For more multimedia resources and activities on economics, visit the Economics CourseMate website.

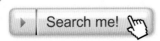

14

Firms in competitive markets

Learning objectives

In this chapter you will:

- learn what characteristics make a market competitive
- examine how competitive firms decide how much output to produce
- examine how competitive firms decide when to shut down production temporarily
- examine how competitive firms decide whether to exit or enter a market
- see how firm behaviour determines a market's short-run and long-run supply curves.

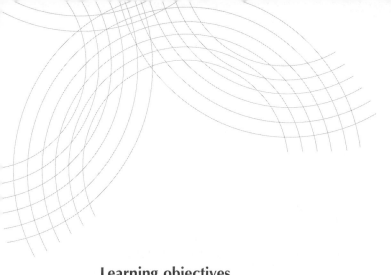

If your local petrol station raised the price it charges for petrol by 20 per cent, it would see a large drop in the amount of petrol it sold. Its customers would quickly switch to buying their petrol at other petrol stations. In contrast, if your local water company raised the price of water by 20 per cent, it would see only a small decrease in the amount of water it sold. People might water their lawns less often and buy more water-efficient shower heads, but they would be hard-pressed to reduce water consumption greatly. The difference between the petrol market and the water market is obvious – there are many firms selling petrol, but there is only one firm selling water. As you might expect, this difference in market structure shapes the pricing and production decisions of the firms that operate in these markets.

In this chapter we examine the behaviour of competitive firms, such as your local petrol station. You may recall that a market is competitive if each buyer and seller is small compared with the size of the market and, therefore, has little ability to influence market prices. In contrast, if a firm can influence the market price of the good it sells, it is said to have market power. In the four chapters that follow this one, we examine the behaviour of firms with market power, such as your local water company.

Our analysis of competitive firms in this chapter will shed light on the decisions that lie behind the supply curve in a competitive market. Not surprisingly, we will find that a market supply curve is tightly linked to firms' costs of production. (Indeed, this general insight should be familiar to you from our analysis in chapter 7.) Less obvious, however, is the question of which among a firm's many types of costs – fixed, variable, average and marginal – are most relevant for its supply decisions. We will see that all these measures of cost play important and interrelated roles.

What is a competitive market?

Our goal in this chapter is to examine how firms make production decisions in competitive markets. As a background for this analysis, we begin by considering what a competitive market is.

The meaning of competition

Search me!
▸ competitive market

Although we have already discussed the meaning of competition in chapter 4, let's review the lesson briefly. A *competitive market*, sometimes called a *perfectly competitive market*, has two characteristics:

- There are many buyers and many sellers in the market.
- The goods offered by the various sellers are largely the same.

As a result of these conditions, the actions of any single buyer or seller in the market have a negligible impact on the market price. Each buyer and seller takes the market price as given.

An example is the market for mowing. Each person offering to mow your lawn for a price has limited control over that price because many other sellers are offering mowing services that are essentially identical. Similarly, no single buyer of mowing services can influence the price of mowing because each buyer purchases a small amount relative to the size of the market. Because sellers can sell all they want at the going price, they have little reason to charge less and if an individual seller charges more, buyers will go elsewhere. Buyers and sellers in competitive markets must accept the price the market determines and, therefore, are said to be price takers.

In addition to the above two conditions for competition, there is a third condition sometimes thought to characterise perfectly competitive markets:

- Firms can freely enter or exit the market.

If, for instance, anyone can decide to start a lawn-mowing business and anyone currently operating a lawn-mowing business can decide to stop, then the lawn-mowing industry would satisfy this condition. Note that much of the analysis of competitive firms does not rely on the assumption of free entry and exit because this condition is not necessary for firms to be price takers. However, as we will see later in this chapter, entry and exit are often powerful forces shaping the long-run outcome in competitive markets.

The revenue of a competitive firm

A firm in a competitive market, like most other firms in the economy, tries to maximise profit, which equals total revenue minus total cost. To see how it does this, we first consider the revenue of a competitive firm. To keep matters concrete, let's consider a specific firm: The Lee Family Lawn-Mowing Business.

The Lee family mows a quantity of lawns Q and receives the market price of P for each lawn mown. The family's total revenue is $P \times Q$. For example, if the market price of mowing a lawn is $20 and the Lee family mows 100 lawns, its total revenue is $2000.

Because the Lee Family Lawn-Mowing Business is only a small part of the total market for mowing, it takes the price as given by market conditions. This means, in particular, that the price of mowing a lawn does not depend on the quantity of lawns that the Lee family mows. If the Lees double the number of lawns they mow, the price of mowing a lawn remains the same and their total revenue doubles. As a result, total revenue is proportional to the amount of output.

Table 14.1 shows the revenue for the Lee Family Lawn-Mowing Business. The first two columns show the amount of output the business produces and the price at which it sells its output. The third column is the total revenue of the business. The table assumes that the price of mowing a lawn is $20, so total revenue is simply $20 times the number of lawns mown.

Just as the concepts of *average* and *marginal* were useful in the last chapter when analysing costs, they are also useful when analysing revenue. To see what these concepts tell us, consider these two questions:

- How much revenue does the business receive for the typical lawn mown?
- How much additional revenue does the business receive if it increases production by mowing one extra lawn?

The last two columns in Table 14.1 answer these questions.

Table 14.1 Total, average and marginal revenue for a competitive firm

Quantity	Price	Total revenue	Average revenue	Marginal revenue
(Q)	(P)	($TR = P \times Q$)	($AR = TR/Q$)	($MR = \Delta TR/\Delta Q$)
1 lawn	$20	$20	$20	—
2	20	40	20	$20
3	20	60	20	20
4	20	80	20	20
5	20	100	20	20
6	20	120	20	20
7	20	140	20	20
8	20	160	20	20

average revenue total revenue divided by the quantity sold

The fourth column in the table shows **average revenue**, which is total revenue (from the third column) divided by the amount of output (from the first column). Average revenue tells us how much revenue a firm receives for the typical unit sold. In Table 14.1, you can see that average revenue equals $20, the price of mowing a lawn. This illustrates a general lesson that applies not only to competitive firms but to other firms as well. Total revenue is the price times the quantity ($P \times Q$), and average revenue is total revenue ($P \times Q$) divided by the quantity (Q). Therefore, for all firms, average revenue equals the price of the good.

marginal revenue the change in total revenue from an additional unit sold

The fifth column shows **marginal revenue**, which is the change in total revenue from the sale of each additional unit of output. In Table 14.1, marginal revenue equals $20, the price of mowing a lawn. This result illustrates a lesson that applies only to competitive firms. Total revenue is $P \times Q$, and P is fixed for a competitive firm. Therefore, when Q rises by one unit, total revenue rises by P dollars. *For competitive firms, marginal revenue equals the price of the good.*

When a competitive firm doubles the amount it sells, what happens to the price of its output and its total revenue?

Profit maximisation and the competitive firm's supply curve

The goal of a competitive firm is to maximise profit, which equals total revenue minus total cost. We have just discussed the firm's revenue and in the last chapter we discussed the firm's costs. We are now ready to examine how the firm maximises profit and how that decision leads to its supply curve.

A simple example of profit maximisation

Let's begin our analysis of the firm's supply decision with the example in Table 14.2. In the first column of the table is the number of lawns mown by the Lee Family Lawn-Mowing Business. The second column shows the family's total revenue, which is $20 times the number of lawns. The third column shows the family's total cost. Total cost includes fixed costs, which are $10 in this example, and variable costs, which depend on the quantity produced.

The fourth column shows the family's profit, which is calculated by subtracting total cost from total revenue. If the family business produces nothing, it has a loss of $10. If it mows one lawn, it has a profit of $6. If it mows two lawns, it has a profit of $18 and so on. To maximise profit, the business chooses the quantity that makes profit as large as possible. In this example, profit is maximised when the Lees mow either four or five lawns, for a profit of $30.

There is another way to look at the business's decision. The Lees can find the profit-maximising quantity by comparing the marginal revenue and marginal cost from each unit produced. The last two columns in Table 14.2 calculate marginal revenue and marginal cost from total revenue and total cost. The first lawn the business mows has a marginal revenue of $20 and a marginal cost of $4; hence, mowing that lawn increases profit by $16 (from negative $10 to positive $6). The second lawn mown has a marginal revenue of $20 and a marginal cost of $8, so that lawn increases profit by $12 (from $6 to $18). As long as marginal revenue exceeds marginal cost, increasing the quantity raises profit. Once the Lee family has reached five lawns, however, the situation is very different. The sixth lawn would have marginal revenue of $20 and marginal cost of $24, so mowing it would reduce profit by $4 (from $30 to $26). As a result, the Lees would not mow more than five lawns.

Table 14.2 Profit maximisation – a numerical example

Quantity (Q)	Total revenue (TR)	Total cost (TC)	Profit (TR – TC)	Marginal revenue ($MR = \Delta TR/\Delta Q$)	Marginal cost ($MC = \Delta TC/\Delta Q$)
0 lawns	\$0	\$10	–\$10	—	—
1	20	14	6	\$20	\$4
2	40	22	18	20	8
3	60	34	26	20	12
4	80	50	30	20	16
5	100	70	30	20	20
6	120	94	26	20	24
7	140	122	18	20	28
8	160	154	6	20	32

One of the *Ten Lessons from Economics* in chapter 1 is that rational people think at the margin. We now see how the Lee Family Lawn-Mowing Business can apply this principle. If marginal revenue is greater than marginal cost – as it is if the family mows only one, two or three lawns – the Lees should increase the number of lawns they mow. If marginal revenue is less than marginal cost – as it is for six, seven or eight lawns – the Lees should decrease production. If the Lees think at the margin and make incremental adjustments to the level of production, they are naturally led to produce the profit-maximising quantity.

The marginal-cost curve and the firm's supply decision

To extend this analysis of profit maximisation, consider the cost curves in Figure 14.1. These cost curves have the three features that, as we discussed in chapter 13, are considered typical: The marginal-cost curve (*MC*) is upward-sloping; the average-total-cost curve (*ATC*) is U-shaped; and the marginal-cost curve crosses the average-total-cost curve at the minimum of average total cost. The figure also shows a horizontal line at the market price (*P*) of the firm's output, which equals the firm's average revenue (*AR*) and its marginal revenue (*MR*). The price line is horizontal because the firm is a price taker – the price is the same regardless of the quantity that the firm decides to produce.

We can use Figure 14.1 to find the quantity of output that maximises profit. Imagine that the firm is producing at Q_1. At this level of output, marginal revenue is greater than marginal cost. That is, if the firm raised its level of production and sales by one unit, the additional revenue (MR_1) would exceed the additional costs (MC_1). Profit, which equals total revenue minus total cost, would increase. Hence, if marginal revenue is greater than marginal cost, as it is at Q_1, the firm can increase profit by raising production.

A similar argument applies when output is at Q_2. In this case, marginal cost is greater than marginal revenue. If the firm reduced production by one unit, the costs saved (MC_2) would exceed the

Figure 14.1 **Profit maximisation for a competitive firm**

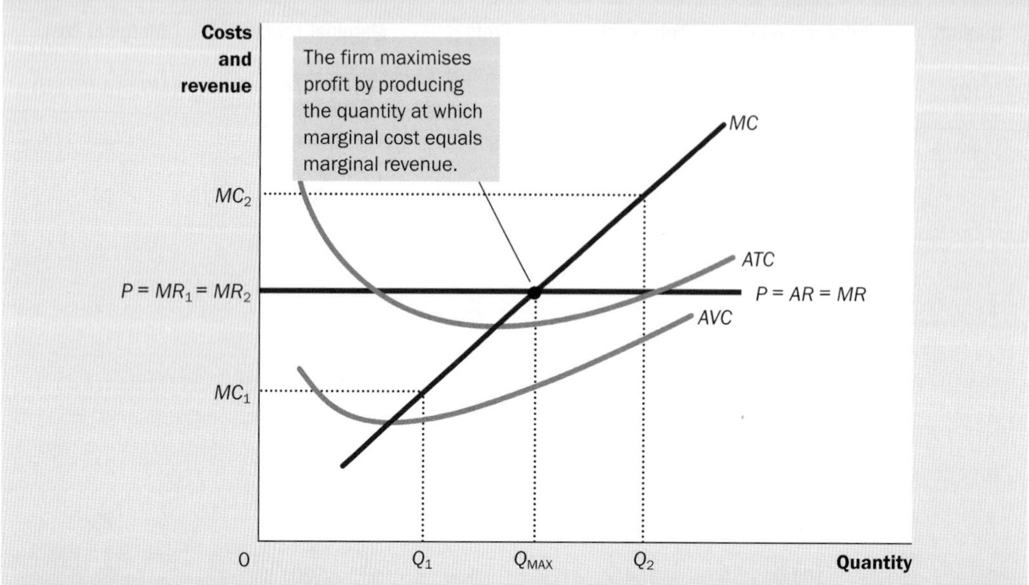

This shows the marginal-cost curve (*MC*), the average-total-cost curve (*ATC*) and the average-variable-cost curve (*AVC*). It also shows the market price (*P*), which equals marginal revenue (*MR*) and average revenue (*AR*). At the quantity Q_1, marginal revenue MR_1 exceeds marginal cost MC_1, so raising production increases profit. At the quantity Q_2, marginal cost MC_2 is above marginal revenue MR_2, so reducing production increases profit. The profit-maximising quantity Q_{MAX} is found where the horizontal price line intersects the marginal-cost curve.

revenue lost (MR_2). Therefore, if marginal revenue is less than marginal cost, as it is at Q_2, the firm can increase profit by reducing production.

Where do these marginal adjustments to level of production end? Regardless of whether the firm begins with production at a low level (such as Q_1) or at a high level (such as Q_2), the firm will eventually adjust production until the quantity produced reaches Q_{MAX}. This analysis shows a general rule for profit maximisation:

- If marginal revenue is greater than marginal cost, the firm should increase its output.
- If marginal cost is greater than marginal revenue, the firm should decrease its output.
- At the profit-maximising level of output, marginal revenue and marginal cost are exactly equal.

These rules are the key to rational decision making by a profit-maximising firm. They apply not only to competitive firms but, as we will see in the next chapter, to other firms as well.

We can now see how the competitive firm decides the quantity of its good to supply to the market. Because a competitive firm is a price taker, its marginal revenue equals the market price. For any given price, the competitive firm's profit-maximising quantity of output is found by looking at the intersection of the price with the marginal-cost curve. In Figure 14.1, that quantity is Q_{MAX}.

Figure 14.2 shows how a competitive firm responds to an increase in the price. When the price is P_1, the firm produces quantity Q_1, which is the quantity that equates marginal cost to the price. When the price rises to P_2, the firm finds that marginal revenue is now higher than marginal cost at the previous level of output, so the firm increases production. The new profit-maximising quantity is Q_2, at which marginal cost equals the new higher price. *In essence, because the firm's*

Figure 14.2 Marginal cost as the competitive firm's supply curve

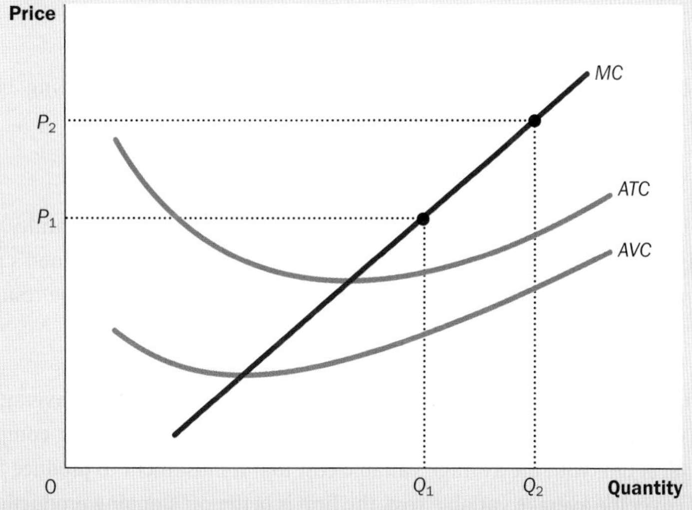

An increase in the price from P_1 to P_2 leads to an increase in the firm's profit-maximising quantity from Q_1 to Q_2. Because the marginal-cost curve shows the quantity supplied by the firm at any given price, it is the firm's supply curve.

marginal-cost curve determines how much the firm is willing to supply at any price, it is the competitive firm's supply curve. There are, however, some caveats to that conclusion, which we examine next.

The firm's short-run decision to shut down

So far we have been analysing the question of how much a competitive firm will produce. In some circumstances, however, the firm will decide to shut down and not produce anything at all.

Here we need to distinguish between a temporary shutdown of a firm and the permanent exit of a firm from the market. A *shutdown* refers to a short-run decision not to produce anything during a specific period of time because of current market conditions. *Exit* refers to a long-run decision to leave the market. The long-run and short-run decisions differ because most firms cannot avoid their fixed costs in the short run but are able to do so in the long run. That is, a firm that shuts down temporarily still has to pay its fixed costs, whereas a firm that exits can save both its fixed and its variable costs.

For example, consider the production decision that a farmer faces. The cost of the land is one of the farmer's fixed costs. If the farmer decides not to produce any crops one season, the land lies fallow and he cannot recover this cost. When making the short-run decision whether to shut down for a season, the fixed cost of land is said to be a *sunk cost.* In contrast, if the farmer decides to leave farming altogether he can sell the land. When making the long-run decision whether to exit the market, the cost of land is not sunk. (We return to the issue of sunk costs shortly.)

Now let's consider what determines a firm's shutdown decision. If the firm shuts down, it loses all revenue from the sale of its product. At the same time, it saves the variable costs of making its product (but still pays the fixed costs). Thus, *the firm shuts down if the revenue that it would earn from producing is less than the variable costs of production.*

A bit of mathematics can make this shutdown criterion more useful. If *TR* stands for total revenue, and *VC* stands for variable costs, then the firm's decision can be written as:

$$\text{Shut down if } TR < VC$$

The firm shuts down if total revenue is less than variable cost. By dividing both sides of this inequality by the quantity *Q*, we can write it as:

$$\text{Shut down if } TR/Q < VC/Q$$

Notice that this can be further simplified. *TR/Q* is total revenue divided by quantity, which is average revenue. As we discussed previously, average revenue for any firm is simply the good's price *P*. Similarly, *VC/Q* is average variable cost *AVC*. Therefore, the firm's shutdown criterion can be restated as:

$$\text{Shut down if } P < AVC$$

That is, a firm chooses to shut down if the price of the good is less than the average variable cost of production. This criterion makes sense – when choosing to produce, the firm compares the price it receives for the typical unit with the average variable cost that it must incur to produce the typical unit. If the price does not cover the average variable cost, the firm is better off stopping production altogether. The firm still loses money (because it has to pay fixed costs) but it would lose even more money by staying open. The firm can reopen in the future if conditions change so that price exceeds average variable cost.

We now have a full description of a competitive firm's profit-maximising strategy. If the firm produces anything, it produces the quantity at which marginal cost equals the price of the good. Yet if the price is less than average variable cost at that quantity, the firm is better off shutting down and not producing anything. These results are illustrated in Figure 14.3. *The competitive firm's short-run supply curve is the portion of its marginal-cost curve that lies above average variable cost.*

Figure 14.3 **The competitive firm's short-run supply curve**

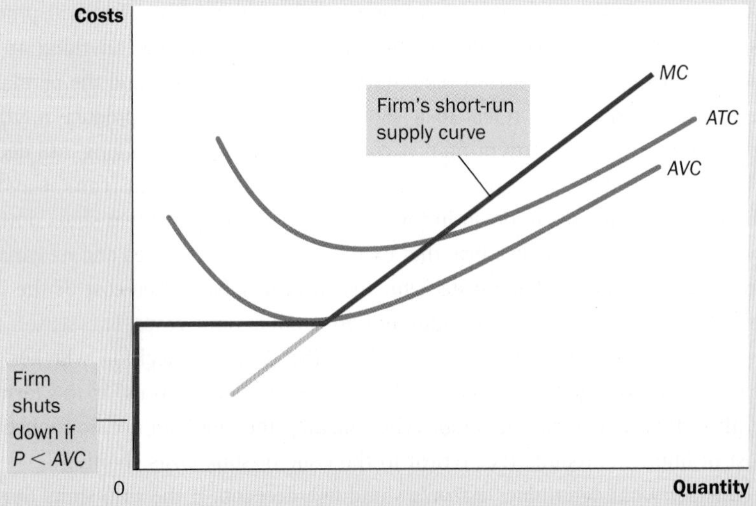

In the short run, the competitive firm's supply curve is its marginal-cost curve (*MC*) above average variable cost (*AVC*). If the price falls below average variable cost, the firm is better off shutting down.

CASESTUDY

Near-empty restaurants and off-season miniature golf

Have you ever walked into a restaurant for lunch and found it almost empty? Why, you might have asked, does the restaurant even bother to stay open? It might seem that the revenue from the few customers could not possibly cover the cost of running the restaurant.

Source: Shutterstock/Rade Kovac.

In making the decision whether to open for lunch, a restaurant owner must keep in mind the distinction between fixed and variable costs. Many of a restaurant's costs – the rent, kitchen equipment, tables, plates, cutlery and so on – are fixed. Shutting down during lunch would not reduce these costs. When the owner is deciding whether to serve lunch, only the variable costs – the price of the additional food and the wages of the extra staff – are relevant. The owner shuts down the restaurant at lunchtime only if the revenue from the few lunchtime customers fails to cover the restaurant's variable costs.

An operator of a miniature-golf course in a summer resort faces a similar decision. Because revenue varies substantially from season to season, the firm must decide when to open and when to close. Once again, the fixed costs – the costs of buying the land and building the course – are irrelevant. The miniature-golf course should be open for business only during those times of year when its revenue exceeds its variable costs.

fyi

Spilt milk and sunk costs

Sometime in your life, you have probably been told, 'Don't cry over spilt milk', or 'Let bygones be bygones'. These sayings hold a deep truth about rational decision making. Economists say that a cost is a sunk cost when it has already been committed and cannot be recovered. In a sense, a sunk cost is the opposite of an opportunity cost: An opportunity cost is what you have to give up if you choose to do one thing instead of another, whereas a sunk cost is one that cannot be avoided, regardless of the choices you make. Because nothing can be done about sunk costs, you can ignore them when making decisions about various aspects of life, including business strategy.

Our analysis of the firm's shutdown decision is one example of the irrelevance of sunk costs. We assume that the firm cannot recover its fixed costs by temporarily stopping production. As a result, the firm's fixed costs are sunk in the short run and the firm can safely ignore these costs when deciding how much to produce. The firm's short-run supply curve is the part of the marginal-cost curve that lies above average variable cost, and the size of the fixed cost does not matter for this supply decision.

The irrelevance of sunk costs explains how real businesses make decisions. In September 2001, following the terrorist attacks in the United States and the collapse of Ansett Airlines in Australia, demand for accommodation in many of Australia's tourist regions declined sharply. Cairns, Port Douglas and other regions that relied on international tourists and air transport were particularly hard hit, and hotels in these areas were operating at a loss. Despite the losses, however, these hotels kept their doors open and continued to serve customers. At first, this decision might seem surprising – if a hotel is losing money by renting rooms, why don't the owners of the hotel just shut down their business?

To understand this behaviour, we must acknowledge that many hotel costs are sunk in the short run. If a hotel owns its building and cannot resell it, then the cost of the building is sunk. Alternatively, if the hotel has a fixed term lease for the building then the cost of the building is sunk until the lease expires. The opportunity cost of a night's accommodation includes only the variable costs such as the wages of the cleaning and administrative staff. As long as the total revenue from renting rooms exceeds these variable costs, the hotels should continue operating. And, in fact, they did.

The irrelevance of sunk costs is also important for personal decisions. Imagine, for instance, that you place a $15 value on seeing a newly released film. You buy a ticket for $10, but before entering the theatre, you lose the ticket. Should you buy another ticket? Or should you now go home and refuse to pay a total of $20 to see the film? The answer is that you should buy another ticket. The benefit of seeing the film ($15) still exceeds the opportunity cost (the $10 for the second ticket). The $10 you paid for the lost ticket is a sunk cost. As with spilt milk, there is no point in crying about it.

The firm's long-run decision to exit or enter a market

The firm's long-run decision to exit a market is similar to its shutdown decision. If the firm exits, it again will lose all revenue from the sale of its product, but now it saves on both fixed and variable costs of production. Thus, *the firm exits if the revenue it would get from producing is less than its total costs.*

We can again make this criterion more useful by writing it mathematically. If *TR* stands for total revenue and *TC* stands for total cost, then the firm's criterion can be written as:

$$\text{Exit if } TR < TC$$

The firm exits if total revenue is less than total cost. By dividing both sides of this inequality by quantity *Q*, we can write it as:

$$\text{Exit if } TR/Q < TC/Q$$

We can simplify this further by noting that *TR*/*Q* is average revenue, which equals the price *P*, and that *TC*/*Q* is average total cost *ATC*. Therefore, the firm's exit criterion is:

$$\text{Exit if } P < ATC$$

That is, a firm chooses to exit if the price of the good is less than the average total cost of production.

A parallel analysis applies to an entrepreneur who is considering starting a firm. The firm will enter a market if such an action would be profitable, which occurs if the price of the good exceeds the average total cost of production. The entry criterion is:

$$\text{Enter if } P > ATC$$

The criterion for entry is exactly the opposite of the criterion for exit.

We can now describe a competitive firm's long-run profit-maximising strategy. If the firm is in the market, it produces the quantity at which marginal cost equals the price of the good. Yet if the price is less than the average total cost at that quantity, the firm chooses to exit (or not enter) the market. These results are illustrated in Figure 14.4. *The competitive firm's long-run supply curve is the portion of its marginal-cost curve that lies above average total cost.*

Measuring profit in our graph for the competitive firm

As we study exit and entry, it is useful to analyse the firm's profit in more detail. Recall that profit equals total revenue (*TR*) minus total cost (*TC*):

$$\text{Profit} = TR - TC$$

We can rewrite this definition by multiplying and dividing the right-hand side by *Q*:

$$\text{Profit} = (TR/Q - TC/Q) \times Q$$

But note that *TR*/*Q* is average revenue, which is the price *P*, and *TC*/*Q* is average total cost *ATC*. Therefore:

$$\text{Profit} = (P - ATC) \times Q$$

This way of expressing the firm's profit allows us to measure profit in our graphs.

Panel (a) of Figure 14.5 shows a firm earning positive profit. As we have already discussed, the firm maximises profit by producing the quantity at which price equals marginal cost. Now look at the

Figure 14.4 **The competitive firm's long-run supply curve**

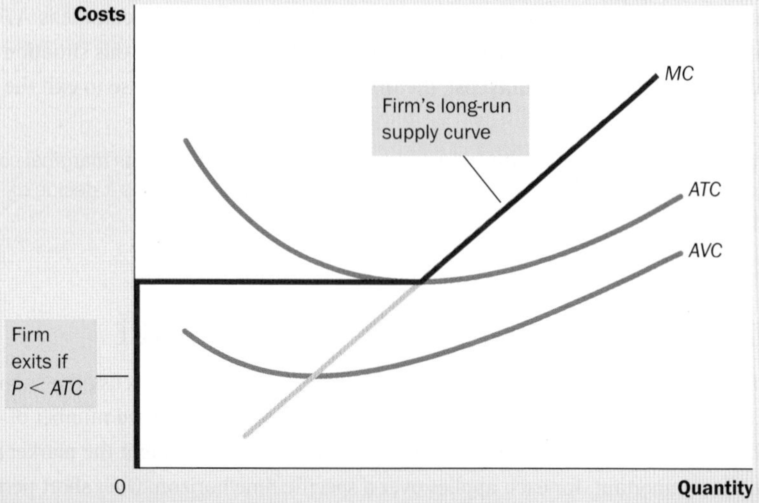

In the long run, the competitive firm's supply curve is its marginal-cost curve (*MC*) above average total cost (*ATC*). If the price falls below average total cost, the firm is better off exiting the market.

Figure 14.5 **Profit as the area between price and average total cost**

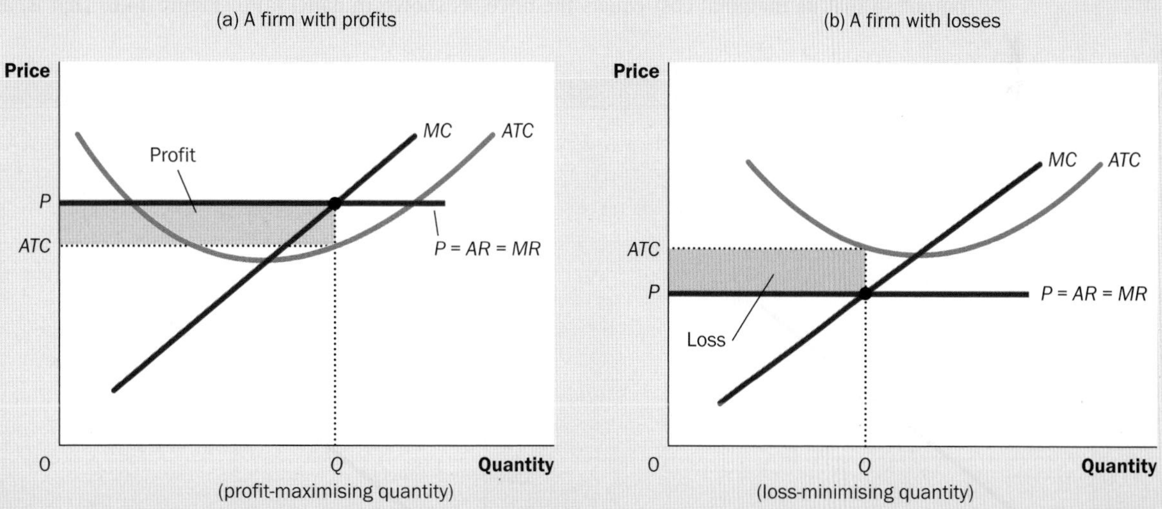

The area of the shaded box between price and average total cost represents the firm's profit. The height of this box is price minus average total cost ($P - ATC$), and the width of the box is the quantity of output (Q). In panel (a), price is above average total cost, so the firm has positive profit. In panel (b), price is less than average total cost, so the firm has losses.

shaded rectangle. The height of the rectangle is $P - ATC$, the difference between price and average total cost. The width of the rectangle is Q, the quantity produced. Therefore, the area of the rectangle is $(P - ATC) \times Q$, which is the firm's profit.

Similarly, panel (b) of this figure shows a firm with losses (negative profit). In this case, maximising profit means minimising losses, a task accomplished once again by producing the quantity at which price equals marginal cost. Now consider the shaded rectangle. The height of the rectangle is *ATC* – *P*, and the width is *Q*. The area is (*ATC* – *P*) × *Q*, which is the firm's loss. Because a firm in this situation is not making enough revenue to cover its average total cost, the firm would eventually choose to exit the market.

How does the price faced by a profit-maximising competitive firm compare with its marginal cost? Explain. When does a profit-maximising competitive firm decide to shut down? When does it decide to exit the market?

The supply curve in a competitive market

Now that we have examined the supply decision of a single firm, we can discuss the supply curve for a market. There are two cases to consider. First, we examine a market with a fixed number of firms. Second, we examine a market in which the number of firms can change as old firms exit the market and new firms enter. Both cases are important, for each applies over a specific time horizon. Over short periods of time, it is often difficult for firms to enter and exit, so the assumption of a fixed number of firms is appropriate. But over long periods of time, the number of firms can adjust to changing market conditions.

The short run: Market supply with a fixed number of firms

Consider first a market with 1000 identical firms. For any given price, each firm supplies a quantity of output so that its marginal cost equals the price, as shown in panel (a) of Figure 14.6. That is, as long

Figure 14.6 **Market supply with a fixed number of firms**

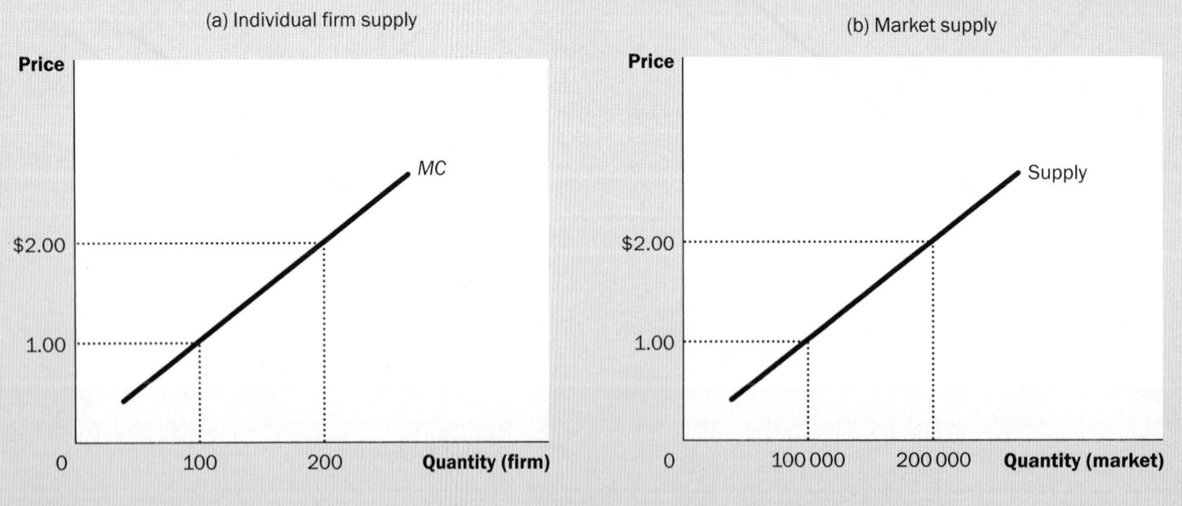

When the number of firms in the market is fixed, the market supply curve, shown in panel (b), reflects the individual firms' marginal-cost curves, shown in panel (a). Here, in a market of 1000 firms, the quantity of output supplied to the market is 1000 times the quantity supplied by each firm.

as price is above average variable cost, each firm's marginal-cost curve is its supply curve. The quantity of output supplied to the market equals the sum of the quantities supplied by each of the individual firms. Thus, to derive the market supply curve, we add the quantity supplied by each firm in the market. As panel (b) of Figure 14.6 shows, because the firms are identical, the quantity supplied to the market is 1000 times the quantity supplied by each firm.

The long run: Market supply with entry and exit

Now consider what happens if firms are able to enter or exit the market. Let's suppose that everyone has access to the same technology for producing the good and access to the same markets to buy the inputs into production. Therefore, all current and potential firms have the same cost curves.

Decisions about entry and exit in a market of this type depend on the incentives facing the owners of existing firms and the entrepreneurs who could start new firms. If firms already in the market are profitable, then new firms will have an incentive to enter the market. This entry will expand the number of firms, increase the quantity of the good supplied and drive down prices and profits. Conversely, if firms in the market are making losses, then some existing firms will exit the market. Their exit will reduce the number of firms, decrease the quantity of the good supplied and drive up prices and profits. *At the end of this process of entry and exit, firms that remain in the market must be making zero economic profit.*

Recall that we can write a firm's profits as:

$$\text{Profit} = (P - ATC) \times Q$$

This equation shows that an operating firm has zero profit if and only if the price of the good equals the average total cost of producing that good. If price is above average total cost, profit is positive, which encourages new firms to enter. If price is less than average total cost, profit is negative, which encourages some firms to exit. *The process of entry and exit ends only when price and average total cost are driven to equality.*

This analysis has a surprising implication. We noted earlier in the chapter that competitive firms produce so that price equals marginal cost. We just noted that free entry and exit forces price to equal average total cost. But if price is to equal both marginal cost and average total cost, these two measures of cost must equal each other. Marginal cost and average total cost are equal, however, only when the firm is operating at the minimum of average total cost. Recall from the preceding chapter that the level of production with lowest average total cost is called the firm's *efficient scale.* Therefore, *in the long-run equilibrium of a competitive market with free entry and exit, firms must be operating at their efficient scale.*

Panel (a) of Figure 14.7 shows a firm in such a long-run equilibrium. In this figure, price P equals marginal cost MC, so the firm is maximising profits. Price also equals average total cost ATC, so profits are zero. New firms have no incentive to enter the market and existing firms have no incentive to leave the market.

From this analysis of firm behaviour, we can determine the long-run supply curve for the market. In a market with free entry and exit, there is only one price consistent with zero profit – the minimum of average total cost. As a result, the long-run market supply curve must be horizontal at this price, as in panel (b) of Figure 14.7. Any price above this level would generate profit, leading to entry and an increase in the total quantity supplied. Any price below this level would generate losses, leading to exit and a decrease in the total quantity supplied. Eventually, the number of firms in the market

Figure 14.7 Market supply with entry and exit

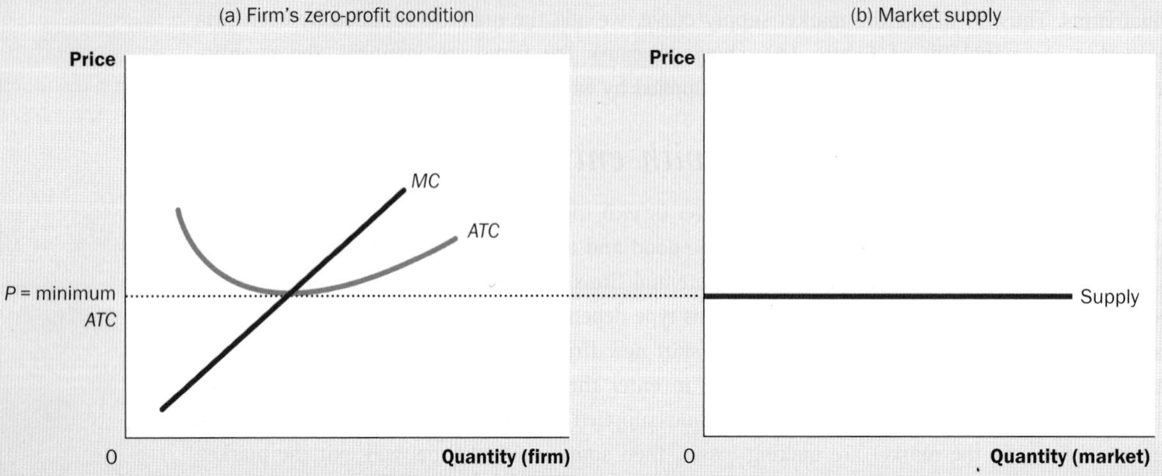

Firms will enter or exit the market until profit is driven to zero. Thus, in the long run, price equals the minimum of average total cost, as shown in panel (a). The number of firms adjusts to ensure that all demand is satisfied at this price. The long-run market supply curve is horizontal at this price, as shown in panel (b).

adjusts so that price equals the minimum of average total cost and there are enough firms to satisfy all the demand at this price.

A shift in demand in the short run and long run

Now that we have a more complete understanding of how firms make supply decisions, we can better explain how markets respond to changes in demand. Because firms can enter and exit a market in the long run but not in the short run, changes in demand have different effects over different time horizons. To see this, let's trace the effects of a shift in demand over time.

Suppose the market for milk begins in long-run equilibrium. Firms are earning zero profit, so price equals the minimum of average total cost. Panel (a) of Figure 14.8 shows this situation. The long-run equilibrium is point A, the quantity sold in the market is Q_1, and the price is P_1.

Now suppose scientists discover that milk has miraculous health benefits. As a result, the demand curve for milk shifts outwards from D_1 to D_2, as in panel (b). The short-run equilibrium moves from point A to point B; as a result, the quantity rises from Q_1 to Q_2, and the price rises from P_1 to P_2. All of the existing firms respond to the higher price by raising the amount produced. Because each firm's supply curve reflects its marginal-cost curve, how much they each increase production is determined by the marginal-cost curve. In the new, short-run equilibrium, the price of milk exceeds average total cost, so the firms are making positive profit.

Over time, the profit generated in this market encourages new firms to enter. Some farmers may switch to milk from other farm products, for example. As the number of firms grows, the short-run supply curve shifts to the right from S_1 to S_2, as in panel (c), and this shift causes the price of milk to fall. Eventually, the price is driven back down to the minimum of average total cost, profits are zero and firms stop entering. Thus, the market reaches a new long-run equilibrium, point C. The price of

Figure 14.8 **An increase in demand in the short run and long run**

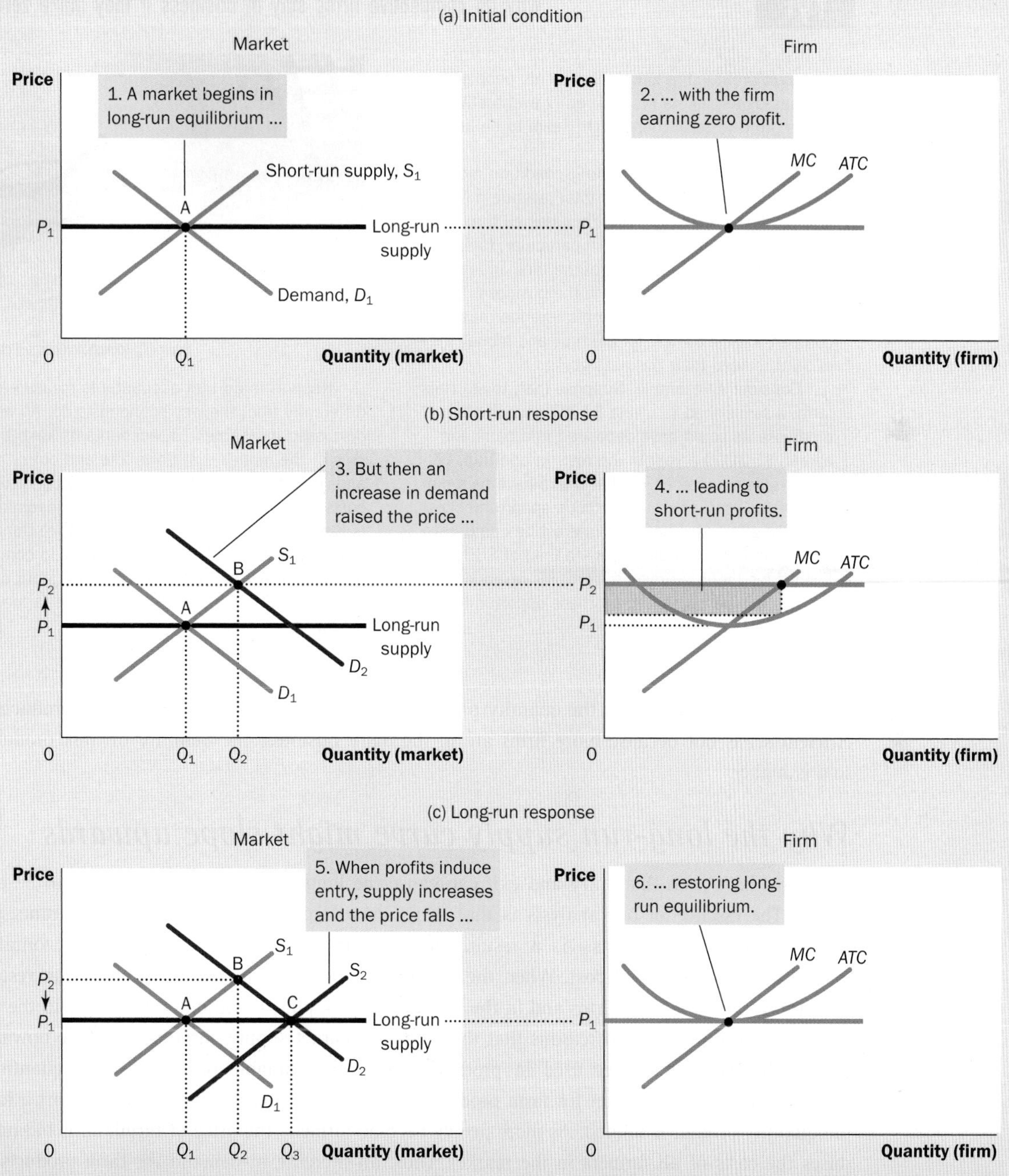

The market starts in a long-run equilibrium, shown as point A in panel (a). In this equilibrium, each firm makes zero profit, and the price equals the minimum average total cost. Panel (b) shows what happens in the short run when demand rises from D_1 to D_2. The equilibrium goes from point A to point B, price rises from P_1 to P_2, and the quantity sold in the market rises from Q_1 to Q_2. Because price now exceeds average total cost, firms make profits, which over time encourage new firms to enter the market. This entry shifts the short-run supply curve to the right from S_1 to S_2, as shown in panel (c). In the new long-run equilibrium, point C, price has returned to P_1, but the quantity sold has increased to Q_3. Profits are again zero, price is back to the minimum of average total cost, but the market has more firms to satisfy the greater demand.

fyi

Why do competitive firms stay in business if they make zero profit?

At first, it might seem odd that competitive firms earn zero profit in the long run. After all, people start businesses to make a profit. If entry eventually drives profit to zero, there might seem to be little reason to stay in business.

To understand the zero-profit condition more fully, recall that profit equals total revenue minus total cost, and that total cost includes all the opportunity costs of the firm. In particular, total cost includes the opportunity cost of the time and money that the firm's owners devote to the business. In the zero-profit equilibrium, the firm's revenue must compensate the owners for the time and money they expend to keep their business going.

Consider an example. Suppose that, to start his farm, a farmer had to invest $1 million, which otherwise he could have deposited in a bank and earned $50 000 a year in interest. In addition, he had to give up another job that would have paid him $30 000 a year. Then the farmer's opportunity cost of farming includes both the interest he could have earned and the forgone wages – a total of $80 000. Even if his profit is driven to zero, his revenue from farming compensates him for these opportunity costs.

Source: iStockphoto/George Pchemyan.

Keep in mind that accountants measure costs differently from the way economists do. As we discussed in chapter 13, accountants keep track only of the money that flows into and out of firms and, therefore, do not include all the opportunity costs. In the zero-profit equilibrium, economic profit is zero, but accounting profit is positive. Our farmer's accountant, for instance, would conclude that the farmer earned an accounting profit of $80 000, which is enough to keep the farmer in business.

milk has returned to P_1, but the quantity produced has risen to Q_3. Each firm is again producing at its efficient scale, but because more firms are in the dairy business, the quantity of milk produced and sold is higher.

Why the long-run supply curve might slope upwards

So far we have seen that entry and exit can cause the long-run market supply curve to be perfectly elastic. The essence of our analysis is that there are a large number of potential entrants, each of which faces the same costs. As a result, the long-run market supply curve is horizontal at the minimum of average total cost. When the demand for the good increases, the long-run result is an increase in the number of firms and in the total quantity supplied, without any change in the price.

There are, however, two reasons that the long-run market supply curve might slope upwards. The first is that some resources used in production may be available only in limited quantities. For example, consider the market for farm produce. Anyone can choose to buy land and start a farm, but the quantity of land is limited. As more people become farmers, the price of farmland is bid up, which raises the costs of all farmers in the market. Thus, an increase in demand for farm products cannot induce an increase in quantity supplied without also inducing a rise in farmers' costs, which in turn means a rise in price. The result is a long-run market supply curve that is upward-sloping, even with free entry into farming.

A second reason for an upward-sloping supply curve is that firms may have different costs. For example, consider the market for painters. Anyone can enter the market for painting services, but not everyone has the same costs. Costs vary in part because some people work faster than others and in part because some people have better alternative uses of their time than others. For any given price, those with lower costs are more likely to enter than those with higher costs. To increase the quantity of painting services supplied, additional entrants must be encouraged to enter the market. Because these new entrants have higher costs, the price must rise to make entry profitable for them. Thus, the market supply curve for painting services slopes upwards even with free entry into the market.

Notice that if firms have different costs, some firms earn profit even in the long run. In this case, the price in the market reflects the average total cost of the marginal firm – the firm that would exit the market if the price were any lower. This firm earns zero profit, but firms with lower costs earn positive profit. Entry does not eliminate this profit because would-be entrants have higher costs than firms already in the market. Higher cost firms will enter only if the price rises, making the market profitable for them.

Thus, for these two reasons, the long-run supply curve in a market may be upward-sloping rather than horizontal, indicating that a higher price is necessary to induce a larger quantity supplied. Nonetheless, the basic lesson about entry and exit remains true. *Because firms can enter and exit more easily in the long run than in the short run, the long-run supply curve is typically more elastic than the short-run supply curve.*

In the long run with free entry and exit, is the price in a market equal to marginal cost, average total cost, both or neither? Explain with a diagram.

Conclusion: Behind the supply curve

We have been discussing the behaviour of profit-maximising firms that supply goods in perfectly competitive markets. You may recall from chapter 1 that one of the *Ten Lessons from Economics* is that rational people think at the margin. This chapter has applied this idea to the competitive firm. Marginal analysis has given us a theory of the supply curve in a competitive market and, as a result, a deeper understanding of market outcomes.

We have learned that when you buy a good from a firm in a competitive market, you can be assured that the price you pay is close to the cost of producing that good. In particular, if firms are competitive and profit-maximising, the price of a good equals the marginal cost of making that good. In addition, if firms can freely enter and exit the market, the price also equals the lowest possible average total cost of production.

Although we have assumed throughout this chapter that firms are price takers, many of the tools developed here are also useful for studying firms in less competitive markets. In the next three chapters we will examine the behaviour of firms with market power. Marginal analysis will again be useful in analysing these firms, but it will have quite different implications.

Summary

- Because a competitive firm is a price taker, its revenue is proportional to the amount of output it produces. The price of the good equals both the firm's average revenue and its marginal revenue.
- To maximise profit, a firm chooses a quantity of output such that marginal revenue equals marginal cost. Because marginal revenue for a competitive firm equals the market price, the firm chooses quantity so that price equals marginal cost. Thus, the firm's marginal-cost curve is its supply curve.
- In the short run when a firm cannot recover its fixed costs, the firm will choose to shut down temporarily if the price of the good is less than average variable cost. In the long run when the firm can recover both fixed and variable costs, it will choose to exit if the price is less than average total cost.
- In a market with free entry and exit, profits are driven to zero in the long run. In this long-run equilibrium, all firms produce at the efficient scale, price equals the minimum of average total cost, and the number of firms adjusts to satisfy the quantity demanded at this price.
- Changes in demand have different effects over different time horizons. In the short run, an increase in demand raises prices and leads to profits, and a decrease in demand lowers prices and leads to losses. But if firms can freely enter and exit the market, then in the long run the number of firms adjusts to drive the market back to the zero-profit equilibrium.

Key concepts

average revenue
marginal revenue

Questions for review

1. What is meant by a competitive firm?
2. Explain the difference between a firm's revenue and its profit. Which do firms maximise?
3. Draw the cost curves for a typical firm. For a given price, explain how the firm chooses the level of output that maximises profit. At that level of output, show on your graph the firm's total revenue and total costs.
4. Under what conditions will a firm shut down temporarily? Explain.
5. Under what conditions will a firm exit a market? Explain.
6. Does a firm's price equal marginal cost in the short run, in the long run or both? Explain.
7. Does a firm's price equal the minimum of average total cost in the short run, in the long run or both? Explain.
8. Are market supply curves typically more elastic in the short run or in the long run? Explain.

Problems and applications

1. What are the characteristics of a competitive market? Which of the following drinks do you think is best described by these characteristics? Why aren't the others?
   a Tap water
   b Bottled mineral water
   c Cola
   d Beer

2 Your room-mate's long hours in the chemistry lab finally paid off – she discovered a secret formula that lets people do an hour's worth of studying in five minutes. So far, she's sold 200 doses and faces the following average-total-cost schedule:

Q	Average total cost
199	$199
200	200
201	201

If a new customer offers to pay her $300 for one dose, should she make one more? Explain.

3 You are thinking of starting a fishing business. The fixed cost of the business is the cost of a fishing rod, which is $15. (The rod cannot be used for anything except fishing.) The variable costs are bait, which is $1 per fish caught, and your time. The opportunity cost of your time is $10 per hour. The following table shows the relationship between hours spent fishing and number of fish caught.

Hours	1	2	3	4	5
Number of fish caught	10	18	24	28	30

a What is the marginal product of each hour spent fishing? Explain why this number changes as the number of fish you catch increases.
b What is the total cost of catching 10 fish? What about the total cost of catching 18 fish? Draw your total cost curve.
c What is the average cost of 10 fish? How about 18 fish? Draw the average-cost curve and explain its shape.
d What is (approximately) the marginal cost of catching the twentieth fish? What about the marginal cost of the twenty-ninth fish? Explain why the marginal cost changes as the number of fish you catch changes.
e Suppose that you can sell fish for $5 each. How many fish will you catch in order to maximise profit? What is the maximum level of profits that you can make?
f Suppose that you purchase your rod and begin fishing. Suddenly, the price of fish drops to $2.10 each. If you continue to fish, how many fish will you catch in order to maximise your profit? What is the maximum level of profit you can make?
g Suppose, as in part (f), that the price of fish has suddenly dropped to $2.10, but you have already bought your fishing rod. The resale price of fishing rods is zero. Will you continue to fish? Why?
h How would your answer to part (g) change (if at all) if you could resell your rod at $5?

4 The licorice industry is competitive. Each firm produces 2 million straps of licorice per year. The straps have an average total cost of $0.20 each and they sell for $0.30.
a What is the marginal cost of a strap?
b Is the industry in long-run equilibrium? Why or why not?

5 You go out to the best restaurant in town and order a lobster dinner for $140. After eating half of the lobster, you realise that you are quite full. Your date wants you to finish your dinner, because you can't take it home and because 'you've already paid for it'. What should you do? Relate your answer to the material in this chapter.

6 'Strong prices traditionally cause expansion in an industry, eventually bringing an end to high prices and manufacturers' prosperity.' Explain, using appropriate diagrams.

7 Many small boats are made of fibreglass, which is derived from petroleum. Suppose that the price of oil rises.
   a Using diagrams, show what happens to the cost curves of an individual boatbuilding firm and to the market supply curve.
   b What happens to the profits of boatbuilders in the short run? What happens to the number of boatbuilders in the long run?

8 Suppose that the Australian textile industry is competitive and there is no international trade in textiles. In long-run equilibrium, the price per unit of cloth is $30.
   a Describe the equilibrium using graphs for the entire market and for an individual producer.
   b Now suppose that textile producers in other countries are willing to sell large quantities of cloth in Australia for only $25 per unit. Assuming that Australian textile producers have large fixed costs, what is the short-run effect of these imports on the quantity produced by an individual producer? What is the short-run effect on profits? Illustrate your answer with a graph.
   c What is the long-run effect on the number of Australian firms in the industry?

9 Suppose there are 100 ice-cream shops operating in Brisbane. Each shop has the usual U-shaped average-total-cost curve. The market demand curve for ice-cream slopes downwards and the market for ice-cream is in long-run competitive equilibrium.
   a Draw the current equilibrium, using graphs for the entire market and for an individual ice-cream shop.
   b Now the city decides to restrict the number of ice-cream shops. The council passes a law that reduces the number of shops to only 80. What effect will this action have on the market and on an individual shop that is still operating? Use graphs to illustrate your answer.
   c Suppose that the council decides to charge the 80 ice-cream shops a licence fee. How will this affect the number of ice-creams sold by an individual shop and the shop's profit? The council wants to raise as much revenue as possible and also wants to ensure that 80 ice-cream shops remain in the city. At what level should the council set the licence fee? Show the answer on your graph.

10 Assume that the gold-mining industry is competitive.
   a Illustrate a long-run equilibrium using diagrams for the gold market and for a representative gold mine.
   b Suppose that an increase in jewellery demand induces a surge in the demand for gold. Using your diagrams, show what happens in the short run to the gold market and to each existing gold mine.
   c If the demand for gold remains high, what would happen to the price over time? Specifically, would the new long-run equilibrium price be above, below or equal to the short-run equilibrium price in part (b)? Is it possible for the new long-run equilibrium price to be above the original long-run equilibrium price? Explain.

Search me!

Search me!

When accessing information about microeconomics use the following keywords in any combinations you require:

- competitive market

CourseMate

CourseMate

For more multimedia resources and activities on economics, visit the Economics CourseMate website.

15

Monopoly

Learning objectives

In this chapter you will:

- learn why some markets have only one seller
- analyse how a monopoly determines the quantity to produce and the price to charge
- see how the monopoly's decisions affect economic wellbeing
- see why monopolies try to charge different prices to different customers.

If you own a personal computer, it probably uses some version of Windows, the operating system sold by the Microsoft Corporation. When Microsoft first designed Windows many years ago, it applied for and received a copyright from the government. The copyright gives Microsoft the exclusive right to make and sell copies of the Windows operating system. So if a person wants to buy a copy of Windows, he or she has little choice but to give Microsoft the approximately $250 that the firm has decided to charge for its product. Microsoft is said to have a *monopoly* in the market for Windows.

Microsoft's competitive environment look very different to the description of the market we developed in chapter 14. In that chapter, we analysed competitive markets, in which there are many firms offering essentially identical products, so each firm has little influence over the price it receives. In contrast, a monopoly such as Microsoft has no close competitors and, therefore, can influence the market price of its product. Whereas a competitive firm is a *price taker*, a monopoly firm is a *price maker*.

In this chapter we examine the implications of this market power. We will see that market power alters the relationship between a firm's price and its costs. A competitive firm takes the price of its output as given and then chooses the quantity supplied so that price equals marginal cost. In contrast, the price charged by a monopoly exceeds marginal cost. This result is clearly true in the case of Microsoft's Windows. The marginal cost of Windows – the extra cost that Microsoft incurs when another buyer downloads a copy of the program – is probably less than a dollar. The market price of Windows is many times the marginal cost.

It is perhaps not surprising that monopolies charge high prices for their products. Customers of monopolies might seem to have little choice but to pay whatever the monopoly charges. But, if so, why does a copy of Windows not cost $1000? Or $10 000? The reason, of course, is that if Microsoft sets the price that high, fewer people would buy the product. People would buy fewer computers, switch to other operating systems (like Android or Apple), or make illegal copies. A monopoly firm can control the price of the good it sells, but because high prices reduce the amount that its customers buy, the monopoly's profits are not unlimited.

As we examine the production and pricing decisions of monopolies, we also consider the implications of monopoly for society as a whole. Monopoly firms, like competitive firms, aim to maximise profit. But this goal has very different ramifications for competitive and monopoly firms. In competitive markets, self-interested consumers and producers behave as if they are guided by an invisible hand to promote general economic wellbeing. By contrast, because monopoly firms are unchecked by competition, the outcome in a market with a monopoly is often not in the best interest of society.

Our study of monopoly firms will have many parallels with competitive firms. As we saw in chapter 14, a competitive firm maximises its profit by setting its output so that marginal revenue equals marginal cost. In this chapter, we show that this same profit-maximisation rule applies to a monopoly firm. However, unlike a competitive firm, a monopoly's marginal revenue is not the same as the market price.

Perfect competition and monopoly provide two ends of a competitive spectrum. For a perfectly competitive firm, competition is so fierce that it has no discretion over the price it charges for its product. It is a price taker. In contrast, a monopoly faces no competition. It sets its output and prices so that output is only subject to market demand. Most firms operate in markets where the level of competition is between these two extremes: they face some (but not perfect) competition. In this respect, our study of perfect competition and monopoly are a first step towards understanding how most firms price their goods and services. As we introduce strategic elements in chapter 16 and product differentiation in chapter 18, the picture will be completed.

Why monopolies arise

monopoly
a firm that is the sole seller of a product without close substitutes

Search me!
▸ monopoly

A firm is a **monopoly** if it is the sole seller of its product and if its product does not have close substitutes. The fundamental cause of monopoly is barriers to entry – a monopoly remains the only seller in its market because other firms cannot enter the market and compete with it. Barriers to entry, in turn, have three main sources:

- *Monopoly resources:* A key resource is owned by a single firm.
- *Government regulation:* The government gives a single firm the exclusive right to produce some good or service.
- *The production process:* A single firm can produce output at a lower cost than can a larger number of producers.

Let's briefly discuss each of these.

Monopoly resources

The simplest way for a monopoly to arise is for a single firm to own a key resource. For example, consider the market for water in a small town in the outback. If dozens of town residents can pump and sell underground bore water, the competitive model discussed in chapter 14 describes the behaviour of sellers. As a result, the price of a litre of water is driven to equal the marginal cost of pumping an extra litre. But if there is only one resident in town who can pump out underground water and it is impossible to get water from anywhere else, then that resident has a monopoly on water. Not surprisingly, the monopolist has much greater market power than any single firm in a competitive market. In the case of a necessity like water, the monopolist could command quite a high price, even if the marginal cost of pumping an extra litre is low.

Although exclusive ownership of a key resource is a potential cause of monopoly, in practice monopolies rarely arise for this reason. Economies are large and resources are owned by many people. Indeed, because many goods are traded internationally, the natural scope of their markets is often world-wide. There are, therefore, few examples of firms that own a resource for which there are no close substitutes.

CASESTUDY

The gas industry in south-eastern Australia

For a firm to be a monopoly, it must be the only seller of a product that does not have any close substitutes. Traditionally, in Victoria, New South Wales and South Australia, single sellers provided almost all natural gas. Natural gas for Victoria came from fields in the Bass Strait, controlled by a joint venture between Esso and BHP Billiton. Gas for New South Wales and South Australia came from the Cooper Basin, which is also controlled by a single joint venture. Although these firms were the only sellers of gas, were they monopolists? In particular, were the prices set by these gas producers constrained by the ability of consumers to substitute other energy sources (such as electricity, coal and oil) for natural gas?

In Victoria, most natural gas is purchased for domestic use such as cooking, central heating and hot water. Although consumers are unlikely to give up their gas stoves or hot-water systems in the short term if the price of gas rises, there will probably be significant substitution of alternative fuels in the longer term. With higher gas prices, households may decide to buy an electric or solar hot-water system rather than a gas system when their current hot-water system needs replacing. Household demand for natural gas may be fairly inelastic over the short term but is likely to be elastic over a five-year or 10-year period. The Esso–BHP Billiton joint venture may have had little ability to raise prices to monopoly levels except in the short term.

In contrast, natural gas in New South Wales is largely used by industry. Many of the firms that rely on natural gas, such as steel smelters and fertiliser companies, have spent large amounts of money building their factories. These factories cannot be easily moved or adapted to other fuels. Often, electricity cannot be used as a substitute for gas and environmental restrictions prevent firms from using oil or coal as a fuel source, particularly if they are located near a major city such as Sydney. These firms are likely to have few alternatives other than to continue to purchase gas even if the price of gas rises significantly. Indeed, a study by the Australian Bureau of Agricultural and Resource Economics found that industrial users of natural gas have a less-elastic demand curve than domestic users. This suggests that the Cooper Basin Partners, who were the only suppliers of gas to New South Wales, may have had more market power than Victorian gas producers.

The ability of electricity and other fuel sources to constrain the price setting of gas producers was a key issue in the reform of the gas sector. Concerns about the monopoly power of gas producers led the state and federal governments to try to introduce more competition into gas supply. In 1998, the Victorian and NSW gas networks were joined by a pipeline between Albury and Wagga Wagga, while in August 2000 a major pipeline linking Sydney to the Bass Strait gas fields was opened. More recently, coal-seam gas has been discovered in Queensland and more gas pipelines have been built connecting Victoria, South Australia, New South Wales and Queensland. As a result, there is now competition in the supply of gas in south-eastern Australia.

Government-created monopolies

In many cases, monopolies arise because the government has given one person or firm the exclusive right to sell some good or service. Sometimes the monopoly arises from the sheer political clout of the would-be monopolist. Kings, for example, once granted exclusive business licences to their friends and allies. In England, this power was taken away from the monarch by parliament in 1624. At other times, the government grants a monopoly because doing so is in the public interest. For instance, until October 2001, the Australian government had given a monopoly to a company called Melbourne IT to issue .com.au Internet addresses. Since then, the monopoly licence has been given to another company, AusRegistry. Having a single company maintain the address database avoids problems such as issuing the same name twice.

Patent and copyright laws are one example of how the government creates a monopoly to serve the public interest. When a pharmaceutical company discovers a new medicine, it can apply to the government for a patent. If the government deems the medicine to be truly original, it approves the patent, which gives the company the exclusive right to manufacture and sell the medicine for a certain number of years. In Australia, patents for medicine last for 20 years. Similarly, when a novelist finishes a book, she can copyright it. The copyright is a government guarantee that no one can print and sell the work without the author's permission. The copyright makes the novelist a monopolist in the sale of her novel.

The effects of patent and copyright laws are easy to see. Because these laws give one producer a monopoly, they lead to higher prices than would occur under competition. But by allowing these monopoly producers to charge higher prices and earn higher profits, the laws also encourage some desirable behaviour. Pharmaceutical companies are allowed to be monopolists in the medicines they discover in order to encourage research by these companies. Authors are allowed to be monopolists in the sale of their books in order to encourage them to write more and better books.

Thus, the laws governing patents and copyrights have both benefits and costs. The benefits of the patent and copyright laws are the increased incentives for creative activity. These benefits are offset, to some extent, by the costs of monopoly pricing, which we examine fully later in this chapter.

Natural monopolies

natural monopoly
a monopoly that arises because a single firm can supply a good or service to an entire market at a smaller cost than could two or more firms

Search me!

▸ natural monopoly

An industry is a **natural monopoly** when a single firm can supply a good or service to an entire market at a lower cost than could two or more firms. For example, an industry is a natural monopoly when there are economies of scale over the relevant range of output. Figure 15.1 shows the average total costs of a firm with economies of scale. In this case, a single firm can produce any amount of output at least cost. That is, for any given amount of output, a larger number of firms leads to less output per firm and higher average total cost.

An example of a natural monopoly is the distribution of water. To provide water to residents of a town, a firm must build a network of pipes throughout the town. If two or more firms were to compete in the provision of this service, each firm would have to pay the fixed cost of building a network. Thus, the average total cost of water is lowest if a single firm serves the entire market.

We saw other examples of natural monopolies when we discussed public goods and common resources in chapter 11. We noted that club goods are excludable but not rival in consumption. An example is a bridge used so infrequently that it is never congested. The bridge is excludable because a toll collector can prevent someone from using it. The bridge is not rival in consumption because use of the bridge by one person does not diminish the ability of others to use it. Because there is a fixed cost of building the bridge and a negligible marginal cost of additional users, the average total cost of a trip across the bridge (the total cost divided by the number of trips) falls as the number of trips rises. Therefore, the bridge is a natural monopoly.

When a firm is a natural monopoly, it is less concerned about new entrants eroding its monopoly power. Normally, a firm has trouble maintaining a monopoly position without ownership of a key

Figure 15.1 Economies of scale as a cause of monopoly

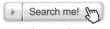

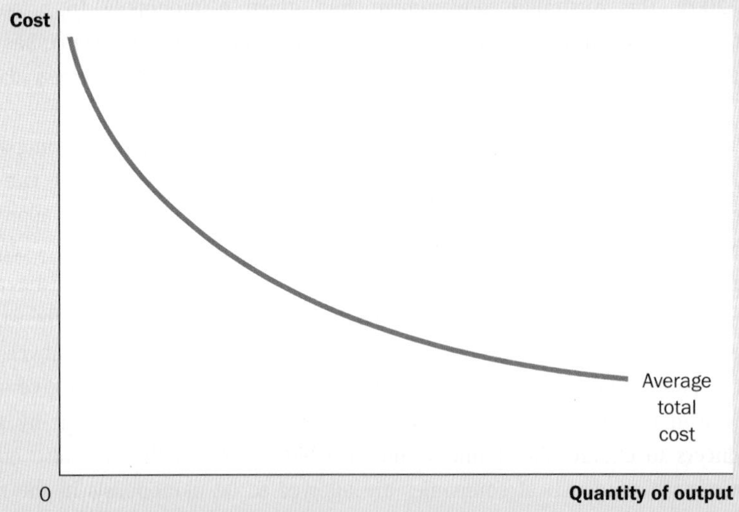

When a firm's average-total-cost curve continually declines, the firm has what is called a natural monopoly. In this case, when production is divided among more firms, each firm produces less, and average total cost rises. As a result, a single firm can produce any given amount at the smallest cost.

resource or protection from the government. The monopolist's profit attracts entrants into the market and these entrants make the market more competitive. In contrast, entering a market in which another firm has a natural monopoly is unattractive. Would-be entrants know that they cannot achieve the same low costs that the monopolist enjoys because, after entry, each firm would have a smaller piece of the market.

In some cases, the size of the market is one determinant of whether an industry is a natural monopoly. Again, consider a bridge across a river. When the population is small, the bridge may be a natural monopoly. A single bridge can satisfy the entire demand for trips across the river at lowest cost. Yet, as the population grows and the bridge becomes congested, satisfying the entire demand may require two or more bridges across the same river. Thus, as a market expands, a natural monopoly can evolve into a competitive market.

Q

What are three reasons a market might have a monopoly? Give two examples of monopolies and explain the reason for each.

How monopolies make production and pricing decisions

Now that we know how monopolies arise, we can consider how a monopoly firm decides how much of its product to make and what price to charge for it. The analysis of monopoly behaviour in this section is the starting point for evaluating whether monopolies are desirable and what policies the government might pursue in monopoly markets.

Monopoly versus competition

The key difference between a competitive firm and a monopoly is the monopoly's ability to influence the price of its output. A competitive firm is small relative to the market in which it operates and, therefore, takes the price of its output as given by market conditions. In contrast, because a monopoly is the sole producer in its market, it can alter the price of its good by adjusting the quantity it supplies to the market.

One way to view this difference between a competitive firm and a monopoly is to consider the demand curve that each firm faces. When we analysed profit maximisation by competitive firms in chapter 14, we drew the market price as a horizontal line. Because a competitive firm can sell as much or as little as it wants at this price, the competitive firm faces a horizontal demand curve, as in panel (a) of Figure 15.2. In effect, because the competitive firm sells a product with many perfect substitutes (the products of all the other firms in its market), the demand curve that any one firm faces is perfectly elastic.

In contrast, because a monopoly is the sole producer in its market, its demand curve is the market demand curve. Thus, the monopolist's demand curve slopes downwards for all the usual reasons, as in panel (b) of Figure 15.2. If the monopolist raises the price of its good, consumers buy less of it. In other words, if the monopolist reduces the quantity of output it sells, the price of its output increases.

The market demand curve provides a constraint on a monopoly's ability to profit from its market power. A monopolist would prefer, if it were possible, to charge a high price and sell a large quantity at that high price. The market demand curve makes that outcome impossible. In particular, the market

Figure 15.2 Demand curves for competitive and monopoly firms

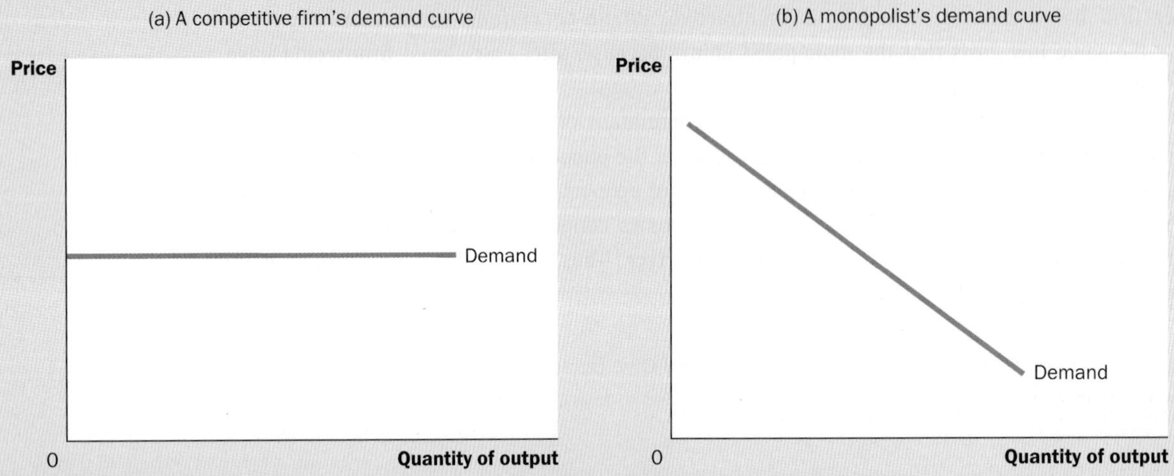

Because competitive firms are price takers, in effect they face horizontal demand curves, as in panel (a). Because a monopoly firm is the sole producer in its market, it faces the downward-sloping market demand curve as in panel (b). As a result, the monopoly has to accept a lower price if it wants to sell more output.

demand curve describes the combinations of price and quantity that are available to a monopoly firm. By adjusting the quantity produced (or, equivalently, the price charged), the monopolist can choose any point on the demand curve, but it cannot choose a point off the demand curve.

What price and quantity of output will the monopolist choose? As with competitive firms, we assume that the monopolist's goal is to maximise profit. Because profit is total revenue minus total costs, our next task in explaining monopoly behaviour is to examine a monopolist's revenue.

A monopoly's revenue

Consider a town with a single producer of water. Table 15.1 shows how the monopoly's revenue might depend on the amount of water produced.

The first two columns show the monopolist's demand schedule. If the monopolist produces 1 litre of water, it can sell that litre for \$10; if it produces 2 litres, it must lower the price to \$9 in order to sell both litres; if it produces 3 litres, it must lower the price to \$8, and so on. If you graphed these two columns of numbers, you would get a typical downward-sloping demand curve.

The third column of the table presents the monopolist's total revenue. It equals the quantity sold (from the first column) times the price (from the second column). The fourth column calculates the firm's average revenue, the amount of revenue the firm receives per unit sold. We calculate average revenue by taking the number for total revenue in the third column and dividing it by the quantity of output in the first column. As we discussed in chapter 14, average revenue always equals the price of the good. This is true for monopolists as well as for competitive firms.

The last column of Table 15.1 calculates the firm's marginal revenue, the amount of revenue that the firm receives for each additional unit of output. We calculate marginal revenue by taking the change in total revenue when output increases by one unit. For example, when the firm is producing

Table 15.1 A monopoly's total, average and marginal revenue

Quantity of water	Price	Total revenue	Average revenue	Marginal revenue
(Q)	(P)	($TR = P \times Q$)	($AR = TR/Q$)	($MR = \Delta TR/\Delta Q$)
0 litres	$11	$0	—	—
1	10	10	$10	$10
2	9	18	9	8
3	8	24	8	6
4	7	28	7	4
5	6	30	6	2
6	5	30	5	0
7	4	28	4	−2
8	3	24	3	−4

3 litres of water, it receives total revenue of $24. Raising production to 4 litres increases total revenue to $28. Thus, marginal revenue is $28 minus $24, or $4.

Table 15.1 shows a result that will be important for understanding monopoly behaviour – *a monopolist's marginal revenue is always less than the price of its good.* For example, if the firm raises production of water from 3 to 4 litres, it will increase total revenue by only $4, even though it will be able to sell each litre for $7. For a monopoly, marginal revenue is lower than price because a monopoly faces a downward-sloping demand curve. To increase the amount sold, a monopoly firm must lower the price of its good. Hence, to sell the fourth litre of water, the monopolist must get less revenue for each of the first 3 litres.

Marginal revenue is very different for monopolies than it is for competitive firms. When a monopoly increases the amount it sells, it has two effects on total revenue ($P \times Q$):

- *The output effect:* more output is sold, so Q is higher, which tends to increase total revenue.
- *The price effect:* the price falls, so P is lower, which tends to decrease total revenue.

Because a competitive firm can sell all it wants at the market price, there is no price effect. When it increases production by one unit, it receives the market price for that unit, and it does not receive any less for the amount it was already selling. That is, because the competitive firm is a price taker its marginal revenue equals the price of its good. In contrast, when a monopoly increases production by one unit, it must reduce the price it charges for every unit it sells, and this cut in price reduces revenue on the units it was already selling. As a result, a monopoly's marginal revenue is less than its price.

Figure 15.3 graphs the demand curve and the marginal-revenue curve for a monopoly firm. (Since the firm's price equals its average revenue, the demand curve is also the average-revenue curve.) These two curves always start at the same point on the vertical axis because the marginal revenue of the first unit sold equals the price of the good. But, for the reason we just discussed, the monopolist's marginal

Figure 15.3 Demand and marginal-revenue curves for a monopoly

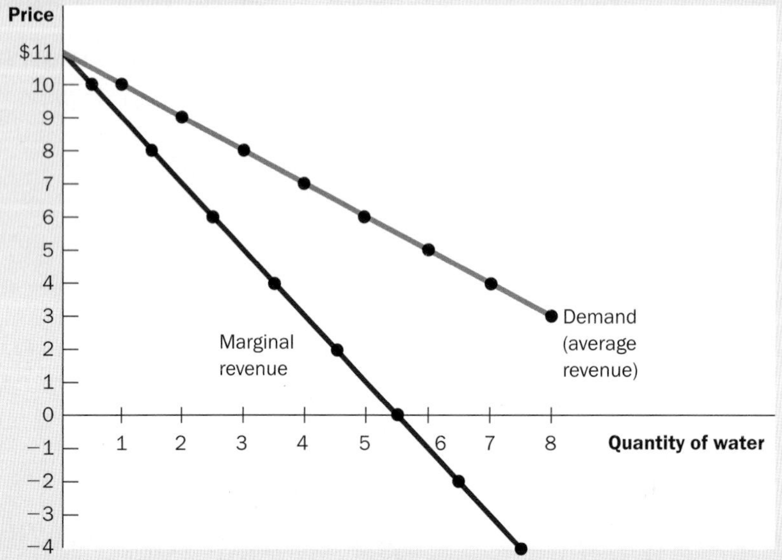

The demand curve shows how the quantity affects the price of the good. The marginal-revenue curve shows how the firm's revenue changes when the quantity increases by one unit. Because the price on all units sold must fall if the monopoly increases production, marginal revenue is always less than the price.

revenue is less than the price of the good. Thus, a monopoly's marginal-revenue curve lies below its demand curve.

You can see in the figure (as well as in Table 15.1) that marginal revenue can even become negative. Marginal revenue is negative when the price effect on revenue is greater than the output effect. In this case, when the firm produces an extra unit of output, the price falls by enough to cause the firm's total revenue to decline, even though the firm is selling more units.

Profit maximisation

Now that we have considered the revenue of a monopoly firm, we are ready to examine how such a firm maximises profit. Recall that one of the *Ten Lessons from Economics* discussed in chapter 1 is that rational people think at the margin. This lesson is as true for monopolists as it is for competitive firms. Here we apply the logic of marginal analysis to the monopolist's problem of deciding how much to produce.

Figure 15.4 graphs the demand curve, the marginal-revenue curve and the cost curves for a monopoly firm. All these curves should seem familiar. The demand and marginal-revenue curves are like those in Figure 15.3, and the cost curves are like those we introduced in chapter 13 and used to analyse competitive firms in chapter 14. These curves contain all the information we need to determine the level of output that a profit-maximising monopolist will choose.

Suppose, first, that the firm is producing at a low level of output, such as Q_1. In this case, marginal cost is less than marginal revenue. If the firm increased production by one unit, the additional revenue

Figure 15.4 **Profit maximisation for a monopoly**

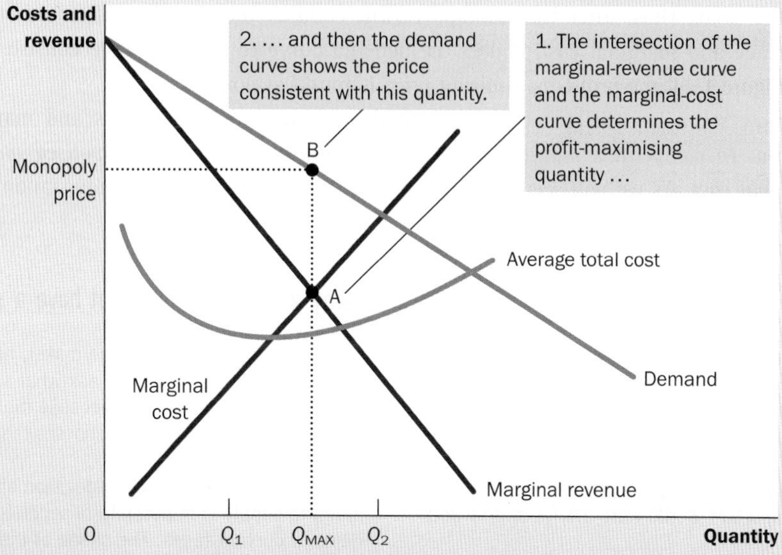
Costs and revenue
2. . . . and then the demand curve shows the price consistent with this quantity.
1. The intersection of the marginal-revenue curve and the marginal-cost curve determines the profit-maximising quantity . . .
B
Monopoly price
Average total cost
A
Demand
Marginal cost
Marginal revenue
0
Q1
QMAX
Q2
Quantity

A monopoly maximises profit by choosing the quantity at which marginal revenue equals marginal cost (point A). It then uses the demand curve to find the price that will induce consumers to buy that quantity (point B).

would exceed the additional costs, and profit would rise. Thus, when marginal cost is less than marginal revenue, the firm can increase profit by producing more units.

A similar argument applies at high levels of output, such as Q_2. In this case, marginal cost is greater than marginal revenue. If the firm reduced production by one unit, the costs saved would exceed the revenue lost. Thus, if marginal cost is greater than marginal revenue, the firm can raise profit by reducing production.

In the end, the firm adjusts its level of production until the quantity reaches Q_{MAX}, at which marginal revenue equals marginal cost. Thus, *the monopolist's profit-maximising quantity of output is determined by the intersection of the marginal-revenue curve and the marginal-cost curve.* In Figure 15.4, this intersection occurs at point A.

You might recall from chapter 14 that competitive firms also choose the quantity of output at which marginal revenue equals marginal cost. In following this rule for profit maximisation, competitive firms and monopolies are alike. But there is also an important difference between these types of firms – the marginal revenue of a competitive firm equals its price, whereas the marginal revenue of a monopoly is less than its price. That is:

$$\text{For a competitive firm: } P = MR = MC$$

$$\text{For a monopoly firm: } P > MR = MC$$

The equality of marginal revenue and marginal cost at the profit-maximising quantity is the same for both types of firm. What differs is how the price is related to marginal revenue and marginal cost.

How does the monopoly find the profit-maximising price for its product? The demand curve answers this question, because the demand curve relates the amount that customers are willing to pay to the quantity sold. Thus, after the monopoly firm chooses the quantity of output that equates marginal revenue and marginal cost, it uses the demand curve to find the price consistent with that quantity. In Figure 15.4, the profit-maximising price is found at point B.

We can now see a key difference between markets with competitive firms and markets with a monopoly firm: *In competitive markets, price equals marginal cost; in monopolised markets, price exceeds marginal cost.* As we will see in a moment, this finding is crucial to understanding the social cost of monopoly.

fyi

Why a monopoly does not have a supply curve

You may have noticed that we have analysed the price in a monopoly market using the market demand curve and the firm's cost curves. We have not made any mention of the market supply curve. In contrast, when we analysed prices in competitive markets beginning in chapter 4, the two most important words were always *supply* and *demand*.

What happened to the supply curve? Although monopoly firms make decisions about what quantity to supply (in the way we have just seen), a monopoly does not have a supply curve. A supply curve tells us the quantity that firms choose to supply at any given price. This concept makes sense when we are analysing competitive firms, which are price takers. But a monopoly firm is a price maker, not a price taker. It is not meaningful to ask what such a firm would produce at any price because the firm sets the price at the same time it chooses the quantity to supply.

Indeed, the monopolist's decision about how much to supply is impossible to separate from the demand curve it faces. The shape of the demand curve determines the shape of the marginal-revenue curve, which in turn determines the monopolist's profit-maximising quantity. In a competitive market, supply decisions can be analysed without knowing the demand curve, but that is not true in a monopoly market. Therefore, we never talk about a monopoly's supply curve.

A monopoly's profit

How much profit does the monopoly make? To see the monopoly's profit, recall that profit equals total revenue (*TR*) minus total costs (*TC*):

$$\text{Profit} = TR - TC$$

We can rewrite this as:

$$\text{Profit} = (TR/Q - TC/Q) \times Q$$

TR/Q is average revenue, which equals the price P, and TC/Q is average total cost ATC. Therefore:

$$\text{Profit} = (P - ATC) \times Q$$

This equation for profit (which is the same as the profit equation for competitive firms) allows us to measure the monopolist's profit in our graph.

Consider the shaded box in Figure 15.5. The height of the box (the segment BC) is price minus average total cost, $P - ATC$, which is the profit on the typical unit sold. The width of the box (the segment DC) is the quantity sold Q_{MAX}. Therefore, the area of this box is the monopoly firm's total profit.

Figure 15.5 The monopolist's profit

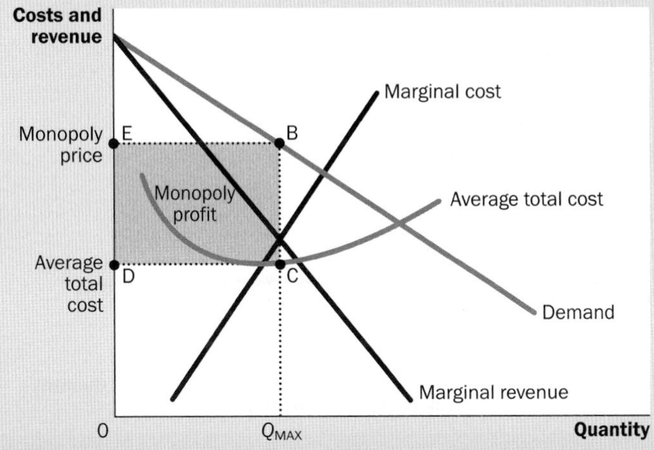

The area of the box BCDE equals the profit of the monopoly firm. The height of the box (BC) is price minus average total cost, which equals profit per unit sold. The width of the box (DC) is the number of units sold.

CASESTUDY

Bell's monopoly and the price of telephone calls

According to our analysis, prices are determined quite differently in monopolised markets from the way they are in competitive markets. A natural way to test this theory is to see what happens when a patent ends. When a company invents a new product, patent law gives the company a monopoly over the sale of that product. But eventually the firm's patent runs out and any company can make and sell the product. At that time, the market switches from being monopolistic to being competitive. By observing what happens to price and output both before and after the patent ends, we can compare monopoly and competitive behaviour.

A good example is provided by the telephone. Alexander Graham Bell invented the telephone and made the first successful transmission on 10 March 1876. Bell's patents over the telephone were held by the American Telephone and Telegraph Company (AT&T) until the patents ended in 1893. When the patents expired, many new firms entered the US telephone industry and it became highly competitive.

What should have happened to the price of telephone calls when the patents ran out? Figure 15.6 shows the market for telephone calls. In this figure, the marginal cost of producing each call is constant. (This is approximately true for many telephone calls.) During the life of the patent, the monopoly firm maximises profit by producing the quantity at which marginal revenue equals marginal cost and charging a price well above marginal cost. But when the patent runs out, the monopoly profit should encourage new firms to enter the market. As the market becomes more competitive, the price should fall to equal marginal cost.

Experience is, in fact, consistent with our theory. While the telephone was protected by a patent, AT&T charged high prices and restricted service to larger towns and cities. In 1893, only 270 000 telephones were installed in the United States. After the patents expired, competition became fierce and prices fell. Within 13 years the number of telephone subscribers had risen to six million. AT&T's profits were reduced by competition and in some states competition was so fierce that AT&T was reported to be making a loss. Just as our analysis predicts, the price of the competitively produced telephone calls was well below the price that the monopolist was charging.

>>

Figure 15.6 Prices and patents

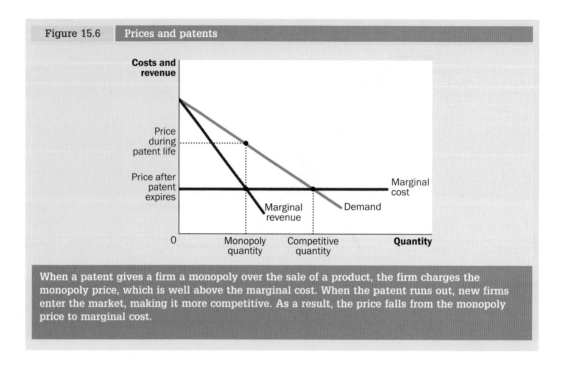

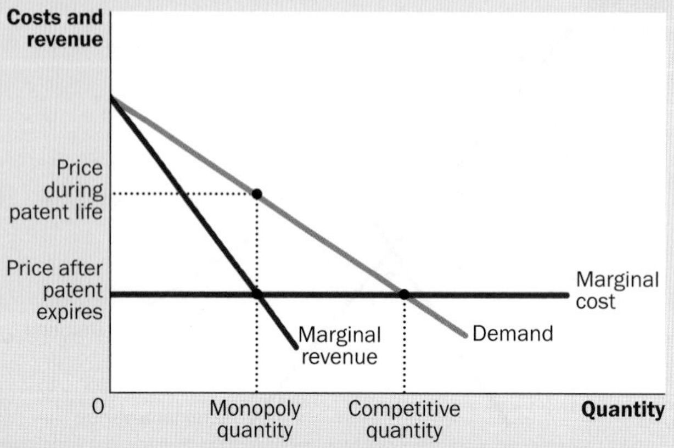

When a patent gives a firm a monopoly over the sale of a product, the firm charges the monopoly price, which is well above the marginal cost. When the patent runs out, new firms enter the market, making it more competitive. As a result, the price falls from the monopoly price to marginal cost.

Explain how a monopolist chooses the quantity of output to produce and the price to charge.

The welfare cost of monopoly

Is monopoly a good way to organise a market? We have seen that a monopoly, in contrast to a competitive firm, charges a price above marginal cost. From the standpoint of consumers, this high price makes monopoly undesirable. At the same time, however, the monopoly is earning profit from charging this high price. From the standpoint of the owners of the firm, the high price makes monopoly very desirable. Is it possible that the benefits to the firm's owners exceed the costs imposed on consumers, making monopoly desirable from the standpoint of society as a whole?

We can answer this question using the type of analysis we first saw in chapter 7. As in that chapter, we use total surplus as our measure of economic wellbeing. Recall that total surplus is the sum of consumer surplus and producer surplus. Consumer surplus is consumers' willingness to pay for a good minus the amount they actually pay for it. Producer surplus is the amount producers receive for a good minus their costs of producing it. In this case, there is a single producer – the monopolist.

You might already be able to guess the result of this analysis. In chapter 7 we concluded that the equilibrium of supply and demand in a competitive market is not only a natural outcome but a desirable one. In particular, the invisible hand of the market leads to an allocation of resources that makes total surplus as large as it can be. Because a monopoly leads to an allocation of resources different from that in a competitive market, the outcome must, in some way, fail to maximise total economic wellbeing.

The deadweight loss

We begin by considering what the monopoly firm would do if it were run by a benevolent social planner. The social planner cares not only about the profit earned by the firm's owners but also about the benefits received by the firm's consumers. The planner tries to maximise total surplus, which equals producer surplus (profit) plus consumer surplus. Keep in mind that total surplus equals the value of the good to consumers minus the costs of making the good incurred by the monopoly producer.

Figure 15.7 analyses what level of output a benevolent social planner would choose. The demand curve reflects the value of the good to consumers, as measured by their willingness to pay for it. The marginal-cost curve reflects the costs of the monopolist. Thus, *the socially efficient quantity is found where the demand curve and the marginal-cost curve intersect.* Below this quantity, the value to consumers exceeds the marginal cost of providing the good, so increasing output would raise total surplus. Above this quantity, the marginal cost exceeds the value to consumers, so decreasing output would raise total surplus. At the optimal quantity, the value of an extra unit to consumers exactly equals the marginal cost of production.

If the social planner were running the monopoly, the firm could achieve this efficient outcome by charging the price found at the intersection of the demand and marginal-cost curves. Thus, like a

Figure 15.7 **The efficient level of output**

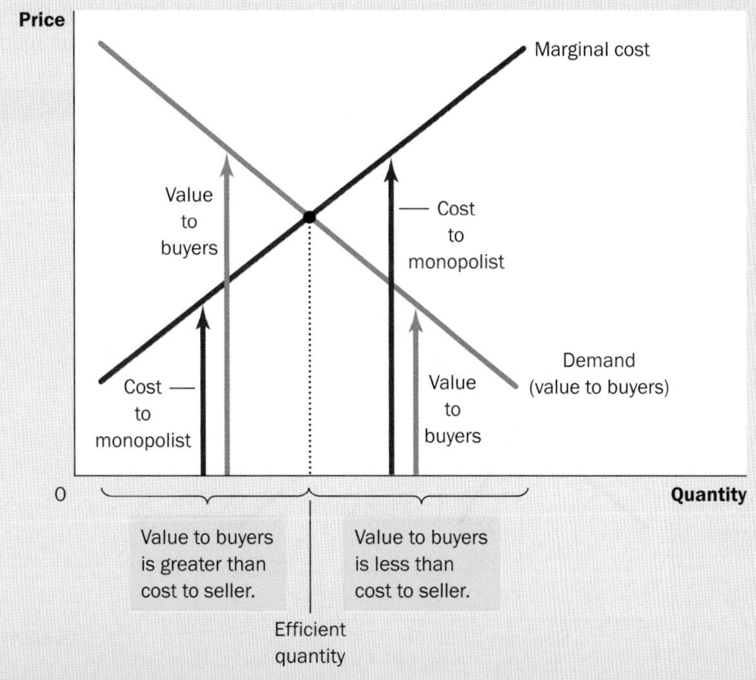

A benevolent social planner who wanted to maximise total surplus in the market would choose the level of output where the demand curve and marginal-cost curve intersect. Below this level, the value of the good to the marginal buyer (as reflected in the demand curve) exceeds the marginal cost of making the good. Above this level, the value to the marginal buyer is less than marginal cost.

competitive firm and unlike a profit-maximising monopoly, a social planner would charge a price equal to marginal cost. Because this price would give consumers an accurate signal about the cost of producing the good, consumers would buy the efficient quantity.

We can evaluate the welfare effects of monopoly by comparing the level of output that the monopolist chooses with the level of output that a social planner would choose. As we have seen, the monopolist chooses to produce and sell the quantity of output at which the marginal-revenue and marginal-cost curves intersect; the social planner would choose the quantity at which the demand and marginal-cost curves intersect. Figure 15.8 shows the comparison. *The monopolist produces less than the socially efficient quantity of output.*

We can also view the inefficiency of monopoly in terms of the monopolist's price. Because the market demand curve describes a negative relationship between the price and quantity of the good, a quantity that is inefficiently low is equivalent to a price that is inefficiently high. When a monopolist charges a price above marginal cost, some potential consumers value the good at more than its marginal cost but less than the monopolist's price. These consumers do not buy the good. Because the value these consumers place on the good is greater than the cost of providing it to them, this result is inefficient. Thus, monopoly pricing prevents some mutually beneficial trades from taking place.

The inefficiency of monopoly can be measured with a deadweight loss triangle, as illustrated in Figure 15.8. Because the demand curve reflects the value to consumers and the marginal-cost curve reflects the costs to the monopoly producer, the area of the deadweight-loss triangle between the demand curve and the marginal-cost curve equals the total surplus lost because of monopoly pricing. It is the reduction in economic wellbeing that results from the monopoly's use of its market power.

Figure 15.8 **The inefficiency of monopoly**

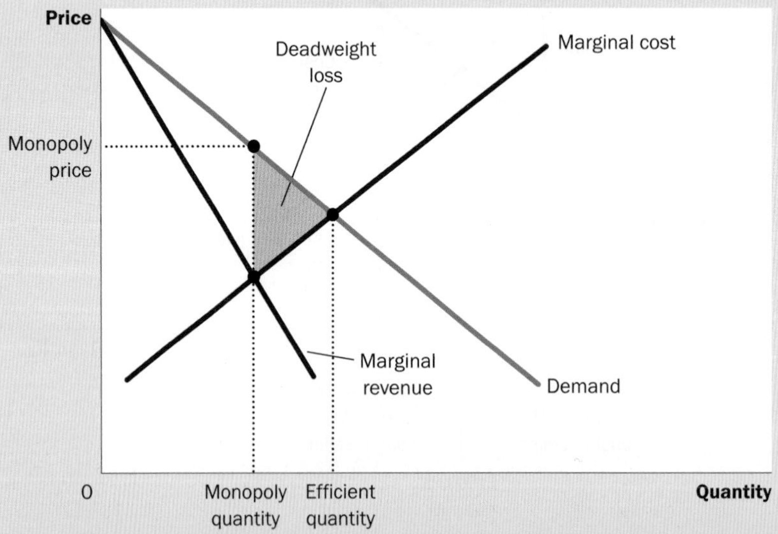

Because a monopoly charges a price above marginal cost, not all consumers who value the good at more than its cost buy it. Thus, the quantity produced and sold by a monopoly is below the socially efficient level. The deadweight loss is represented by the area of the triangle between the demand curve (which reflects the value of the good to consumers) and the marginal-cost curve (which reflects the costs of the monopoly producer).

The deadweight loss caused by monopoly is similar to the deadweight loss caused by a tax. Indeed, a monopolist is like a private tax collector. As we saw in chapter 8, a tax on a good places a wedge between consumers' willingness to pay (as reflected in the demand curve) and producers' costs (as reflected in the supply curve). Because a monopoly exerts its market power by charging a price above marginal cost, it creates a similar wedge. In both cases, the wedge causes the quantity sold to fall short of the social optimum. The difference between the two cases is that the government gets the revenue from a tax, whereas a private firm gets the monopoly profit.

The monopoly's profit: A social cost?

It is tempting to decry monopolies for 'profiteering' at the expense of the public. And, indeed, a monopoly firm does earn a higher profit by virtue of its market power. According to the economic analysis of monopoly, however, the firm's profit is not in itself necessarily a problem for society.

Welfare in a monopolised market, like all markets, includes the welfare of both consumers and producers. Whenever a consumer pays an extra dollar to a producer because of a monopoly price, the consumer is worse off by a dollar, and the producer is better off by the same amount. This transfer from the consumers of the good to the owners of the monopoly does not affect the market's total surplus – the sum of consumer and producer surplus. In other words, the monopoly profit itself does not represent a reduction in the size of the economic pie; it merely represents a bigger slice for producers and a smaller slice for consumers. Unless consumers are for some reason more deserving than producers – a judgement that goes beyond the realm of economic efficiency – the monopoly profit is not a social problem.

The problem in a monopolised market arises because the firm produces and sells a quantity of output below the level that maximises total surplus. The deadweight loss measures how much the economic pie shrinks as a result. This inefficiency is inextricably connected to the monopoly's high price – consumers buy fewer units when the firm raises its price above marginal cost. But keep in mind that the profit earned on the units that continue to be sold is not the problem. The problem stems from the inefficiently low quantity of output. Put differently, if the high monopoly price did not discourage some consumers from buying the good, it would raise producer surplus by exactly the amount it reduced consumer surplus, leaving total surplus the same as could be achieved by a benevolent social planner.

There is, however, a possible exception to this conclusion. Suppose that a monopoly firm has to incur additional costs to maintain its monopoly position. For example, a firm with a government-created monopoly might need to hire lobbyists to convince politicians to continue its monopoly. In this case, the monopoly may use up some of its monopoly profits paying for these additional costs. If so, the social loss from monopoly includes both these costs and the deadweight loss resulting from a price above marginal cost.

fyi **Measuring the cost of monopoly**

How large is the social cost from monopoly? A number of studies have tried to measure the size of monopoly deadweight loss, but the results from this research have been inconclusive. US researchers, for example, have argued that monopoly deadweight loss represents as little as 0.1 per cent or as much as 6 per cent of total US production. Robert Dixon and John Creedy, at the University of Melbourne, estimate that the size of monopoly deadweight loss in Australia is approximately 1 per cent of total production. Dixon and Creedy also look at how the burden of monopoly deadweight loss is shared over society. They conclude that monopoly has a greater impact on lower-income households. Not only does abuse of monopoly power lead to a general social cost, it also tends to increase social inequality.

Q How does a monopolist's quantity of output compare with the quantity of output that maximises total surplus?

Price discrimination

So far we have been assuming that the monopoly firm charges the same price to all customers. Yet in many cases firms try to sell the same good to different customers for different prices. This practice is called **price discrimination**.

price discrimination
the business practice of selling the same good at different prices to different customers

Search me!
▸ price discrimination

Before discussing the behaviour of a price-discriminating monopolist, we should note that price discrimination is not possible when a good is sold in a competitive market. In a competitive market, there are many firms selling the same good at the market price. No firm is willing to charge a lower price to any customer because the firm can sell all it wants at the market price. And if any firm tried to charge a higher price to a customer, that customer would buy from another firm. For a firm to price discriminate, it must have some market power.

A parable about pricing

To understand why a monopolist would want to price discriminate, let's consider a simple example. Imagine that you are the managing director of Readalot Publishing Company. Readalot's best-selling author has just written her latest novel. To keep things simple, let's imagine that you pay the author a flat $2 million for the exclusive rights to publish the book. Let's also assume that the cost of printing the book is zero. Readalot's profit, therefore, is the revenue it gets from selling the book minus the $2 million it has paid to the author. Given these assumptions, how would you, as Readalot's managing director, decide what price to charge for the book?

Your first step in setting the price is to estimate what the demand for the book is likely to be. Readalot's marketing department tells you that the book will attract two types of readers. The book will appeal to the author's 100 000 loyal fans. These fans will be willing to pay as much as $30 for the book. In addition, the book will appeal to about 400 000 less-enthusiastic readers who will be willing to pay up to $5 for the book.

What price maximises Readalot's profit? There are two natural prices to consider: $30 is the highest price Readalot can charge and still get the 100 000 loyal fans, and $5 is the highest price it can charge and still get the entire market of 500 000 potential readers. It is a matter of simple arithmetic to solve Readalot's problem. At a price of $30, Readalot sells 100 000 copies, has revenue of $3 million and makes a profit of $1 million. At a price of $5, it sells 500 000 copies, has revenue of $2.5 million and makes a profit of $500 000. Thus, Readalot maximises profit by charging $30 and forgoing the opportunity to sell to the 400 000 less-enthusiastic readers.

Notice that Readalot's decision causes a deadweight loss. There are 400 000 readers willing to pay $5 for the book and the marginal cost of providing it to them is zero. Thus, $2 million of total surplus is lost when Readalot charges the higher price. This deadweight loss is the usual inefficiency that arises whenever a monopolist charges a price above marginal cost.

Now suppose that Readalot's marketing department makes an important discovery – these two groups of readers are in separate markets. All the loyal fans live in Australia and all the other readers live in the United States. Moreover, it is difficult for readers in one country to buy books in the other.

In response to this discovery, Readalot can change its marketing strategy and increase profits. To the 100 000 Australian readers, it can charge $30 for the book. To the 400 000 American readers, it can charge $5 for the book. In this case, revenue is $3 million in Australia and $2 million in the United States, for a total of $5 million. Profit is then $3 million, which is substantially greater than the $1 million the company could earn charging the same $30 price to all customers. Not surprisingly, Readalot chooses to follow this strategy of price discrimination.

Although the story of Readalot Publishing is hypothetical, it describes accurately the business practice of many publishing companies. Textbooks, for example, are often sold at a lower price in Indonesia than in Australia. Even more important is the price differential between hardcover books and paperbacks. When a publisher has a new novel, it initially releases an expensive hardcover edition and later releases a cheaper paperback edition. The difference in price between these two editions far exceeds the difference in printing costs. The publisher's goal is just as in our example. By selling the hardcover to loyal fans and the paperback to less-enthusiastic readers, the publisher price discriminates and raises its profit.

The moral of the story

Like any parable, the story of Readalot Publishing is stylised. Yet, also like any parable, it teaches some important and general lessons. In this case, there are three lessons to be learned about price discrimination.

The first and most obvious lesson is that price discrimination is a rational strategy for a profit-maximising monopolist. In other words, by charging different prices to different customers, a monopolist can increase its profit. In essence, a price-discriminating monopolist charges each customer a price closer to his or her willingness to pay than is possible with a single price.

The second lesson is that price discrimination requires the ability to separate customers according to their willingness to pay. In our example, customers were separated geographically. But sometimes monopolists choose other differences, such as age or income, to distinguish among customers.

A corollary to this second lesson is that certain market forces can prevent firms from price discriminating. In particular, one such force is *arbitrage*, the process of buying a good in one market at a low price and selling it in another market at a higher price in order to profit from the price difference. In our example, suppose that Australian bookstores could buy the book in the United States and resell it to Australian readers. This arbitrage would prevent Readalot from price discriminating because no Australian would buy the book at the higher price.

The third lesson from our parable is the most surprising – price discrimination can raise economic welfare. Recall that a deadweight loss arises when Readalot charges a single $30 price, because the 400 000 less-enthusiastic readers do not end up with the book, even though they value it at more than its marginal cost of production. In contrast, when Readalot price discriminates, all readers end up with the book and the outcome is efficient. Thus, price discrimination can eliminate the inefficiency inherent in monopoly pricing.

Note that the increase in welfare from price discrimination shows up as higher producer surplus rather than higher consumer surplus. In our example, consumers are no better off for having bought the book, because the price they pay exactly equals the value they place on the book. The entire increase in total surplus from price discrimination accrues to Readalot Publishing in the form of higher profit.

IN THE NEWS . . .

MONOPOLIES AND GOVERNMENT POLICY

In the 1990s and 2000s, Australia privatised many government-owned infrastructure monopolies with the hope of opening up competition or relying on regulation to keep prices in check. This included Telstra, Australia's main telephone company. In this article from 2006, John Quiggin makes the case for reversing this process. And it is now occurring. As this chapter is being written, the government is re-buying part of Telstra in order to build a National Broadband Network (NBN). The NBN will be a new, government-owned telecommunications monopoly.

Make Telstra public again

by John Quiggin

Following Australian telecommunications policy is like watching one of those horror movies where the protagonist insists on going down the staircase into the cellar, even though everyone in the audience can see that disaster awaits. Or perhaps it's more like *Groundhog Day*, where the hero relives the same bad day over and over again. Looking at the current crisis over Telstra, it's striking that, despite the massive technological changes of the past decade, the same policy issues are being debated and the same mistakes are made.

The most salient example is the protracted saga of Telstra's proposed privatisation. It was obvious to anyone who cared to look that the idea of partial privatisation, commenced by the Howard government in 1997 (in emulation of previous privatisations on this model undertaken by Labor) was a recipe for conflicts of interest, and for the creation of a regulatory nightmare.

As Treasurer Peter Costello said in early 2000, barely two years after the T1 sale,

> If Telstra is going to be caught in a position where it is half privately owned and half government-owned, I don't think that is going to be a good outcome. Telstra should all be either privately owned, or if people really think that nationalisation and government ownership is necessary they ought to have the courage of their convictions and nationalise it.

More than six years later, Telstra is still half-private and half-public and it seems inevitable that, even if a sale goes ahead, a substantial share of Telstra will remain in public ownership through the future fund. Certainly, there is nothing in the record of regulatory policy to suggest that full privatisation would work well. So Costello's own logic would suggest that he should be advocating renationalisation.

But the debate over Telstra's ownership is of secondary importance compared to the more fundamental problem that telecommunications policy has failed to meet the needs of telecommunications consumers of Australia as a nation. We lagged badly in the initial provision and take-up of broadband, and now seem certain to fall even further behind as other countries move to high-speed Internet technologies based on optical fibre all the way to the home.

More than ten years and several communications ministers ago, it was evident that poorly designed telecommunications policy was promoting investment decisions driven by considerations of corporate and regulatory strategy, yielding outcomes that were not in the national interest. The biggest example then was the race between Telstra and Optus to roll out duplicate hybrid-fibre coax cable networks, covering half the country, leaving everyone else to wait a decade or more for decent broadband access.

As I wrote at the time, the future of communications, and most notably the rapidly developing Internet, lies in digital networks based on optical fibre … the more progressive telecommunications companies in the United States are already discarding HFC in favor of building optical fibre 'up to the curb … The resources being wasted in providing duplicate analog networks could have made Australia a world leader in the development of digital telecommunications networks.' ('Pay TV's wasted billions', *Australian Financial Review*, 8 January 1996.)

A decade later, with Japan and other countries already delivering fibre to the home, allowing high-speed Internet traffic for both uploads and downloads, Telstra finally came up with a proposal to roll fibre out, but only as far as local nodes. But, this was a mere bargaining chip in Telstra's corporate regulatory strategy, to be withdrawn when the regulator did not give the right outcome.

So, apparently, we are supposed to rely on the second-class option of stretching ADSL technology to its limits, in the hope (contradicted by Telstra's own statements on the subject) that the copper-wire network will stand up to the strain.

It's time for the government to face up to its responsibilities for our national infrastructure. Telstra should be brought back into public ownership, and required to construct telecommunications infrastructure to meet national needs.

The first step in this process is that the government should take its role as majority owner seriously, and appoint a board and CEO committed to acting in the national interest. Peripheral assets like the Foxtel stake should be sold off. And the Future Fund could be used to buy out shareholders who would prefer a company more focused on short-term profits.

Australian telecommunications policy has been stuck in the same endless loop for a decade or more. If the horror movie we've seen so far is to have a happy ending, we need to turn around and head back upstairs.

Source: John Quiggin/*Australian Financial Review*, 17 August 2006.

The analytics of price discrimination

Let's consider a bit more formally how price discrimination affects economic welfare. We begin by assuming that the monopolist can price discriminate perfectly. *Perfect price discrimination* describes a situation in which the monopolist knows exactly each customer's willingness to pay and can charge each customer a different price. In this case, the monopolist charges each customer exactly his or her willingness to pay and the monopolist gets the entire surplus in every transaction.

Figure 15.9 shows producer and consumer surplus with and without price discrimination. Without price discrimination, the firm charges a single price above marginal cost, as shown in panel (a). Because some potential customers who value the good at more than marginal cost do not buy it at this high price, the monopoly causes a deadweight loss. Yet when a firm can perfectly price discriminate, as shown in panel (b), customers who value the good at more than marginal cost buy the good and are charged their willingness to pay. All mutually beneficial trades take place, there is no deadweight loss, and the entire surplus derived from the market goes to the monopoly producer in the form of profit.

In reality, of course, price discrimination is not perfect. Customers do not walk into shops with signs displaying their willingness to pay. Instead, firms price discriminate by dividing customers into groups: young versus old, weekday versus weekend shoppers, Australians versus Americans and so on. Unlike those in our parable of Readalot Publishing, customers within each group differ in their willingness to pay for the product, making perfect price discrimination impossible.

How does this imperfect price discrimination affect welfare? The analysis of these pricing schemes is quite complicated and it turns out that there is no general answer to this question. Compared with

Figure 15.9 Welfare with and without price discrimination

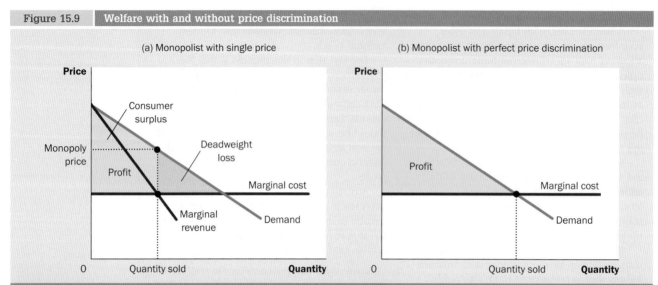

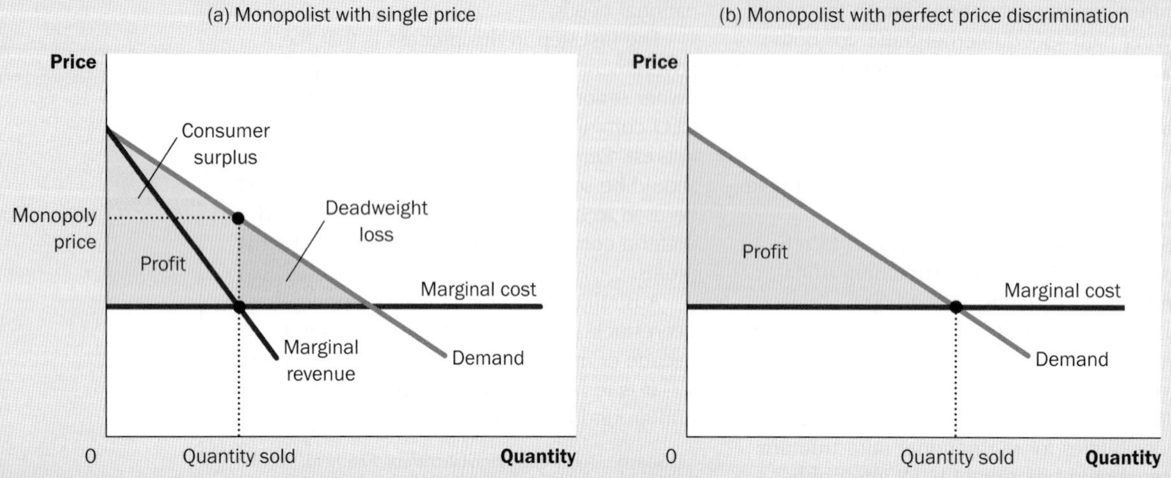

Panel (a) shows a monopolist that charges the same price to all customers. Total surplus in this market equals the sum of profit (producer surplus) and consumer surplus. Panel (b) shows a monopolist that can perfectly price discriminate. Because consumer surplus equals zero, total surplus now equals the firm's profit. Comparing these two panels, you can see that perfect price discrimination raises profit, raises total surplus and lowers consumer surplus.

the monopoly outcome with a single price, imperfect price discrimination can raise, lower or leave unchanged total surplus in a market. The only certain conclusion is that price discrimination raises the monopoly's profit – otherwise the firm would choose to charge all customers the same price.

Examples of price discrimination

Firms in our economy use various business strategies aimed at charging different prices to different customers. Now that we understand the economics of price discrimination, let's consider some examples.

Movie tickets

Many movie theatres charge a lower price for children, students and senior citizens than for other patrons. This fact is hard to explain in a competitive market. In a competitive market, price equals marginal cost, and the marginal cost of providing a seat for a child, student or senior citizen is the same as the marginal cost of providing a seat for anyone else. Yet this fact is easily explained if movie theatres have some local monopoly power and if children, students and senior citizens have a lower willingness to pay for a ticket. In this case, movie theatres raise their profit by price discriminating.

Airline prices

Seats on aeroplanes are sold at many different prices. Most airlines charge a lower price for a ticket if it has less flexible conditions, such as limits on the ability to change flights or cancel the booking at the last minute. The difference in prices generally is far higher than the difference in cost to the airline of the flexible conditions. So why do airlines price in this way? The reason is that charging a higher price for a flexible ticket provides a way to separate business travellers and personal travellers. A passenger on a business trip has a high willingness to pay and, most likely, wants the flexibility to change their flight at the last minute, for example, if a meeting is rescheduled or runs over time. In contrast, a passenger travelling for personal reasons has a lower willingness to pay and is less likely to need to vary their flight at the last minute. Thus, the airlines can successfully price discriminate by charging a higher price for passengers who want a ticket with flexible conditions.

'Would it bother you to hear how little I paid for this flight?'

Source: © William Hamilton

Store brands

Many large shops have a store brand. The store-brand products are shelved next to well-known brands and are often cheaper than these well-known products. In some cases the store brand and the well-known brand are essentially the same product, produced by the same firm. Why would shops stock the same product but in two different packages with two different prices?

The answer is that store brands allow shops to price discriminate. Some customers are willing to pay a premium to buy a product produced by a well-known manufacturer. These customers are willing to pay more for a product sold with the manufacturer's brand. Other customers do not care about the brand of the product and are simply interested in buying the cheapest product available. By offering a store-brand product as well as the product with the manufacturer's brand, shops are able to price discriminate between these two types of buyers.

Quantity discounts

So far in our examples of price discrimination, the monopolist charges different prices to different customers. Sometimes, however, monopolists price discriminate by charging different prices to the same customer for different units that the customer buys. For example, many firms offer lower prices to customers who buy large quantities. A bakery might charge $0.50 for each doughnut, but $5 for a dozen. This is a form of price discrimination because the customer pays a higher price for the first unit bought than for the twelfth. Quantity discounts are often a successful way of price discriminating because a customer's willingness to pay for an additional unit declines as the customer buys more units.

Q

Telephone and Internet line rentals are often more expensive in rural areas than in urban areas. Is that enough information to conclude that telecommunication firms price discriminate rural consumers?

IN THE NEWS ...

PRICE DISCRIMINATION ON BROADWAY

Theatre producers often use price discrimination to try and raise profits. But how well do they go? This article looks at a study of price discrimination on Broadway by Hal R. Varian. His conclusion is that the producers price discriminate pretty well.

The dynamics of pricing tickets for Broadway shows

by Hal R. Varian

Every night in New York, about 25 000 people, on average, attend Broadway shows.

As avid theatregoers know, ticket prices have been rising inexorably. The top ticket price for Broadway shows has risen 31 per cent since 1998. But the actual price paid has gone up by only 24 per cent.

The difference is a result of discounting. Savvy fans know that there are deals available for even the most popular shows, with the most popular discounts being offered through coupons, two-for-one deals, special prices for students, and through the TKTS booth in Times Square.

Why so much discounting? The value of a seat in a theatre, like a seat on an airplane, is highly perishable. Once the show starts or the plane takes off, a seat is worth next to nothing.

In both industries, sellers use a variety of strategies to try to ensure that the seats are sold to those who are willing to pay the most. This phenomenon was examined by a Stanford economist, Phillip Leslie, in an article, 'Price Discrimination in Broadway Theater', published in the autumn 2004 issue of the *RAND Journal of Economics*.

Mr. Leslie was able to collect detailed data on a 1996 Broadway play, 'Seven Guitars'. Over 140 000 people saw this play, and they bought tickets in 17 price categories. Some price variation was due to the quality of the seats – orchestra, mezzanine, balcony and so on – while other price differences were a result of various forms of discounting.

The combination of quality variation and discounts led to widely varying ticket prices. The average difference of two tickets chosen at random on a given night was about 40 per cent of the average price. This is comparable to the price variation in airline tickets ...

The ticket promotions also varied over the 199 performances of the show. Targeted direct mail was used early on, while two-for-one tickets were not introduced until about halfway through the run.

The tickets offered for sale at the TKTS booth in Times Square are typically orchestra seats, the best category of seats available. But the discounted tickets at TKTS tend to be the lower-quality orchestra seats. They sell at a fixed discount of 50 per cent, but are offered only for performances that day.

Mr. Leslie's goal was primarily to model the behavior of the theatregoer. The audience for Broadway shows is highly diverse. About 10 per cent, according to a 1991 survey conducted by Broadway producers, had household incomes of \$25 000 or \$35 000 while an equal number had incomes over \$150 000 (in 1990 dollars).

The prices and discounting policy set by the producers of Broadway shows try to use this heterogeneity to get people to sort themselves by their willingness to pay for tickets.

You probably will not see Donald Trump waiting in line at TKTS; presumably, those in his income class do not mind paying full price. But a lot of students, unemployed actors and tourists do use TKTS.

Yes, it is inconvenient to wait in line at TKTS. But that is the point. If it weren't inconvenient, everyone would do it, and this would result in substantially lower revenues for Broadway shows.

Mr. Leslie uses some advanced econometric techniques to estimate the values that different income groups put on the various categories of tickets. He finds that Broadway producers do a pretty good job, in general, at maximizing revenue ...

We are likely to see more and more goods and services sold using the same sort of differential pricing. As more and more transactions become computer-mediated, it becomes easier for sellers to collect data, to experiment with pricing and to analyze the results of those experiments.

This, of course, makes life more complicated for us consumers. The flip side is that pricing variations make those good deals more likely.

Last time I was in New York, I was pleased that I managed to get a ticket to 'The Producers' for half price. It almost made up for the fact that I had to book my airline ticket two weeks in advance and stay over a Saturday night.

Give two examples of price discrimination. How does perfect price discrimination affect consumer surplus, producer surplus and total surplus?

Conclusion: The prevalence of monopoly

This chapter has discussed the behaviour of firms who have control over the prices they charge. We have seen that these firms behave very differently from the competitive firms studied in the previous chapter. Table 15.2 summarises some of the key similarities and differences between competitive and monopoly markets.

From the standpoint of public policy, a crucial result is that monopolists produce less than the socially efficient quantity and charge prices above marginal cost. As a result, they cause deadweight losses. In some cases, these inefficiencies can be mitigated through price discrimination by the monopolist, but other times they call for policymakers to take an active role. What actions policymakers might take is the subject of chapter 17.

Table 15.2 Competition versus monopoly: A summary comparison

	Competition	Monopoly
Similarities		
Goals of firms	Maximise profits	Maximise profits
Rule for maximising profit	$MR = MC$	$MR = MC$
Can earn economic profits in the short run?	Yes	Yes
Differences		
Number of firms	Many	One
Marginal revenue	$MR = P$	$MR < P$
Price	$P = MC$	$P > MC$
Produce welfare-maximising level of output	Yes	No
Entry in the long run?	Yes	No
Can earn economic profits in the long run?	No	Yes
Price discrimination profitable	No	Yes

How prevalent are the problems of monopoly? There are two answers to this question.

In one sense, monopolies are common. Most firms have some control over the prices they charge. They are not forced to charge the market price for their goods, because their goods are not exactly the same as those offered by other firms. A Toyota Camry is not the same as a Ford Falcon. Heinz tomato soup is not the same as Campbell's. Each of these goods has a downward-sloping demand curve, which gives each producer some degree of monopoly power.

Yet firms with substantial monopoly power are quite rare. Few goods are unique. Most have substitutes that, even if not exactly the same, are very similar. Heinz can raise the price of its tomato soup a little without losing all its sales, but if it raises it very much, sales will fall substantially.

In the end, monopoly power is a matter of degree. It is true that many firms have some monopoly power. It is also true that their monopoly power is usually quite limited. In these cases, we will not go far wrong assuming that firms operate in competitive markets, even if that is not precisely the case.

Summary

- A monopoly is a firm that is the sole seller in its market. A monopoly arises when a single firm owns a key resource, when the government gives a firm the exclusive right to produce a good, or when a single firm can supply the entire market at a smaller cost than many firms could.
- Because a monopoly is the sole producer in its market, it faces a downward-sloping demand curve for its product. When a monopoly increases production by one unit, it causes the price of its good to fall, which reduces the amount of revenue earned on all units produced. As a result, a monopoly's marginal revenue is always below the price of its good.
- Like a competitive firm, a monopoly firm maximises profit by producing the quantity at which marginal revenue equals marginal cost. The monopoly then chooses the price at which that quantity is demanded. Unlike a competitive firm, a monopoly firm's price exceeds its marginal revenue, so its price exceeds marginal cost.
- A monopolist's profit-maximising level of output is below the level that maximises the sum of consumer and producer surplus. That is, when the monopoly charges a price above marginal cost, some consumers who value the good more than its cost of production do not buy it. As a result, monopoly causes deadweight losses similar to the deadweight losses caused by taxes.
- Monopolists often can raise their profits by charging different prices for the same good based on a buyer's willingness to pay. This practice of price discrimination can raise economic welfare by getting the good to some consumers who otherwise would not buy it. In the extreme case of perfect price discrimination, the deadweight losses of monopoly are completely eliminated. More generally, when price discrimination is imperfect, it can either raise or lower welfare compared with the outcome with a single monopoly price.

Key concepts

monopoly | natural monopoly | price discrimination

Questions for review

1. Give an example of a government-created monopoly. Is creating this monopoly necessarily bad public policy? Explain.
2. Define natural monopoly. What does the size of a market have to do with whether an industry is a natural monopoly?
3. Why is a monopolist's marginal revenue less than the price of its good?
4. Draw the demand, marginal-revenue and marginal-cost curves for a monopolist. Show the profit-maximising level of output. Show the profit-maximising price.
5. In your diagram from the previous question, show the level of output that maximises total surplus. Show the deadweight loss from the monopoly. Explain your answer.
6. Give two examples of price discrimination. In each case, explain why the monopolist chooses to follow this business strategy.

Problems and applications

1 Define a firm's marginal revenue. If the price of a good is always greater than zero, can a monopolist's marginal revenue ever be negative? Explain.

2 Does a monopolist or a competitive firm face a more elastic demand curve? What characteristic of the good being sold leads to a larger elasticity? Explain.

3 Suppose that a natural monopolist were required by law to charge average total cost. On a diagram, label the price charged and the deadweight loss to society relative to marginal-cost pricing.

4 Max is a magazine monopolist. His marginal cost of production (per magazine) is constant at $5. His demand information is as follows:

Price ($)	Q^D
50	0
40	5
30	10
20	20
15	30
10	50
5	102
2.50	200

a Calculate the total revenue for Max at each price.

b Calculate the (approximate) marginal revenue for Max at each price.

c What is Max's profit-maximising output level and price? Compare this with the perfectly competitive equilibrium level of output and price.

5 Consider the delivery of mail. In general, what is the shape of the average-total-cost curve? How might the shape differ between isolated rural areas and densely populated urban areas? How might the shape have changed over time? Explain.

6 Suppose the Go-for-it Gas company has a monopoly on natural gas sales. If the price of electricity increases, what is the change in Go-for-it's profit-maximising levels of output, price and profit? Explain in words and with a graph.

7 A small town is served by many competing supermarkets, which have constant marginal cost.

a Using a diagram of the market for groceries, show the consumer surplus, producer surplus and total surplus.

b Now suppose that the independent supermarkets combine to form one chain. Using a new diagram, show the new consumer surplus, producer surplus and total surplus. Relative to the competitive market, what is the transfer from consumers to producers? What is the deadweight loss?

8 Ted Grunge has just finished recording his latest CD. His record company's marketing department determines that the demand for the CD is as follows:

Price ($)	Number of CDs
24	10 000
22	20 000
20	30 000
18	40 000
16	50 000
14	60 000

The company can produce the CD with no fixed cost and a variable cost of $5 per CD.

a Find total revenue for quantity equal to 10 000, 20 000 and so on. What is the marginal revenue for each 10 000 increase in the quantity sold?

b What quantity of CDs would maximise profit? What would the price be? What would the profit be?

c If you were Ted's agent, what recording fee would you advise Ted to demand from the record company? Why?

9 A company is considering building a bridge across a river. The bridge would cost $2 million to build and nothing to maintain. The following table shows the company's anticipated demand over the lifetime of the bridge:

P (per crossing)	*Q* (number of crossings, in thousands)
$8	0
7	100
6	200
5	300
4	400
3	500
2	600
1	700
0	800

a If the company were to build the bridge, what would be its profit-maximising price? Would that be the efficient level of output? Why or why not?

b If the company is interested in maximising profit, should it build the bridge? What would be its profit or loss?

c If the government were to build the bridge, what price should it charge?

d Should the government build the bridge? Explain.

10 The Placebo Drug Company holds a patent on one of its discoveries.

a Assuming that the production of the drug involves rising marginal cost, illustrate Placebo's profit-maximising price and quantity. Also show Placebo's profits.

b Now suppose that the government imposes a tax on each bottle of the drug produced. On a new diagram, illustrate Placebo's new price and quantity. How does each compare with your answer in part (a)?

c Although it is not easy to see in your diagrams, the tax reduces Placebo's profit. Explain why this must be true.

d Instead of the tax per bottle, suppose that the government imposes a tax on Placebo of $10 000 regardless of how many bottles are produced. How does this tax affect Placebo's price, quantity and profits? Explain.

11 Larry, Curly and Moe run the only pub in town. Larry wants to sell as many drinks as possible without losing money. Curly wants the pub to bring in as much revenue as possible. Moe wants to make the largest possible profits. Using a single diagram of the pub's demand curve and cost curves, show the price and quantity combinations favoured by each of the three partners. Explain.

12 The Best Computer Company just developed a new computer chip, on which it immediately acquires a patent.

a Draw a diagram that shows the consumer surplus, producer surplus and total surplus in the market for this new chip.

b What happens to these three measures of surplus if the firm can perfectly price discriminate? What is the change in deadweight loss? What transfers occur?

13 Explain why a monopolist will always produce a quantity at which the demand curve is elastic. (*Hint:* If demand is inelastic and the firm raises its price, what happens to total revenue and total costs?)

14 Many schemes for price discriminating involve some cost. For example, discount coupons in newspapers and magazines take time to cut out. Impatient buyers who cannot afford the time end up paying a higher price. But the coupons also take up time and resources from both the buyers who do cut them out and the seller. This question considers the implications of costly price discrimination. To keep things simple, let's assume that our monopolist's production costs are simply proportional to output, so that average total cost and marginal cost are constant and equal to each other.

a Draw the cost, demand and marginal-revenue curves for the monopolist. Show the price the monopolist would charge without price discrimination.

b In your diagram, mark the area equal to the monopolist's profit and call it *X*. Mark the area equal to consumer surplus and call it *Y*. Mark the area equal to the deadweight loss and call it *Z*.

c Now suppose that the monopolist can perfectly price discriminate. What is the monopolist's profit? (Give your answer in terms of *X*, *Y* and *Z*.)

d What is the change in the monopolist's profit from price discrimination? What is the change in total surplus from price discrimination? Which change is larger? Explain. (Give your answer in terms of *X*, *Y* and *Z*.)

e Now suppose that there is some cost of price discrimination. To model this cost, let's assume that the monopolist has to pay a fixed cost *C* in order to price discriminate. How would a monopolist make the decision whether to pay this fixed cost? (Give your answer in terms of *X*, *Y*, *Z* and *C*.)

f How would a benevolent social planner, who cares about total surplus, decide whether the monopolist should price discriminate? (Give your answer in terms of *X*, *Y*, *Z* and *C*.)

g Compare your answers to parts (e) and (f). How does the monopolist's incentive to price discriminate differ from the social planner's? Is it possible that the monopolist will price discriminate even though it is not socially desirable?

Search me!

Search me!

When accessing information about microeconomics use the following keywords in any combinations you require:

- monopoly
- natural monopoly
- price discrimination

CourseMate

CourseMate

For more multimedia resources and activities on economics, visit the Economics CourseMate website.

16

Business strategy

Learning objectives

In this chapter you will:

- see what market structures lie between monopoly and competition
- examine what outcomes are possible when a market is an oligopoly
- learn about the prisoners' dilemma and how it applies to oligopoly and other issues.

If you go to a shop to buy tennis balls, it is likely that you will come home with one of four brands: Wilson, Penn, Dunlop or Spalding. These four companies make almost all of the tennis balls sold in Australia. Together these firms determine the quantity of tennis balls produced and, given the market demand curve, the price at which they are sold.

How can we describe the market for tennis balls? The previous two chapters discussed two types of market structure. In a competitive market, each firm is so small compared with the market that it cannot influence the price of its product and, therefore, takes the price as given by market conditions. In a monopolised market, a single firm supplies the entire market for a good, and that firm can choose any price and quantity on the market demand curve.

The market for tennis balls fits neither the competitive nor the monopoly model. Competition and monopoly are extreme forms of market structure. Competition occurs when there are many firms in a market offering essentially identical products; monopoly occurs when there is only one firm in a market. It is natural to start the study of industrial organisation with these polar cases, for they are the easiest cases to understand. Yet many industries, including the tennis ball industry, fall somewhere between these two extremes. Firms in these industries have competitors but, at the same time, do not face so much competition that they are price takers. Economists call this situation *imperfect competition.*

In this chapter we discuss the types of imperfect competition and examine a particular type called **oligopoly**. The essence of an oligopolistic market is that there are only a few sellers. As a result, the actions of any one seller in the market can have a large impact on the profits of all the other sellers. Oligopolistic firms are interdependent in a way that competitive firms are not. Our goal in this chapter is to see how this interdependence shapes firms' behaviour.

oligopoly
a market structure in which only a few sellers offer similar or identical products

Search me!
▸ oligopoly

The analysis of oligopoly offers an opportunity to introduce **game theory**, the study of how people behave in strategic situations. By 'strategic' we mean a situation in which a person, when choosing among alternative courses of action, must consider how others might respond to the action he takes. Strategic thinking is crucial not only in checkers, chess and noughts-and-crosses but in many business decisions. Because oligopolistic markets have only a small number of firms, each firm must act strategically. Each firm knows that its profit depends not only on how much it produces but also on how much the other firms produce. In making its production decision, each firm in an oligopoly should consider how its decision might affect the production decisions of all the other firms.

game theory
the study of how people behave in strategic situations

Game theory is not necessary for understanding competitive or monopoly markets. In a market that is either perfectly competitive or monopolistically competitive, each firm is so small compared to

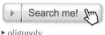

Source: DILBERT © 2005 Scott Adams. Used by permission of UNIVERSAL UCLICK. All rights reserved.

the market that strategic interactions with other firms are not important. In a monopolised market, strategic interactions are absent because the market has only one firm. But, as we will see, game theory is useful for understanding oligopolies and many other situations in which a small number of players interact with one another. Game theory helps explain the strategies that people choose, whether they are playing tennis or selling tennis balls.

Between monopoly and perfect competition

The previous two chapters analysed markets with many competitive firms and markets with a single monopoly firm. In chapter 14, we saw that the price in a perfectly competitive market always equals the marginal cost of production. We also saw that, in the long run, entry and exit drive economic profit to zero, so the price also equals average total cost. In chapter 15, we saw how monopoly firms can use their market power to keep prices above marginal cost, leading to a positive economic profit for the firm and a deadweight loss for society.

The cases of perfect competition and monopoly illustrate some important ideas about how markets work. Most markets in the economy, however, include elements of both these cases and, therefore, are not completely described by either of them. The typical firm in the economy faces competition, but the competition is not so rigorous as to make the firm exactly fit the description of the price-taking firm analysed in chapter 14. The typical firm also has some degree of market power, but its market power is not so great that the firm can exactly fit the description of the monopoly firm analysed in chapter 15. In other words, the typical firm in our economy is imperfectly competitive.

One type of imperfect competition is an oligopoly, which is a market with only a few sellers, each offering a product similar or identical to the others. One example is the market for tennis balls. Another is the market for retail groceries. Two large sellers, Coles and Woolworths, together supply around 70 per cent of all dry groceries sold to Australian consumers.

A second type of imperfectly competitive market is called *monopolistic competition*. This describes a market structure in which there are many firms selling products that are similar but not identical. Examples include the markets for novels, films, CDs and computer games. In a monopolistically competitive market, each firm has a monopoly over the product it makes, but many other firms make similar products that compete for the same customers.

Figure 16A. summarises the four types of market structure. The first question to ask about any market is how many firms there are. If there is only one firm, the market is a monopoly. If there are only a few firms, the market is an oligopoly. If there are many firms, we need to ask another question: Do the firms sell identical or differentiated products? If the many firms sell differentiated products, the market is monopolistically competitive. If the many firms sell identical products, the market is perfectly competitive.

Because reality is never as simple as theory, at times you may find it hard to decide what structure best describes a market. There is, for instance, no single number that separates 'few' from 'many' when counting the number of firms. (Do the dozen or so companies that sell cars in Australia make this market an oligopoly or more competitive? The answer is open to debate.) Similarly, there is no sure way to determine when products are differentiated and when they are identical. (Are different brands of milk really the same? Again, the answer is debatable.) When analysing actual markets, economists have to keep in mind the lessons learned from studying all types of market structure and then apply each lesson as it seems appropriate.

Figure 16.1 The four types of market structure

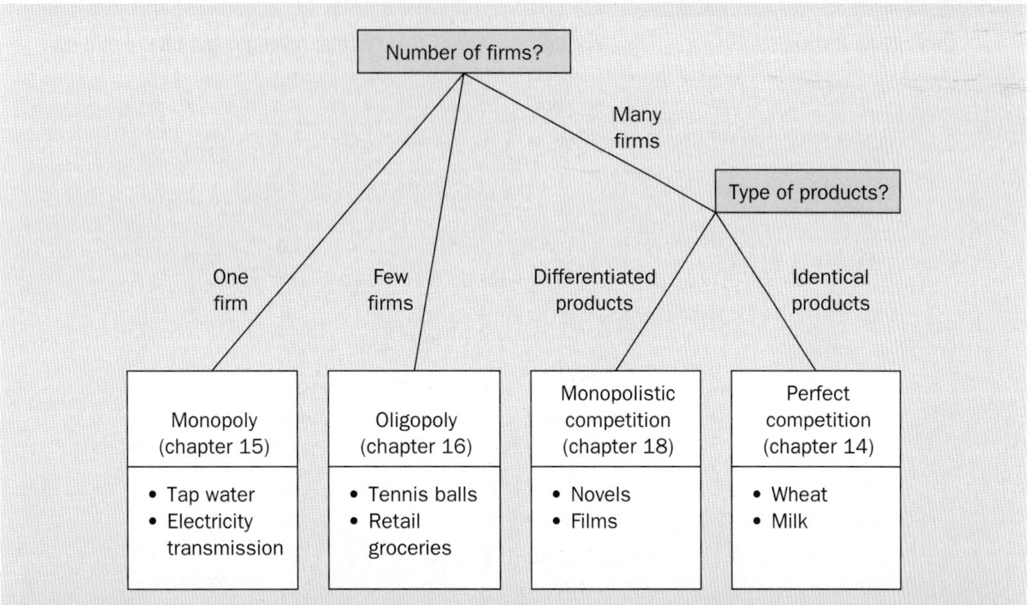

Economists who study industrial organisation divide markets into four types – monopoly, oligopoly, monopolistic competition and perfect competition.

Now that we understand how economists define the various types of market structure, we can continue our analysis of them. In chapter 18, we analyse monopolistic competition. In this chapter we examine the business strategy of oligopolists.

Q Define oligopoly and monopolistic competition and give an example of each.

Markets with only a few sellers

Because an oligopolistic market has only a small group of sellers, a key feature of oligopoly is the tension between cooperation and self-interest. The oligopolists are best off when they cooperate and act like a monopolist – producing a small quantity of output and charging a price above marginal cost. Yet because each oligopolist cares about only its own profit, there are powerful incentives at work that hinder a group of firms from maintaining the monopoly outcome.

A duopoly example

To understand the behaviour of oligopolies, let's consider an oligopoly with only two members, called a duopoly. Duopoly is the simplest type of oligopoly. Oligopolies with three or more members face the same problems as oligopolies with only two members, so we do not lose much by starting with the case of duopoly.

Table 16.1 The demand schedule for water

Quantity (in litres)	Price ($)	Total revenue (and total profit) ($)
0	120	0
10	110	1100
20	100	2000
30	90	2700
40	80	3200
50	70	3500
60	60	3600
70	50	3500
80	40	3200
90	30	2700
100	20	2000
110	10	1100
120	0	0

Imagine a town in which only two residents – Jack and Jill – own wells that produce water safe for drinking. Each Saturday, Jack and Jill decide how many litres of water to pump, bring the water to town and sell it for whatever price the market will bear. To keep things simple, suppose that Jack and Jill can pump as much water as they want without cost; that is, the marginal cost of water equals zero.

Table 16.1 shows the town's demand schedule for water. The first column shows the total quantity demanded and the second column shows the price. If the two well owners sell a total of 10 litres of water, water goes for $110 a litre. If they sell a total of 20 litres, the price falls to $100 a litre. And so on. If you graphed these two columns of numbers, you would get a standard downward-sloping demand curve.

The last column in Table 16.1 shows the total revenue from the sale of water. It equals the quantity sold times the price. Because there is no cost to pumping water, the total revenue of the two producers equals their total profit.

Let's now consider how the organisation of the town's water industry affects the price of water and the quantity of water sold.

Competition, monopolies and cartels

Before considering the price and quantity of water that would result from the duopoly of Jack and Jill, let's discuss briefly what the outcome would be if the water market were either perfectly competitive or a monopoly. These two polar cases are natural benchmarks.

If the market for water were perfectly competitive, the production decisions of each firm drive price equal to marginal cost. Because we have assumed that the marginal cost of pumping additional water is zero, the equilibrium price of water under perfect competition would be zero as well. The equilibrium quantity would be 120 litres. The price of water would reflect the cost of producing it and the efficient quantity of water would be produced and consumed.

Now consider how a monopoly would behave. Table 16.1 shows that total profit is maximised at a quantity of 60 litres and a price of $60 a litre. A profit-maximising monopolist, therefore, would produce this quantity and charge this price. As is standard for monopolies, price would exceed marginal cost. The result would be inefficient, for the quantity of water produced and consumed would fall short of the socially efficient level of 120 litres.

What outcome should we expect from our duopolists? One possibility is that Jack and Jill get together and agree on the quantity of water to produce and the price to charge for it. Such an agreement among firms over production and price is called **collusion** and the group of firms acting in unison is called a **cartel**. Once a cartel is formed, the market is in effect served by a monopoly and we can apply our analysis from chapter 15. That is, if Jack and Jill were to collude, they would agree on the monopoly outcome because that outcome maximises the total profit that the producers can get from the market. Our two producers would produce a total of 60 litres, which would be sold at a price of $60 a litre. Once again, price exceeds marginal cost and the outcome is socially inefficient.

collusion
an agreement among firms in a market about quantities to produce or prices to charge

cartel
a group of firms acting in unison

Search me!

▸ cartel

A cartel must agree not only on the total level of production but also on the amount produced by each member. In our case, Jack and Jill must agree how to split between themselves the monopoly production of 60 litres. Each member of the cartel will want a larger share of the market because a larger market share means larger profit. If Jack and Jill agreed to split the market equally, each would produce 30 litres, the price would be $60 a litre and each would get a profit of $1800.

The equilibrium for an oligopoly

Oligopolists would like to form cartels and earn monopoly profits, but that is often impossible. As we discuss in the next chapter, competition laws prohibit explicit agreements among oligopolists as a matter of public policy. In addition, squabbling among cartel members over how to divide the profit in the market can make agreement among members difficult. Let's therefore consider what happens if Jack and Jill decide separately how much water to produce.

At first, one might expect Jack and Jill to reach the monopoly outcome on their own, because this outcome maximises their joint profit. In the absence of a binding agreement, however, the monopoly outcome is unlikely. To see why, imagine that Jack expects Jill to produce only 30 litres (half of the monopoly quantity). Jack would reason as follows:

'I could produce 30 litres as well. In this case, a total of 60 litres of water would be sold at a price of $60 a litre. My profit would be $1800 (30 litres × $60 a litre). Alternatively, I could produce 40 litres. In this case, a total of 70 litres of water would be sold at a price of $50 a litre. My profit would be $2000 (40 litres × $50 a litre). Even though total profit in the market would fall, my profit would be higher, because I would have a larger share of the market.'

Of course, Jill might reason the same way. If so, Jack and Jill would each bring 40 litres to town. Total sales would be 80 litres and the price would fall to $40. Thus, if the duopolists individually pursue their own self-interest when deciding how much to produce, they produce a total quantity greater than the monopoly quantity, charge a price lower than the monopoly price and earn total profit less than the monopoly profit.

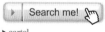

Although the logic of self-interest increases the duopoly's output above the monopoly level, it does not push the duopolists to reach the competitive allocation. Consider what happens when each duopolist is producing 40 litres. The price is $40, and each duopolist makes a profit of $1600. In this case, Jack's self-interested logic leads to a different conclusion:

'Right now, my profit is $1600. Suppose I increase my production to 50 litres. In this case, a total of 90 litres of water would be sold, and the price would be $30 a litre. Then my profit would be only $1500. Rather than increasing production and driving down the price, I am better off keeping my production at 40 litres.'

Nash equilibrium
a situation in which economic actors interacting with one another each choose their best strategy given the strategies that all the other actors have chosen

Search me!

▸ Nash equilibrium

The outcome in which Jack and Jill each produce 40 litres looks like some sort of equilibrium. In fact, this outcome is called a **Nash equilibrium** (named after mathematician John Nash, whose life was portrayed in the book and movie *A Beautiful Mind*). A Nash equilibrium is a situation in which economic actors interacting with one another each choose their best strategy given the strategies the others have chosen. In this case, given that Jill is producing 40 litres, the best strategy for Jack is to produce 40 litres. Similarly, given that Jack is producing 40 litres, the best strategy for Jill is to produce 40 litres. Once they reach this Nash equilibrium, neither Jack nor Jill has an incentive to make a different decision.

This example illustrates the tension between cooperation and self-interest. Oligopolists would be better off cooperating and reaching the monopoly outcome. Yet because they pursue their own self-interest, they do not end up reaching the monopoly outcome and maximising their joint profit. Each oligopolist is tempted to raise production and capture a larger share of the market. As each of them tries to do this, total production rises and the price falls.

At the same time, self-interest does not drive the market all the way to the competitive outcome. Like monopolists, oligopolists are aware that increases in the amount they produce reduce the price of their product. Therefore, they stop short of following the competitive firm's rule of producing up to the point where price equals marginal cost.

In summary, *when firms in an oligopoly individually choose production to maximise profit, they produce a quantity of output greater than the level produced by monopoly and less than the level produced by competition. The oligopoly price is less than the monopoly price but greater than the competitive price (which equals marginal cost).*

How the size of an oligopoly affects the market outcome

We can use the insights from this analysis of duopoly to discuss how the size of an oligopoly is likely to affect the outcome in a market. Suppose, for instance, that John and Joan suddenly discover water sources on their property and join Jack and Jill in the water oligopoly. The demand schedule in Table 16.1 remains the same, but now more producers are available to satisfy this demand. How would an increase in the number of sellers from two to four affect the price and quantity of water in the town?

If the sellers of water could form a cartel, they would once again try to maximise total profit by producing the monopoly quantity and charging the monopoly price. Just as when there were only two sellers, the members of the cartel would need to agree on production levels for each member and find some way to enforce the agreement. As the cartel grows larger, however, this outcome is less likely. Reaching and enforcing an agreement become more difficult as the size of the group increases.

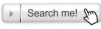

If the oligopolists do not form a cartel – perhaps because the competition laws prohibit it – they must each decide on their own how much water to produce. To see how the increase in the number of sellers affects the outcome, consider the decision facing each seller. At any time, each well owner has the option to raise production by one litre. In making this decision, the well owner weighs two effects:

- *the output effect* – because price is above marginal cost, selling one more litre of water at the going price will raise profit
- *the price effect* – raising production will increase the total amount sold, which will lower the price of water and lower the profit on all the other litres sold.

If the output effect is larger than the price effect, the well owner will increase production. If the price effect is larger than the output effect, the owner will not raise production. (In fact, in this case, it is profitable to reduce production.) Each oligopolist continues to increase production until these two marginal effects exactly balance, taking the other firms' production as given.

Now consider how the number of firms in the industry affects the marginal analysis of each oligopolist. The larger the number of sellers, the less concerned each seller is about its own impact on the market price. That is, as the oligopoly grows in size, the magnitude of the price effect falls. When the oligopoly grows very large, the price effect disappears altogether. The production decision of an individual firm no longer affects the market price. In this extreme case, each firm takes the market price as given when deciding how much to produce. It increases production as long as price is above marginal cost.

We can now see that a large oligopoly is essentially a group of competitive firms. A competitive firm considers only the output effect when deciding how much to produce – because a competitive firm is a price taker, the price effect is absent. Thus, *as the number of sellers in an oligopoly grows larger, an oligopolistic market looks more and more like a competitive market. The price approaches marginal cost and the quantity produced approaches the socially efficient level.*

This analysis of oligopoly offers a new perspective on the effects of international trade. Imagine that Toyota and Honda are the only car makers in Japan, Volkswagen and Mercedes-Benz are the only car makers in Germany, and Ford and Holden are the only car makers in Australia. If these nations prohibited international trade in cars, each would have a car oligopoly with only two members, and the market outcome would be likely to depart substantially from the competitive ideal. With international trade, however, the car market is a world market, and the oligopoly in this example has six members. Allowing free trade increases the number of producers from which each consumer can choose and this increased competition keeps prices closer to marginal cost. Thus, the theory of oligopoly provides another reason, in addition to the theory of comparative advantage discussed in chapter 3, that all countries can benefit from free trade.

CASESTUDY

OPEC and the world oil market

Our story about the town's market for water is fictional, but if we change water to crude oil, and Jack and Jill to Iran and Iraq, the story is quite close to being true. Much of the world's oil is produced by a few countries, mostly in the Middle East. These countries together make up an oligopoly. Their decisions about how much oil to pump are much the same as Jack and Jill's decisions about how much water to pump.

The countries that produce most of the world's oil have formed a cartel, called the Organization of Petroleum Exporting Countries (OPEC). As originally formed in 1960, OPEC included Iran, Iraq, Kuwait, Saudi Arabia and Venezuela. By 1973, eight other nations had joined: Qatar, Indonesia, Libya, the United Arab Emirates, Algeria, Nigeria, Ecuador and Gabon. These countries control about three-quarters of the world's oil reserves. Like any cartel, OPEC tries to raise the price of its product through a coordinated reduction in quantity produced. OPEC tries to set production levels for each of the member countries.

The problem that OPEC faces is much the same as the problem that Jack and Jill face in our story.

>>

The OPEC countries would like to maintain a high price for oil. But each member of the cartel is tempted to increase production in order to get a larger share of the total profit. OPEC members frequently agree to reduce production but then cheat on their agreements.

OPEC was most successful at maintaining cooperation and high prices in the period from 1973 to 1985. The price of crude oil rose from US$2.64 a barrel in 1972 to US$11.17 in 1974 and then to US$35.10 in 1981. But in the early 1980s member countries began arguing about production levels, and OPEC became ineffective at maintaining cooperation. By 1986 the price of crude oil had fallen back to US$12.52 a barrel.

During the 1990s, the members of OPEC met about twice a year, but the cartel failed to reach and enforce agreement. The members of OPEC made production decisions largely independent of one another and the world market for oil was fairly competitive. Throughout most of the decade, the price of crude oil, adjusted for overall inflation, remained less than half the level OPEC had achieved in 1981. In 1999, however, cooperation among oil-exporting nations started to pick up. Prices soared in early 2001 but then fell rapidly late in 2001. Prices rose again in 2004 above US$50 per barrel but this was triggered by the war in Iraq rather than OPEC.

Since then prices have remained relatively high driven by both demand from the rapidly growing economies of China and India and by restrictions on supply from OPEC countries. In 2008, oil prices reached US$147 per barrel, before falling back due to slower economic growth in Europe and the US. As this book goes to press, oil prices are around US$85 per barrel. Only time will tell how effective OPEC is at keeping oil prices up in the future.

Q

If the members of an oligopoly could agree on a total quantity to produce, what quantity would they choose? If the oligopolists do not act together but instead make production decisions individually, do they produce a total quantity more or less than in your answer to the previous question? Why?

Game theory and the economics of cooperation

As we have seen, oligopolies would like to reach the monopoly outcome, but doing so requires cooperation, which at times is difficult to maintain. In this section we look more closely at the problems that people face when cooperation is desirable but difficult. To analyse the economics of cooperation, we need to learn a little about game theory.

prisoners' dilemma
a particular 'game' between two captured prisoners that illustrates why cooperation is difficult to maintain even when it is mutually beneficial

In particular, we focus on an important 'game' called the **prisoners' dilemma**. This game provides insight into why cooperation is difficult. In many situations, people fail to cooperate with one another even when cooperation would make them all better off. An oligopoly is just one example. The story of the prisoners' dilemma contains a general lesson that applies to any group trying to maintain cooperation among its members.

The prisoners' dilemma

The prisoners' dilemma is a story about two criminals who have been captured by the police. Let's call them Ned and Kelly. The police have enough evidence to convict both Ned and Kelly of the minor crime of possessing an unlicensed gun, so that each would spend a year in jail. The police also suspect that the two criminals have committed a bank robbery together, but they lack hard evidence to convict them of this major crime. The police question Ned and Kelly in separate rooms and they offer each of them the following deal:

> Right now, we can lock you up for one year. If you confess to the bank robbery and implicate your partner, however, we'll give you immunity, and

Figure 16.2 The prisoners' dilemma

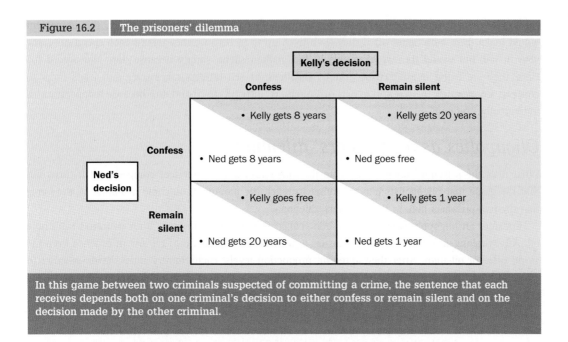

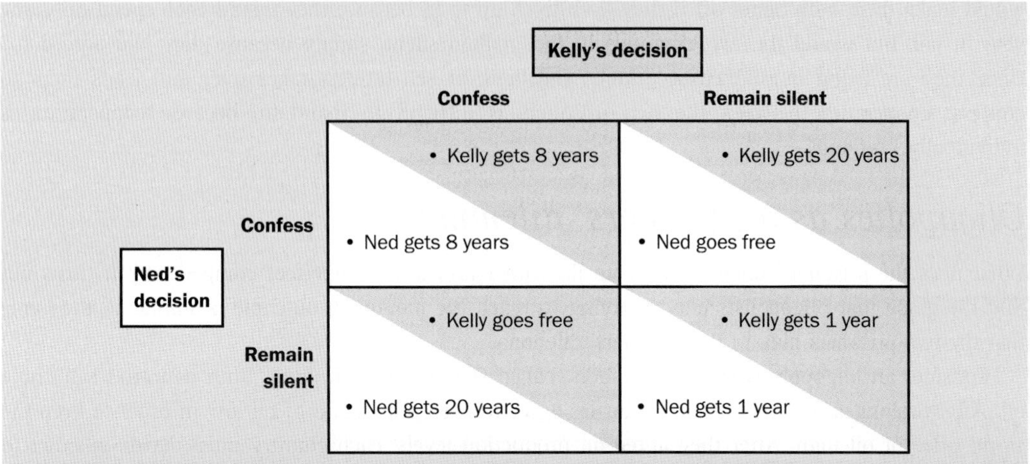

In this game between two criminals suspected of committing a crime, the sentence that each receives depends both on one criminal's decision to either confess or remain silent and on the decision made by the other criminal.

> you can go free. Your partner will get 20 years in jail. But if you both confess to the crime, we won't need your testimony and we can avoid the cost of a trial, so you will each get an intermediate sentence of eight years.

If Ned and Kelly, heartless bank robbers that they are, care only about their own sentences, what would you expect them to do? Would they confess or remain silent? Figure 16.2 shows their choices. Each prisoner has two strategies: Confess or remain silent. The sentence each prisoner gets depends on the strategy he or she chooses and the strategy chosen by his or her partner in crime.

Consider first Kelly's decision. She reasons as follows:

> I don't know what Ned is going to do. If he remains silent, my best strategy is to confess, since then I'll go free rather than spending a year in jail. If he confesses, my best strategy is still to confess, since then I'll spend eight years in jail rather than 20. So, regardless of what Ned does, I am better off confessing.

In the language of game theory, a strategy is called a **dominant strategy** if it is the best strategy for a player to follow regardless of the strategies pursued by other players. In this case, confessing is a dominant strategy for Kelly. She spends less time in jail if she confesses, regardless of whether Ned confesses or remains silent.

dominant strategy
a strategy that is best for a player in a game regardless of the strategies chosen by the other players

Now consider Ned's decision. He faces exactly the same choices as Kelly and he reasons in much the same way. Regardless of what Kelly does, Ned can reduce his time in jail by confessing. In other words, confessing is also a dominant strategy for Ned.

In the end, both Ned and Kelly confess and both spend eight years in jail. Yet, from their standpoint, this is a terrible outcome. If they had both remained silent, both of them would have been better off, spending only one year in jail on the gun charge. By each pursuing his or her own interests, the two prisoners together reach an outcome that is worse for each of them.

You might have thought that Ned and Kelly would have foreseen this situation and planned ahead. But even with advance planning, they would still run into problems. Imagine that, before the police captured Ned and Kelly, the two criminals had made a pact not to confess. Clearly, this agreement would make them both better off if they both lived up to it, because they would each spend only one year in jail. But would the two criminals in fact remain silent, simply because they had agreed to? Once they are being questioned separately, the logic of self-interest takes over and leads them to confess. Cooperation between the two prisoners is difficult to maintain, because cooperation is individually irrational.

Oligopolies as a prisoners' dilemma

What does the prisoners' dilemma have to do with markets and imperfect competition? It turns out that the game that oligopolists play in trying to reach the monopoly outcome is similar to the game that the two prisoners play in the prisoners' dilemma.

Consider an oligopoly with two members, called Oilania and Slickland. Both countries sell crude oil. After prolonged negotiation, the countries agree to keep production of oil low in order to keep the world price of oil high. After they agree on production levels, each country must decide whether to cooperate and live up to this agreement or to ignore it and produce at a higher level. Figure 16.3 shows how the profits of the two countries depend on the strategies they choose.

Suppose you are the prime minister of Slickland. You might reason as follows:

> I could keep production low as we agreed, or I could raise my production and sell more oil on world markets. If Oilania lives up to the agreement and keeps its production low, then my country earns profit of $60 billion with high production and $50 billion with low production. In this case, Slickland is better off with high production. If Oilania fails to live up to the agreement and produces at a high level, then my country earns $40 billion with high production and $30 billion with low production. Once again, Slickland is better off with high production. So, regardless of what Oilania chooses to do, my country is better off reneging on our agreement and producing at a high level.

Figure 16.3 An oligopoly game

Oilania's decision \ Slickland's decision	High production	Low production
High production	• Slickland gets $40 billion • Oilania gets $40 billion	• Slickland gets $30 billion • Oilania gets $60 billion
Low production	• Slickland gets $60 billion • Oilania gets $30 billion	• Slickland gets $50 billion • Oilania gets $50 billion

In this game between members of an oligopoly, the profit that each earns depends both on one member's production decision and on the production decision made by the other member.

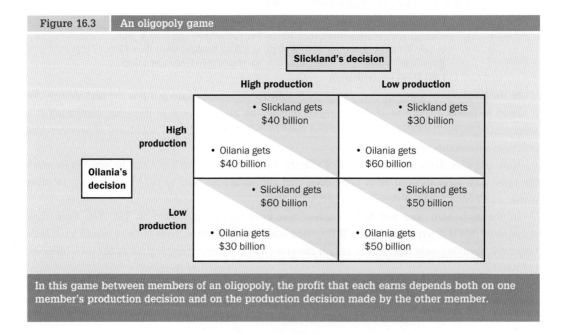

Producing at a high level is a dominant strategy for Slickland. Of course, Oilania reasons in exactly the same way and so both countries produce at a high level. The result is the inferior outcome (from Oilania's and Slickland's standpoints) with low profits for each country.

This example illustrates why oligopolies have trouble maintaining monopoly profits. The monopoly outcome is jointly rational for the oligopoly, but each oligopolist has an incentive to cheat. Just as self-interest drives the prisoners in the prisoners' dilemma to confess, self-interest makes it difficult for the oligopoly to maintain the cooperative outcome with low production, high prices and monopoly profits.

Other examples of the prisoners' dilemma

We have seen how the prisoners' dilemma can be used to understand the problem facing oligopolies. The same logic applies to many other situations as well. Here we consider three examples in which self-interest prevents cooperation and leads to an inferior outcome for the parties involved.

Arms races

In the decades after the Second World War, the world's two superpowers – the United States and the Soviet Union – were engaged in a prolonged competition over military power. This topic motivated some of the early work on game theory. The game theorists pointed out that an 'arms race' is much like the prisoners' dilemma.

To see why, consider the decisions of the United States and the Soviet Union about whether to build new weapons or to disarm. Each country prefers to have more arms than the other because a larger arsenal gives it more influence in world affairs. But each country also prefers to live in a world safe from the other country's weapons.

Figure 16.4 shows the deadly game. If the Soviet Union chooses to arm, the United States is better off doing the same to prevent the loss of power. If the Soviet Union chooses to disarm, the

Figure 16.4 An arms-race game

Decision of the Soviet Union (USSR)	Decision of the United States (US): Arm	Decision of the United States (US): Disarm
Arm	• US at risk • USSR at risk	• US at risk and weak • USSR safe and powerful
Disarm	• US safe and powerful • USSR at risk and weak	• US safe • USSR safe

In this game between two countries, the safety and power of each depends both on one country's decision whether to arm and on the decision made by the other country.

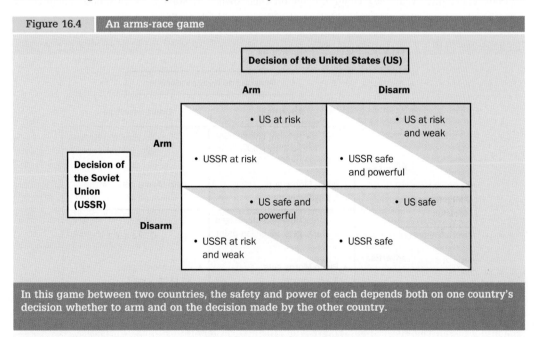

United States is better off arming because doing so would make it more powerful. For each country, arming is a dominant strategy. Thus, each country chooses to continue the arms race, resulting in the inferior outcome in which both countries are at risk.

Throughout the era of the Cold War, from the late 1940s through to about 1990, the United States and the Soviet Union attempted to solve this problem through negotiation and agreements over arms control. The problems that the two countries faced were similar to those that oligopolists encounter in trying to maintain a cartel. Just as oligopolists argue over production levels, the United States and the Soviet Union argued over the amount of arms that each country would be allowed. And just as cartels have trouble enforcing production levels, the United States and the Soviet Union each feared that the other country would cheat on any agreement. In both arms races and oligopolies, the relentless logic of self-interest drives the participants toward a non-cooperative outcome that is worse for each party.

Advertising

When two firms advertise to attract the same customers, they face a problem similar to the prisoners' dilemma. For example, consider the decisions facing two cigarette companies, Benson and Hedges and Philip Morris. If neither company advertises, the two companies split the market. If both advertise, they again split the market, but profits are lower, since each company must bear the cost of advertising. Yet if one company advertises while the other does not, the one that advertises attracts customers from the other.

Figure 16.5 shows how the profits of the two companies depend on their actions. You can see that advertising is a dominant strategy for each firm. Thus, both firms choose to advertise, even though both firms would be better off if neither firm advertised.

A test of this theory of advertising occurred in the 1970s, when a number of countries, including Australia, passed laws banning cigarette advertisements on television. When these laws went into effect, cigarette advertising fell and the profits of cigarette companies rose. The law did for the cigarette companies what they could not do on their own – it solved the prisoners' dilemma by enforcing the cooperative outcome with low advertising and high profit.

Figure 16.5 **An advertising game**

		Benson and Hedges' decision	
		Advertise	**Don't advertise**
Philip Morris's decision	**Advertise**	• Benson and Hedges gets \$3 billion profit • Philip Morris gets \$3 billion profit	• Benson and Hedges gets \$2 billion profit • Philip Morris gets \$5 billion profit
	Don't advertise	• Benson and Hedges gets \$5 billion profit • Philip Morris gets \$2 billion profit	• Benson and Hedges gets \$4 billion profit • Philip Morris gets \$4 billion profit

In this game between firms selling similar products, the profit that each earns depends both on one firm's advertising decision and on the advertising decision of the other firm.

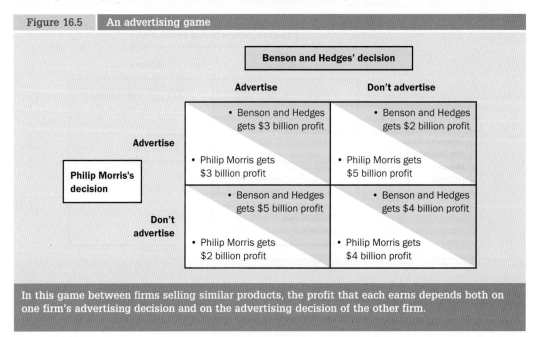

Common resources

In chapter 11 we saw that people tend to overuse common resources. One can view this problem as an example of the prisoners' dilemma.

Imagine that two gas companies – Queensland Gas Company (QGC) and Santos – own adjacent gas fields. Under the fields is a common reserve of gas worth \$12 million. Drilling a well to recover the gas costs \$1 million. If each company drills one well, each will get half of the oil and earn a \$5 million profit (\$6 million in revenue minus \$1 million in costs).

Because the oil deposit is a common resource, the companies will not use it efficiently. Suppose that either company could drill a second well. If one company has two of the three wells, that company gets two-thirds of the oil, which yields a profit of \$6 million. Yet if each company drills a second well, the two companies again split the oil. In this case, each bears the cost of a second well, so profit is only \$4 million for each company.

Figure 16.6 shows the game. Drilling two wells is a dominant strategy for each company. Once again, the self-interest of the two players leads them to an inferior outcome.

The prisoners' dilemma and the welfare of society

The prisoners' dilemma describes many of life's situations and it shows that cooperation can be difficult to maintain, even when cooperation would make both players in the game better off. Clearly, this lack of cooperation is a problem for those involved in these situations. But is lack of cooperation a problem from the standpoint of society as a whole? The answer depends on the circumstances.

In some cases, the non-cooperative equilibrium is bad for society as well as the players. In the arms-race game in Figure 16.4, both the United States and the Soviet Union end up at risk. In the common-resources game in Figure 16.6, the extra wells dug by QGC and Santos are pure waste. In both cases, society would be better off if the two players could reach the cooperative outcome.

Figure 16.6 A common-resources game

Santos's decision \ QGC's decision	Drill two wells	Drill one well
Drill two wells	• QGC gets \$4 million profit • Santos gets \$4 million profit	• QGC gets \$3 million profit • Santos gets \$6 million profit
Drill one well	• QGC gets \$6 million profit • Santos gets \$3 million profit	• QGC gets \$5 million profit • Santos gets \$5 million profit

In this game between firms pumping oil from a common pool, the profit that each earns depends both on the number of wells one firm drills and on the number of wells drilled by the other firm.

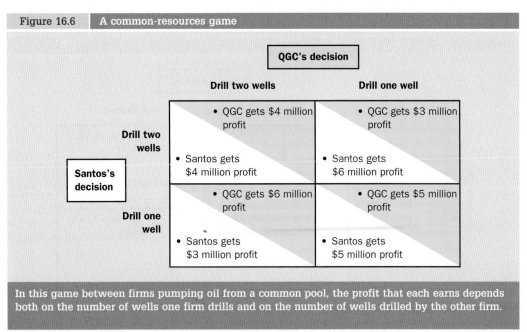

In contrast, in the case of oligopolists trying to maintain monopoly profits, lack of cooperation is desirable from the standpoint of society as a whole. The monopoly outcome is good for the oligopolists, but it is bad for the consumers of the product. As we first saw in chapter 7, the competitive outcome is best for society because it maximises total surplus. When oligopolists fail to cooperate, the quantity they produce is closer to this optimal level. Put differently, the invisible hand guides markets to allocate resources efficiently only when markets are competitive, and markets are competitive only when firms in the market fail to cooperate with one another.

Similarly, consider the case of the police questioning two suspects. Lack of cooperation between the suspects is desirable, for it allows the police to convict more criminals. The prisoners' dilemma is a dilemma for the prisoners, but it can be a boon to everyone else.

Why people sometimes cooperate

The prisoners' dilemma shows that cooperation is difficult. But is it impossible? Not all prisoners, when questioned by the police, decide to turn in their partners in crime. Cartels sometimes do manage to maintain collusive arrangements, despite the incentive for individual members to defect. Very often, the reason that players can solve the prisoners' dilemma is that they play the game not once but many times.

To see why cooperation is easier to enforce in repeated games, let's return to our duopolists, Jack and Jill. Recall that Jack and Jill would like to maintain the monopoly outcome in which each produces 30 litres, but self-interest drives them to an equilibrium in which each produces 40 litres. Figure 16.7 shows the game they play. Producing 40 litres is a dominant strategy for each player in this game.

Imagine that Jack and Jill try to form a cartel. To maximise total profit, they would agree to the cooperative outcome in which each produces 30 litres. Yet, if Jack and Jill are to play this game only once, neither has any incentive to live up to this agreement. Self-interest drives each of them to renege and produce 40 litres.

Now suppose that Jack and Jill know that they will play the same game every week. When they make their initial agreement to keep production low, they can also specify what happens if one party

Figure 16.7 **Jack and Jill's oligopoly game**

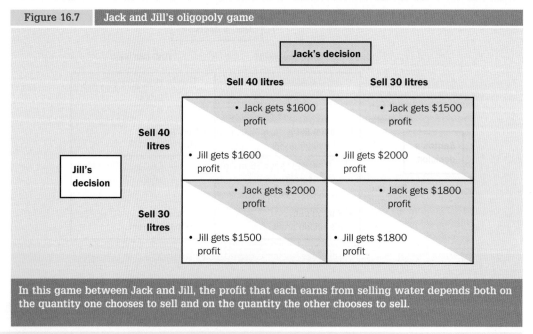

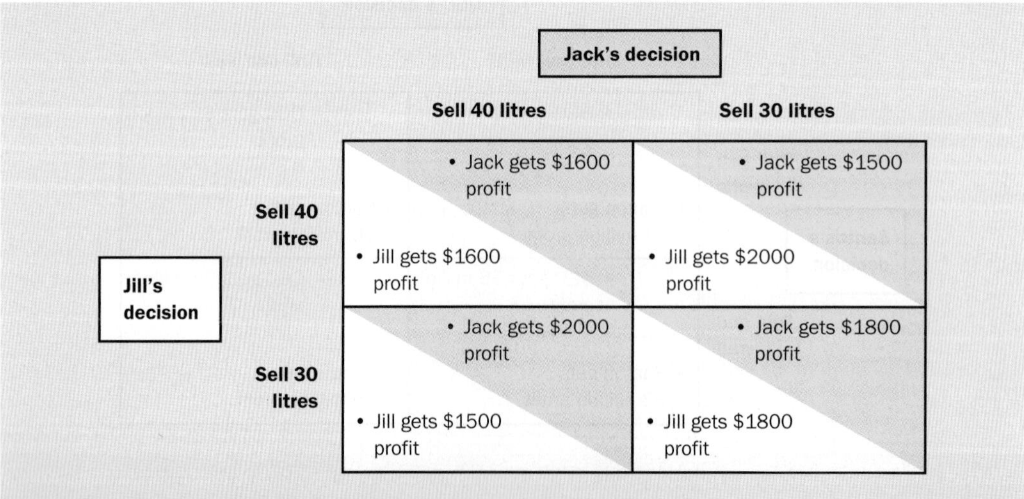

In this game between Jack and Jill, the profit that each earns from selling water depends both on the quantity one chooses to sell and on the quantity the other chooses to sell.

reneges. They might agree, for instance, that once one of them reneges and produces 40 litres, both of them will produce 40 litres forever after. This penalty is easy to enforce, for if one party is producing at a high level, the other has every reason to do the same.

The threat of this penalty may be all that is needed to maintain cooperation. Each person knows that defecting would raise his or her profit from $1800 to $2000. But this benefit would last for only one week. Thereafter, profit would fall to $1600 and stay there. As long as the players care enough about future profits, they will choose to forgo the one-time gain from defection. Thus, in a game of repeated prisoners' dilemma, the two players may well be able to reach the cooperative outcome.

CASESTUDY

The prisoners' dilemma tournament

Imagine that you are playing a game of prisoners' dilemma with a person being 'questioned' in a separate room. Moreover, imagine that you are going to play not once but many times. Your score at the end of the game is the total number of years in jail. You would like to make this score as small as possible. What strategy would you play? Would you begin by confessing or remaining silent? How would the other player's actions affect your subsequent decisions about confessing?

Repeated prisoners' dilemma is quite a complicated game. To encourage cooperation, players must penalise each other for not cooperating. Yet the strategy described earlier for Jack and Jill's water cartel – defect forever as soon as the other player defects – is not very forgiving. In a game repeated many times, a strategy that allows players to return to the cooperative outcome after a period of non-cooperation may be preferable.

To see what strategies work best, political scientist Robert Axelrod held a tournament. People entered by sending computer programs designed to play repeated prisoners' dilemma. Each program then played the game against all the other programs. The 'winner' was the program that received the fewest total years in jail.

The winner turned out to be a simple strategy called tit-for-tat. According to tit-for-tat, a player should start by cooperating and then do whatever the other player did last time. Thus, a tit-for-tat player cooperates until the other player defects; he then defects until the other player cooperates again. In other words, this strategy starts out friendly, penalises unfriendly players and forgives them if warranted. To Axelrod's surprise, this simple strategy did better than all the more complicated strategies that people had sent in.

The tit-for-tat strategy has a long history. It is essentially the biblical strategy of 'an eye for an eye, a tooth for a tooth'. The prisoners' dilemma tournament suggests that this may be a good rule of thumb for playing some of the games of life.

Q

Tell the story of the prisoners' dilemma. Write down a table showing the prisoners' choices and explain what outcome is likely. What does the prisoners' dilemma teach us about oligopolies?

Conclusion

Oligopolies would like to act like monopolies, but self-interest drives them closer to competition. Thus, oligopolies can end up looking either more like monopolies or more like competitive markets, depending on the number of firms in the oligopoly and how cooperative the firms are. The story of the prisoners' dilemma shows why oligopolies can fail to maintain cooperation, even when cooperation is in their best interest.

Of course, as the chapter shows, while firms may benefit from cooperation, such cooperation causes deadweight losses. This provides a motive for policymakers to regulate the behaviour of oligopolists through competition laws. In the next chapter, we look at the types of behaviour that concern policymakers and the tools they use to regulate oligopolists.

Summary

- Oligopolists maximise their total profits by forming a cartel and acting like a monopolist. Yet, if oligopolists make decisions about production levels individually, the result is a greater quantity and a lower price than under the monopoly outcome. The larger the number of firms in the oligopoly, the closer the quantity and price will be to the levels that would prevail under competition.
- The prisoners' dilemma shows that self-interest can prevent people from maintaining cooperation, even when cooperation is in their mutual interest. The logic of the prisoners' dilemma applies in many situations, including arms races, advertising, common-resource problems and oligopolies.

Key concepts

cartel
collusion
dominant strategy
game theory
Nash equilibrium
oligopoly
prisoners' dilemma

Questions for review

1 If a group of sellers could form a cartel, what quantity and price would they try to set?
2 Compare the quantity and price of an oligopoly with those of a monopoly.
3 Compare the quantity and price of an oligopoly with those of a competitive market.
4 How does the number of firms in an oligopoly affect the outcome in its market?
5 What is the prisoners' dilemma and what does it have to do with oligopoly?
6 Give two examples other than oligopoly to show how the prisoners' dilemma helps to explain behaviour.

Problems and applications

1 *The New York Times* (30 November 1993) reported: 'The inability of OPEC to agree last week to cut production has sent the oil market into turmoil … [leading to] the lowest price for domestic crude oil since June 1990'.
   a Why were the members of OPEC trying to agree to cut production?
   b Why do you suppose OPEC was unable to agree on cutting production? Why did the oil market go into 'turmoil' as a result?
   c The newspaper also noted OPEC's view 'that producing nations outside the organization, like Norway and Britain, should do their share and cut production'. What does the phrase 'do their share' suggest about OPEC's desired relationship with Norway and Britain?

2 A large share of the world's supply of diamonds comes from Russia and South Africa. Suppose that the marginal cost of mining diamonds is $1000 per diamond, and the demand for diamonds is described by the following schedule:

Price ($)	Quantity
8000	5000
7000	6000
6000	7000
5000	8000
4000	9000
3000	10 000
2000	11 000
1000	12 000

a If there were many suppliers of diamonds, what would be the price and quantity?

b If there were only one supplier of diamonds, what would be the price and quantity?

c If Russia and South Africa formed a cartel, what would be the price and quantity? If the countries split the market evenly, what would be South Africa's production and profit? What would happen to South Africa's profit if it increased its production by 1000 while Russia stuck to the cartel agreement?

d Use your answer to part (c) to explain why cartel agreements are often not successful.

3 This chapter discusses companies that are oligopolists in the market for the goods they sell. Many of the same ideas apply to companies that are oligopolists in the market for the inputs they buy.

a If sellers who are oligopolists try to increase the price of goods they sell, what is the goal of buyers who are oligopolists?

b Australian football teams have an oligopoly in the market for football players. What is the teams' goal regarding players' salaries? Why is this goal difficult to achieve?

c Football leagues often decide to set a salary cap for each football team in their league. This limits the amount each team can pay its players. If football teams are already colluding over salaries, why might they still feel the need for a salary cap?

4 Why is game theory helpful for understanding markets with a few firms, but not markets with many firms?

5 Describe several activities in your life in which game theory could be useful. What is the common link among these activities?

6 Consider trade relations between Australia and New Zealand. Assume that the leaders of the two countries believe the pay-offs to alternative trade policies are as follows:

		Australia's decision	
		High tariffs	Low tariffs
New Zealand's decision	Low tariffs	• Australia gains $10 billion • New Zealand gains $10 billion	• Australia gains $20 billion • New Zealand gains $2 billion
	High tariffs	• Australia gains $2 billion • New Zealand gains $20 billion	• Australia gains $4 billion • New Zealand gains $4 billion

a What is the dominant strategy for Australia? For New Zealand? Explain.
b Define *Nash equilibrium*. What is the Nash equilibrium for trade policy?
c Under the Closer Economic Relations agreement, Australia and New Zealand both agreed to allow free trade in goods and services between the two countries. Do the perceived pay-offs as shown here justify this move to a bilateral free trade policy?
d Based on your understanding of the gains from trade (discussed in chapters 3 and 9), do you think that these pay-offs actually reflect a nation's welfare under the four possible outcomes?

7 Suppose that you and a classmate are assigned a project on which you will receive one combined mark. You each want to receive a good mark, but you also want to do as little work as possible. The decision box and pay-offs are as follows:

Classmate's decision		Your decision: Work	Your decision: Shirk
	Work	• You: 85%, no fun • Classmate: 85%, no fun	• You: 65%, fun • Classmate: 65%, no fun
	Shirk	• You: 65%, no fun • Classmate: 65%, fun	• You: 40%, fun • Classmate: 40%, fun

Assume that having fun is your normal state, but having no fun is as unpleasant as a reduction in your assignment mark of 40 per cent.
a Write out the decision box that combines the mark and the amount of fun you have into a single pay-off for each outcome.
b If neither you nor your classmate knows how much work the other person is doing, what is the likely outcome? Does it matter whether you are likely to work with this person again? Explain your answer.

8 The chapter states that the ban on cigarette advertising on television increased the profits of cigarette companies. Could the ban still be good public policy? Explain your answer.

9 Farmer Jones and Farmer Smith graze their cattle on the same field. If there are 20 cows grazing in the field, each cow produces $4000 of milk over its lifetime. If there are more cows in the field, then each cow can eat less grass and its milk production falls. With 30 cows on the field, each produces $3000 of milk; with 40 cows, each produces $2000 of milk. Cows cost $1000 each.
a Assume that Farmer Jones and Farmer Smith can each purchase either 10 or 20 cows, but that neither knows how many the other is buying when she makes her purchase. Calculate the pay-offs of each outcome.
b What is the likely outcome of this game? What would be the best outcome? Explain.
c There used to be more common grazing land than there is today. Why? (For more discussion of this topic, re-read chapter 11.)

10 Little Kona is a small coffee company that is considering entering a market dominated by Big Brew. Each company's profit depends on whether Little Kona enters and whether Big Brew sets a high price or a low price:

		Big Brew	
		High price	Low price
Little Kona	Enter	Brew makes $3 million Kona makes $2 million	Brew makes $1 million Kona loses $1 million
	Don't enter	Brew makes $7 million Kona makes zero	Brew makes $2 million Kona makes zero

Big Brew threatens Little Kona by saying, 'If you enter, we're going to set a low price, so you had better stay out'. Do you think Little Kona should believe the threat? Why or why not? What do you think Little Kona should do?

11 Jeff and Steve are playing tennis. Every point comes down to whether Steve guesses correctly whether Jeff will hit the ball to Steve's left or right. The outcomes are:

		Steve guesses	
		Left	Right
Jeff hits	Left	Steve wins point Jeff loses point	Steve loses point Jeff wins point
	Right	Steve loses point Jeff wins point	Steve wins point Jeff loses point

Does either player have a dominant strategy? If Jeff chooses a particular strategy (Left or Right) and sticks with it, what will Steve do? So, can you think of a better strategy for Jeff to follow?

Search me!

Search me!

When accessing information about microeconomics use the following keywords in any combinations you require:

- cartel
- oligopoly
- Nash equilibrium

CourseMate

CourseMate

For more multimedia resources and activities on economics, visit the Economics CourseMate website.

APPENDIX

Types of oligopolistic competition

In the chapter, we described oligopolistic competition in relatively simple terms. Rival firms could choose between colluding or competing, or between advertising and not advertising. In reality, competition in an oligopoly is more complex. This is because firms can choose from a wide range of prices and production decisions.

Game theory is equipped to handle these more complex situations. This appendix will introduce you to two game-theoretic models that capture the interaction between firms in an oligopoly.

Anticipating your competitor's response

To understand the behaviour of a firm in an oligopoly, consider our water duopolists, Jack and Jill. Suppose they are initially producing 40 litres each, so that the market price is $40 per litre. Jack is considering producing more.

However, this will be profitable only if price does not fall by too much. This depends on how Jill might react to Jack's increased production. Jack conjectures that there are two ways Jill may react:

- *Reducing price to maintain quantity sold.* Jill might be concerned about the reduction in her sales quantity as a result of Jack's increased production. In order to maintain her existing volume, Jill could reduce her price.
- *Reducing production to maintain market price.* Alternatively, Jill might be worried about the potential drop in the market price of water when Jack increases his output. She realises that if she cuts back production, she can maintain the existing price in the market.

It is possible that Jill's reactions might be more complicated. Economists, however, have found that focusing on reactions that maintain price or quantity simplifies the analysis of oligopoly. In effect, they define two distinct theories of competition – *Cournot quantity competition* and *Bertrand price competition.* We will examine each in turn. As we will see, because Jack anticipates price matching by Jill under Cournot competition but not Bertrand competition, the former results in higher equilibrium prices than does the latter.

Cournot quantity competition

Suppose that Jack believes that Jill will always maintain her current level of output. That is, he believes that Jill will let the price of water fall rather than reduce her output.

This belief is the basis of Cournot quantity competition. This competition is named after Augustin Cournot who, in 1838, was the first person to attempt to model oligopolistic competition. It is called

Table 16A.1 Jack's profit maximisation decision when Jill produces 20 litres

Market quantity	Jill's quantity	Jack's quantity	Price ($)	Jack's total revenue (and total profit) ($)
20 litres	20 litres	0 litres	100	0
30	20	10	90	900
40	20	20	80	1600
50	20	30	70	2100
60	20	40	60	2400
70	20	50	50	2500
80	20	60	40	2400
90	20	70	30	2100
100	20	80	20	1600
110	20	90	10	900
120	20	100	0	0

quantity competition because each firm believes that its rivals will always act to maintain their current quantity.

When we talked about oligopolistic competition between Jack and Jill in the chapter, we were really talking about Cournot quantity competition. To see this, let's modify the demand schedule for water given in Table 16.1 to focus on Jack's behaviour, given his belief about Jill's output.

Table 16A.1 highlights the decision facing Jack. If Jill is producing 20 litres of water, then Jack knows that demand for his water is simply the market demand less a quantity of 20 litres. This is because for every level of production he chooses, Jill will adjust her price so that the difference between market demand at that price and Jack's production is exactly 20 litres. The individual demand schedule for Jack's water is simply the market schedule less 20 litres.

To maximise profits, Jack will follow the same rule we discussed in chapter 15 for a monopolist – he will choose a quantity that equates his marginal revenue and marginal cost. As Jack's marginal cost is zero in this example, he will maximise profits by maximising total revenue. From Table 16A.1, if Jill is producing 20 litres, Jack will produce 50 litres to maximise his profit.

What if Jack believes that Jill will produce 60 litres of water? This is shown in Table 16A.2. Because Jill is producing more, Jack has to produce less to maintain a given market price. The individual demand schedule facing Jack is lower and Jack's profit-maximising output level is now only 30 litres of water.

Notice that, when Jack believes that Jill is going to produce more, he will react by producing less. The more Jill is going to produce, the smaller the share of the market available to Jack. So Jack reacts by limiting his own output to maintain the market price and maximise his own profits. Figure 16A.1

Table 16A.2 Jack's profit maximisation decision when Jill produces 60 litres

Market quantity	Jill's quantity	Jack's quantity	Price ($)	Jack's total revenue (and total profit) ($)
60 litres	60 litres	0 litres	60	0
70	60	10	50	500
80	60	20	40	800
90	60	30	30	900
100	60	40	20	800
110	60	50	10	500

shows how Jack's output choice will alter with Jill's production decision. The upper part shows how Jack's individual demand curve depends on Jill's output choice. If Jill produces 20 litres then Jack's individual demand curve is given by D_1 – the market demand shifted left by 20 litres. Jack will maximise profits by producing 50 litres of water. This is where the relevant marginal revenue curve MR_1 intersects with marginal cost. Remember that marginal cost is zero in this example. The lower part then plots this decision. Jack produces 50 litres when Jill produces 20 litres.

If Jill increases production to 60 litres, then this reduces Jack's individual demand curve. This is shown by curve D_2. Again Jack maximises profits by producing where marginal revenue equals marginal cost. But because Jill is producing more, Jack's marginal revenue at each level of output is less. This is shown by the curve MR_2. Jack's profit-maximising response to Jill's production is then shown in the lower part. When Jill produces 60 litres of water Jack wants to produce only 30 litres.

Jack's reaction curve, shown in the lower part of Figure 16A.1, shows Jack's profit-maximising level of output for every output level chosen by Jill. If Jill produces nothing, then Jack is a monopolist and will produce the monopoly output, 60 litres. If Jack expects Jill to flood the market and sell 120 litres, then it is not worthwhile for Jack to produce anything. In between, if Jill produces 20 litres, Jack will produce 50, and if Jill produces 60 litres, Jack will produce 30.

If Jill holds similar beliefs to Jack – that is, that Jack will always act to maintain his existing output level – then she will have a reaction curve with a similar property to Jack's. That is, Jill will always want to decrease (increase) her output as Jack increases (decreases) his.

We can place Jack's and Jill's reaction curves on the same diagram. This is done in Figure 16A.2. This allows us to determine the Nash equilibrium in Cournot quantity competition. Recall that the choice of strategies for two players is a Nash equilibrium if neither player can gain by changing to another strategy. In this case, in the choice of quantities, a Nash equilibrium occurs if neither Jack nor Jill wishes to change his or her output, assuming that the other acts to keep his or her output the same.

In Figure 16A.2, the only Nash equilibrium is where Jack and Jill both choose 40 litres of water each. This is the same equilibrium as we found by trial and error in the chapter. If Jack were to choose 20 litres, Jill will want to choose 50 litres – the corresponding point on her reaction curve. These choices of output are not a Nash equilibrium, however, because, while Jill is happy with her

Figure 16A.1 Jack's output choice will alter with Jill's production decision

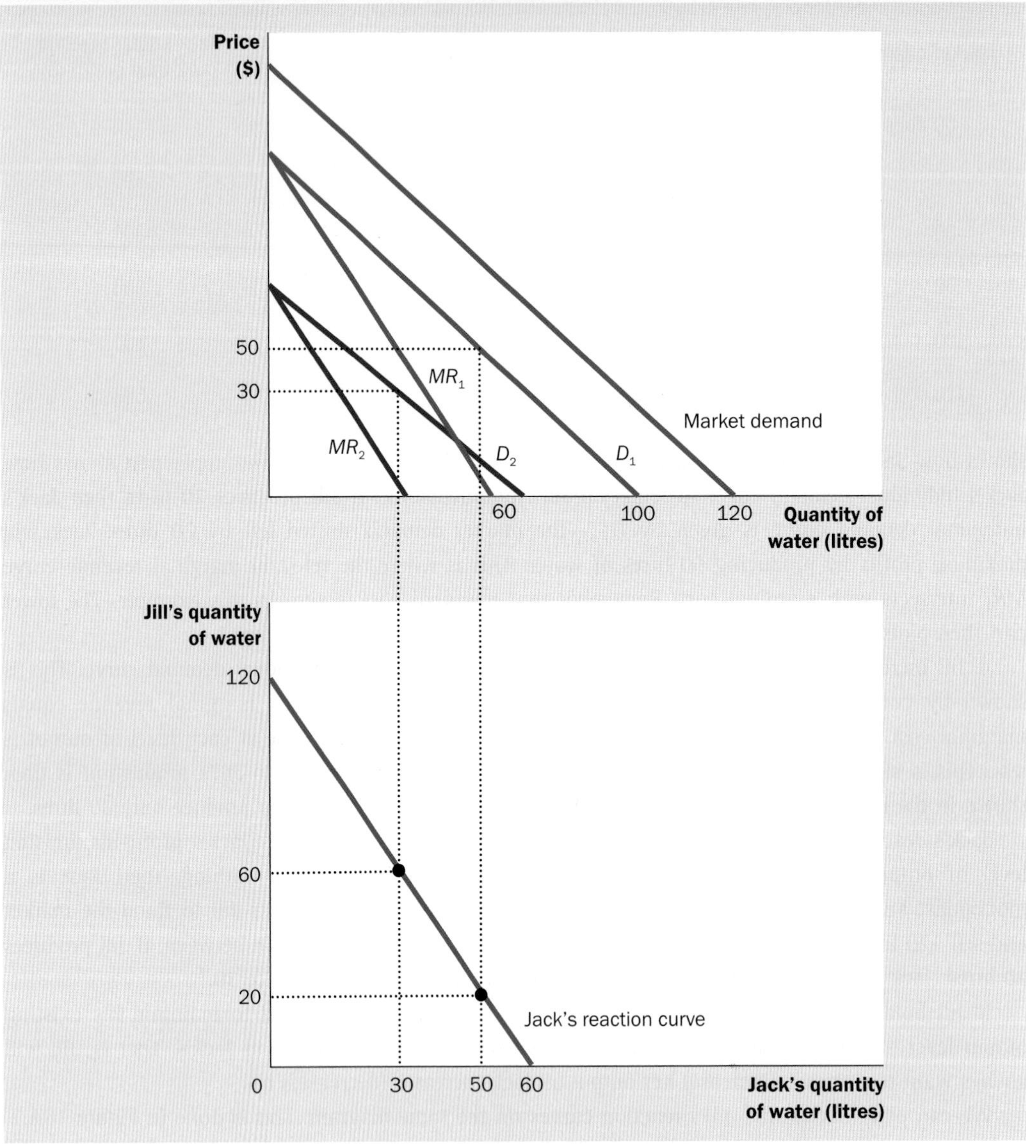

choice, Jack can improve his profits by choosing an output of 35 litres. This corresponds to a point on his reaction curve. Unless both Jack and Jill are choosing outputs on their reaction curves, each is not maximising profits given the choice of the other. Hence, only points where reaction curves coincide represent a Nash equilibrium.

As we noted in the chapter, the Cournot equilibrium involves total production of 80 litres, more than the monopoly output of 60 litres. It also involves less production than under perfect

Figure 16A.2 Jack's and Jill's reaction curves

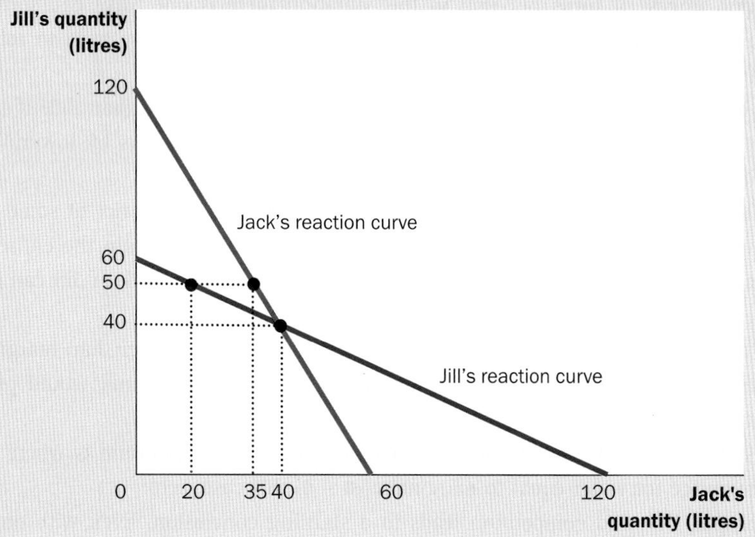

competition. In this example, the perfectly competitive output would be 120 litres with a price equal to the marginal cost of zero.

Bertrand price competition

What if Jack believes that Jill will always act to maintain her price rather than her quantity of sales? This situation is illustrated by Bertrand price competition. Joseph Bertrand, when reviewing Cournot's work in 1883, noticed that a different conclusion could arise when firms believe that rivals will act to maintain price rather than output. It is called price competition for this reason. Indeed, it is easier to analyse Bertrand price competition by examining firms' pricing choices rather than their output choices.

To see what happens in price competition, imagine that Jill currently sells water for $50 per litre. She will sell as much or as little as she needs to maintain this price. Now if Jack sets his price at, say, $60, he will find himself unable to sell any water. This is because water, from the point of view of consumers, is a homogeneous product. Hence, consumers will purchase from the firm that sells at the lowest price. With Jack setting his price at $60, Jill is able to capture the entire market (a quantity of 70 litres). Jack earns no profits.

Can Jack do better than this by changing his price, given that he believes that Jill will maintain her price at $50? Suppose that Jack lowers his price and undercuts Jill. For example, Jack could lower his price to $40. As Jack is selling water more cheaply than Jill, he will capture the entire market. Jack will sell 80 litres and make $3200 in profit. Jill, in contrast, will make no sales and earn no profit. Jack is better off undercutting Jill than by pricing above her.

What is true for Jack is true for Jill. If she prices below Jack, she earns more than if she prices above him. What this means is that both Jack and Jill will find it advantageous to react to the other's price by lowering their own price.

When Jack and Jill have reactions that involve undercutting each other's price, what will be the Nash equilibrium prices? It turns out that in this situation there is one Nash equilibrium price – a price equal to marginal cost which is zero. To see why this is the case, we need to reason in steps. Consider the following:

1. It cannot be a Nash equilibrium for Jack to charge a different price than Jill. If this were to occur, the person with the higher price could always earn more profits by lowering price and undercutting rivals.
2. It cannot be a Nash equilibrium for Jack and Jill to charge the same price at some level above marginal cost. If this were to happen, then either Jack or Jill could gain the entire market by charging a slightly lower price. By making a small price cut, either Jack or Jill can steal all the other water seller's customers and increase his or her own profit.
3. It cannot be a Nash equilibrium for Jack or Jill to charge a price lower than marginal cost (in this case, zero). They would make a loss by selling at such a price and would prefer not to produce at all.

Given these three steps, we must conclude that the only Nash equilibrium is where Jack and Jill charge the same price for water equal to marginal cost – in this case, zero.

In our example, Bertrand competition leads to a startling conclusion. Even with only two firms, each firm in equilibrium will set a price equal to marginal cost – the same as under perfect competition. This result holds whenever production involves constant marginal costs. Bertrand price competition will always lead to the same outcome as perfect competition in this case.

Comparing Cournot and Bertrand competition

Cournot and Bertrand competition yield markedly different outcomes. Bertrand price competition leads to outcomes close to those of perfect competition. In contrast, Cournot pricing outcomes are in between perfect competition and monopoly pricing.

Both types of competition are theoretical possibilities. Which one is more applicable depends on the situation. Remember that each involves firms having a different type of belief about their competitors. In Cournot, firms believe rivals will act to maintain output, whereas in Bertrand, they believe that their rivals' price will remain fixed.

Cournot beliefs will be more appropriate in industries where it is difficult for firms to actually change their output levels. This could occur when firms have limited production capacities, face rigid production technologies or manufacture to maintain an inventory stock rather than to supply customers' orders.

Bertrand competition is more likely when firms compete directly over price before setting output. For example, when tendering for a one-off project, like building a major highway in Melbourne or Sydney, competitors face a situation like Bertrand price competition. The firm with the lowest bid wins the tender and gets to build the project and the losers get nothing.

17

Competition policy

Learning objectives

In this chapter you will:

- consider the various public policies aimed at solving the problem of monopoly
- consider how competition laws try to foster competition in oligopolistic markets
- examine various business strategies such as resale price maintenance and tying
- consider why competition laws are often controversial.

One of the *Ten Lessons from Economics* presented in chapter 1 is that governments can sometimes improve market outcomes. We have already seen how this idea can work when there are externalities or public goods. In this chapter, we show how governments can sometimes improve market outcomes when there is either monopoly or oligopoly.

Monopoly firms, like competitive firms, aim to maximise profit. But this goal has very different ramifications for competitive and monopoly firms. As we first saw in chapter 7, self-interested buyers and sellers in competitive markets are unwittingly led by an invisible hand to promote general economic wellbeing. In contrast, because monopoly firms are unchecked by competition, the outcome in a market with a monopoly is often not in the best interest of society. As we saw in chapter 15, a monopoly will increase its profit by restricting output and raising the price that it charges above marginal cost. This results in a deadweight loss because the monopolist produces less than the socially efficient quantity of output.

Oligopoly can also lead to a deadweight loss. However, oligopoly can lead to a range of market outcomes. If there are many oligopolists then competition can be intense. As we noted in chapter 16, as the number of sellers in an oligopoly grows, an oligopolistic market looks more and more like a competitive market. The price approaches marginal cost and the quantity produced approaches the socially efficient level. In contrast, if there are few oligopolists or if the firms in an oligopoly cooperate and form a cartel, then the market outcome will look like a monopoly. The oligopoly raises profits by producing less and charging more.

Governments around the world have responded by enacting laws that restrict the behaviour of monopolies and oligopolies. In extreme situations, governments have nationalised monopoly and oligopoly firms in the belief that direct government control will lead to a more efficient market outcome. In other situations, governments have acted to break up monopolies. For example, in 1984, the US telephone monopolist, AT&T, was broken into a number of smaller companies due to government action. Similarly, as part of the development of a government-owned National Broadband Network (NBN) in Australia, the main telecommunications company, Telstra, will be broken up. The NBN will use some assets that are separated from Telstra and the break up aims to improve competition in telecommunications.

competition laws
laws that restrict the behaviour of firms with market power, such as monopolies or firms in a small oligopoly

More generally, firms that are either monopolies or oligopolies face a variety of **competition laws** that restrict their behaviour. These laws, which are also called antitrust laws in the US, prevent one firm buying another firm if it is likely to lead to a monopoly or a small oligopoly. They also make it illegal for firms to form a cartel or to use certain tactics to undermine competitors and force them out of the market. In Australia, the key competition regulator, the Australian Competition and Consumer Commission (ACCC), keeps a close eye on firms that either are monopolies or compete in a small oligopoly. For example, in 2009 the ACCC objected to the petrol retailer Caltex buying another petrol retailer, Mobil. Caltex and Mobil were two of the main petrol retailers in Australia at the time and, while there were a number of other major retailers, the ACCC argued that petrol retailing was an oligopoly. The ACCC argued that if Caltex was allowed to purchase Mobil, then competition would be significantly harmed As a result, Caltex decided to pull out of the deal.

competition policy
the laws and procedures that aim to improve social efficiency in oligopolistic and monopolistic markets

Search me!
▸ competition policy

Government policies, including competition laws, that aim to improve the efficiency of oligopolistic and monopoly markets are called **competition policy**. In this chapter we consider some of these policies, and look at how they can improve market efficiency.

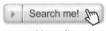

Public policy towards monopolies

We have seen that monopolies, in contrast to competitive markets, fail to allocate resources efficiently. Monopolies produce less than the socially desirable quantity of output and, as a result, charge prices above marginal cost.

Policymakers in the government can respond to the problem of monopoly in one of four ways:

- by trying to make monopolised industries more competitive
- by regulating the behaviour of the monopolies
- by turning some private monopolies into public enterprises
- by doing nothing at all.

Using the law to increase competition

If the two largest Australian banks wanted to merge, the deal would be closely examined by the federal government before it went into effect. The lawyers and economists at the ACCC might well decide that a merger between two large banking corporations would make the Australian banking market substantially less competitive and, as a result, would reduce the economic wellbeing of the country as a whole. If so, the ACCC would challenge the merger in court and, if the judge agreed, the two companies would not be allowed to merge. The main competition law in Australia to control mergers and prevent monopolists from abusing their market power is the ***Competition and Consumer Act***. This law, previously called the *Trade Practices Act*, was enacted by parliament in 1974. It has been added to and amended since 1974 to broaden the government's power to prevent anti-competitive behaviour.

Competition and Consumer Act
Australia's main competition laws (formerly the *Trade Practices Act*)

Search me!

▸ *Competition and Consumer Act*

The *Competition and Consumer Act* gives the government various ways to promote competition. The Act allows the government to prevent a merger that will substantially lessen competition. The government has used this law in recent years to challenge mergers in the petrol, banking, retail groceries and paint industries. The Act also makes it illegal for a firm with substantial market power to use that power to restrict or harm competition. In one case, BHP Billiton, the big steel and mining company, was found to have breached this section of the Act when it refused to sell a crucial input to a competitor, Queensland Wire Industries.

Amendments to the Act in the 1990s extended the federal government's ability to control firms with market power. Local telephone services are often viewed as a natural monopoly and new sections were added to the Act in 1997 to regulate telecommunications. Part IIIA of the Act was added in 1995 to regulate firms that control important monopoly facilities, such as a pipeline or a rail track.

Competition laws, like the *Competition and Consumer Act*, have costs as well as benefits. Sometimes companies merge not to reduce competition but to lower costs through more efficient joint production. These benefits from mergers are sometimes called *synergies*. By merging, two banks may be able to economise on branch and electronic networks such as EFTPOS and ATMs.

If competition laws are to raise social welfare, the government must be able to determine which mergers are desirable and which are not. That is, it must be able to measure and compare the social benefit from synergies with the social costs of reduced competition. Critics of competition laws are sceptical that governments, through agencies such as the ACCC, can perform the necessary cost–benefit analysis to get it right every time. As an example, in 2003 Qantas and Air New Zealand wanted to form a joint venture that would allow them to cooperate on flight schedules and pricing.

Both the ACCC and the Commerce Commission, the competition regulator in New Zealand, decided that the joint venture would result in a loss of social welfare. The airlines appealed this decision to the courts in both Australia and New Zealand. In 2004, the New Zealand High Court upheld the Commerce Commission's decision. The High Court recognised that the joint venture would result in some benefits but concluded that the social loss from reduced competition between the airlines would more than outweigh any benefits. In contrast, the Australian Competition Tribunal upheld the appeal by the airlines. The Tribunal believed that growing competition from other airlines, such as Virgin and Emirates, flying between Australia and New Zealand, would be adequate to prevent the joint venture from reducing competition.

"BUT IF WE DO MERGE WITH AMALGAMATED, WE'LL HAVE ENOUGH RESOURCES TO FIGHT THE ANTI-TRUST VIOLATION CAUSED BY THE MERGER."

Source: ScienceCartoonsPlus.com.

Regulation

Another way in which the government deals with the problem of monopoly is by regulating the behaviour of monopolists. This solution is common in the case of natural monopolies, such as privately owned gas and electric companies. These companies are not allowed to charge any price they want. Instead, government agencies regulate their prices.

What price should the government set for a natural monopoly? This question is not as easy as it might at first appear. One might conclude that the price should equal the monopolist's marginal cost. If price equals marginal cost, customers will buy the quantity of the monopolist's output that maximises total surplus and the allocation of resources will be efficient.

Figure 17.1 Marginal-cost pricing for a natural monopoly

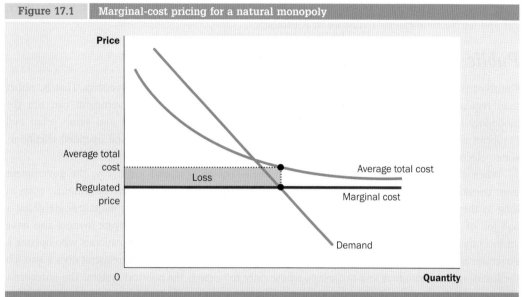

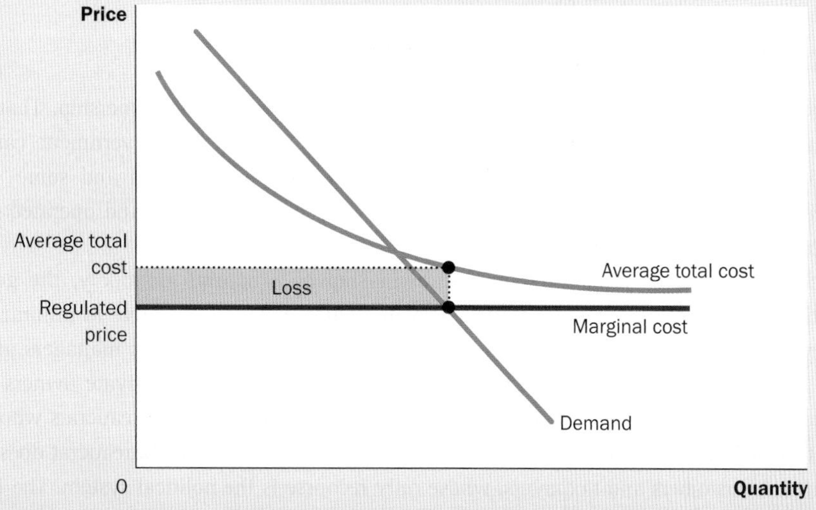

Because a natural monopoly usually has declining average total cost, marginal cost is less than average total cost. Therefore, if regulators require a natural monopoly to charge a price equal to marginal cost, price will be below average total cost and the monopoly will lose money.

There are, however, two practical problems with marginal-cost pricing as a regulatory system. The first is illustrated in Figure 17.1. Natural monopolies usually have declining average total cost. As we discussed in chapter 13, when average total cost is declining, marginal cost is less than average total cost. If regulators are to set a price equal to marginal cost, that price will be less than the firm's average total cost and the firm will lose money. Instead of charging such a low price, the monopoly firm would just exit the industry.

Regulators can respond to this problem in various ways, none of which is perfect. One way is to subsidise the monopolist. In essence, the government picks up the losses inherent in marginal-cost pricing. Yet to pay for the subsidy, the government needs to raise money through taxation, which involves its own deadweight losses. Alternatively, the regulators can allow the monopolist to charge a price higher than marginal cost. If the regulated price equals average total cost, the monopolist earns exactly zero profit. Yet average-cost pricing leads to deadweight losses, because the monopolist's price no longer reflects the marginal cost of producing the good. In essence, average-cost pricing is like a tax on the good the monopolist is selling.

The second problem with marginal-cost pricing as a regulatory system (and with average-cost pricing as well) is that it gives the monopolist no incentive to reduce costs. Each firm in a competitive market tries to reduce its costs because lower costs mean higher profits. But if a regulated monopolist knows that regulators will reduce prices whenever costs fall, the monopolist will not benefit from any reduction in costs and so will not work to reduce costs. The monopolist's failure to reduce costs hurts total welfare.

In practice, regulators deal with both problems by allowing monopolists to keep some of the benefits from lower costs in the form of higher profit, a practice that requires some departure from marginal-cost pricing. Price cap regulation allows the regulated firm to keep all the benefits from lower costs for a fixed period of time. This regulation is used to control market power in the electricity, gas and telecommunications industries in Australia.

Public ownership and privatisation

The third policy used by the government to deal with monopoly is public ownership. That is, rather than regulating a natural monopoly that is run by a private firm, the government can run the monopoly itself. This solution has been common in Australia, New Zealand and some Asian and European countries. In these countries, the government has, at times, owned and operated telephone, water, electricity and rail companies.

When choosing between public and private ownership of a natural monopoly, the government must consider how ownership alters incentives. Private owners have an incentive to minimise costs as long as they reap part of the benefit in the form of higher profit. If the firm's managers are doing a bad job of keeping costs down, the firm's owners will fire them. However, private owners also have an incentive to abuse market power if this raises profits. In contrast, public bureaucrats who operate a government-owned monopoly may have little incentive to lower costs. If the bureaucrat does a bad job the losers are the customers and taxpayers, whose only recourse is the political system. The bureaucrat also has little incentive to abuse market power.

Reducing costs raises economic wellbeing but using market power to increase prices leads to an economic loss. The government's ownership choice will depend on which incentives are stronger and have the biggest effect on economic wellbeing. The best form of ownership will also depend on whether the government can effectively control the actions of a private owner or a public bureaucrat. If a private firm can be effectively regulated to avoid abuse of market power, then private ownership with regulation may be preferred to public ownership. However, as noted above, regulation of natural monopolies often creates a deadweight loss and may reduce the owner's incentives to keep costs low.

Public bureaucrats may be given incentives to lower costs. The government can set cost targets for a public manager and the manager may face demotion or dismissal if these targets are not met. This process of providing incentives to public managers to make them behave more like private owners is called corporatisation.

In recent years, governments in Australia and around the world have been relying more on private ownership and regulation and less on public ownership to control natural monopolies. In Australia, the New South Wales government recently sold some of their publicly owned electricity companies to private firms, while the Queensland government privatised QR National, the state's main railway company. The federal government sold Telstra, Australia's largest telecommunications company, to private owners in the 1990s and 2000s. Critics of **privatisation** argue that the motive behind these public sell-offs is to raise funds to control government debt (rather than resorting to unpopular tax increases). Although there is significant debate about the motives behind privatisation, the trend from public to private ownership in part reflects the view that the profit motive is the best way to guarantee that firms are well run.

privatisation
the sale of a government-owned business to private owners

Doing nothing

Each of the foregoing policies aimed at reducing the problem of monopoly has drawbacks. As a result, some economists argue that it is often best for the government not to try to remedy the inefficiencies of monopoly pricing. Here is the assessment of economist George Stigler, who won the Nobel Prize for his work in industrial organisation, writing in the *Fortune Encyclopedia of Economics*:

> A famous theorem in economics states that a competitive enterprise economy will produce the largest possible income from a given stock of resources. No real economy meets the exact conditions of the theorem, and all real economies will fall short of the ideal economy – a difference called 'market failure'. In my view, however, the degree of 'market failure' for the American economy is much smaller than the 'political failure' arising from the imperfections of economic policies found in real political systems.

As this quotation makes clear, determining the proper role of the government in the economy requires judgements about politics as well as economics.

CASESTUDY

The ACCC – Australia's competition regulator

There is no general law in Australia that prevents monopoly pricing. If a firm has a lot of market power and might abuse this power by raising its prices to monopoly levels, then state or federal governments may intervene to control the firm's prices. For example, there are price controls in Australia covering telephone calls and electricity prices. Generally, however, the law is aimed at preventing firms from becoming monopolies by mergers or takeovers and stopping firms that have a lot of market power from harming their competitors. These laws make up part of the *Competition and Consumer Act*, and the regulator with the responsibility of upholding these laws is the Australian Competition and Consumer Commission (ACCC).

The ACCC, which was formed in November 1995, has a wide range of responsibilities. Roughly speaking, its tasks fall into two categories – consumer protection and competition protection. Consumer protection laws punish firms if they mislead consumers over products. To give one example, it is the ACCC that protects customers from false claims or omissions in advertisements. In November 2010, following an ACCC investigation, the Federal Court ordered Optus, a telecommunications company, to stop advertising its Internet services in a way that was likely to mislead customers. Consumer protection laws also make certain undesirable selling practices illegal and protect consumers from shoddy goods and defective products.

The competition protection laws prevent firms from agreeing not to compete and stop firms from writing contracts that might limit competition. We discuss these laws in more detail below. It is also illegal under the *Competition and Consumer Act* for firms with market power to use this power to undermine competition. In 1994 and 1995, for example, Woolworths stores in Victoria retaliated against bakers who supplied cheap bread to Woolworth's retail competitors by removing the bakers' bread from Woolworths stores and refusing to accept any further deliveries. Woolworths argued that their actions were simply an attempt to negotiate a better deal from the bakers. The ACCC believed that Woolworth's real motive was to force the bakers to raise their supply prices to competitor stores, making it harder for those stores to compete against Woolworths. In 2004, the Full Federal Court handed down its decision, agreeing with the ACCC that Woolworth's actions were anti-competitive.

One of the most important laws deals with the creation of monopoly. As we noted earlier in this chapter, the *Competition and Consumer Act* prevents mergers or takeovers that will substantially lessen competition. The ACCC plays an important part in determining which mergers are legal and which are illegal. Before firms merge, they can approach the ACCC for 'approval'. The ACCC can grant this approval if they believe that the merger is legal or if they believe that there are public benefits from the merger that more than outweigh any likely anti-competitive effects. Sometimes, the ACCC will require the merging firms to undertake to reduce their market power before the merger is approved. This might include selling some assets to another competitor, such as when Macquarie Media purchased Southern Cross Broadcasting in 2007. Macquarie was required to sell some of its radio stations around Australia to prevent a reduction in competition.

It is sometimes argued that Australia's merger laws are too restrictive. See for example the 'In the news' article on 'Should merging be easier' in this chapter. Most mergers, however, pass the eye of the ACCC with no problems. Around 3 per cent to

>>

5 per cent of mergers involve the firms making undertakings that offset any competition concerns while only about 2 per cent of mergers are opposed outright by the ACCC.

The ACCC, and its chairman Rod Sims, are often unpopular with firms – particularly those that it is investigating. But, if the competition regulator is doing its job then it should be unpopular with business. The aim of a competition regulator is to prevent firms from acting in ways that raise their own profits but, overall, lower the welfare of society. As a previous head of the ACCC noted, unpopularity goes with the job.

IN THE NEWS . . .

SHOULD MERGING BE EASIER?

Business often argues that Australia's merger laws are too strict and that the *Competition and Consumer Act* (formally the *Trade Practices Act*) needs to be updated. In this article, Ross Gittins considers the argument for relaxing merger laws in Australia – and finds that the main arguments have poor foundations.

CEOs hanker for a hand-up

by Ross Gittins

With the Howard Government on the ropes in an election year, don't think it's only small business and the bush that are getting in for their chop. Big business has just presented its own log of claims.

The Business Council of Australia held its annual 'strategy forum' last week and addressed this grand question: What does Australia need to do to ensure the country remains relevant and vital with an economy capable of growing and delivering work and better living standards into the future?

After deep deliberation, it came up with five issues it claimed were fundamental to achieving that aim: e-transformation, education and training, modernisation of the *Trade Practices Act*, tax breaks for companies with overseas operations and a 'balanced' approach to greenhouse gas emissions.

Not bad, eh? Two parts trendy motherhood to three parts straight self-interest. What's the best we can do to keep Australia wonderful? Make life easier for big business.

When the CEOs of our biggest companies can come up with nothing more inspiring than that in the way of further economic reform, it suggests they're riven by conflicting interests. All they can agree on is tax cuts all round and open slather on company takeovers.

Huh? Yes, that's right. When they talk about the need for 'a regulatory system which is consistent with international trends' and the need to 'modernise' the *Trade Practices Act*, that's what they're on about: making it easier for them to keep playing the takeover game.

See if you can deduce that from this coded message: 'the forum recognised that the existing *Trade Practices Act*, which was enacted in the early 1970s in very different circumstances, had failed to take account of international trends and needed to be modernised to ensure Australian companies are able to compete'.

If you can't quite see how allowing Australian companies to swallow their competitors will 'ensure they are able to compete', you're obviously not up with the latest 'international trends'.

This is an allusion to a CEOs' special, the National Champion argument. It says that if we want our big companies to be able to expand abroad, we have to allow them to become near-monopolies in our market so they can attain critical mass.

It's a silly argument that will always be more appealing to a CEO than to the rest of us. Why should we put up with an uncompetitive local market just so NAB or Pioneer Concrete can be big in North America? What's in it for us?

And how is allowing our biggest companies to become fat and lazy monopolists in their local market going to make them fit enough to compete in other people's markets?

As for the line that the *Trade Practices Act*, having been passed in 1974, is now terribly out of date, it's nonsense too. The merger provisions of the act were amended in 1993, following two public inquiries.

From the way the CEOs are carrying on, you'd think the present law was greatly inhibiting their takeover plans – but it isn't (more's the pity). Only about 5 per cent of the takeover proposals notified to the ACCC are blocked – and about half of those are subsequently approved after the proposal's been modified to reduce its anti-competitive elements.

The main area where restrictions on takeovers could be contrary to the public interest is in markets for internationally 'tradable' goods (mainly manufactures), where domestic producers may need to consolidate their activities so as to gain the economies of scale needed to compete effectively against imports or on export markets.

But the ACCC has long acknowledged the merits of this case. Domestic consumers' interests are protected by competition from imports, so where imports have at least 10 per cent of the local market, merger proposals are given the tick.

No, the main area of contention is in markets for 'non-tradable' goods or services, where there's no possibility of competition from imports and little likelihood that achieving scale economies in the local market could assist the merged companies' attempts to gain a foothold in overseas markets.

But whereas the economic rationalists' opposition to such mergers assumes the companies' motive is to gain monopoly power in the domestic market, experience suggests motives are often far less rational.

For CEOs who're finding it hard going to gain market share or increase profits by being better than their competitors, taking over other firms is a lazy way of giving the appearance of progress, growth and general busyness. And expanding the empire always justifies an executive pay rise.

The wealth of research showing that shareholders rarely end up benefiting from takeovers lends support to this more cynical interpretation.

Be that as it may, it's clear that while One Nation is attacking national competition policy from one end, the Business Council is now attacking it from the other. A most unedifying spectacle.

Source: Ross Gittins/*Sydney Morning Herald*, 26 February 2001.

Q

Describe the ways policymakers can respond to the inefficiencies caused by monopolies. Give a potential problem with each of these policy responses.

Public policy towards oligopolies

As we saw in chapter 16, cooperation among oligopolists is undesirable from the standpoint of society as a whole, because it leads to production that is too low and prices that are too high. To move the allocation of resources closer to the socially desirable level, policymakers should try to induce firms in an oligopoly to compete rather than cooperate. Let's consider how policymakers do this and then examine the controversies that arise in this area of public policy.

Doonesbury
BY
G.B. TRUDEAU
WOW... WHAT'S THAT, ALEX?
ACTUALLY, IT'S A WHOLE NEW PARADIGM, LISA.
GET OUT! YOU GO, GIRLFRIEND!
OKAY, ANYONE HAVE A QUESTION FOR ME?
I DO, MR. GATES.
MY UNCLE BERNIE SAYS NOBODY CAN COMPETE AGAINST YOU, THAT ANYONE WHO TRIES GETS SQUASHED LIKE A BUG...
x3 = 43 + 7 = ?
IS THAT TRUE? I MEAN, I WANT TO BE AN ENGINEER LIKE YOU, BUT I DON'T WANT TO BE SQUASHED LIKE A BUG!
UNIVERSAL PRESS SYNDICATE © 1998 G.B. Trudeau
WELL, YOUNG LADY...
LIKE, I HAVE THIS COOL IDEA THAT WOULD MAKE WINDOWS OBSOLETE, BUT I'M WORRIED ABOUT WHAT YOU GUYS'LL DO!
HMM... WELL, YES, THAT WOULD PRESENT US WITH A PROBLEM...
HOW ABOUT IF I PAY YOU $10 MILLION TO BECOME A DENTIST?
43 + 7 = ?
DEAL.
VERY GOOD, DEAR.
GO DOONESBURY@http://www.doonesbury.com

Restraint of trade and competition laws

One way that policy discourages cooperation is through the common law. Normally, freedom of contract is an essential part of a market economy. Businesses and households use contracts to arrange mutually advantageous trades. In doing this, they rely on the court system to enforce contracts. Yet, for many centuries, judges in England and Australia have deemed agreements among competitors to reduce quantities and raise prices to be contrary to the public good. They therefore refused to enforce such agreements.

Australia's competition laws reinforce this policy. The *Competition and Consumer Act* makes it illegal for corporations to make a contract or arrangement that would substantially lessen competition. It is also illegal for firms to form a cartel so that they can agree to set prices above a competitive level. This law means that oligopolists cannot agree to act together and make their markets less competitive. The law has been used to prevent collusive behaviour in a number of industries including pre-mixed concrete, steel products and car windscreens. In 2007, Visy Industries was fined $36 million for its role in a cartel with Amcor, the two main suppliers of cardboard boxes in Australia.

IN THE NEWS ...

HOW TO FORM A CARTEL

In 2007, the Australian Competition and Consumer Commission (ACCC) successfully prosecuted Visy for its part in a cartel that fixed the price of cardboard boxes. The court fined Visy $36 million with individual executives also being fined a total of $4 million. This was the largest cartel fine in Australia's history and one of the largest for a domestic cartel anywhere in the world. This article looks at how the cartel was formed.

Cartel's dirty box of tricks

by Blair Speedy and Cameron Stewart

It was a chance meeting during a lazy beach walk in early 2000 that sowed the seeds of Australia's largest cartel scandal. Walking in one direction along the beach on Queensland's Sunshine Coast was Peter Brown, the manager of the Australian and New Zealand divisions of packaging group Amcor, one of the country's best-known and oldest public companies. Walking the other way was Harry Debney, who ran the cardboard division of arch-rival Visy, owned by billionaire Richard Pratt.

'My wife went to the same school originally that Harry went to, so there was a sort of connection,' Brown recalls. 'We met each other on a beach walk one day and arranged to meet in Melbourne.'

It was to be the last accidental encounter between these two men. Seven years on, these two architects of the cartel are in disgrace, Amcor, Visy and Pratt have been shamed, and Australians are an estimated $700 million poorer as a result of a ruthless price-fixing deal in the nation's $2 billion box market ...

According to Brown's testimony, [in early 2000] Debney called his home and 'had a chat to my wife' and then asked Brown if he could drop by in the morning.

'It wasn't some sort of spur-of-the-moment thing,' he told the ACCC. 'It was planned and he laid out what he would like to do in terms of managing the marketplace.'

In the agreed statement of facts between the ACCC and Visy, tendered to the Federal Court last month, Debney is portrayed as the prime proposer of the cartel, a position at odds with Pratt's public claim that Amcor was the initiator of the illegal deal.

The transcripts show that far from being shocked by Debney's approach, Brown embraced it, believing it to be a lifeline for Amcor as well as for his own future.

>>

'At about that time Russell Jones started to put a lot of pressure on me about the performance of the business in terms of price levels, and I certainly felt I had no alternative but to enter into some sort of pricing arrangement, and I wasn't unenthusiastic,' Brown told the ACCC. 'I mean, I don't think I complained bitterly about the process because I could see that, if it worked, it would lead to better outcomes.'

And it did. Brown said that once prices started to rise under the cartel arrangement, the Amcor board was pleased: 'They said they held me in high regard.'

If Brown's motivation to enter the cartel was to save his ailing company and his career, Visy's motivation – at a time when it was already trouncing Amcor – appears to be a blend of naked greed and Machiavellian intent. Pratt has claimed the cartel agreement was a ruse by Visy to make Amcor relax and then go behind its back to steal market share.

In handing down a record $36 million fine last month to Visy, and through it to Pratt, Federal Court judge Peter Heerey ridiculed this claim, describing it as a 'John le Carré defence'. However, the transcripts reveal Amcor believed Pratt was trying to double-cross it even while setting up the cartel.

'All the advice I was getting from people within Amcor was, "Look, these guys will talk peace with you and then turn around and take a great slab of business from you overnight",' Brown told the ACCC. He revealed that Debney kept warning him he wouldn't be able to control Pratt.

'He (Debney) would make a commitment and something would go wrong and he would say, "Well, you know Richard Pratt, nobody controls Richard".'

Brown revealed that Pratt tried to swipe an Arnott's contract from Amcor despite the cartel agreement forbidding the conspirators from poaching each other's customers.

'The CEO of Arnott's rang me up and said, "I have just had Richard Pratt in here telling me he wants all the business", and I said, "Well, that is a bit of a worry."'

'The guy (Pratt) is a loose cannon: When it suited him, he would go and do what he wanted to do. I mean, when you are worth $3 billion or whatever it is, you can do what you like, pretty well, can't you?'

It was the suspicion that Visy was double-crossing Amcor on the cartel that led Brown to ask Jones to meet Pratt at the All Nations Hotel in Melbourne in May 2001 to reaffirm Visy's commitment to the illegal deal.

According to the transcripts, Jones knew what he was doing was illegal. He said the meeting with Pratt lasted 75 minutes but they talked about the cartel for only about 60 seconds. He took notes of the meeting but made no mention of the cartel discussions in those notes. However, it is Jones's claim about what took place in these crucial 60 seconds that would lead to Pratt's undoing and directly contradict his public claim that he did not know the details of the cartel arrangement with Amcor.

In his ACCC interview, Jones said his cartel discussion with Pratt, though brief, was detailed, with specific contracts being discussed.

'Just to be clear, the matter of the contracts was discussed on the first meeting with Mr Pratt, and Mr Pratt alone,' Jones said. 'I referred to these lists of three or four (contracts). He was aware of them and aware that they were under some sort of negotiation, or likely to be.'

Jones said Pratt 'clearly understood the contents of the discussion' and agreed it 'should be adhered to by both parties'.

Jones told the ACCC he realised the gravity of the game that was being played between two of the country's most powerful companies.

'I was asked to do something which clearly I should not have done,' he said. Later on in the interview, Jones conceded that 'my mistake was that I didn't stop it'.

Source: Blair Speedy & Cameron Stewart/ *The Australian*, 16 November 2007.

Controversies over competition policy

Over time, much controversy has centred on the question of what kinds of behaviour competition laws should prohibit. Most economists agree that price-fixing agreements among competing firms should be illegal. Yet competition laws have been used to condemn some business practices whose effects are not obvious. Competition laws, if poorly designed, may also harm rather than help competition. Here we consider three examples of controversial competition laws.

Resale price maintenance

One example of a controversial business practice is **resale price maintenance**. Imagine that Superduper Electronics sells DVD players to retail stores for $300. If Superduper requires the retailers to charge customers $350, it is said to engage in resale price maintenance. Any retailer that charged less than $350 would have violated its contract with Superduper.

resale price maintenance
when a wholesaler requires that its retailers do not sell its products to their customers below a specified retail price

At first, resale price maintenance might seem anti-competitive and, therefore, detrimental to society. Like an agreement among members of a cartel, it prevents the retailers from competing on price. For this reason, resale price maintenance is illegal under the *Competition and Consumer Act*. Yet some economists have defended resale price maintenance on two grounds.

First, they deny that it is aimed at reducing competition. To the extent that Superduper Electronics has any market power, it can exert that power through the wholesale price, rather than through resale price maintenance. Moreover, Superduper has no incentive to discourage competition among its retailers. Indeed, because a cartel of retailers sells less than a group of competitive retailers, Superduper would be worse off if its retailers were a cartel.

Second, economists have argued that resale price maintenance has a legitimate goal. Superduper may want its retailers to provide customers with a pleasant showroom and a knowledgeable sales force. Yet, without resale price maintenance, some customers would take advantage of one store's service to learn about the DVD player's special features and then buy the DVD player at a discount retailer that does not provide this service. To some extent, good service is a public good among the retailers that sell Superduper DVD players. As we discussed in chapter 11, when one person provides a public good, others are able to enjoy it without paying for it. In this case, discount retailers would free ride on the service provided by other retailers, leading to less service than is desirable. Resale price maintenance is one way for Superduper to solve this free-rider problem.

The example of resale price maintenance illustrates an important principle – *business practices that appear to reduce competition may in fact have legitimate purposes.* This principle makes the application of the competition laws all the more difficult. The economists, lawyers and judges in charge of enforcing these laws must determine what kinds of behaviour public policy should prohibit as impeding competition and reducing economic wellbeing. Often that job is not easy.

Predatory pricing

Firms with market power normally use that power to raise prices above the competitive level. But should policymakers ever be concerned that firms with market power might charge prices that are too low? This question is at the heart of a second debate over competition policy.

Imagine a large airline, call it Aussie Air, has a monopoly on some route. Then Rural Express enters and takes 20 per cent of the market, leaving Aussie with 80 per cent. In response to this competition, Aussie starts slashing its fares. Some competition analysts argue that Aussie's move

predatory pricing
when a firm sells its product at an artificially low price in order to drive out an efficient competitor and reduce long-run competition

Search me!

▸ predatory pricing

could be anti-competitive: The price cuts may be intended to drive Rural Express out of the market so Aussie can recapture its monopoly and raise prices again. Such behaviour is called **predatory pricing**.

Predatory pricing is a common claim in airlines, groceries and other industries. However, some economists are sceptical of this argument and believe that predatory pricing is rarely, and perhaps never, a profitable business strategy. Why? For a price war to drive out a rival, prices have to be driven below cost. Yet if Aussie starts selling cheap tickets at a loss, it had better be ready to fly more planes, because low fares will attract more customers. Rural Express, meanwhile, can respond to Aussie's predatory move by cutting back on flights. As a result, Aussie ends up bearing more than 80 per cent of the losses, putting Rural Express in a good position to survive the price war. If the 'predator' suffers more than the 'prey' then using predatory pricing to harm competition makes no sense.

Economists continue to debate whether predatory pricing should be a concern for competition policymakers. Various questions remain unresolved. Is predatory pricing ever a profitable business strategy? If so, when? Are the courts capable of telling which price cuts are competitive and thus good for consumers and which are predatory? There are no easy answers.

Tying

tying
when a firm will only sell customers one product if they also buy another product

Another example of a controversial business practice is **tying** or bundling. Suppose that Makemoney Movies produces two new films – *Spiderman* and *Hamlet*. If Makemoney offers theatres the two films together at a single price, rather than separately, the studio is said to be tying (or bundling) its two products.

Some tying arrangements can violate competition laws. The reasoning behind the laws against tying – or, as the legal profession calls it, full-line forcing – is as follows. Imagine that *Spiderman* is a blockbuster, whereas *Hamlet* is an unprofitable art film. Then the studio could use the high demand for *Spiderman* to force theatres to buy *Hamlet*. It seemed that the studio could use tying as a mechanism for expanding its market power.

Economists have been sceptical of this argument. Imagine that theatres are willing to pay $20 000 for *Spiderman* and nothing for *Hamlet*. Then the most that a theatre would pay for the two movies together is $20 000 – the same as it would pay for *Spiderman* by itself. Forcing the theatre to accept a worthless movie as part of the deal does not increase the theatre's willingness to pay. Makemoney cannot increase its market power simply by bundling the two movies together.

Why, then, does tying exist? One possibility is that it is a form of price discrimination. Suppose there are two theatres. City Theatre is willing to pay $16 000 for *Spiderman* and $5000 for *Hamlet*. Country Theatre is willing to pay $14 000 for *Spiderman* and $6000 for *Hamlet*. If Makemoney charges separate prices for the two films, its best strategy is to charge $14 000 for *Spiderman* and $5000 for *Hamlet*, for a total of $19 000 from each theatre. Yet if Makemoney offers the two movies as a bundle, it can charge each theatre $20 000 for the movies. Thus, if different theatres value the films differently, tying allows the studio to increase profit by charging a combined price closer to the buyers' total willingness to pay.

Tying remains a controversial business practice. The argument that tying allows a firm to extend its market power to other goods is not well founded, at least in its simplest form. Yet economists have proposed more elaborate theories for how tying can impede competition. Given our current economic knowledge, it is unclear whether tying has adverse effects for society as a whole.

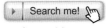

CASESTUDY

The Baxter case

Between 1998 and 2001, Baxter Healthcare, a major pharmaceutical company, offered the following deal to state hospitals. If the hospitals purchased two products, called 'sterile fluids' and 'PD products', separately from Baxter, then each product would have a high price. But if the hospitals bought both products as a bundle, exclusively from Baxter, then they would receive a significant price discount.

Baxter was the only Australian manufacturer of sterile fluids at the time and the cost of importing these fluids was high. In contrast, other pharmaceutical companies could supply PD products. However, hospitals need both of these products and Baxter won all of the contracts.

The ACCC commenced legal action against Baxter in 2002, arguing that Baxter's bundling was a deliberate attempt by the company to use its market power in sterile fluids to reduce competition in the supply of PD products. The court proceedings were controversial, raising difficult economic and legal questions.

The economists who gave evidence in the case, including Barry Nalebuff, from Yale University, provided very different interpretations of Baxter's behaviour. Economists for Baxter argued that the bundled price was simply a legitimate competitive attempt by the company to win as much business as possible. The low bundled price benefitted the hospitals that purchased the products. In contrast, the economists for the ACCC considered that the bundled price was below a competitive level. Baxter was attempting to damage its competitors by setting such a low bundled price.

On the legal side, Baxter argued that it could not violate Australia's competition laws because it was selling products to the government, and these laws do not cover government transactions. The ACCC argued that, while the government could not itself breach the competition laws, the laws still applied when the government was a consumer and the seller engaged in anticompetitive behaviour.

The legal dispute went all the way to the High Court before, in 2008, the Full Federal Court ruled that Baxter's bundling was anti-competitive and illegal. The proceedings were finalised in 2010 with Baxter being fined $4.9 million.

Transparent pricing

Competition authorities in many countries support laws that make prices more transparent. Before July 1997, the dominant telecommunications company in Australia, Telstra, was required by law to report its prices to a regulator. Telstra's competitors could see this price list and it was illegal for Telstra to charge any customer a price that differed from the list price.

These laws were supposed to help competition in telecommunications by making prices clear. If customers know the prices being charged then it makes it easier for them to shop around for the cheapest deal.

Economists were sceptical of this argument. Rather than encouraging competition, requiring firms to list their prices may make it easier for firms to collude. Consider our example from chapter 16 of Jack and Jill, the water duopolists. One reason Jack and Jill might find it difficult to form a cartel is that each producer has an incentive to cheat on any cartel agreement, raise output and push down the price. If the law requires them to list their output level or price in advance then this makes it harder for any firm to successfully cheat on the cartel. As soon as Jack tries to increase his output and lower his price, Jill is informed of this cheating by the competition authorities. Jill can then immediately respond, raising her output and lowering her price. This reduces the short-term benefit Jack gets from cheating. Because Jill is able to immediately detect any attempt by Jack to cheat on the cartel, cheating becomes unprofitable for Jack. The competition laws have helped the cartel to sustain high prices.

A test of the effects of transparent pricing rules comes from experience in Denmark. In 1993, the Danish Competition Council decided to collect and publish the prices that different firms were charging in the ready-mixed concrete industry. By publishing this information, the Council hoped to make prices more transparent for customers. The Council believed that this would make the market more competitive by making it easier for customers to shop around. When economists analysed the Council's action they showed that, rather than making the market more competitive, publishing price data helped the firms to cooperate and set higher prices. Before the Council published the price information, different companies charged different prices for ready-mixed concrete. After the Council began to publish information about prices, however, each company quickly moved to set a price almost identical to that of its competitors. Most importantly, companies that initially charged a low price quickly raised their price to match the high price set by competitors. The Council's attempt to help competition by publishing prices helped the firms to avoid competition. As a result, the Council stopped publishing the price information in December 1996.

IN THE NEWS . . .

DO LOW PRICES HURT OR HELP COMPETITION?

Applying competition laws is never easy. What to one person looks like reasonable competitive behaviour may look to another like an attempt to harm competition. Laws which make low prices illegal are particularly controversial. Competition reduces prices to the benefit of society. But if a firm sets prices too low, it may be viewed as a deliberate attempt to bankrupt competitors and reduce competition. In many countries this 'predatory pricing' is illegal. But rules aimed at preventing predatory pricing may stifle socially desirable competition. This article shows how rules aimed at preventing predatory pricing in Ireland acted like a resale price maintenance scheme. It is argued that this led to higher prices for consumers, without any offsetting benefits.

Competition authority faults grocery order

by Sean MacCarthaigh

The Competition Authority has ... called on the Government not to renew the Groceries Order, which bans all below-cost selling by food retailers. In a discussion paper, the authority said its new powers allowed it to stop predatory pricing, which would include all below-cost selling that was damaging to the consumer, whereas the Groceries Order actually contributed to stifling real competition.

The suggestion met with strong criticism from retailers, who said allowing below-cost selling would put smaller shops out of business. The grocery and dairy lobby group ... said the authority was irresponsible and remote from commercial reality. The business lobby IBEC said a change could mean 23 000 job losses ...

'The Groceries Order has had its day,' said the chairman of the authority, Professor McNutt. In its submission to the Government, the authority says the ban on below-cost selling in effect allows suppliers to set the minimum price at which retailers can sell their goods, a practice prohibited under the competition laws of virtually all developed countries. Under the Groceries Order, the Competition Authority argues, supermarket chains get significant discounts on goods, but keep these off the invoice sheet. This allows them not to pass the savings on to customers.

'The view of the authority is that the order actually has anticompetitive effects,' said Mr Pat Massey, the body's chief executive. Professor McNutt rejected IBEC's suggestion that 23 000 people could lose their jobs in the grocery sector if the laws were changed, adding 'there was no evidence for this and that competition was usually good for employment'.

Source: Sean MacCarthaigh/*The Irish Times*, 9 July 1997.

Q What kind of agreement is illegal for businesses to make? Why are competition laws controversial?

Conclusion

Policymakers regulate the behaviour of oligopolists and monopolists through competition laws. While some of these policies are relatively uncontroversial, such as laws that prevent mergers that create a monopoly and laws that break up cartels, other parts of competition policy are the subject of ongoing debate.

Since first enacted in 1974, Australia's competition laws have been the subject of five major reviews, the most recent being the 'Dawson Review' in 2003. This review recommended a number of changes to the laws which fit in with our discussion above. For example, the review recognised that tying can be a legitimate business strategy and recommended that it should only be illegal when it can be shown that the tying leads to a substantial reduction in competition.

The debate on competition policy will continue in the future, reflecting the economic issues presented in this chapter. Some business practices that appear to reduce competition may have legitimate if subtle business purposes. As a result, policymakers need to be careful when using the substantial powers of competition laws to place limits on firm behaviour.

Summary

- Policymakers can respond to the inefficiency of monopoly behaviour in four ways. They can use the competition laws to try to make the industry more competitive. They can regulate the prices that the monopoly charges. They can turn the monopolist into a government-run enterprise. Or, if the market failure is deemed small compared with the inevitable imperfections of policies, they can do nothing at all.
- Policymakers use competition laws to prevent oligopolies from engaging in behaviour that reduces competition. If firms in an oligopoly form a cartel to reduce competition and raise profits, then authorities, such as the ACCC, can prosecute those firms under the competition laws.
- The application of these competition laws and competition policy more generally can be controversial. Some behaviour that may seem to reduce competition may in fact have legitimate business purposes.

Key concepts

Competition and Consumer Act
competition laws
competition policy
predatory pricing
privatisation
resale price maintenance
tying

Questions for review

1 What gives the government the power to regulate mergers between firms? From the standpoint of the welfare of society, give a good reason and a bad reason that two firms might want to merge.
2 Describe the two problems that arise when regulators tell a natural monopoly that it must set a price equal to marginal cost.
3 What is resale price maintenance and why is it controversial?
4 Describe the problems facing a firm if it decides to use predatory pricing to eliminate a competitor.
5 How can tying or bundling be used by a firm to raise its profits? Why is this business strategy controversial?
6 Explain how rules that create transparent pricing might also encourage cartels.

Problems and applications

1 Natural monopoly firms are often regulated so that they can only charge prices set by the authorities. Under one approach, prices are based on the monopolist's costs so that for any given quantity of sales, the monopolist can only set prices equal to its average costs.
   a Why might regulators believe that forcing the monopoly to charge a price equal to average cost is a good outcome? Does this price regulation maximise social welfare? What problems do you see with this form of price regulation?
   b Suppose the monopolist can undertake innovation that will lower its average cost. If the monopolist faces average-cost price regulation, does it face strong or weak incentives to innovate?
   c An alternative to average-cost price regulation is to set a 'price cap' for the natural monopoly firm. With a price cap, the regulator does not adjust the regulated price as soon as monopolist's costs change but keeps the same regulated prices for a number of years. It is argued that price-cap regulation encourages innovation. Do you agree with this and why?

2 The singer Pink has a monopoly over a scarce resource: herself. She is the only person who can produce a Pink concert. Does this fact imply that the government should regulate the prices of her concerts? Why or why not?

3 While cartels are illegal, companies often have big incentives to form a cartel and raise prices. To understand these incentives, let's analyse a game between the two competing companies. Suppose that each company can charge either a high price for its product or a low price. If one company charges $100, it earns low profits if the other company charges $100 also, and high profits if the other company charges $200. On the other hand, if the company charges $200, it earns very low profits if the other company charges $100, and medium profits if the other company charges $200 also. (You may need to refer to chapter 16 and the prisoners' dilemma to complete this activity.)

   a Draw the decision box for this game.

   b What is the Nash equilibrium in this game? Explain.

   c Is there an outcome that would be better than the Nash equilibrium for both companies? How could it be achieved? Who would lose if it were achieved?

4 Suppose that there are currently four producers of tyres in Australia – Allcar, Bootstone, Carstuff and Duddos. There are no imported tyres in Australia and there are significant barriers to new entry. Allcar has 25 per cent of all tyre sales, Bootstone has 10 per cent of all tyre sales, Carstuff has 40 per cent of all tyre sales and Duddos has 25 per cent of all tyre sales. The marginal cost of producing a tyre is constant and equal to $20 per tyre. The current market price of a tyre is $50. One million tyres are sold each year. Industry estimates suggest that a $10 increase in the market price of tyres will result in a reduction of sales by 100 000 each year. Allcar and Bootstone wish to merge. They claim that their merger will lead to a $10 reduction in the marginal cost of each tyre that they produce (i.e., the marginal cost for the merged firm will fall from $20 per tyre to $10 per tyre). Assume that Allcar and Bootstone are making a correct claim about the reduction in marginal cost but that the merger will also lead to a $10 rise in the market price of tyres.

   a Draw a diagram showing the deadweight loss associated with the oligopoly in the Australian tyre market before any merger between Allcar and Bootstone.

   b Show how the deadweight loss will change if Allcar and Bootstone are allowed to merge. Give an estimate of the size of the change in the deadweight loss.

   c What are the cost savings that will be created by the merger? What factors might affect the total size of these cost savings?

   d Do you think that the merger between Allcar and Bootstone will increase or decrease social surplus? Why?

5 Businesses are often accused of engaging in predatory pricing. However, competition regulators often have difficulties separating predatory pricing from vigorous competition. The Areeda–Turner test for predatory pricing states that if a firm sets its price above its marginal cost then it is probably not predatory pricing, but if it sets its price below marginal cost then it is probably predatory. Remembering our analysis of profit-maximising firms from chapters 14 and 15, explain why pricing below marginal cost might be viewed as a deliberate attempt to drive out a competitor rather than vigorous competitive pricing. Can you think of any situations where a firm might set a price below marginal cost but not be predatory pricing?

6 The Baxter case study presented in this chapter discussed how Baxter Healthcare was prosecuted under Australian competition laws for bundling two types of pharmaceutical products. But many products come as bundles. Car bodies and engines are sold as a bundle. Mobile phones and calling plans are often sold as a package. Even shoes and shoe laces are usually sold together. Think of reasons why bundling might be good for consumers and business. Under what circumstances could bundling create competition concerns? In particular, why might government be concerned if the firm that bundles the products has a monopoly in part of the bundle?

7 In 2004, the ACCC successfully prosecuted a number of petrol sellers in a Victorian town for collusion. These petrol sellers advertised their prices on boards outside their petrol stations. When one of the sellers wanted to raise petrol prices in the town, they would increase the price on their own board and then ring the other sellers suggesting that they 'go for a drive'.

a Why was it important for the cartel to have the petrol prices easily visible on boards outside their petrol stations?

b Should the government prevent this type of collusion by banning the advertising of petrol prices?

c What would be the costs and benefits of such a policy?

d More recently, some politicians have been concerned about banks telling their customers about plans to raise the interest rates on home loans. The politicians have argued that these statements allow the banks to signal rate increases to each other, helping them to collude and maintain higher interest rates. Do you think that banks should be banned from telling customers about planned interest rate changes? Why or why not?

Search Me!

Search me!

When accessing information about microeconomics use the following keywords in any combinations you require:

- *Competition and Consumer Act*
- competition policy
- predatory pricing

CourseMate

CourseMate

For more multimedia resources and activities on economics, visit the Economics CourseMate website.

18

Monopolistic competition

Learning objectives

In this chapter you will:

- analyse competition among firms that sell differentiated products
- compare the outcome under monopolistic competition and under perfect competition
- consider the desirability of outcomes in monopolistically competitive markets
- examine the debate over the effects of advertising
- examine the debate over the role of brand names.

You walk into a bookshop to buy a book to read during your next holiday. On the shelves you find a Sue Grafton mystery, a Stephen King thriller, a Meg Cabot romance, a Stephenie Meyer fantasy and many other choices. When you pick out a book and buy it, what kind of market are you participating in?

On the one hand, the market for books seems quite competitive. As you look over the shelves at your bookshop, you find many authors and many publishers vying for your attention. A buyer in this market has thousands of competing products from which to choose. And because anyone can enter the industry by writing and publishing a book, the book business is not very profitable. For every highly paid novelist, there are hundreds of struggling ones.

On the other hand, the market for books seems quite monopolistic. Because each book is unique, publishers have some latitude in choosing what price to charge. The sellers in this market are price makers rather than price takers. And, indeed, the price of books greatly exceeds marginal cost. The price of a typical hardcover novel, for instance, is about $35, whereas the cost of printing one additional copy of the novel is less than $10.

In this chapter we examine markets that have some features of competition and some features of monopoly. This market structure is called **monopolistic competition**. In a monopolistically competitive market, each firm has a monopoly over the product it makes, but many other firms make similar products that compete for the same customers. To be more precise, monopolistic competition describes a market with the following attributes:

monopolistic competition
a market structure in which many firms sell products that are similar but not identical

Search me!
▸ monopolistic competition

- *Many sellers:* There are many firms competing for the same group of customers.
- *Product differentiation:* Each firm produces a product that is at least slightly different from those of other firms. Thus, rather than being a price taker, each firm faces a downward-sloping demand curve.
- *Free entry:* Firms can enter (or exit) the market without restriction. Thus, the number of firms in the market adjusts until economic profits are driven to zero.

A moment's thought reveals a long list of markets with these attributes – books, CDs, films, computer games, restaurants, piano lessons, furniture and so on.

Monopolistic competition, like oligopoly, is a market structure that lies between the extreme cases of competition and monopoly. But oligopoly and monopolistic competition are quite different. Oligopoly departs from the perfectly competitive ideal of chapter 14 because there are only a few sellers in the market. The small number of sellers makes vigorous competition less likely and it makes strategic interactions among them vitally important. In contrast, under monopolistic competition, there are many sellers, each of which is small compared with the market. A monopolistically competitive market departs from the perfectly competitive ideal because each of the sellers offers a somewhat different product.

Competition with differentiated products

To understand monopolistically competitive markets, we first consider the decisions facing an individual firm. We then examine what happens in the long run as firms enter and exit the industry. Next, we compare the equilibrium under monopolistic competition with the equilibrium under perfect competition that we examined in chapter 14. Finally, we consider whether the outcome in a monopolistically competitive market is desirable from the standpoint of society as a whole.

The monopolistically competitive firm in the short run

Each firm in a monopolistically competitive market is, in many ways, like a monopoly. Because its product is different from those offered by other firms, it faces a downward-sloping demand curve. (In contrast, a perfectly competitive firm faces a horizontal demand curve at the market price.) Thus, the monopolistically competitive firm follows a monopolist's rule for profit maximisation – it chooses the quantity at which marginal revenue equals marginal cost and then uses its demand curve to find the price consistent with that quantity.

Figure 18.1 shows the cost, demand and marginal-revenue curves for two typical firms, each in a different monopolistically competitive industry. In both panels of this figure, the profit-maximising quantity is found at the intersection of the marginal-revenue and marginal-cost curves. The two panels in this figure show different outcomes for the firm's profit. In panel (a), price exceeds average total cost, so the firm makes a profit. In panel (b), price is below average total cost. In this case, the firm is unable to make a positive profit, so the best the firm can do is to minimise its losses.

All this should seem familiar. A monopolistically competitive firm chooses its quantity and price just as a monopoly does. In the short run, these two types of market structure are similar.

The long-run equilibrium

The situations depicted in Figure 18.1 do not last long. When firms are making profits, as in panel (a), new firms have an incentive to enter the market. This entry increases the number of products from which customers can choose and, therefore, reduces the demand faced by each firm already in the market. In other words, profit encourages entry, and entry shifts the demand curves faced by the

Figure 18.1 **Monopolistic competitors in the short run**

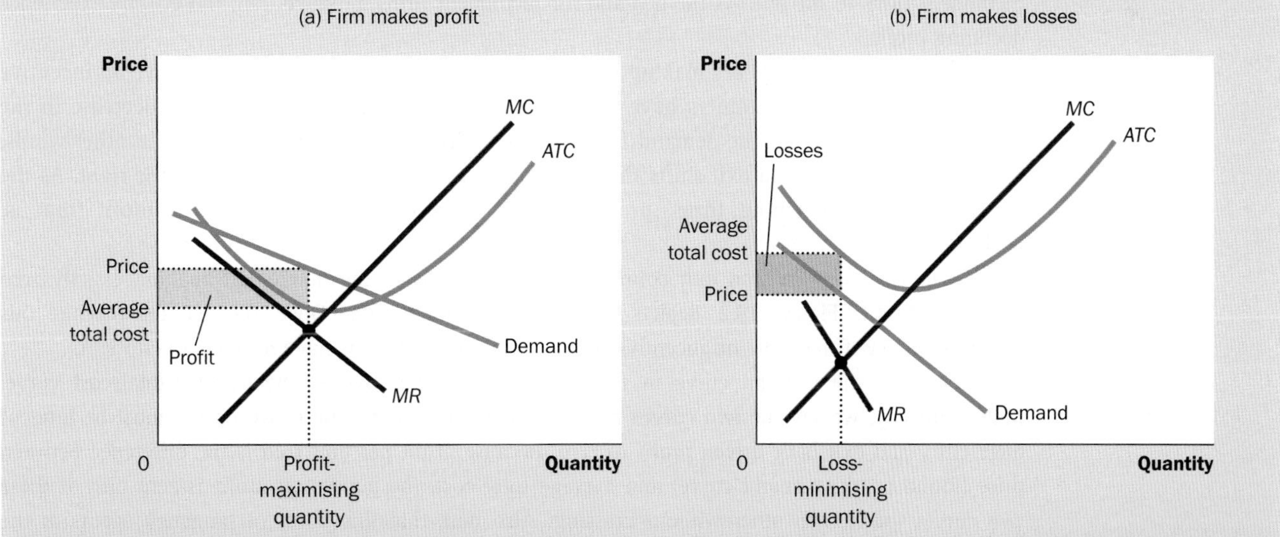

Monopolistic competitors, like monopolists, maximise profit by producing the quantity at which marginal revenue equals marginal cost. The firm in panel (a) makes a profit because, at this quantity, price is above average total cost. The firm in panel (b) makes losses because, at this quantity, price is less than average total cost.

Figure 18.2 A monopolistic competitor in the long run

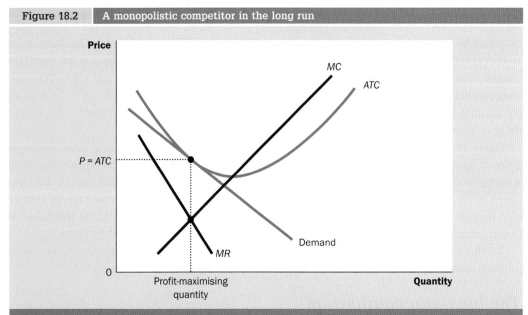

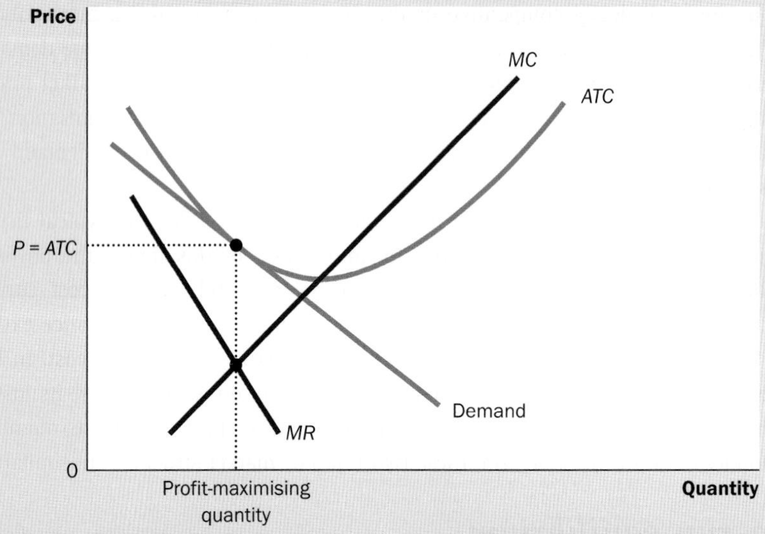

In a monopolistically competitive market, if firms are making a profit, new firms enter and the demand curves for the incumbent firms shift to the left. Similarly, if firms are making losses, old firms exit and the demand curves of the remaining firms shift to the right. Because of these shifts in demand, a monopolistically competitive firm eventually finds itself in the long-run equilibrium shown here. In this long-run equilibrium, price equals average total cost and the firm earns zero profit.

incumbent firms to the left. As the demand for incumbent firms' products fall, these firms experience declining profit.

Conversely, when firms are making losses, as in panel (b), firms in the market have an incentive to exit. As firms exit, customers have fewer products from which to choose. This decrease in the number of firms expands the demand faced by those firms that stay in the market. In other words, losses encourage exit, and exit shifts the demand curves of the remaining firms to the right. As the demand for the remaining firms' products rises, these firms experience rising profit (that is, declining losses).

This process of entry and exit continues until the firms in the market are making exactly zero economic profit. Figure 18.2 depicts the long-run equilibrium. Once the market reaches this equilibrium, new firms have no incentive to enter and existing firms have no incentive to exit.

Notice that the demand curve in this figure just barely touches the average-total-cost curve. Mathematically, we say the two curves are tangent to each other. These two curves must be tangent once entry and exit have driven profit to zero. Because profit per unit sold is the difference between price (found on the demand curve) and average total cost, the maximum profit is zero only if these two curves touch each other without crossing. Also note that this point of tangency occurs at the same quantity where marginal revenue equals marginal cost. That these two points line up is not a coincidence. It is required because this particular quantity maximises profit and the maximum profit is exactly zero in the long run.

To sum up, two characteristics describe the long-run equilibrium in a monopolistically competitive market:

- As in a monopoly market, price exceeds marginal cost. This conclusion arises because profit maximisation requires marginal revenue to equal marginal cost and because the downward-sloping demand curve makes marginal revenue less than the price.
- As in a competitive market, price equals average total cost. This conclusion arises because free entry and exit drive economic profit to zero.

The second characteristic shows how monopolistic competition differs from monopoly. Because a monopoly is the sole seller of a product without close substitutes, it can earn positive economic profit, even in the long run. In contrast, because there is free entry into a monopolistically competitive market, the economic profit of a firm in this type of market is driven to zero.

'Given the downward slope of our demand curve, and the ease with which other firms can enter the industry, we can strengthen our profit position only by equating marginal cost and marginal revenue. Order more jelly beans.'

Source: ScienceCartoonsPlus.com.

Monopolistic versus perfect competition

Figure 18.3 compares the long-run equilibrium under monopolistic competition with the long-run equilibrium under perfect competition. (Chapter 14 discussed the equilibrium with perfect competition.) There are two noteworthy differences between monopolistic and perfect competition – excess capacity and the mark-up.

Excess capacity

As we have just seen, entry and exit drive each firm in a monopolistically competitive market to a point of tangency between its demand and average-total-cost curves. Panel (a) of Figure 18.3 shows that the quantity of output at this point is smaller than the quantity that minimises average total cost. Thus, under monopolistic competition, firms produce on the downward-sloping portion of their average-total-cost curves. In this way, monopolistic competition contrasts starkly with perfect competition. As panel (b) of Figure 18.3 shows, free entry in competitive markets drives firms to produce at the minimum of average total cost.

The quantity that minimises average total cost is called the *efficient scale* of the firm. In the long run, perfectly competitive firms produce at the efficient scale, whereas monopolistically competitive firms produce below this level. Firms are said to have *excess capacity* under monopolistic competition. In other words, a monopolistically competitive firm, unlike a perfectly competitive firm, could increase the quantity it produces and lower the average total cost of production. The firm forgoes this

Figure 18.3 **Monopolistic versus perfect competition**

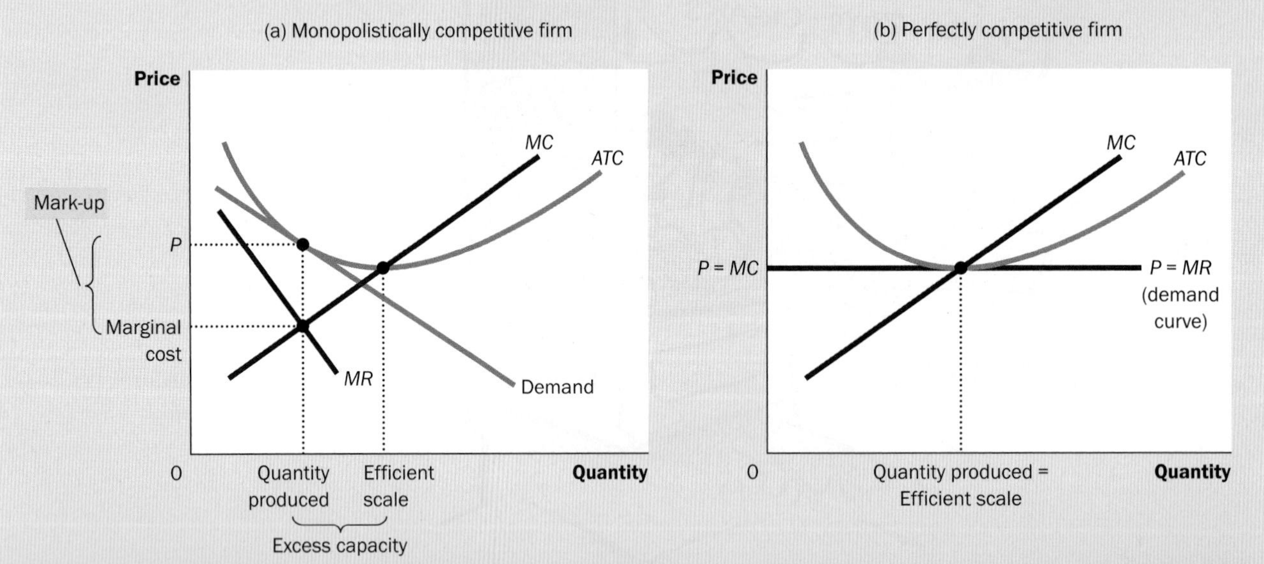

Panel (a) shows the long-run equilibrium in a monopolistically competitive market and panel (b) shows the long-run equilibrium in a perfectly competitive market. Two differences are notable: (1) the perfectly competitive firm produces at the efficient scale, where average total cost is minimised – in contrast, the monopolistically competitive firm produces at less than the efficient scale; (2) price equals marginal cost under perfect competition, but price is above marginal cost under monopolistic competition.

opportunity because it would need to cut its price to sell the additional output. It is more profitable for a monopolistic competitor to continue operating with excess capacity.

Mark-up over marginal cost

A second difference between perfect competition and monopolistic competition is the relationship between price and marginal cost. For a competitive firm, such as that shown in panel (b) of Figure 18.3, price equals marginal cost. For a monopolistically competitive firm, such as that shown in panel (a), price exceeds marginal cost, because the firm always has some market power.

How is this mark-up over marginal cost consistent with free entry and zero profit? The zero-profit condition ensures only that price equals average total cost. It does not ensure that price equals marginal cost. Indeed, in the long-run equilibrium, monopolistically competitive firms operate on the declining portion of their average-total-cost curves, so marginal cost is below average total cost. Thus, for price to equal average total cost, price must be above marginal cost.

In this relationship between price and marginal cost, we see a key behavioural difference between perfect competitors and monopolistic competitors. Imagine that you were to ask a firm the following question: Would you like to see another customer come through your door ready to buy from you at your current price? A perfectly competitive firm would answer that it didn't care. Because price exactly equals marginal cost, the profit from an extra unit sold is zero. In contrast, a monopolistically competitive firm is always eager to get another customer. Because its price exceeds marginal cost, an extra unit sold at the posted price means more profit.

Monopolistic competition and the welfare of society

Is the outcome in a monopolistically competitive market desirable from the standpoint of society as a whole? Can policymakers improve on the market outcome? In previous chapters we evaluated markets from the standpoint of efficiency – that is, whether society is getting the most it can out of its scarce resources. We learned that competitive markets lead to efficient outcomes, unless there are externalities, and that monopoly markets lead to deadweight losses. Monopolistically competitive markets are more complex than either of these polar cases, so evaluating welfare in these markets is a more subtle exercise.

One source of inefficiency is the mark-up of price over marginal cost. Because of the mark-up, some consumers who value the good at more than the marginal cost of production (but less than the price) will be deterred from buying it. Thus, a monopolistically competitive market has the normal deadweight loss of monopoly pricing.

Although this outcome is clearly undesirable compared with the first-best outcome of price equal to marginal cost, there is no easy way for policymakers to fix the problem. To enforce marginal-cost pricing, policymakers would need to regulate all firms that produce differentiated products. Because such products are so common in the economy, the administrative burden of such regulation would be overwhelming.

Moreover, regulating monopolistic competitors would entail all the problems of regulating natural monopolies. In particular, because monopolistic competitors are making zero profits already, requiring them to lower their prices to equal marginal cost would cause them to make losses. To keep these firms in business, the government would need to help them cover these losses. Rather than raising taxes to pay for these subsidies, policymakers may decide it is better to live with the inefficiency of monopolistic pricing.

Another way in which monopolistic competition may be socially inefficient is that the number of firms in the market may not be 'ideal'. That is, there may be too much or too little entry. One way to think about this problem is in terms of the externalities associated with entry. Whenever a new firm considers entering the market with a new product, it considers only the profit it would make. Yet its entry would also have two effects that are external to the firm:

- *The product-variety externality:* Because consumers get some consumer surplus from the introduction of a new product, entry of a new firm conveys a positive externality on consumers.
- *The business-stealing externality:* Because other firms lose customers and profits from the entry of a new competitor, entry of a new firm imposes a negative externality on existing firms.

Thus, in a monopolistically competitive market, there are both positive and negative externalities associated with the entry of new firms. Depending on which externality is larger, a monopolistically competitive market could have either too few or too many products.

Both of these externalities are closely related to the conditions for monopolistic competition. The product-variety externality arises because a new firm would offer a product different from those of the existing firms. The business-stealing externality arises because firms post a price above marginal cost and, therefore, are always eager to sell additional units. Conversely, because perfectly competitive firms produce identical goods and charge a price equal to marginal cost, neither of these externalities exists under perfect competition.

In the end, we can conclude only that monopolistically competitive markets do not have all the desirable welfare properties of perfectly competitive markets. That is, the invisible hand does not ensure that total surplus is maximised under monopolistic competition. Yet because the inefficiencies are subtle, hard to measure and hard to fix, there is no easy way for public policy to improve the market outcome.

Q

List the three key attributes of monopolistic competition. Draw and explain a diagram to show the long-run equilibrium in a monopolistically competitive market. How does this equilibrium differ from that in a perfectly competitive market?

Advertising

It is nearly impossible to go through a typical day in a modern economy without being bombarded with advertising. Whether you are reading a newspaper, watching television, surfing the Internet or driving down the highway, some firm will try to convince you to buy its product. Such behaviour is a natural feature of monopolistic competition (as well as some oligopolistic industries). When firms sell differentiated products and charge prices above marginal cost, each firm has an incentive to advertise in order to attract more buyers to its particular product.

The amount of advertising varies substantially across products. Firms that sell highly differentiated consumer goods, such as over-the-counter medicines, perfumes, soft drinks, razor blades, breakfast cereals and dog food, typically spend between 10 and 20 per cent of revenue for advertising. Firms that sell industrial products, such as drill presses and communications satellites, typically spend very little on advertising. And firms that sell homogeneous products, such as wheat, peanuts or crude oil, spend nothing at all.

For the economy as a whole, about 1 to 2 per cent of total firm revenue is spent on advertising. This spending takes many forms, including commercials on television and radio, space in newspapers and magazines, direct mail, the yellow pages, billboards and the Internet.

The debate about advertising

Is society wasting the resources it devotes to advertising? Or does advertising serve a valuable purpose? Assessing the social value of advertising is difficult and often generates heated argument among economists. Let's consider both sides of the debate.

The critique of advertising

Critics of advertising argue that firms advertise in order to manipulate people's tastes. Much advertising is psychological rather than informational. Consider, for example, the typical television commercial for some brand of soft drink. The commercial probably does not tell the viewer about the product's price or quality. Instead, it might show a group of happy people at a party on a beach on a beautiful sunny day. In their hands are cans of the soft drink. The goal of the commercial is to convey a subconscious (if not subtle) message: 'You too can have many friends and be happy, if only you drink our product'. Critics of advertising argue that such a commercial creates a desire that otherwise might not exist.

Critics also argue that advertising impedes competition. Advertising often tries to convince consumers that products are more different than they truly are. By increasing the perception of product differentiation and fostering brand loyalty, advertising makes buyers less concerned with price differences among similar goods. With a less elastic demand curve, each firm charges a larger mark-up over marginal cost.

The defence of advertising

Defenders of advertising argue that firms use advertising to provide information to customers. Advertising conveys the prices of the goods being offered for sale, the existence of new products and the locations of retail outlets. This information allows customers to make better choices about what to buy and, thus, enhances the ability of markets to allocate resources efficiently.

Defenders also argue that advertising fosters competition. Because advertising allows customers to be more fully informed about all the firms in the market, customers can more easily take advantage of price differentials. Thus, each firm has less market power. In addition, advertising allows new firms to enter more easily, because it gives entrants a means of attracting customers from existing firms.

CASESTUDY

Advertising and the price of glasses

What effect does advertising have on the price of a good? On the one hand, advertising might make consumers view products as being more different than they otherwise would. If so, it would make markets less competitive and firms' demand curves less elastic, and this would lead firms to charge higher prices. On the other hand, advertising might make it easier for consumers to find the firms offering the best prices. In this case, it would make markets more competitive and firms' demand curves more elastic, and this would lead to lower prices.

In an article published in the *Journal of Law and Economics* in 1972, economist Lee Benham tested these two views of advertising. In the United States during the 1960s, the various state governments had vastly different rules about advertising by optometrists. Some states allowed advertising for glasses and eye examinations. Many states, however, prohibited it. For example, the Florida law read as follows:

> It is unlawful for any person, firm, or corporation to ... advertise either directly or indirectly by any

>>

> means whatsoever any definite or indefinite price or credit terms on prescriptive or corrective lens, frames, complete prescriptive or corrective glasses, or any optometric service ... This section is passed in the interest of public health, safety, and welfare, and its provisions shall be liberally construed to carry out its objects and purposes.

Professional optometrists enthusiastically endorsed these restrictions on advertising.

Benham used the differences in US state laws as a natural experiment to test the two views of advertising. The results were striking. In those states that prohibited advertising, the average price paid for a pair of glasses was $33. (This was 1963, when prices were much lower than they are today.) In those states that did not restrict advertising, the average price was $26. Thus, advertising reduced average prices by more than 20 per cent. In the market for glasses, and probably in many other markets as well, advertising fosters competition and leads to lower prices for consumers.

fyi

Galbraith versus Hayek

Two great economists of the twentieth century were John Kenneth Galbraith (bottom left) and Friedrich Hayek. They held very different views about advertising, which reflected their views about the capitalist system more broadly.

John Kenneth Galbraith's most famous book was *The Affluent Society*, published in 1958. In it, he argued that corporations use advertising to create demand for products that people otherwise do not want or need. The market system should not be applauded, he believed, for satisfying desires that it has itself created. Galbraith was sceptical that economic growth was leading to higher levels of wellbeing, because people's aspirations were being made to keep pace with their increased material prosperity. He worried that as advertising and salesmanship artificially enhanced the desire for private goods, public spending on such items as better schools and better parks suffered. The result, according to Galbraith, was 'private opulence and public squalor'. Galbraith's policy recommendation was clear: increase the size of government.

Friedrich Hayek's most famous book was *The Road to Serfdom*, published in 1944. It argued that an expansive government inevitably means a sacrifice of personal freedoms. Hayek also wrote a well-known critique of Galbraith in 1961, addressing specifically Galbraith's view of advertising. Hayek observed that advertising was merely one example of a larger phenomenon: Our social environment creates many of our preferences. Literature, art and music are all acquired tastes. A person's demand for hearing a Mozart concerto may have been created in a music appreciation class, but this fact does not make the desire less legitimate or the music professor a sinister influence. Hayek concluded, 'It is because each individual producer thinks that the consumers can be persuaded to like his products that he endeavors to influence them. But though this effort is part of the influences which shape consumers' taste, no producer can in any real sense "determine" them'.

These two economists disagreed about the roles of advertising, markets and government, but they did have one thing in common: great acclaim. In 1974, Hayek won the Nobel Prize in economics. In 2000, Galbraith won the US National Medal of Freedom. And even though their books are now many decades old, they are still well worth reading. The issues that Hayek and Galbraith addressed are timeless and their insights apply as well to our economy as to their own.

Source: Getty Images.

Source: Corbis Australia.

Advertising as a signal of quality

Many types of advertising contain little apparent information about the product being advertised. Consider a firm introducing a new breakfast cereal. A typical advertisement might have some highly paid actor eating the cereal and exclaiming how wonderful it tastes. How much information does the advertisement really provide?

The answer is: more than you might think. Defenders of advertising argue that even advertising that appears to contain little hard information may, in fact, tell consumers something about product quality. The willingness of the firm to spend a large amount of money on advertising can itself be a signal to consumers about the quality of the product being offered.

Consider the problem facing two firms – SuperGrain and Sunshine Wheat Co. Each company has just come up with a recipe for a new cereal, which it would sell for $5 a box. To keep things simple, let's assume that the marginal cost of making cereal is zero, so the $5 is all profit. Each company knows that if it spends $10 million on advertising, it will get one million consumers to try its new cereal. And each company knows that if consumers like the cereal, they will buy it not once but many times.

Consider first SuperGrain's decision. Based on market research, SuperGrain knows that its cereal is only mediocre. Although advertising would sell one packet to each of one million consumers, the consumers would quickly learn that the cereal is not very good and stop buying it. SuperGrain decides it is not worth paying $10 million in advertising to get only $5 million in sales. So it does not bother to advertise. It sends its cooks back to the drawing board to find another recipe.

Sunshine Wheat, on the other hand, knows that its cereal is great. Each person who tries it will buy a box a month for the next year. Thus, the $10 million in advertising will bring in $60 million in sales. Advertising is profitable here because Sunshine Wheat has a good product that consumers will buy repeatedly. Thus, Sunshine Wheat chooses to advertise.

Now that we have considered the behaviour of the two firms, let's consider the behaviour of consumers. We began by asserting that consumers are inclined to try a new cereal that they see advertised. But is this behaviour rational? Should a consumer try a new cereal just because the seller has chosen to advertise it?

In fact, it may be completely rational for consumers to try new products that they see advertised. In our story, consumers decide to try Sunshine Wheat's new cereal because Sunshine Wheat advertises. Sunshine Wheat chooses to advertise because it knows that its cereal is quite good, whereas SuperGrain chooses not to advertise because it knows that its cereal is only mediocre. By its willingness to spend money on advertising, Sunshine Wheat signals to consumers the quality of its cereal. Each consumer thinks, quite sensibly: 'If Sunshine Wheat is willing to spend so much money advertising this new cereal, it must be really good'.

What is most surprising about this theory of advertising is that the content of the advertisement is irrelevant. Sunshine Wheat signals the quality of its product by its willingness to spend money on advertising. What the advertisements say is not as important as the fact that consumers know ads are expensive. In contrast, cheap advertising cannot be effective at signalling quality to consumers. In our example, if an advertising campaign costs less than $5 million, both SuperGrain and Sunshine Wheat would use it to market their new cereals. Because both good and mediocre cereals would be advertised, consumers could not infer the quality of a new cereal from the fact that it is advertised. Over time, consumers would learn to ignore such cheap advertising.

This theory can explain why firms pay famous actors large amounts of money to make advertisements that, on the surface, appear to convey no information at all. The information is not in the advertisement's content, but simply in its existence and expense.

Brand names

Advertising is closely related to the existence of brand names. In many markets, there are two types of firms. Some firms sell products with widely recognised brand names and other firms sell generic substitutes. For example, in a typical pharmacy, you can find Panadol headache tablets on the shelf next to a generic tablet. In a typical grocery store, you can find Pepsi next to less familiar colas. Most often, the firm with the brand name spends more on advertising and charges a higher price for its product.

Just as there is disagreement about the economics of advertising, there is disagreement about the economics of brand names. Let's consider both sides of the debate.

Critics of brand names argue that brand names cause consumers to perceive differences that do not really exist. In many cases, the generic good is almost indistinguishable from the brand-name good. Consumers' willingness to pay more for the brand-name good, these critics assert, is a form of irrationality fostered by advertising. Economist Edward Chamberlin, one of the early developers of the theory of monopolistic competition, concluded from this argument that brand names were bad for the economy. He proposed that governments discourage their use by refusing to enforce the exclusive trademarks that companies use to identify their products.

More recently, economists have defended brand names as a useful way for consumers to ensure that the goods they buy are of high quality. There are two related arguments. First, brand names provide consumers with information about quality when quality cannot be easily judged in advance of purchase. Second, brand names give firms an incentive to maintain high quality, since firms have a financial stake in maintaining the reputation of their brand names.

To see how these arguments work in practice, consider a famous brand name, McDonald's hamburgers. Imagine that you are driving through an unfamiliar town and want to stop for lunch. You see a McDonald's and a local restaurant next to it. Which do you choose? The local restaurant may in fact offer better food at lower prices, but you have no way of knowing that. In contrast, McDonald's offers a consistent product across many cities. Its brand name is useful to you as a way of judging the quality of what you are about to buy.

The McDonald's brand name also ensures that the company has an incentive to maintain quality. For example, if some customers were to become ill from bad food sold at a McDonald's, the news would be disastrous for the company. McDonald's would lose much of the valuable reputation that it has built up with years of expensive advertising. As a result, it would lose sales and profit not just in the outlet that sold the bad food but in its many outlets throughout the country. In contrast, if some customers were to become ill from bad food at a local restaurant, that restaurant might have to close down, but the lost profits would be much smaller. Hence, McDonald's has a greater incentive to ensure that its food is safe.

The debate over brand names thus centres on the question of whether consumers are rational in preferring brand names over generic substitutes. Critics of brand names argue that brand names are the result of an irrational consumer response to advertising. Defenders of brand names argue that consumers have good reason to pay more for brand-name products because they can be more confident in the quality of these products.

How might advertising make markets less competitive? How might it make markets more competitive? Give the arguments for and against brand names.

Conclusion

Monopolistic competition is true to its name; it is a hybrid of monopoly and competition. Like a monopoly, each monopolistic competitor faces a downward-sloping demand curve and, as a result, charges a price above marginal cost. As in a competitive market, however, there are many firms, and entry and exit drive the profit of each monopolistic competitor towards zero. Table 18.1 summarises these lessons.

Because monopolistically competitive firms produce differentiated products, each firm advertises in order to attract customers to its own brand. To some extent, advertising manipulates consumers' tastes,

Table 18.1 Monopolistic competition: Between perfect competition and monopoly

	Market structure		
	Perfect competition	Monopolistic competition	Monopoly
Features that all three market structures share			
Goal of firms	Maximise profits	Maximise profits	Maximise profits
Rule for maximising	$MR = MC$	$MR = MC$	$MR = MC$
Can earn economic profits in the short run?	Yes	Yes	Yes
Features that monopoly and monopolistic competition share			
Price take?	Yes	No	No
Price	$P = MC$	$P > MC$	$P > MC$
Produces welfare-maximising level of output?	Yes	No	No
Features that perfect competition and monopolistic competition share			
Number of firms	Many	Many	One
Entry in long run?	Yes	Yes	No
Can earn economic profits in long run?	No	No	Yes

promotes irrational brand loyalty and impedes competition. To a larger extent, advertising provides information, establishes brand names of reliable quality and fosters competition.

The theory of monopolistic competition seems to describe many markets in the economy. It is somewhat disappointing, therefore, that the theory does not yield simple and compelling advice for public policy. From the standpoint of the economic theorist, the allocation of resources in monopolistically competitive markets is not perfect. Yet, from the standpoint of a practical policymaker, there may be little that can be done to improve it.

Summary

- A monopolistically competitive market is characterised by three attributes: many firms, differentiated products and free entry.
- The equilibrium in a monopolistically competitive market differs from that in a perfectly competitive market in two related ways. First, each firm has higher average costs; that is, it operates on the downward-sloping portion of the average-total-cost curve. Second, each firm charges a price above marginal cost.
- Monopolistic competition does not have all the desirable properties of perfect competition. There is the standard deadweight loss of monopoly caused by the mark-up of price over marginal cost. In addition, the number of firms (and thus the variety of products) can be too large or too small. In practice, the ability of policymakers to correct these inefficiencies is limited.
- The product differentiation inherent in monopolistic competition leads to the use of advertising and brand names. Critics of advertising and brand names argue that firms use them to take advantage of consumer irrationality and to reduce competition. Defenders of advertising and brand names argue that firms use them to inform consumers and to compete more vigorously on price and product quality.

Key concept

monopolistic competition

Questions for review

1 Describe the three attributes of monopolistic competition. How is monopolistic competition like monopoly? How is it like perfect competition?

2 Draw a diagram of the long-run equilibrium in a monopolistically competitive market. How is price related to average total cost? How is price related to marginal cost?

3 Does a monopolistic competitor produce too much or too little output compared with the most efficient level? What practical considerations make it difficult for policymakers to solve this problem?

4 How might advertising reduce economic wellbeing? How might advertising increase economic wellbeing?

5 How might advertising with no apparent informational content in fact convey information to consumers?

6 Explain two benefits that might arise from the existence of brand names.

Problems and applications

1 Classify the following markets as perfectly competitive, monopolistic or monopolistically competitive, and explain your answer:

a wooden HB pencils
b bottled mineral water
c copper
d local telephone calls

e peanut butter
f lipstick.

2 What feature of the product being sold distinguishes a monopolistically competitive firm from a monopolistic firm?
3 The chapter states that monopolistically competitive firms could increase the quantity they produce and lower the average total cost of production. Why don't they do so?
4 Sparkle is one firm of many in the market for toothpaste, which is in long-run equilibrium.
a Draw a diagram showing Sparkle's demand curve, marginal-revenue curve, average-total-cost curve and marginal-cost curve. Label Sparkle's profit-maximising output and price.
b What is Sparkle's profit? Explain.
c On your diagram, show the consumer surplus derived from the purchase of Sparkle toothpaste. Also show the deadweight loss relative to the efficient level of output.
d If the government forced Sparkle to produce the efficient level of output, what would happen to the firm? What would happen to Sparkle's customers?
5 Do monopolistically competitive markets typically have the socially desirable number of products? Explain.
6 If you were thinking of entering the ice-cream business, would you try to make ice-cream that is just like one of the existing brands? Explain your decision using the ideas of this chapter.
7 Describe three commercials that you have seen on television. In what ways, if any, were each of these commercials socially useful? In what ways were they socially wasteful? Did the commercials affect the likelihood of your buying the product? Why?
8 For each of the following pairs of firms, explain which firm would be more likely to engage in advertising:
a a family-owned farm or a family-owned restaurant
b a manufacturer of forklifts or a manufacturer of cars
c a company that invented a very reliable watch or a company that invented a less-reliable watch that costs the same amount to make.
9 The makers of Aspro pain reliever do a lot of advertising and have very loyal customers. In contrast, the makers of generic aspirin do no advertising and their customers shop only for the lowest price. Assume that the marginal costs of Aspro and generic aspirin are the same and constant.
a Draw a diagram showing Aspro's demand, marginal-revenue and marginal-cost curves. Label Aspro's price and mark-up over marginal cost.
b Repeat part (a) for a producer of generic aspirin. How do the diagrams differ? Which company has the bigger mark-up? Explain.
c Which company has the bigger incentive for careful quality control? Why?
10 In 2010, newspapers reported that Lavazza coffee paid the actress Julia Roberts around $1.5 million for an Italian advertisement where she drank a cup of coffee, smiled, but said nothing. This was a payment of around $33 000 per second. Why would Lavazza pay Ms Roberts such a high amount for an advertisement? Can such a payment be consistent with rational consumer behaviour? Do you think that this payment is justified?

Search me!

Search me!

When accessing information about microeconomics use the following keywords in any combinations you require:

- monopolistic competition

CourseMate

CourseMate

For more multimedia resources and activities on economics, visit the Economics CourseMate website.

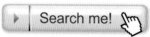

PART SIX
The economics of labour markets

19

The markets for the factors of production

Learning objectives

In this chapter you will:

- analyse the labour demand of competitive, profit-maximising firms
- consider the household decisions that lie behind labour supply
- learn why equilibrium wages equal the value of the marginal product of labour
- consider how the other factors of production – land and capital – are compensated
- examine how a change in the supply of one factor alters the earnings of all the factors.

When you finish university, your income will be determined largely by what kind of job you take. If you become a computer programmer, you will earn more than if you become a petrol station attendant. This fact is not surprising, but it is not obvious why it is true. No law requires that computer programmers be paid more than petrol station attendants. No ethical principle says that programmers are more deserving. What, then, determines which job will pay you the higher wage?

Your income, of course, is a small piece of a larger economic picture. In 2009–10, the total income of all Australian residents was about $1284 billion. People earned this income in various ways. Workers earned over half of it in the form of wages and fringe benefits. The rest went to landowners and to the owners of capital – the economy's stock of equipment and structures – in the form of rent, profit and interest. What determines how much goes to workers? To landowners? To the owners of capital? Why do some workers earn higher wages than others, some landowners higher rental income than others and some capital owners greater profit than others? Why, in particular, do computer programmers earn more than petrol station attendants?

The answers to these questions, like most in economics, hinge on supply and demand. The supply of and demand for labour, land and capital determine the prices paid to workers, landowners and capital owners. To understand why some people have higher incomes than others, therefore, we need to look more deeply at the markets for the services they provide. That is our job in this and the next two chapters.

This chapter provides the basic theory for the analysis of factor markets. As you may recall from chapter 2, the **factors of production** are the inputs used to produce goods and services. Labour, land and capital are the three most important factors of production. When a computer firm produces a new software program, it uses programmers' time (labour), the physical space on which its offices sit (land) and an office building and computer equipment (capital). Similarly, when a petrol station sells petrol, it uses attendants' time (labour), the physical space (land) and the petrol tanks and pumps (capital).

factors of production
the inputs used to produce goods and services

In many ways factor markets resemble the goods markets we have analysed in previous chapters, but they are different in one important way – the demand for a factor of production is a *derived demand*. That is, a firm's demand for a factor of production is derived from its decision to supply a good in another market. The demand for computer programmers is inextricably tied to the supply of computer software, and the demand for petrol station attendants is inextricably tied to the supply of petrol.

Search me!
▸ factors of production

In this chapter we analyse factor demand by considering how a competitive, profit-maximising firm decides how much of any factor to buy. We begin our analysis by examining the demand for labour. Labour is the most important factor of production, because workers receive most of the total income earned in the economy. Later in the chapter, we see will see that our analysis of the labour market also applies to the markets for the other factors of production.

The basic theory of factor markets developed in this chapter takes a large step towards explaining how the income of the economy is distributed among workers, landowners and owners of capital. Chapter 20 builds on this analysis to examine in more detail why some workers earn more than others. Chapter 21 examines how much income inequality results from the functioning of factor markets and considers what role the government should and does play in altering the distribution of income.

The demand for labour

Labour markets, like other markets in the economy, are governed by the forces of supply and demand. This is illustrated in Figure 19.1. In panel (a) the supply of and demand for apples determine the price of apples. In panel (b) the supply of and demand for apple pickers determine the price, or wage, of apple pickers.

As we have already noted, however, labour markets are different from most other markets because labour demand is a derived demand. Most labour services, rather than being final goods ready to be enjoyed by consumers, are inputs into the production of other goods. To understand labour demand, we need to focus on the firms that hire the labour and use it to produce goods for sale. By examining the link between the production of goods and the demand for labour, we gain insight into the determination of equilibrium wages.

The competitive profit-maximising firm

Let's look at how a typical firm, such as an apple producer, decides the quantity of labour to demand. The firm owns an apple orchard and each week must decide how many apple pickers to hire to harvest its crop. After the firm makes its hiring decision, the workers pick as many apples as they can. The firm then sells the apples, pays the workers and keeps what is left as profit.

We make two assumptions about our firm. First, we assume that our firm is *competitive* both in the market for apples (where the firm is a seller) and in the market for apple pickers (where the firm is a buyer). Recall from chapter 14 that a competitive firm is a price taker. Because there are many other firms selling apples and hiring apple pickers, a single firm has little influence over the price it gets for apples or the wage it pays apple pickers. The firm takes the price and the wage as given by market

Figure 19.1 **The versatility of supply and demand**

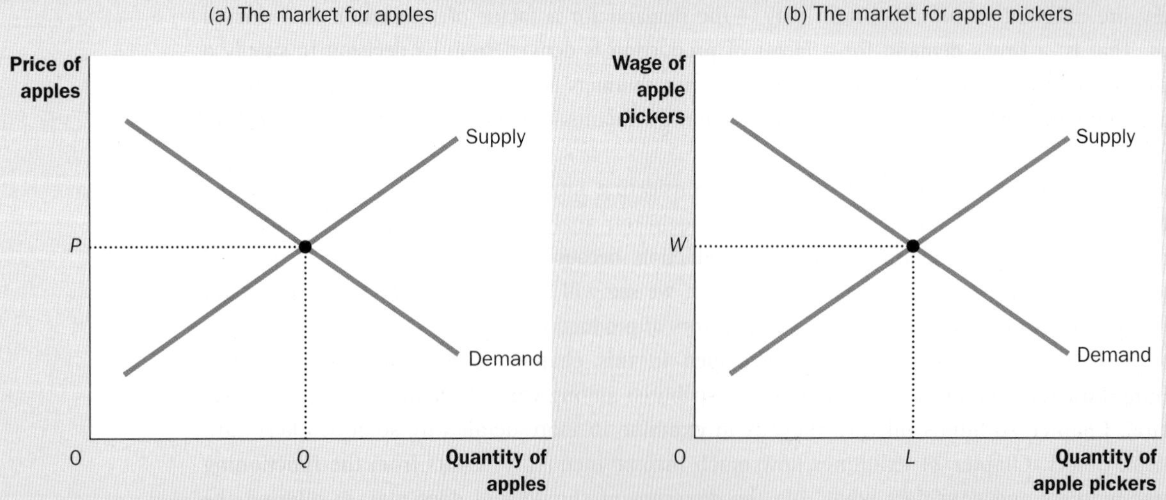

The basic tools of supply and demand apply to goods and to labour services. Panel (a) shows how the supply of and demand for apples determine the price of apples. Panel (b) shows how the supply of and demand for apple pickers determine the wage of apple pickers.

conditions. It only has to decide how many workers to hire and how many apples to sell. (In the appendix, we will consider what happens in the case of monopoly and imperfect competition.)

Second, we assume that the firm is *profit-maximising*. Thus, the firm does not directly care about the number of workers it has or the number of apples it produces. It cares only about profit, which equals the total revenue from the sale of apples minus the total cost of producing them. The firm's supply of apples and its demand for workers are derived from its primary goal of maximising profit.

The production function and the marginal product of labour

To make its hiring decision, the firm must consider how the size of its workforce affects the amount of output produced. In other words, it must consider how the number of apple pickers affects the quantity of apples it can harvest and sell. Table 19.1 gives a numerical example. In the first column is the number of workers. In the second column is the quantity of apples the workers harvest each week.

These two columns of numbers describe the firm's ability to produce. As we noted in chapter 13, economists use the term *production function* to describe the relationship between the quantity of the inputs used in production and the quantity of output from production. Here the 'input' is the apple pickers and the 'output' is the apples. The other inputs – the trees themselves, the land, the firm's trucks and tractors, and so on – are held fixed for now. This firm's production function shows that if the firm hires one worker, that worker will pick 100 boxes of apples per week. If the firm hires two workers, the two workers together will pick 180 boxes per week and so on.

Figure 19.2 graphs the data on labour and output presented in Table 19.1. The number of workers is on the horizontal axis and the amount of output is on the vertical axis. This figure illustrates the production function.

marginal product of labour
the increase in the amount of output from an additional unit of labour

One of the *Ten Lessons from Economics* introduced in chapter 1 is that rational people think at the margin. This idea is the key to understanding how firms decide what quantity of labour to hire. To take a step towards this decision, the third column in Table 19.1 gives the **marginal product of labour**, the increase in the amount of output from an additional unit of labour. When the firm increases the number of workers from one to two, for example, the amount of apples produced rises from 100 to 180 boxes. Therefore, the marginal product of the second worker is 80 boxes.

Notice that as the number of workers increases, the marginal product of labour declines. That is, the production process exhibits *diminishing marginal product*. At first, when only a few workers are hired, they can pick the low-hanging fruit. As the number of workers increases, additional workers have to climb higher up the ladders to find apples to pick. Hence, as more and more workers are hired, each additional worker contributes less to the production of apples. For this reason, the production function in Figure 19.2 becomes flatter as the number of workers rises.

The value of the marginal product and the demand for labour

Our profit-maximising firm is concerned more with money than with apples. As a result, when deciding how many workers to hire, the firm considers how much profit each worker would bring in. Because profit is total revenue minus total cost, the profit from an additional worker is the worker's contribution to revenue minus the worker's wage.

To find the worker's contribution to revenue, we must convert the marginal product of labour (which is measured in boxes of apples) into the value of the marginal product (which is measured in dollars). We do this using the price of apples. To continue our example, if a box of apples sells for $10 and if an additional worker produces 80 boxes of apples, then the worker produces $800 of revenue.

Figure 19.2 **The production function**

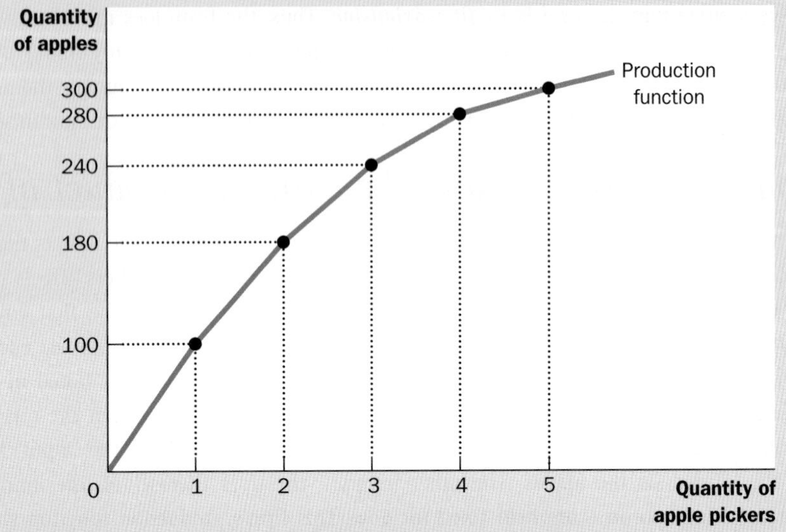

The production function is the relationship between the inputs into production (apple pickers) and the output from production (apples). As the quantity of the input increases, the production function gets flatter, reflecting the property of diminishing marginal product.

Table 19.1 **How the competitive firm decides how much labour to hire**

Labour (number of workers)	Output (boxes per week)	Marginal product of labour	Value of the marginal product of labour	Wage	Marginal profit
(*L*)	(*Q*)	($MPL = \Delta Q/\Delta L$)	($VMPL = P \times MPL$)	(*W*)	(ΔProfit = $VMPL - W$)
0	0	—	—	—	—
1	100	100	$1000	$500	$500
2	180	80	800	500	300
3	240	60	600	500	100
4	280	40	400	500	–100
5	300	20	200	500	–300

value of the marginal product
the marginal product of an input times the price of the output

The **value of the marginal product** of any input is the marginal product of that input multiplied by the market price of the output. The fourth column in Table 19.1 shows the value of the marginal product of labour in our example, assuming the price of apples is $10 per box. Because the market price is constant for a competitive firm, the value of the marginal product (like the marginal product itself) diminishes as the number of workers rises. Economists sometimes call this column of numbers the firm's *marginal revenue product*: It is the extra revenue the firm gets from hiring an additional unit of a factor of production.

Now consider how many workers the firm will hire. Suppose that the market wage for apple pickers is $500 per week. In this case, the first worker that the firm hires is profitable; the first worker yields $1000 in revenue or $500 in profit. Similarly, the second worker yields $800 in additional revenue or $300 in profit. The third worker produces $600 in additional revenue or $100 in profit. After the third worker, however, hiring workers is unprofitable. The fourth worker would yield only $400 of additional revenue. Because the worker's wage is $500, hiring the fourth worker would mean a $100 reduction in profit. Thus, the firm hires only three workers.

It is instructive to consider the firm's decision graphically. Figure 19.3 graphs the value of the marginal product. This curve slopes downwards because the marginal product of labour diminishes as the number of workers rises. The figure also includes a horizontal line at the market wage. To maximise profit, the firm hires workers up to the point where these two curves cross. Below this level of employment, the value of the marginal product exceeds the wage, so hiring another worker would increase profit. Above this level of employment, the value of the marginal product is less than the wage, so the marginal worker is unprofitable. Thus, *a competitive, profit-maximising firm hires workers up to the point where the value of the marginal product of labour equals the wage.*

Having explained the profit-maximising hiring strategy for a competitive firm, we can now offer a theory of labour demand. Recall that a firm's labour demand curve tells us the quantity of labour that a firm demands at any given wage. We have just seen in Figure 19.3 that the firm makes that decision

Figure 19.3 The value of the marginal product of labour

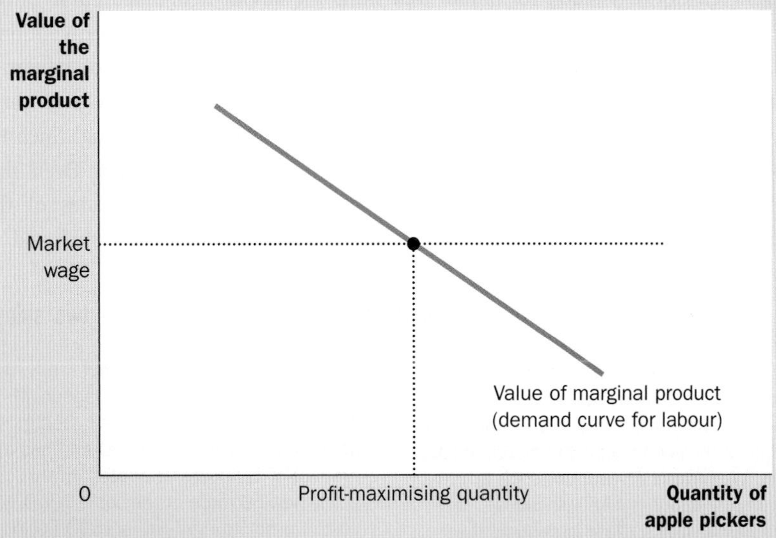

This shows how the value of the marginal product (the marginal product times the price of the output) depends on the number of workers. The curve slopes downwards because of diminishing marginal product. For a competitive, profit-maximising firm, this value-of-marginal-product curve is also the firm's labour demand curve.

by choosing the quantity of labour at which the value of the marginal product equals the wage. As a result, *the value-of-marginal-product curve is the labour demand curve for a competitive, profit-maximising firm.*

What causes the labour demand curve to shift?

We now understand the labour demand curve: It reflects the value of marginal product of labour. With this insight in mind, let's consider a few of the things that might cause the labour demand curve to shift.

The output price

The value of the marginal product is marginal product times the price of the firm's output. Thus, when the output price changes, the value of the marginal product changes and the labour demand curve shifts. An increase in the price of apples, for instance, raises the value of the marginal product of each worker that picks apples and, therefore, increases labour demand from the firms that supply apples. Conversely, a decrease in the price of apples reduces the value of the marginal product and decreases labour demand.

Technological change

Between 2001–02 and 2009–10, the amount of output a typical Australian worker produced in an hour increased by about one-third. Why? The most important reason is technological progress: Scientists and engineers are constantly figuring out new and better ways of doing things. This has profound implications for the labour market. Technological advance raises the marginal product of labour, which in turn increases the demand for labour and shifts the labour-demanded curve to the right.

It is also possible for technological change to reduce labour demand. The invention of a cheap industrial robot, for instance, could conceivably reduce the marginal product of labour, shifting the labour-demanded curve to the left. Economists call this labour-saving technological change. History suggests, however, that most technological progress is instead labour-augmenting. Such technological advance explains persistently rising employment in the face of rising wages. Even though wages (adjusted for inflation) increased by 131 per cent during the last four decades of the twentieth century, firms nonetheless increased by 80 per cent the amount of labour they employed.

fyi

Input demand and output supply – two sides of the coin

In chapter 14 we discussed how a competitive, profit-maximising firm decides how much of its output to sell – it chooses the quantity of output at which the price of the good equals the marginal cost of production. We have just seen how such a firm decides how much labour to hire – it chooses the quantity of labour at which the wage equals the value of the marginal product. Because the production function links the quantity of inputs to the quantity of output, you should not be surprised to learn that the firm's decision about input demand is closely linked to its decision about output supply. In fact, these two decisions are two sides of the same coin.

To see this relationship more fully, let's consider how the marginal product of labour (*MPL*) and marginal cost (*MC*) are related. Suppose an additional worker costs $500 and has a marginal product of 50 boxes of apples. In this case, producing 50 more boxes costs $500; the marginal cost of a box to the firm is $500/50, or $10. More generally, if W is the wage and an extra unit of labour produces MPL units of output, then the marginal cost of a unit of output is $MC = W/MPL$.

This analysis shows that diminishing marginal product is closely related to increasing marginal cost. When our apple orchard grows crowded with workers, each additional worker adds less to the production of apples (*MPL* falls). Similarly, when the apple firm is producing a large quantity of apples, the orchard is already crowded with workers, so it is more costly to produce an additional box of apples (*MC* rises).

Now consider our criterion for profit maximisation. We determined earlier that a profit-maximising firm chooses the quantity of labour so that the value of the marginal product ($P \times MPL$) equals the wage (W). We can write this mathematically as:

$$P \times MPL = W$$

If we divide both sides of this equation by *MPL*, we obtain:

$$P = W/MPL$$

We just noted that *W/MPL* equals marginal cost *MC*. Therefore, we can substitute to obtain:

$$P = MC$$

This equation states that the price of the firm's output is equal to the marginal cost of producing a unit of output. Thus, when a competitive firm hires labour up to the point at which the value of the marginal product equals the wage, it also produces up to the point at which the price equals marginal cost. Our analysis of labour demand in this chapter is just another way of looking at the production decision we first saw in chapter 14.

The supply of other factors

The quantity available of one factor of production can affect the marginal product of other factors. A fall in the supply of ladders, for instance, will reduce the marginal product of apple pickers and thus the demand for apple pickers. We consider this linkage among the factors of production more fully later in the chapter.

fyi — The Luddite revolt

Over the long span of history, technological progress has been the worker's friend. It has increased productivity, labour demand and wages. Yet there is no doubt that workers sometimes see technological progress as a threat to their standard of living.

The Luddites

Source: Photolibrary.

One famous example occurred in England in the early nineteenth century, when skilled knitters saw their jobs threatened by the invention and spread of machines that could produce textiles using less skilled workers and at much lower cost. The displaced workers organised violent revolts against the new technology. They smashed the weaving machines used in the wool and cotton mills and, in some cases, set the homes of the mill owners on fire. Because the workers claimed to be led by General Ned Ludd (who may have been a legendary figure rather than a real person), they were called Luddites.

The Luddites wanted the British government to save their jobs by restricting the spread of the new technology. Instead, the Parliament took action to stop the Luddites. Thousands of troops were sent to suppress the Luddite riots. The Parliament eventually made destroying machines a capital crime. After a trial in York in 1813, 17 men were hanged for the offence. Many others were convicted and sent to Australia, as prisoners.

Today, the term *Luddite* refers to anyone who opposes technological progress.

Define marginal product of labour and value of the marginal product of labour. Describe how a competitive, profit-maximising firm decides how many workers to hire.

The supply of labour

Having analysed labour demand in detail, let's turn to the other side of the market and consider labour supply. A formal model of labour supply is included in chapter 22, where we develop the theory of household decision making. Here we discuss briefly and informally the decisions that lie behind the labour supply curve.

The trade-off between work and leisure

One of the *Ten Lessons from Economics* in chapter 1 is that people face trade-offs. Probably no trade-off is more obvious or more important in a person's life than the trade-off between work and leisure. The more hours you spend working, the fewer hours you have to watch television, enjoy dinner with friends or pursue your favourite hobby. The trade-off between labour and leisure lies behind the labour supply curve.

Another one of the *Ten Lessons from Economics* is that the cost of something is what you give up to get it. What do you give up to get an hour of leisure? You give up an hour of work, which in turn means an hour of wages. Thus, if your wage is $15 per hour, the opportunity cost of an hour of leisure is $15. And when you get a raise to $20 per hour, the opportunity cost of enjoying leisure goes up.

The labour supply curve reflects how workers' decisions about the labour–leisure trade-off respond to a change in that opportunity cost. An upward-sloping labour supply curve means that an increase in the wage induces workers to increase the quantity of labour they supply. Because time is limited, more hours of work means that workers are enjoying less leisure. That is, workers respond to the increase in the opportunity cost of leisure by taking less of it.

It is worth noting that the labour supply curve need not be upward sloping. Imagine you got that raise from $15 to $20 per hour. The opportunity cost of leisure is now greater, but you are also richer than you were before. You might decide that with your extra wealth you can now afford to enjoy more leisure; in this case, your labour supply curve would slope backwards. In chapter 22, we discuss this possibility in terms of conflicting effects on your labour supply decision (called income and substitution effects). For now, we ignore the possibility of backward-sloping labour supply and assume that the labour supply is upward sloping.

What causes the labour supply curve to shift?

The labour supply curve shifts whenever people change the amount they want to work at a given wage. Let's now consider some of the events that might cause such a shift.

Changes in tastes

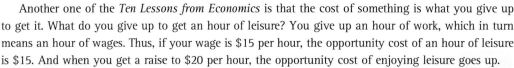

In 1954, 29 per cent of women aged 15 to 64 were employed at paid jobs or looking for work. In 2009, the number had risen to 59 per cent. There are, of course, many explanations for this development, but one of them is changing tastes, or attitudes towards work. A generation or two ago, it was the norm for women to stay at home while raising children. Today, family sizes are smaller and more mothers choose to work. The result is an increase in the supply of labour.

Changes in alternative opportunities

The supply of labour in any one labour market depends on the opportunities available in other labour markets. If the wage earned by pear pickers suddenly rises, some apple pickers may choose to switch occupations. The supply of labour in the market for apple pickers falls.

Immigration

Movement of workers from region to region, or country to country, is an obvious and often important source of shifts in labour supply. When immigrants come to Australia, for instance, the supply of labour in Australia increases and the supply of labour in immigrants' home countries contracts. In fact, much of the policy debate about immigration centres on its effect on labour supply and, thereby, on equilibrium in the labour market.

IN THE NEWS . . .

THE ECONOMY NEEDS YOU

This article shows that in times of low unemployment, immigrants play a critical role in keeping the economy going.

You can come in now

Sydney: The Japanese-owned abattoir at Oakey, in south-east Queensland, seems to have everything going for it. There is no shortage of cattle to feed a booming market that has made Australia the world's biggest beef exporter by value. Yet it has been unable to find enough skilled workers to process the beasts. By June, it expects to import workers from Brazil, Australia's main competitor.

After 14 years of boom, the story of scarce skills is being repeated all over Australia. Under pressure from business leaders, John Howard's conservative coalition government has decided to look beyond Australia to curb the crisis. On April 14th Amanda Vanstone, the immigration minister, said that Australia would take in 140 000 immigrants in 2005–06, 20 000 more than last year and the biggest number for 35 years. Rules on ages and English proficiency will be relaxed. Backpackers who spend at least three months picking fruit or working on farms will qualify automatically for a second year's visa.

From a government that cut immigration sharply in its earlier years, and has since been noted for its tough approach to asylum-seekers, the latest increase suggests how much the economy needs immigration. To a list of 38 skills the country says it is short of, including those of doctors, chefs and hairdressers, Ms Vanstone added 18, including the trades of bricklayers, plumbers, electricians and carpenters.

Official figures show that almost 150 000 jobs cannot be filled for lack of the right skills. A recent survey by the Australian Chamber of Commerce and Industry found that almost 80 per cent of employers were worried about finding people with the needed skills. More than half the firms surveyed last year by two of the country's biggest banks said that a shortage of suitable recruits was hampering their growth.

With unemployment hovering just above 5 per cent, these trends have worried the central bank because of inflationary pressures stoked by higher wage demands. But not everyone is welcoming the new recruits. The opposition Labor Party, and the trade unions, say boosting immigration is no substitute for spending more on equipping Australians themselves with the skills they need to find work more readily.

Source: *The Economist*, 28 April 2008.

Who has a greater opportunity cost of enjoying leisure – a cleaner or a brain surgeon? Explain. Can this help explain why doctors work such long hours?

Equilibrium in the labour market

So far we have established two facts about how wages are determined in competitive labour markets:

- the wage adjusts to balance the supply and demand for labour
- the wage equals the value of the marginal product of labour.

At first, it might seem surprising that the wage can do both these things at once. In fact, there is no real puzzle here, but understanding why there is no puzzle is an important step to understanding wage determination.

Figure 19.4 shows the labour market in equilibrium. The wage and the quantity of labour have adjusted to balance supply and demand. When the market is in this equilibrium, each firm has bought as much labour as it finds profitable at the equilibrium wage. That is, each firm has followed the rule for profit maximisation – it has hired workers until the value of the marginal product equals the wage. Hence, the wage must equal the value of the marginal product of labour once it has brought supply and demand into equilibrium.

This brings us to an important lesson: *any event that changes the supply of labour or demand for labour must change the equilibrium wage and the value of the marginal product by the same amount, because these must always be equal.* To see how this works, let's consider some events that shift these curves.

Figure 19.4 Equilibrium in a labour market

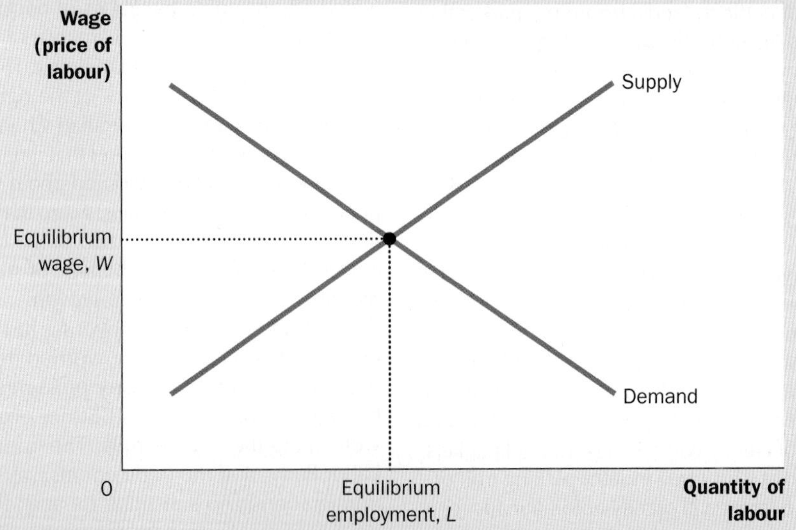

Like all prices, the price of labour (the wage) depends on supply and demand. Because the demand curve reflects the value of the marginal product of labour, in equilibrium workers receive the value of their marginal contribution to the production of goods and services.

Shifts in labour supply

Suppose that immigration increases the number of workers willing to pick apples. As Figure 19.5 shows, the supply of labour shifts to the right from S_1 to S_2. At the initial wage W_1, the quantity of labour supplied now exceeds the quantity demanded. This surplus of labour puts downward pressure on the wage of apple pickers and the fall in the wage in turn makes it profitable for firms to hire more workers. As the number of workers employed in each apple orchard rises, the marginal product of a worker falls and so does the value of the marginal product. In the new equilibrium, both the wage and the value of the marginal product of labour are lower than they were before the influx of new workers.

An episode from Israel illustrates how a shift in labour supply can alter the equilibrium in a labour market. During most of the 1980s, many thousands of Palestinians regularly commuted from their homes in the Israeli-occupied West Bank and Gaza Strip to jobs in Israel, primarily in the construction and agriculture industries. In 1988, however, political unrest in these occupied areas induced the Israeli government to take steps that, as a by-product, reduced this supply of workers. Curfews were imposed, work permits were checked more thoroughly and a ban on overnight stays of Palestinians in Israel was enforced more rigorously. The economic impact of these steps was exactly as theory predicts – the number of Palestinians with jobs in Israel fell by half and those who continued to work in Israel enjoyed wage increases of about 50 per cent. With a reduced number of Palestinian workers in Israel, the value of the marginal product of the remaining workers was much higher.

Figure 19.5 A shift in labour supply

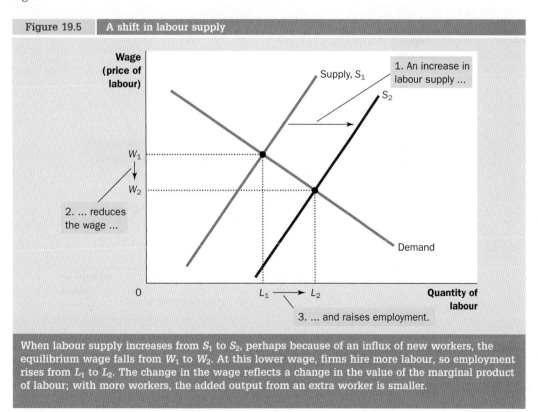

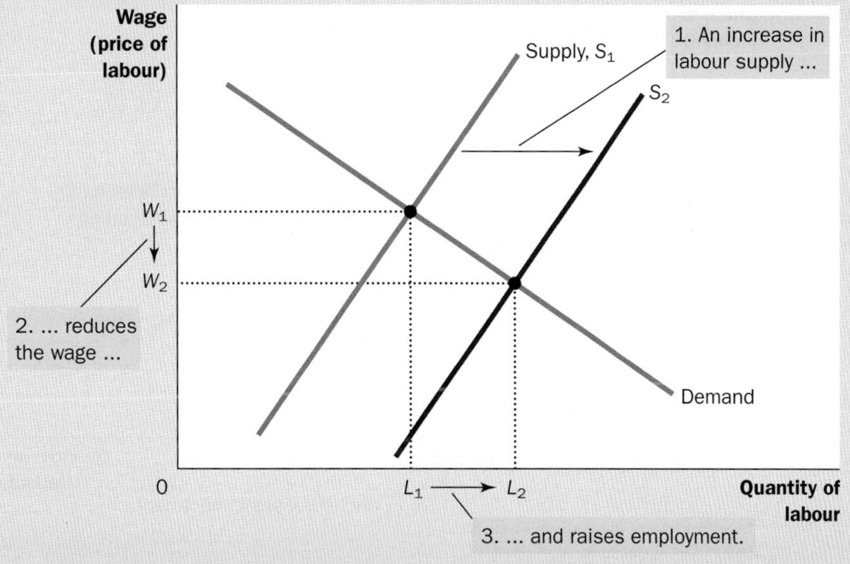

When labour supply increases from S_1 to S_2, perhaps because of an influx of new workers, the equilibrium wage falls from W_1 to W_2. At this lower wage, firms hire more labour, so employment rises from L_1 to L_2. The change in the wage reflects a change in the value of the marginal product of labour; with more workers, the added output from an extra worker is smaller.

Shifts in labour demand

Now suppose that an increase in the popularity of apples causes their price to rise. This price increase does not change the marginal product of labour for any given number of workers, but it does raise the value of the marginal product. With a higher price for apples, hiring more apple pickers is now profitable. As Figure 19.6 shows, when the demand for labour shifts to the right from D_1 to D_2, the equilibrium wage rises from W_1 to W_2, and equilibrium employment rises from L_1 to L_2. Once again, the wage and the value of the marginal product of labour move together.

This analysis shows that prosperity for firms in an industry is often linked to prosperity for workers in that industry. When the price of apples rises, apple producers make greater profit and apple pickers earn higher wages. When the price of apples falls, apple producers earn smaller profit and apple pickers earn lower wages. This lesson is well known to workers in industries with highly volatile prices. Workers in oilfields, for instance, know from experience that their earnings are closely linked to the world price of crude oil.

From these examples, you should now have a good understanding of how wages are set in competitive labour markets. Labour supply and labour demand together determine the equilibrium wage and shifts in the supply or demand curve for labour cause the equilibrium wage to change. At the same time, profit maximisation by the firms that demand labour ensures that the equilibrium wage always equals the value of the marginal product of labour.

Figure 19.6 **A shift in labour demand**

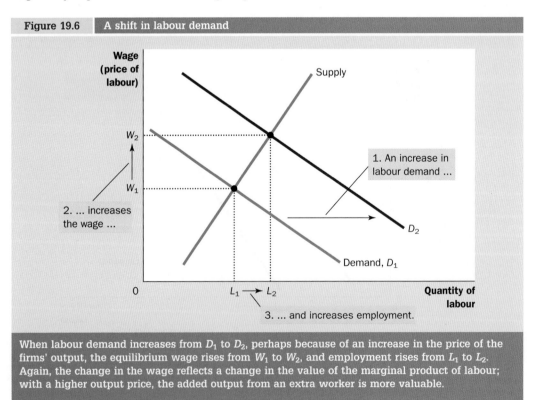

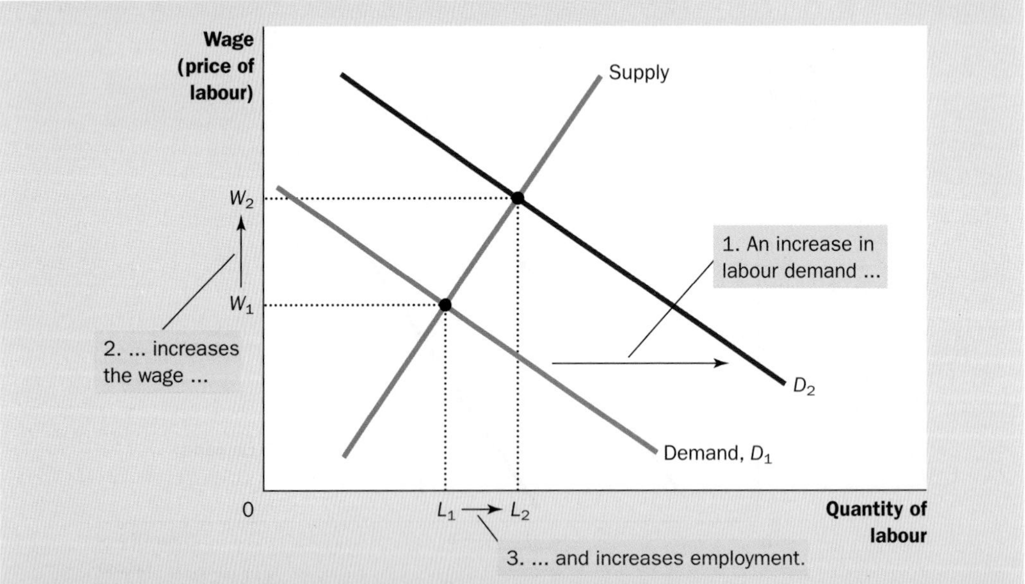

When labour demand increases from D_1 to D_2, perhaps because of an increase in the price of the firms' output, the equilibrium wage rises from W_1 to W_2, and employment rises from L_1 to L_2. Again, the change in the wage reflects a change in the value of the marginal product of labour; with a higher output price, the added output from an extra worker is more valuable.

How does an influx of workers affect labour supply, labour demand, the marginal product of labour and the equilibrium wage?

CASESTUDY

Productivity and wages

One of the *Ten Lessons from Economics* in chapter 1 is that our standard of living depends on our ability to produce goods and services. We can now see how this principle works in the market for labour. In particular, our analysis of labour demand shows that wages equal productivity as measured by the value of the marginal product of labour. Put simply, highly productive workers are highly paid, and less-productive workers are less highly paid.

This lesson is key to understanding why workers today are better off than workers in previous generations. In Australia, up until the early 1970s, productivity growth was relatively high (3 per cent per annum). However, after this time there was a decline in the rate of growth in productivity (to 1 per cent per annum during the 1980s). Corresponding to this slowdown in productivity was a reduction in the growth rate in wages (adjusted for inflation) from about 3 per cent per annum to less than 0.5 per cent per annum growth during the 1980s. Australia's productivity growth then rose to over 2 per cent per annum in the 1990s before falling back to about 1.5 per cent in the 2000s. Wages followed the same pattern.

The link between productivity and wages also sheds light on international experience. Table 19.2 presents some data on productivity growth and wage growth for a representative group of countries between 1950 and 1990, ranked in order of their productivity growth. Although these international data are far from precise, a close link between the two variables is apparent. In South Korea, Hong Kong and Singapore, productivity has grown rapidly and so have wages. In Mexico and Argentina, productivity has fallen and so have wages. Australia falls in the middle of the distribution. So over the longer term, by international standards, Australian productivity growth and wage growth have been neither exceptionally bad nor exceptionally good.

Table 19.2 Productivity and wage growth around the world

Country	Growth rate of productivity (%)	Growth rate of wages (%)
South Korea	6.9	7.9
Hong Kong	6.0	4.9
Singapore	4.9	5.0
Japan	3.0	2.0
Indonesia	2.3	4.4
United Kingdom	2.7	2.4
United States	2.3	0.5
Australia	1.6	0.3
New Zealand	0.9	–0.3
Malaysia	0.8	2.4
Brazil	–0.2	–2.4
Argentina	–1.7	–1.3
Mexico	–1.8	–3.0

Source: Robert Summers and Alan Heston, 'The Penn World Tables (Mark 5): an expanded set of international comparisons, 1950–88', *Quarterly Journal of Economics*, vol. 106, no. 2, 1991, pp. 327–68, and *World Development Report 1994*, Table 7, pp. 174–5. Growth in productivity is measured here as the annualised rate of change in gross national product per person from 1980 to 1988. Growth in wages is measured as the annualised change in earnings per employee in manufacturing from 1980 to 1991.

The other factors of production: Land and capital

We have seen how firms decide how much labour to hire and how these decisions determine workers' wages. At the same time that firms are hiring workers, they are also deciding about other inputs to production. For example, our apple-producing firm might have to choose the size of its apple orchard and the number of ladders to make available to its apple pickers. We can think of the firm's factors of production as falling into three categories: labour, land and capital.

capital
the equipment and structures used to produce goods and services

Search me!

▸ capital

The meaning of the terms *labour* and *land* is clear, but the definition of *capital* is somewhat tricky. Economists use the term **capital** to refer to the stock of equipment and structures used for production. That is, the economy's capital represents the accumulation of goods produced in the past that are being used in the present to produce new goods and services. For our apple firm, the capital stock includes the ladders used to climb the trees, the trucks used to transport the apples, the buildings used to store the apples and even the trees themselves.

Equilibrium in the markets for land and capital

What determines how much the owners of land and capital earn for their contribution to the production process? Before answering this question, we need to distinguish between two prices, the purchase price and the rental price. The *purchase price* of land or capital is the price a person pays to own that factor of production indefinitely. The *rental price* is the price a person pays to use that factor for a limited period of time. It is important to keep this distinction in mind because, as we will see, these prices are determined by somewhat different economic forces.

Having defined these terms, we can now apply the theory of factor demand we developed for the labour market to the markets for land and capital. The wage is, after all, simply the rental price of labour. Therefore, much of what we have learned about wage determination applies also to the rental prices of land and capital. As Figure 19.7 illustrates, the rental price of land, shown in panel (a), and the rental price of capital, shown in panel (b), are determined by supply and demand. Moreover, the demand for land and capital is determined just like the demand for labour. That is, when our

Figure 19.7 **The markets for land and capital**

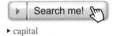

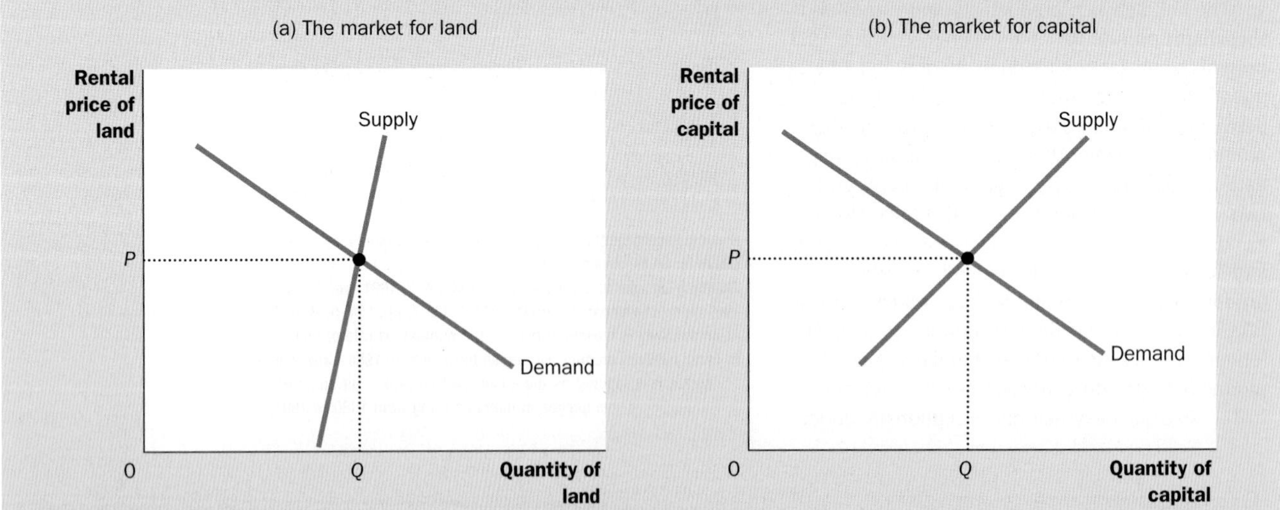

Supply and demand determine the compensation paid to the owners of land, as shown in panel (a), and the compensation paid to the owners of capital, as shown in panel (b). The demand for each factor, in turn, depends on the value of the marginal product of that factor.

apple-producing firm is deciding how much land and how many ladders to rent, it follows the same logic as when deciding how many workers to hire. For both land and capital, the firm increases the quantity hired until the value of the factor's marginal product equals the factor's price. Thus, the demand curve for each factor reflects the marginal productivity of that factor.

We can now explain how much income goes to labour, how much goes to landowners and how much goes to the owners of capital. As long as the firms using the factors of production are competitive and profit-maximising, each factor's rental price must equal the value of the marginal product for that factor. *Labour, land and capital each earn the value of their marginal contribution to the production process.*

Now consider the purchase price of land and capital. The rental price and the purchase price are obviously related; buyers are willing to pay more to buy a piece of land or capital if it produces a valuable stream of rental income. And, as we have just seen, the equilibrium rental income at any point in time equals the value of that factor's marginal product. Therefore, the equilibrium purchase price of a piece of land or capital depends on both the current value of the marginal product and the value of the marginal product expected to prevail in the future.

fyi

What is capital income?

Labour income is an easy concept to understand: it is the pay cheque that workers get from their employers. The income earned by capital, however, is less obvious.

In our analysis, we have been implicitly assuming that households own the economy's stock of capital – ladders, drill presses, warehouses, etc. – and rent it to the firms that use it. Capital income, in this case, is the rent that households receive for the use of their capital. This assumption simplified our analysis of how capital owners are compensated, but it is not entirely realistic. In fact, firms usually own the capital they use and, therefore, they receive the profits from this capital.

These earnings from capital, however, eventually get paid to households. Some of it gets paid in the form of interest to those households who have lent money to firms. Bond holders and bank depositors are two examples of recipients of interest. Thus, when you receive interest on your bank account, that income is part of the economy's capital income.

In addition, some of the profits from capital are paid to households in the form of dividends. Dividends are payments by a firm to the firm's shareholders. A shareholder is a person who has bought a share in the ownership of the firm and, therefore, is entitled to share in the firm's profits.

A firm does not have to pay out all of its earnings to households in the form of interest and dividends. Instead, it can retain some earnings within the firm and use these earnings to buy additional capital. Although these retained earnings do not get paid to the firm's shareholders, the shareholders benefit from them nonetheless. Because retained earnings increase the amount of capital the firm owns, they tend to increase future earnings and, thereby, the value of the firm's shares.

These institutional details are interesting and important, but they do not alter our conclusion about the income earned by the owners of capital. Capital is paid according to the value of its marginal product, regardless of whether this income gets transmitted to households in the form of interest or dividends or whether it is kept within firms as retained earnings.

Linkages among the factors of production

We have seen that the price paid to any factor of production – labour, land or capital – equals the value of the marginal product of that factor. The marginal product of any factor, in turn, depends on the quantity of that factor that is available. Because of diminishing returns, a factor in abundant supply has a low marginal product and thus a low price, and a factor in scarce supply has a high marginal product and a high price. As a result, when the supply of a factor falls, its equilibrium factor price rises.

When the supply of any factor changes, however, the effects are not limited to the market for that factor. In most situations, factors of production are used together in a way that makes the productivity of each factor dependent on the quantities of the other factors available to be used in the production process. As a result, a change in the supply of any one factor alters the earnings of all the factors.

For example, suppose that a storm destroys many of the ladders that workers use to pick apples from the orchards. What happens to the earnings of the various factors of production? Most obviously, the supply of ladders falls and, therefore, the equilibrium rental price of ladders rises. Those owners who were lucky enough to avoid damage to their ladders now earn a higher return when they rent out their ladders to the firms that produce apples.

Yet the effects of this event do not stop at the ladder market. Because there are fewer ladders with which to work, the workers who pick apples have a smaller marginal product. Thus, the reduction in the supply of ladders reduces the demand for apple pickers and this causes the equilibrium wage to fall.

This story shows a general lesson – an event that changes the supply of any factor of production can alter the earnings of all the factors. The change in earnings of any factor can be found by analysing the impact of the event on the value of the marginal product of that factor.

CASESTUDY

The economics of the Black Death

In fourteenth-century Europe, the bubonic plague wiped out about one-third of the population within a few years. This event, called the Black Death, provides a grisly natural experiment to test the theory of factor markets that we have just developed. Consider the effects of the Black Death on those who were lucky enough to survive. What do you think happened to the wages earned by workers and the rents earned by landowners?

To answer this question, let's examine the effects of a reduced population on the marginal product of labour and the marginal product of land. With a smaller supply of workers, the marginal product of labour rises. (This is simply diminishing marginal product working in reverse.) Thus, we would expect the Black Death to raise wages.

Because land and labour are used together in production, a smaller supply of workers also affects the market for land, the other major factor of production in medieval Europe. With fewer workers available to farm the land, an additional unit of land produced less additional output. In other words, the marginal product of land fell. Thus, we would expect the Black Death to lower rents.

The surviving workers were lucky in more ways than one.

Source: © photos.com/Getty Images.

In fact, both predictions are consistent with the historical evidence. Wages approximately doubled during this period and rents declined 50 per cent or more. The Black Death led to economic prosperity for the peasant classes and reduced incomes for the landed classes.

What determines the income of the owners of land and capital? How would an increase in the quantity of capital affect the incomes of those who already own capital? How would it affect the incomes of workers?

Conclusion

This chapter explained how labour, land and capital are compensated for the roles they play in the production process. The theory developed here is called the *neoclassical theory of distribution.* According to the neoclassical theory, the amount paid to each factor of production depends on the supply of and demand for that factor. The demand, in turn, depends on that particular factor's marginal productivity. In equilibrium, each factor of production earns the value of its marginal contribution to the production of goods and services.

The neoclassical theory of distribution is widely accepted. Most economists begin with the neoclassical theory when trying to explain how the Australian economy's $854 billion of income is distributed among the economy's various members. In the following two chapters, we consider the distribution of income in more detail. As you will see, the neoclassical theory provides the framework for this discussion.

Even at this point you can use the theory to answer the question that began this chapter: Why are computer programmers paid more than petrol station attendants? It is because programmers can produce a good of greater market value than can a petrol station attendant. People are willing to pay dearly for a good computer game, but they are willing to pay little to have their petrol pumped and their windscreens washed. The wages of these workers reflect the market prices of the goods they produce. If people suddenly got tired of using computers and decided to spend more time driving, the prices of these goods would change and so would the equilibrium wages of these two groups of workers.

Summary

- The economy's income is distributed in the markets for the factors of production. The three most important factors of production are labour, land and capital.
- The demand for factors is a derived demand that comes from firms that use the factors to produce goods and services. Competitive, profit-maximising firms hire each factor up to the point at which the value of the marginal product of the factor equals its price.
- The supply of labour arises from individuals' trade-off between work and leisure. An upward-sloping labour supply curve means that people respond to an increase in the wage by enjoying less leisure and working more hours.
- The price paid to each factor adjusts to balance the supply and demand for that factor. Because factor demand reflects the value of the marginal product of that factor, in equilibrium each factor is compensated according to its marginal contribution to the production of goods and services.
- Because factors of production are used together, the marginal product of any one factor depends on the quantities of all factors that are available. As a result, a change in the supply of one factor alters the equilibrium earnings of all the factors.

Key concepts

capital
factors of production
marginal product of labour
value of the marginal product

Questions for review

1. Explain how a firm's production function is related to its marginal product of labour, how a firm's marginal product of labour is related to the value of its marginal product, and how a firm's value of marginal product is related to its demand for labour.
2. Give two examples of events that could shift the demand for labour.
3. Give two examples of events that could shift the supply of labour.
4. Explain how wages can adjust to balance the supply and demand for labour while simultaneously equalling the value of the marginal product of labour.
5. If the population of Australia suddenly grew because of a large immigration, what would happen to wages? What would happen to the rents earned by the owners of land and capital?

Problems and applications

1. Suppose that the government proposes a new law aimed at reducing health-care costs – all Australians are to be required to eat one apple daily.
   a. How would this apple-a-day law affect the demand for and equilibrium price of apples?
   b. How would the law affect the marginal product and the value of the marginal product of apple pickers?
   c. How would the law affect the demand and equilibrium wage for apple pickers?
2. Henry Ford once said: 'It is not the employer who pays wages – he only handles the money. It is the product that pays wages'. Explain.

3 Show the effect of each of the following events on the market for labour in the computer manufacturing industry.

a The federal government buys personal computers for all Australian university students.

b More university students study engineering and computer science.

c Computer firms build new manufacturing plants.

4 Your uncle opens a sandwich shop that employs seven people. The employees are paid $6 per hour and a sandwich sells for $3. If your uncle is maximising his profit, what is the value of the marginal product of the last worker he hired? What is that worker's marginal product?

5 Imagine a firm that hires two types of workers – some with computer skills and some without. If technology advances, so that computers become more useful to the firm, what happens to the marginal product of the two types? What happens to equilibrium wages? Explain, using appropriate diagrams.

6 During the 1980s Australia experienced a significant inflow of capital from other countries. For example, Japanese car makers Toyota and Mitsubishi invested in new and upgraded factories in Australia.

a Using a diagram of the Australian capital market, show the effect of this inflow on the rental price of capital in Australia and on the quantity of capital in use.

b Using a diagram of the Australian labour market, show the effect of the capital inflow on the average wage paid to Australian workers.

7 Suppose that labour is the only input used by a perfectly competitive firm that can hire workers for $50 per day. The firm's production function is as follows:

Days of labour	Units of output
0	0
1	7
2	13
3	19
4	25
5	28

Each unit of output sells for $10. Plot the firm's demand for labour. How many days of labour should the firm hire? Show this point on your graph.

8 (This question requires knowledge of the appendix to this chapter.) Using the production function described in the previous question, suppose that the firm is a monopolist. Its demand schedule is as follows:

Price	Units of output
20	0
15	7
12	13
10	19
9	25
8	28
7	29

Plot the firm's demand for labour. How many days of labour should the firm hire? Show this point on your graph.

9 (This question is challenging.) In recent years, some policymakers have proposed requiring firms to improve safety standards. For example, there are laws requiring additional safety training and equipment to be provided to each worker. Let's consider the effects of such a policy on the labour market.

   a Suppose that a law required firms to give each worker $3 of safety-related training for every hour that the worker is employed by the firm. How does this law affect the marginal profit that a firm earns from each worker? How does the law affect the demand curve for labour? Draw your answer on a graph with the cash wage on the vertical axis.

   b If there is no change in labour supply, how would this law affect employment and wages?

   c Why might the labour supply curve shift in response to this law? Would this shift in labour supply raise or lower the impact of the law on wages and employment?

   d As chapter 6 discussed, the wages of some workers, particularly the unskilled and inexperienced, are kept above the equilibrium level by minimum-wage laws. What effect would such an occupational safety policy have for these workers?

Search me!

Search me!

When accessing information about microeconomics use the following keywords in any combinations you require:

- capital
- factors of production

CourseMate

CourseMate

For more multimedia resources and activities on economics, visit the Economics CourseMate website.

APPENDIX

The demand for labour under imperfect competition and monopoly

In the chapter, we demonstrated how the demand for labour was determined in a perfectly competitive market. A competitive, profit-maximising firm hires workers up to the point where the value of the marginal product of labour equals the wage. As we will see here, a similar rule applies when market conditions are not perfectly competitive. However, in this case, firms hire workers up to the point where the marginal revenue product of labour equals the wage. This involves reasoning akin to the competitive firm case. The firm evaluates the effect of an additional worker on total revenue when making its labour quantity choice.

To consider this, let us re-examine the case of the water producer in chapter 15. It was the only producer of water in its town – a monopoly. We learnt in chapter 15 that the monopolist faces demand conditions identical to market demand for water in the town. This demand schedule is reproduced in Table 19A.1. Also listed in that table is the firm's total and marginal revenue.

Recall that the critical feature of the monopolist's demand that distinguishes it from demand faced by a perfectly competitive firm is that it is less elastic. Whereas the demand curve for a firm under perfect competition is perfectly elastic and equal to price, under monopoly (and, indeed, oligopoly and monopolistic competition), price falls as the firm produces more output. This is the price effect we discussed in chapter 15. So as output is increased, marginal revenue is not simply equal to price. As depicted in Table 19A.1, as output rises from, say, 1 to 2 litres per day, total revenue rises by $8. Although the firm sells more litres, it receives less per litre.

Table 19A.1 A monopoly's total and marginal revenue

Quantity of water (Q)	Price (P)	Total revenue ($TR = P \times Q$)	Marginal revenue ($MR = \Delta TR/\Delta Q$)
0 litres	$11	$0	—
1	10	10	$10
2	9	18	8
3	8	24	6

Quantity of water (Q)	Price (P)	Total revenue ($TR = P \times Q$)	Marginal revenue ($MR = \Delta TR/\Delta Q$)
4	7	28	4
5	6	30	2
6	5	30	0
7	4	28	–2
8	3	24	–4

By adding more workers, the firm can supply more water to the town. However, each additional worker causes output to rise by a diminished amount – that is, the marginal product of labour declines with output. This is depicted in Table 19A.2. Note that although output is 4 litres per day when there is a single worker, it is 6 litres per day when there are two workers. Thus, the marginal product of the second worker is 2 litres per day.

To calculate whether it should put the second worker on, however, the firm must calculate the effect on firm profits. In particular, what happens to total revenue? As output rises from 4 to 6 litres per day, price falls from \$7 to \$5 and revenue rises from \$28 to \$30. So the addition to revenue from employing a second worker is \$2. This is the marginal revenue product of labour for two workers. Table 19A.2 makes this calculation for all quantities of labour employed by the firm. Marginal revenue product is the addition to total revenue created by the addition of another worker.

Suppose that, unlike the market for water, the labour market is competitive and that the prevailing wage is \$1 per day. Then a firm will improve its profits by adding another worker if and only if the marginal revenue product of labour from that worker exceeds the worker's wage. For the firm in Table 19A.2, this condition holds true for two workers but not for three. Hence, the firm will choose

Table 19A.2 How a monopolistic firm decides how much labour to hire

Labour (number of workers) (L)	Output (litres per day) (Q)	Total revenue	Marginal product of labour ($MPL = \Delta Q/\Delta L$)	Marginal revenue product of labour ($MRPL = \Delta TR/\Delta L$)	Wage (W)	Marginal profit ($\Delta Profit = MRPL - W$)
0	0	\$0	-	\$28	\$1	-
1	4	28	4	2	1	\$27
2	6	30	2	–2	1	1
3	7	28	1	–4	1	–3
4	8	24	1			–5

to employ two workers and produce an output of 6 litres per day. Thus, any profit-maximising firm hires workers up to the point where the marginal revenue product of labour equals the wage.

Notice that this same rule guides the labour-hiring decision for a competitive firm. In that case, when an additional worker produces more output, each new unit sold earns the prevailing market price. That price is the marginal revenue for each additional unit of output produced. So the value of the marginal product is the same as the marginal revenue product for a competitive firm.

For the monopolist, however, when it adds another worker, that worker produces more output (its marginal product) but earns the firm additional revenue of an amount less than price. The firm must consider this price effect as well as the output effect when deciding to hire another worker. For each extra unit produced, the additional revenue the firm earns is its marginal revenue. Therefore, the marginal revenue product of labour ($\Delta TR/\Delta L$) is the additional revenue over all of the additional output that worker produces or marginal revenue times its marginal product ($\Delta TR/\Delta Q \times \Delta Q/\Delta/L$). This is the value an additional worker adds to the firm.

As we mentioned in the chapter, the idea that the firm hires up until the point where the value of the marginal product of labour equals the wage is just another way of looking at the firm's profit-maximising output decision. Recall from chapter 15 that a monopolist wishes to produce an output quantity such that marginal revenue equals marginal cost. In the chapter we demonstrated that marginal cost is the wage divided by the marginal product of labour. Because the value of the marginal product of labour equals marginal revenue multiplied by marginal product, then mathematically we have:

$$MR \times MPL = W \text{ or } MR = W/MPL = MC$$

So when a firm hires labour up to the point where the marginal revenue product equals the wage, it is choosing output such that marginal revenue equals marginal cost.

Thus, the theory of labour demand we introduced in the chapter remains essentially unchanged for situations where markets are not perfectly competitive. In general, the firm chooses its quantity of labour by looking at the point at which the marginal revenue product of labour equals the wage. Hence, *the marginal revenue product curve is the labour demand curve for any firm.*

20

Earnings, unions and discrimination

Learning objectives

In this chapter you will:

- examine how wages compensate for differences in job characteristics
- learn about and compare the human-capital and signalling theories of education
- examine why in some occupations a few superstars earn tremendous incomes
- evaluate the role of unions in labour markets
- examine how information asymmetries might result in efficiency wages
- consider why it is difficult to measure the impact of discrimination on wages
- see when market forces can and cannot provide a natural remedy for discrimination.

Sports stars and musicians can earn incomes in the millions of dollars per year. Most surgeons earn salaries over $250 000 and the average person working in manufacturing earns about $35 000 per year. This illustrates the large differences in earnings that are so common in our economy. These differences explain why some people live in mansions, drive BMWs and holiday on the French Riviera, and other people live in small flats, take the bus and holiday in their own backyards.

What causes earnings to vary so much from person to person? Chapter 19, which developed the basic neoclassical theory of the labour market, offers an answer to this question. There we saw that wages are governed by labour supply and labour demand. Labour demand, in turn, reflects the marginal productivity of labour. In equilibrium, each worker is paid the value of his or her marginal contribution to the economy's production of goods and services.

This theory of the labour market, though widely accepted by economists, is only the beginning of the story. To understand the wide variation in earnings that we observe, we must go beyond this general framework and examine more precisely what determines the supply and demand for different types of labour. That is our goal in this chapter.

Some determinants of equilibrium wages

Workers differ from one another in many ways. Jobs also have differing characteristics – both in terms of the wages they pay and in terms of their non-monetary attributes. In this section we consider how the characteristics of workers and jobs affect labour supply, labour demand and equilibrium wages.

Compensating differentials

When a worker is deciding whether to take a job, the wage is only one of many job attributes that the worker takes into account. Some jobs are easy, fun and safe; others are hard, dull and dangerous. The better the job as gauged by these non-monetary characteristics, the more people there are who are willing to do the job at any given wage. In other words, the supply of labour for easy, fun and safe jobs is greater than the supply of labour for hard, dull and dangerous jobs. As a result, 'good' jobs will tend to have lower equilibrium wages than 'bad' jobs.

For example, imagine you are looking for a job during university orientation week. Two kinds of jobs are available. You can take a job as a new-student assistant, or you can take a job as a cleaner. The assistants leisurely stroll around the campus during the day and help any new students who need directions or other assistance. The cleaners must report to work at 4.30 each morning and clean up the mess left after orientation week parties. Which job would you want? Most people would prefer to be a new-student assistant if the wages were the same. In order to get people to become campus cleaners, the university has to offer higher wages to cleaners than to student assistants.

Economists use the term **compensating differential** to refer to a difference in wages that arises from non-monetary characteristics of different jobs. Compensating differentials are prevalent in the economy. Here are some examples:

compensating differential
a difference in wages that arises to offset the non-monetary characteristics of different jobs

- Coalminers are paid more than other workers with similar levels of education. Their higher wage compensates them for the dirty and dangerous nature of coalmining, as well as the long-term health problems that coalminers experience.
- Workers who work the night shift at factories are paid more than similar workers who work the day shift. The higher wage compensates them for having to work at night and sleep during the day, a lifestyle that most people find undesirable.

- University lecturers are paid less than lawyers and doctors, who have similar amounts of education. Lecturers' lower wages compensate them for the great intellectual and personal satisfaction that their jobs offer. (Indeed, teaching economics is so much fun that it is surprising that economics lecturers get paid anything at all!)

'On the one hand, I know I could make more money if I left public service for the private sector, but, on the other hand, I couldn't chop off heads.'

Source: Fradon, Dana © 1985 Dana Fradon/The New Yorker Collection/www.cartoonbank.com.

CASESTUDY

Paying for work quality

It is sometimes difficult to tell whether wages employees receive are driven by productivity (implying high wages) or job satisfaction (implying lower wages). This is true of some scientific professions where people like to be able to publish their work while their employers may or may not approve of this. One reason for disapproval is that publication gives their competitors an insight into their strategy. But against this are suggestions that publication may make a firm's scientists more connected and able to absorb developments elsewhere, increasing productivity.

So does job satisfaction drive a scientist's wage? It is hard to tell because a high-quality employee will command both a high wage because of productivity reasons and also potentially be able to insist on work conditions. Scott Stern, in a paper published in *Management Science* in 2004, surveyed job candidates to tease all of this out. To take into account the quality of the candidate, Stern not only compared candidates but also compared the group of job offers each received. He showed that candidates with multiple job offers (some with publication rights and others without), would accept 20 per cent lower salaries for the jobs where they could publish. This suggested that personal job satisfaction rather than productivity was driving those rights. People really do 'pay' for job satisfaction.

Human capital

As we discussed in the previous chapter, the word *capital* usually refers to the economy's stock of equipment and structures. The capital stock includes the farmer's tractor, the manufacturer's factory and the teacher's blackboard. The essence of capital is that it is a factor of production that itself has been produced.

There is another type of capital that, although less tangible than physical capital, is just as important to the economy's production. **Human capital** is the accumulation of investments in people. The most important type of human capital is education. Like all forms of capital, education represents an expenditure of resources at one point in time to raise productivity in the future. But, unlike an investment in other forms of capital, an investment in education is tied to a specific person and this linkage is what makes it human capital.

human capital
the accumulation of investments in people, such as education and on-the-job training

Search me!
▸ human capital

Not surprisingly, workers with more human capital on average earn more than those with less human capital. University graduates in Australia, for example, earn about 36 per cent more than those workers who end their education with a secondary school certificate. This large difference has been documented in many countries around the world. It tends to be even larger in less-developed countries, where educated workers are in scarce supply.

It is easy to see why education raises wages from the perspective of supply and demand. Firms – the demanders of labour – are willing to pay more for the highly educated because highly educated workers have higher marginal products. Workers – the suppliers of labour – are willing to pay the cost of becoming educated only if there is a reward for doing so. In essence, the difference in wages between highly educated workers and less-educated workers may be considered a compensating differential for the cost of becoming educated.

CASESTUDY

The changing value of skills

In Australia, consistent with human capital theory, workers with skills command higher salaries than those without. A 2010 study by the Productivity Commission looked at how wages change with an individual's level of education. Their results showed that, compared with a worker who finished school at or before year 11, a university degree led to around a 38 per cent increase in wages. The relative wage increase was slightly higher for men than for women. Compared to a worker whose education finished at the end of high school, a worker with a university degree earned around 26 per cent higher wages.

While higher education typically leads to higher earnings, the size of the wage premium changes over time. In Australia, the wage premium for a worker with a university degree relative to a worker with just a high school education fell in the 1970s and early 1980s. The premium then rose in the 1990s and early 2000s before falling again in the late 2000s.

What explains these patterns? A study by Jeff Borland, published in the *Economic Record* in 1996, identifies shifts in both the relative demand and relative supply of skilled to unskilled workers. Increased access to education and higher labour force participation rates for women have raised the proportion of workers with university education in the workforce. On the other hand, the relative demand for skilled workers has also been growing.

When both demand and supply increase in a market, the result is an increase in quantity although price may increase or decrease. In the case of the market for skilled workers in Australia, in the 1970s the relative number of skilled workers employed increased and the relative earnings of those workers decreased. Since then, the relative number of skilled workers employed has continued to increase and strong growth in demand for these workers has meant that their relative earnings have also increased. The mining boom in Australia in the late 2000s reversed this trend, at least temporarily.

The value of an education is not simply measured by the earnings of workers in full-time employment. Their employment prospects must also be taken into account. In 1997, for instance,

>>

male workers with a degree were 50 per cent less likely to find themselves without a job compared with those with secondary school education. For women, the improvement in employment prospects from education was even greater.

Taking both relative earnings and the relative likelihood of finding employment into account, there is probably an increasing value to having skills in the workforce.

Ability, effort and chance

Why do top sporting professionals get paid more than minor players? Certainly, the higher wages are not a compensating differential. Playing in top-level sporting competitions is not necessarily a less pleasant task than playing in minor competitions; in fact, the opposite is often true. Top sporting professionals do not require more years of schooling and are not always more experienced. To a large extent, top sporting professionals earn more just because they have greater natural ability.

Natural ability is important for workers in all occupations. Because of heredity and upbringing, people differ in their physical and mental attributes. Some people are strong, others weak. Some people are smart, others less so. Some people are outgoing, others awkward in social situations. These and many other personal characteristics determine how productive workers are and, therefore, play a role in determining the wages they earn.

Closely related to ability is effort. Some people work hard, others are lazy. We should not be surprised to find that those who work hard are more productive and earn higher wages. To some extent, firms reward workers directly by paying people on the basis of what they produce. Salespeople, for instance, are often paid a percentage of the sales they make. At other times, hard work is rewarded less directly in the form of a higher annual salary or a bonus.

Chance also plays a role in determining wages. If a person attended a trade school to learn how to repair televisions with vacuum tubes and then found this skill made obsolete by the invention of solid-state electronics, this worker would end up earning a low wage compared with others with similar years of training. The low wage of this worker is due to chance – a phenomenon that economists recognise but do not shed much light on.

How important are ability, effort and chance in determining wages? It is hard to say, because ability, effort and chance are hard to measure. But indirect evidence suggests that they are very important. When labour economists study wages, they relate a worker's wage to those variables that can be measured – years of schooling, years of experience, age and job characteristics. Although all of these measured variables affect a worker's wage as theory predicts, they account for less than half of the variation in wages in our economy. Because so much of the variation in wages is left unexplained, omitted variables, including ability, effort and chance, must play an important role.

CASESTUDY

The benefits of beauty

People differ in many ways. One difference is how attractive they are. The actor Brad Pitt, for instance, is good-looking. In part for this reason, his films attract large audiences. Not surprisingly, the large audiences mean a large income for him.

How prevalent are the economic benefits of beauty? Labour economists Daniel Hamermesh and Jeff Biddle tried to answer this question in a study published in the December 1994 issue of the *American Economic Review*. Hamermesh and Biddle examined data from surveys of individuals in the United States and Canada. The interviewers who conducted the survey were asked to rate each respondent's physical appearance. Hamermesh and

Biddle then examined how much the wages of the respondents depended on the standard determinants – education, experience and so on – and how much they depended on physical appearance.

Hamermesh and Biddle found that beauty pays. People who are deemed to be more attractive than average earn 5 per cent more than people of average looks. People of average looks earn 5 per cent to 10 per cent more than people considered less attractive than average. Similar results were found for men and women.

What explains these differences in wages? There are several ways to interpret the 'beauty premium'.

One interpretation is that good looks are themselves a type of innate ability determining productivity and wages. Some people are born with the attributes of a movie star; other people are not. Good looks are useful in any job in which workers present themselves to the public – such as acting, sales and waiting on tables. In this case, an attractive worker is more valuable to the firm than an unattractive worker. The firm's willingness to pay more to attractive workers reflects its customers' preferences.

A second interpretation is that reported beauty is an indirect measure of other types of ability. How attractive a person appears depends on more than just heredity. It also depends on dress, hairstyle, personal conduct and other attributes that a person can control. Perhaps a person who successfully projects an attractive image in a survey interview is more likely to be an intelligent person who succeeds at other tasks as well.

A third interpretation is that the beauty premium is a type of discrimination, a topic to which we return later.

Good looks pay.

Source: iStockphoto/Jacob Wackerhausen.

An alternative view of education: Signalling

Earlier we discussed the human-capital view of education, according to which schooling raises workers' wages because it makes them more productive. Although this view is widely accepted, some economists have proposed an alternative theory, which emphasises that firms use educational attainment as a way of differentiating between high-ability and low-ability workers. According to this alternative view, when people get a university degree, for instance, they do not become more productive, but they do *signal* their high ability to prospective employers. Because it is easier for high-ability people to get a degree than it is for low-ability people, more high-ability people get degrees. As a result, it is rational for firms to interpret a degree as a signal of ability.

The signalling theory of education is similar to the signalling theory of advertising discussed in chapter 18. In the signalling theory of advertising, the advertisement itself contains no real information, but the firm signals the quality of its product to consumers by its willingness to spend money on advertising. In the signalling theory of education, schooling has no real productivity benefit, but the worker signals innate productivity to employers by being willing to spend years at university. In both cases, an action is being taken not for its intrinsic benefit but because the willingness to take that action conveys private information to someone observing it.

Thus, we now have two views of education: the human-capital theory and the signalling theory. Both views can explain why better educated workers tend to earn more than less-educated workers. According to the human-capital view, education makes workers more productive; according to the signalling view, education is correlated with natural ability. But the two views have radically different predictions for the effects of policies that aim to increase educational attainment. According to the human-capital view, increasing educational levels for all workers would raise all workers' productivity and thereby their wages. According to the signalling view, education does not enhance productivity, so raising all workers' educational levels would not affect wages.

Most likely, the truth lies somewhere between these two extremes. The benefits to education are probably a combination of productivity-enhancing effects of human capital and the productivity-revealing effects of signalling. The open question is the relative size of these two effects.

The superstar phenomenon

Although most actors earn very little and often have to take jobs as waiters to support themselves, actor Sandra Bullock earned just over $60 million in 2009–10. Similarly, while most people who play tennis do it for free as a hobby, Roger Federer professionally earned over $60 million in 2009–10. Sandra Bullock and Roger Federer are superstars in their fields and their great public appeal is reflected in astronomical incomes.

Why do Bullock and Federer earn so much? It is not surprising that there are differences in incomes within occupations. Good carpenters earn more than mediocre carpenters and good plumbers earn more than mediocre plumbers. People vary in ability and effort, and these differences lead to differences in income. Yet the best carpenters and plumbers do not earn the millions that are common among the best actors and athletes. What explains the difference?

To understand the tremendous incomes of Bullock and Federer, we must examine the special features of the markets in which they sell their services. Superstars arise in markets that have two characteristics:

- Every customer in the market wants to enjoy the good supplied by the best producer.
- The good is produced with a technology that makes it possible for the best producer to supply every customer at low cost.

If Sandra Bullock is the finest actor around, then everyone will want to see her next film; seeing twice as many films by an actor half as talented is not a good substitute. Moreover, it is possible for everyone to enjoy a performance by Sandra Bullock. Because it is easy to make multiple copies of a film, Bullock can provide her service to millions of people simultaneously. Similarly, because tennis tournaments are broadcast on television, millions of fans can enjoy the extraordinary athletic skills of Roger Federer.

We can now see why there are no superstar carpenters and plumbers. Other things being equal, everyone may prefer to employ the best carpenter, but a carpenter, unlike a film actor, can provide his services to only a limited number of customers. Although the best carpenter will be able to command a somewhat higher wage than the average carpenter, the average carpenter will still be able to earn a good living.

Source: Getty Images.

Source: Getty Image.

Define *compensating differential* and give an example. Give two reasons why better educated workers earn more than less-educated workers.

Unions and imperfect competition in labour markets

In some industries, labour markets do not operate according to the simple principles of supply and demand. In industries such as transport, teaching and mining, wages are determined by negotiations between unions and employers. A **union** is a type of cartel. Like any cartel, a union is a group of sellers acting together in the hope of exerting their joint market power. Many workers in the economy discuss their wages, benefits and working conditions with their employers as individuals. In contrast, workers in a union do so as a group. The process by which unions and firms agree on the terms of employment is called **collective bargaining**.

union
a worker association that bargains with employers over wages and working conditions

collective bargaining
the process by which unions and firms agree on the terms of employment

Unions are an example of imperfect competition in labour markets. But large employers can also exercise market power. Like product markets, these imperfections in competition in labour markets have an effect on prices and quantity – in this case, wages and levels of employment.

The role of unions has been the source of considerable debate in Australia. Every year it seems that workers and employers in another industry, whether it be air transport, brewing or the ports, are in a dispute. Unionisation was partly a response to very poor working conditions in those industries. There was a time when being a member of a union was seen as very important to maintaining better work conditions. Recently, however, economic changes have altered this pattern. As depicted in Table 20.1, trade union membership rates have been declining in Australia.

Here we will look at how an economist might analyse union behaviour. This will allow us to pinpoint employer concerns about unions and to also evaluate their overall economic impact.

Table 20.1 Unionisation rate – union members as a percentage of employees

Year	Unionisation rate (%)
1976	53
1982	54
1986	46
1990	41
1994	35
1998	28
2000	25
2003	23
2006	20
2009	20

Source: Anne Hawke and Mark Wooden, 'The changing face of Australian industrial relations', *Economic Record*, vol. 74, no. 224, 1998, pp. 74–88; Australian Bureau of Statistics, Cat. No. 310.0, 6325.0 and 6310.0 (various years).

Unions as monopolists

One way to view a union is as a wage-setting monopolist. To see this, consider the hypothetical example of the strawberry picking industry in the region of Bargainland. For decades, strawberry picking had been one of the lowest paid jobs in the region. Strawberry picking did not require many specialised skills so it could be performed by many workers in Bargainland.

One day, one particularly savvy strawberry picker decided to think more carefully about the market for strawberry pickers. She reasoned that strawberry pickers may be paid so little because owners of strawberry patches could play them off against one another. Pickers who want higher wages have little bargaining power with a patch owner who can simply fire them and hire other pickers at the prevailing wage. To this person, it is not strawberry pickers' lack of skills that is the problem but their lack of market power.

Our smart strawberry picker was skilled in the economics of chapter 15. She reckoned that if all the strawberry pickers in Bargainland were to get together and form an organisation – the Bargainland Strawberry Pickers' Union (BSPU) – they could act more like a monopolist and, hence, increase their wages. 'Pickers need not be at the bottom of the heap in Bargainland', proclaimed the new leader of the union. 'Join the BSPU and together we will ensure a decent income and better working conditions.' All the strawberry pickers in Bargainland agreed to join. In addition, the BSPU ensured that only workers who were members could pick strawberries. This created an entry barrier into strawberry picking. This was an important condition that would allow the union to exercise market power.

But here the union leader found a problem. Although the BSPU could choose a wage, it was constrained to choose a point on the market demand curve for strawberry pickers. Remember that this curve was determined by the value of the marginal product of strawberry pickers. This had not changed, so the BSPU through its actions could only move along this curve.

Figure 20.1 Labour demand and union monopoly power

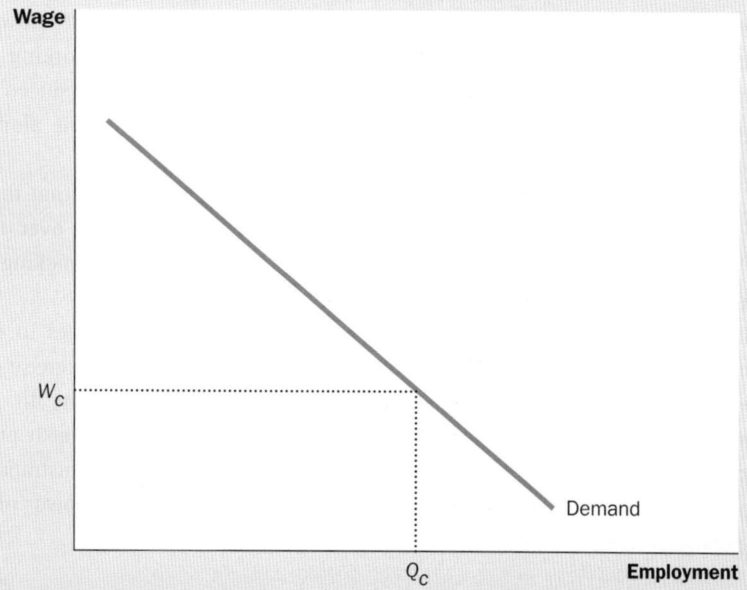

Unions might wish to increase the wages of their members. However, when firms in the industry are perfectly competitive, their demand for labour will be represented by a curve such as the one in the diagram. If the union wishes to raise wages above the competitive wage of W_C, it must accept an employment level lower than Q_C. A union that cares about both wage and employment levels faces a dilemma and may not wish to exercise its monopoly power.

In Figure 20.1, you can see that for the wages of strawberry pickers to rise, the number of pickers employed has to fall. For the BSPU leader this was a dilemma; the idea of the BSPU was to raise wages of all of its members, not send them to unemployment or a lower paid job.

This illustrates our first point regarding the interpretation of unions as monopolists – they can raise wages but only at the expense of employment levels. Our examination of monopoly behaviour in chapter 15 was based on the assumption that these firms attempted to maximise profits. They did not care if they sold less, if this led to higher profits. For a union, however, such choices are not so easy. It faces a different set of objectives than does a monopolist in a product market. A union can restrict employment and raise wages and, thereby, raise total income received by workers in the industry. However, in order to do this, the union must also restrict access to employment in the industry. This must harm some workers.

Unions face the same dilemma in asking for better working conditions – such as improved safety, better working hours, annual leave and a healthier work environment. Better working conditions usually mean more costs associated with employing workers. Firms will take such costs into account when determining the quantity of labour they hire. For them, every dollar spent per worker on improved conditions is equivalent to another dollar in wages. Hence, the union, in asking for better working conditions, is constrained by the market demand curve for labour.

Therefore, the union's ability to extract better pay or working conditions is limited by industry conditions. Whether unionised labour is paid more is contingent upon union objectives. If the union is concerned about keeping all its members employed, this will limit its ability to raise wages. There are, however, some situations in which union goals may be compatible with higher wages:

- It may be possible for the workers to agree to shorter working hours. In our strawberry picking story, the union leader could propose that all workers agree to limit their working hours and, in effect, share work. The total quantity of hours worked could then be reduced without any corresponding reduction in employment. The result would be a movement along the labour demand curve to a point where each worker received a higher hourly wage.
- Sometimes it is argued that unions favour members over outsiders. Suppose that the BSPU could insist that no new workers were employed as strawberry pickers. Then, over time, through retirement or other circumstances, some workers will leave strawberry picking. This would reduce total employment and increase wages earned by 'insiders'.

In some industries, it is conceivable that union goals will allow higher wages to occur through the exercise of monopoly power. Recall, however, that a union's ability to exercise this power is contingent upon the same conditions underlying a product market monopoly. In particular, by restricting strawberry pickers to union members, the BSPU was able to ensure that it prevented firms from bypassing the union's attempts at wage setting. In recent times, laws in Australia have limited the ability of unions to insist on compulsory membership. This has eroded the power of some unions to exercise monopoly power.

Bilateral monopoly

monopsony
a market situation where there is a single buyer for a product

In many industries, employers have the ability to negotiate and influence wages. An extreme example of this is called **monopsony**, that is, where there is a single employer in an industry. For instance, mines in outlying towns, steelworks and other firms in large-scale manufacturing industries could be considered monopsonists. When a union confronts a monopsonist, the outcomes can be very different from those for a union whose workers are employed by competitive firms.

Returning to our hypothetical example of the Bargainland strawberry industry, suppose that strawberry-patch owners become concerned about the monopoly power of the BSPU. This is not surprising as higher wages might cause some patches to go out of business. The patches decide to merge and form a single company. This gives them a monopoly over strawberry production in Bargainland and also allows them to negotiate directly with the BSPU over wages and employment. The managing director of the new company is known for tough negotiating.

bilateral monopoly
a market situation where there are both a single buyer and a single seller for a product

The union leader and employer meet to negotiate directly with one another on behalf of their respective organisations. This situation is referred to as a **bilateral monopoly**. We want to consider the type of agreements they might arrive at. Both parties realise one very important thing – any deal that does not maximise industry profit (after considering labour costs) will not be in either party's interests. For instance, suppose that the union leader was concerned that, during harvest season before unionisation, pickers were required to work on weekends. This loss of leisure time had a high opportunity cost to the strawberry pickers. The employer could explain that it was efficient to harvest strawberries quickly. If harvesting did not continue over weekends, this would cost the company a sizeable amount of money in lost strawberries. So the employer proposes to increase weekend wages and share the increased profits created by a speedy harvest with the workers. If the increase in wages is worth the loss of a few weekends' worth of leisure, the union leader accepts the proposal. If adequate compensation is offered, it would not be sensible for the union leader to insist on a work practice that raises production costs.

However, when it comes to negotiations over total wages, both parties are at an impasse. An increase in wages does not itself influence the strawberry company's ability to earn additional revenue. It is simply a transfer from company shareholders to employees. The union leader digs her heels in on this issue and threatens to take industrial action, such as a **strike**, if total wages are not increased. But the BSPU cannot demand too much. If the strawberry company fails to make any profits above total wages paid, its owners might shut it down. Eventually, however, the employer advocate considers the losses from a strike and makes the BSPU a wage offer – lucrative enough so that a strike really is not worthwhile.

strike
the organised withdrawal of labour from a firm by a union

These outcomes, over working time and wages, reflect the type of agreements that can arise in bilateral monopoly. The issue of wages is purely distributional. In fact, there are many agreements that can arise that give workers more or less money relative to shareholders. These agreements can be depicted using a **possibilities frontier**. One such frontier is depicted in Figure 20.2. The possibilities frontier depicts all agreements that can be made that maximise the strawberry industry's profits. At some agreements (such as point A), the union is ineffectual and receives a minimal wage payout. There are others (such as point B) in which the union has all of the bargaining power and so shareholders earn a minimal profit level – just enough to make it worthwhile to continue the business. Finally, there are agreements (such as point C) where both the union and company can be better off by agreeing to a point closer to the possibilities frontier. An example of this was the decision over whether to work weekends during harvest season. By agreeing to do that, both the workers and shareholders were better off.

possibilities frontier
a graph depicting all the outcomes that maximise the sum of profits plus wages to workers

Figure 20.2 **Possibilities frontier between a union and employer**

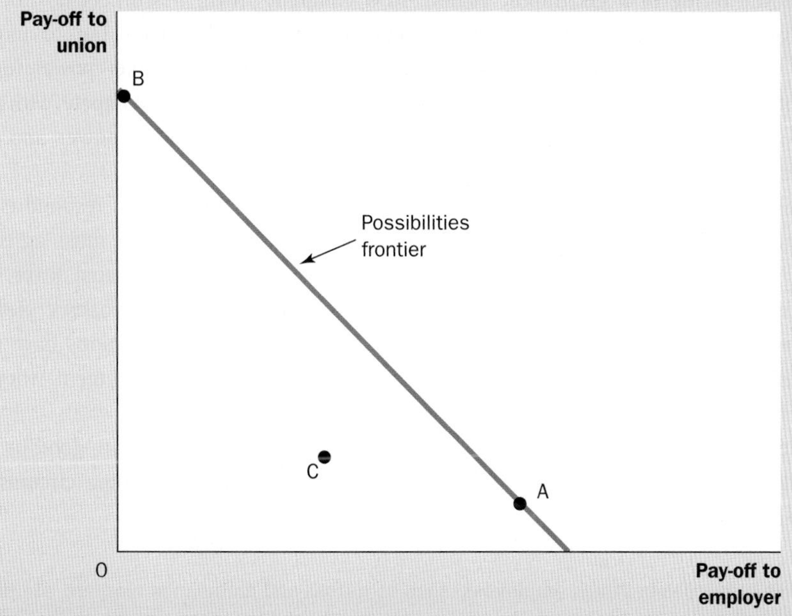

This figure depicts the possibilities frontier between a union and a single industry-wide employer. The figure depicts the pay-offs that the employer and union receive from any given agreement. Only pay-off combinations inside the possibilities frontier can actually be achieved. Both the union and employer will prefer to come to agreements that lie on the possibilities frontier. If they agree to a point such as C, each could be made better off by moving closer to the frontier.

Reasonable negotiators will agree to points on the possibilities frontier. Any point outside the frontier is simply not possible. Any point within the frontier can be improved on to the benefit of both parties, so there is no inherent conflict. The actual point on the frontier where negotiators, such as the union leader and the employer, end up depends on their relative bargaining power. For example, if the BSPU can hold out for a long strike, this improves its bargaining position. However, if the strawberry company can easily find other workers who can pick during the strike, this reduces the union's bargaining position. There are many factors that influence bargaining power, so the earnings of unionised workers will differ from industry to industry.

Are unions good or bad for the economy?

Economists disagree about whether unions are good or bad for the economy as a whole. Let's consider both sides of the debate.

Critics argue that unions are merely a type of cartel. When unions raise wages above the level that would prevail in competitive markets, they reduce the quantity of labour demanded, cause some workers to be unemployed and reduce the wages in the rest of the economy. The resulting allocation of labour is, critics argue, both inefficient and inequitable. It is inefficient because high union wages reduce employment in unionised firms below the efficient, competitive level. It is inequitable because some workers benefit at the expense of other workers.

Advocates of unions contend that unions are a necessary antidote to the market power of the firms that hire workers. The extreme case of this market power is the 'company town', where a single firm does most of the hiring in a geographic region. In a company town, if workers do not accept the wages and working conditions that the firm offers, they have little choice but to move or stop working. In the absence of a union, therefore, the firm could use its market power to pay lower wages and offer worse working conditions than would prevail if it had to compete with other firms for the same workers. In this case, a union may balance the firm's market power and protect the workers from being at the mercy of the firm owners.

Advocates of unions also claim that unions are important for helping firms respond efficiently to workers' concerns. Whenever a worker takes a job, the worker and the firm must agree on many attributes of the job in addition to the wage – hours of work, overtime, annual leave, sick leave, health benefits, promotion schedules, job security and so on. By representing workers' views on these issues, unions allow firms to provide the right mix of job attributes. Even if unions have the adverse effect of pushing wages above the equilibrium level and causing unemployment, they have the benefit of helping firms keep a happy and productive workforce.

In the end, there is no consensus among economists about whether unions are good or bad for the economy. Like many institutions, their influence is probably beneficial in some circumstances and adverse in others.

Q

There are some industries in which employees, such as nurses and ambulance workers, are particularly concerned about the consequences of industrial action on others. How does this concern influence their bargaining power?

The theory of efficiency wages

One explanation for different earnings might come from different practices designed to improve workplace performance. Firms may set wages high so as to motivate workers to perform well in their jobs. This wage is called an **efficiency wage**. Efficiency wages are wages above the equilibrium wages that would result when supply equals demand. Thus, efficiency wages can potentially explain unemployment as well as earnings.

efficiency wages
above-equilibrium wages paid by firms in order to increase worker productivity

Why should firms want to keep wages high? In some ways, this decision seems odd, for wages are a large part of firms' costs. Normally, we expect profit-maximising firms to want to keep costs – and therefore wages – as low as possible. The novel insight of efficiency-wage theory is that paying high wages might be profitable because they might raise the efficiency of a firm's workers.

Search me!
▸ efficiency wages

There are several types of efficiency-wage theory. Each type suggests a different explanation for why firms may want to pay high wages. Let's now consider four of these theories.

Worker health

The first and simplest type of efficiency-wage theory emphasises the link between wages and worker health. Better paid workers eat a more nutritious diet and workers who eat a better diet are healthier and more productive. A firm may find it more profitable to pay high wages and have healthy, productive workers than to pay lower wages and have less-healthy, less-productive workers.

This type of efficiency-wage theory is not relevant for firms in rich countries such as Australia. In these countries, the equilibrium wages for most workers are well above the level needed for an adequate diet. Firms are not concerned that paying equilibrium wages would place their workers' health in jeopardy.

Paying higher wages to raise worker health is more relevant for firms in less-developed countries where inadequate nutrition is a more common problem. Unemployment is high in the cities of many poor African countries, for example. In these countries, firms may fear that cutting wages would adversely influence their workers' health and productivity. Concern over nutrition may explain why firms do not cut wages despite a surplus of labour.

fyi **Why do strikes occur?**

Strikes are costly to both firms and workers. To firms they represent lost output; to workers, lost income. The longer the strike, the more costly to both parties. So why do they occur?

Our discussion of bilateral monopoly contended that if unions and management were reasonable, they would see the harm from costly actions and agree to outcomes on the possibilities frontier. The threat of a strike might influence the eventual outcome negotiated, but the strikes themselves should not occur for this would not be in the interests of unions or management.

In reality, strikes occur because negotiations do not always run so smoothly. Negotiations break down. During times of disagreement, unions wish to demonstrate their resolve by striking and being willing to forgo income. Management also wants to demonstrate to the union that it can weather a strike and hold out as well. In this case, disagreements are the result of 'brinkmanship' – an attempt by both parties to temporarily use threats to demonstrate the value of their work to the firm.

If both unions and management had a better understanding of the costs of strike action, brinkmanship might not occur. In this way, strikes can be seen as the result of a lack of information. Unions might believe that a company does not appreciate their full value. Management might believe that unions do not appreciate the willingness of their company's shareholders to hold out and earn high profits.

>>

Nonetheless, in the past – whether because of simple misunderstandings or differences in information – many workdays were lost to industrial action in Australia. Australia has always had government involvement in the resolution of industrial disputes. At its core is a dispute resolution body – the Industrial Relations Commission. Whenever a union contemplated strike action, the Commission's task was to step in and arbitrate the dispute. Its rulings were binding.

The arbitration system was strengthened considerably during the 1980s. Also during that time, the Labor government struck an Accord with the trade unions to agree to wage restraint. The result of this was a dramatic reduction in strike action. As depicted in Figure 20.3, this resulted in a reduction in workdays lost due to industrial disputes.

Figure 20.3 Industrial disputes in Australia

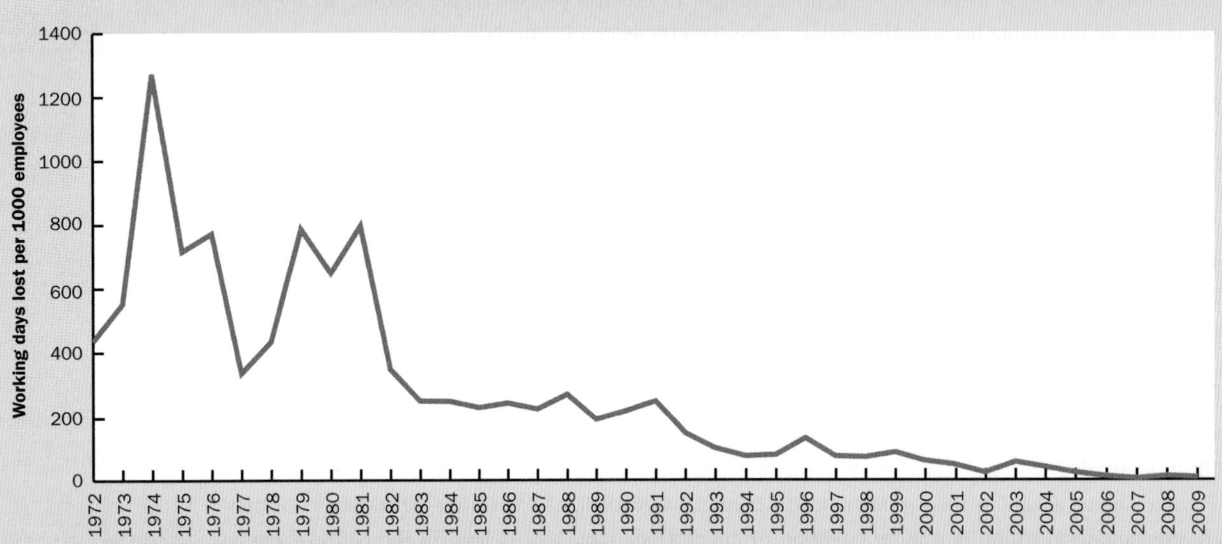

Source: Reserve Bank of Australia and Australian Bureau of Statistics, Cat. No. 6321.0.

Worker turnover

A second type of efficiency-wage theory emphasises the link between wages and worker turnover. Workers quit jobs for many reasons – to take jobs in other firms, to move to other parts of the country, to leave the labour force and so on. The frequency with which they quit depends on the entire set of incentives they face, including the benefits of leaving and the benefits of staying with their current employer. The more a firm pays its workers, the less often its workers will choose to leave. Thus, a firm can reduce turnover among its workers by paying them a high wage.

Why do firms care about turnover? The reason is that it is costly for firms to hire and train new workers. Moreover, even after they are trained, newly hired workers are not as productive as experienced workers. Firms with higher turnover, therefore, will tend to have higher production costs. Firms may find it profitable to pay wages above the equilibrium level in order to reduce turnover.

Worker effort

A third type of efficiency-wage theory emphasises the link between wages and worker effort. In many jobs, workers have some discretion over how hard to work. As a result, firms monitor the efforts of their workers and workers caught shirking their responsibilities are fired. But not all shirkers are caught immediately because monitoring workers is costly and imperfect. A firm can respond to this problem by paying wages above the equilibrium level. High wages make workers more eager to keep their jobs and, thereby, give workers an incentive to put forward their best effort.

This particular type of efficiency-wage theory is similar to the old Marxist idea of the 'reserve army of the unemployed'. Marx thought that employers benefited from unemployment because the threat of unemployment helped to discipline those workers who had jobs. In the worker-effort variant of efficiency-wage theory, unemployment fills a similar role. If the wage were at the level that balanced supply and demand, workers would have less reason to work hard, because if they were fired they could quickly find new jobs at the same wage. Therefore, firms find it profitable to raise wages above the equilibrium level. This causes unemployment while providing an incentive for workers not to shirk their responsibilities.

Worker quality

A fourth and final type of efficiency-wage theory emphasises the link between wages and worker quality. When a firm hires new workers, it cannot perfectly gauge the quality of the applicants. By paying a high wage, the firm attracts a better pool of workers to apply for its jobs.

To see how this might work, consider a simple example. Waterwell Company owns one well and needs one worker to pump water from the well. Two workers, Bill and Ben, are interested in the job. Bill, a proficient worker, is willing to work for $10 per hour. Below that wage, he would rather start his own lawn-mowing business. Ben, a complete incompetent, is willing to work for anything above $2 per hour. Below that wage, he would rather sit on the beach. Economists say that Bill's *reservation wage* – the lowest wage he would accept – is $10, and Ben's reservation wage is $2.

What wage should the firm set? If the firm were interested in minimising labour costs, it would set the wage at $2 per hour. At this wage, the quantity of workers supplied (one) would balance the quantity demanded. Ben would take the job, and Bill would not apply for it. Yet suppose Waterwell knows that only one of these two applicants is competent, but it does not know whether it is Bill or Ben. If the firm hires the incompetent worker, he will damage the well, causing the firm huge losses. In this case, the firm has a better strategy than paying the equilibrium wage of $2 and hiring Ben. It can offer $10 per hour, inducing both Bill and Ben to apply for the job. By choosing randomly between these two applicants and turning the other away, the firm has a fifty-fifty chance of hiring the competent worker. In contrast, if the firm offers any lower wage, it is sure to hire the incompetent worker.

This story illustrates a general phenomenon. When a firm has an excess supply of workers, it might seem profitable to reduce the wage it is offering. But by reducing the wage, the firm induces an adverse change in the mix of workers. In this case, at a wage of $10, Waterwell has two workers applying for one job. But if Waterwell responds to this excess supply by reducing the wage, the competent worker (who has better alternative opportunities) will not apply. Thus, it is profitable for the firm to pay a wage above the level that balances supply and demand.

CASESTUDY

Henry Ford and the generous $5-a-day wage

Henry Ford was an industrial visionary. As founder of the Ford Motor Company, he was responsible for introducing modern techniques of production. Rather than building cars with small teams of skilled craftsmen, Ford built cars on assembly lines in which unskilled workers were taught to perform the same simple tasks over and over again. The output of this assembly process was the Model T Ford, one of the most famous early cars.

In 1914, Ford introduced another innovation – the $5 workday. This might not seem like much today, but back then $5 was about twice the going wage. It was also far above the wage that balanced supply and demand. When the new $5-a-day wage was announced, long lines of job seekers formed outside the Ford factories. The number of workers willing to work at this wage far exceeded the number of workers Ford needed.

Ford's high-wage policy had many of the effects predicted by efficiency-wage theory. Staff turnover fell, absenteeism fell and productivity rose. Workers were so much more efficient that Ford's production costs were lower even though wages were higher. Thus, paying a wage above the equilibrium level was profitable for the firm. Henry Ford himself called the $5-a-day wage 'one of the finest cost-cutting moves we ever made'.

Historical accounts of this episode are also consistent with efficiency-wage theory. A historian of the early Ford Motor Company wrote:

> Ford and his associates freely declared on many occasions that the high-wage policy turned out to be good business. By this they meant that it had improved the discipline of the workers, given them a more loyal interest in the institution, and raised their personal efficiency.

An early Ford assembly line

Source: Library of Congress Prints and Photographs Division, Washington D.C. 20540 USA.

Why did it take Henry Ford to introduce this efficiency wage? Why were other firms not already taking advantage of this seemingly profitable business strategy? According to some analysts, Ford's decision was closely linked to his use of the assembly line. Workers organised in an assembly line are highly interdependent. If one worker is absent or works slowly, other workers are less able to complete their own tasks. Thus, while assembly lines made production more efficient, they also raised the importance of low worker turnover, high worker quality and high worker effort. As a result, paying efficiency wages may have been a better strategy for the Ford Motor Company than for other businesses at the time.

Give four explanations for why firms might find it profitable to pay wages above the level that balances quantity of labour supplied and quantity of labour demanded.

The economics of discrimination

discrimination
the offering of different opportunities to similar individuals who differ only by race, ethnic group, sex, age or other personal characteristics

Another source of differences in wages is discrimination. **Discrimination** occurs when the marketplace offers different opportunities to similar individuals who differ only by race, ethnic group, sex, age or other personal characteristics. Discrimination reflects some people's prejudice against certain groups in society. Although discrimination is an emotionally charged topic that often generates heated debate, economists try to study the topic objectively in order to separate myth from reality.

Measuring labour-market discrimination

How much does discrimination in labour markets affect the earnings of different groups of workers? This question is important, but answering it is not easy.

It might seem natural to gauge the amount of discrimination in labour markets by looking at the average wages of different groups. For instance, in recent years the income of the average Indigenous worker in Australia has been about 55 per cent to 65 per cent of the income of the average worker in the rest of the population. The wage of the average female worker has been about 25 per cent less than the wage of the average male worker. These wage differentials are sometimes presented in political debate as evidence that many employers discriminate against Indigenous people and women.

Yet there is an obvious problem with this approach. Even in a labour market free of discrimination, different people have different wages. People differ in the amount of human capital they have and in the kinds of work they are able and willing to do. The wage differences we observe in the economy are, to a large extent, attributable to the determinants of equilibrium wages we discussed in the last section. Simply observing differences in wages among broad groups says little about the prevalence of discrimination.

Consider, for example, the role of human capital. A study by Alison Preston, published in the *Economic Record* in 1997, estimated that about 27 per cent of the wage gap could be explained by human capital factors such as qualifications and experience. That is, part of the reason men appeared to earn more than women was due to the fact that women were less likely to gain higher education qualifications. Similar gaps in education have been reported for Aborigines.

Human capital acquired in the form of job experience also leads to wage differences. Women tend to have less job experience on average compared to men. One reason is that female labour force participation has increased over the past few decades. Because of this historic change, the average female worker today is younger than the average male worker. In addition, women are more likely to interrupt their careers to raise children. For both reasons, the experience of the average female worker is less than the experience of the average male worker.

Yet another source of wage differences is compensating differentials. Men and women do not always choose the same type of work and this fact may help explain some of the earnings differential between men and women. For example, women are more likely to be secretaries and men are more likely to be truck drivers. The relative wages of secretaries and truck drivers depend in part on the working conditions of each job. Because these non-monetary aspects are hard to measure, it is difficult to gauge the practical importance of compensating differentials in explaining the wage differences that we observe.

In the end, the study of wage differences among groups does not establish any clear conclusion about the prevalence of discrimination in Australian labour markets. Most economists believe that some of the observed wage differentials are attributable to discrimination, but there is no consensus about how much. The only conclusion about which economists are in consensus is a negative one – because the differences in average wages among groups in part reflect differences in human capital and job characteristics, they do not by themselves say anything about how much discrimination there is in the labour market.

Of course, differences in human capital among groups of workers may themselves reflect discrimination. The inferior schooling historically available to Indigenous students, for instance, may be traced to prejudice on the part of governments and to regional funding differences. But this kind of discrimination occurs long before the worker enters the labour market. In this case, the disease is political, even if the symptom is economic.

Discrimination by employers

Let's now turn from measurement to the economic forces that lie behind discrimination in labour markets. If one group in society receives a lower wage than another group, even after controlling for human capital and job characteristics, who is to blame for this differential?

The answer is not obvious. It might seem natural to blame employers for discriminatory wage differences. After all, employers make the hiring decisions that determine labour demand and wages. If some groups of workers earn lower wages than we would otherwise expect, then it seems that employers are responsible. Yet many economists are sceptical of this easy answer. They believe that competitive market economies provide a natural antidote to employer discrimination. That antidote is called the profit motive.

Imagine an economy in which workers are differentiated by their hair colour. Blondes and brunettes have the same skills, experience and work ethic. Yet, because of discrimination, employers prefer not to hire workers with blonde hair. Thus, the demand for blondes is lower than it otherwise would be. As a result, blondes earn a lower wage than brunettes.

How long can this wage differential persist? In this economy, there is an easy way for a firm to beat its competitors – it can hire blonde workers. By hiring blondes, a firm pays lower wages and thus has lower costs than firms that hire brunettes. Over time, more and more 'blonde' firms enter the market to take advantage of this cost advantage. The existing 'brunette' firms have higher costs and, therefore, begin to lose money when faced with the new competitors. These losses induce the brunette firms to go out of business. Eventually, the entry of blonde firms and the exit of brunette firms cause the demand for blonde workers to rise and the demand for brunette workers to fall. This process continues until the wage differential disappears.

Put simply, business owners who care only about making money are at an advantage when competing against those who also care about discriminating. As a result, firms that do not discriminate tend to replace those that do. In this way, competitive markets have a natural remedy for employer discrimination.

CASESTUDY

Segregated streetcars and the profit motive

In the early twentieth century, streetcars in many southern US cities were segregated by race. White passengers sat in the front of the streetcars, and black passengers sat in the back. What do you suppose caused and maintained this discriminatory practice? And how was this practice viewed by the firms that ran the streetcars?

In a 1986 article in the *Journal of Economic History*, economic historian Jennifer Roback looked at these questions. Roback found that the segregation of races on streetcars was the result of laws that required such segregation. Before these laws were passed, racial discrimination in seating was rare. It was far more common to segregate smokers and non-smokers.

Moreover, the firms that ran the streetcars often opposed the laws requiring racial segregation. Providing separate seating for different races raised the firms' costs and reduced their profit. One railroad company manager complained to the city council that, under the segregation laws, 'the company has to haul around a good deal of empty space'.

Here is how Roback describes the situation in one southern US city:

> The railroad company did not initiate the segregation policy and was not at all eager to abide by it. State legislation, public agitation, and a threat to arrest the president of the railroad were all required to induce them to separate the races on their cars ... There is no indication that the management was motivated by belief in civil rights or racial equality. The evidence indicates their primary motives were economic; separation was costly ... Officials of the company may or may not have disliked blacks, but they were not willing to forgo the profits necessary to indulge such prejudice.

The story of southern streetcars illustrates a general lesson – business owners are usually more interested in making profit than in discriminating against a particular group. When firms engage in discriminatory practices, the ultimate source of the discrimination often lies not with the firms themselves but elsewhere. In this particular case, the streetcar companies segregated whites and blacks because discriminatory laws, which the companies opposed, required them to do so.

Discrimination by customers and governments

Although the profit motive is a strong force acting to eliminate discriminatory wage differentials, there are limits to its corrective abilities. Here we consider two of the most important limits: *customer preferences* and *government policies*.

To see how customer preferences for discrimination can affect wages, consider again our imaginary economy with blondes and brunettes. Suppose that restaurant owners discriminate against blondes when hiring waiters. As a result, blonde waiters earn lower wages than brunette waiters. In this case, a restaurant could open up with blonde waiters and charge lower prices. If customers cared only about the quality and price of their meals, the discriminatory firms would be driven out of business and the wage differential would disappear.

On the other hand, it is possible that customers prefer being served by brunette waiters. If this preference for discrimination is strong, the entry of blonde restaurants need not succeed in eliminating the wage differential between brunettes and blondes. That is, if customers have discriminatory preferences, a discriminatory wage differential is consistent with a competitive market. An economy with such discrimination would contain two types of restaurants. Restaurants that hire blonde-haired waiters have lower costs and charge lower prices, and restaurants that hire brunettes have higher costs and charge higher prices. Customers who did not care about the hair colour of their waiters would be attracted to the lower prices at the blonde restaurants. Bigoted customers would go to the brunette restaurants. They would pay for their discriminatory preference in the form of higher prices.

Another way for discrimination to persist in competitive markets is for the government to prescribe discriminatory practices. If, for instance, the government passed a law stating that blondes could wash dishes in restaurants but could not work as waiters, then a wage differential could persist in a competitive market. The example of segregated streetcars in the forgoing case study is one example of government-decreed discrimination. More recently, before South Africa abandoned its system of apartheid, blacks were prohibited from working in some jobs. Discriminatory governments pass such laws in order to suppress the normal equalising force of free and competitive markets.

To sum up – *competitive markets contain a natural remedy for employer discrimination. The entry of firms that care only about profit tends to eliminate discriminatory wage differentials. These wage differentials persist in competitive markets only when customers are willing to pay to maintain the discriminatory practice or when the government mandates it.*

CASESTUDY

Can asymmetric information explain discrimination?

Economic theorists have argued that asymmetric information can sometimes explain discrimination. For instance, employers might be uncertain about the quality of workers. In the absence of other information, employers might use the worker's sex, ethnicity or racial group as an indicator of ability. For instance, an employer might believe workers from a minority group have a lower education level and pay them less. Workers from that group considering investing in more education are deterred from so doing because of this discrimination. They refrain from education, thus reinforcing the negative stereotype.

In a 1998 article in the *Journal of Public Economics*, Patrick Francois argued that such statistical discrimination may explain gender-based earning differences. He supposes that when men and women form households they can either reap the benefits of household trade with one person staying at home while the other works, or hire outsiders to do those jobs, for example, a nanny or cleaning service. The question he then examines is: How does this affect efficiency wages that might be paid to men or women? Suppose that employers believe (rightly or wrongly) that women's partners are more likely to be working as well. When those employers set wages, they set them high enough to make those workers wish to expend effort in their jobs rather than shirk and risk being fired. However, for a person with a partner at home, the costs of being fired are greater – the family loses all its household income. This means that an employer can pay that worker a lower efficiency wage.

The consequence of this is that, if employers believe that it is more likely that men have partners at home than women do, and it is hard for them to observe this for individuals prior to hiring, then men will be less risky to hire than women. This means that women will have less chance of being hired in high-paying efficiency-wage jobs.

Statistical discrimination based on asymmetric information can explain why earnings differentials between different groups arise, even if there is competition between firms and there are no intrinsic differences between workers from distinct groups. As such, it can rationalise policies of affirmative action designed to redress negative stereotypes.

Problems of asymmetric information occur in a variety of markets. We discuss asymmetric information and the economic issues that it raises in detail in chapter 23.

Q Why is it hard to establish whether a group of workers is being discriminated against? Explain how profit-maximising firms tend to eliminate discriminatory wage differentials. How might a discriminatory wage differential persist?

Conclusion

In competitive markets, workers earn a wage equal to the value of their marginal contribution to the production of goods and services. There are, however, many things that affect the value of the marginal product. Firms pay more for workers who are more talented, more diligent, more experienced and more educated because these workers are more productive. Firms might also pay more to workers who are members of unions. In the absence of complete information, firms may give workers more pay to attract those of high ability or motivate them to work hard. Firms pay less to those workers against whom customers discriminate. They pay them less because these workers contribute less to revenue.

The theory of the labour market we have developed in the last two chapters explains why some workers earn higher wages than other workers. The theory does not say that the resulting distribution of income is equitable, fair or desirable in any way. That is the topic we take up in chapter 21.

Summary

- Workers earn different wages for many reasons. To some extent, wage differentials compensate workers for job attributes. Other things being equal, workers in hard, unpleasant jobs get paid more than workers in easy, pleasant jobs.
- Workers with more human capital get paid more than workers with less human capital. The return to accumulating human capital is high and has increased over the past decade.
- Although years of education, experience and job characteristics affect earnings as theory predicts, there is much variation in earnings that cannot be explained by things that economists can measure. The unexplained variation in earnings is largely attributable to natural ability, effort and chance.
- Some economists have suggested that better educated workers earn higher wages not because education raises productivity but because workers with high natural ability use education as a way to signal their high ability to employers. If this signalling theory were correct, then increasing the educational attainment of all workers would not raise the overall level of wages.
- Whether a workforce is unionised or not can have an impact on wages. Unions can act like a monopolist in the labour market, restricting employment to raise wages. However, unlike product market monopolists, unions might be concerned about the lost employment. Such concern limits their ability to control wages.
- When a union negotiates with a single firm – a monopsonist – we have a situation called bilateral monopoly. Resulting negotiations over wages and work conditions are likely to lead to agreements on the possibilities frontier. However, where on the frontier the union and management end up depends on their relative bargaining power.
- Efficiency wages can explain why workers earn above-equilibrium wages. According to this theory, firms find it profitable to pay wages above the equilibrium level. High wages can improve worker health, lower worker turnover, increase worker effort and raise worker quality.
- Some differences in earnings are attributable to discrimination on the basis of race, sex or other factors. Measuring the amount of discrimination is difficult, however, because one must correct for differences in human capital and job characteristics.
- Competitive markets tend to limit the impact of discrimination on wages. If the wages of a group of workers are lower than those of another group for reasons not related to marginal productivity, then non-discriminatory firms will be more profitable than discriminatory firms. Profit-maximising behaviour, therefore, can act to reduce discriminatory wage differentials. Discrimination can persist in competitive markets if customers are willing to pay more to discriminatory firms or if the government passes laws requiring firms to discriminate.

Key concepts

bilateral monopoly
collective bargaining
compensating differential
discrimination
efficiency wages
human capital
monopsony
possibilities frontier
strike
union

Questions for review

1. Why do coalminers get paid more than other workers with similar amounts of education?
2. In what sense is education a type of capital?
3. How might education raise a worker's wage without raising the worker's productivity?
4. What limits a union's ability to exercise monopoly power over wages?
5. Why is it unlikely the parties in a bilateral monopoly will agree to outcomes inside the possibilities frontier?
6. What claims do advocates of unions make to argue that unions are good for the economy?
7. Explain four ways in which a firm might increase its profits by raising the wages it pays.
8. What difficulties arise in deciding whether a group of workers has a lower wage because of discrimination?
9. Do the forces of economic competition tend to intensify or reduce discrimination on the basis of race?
10. Give an example of how discrimination might persist in a competitive market.

Problems and applications

1. University students sometimes work during their holidays for private firms or the government in areas relating to their chosen careers. Many of these positions are menial and pay little.
   a. What is the opportunity cost of taking such a job?
   b. Explain why students are willing to take these low-paying jobs.
   c. If you were to compare the earnings later in life of workers who as students had worked at menial jobs in the industry that interested them and those who had taken holiday jobs that paid more, what would you expect to find?
2. A basic finding of labour economics is that workers who have more experience in the labour force are paid more than workers who have less experience but the same amount of formal education. Why might this be so? Some studies have also found that experience at the same job has an extra positive influence on wages. Explain.
3. The wages of university-educated workers dropped during the 1970s, rose in the early 1980s, and then dropped and rose again towards the end of the 1980s. Yet economists believe that the demand for university-educated workers increased fairly steadily during this time. What could explain the pattern of wage changes?
4. Relative to the industrialised countries, developing countries have more unskilled workers and fewer skilled workers. Would you expect the value of skills to be relatively higher or lower in developing countries than in industrialised countries? Explain.
5. At some universities, academics in business-related disciplines receive higher salaries than academics in some other fields.
   a. Why might this be true?
   b. Some other universities have a policy of paying equal salaries to academics in all fields. At some of these universities, academics in business-related disciplines have lighter teaching loads than academics in some other fields. What role do the differences in teaching loads play?
6. Sara works for Steve, whom she hates because of his snobbish attitude. Yet when she looks for other jobs, the best she can do is find a job paying $10 000 less than her current salary. Should she take the job? Analyse Sara's situation from an economic point of view.

7 When recording devices were first invented almost 100 years ago, musicians could suddenly supply their music to large audiences at low cost. How do you suppose this event affected the income of the best musicians? How do you suppose it affected the income of average musicians?

8 A union and a mining company are negotiating over wages and conditions. The mining company would like to run the mine over a longer period of the day. This would require 10 miners to work at night. The company argues that the increased productivity would result in $100 000 additional yearly profits for the firm. The miners, however, believe that being able to work during the day rather than at night is worth about $8000 a year to each. This is the value of being able to spend more time with their families.

a What will happen in negotiations over night work? Can the company convince the union to accept this?

b How would your answer change if the relative value of day work was $12 000 for each miner?

9 Do you think that firms in small towns or cities have more market power in hiring? Do you think that firms generally have more market power in hiring today than 50 years ago or less? How do you think this change over time has affected the role of unions in the economy? Explain.

10 Alan runs a management consulting firm. He hires primarily female economists because, he says, 'they will work for less than comparable men because women have fewer job options'. Is Alan's behaviour admirable or despicable? If more employers were like Alan, what would happen to the wage differential between men and women?

11 Suppose that all of the difference in earnings between Indigenous workers and other Australian workers could be attributed to the difference in years of schooling and school quality. Would this imply that discrimination plays no role in the difference in earnings across racial groups? Why or why not?

12 Suppose that all young women were channelled into careers as secretaries, nurses and teachers; at the same time, young men were encouraged to consider these three careers and many others as well.

a Draw a diagram showing the combined labour market for secretaries, nurses and teachers. Draw a diagram showing the combined labour market for all other fields. In which market is the wage higher? Do men or women receive higher wages on average?

b Now suppose that society changed and encouraged both young women and young men to consider a wide range of careers. Over time, what effect would this change have on the wages in the two markets you illustrated in part (a)? What effect would the change have on the average wages of men and women?

13 This chapter considers the economics of discrimination by employers, customers and governments. Now consider discrimination by workers. Suppose that some brunette workers did not like working with blonde workers. Do you think this worker discrimination could explain lower wages for blonde workers? If such a wage differential existed, what would a profit-maximising entrepreneur do? If there were many such entrepreneurs, what would happen over time?

Search me!

Search me!

When accessing information about microeconomics use the following keywords in any combinations you require:

- efficiency wages
- human capital

CourseMate

CourseMate

For more multimedia resources and activities on economics, visit the Economics CourseMate website.

21

Income inequity and poverty

Learning objectives

In this chapter you will:

- examine the degree of economic inequality in our society
- consider some problems that arise when measuring economic inequality
- see how political philosophers view the government's role in redistributing income
- consider the various policies aimed at helping poor families escape poverty.

'The only difference between the rich and other people is that the rich have more money', Mary Colum, the Irish critic and short-story writer, once said to novelist Ernest Hemingway. Maybe so. But this claim leaves many questions unanswered. The gap between rich and poor is a fascinating and important topic of study – for the comfortable rich, for the struggling poor and for the aspiring and worried middle class.

From the previous two chapters you should have some understanding about why different people have different incomes. A person's earnings depend on the supply of and demand for that person's labour, which in turn depend on natural ability, human capital, compensating differentials, union membership, incentive effects, discrimination and so on. Because wages and salaries make up about two-thirds of the total income in the Australian economy, the factors that determine wages are also largely responsible for determining how the economy's total income is distributed among the various members of society. In other words, they determine who is rich and who is poor.

In this chapter we discuss the distribution of income. As we shall see, this topic raises some fundamental questions about the role of economic policy. One of the *Ten Lessons from Economics* in chapter 1 is that governments can sometimes improve market outcomes. This possibility is particularly important when considering the distribution of income. The invisible hand of the marketplace acts to allocate resources efficiently, but it does not necessarily ensure that resources are allocated fairly. As a result, many economists – though not all – believe that the government should redistribute income to achieve greater equality. In doing so, however, the government runs into another of the *Ten Lessons from Economics* – people face trade-offs. When the government introduces policies to make the distribution of income more equitable, it distorts incentives, alters behaviour and makes the allocation of resources less efficient.

Our discussion of the distribution of income proceeds in three steps. First, we assess how much inequality there is in our society. Second, we consider some different views about what role the government should play in altering the distribution of income. Third, we discuss various public policies aimed at helping society's poorest members.

The measurement of inequality

We begin our study of the distribution of income by considering four questions of measurement:

- How much inequality is there in our society?
- How many people live in poverty?
- What problems arise in measuring the amount of inequality?
- How often do people move among income classes?

These measurement questions are the natural starting point from which to discuss public policies aimed at changing the distribution of income.

Australian income inequality

There are various ways to describe the distribution of income in the economy. Table 21.1 presents a particularly simple way. It shows the percentage of households that fall into each of nine income categories. You can use this table to find where your household lies in the income distribution.

For examining differences in the income distribution over time or across countries, economists find it more useful to present the income data as in Table 21.2. To see how to interpret this table, consider

Table 21.1 Distribution of income in Australia, 2007–08

Gross weekly income	% of households
Under $199	2.15
$200–$399	10.70
$400–$599	10.18
$600–$799	9.10
$800–$999	7.43
$1000–$1199	7.32
$1200–$1599	13.73
$1600–$1999	11.03
$2000–$2499	10.20
$2500 and over	18.16

Source: Australian Bureau of Statistics, Cat. No. 6523.0, 2007–08.

Table 21.2 Income inequity in Australia

Year	Bottom fifth	Second fifth	Third fifth	Fourth fifth	Top fifth
1999–2000	3.8	9.0	15.0	23.8	48.5
1994–95	3.6	9.3	15.2	24.0	47.9
1990	4.8	9.7	15.5	23.9	46.2
1986	4.8	9.7	15.9	24.4	45.3
1981–82	4.6	9.8	16.6	24.8	44.2

This table shows the percentage of total before-tax income received by families in each fifth of the income distribution.

Sources: *Income Distribution, Australia, 1999–2000*, ABS 6523.0; Income Distribution, Australia, various (ABS 6523.0) in 'Are incomes becoming more unequal? Are real incomes rising?' Parliament of Australia, Current Issues Brief 15, 1999–2000, and United Nations University, World Institute for Development Economics Research (2004).

the following thought experiment. Imagine that you lined up all the families in the economy according to their annual income. Then you divided the families into five equal groups: the bottom fifth, the second fifth, the middle fifth, the fourth fifth and the top fifth. Next you calculated the share of total income that each group of families received. In this way, you could produce the numbers in Table 21.2.

These numbers give us a way of gauging how the economy's total income is distributed. If income were equally distributed across all families, each one-fifth of families would receive one-fifth

(20 per cent) of income. If all income were concentrated among just a few families, the top fifth would receive 100 per cent and the other fifths would receive 0 per cent. The actual economy, of course, is between these two extremes. The table shows that in 1999–2000 the bottom fifth of all families received 3.8 per cent of all income and the top fifth of all families received 48.5 per cent of all income. In other words, even though the top and bottom fifths include the same number of families, the top fifth has more than 10 times as much income as the bottom fifth.

Table 21.2 also shows the distribution of income in various years beginning in 1981–82. At first glance, the distribution of income appears to have been stable. Over this time, the bottom fifth of families has received about 4 per cent to 5 per cent of income and the top fifth has received about 40 per cent to 44 per cent of income. Closer inspection of the table reveals a trend in the degree of inequality. From 1981 to 2000, the share of the bottom fifth fell from 4.6 per cent to 3.8 per cent and the share of the top fifth rose from 44.2 per cent to 48.5 per cent.

In chapter 20 we discussed some of the reasons for this increase in inequality. Increases in international trade with low-wage countries and changes in technology have tended to reduce the demand for unskilled labour and raise the demand for skilled labour. As a result, the wages of unskilled workers have fallen relative to the wages of skilled workers and this change in relative wages has increased inequality in family incomes.

IN THE NEWS . . .

EMPLOYMENT PROSPECTS FOR INDIGENOUS AUSTRALIANS

Indigenous Australians are one of our most disadvantaged groups. Official unemployment among Indigenous Australians is approximately three times higher than for the rest of the population. But research from the 1990s showed that unofficial unemployment is much higher. This article looks at the gap between official and real unemployment. While the research is almost 20 years old, and the CDEP scheme discussed in the article has been operating for more than 30 years, there has been little (if any) improvement since the article was written.

Indigenous and invisible

by Mark Davis

Aborigines are the most disadvantaged group in the Australian labour market. Their real rate of unemployment is 34 per cent – and expected to rise to 48 per cent by 2006.

It has been called a demographic time bomb ticking away in Australia's Aboriginal and Torres Strait Islander communities.

While the Australian population as a whole is rapidly ageing, the reverse is true for the country's indigenous population, a fact with profound implications for the welfare of Aboriginal Australians.

Aborigines are already the most disadvantaged group in the Australian labour market.

In 1996, the latest available statistics, Aboriginal unemployment stood at 23 per cent. But the real unemployment rate for the indigenous population – when those in work-for-the-dole programs were included – was 34 per cent.

It was figures like these which prompted the Workplace Relations Minister, Peter Reith, to warn the Prime Minister, John Howard, last December that Aborigines were in danger of being permanently marginalised from the labour market, with high social costs.

Yet as bad as the current Aboriginal unemployment numbers are, on the Federal Government's own policy settings for indigenous labour market programs they are set to get much worse.

Recent demographic research shows that the Aboriginal working-age population is growing more than twice as fast as the non-indigenous working-age population.

>>

And with the Government winding back growth in the main Aboriginal labour market program, the number of new jobs created for Aborigines is not expected to keep pace with population growth.

A report by the Australian National University's Centre for Aboriginal Economic Policy Research estimates that 64 000 young Aborigines will reach working age over the decade from 1996 to 2006.

This will boost the size of the indigenous workforce by 28 per cent, compared with expected growth in the entire labour force of 11.6 per cent over the same period.

The authors of the ANU report – Dr John Taylor and Dr Boyd Hunter, two of the country's leading experts on Aboriginal labour-market programs – forecast that on current trends the official Aboriginal unemployment rate will reach 28 per cent by 2006.

They estimate that the real unemployment rate will reach a chilling 48 per cent in 2006 (when Aborigines in work-for-the-dole programs are classed as unemployed, consistent with the treatment of non-Aborigines in similar programs).

These are difficult figures to comprehend. To grasp the magnitude of the unemployment problem in Australia's 390 000-strong indigenous population, project the statistics across the whole of the Australian population – then the jobless figure would stand at around 4.5 million.

The grim outlook for Aboriginal labour-market outcomes stems from three factors: Demographics, disadvantage and discrimination.

The demographic trend reflects their relatively high birth rates, coupled with a relatively low life expectancy.

According to demographers Dr Habtemariam Tesfaghiorghis and Dr Alan Gray, virtually all population growth in the Aboriginal community from the 1980s into the new millennium will be concentrated in the 15- to 64-year-old working-age bracket.

'The implications in terms of employment have been shown to be enormous,' they wrote in one of the first research papers to identify the looming demographic shift in the Aboriginal population.

And while demography boosts the number of Aborigines entering the workforce, disadvantage makes it difficult for them to find jobs.

Aborigines are disadvantaged on virtually all the dimensions affecting people's chances of prospering in the labour market – health, education, training, vocational skills and work experience, all the elements making up what economists call the 'human capital' that individuals bring to the labour market.

In labour-market terms, Aborigines also suffer from so-called 'locational disadvantage' – they are relatively concentrated in remote areas and country towns where there are few jobs.

The 1996 census shows that only 30 per cent of the indigenous population live in major urban areas, compared with 63 per cent of the total Australian population.

Then there is the reality of discrimination against Aborigines.

Sophisticated econometric analysis has shown that locational and human-capital disadvantages do not fully account for the poor labour-market outcomes experienced by Aborigines.

A University of Canberra economist, Dr Anne Daly, analysed data from the 1986 census and found that the probability of working-age Aboriginal males being in jobs was 35 percentage points lower than for non-Aboriginal males.

However, her statistical analysis showed that only 7 percentage points of this 35-point gap could be explained by the differences between the two groups in education, age, marital status, location and language.

In a second study, using data from the 1991 census, Daly compared earnings of Aborigines and non-Aborigines in full-time jobs. After allowing for the effect of differences in 'human capital', she still found that Aboriginal males earned 9 per cent less than their non-Aboriginal counterparts.

A recent paper by ANU's Jeff Borland and Boyd Hunter, using data collected in 1994, found that some of the unexplained disparity in labour-market outcomes could be accounted for by the higher arrest rates among Aborigines.

But Borland and Hunter's statistical analysis still concluded that about two-thirds of the difference in employment-to-population rates resulted from different treatment rather than different attributes.

Peter Reith is concerned about the ability of labour-market 'insiders' – people already in secure jobs – to negotiate wages and employment costs up to levels that bar unemployed 'outsiders' from getting jobs.

Aborigines may well be the ultimate labour-market outsiders in Australia.

Yet despite the magnitude of the problem, Aborigines have been largely invisible in the public debate over unemployment. This is because the monthly 'headline' labour-force statistics do not measure labour-market outcomes for Aborigines, leaving the five-yearly census as the only reliable source of data.

In a letter to Howard in December, Reith identified Aborigines as one of the groups needing tailored government assistance.

'It is clear that the present labour-market programs are not providing satisfactory outcomes,' Reith wrote of indigenous unemployment.

He plans to visit Aboriginal communities to discuss the issue and has asked his department to prepare a report on indigenous employment initiatives.

Whether this produces any shift in the Government's approach to indigenous labour-market issues remains to be seen. The reality is that since coming to office, the Government's main policy change in this area has worsened the indigenous employment problem.

Since 1996 the Government has significantly slowed down the rate of expansion in a key Aboriginal labour-market program, the Community Development Employment Projects (CDEP).

CDEP is a work-for-the-dole or 'workfare' scheme in which unemployment and welfare benefits formerly paid to individual Aborigines are instead pooled and paid to local Aboriginal community groups. These funds are then used to pay wages to individuals for working on projects such as infrastructure construction and in ventures including tourism, contracting, retailing, and textile and artefact production.

CDEP was established by the Fraser Government in 1977. It grew dramatically in the late 1980s and early 1990s. At the time of the 1996 census it accounted for around 12 000 of the 82 000 Aborigines officially classified as being in employment.

But once the Howard Government came to office in 1996, it halted the expansion of CDEP and only funded so-called 'natural growth' in the number of places in the scheme.

In last year's Budget, the Government rejected calls by the Aboriginal and Torres Strait Islander Commission to fund an extra 3200 places by 2001–02.

The Government's lack of enthusiasm defies a glowing report on the program by the former chief of Australia's peak employer group, Ian Spicer.

Commissioned by the Government to review CDEP, Spicer concluded: 'Across Australia CDEP has been critical to developing an improved sense of pride in community and culture, and has provided the basis for acquiring greater skills, employment and enterprise development resulting in ongoing social and economic growth.

'In each of the regions where CDEP exists it has made a significant contribution to addressing the unemployment situation of indigenous people. It has, in recent years, been responsible for two-thirds of the jobs created for indigenous Australians.'

The Government's attitude, together with the secular trend for reduced employment growth in the public sector, throws the burden of Aboriginal job creation onto the private sector.

ATSIC has recently forged new links between its labour-market and training programs and private sector employers such as Rio Tinto and Pasminco.

But ANU's John Taylor and Boyd Hunter argue that the major policy hurdle in promoting private-sector employment of Aborigines is geography.

'This is because the majority of indigenous people remain widely scattered across non-metropolitan regions, while new business activity and growth in private-sector employment is increasingly focused on a few mega-metropolitan areas.'

Source: Mark Davis/*Australian Financial Review*, 29 March 1999.

CASESTUDY

The women's movement and income distribution

Over the past several decades, there has been a dramatic change in women's roles in the Australian economy. The percentage of married women who hold jobs has risen from about 12 per cent in the 1950s to around 70 per cent in the late 2000s. As full-time homemakers have become less common, a woman's earnings have become a more important determinant of the total income of a typical family.

Although the women's movement has led to more equality between men and women regarding access to education and jobs, it has also led to less equality in family incomes. The reason is that the rise in women's labour force participation has not been the same across all income groups. In particular, the women's movement has had its greatest impact on younger women and women from high-income households. Married women over 50 years old are much less likely to have a job than younger married women. Women from low-income households have long had high rates of participation in the labour force, even in the 1950s, and their behaviour has changed much less.

In this sense, the women's movement has changed the behaviour of the partners of high-income men. In the 1950s, a male executive or doctor was likely to marry a woman who would stay at home and raise the children. Today, the partner of a male executive or doctor is more likely to be an executive or doctor herself. The result is that rich households have become even richer, a pattern that raises inequality in family incomes.

As this example shows, there are social as well as economic determinants of the distribution of income. Moreover, the simplistic view that 'income inequality is bad' can be misleading. Increasing the opportunities available to women was a good change for society, even if one effect was greater inequality in family incomes. When evaluating any change in the distribution of income, policymakers must look at the reasons for that change before deciding whether it presents a problem for society.

Equality for women has meant less equality for family incomes

Source: iStockphoto/Jacob Wackerhausen.

CASESTUDY

Income inequality around the world

How does the amount of income inequality in Australia compare with that in other countries? This question is interesting, but answering it is problematic. Not every country in the world collects data in the same way; for example, some countries collect data on individual incomes, whereas other countries collect data on family incomes. As a result, data from one country may not be strictly comparable with data from another. Whenever we find a difference between two countries, we can never be sure whether it reflects a true difference in the economies or merely a difference in the way data are collected.

With this warning in mind, consider Table 21.3, which compares the income distribution of Australia with that of eight other countries. The countries are ranked from the most equitable to the most inequitable. On the top of the list is Japan, where the richest fifth of the population has income only about three times that of the poorest fifth. On the bottom of the list is Brazil, where the richest fifth has income more than 25 times that of the poorest fifth. Although all countries have substantial inequality in income, the degree of inequality is not the same everywhere.

When countries are ranked by inequality, Australia ends up in the middle of the pack. The poorest fifth of the Australian population earns 3.8 per cent of total income, compared with 10.6 per cent in Japan and 2.45 per cent in Brazil.

The income distribution of Australia is almost the same as the income distribution in the United States. The similarity in the economic systems of these two countries is reflected in a similar distribution of income.

Table 21.3 Income inequality around the world

Country	Bottom fifth	Second fifth	Third fifth	Fourth fifth	Top fifth
Japan	10.6	14.2	17.6	22.0	35.7
South Korea	7.5	12.9	17.4	22.9	39.3
United Kingdom	6.6	11.3	15.9	22.4	43.8
China	5.9	10.2	15.1	22.2	46.6
New Zealand	2.7	10.0	16.3	24.1	46.9
Australia	3.8	9.0	15.0	23.8	48.5
United States	3.6	8.9	14.8	23.0	49.6
Malaysia	4.2	8.0	12.4	20.1	55.3
Brazil	2.4	5.6	9.4	16.8	65.7

This shows the percentage of total before-tax income received by families in each fifth of the income distribution.

Source: United Nations University, World Institute for Development Economics Research, World Income Inequality Database (WIID2 beta).

The poverty rate

A commonly used gauge of the distribution of income is the **poverty rate**. The poverty rate is the percentage of the population whose family income falls below an absolute level called the **poverty line**. Although there are many ways of measuring the poverty line, the most commonly used approach in Australia is that defined by the Commission of Inquiry into Poverty – or Henderson Commission – conducted in 1975. This measure was initially set at 56.5 per cent of average weekly earnings. This line is adjusted every year to account for changes in average earnings and it depends on family size. For instance, in 1973, the poverty line was set at $62.70 for a family consisting of two adults and two children. In 2008, the poverty line for such families was $710.14 per week.

poverty rate
the percentage of the population whose family income falls below an absolute level called the poverty line

poverty line
an absolute level of income set by the federal government for each family size below which a family is deemed to be in poverty

Search me!

▸ poverty line

To get some idea about what the poverty rate tells us, consider the data for 1972–73. In that year, the typical family had an income of about $111 per week and the poverty line for a family of four was $62.70. The poverty rate was 8.2 per cent. In other words, 8.2 per cent of the population were members of families with incomes below the poverty line for their family size.

The poverty rate has been rising over time. In 1981–82, the poverty rate was 9.2 per cent, rising to 12.8 per cent in 1989–90. Despite continued growth in average income, the poverty rate has drifted

Table 21.4 Poverty rates for income units, 1990 and 2000

	Below the before-housing half average income poverty line (Henderson equivalence scale)	
Income unit type	1990	2000
All units	11.3%	13.0%
Single people	13.7	18.3
Aged 15–24	16.2	15.9
25–49	9.2	11.5
50–64	10.6	11.5
65+	7.3	11.2
Couples without children	6.6	6.4
Couples with children	10.4	12.2
Sole one-parents with children	28.0	21.4

Source: Ann Harding, Rachel Lloyd & Harry Greenwell, Financial Disadvantage in Australia 1990 to 2000: The persistence of poverty in a decade of growth, NATSEM National Centre for Social and Economic Modelling, University of Canberra.

upwards to some extent. This lack of progress in reducing poverty in recent years is closely related to the increasing inequality we saw in Table 21.2. Although economic growth has raised the income of the typical family, the increase in inequality has prevented the poorest families from gaining an equal share in this greater economic prosperity.

Poverty is an economic malady that affects all groups within the population, but it does not affect all groups with equal frequency. Table 21.4 shows the poverty rates for types of family units. It reveals that poverty is related to the number of earners in a household and to age. In addition, it is well known that Indigenous Australians are much more likely to be poor, as are single mothers.

Problems in measuring inequality

Although data on the income distribution and the poverty rate help to give us some idea about the degree of inequality in our society, interpreting these data is not as straightforward as it might first appear. The data are based on households' annual incomes. What people care about, however, is not their incomes but their ability to maintain a good standard of living. For various reasons, data on the income distribution and the poverty rate give an incomplete picture of inequality in living standards. We examine these reasons below.

Expenditure-based versus income-based measures

In Australia, the poverty line is based on income. A better measure, some say, would be expenditure-based, providing a direct measure of living standards. This is done in the United States. There the poverty line is set at roughly three times the cost of providing an adequate diet. This line is adjusted every year to account for changes in the level of prices and, as in Australia, it is based on family size. However, the collection of data on expenditure is a difficult exercise and its use is the subject of considerable controversy.

The economic life cycle

Incomes vary predictably over people's lives. A young worker, especially one at university, has a low income. Income rises as the worker gains maturity and experience, peaks at around age 50, and then falls sharply when the worker retires at around age 65. This regular pattern of income variation is called the **life cycle**.

life cycle
the regular pattern of income variation over a person's life

Because people can borrow and save to smooth out life cycle changes in income, their standard of living in any year depends more on lifetime income than on that year's income. The young often borrow, perhaps to buy a house or car, and then repay the majority of the loan later when their incomes rise. People have their highest saving rates when they are middle-aged. Because people can save in anticipation of retirement, for example, through superannuation, the large declines in incomes at retirement need not lead to similar declines in the standard of living.

This normal life cycle pattern causes inequality in the distribution of annual income, but it does not represent true inequality in living standards. To gauge the inequality of living standards in our society, the distribution of lifetime incomes is more relevant than the distribution of annual incomes. Unfortunately, data on lifetime incomes are not readily available. When looking at any data on inequality, however, it is important to keep the life cycle in mind. Because a person's lifetime income smoothes out the highs and lows of the life cycle, lifetime incomes are more evenly distributed across the population than are annual incomes.

Transitory versus permanent income

Incomes vary over people's lives not only because of predictable life cycle variation but also because of random and transitory forces. One year disease kills off the South Australian grape crop and South Australian vineyards see their incomes fall temporarily. At the same time, the South Australian disease drives up the price of wine and Victorian vineyards see their incomes temporarily rise. The next year the reverse might happen.

Just as people can borrow and lend to smooth out life cycle variation in income, they can also borrow and lend to smooth out transitory variation in income. When Victorian vineyards experience a good year, they would be foolish to spend all of their additional income. Instead, they save some of it, knowing that their good fortune is unlikely to persist. Similarly, the South Australian vineyards respond to their temporarily low incomes by drawing on their savings or by borrowing. To the extent that a family saves and borrows to buffer itself from transitory changes in income, these changes do not affect its standard of living. A family's ability to buy goods and services depends largely on its **permanent income**, which is its normal, or average, income.

permanent income
a person's normal income

To gauge inequality of living standards, the distribution of permanent income is more relevant than the distribution of annual income. Although permanent income is hard to measure, it is an important concept. Because permanent income excludes transitory changes in income, permanent income is more evenly distributed than is current income.

Economic mobility

People sometimes speak of 'the rich' and 'the poor' as if these groups consisted of the same families year after year. In fact, this is not at all the case. Economic mobility, the movement of people among income classes, is substantial in modern economies. Movements up the income ladder can be due to good luck or hard work and movements down the ladder can be due to bad luck or laziness. Some of this mobility reflects transitory variation in income, while some reflects more persistent changes in income.

Because economic mobility is so great, many of those below the poverty line are there only temporarily. Poverty is a long-term problem for relatively few families. In a typical 10-year period, about one in four families falls below the poverty line in at least one year. Yet fewer than 3 per cent of families are poor for eight or more years. Because it is likely that the temporarily poor and the persistently poor face different problems, policies that aim to combat poverty need to distinguish between these groups.

Another way to gauge economic mobility is the persistence of economic success from generation to generation. Andrew Leigh, who has studied this topic in Australia, finds substantial mobility. If a father earns 10 per cent above his generation's average income, his son will most likely earn 2–3 per cent above his generation's average income. Australia appears to be more socially mobile than the United States, but not as socially mobile as the Scandinavian countries.

Q

What does the poverty rate measure? Describe three potential problems in interpreting the measured poverty rate.

The political philosophy of redistributing income

We have just seen how the economy's income is distributed and have discussed some of the problems encountered in interpreting measured inequality. We now turn to the policy question: What should the government do about economic inequality?

This question is not just about economics. Economic analysis alone cannot tell us whether policymakers should try to make our society more egalitarian. Our views on this question are, to a large extent, a matter of political philosophy. Yet because the government's role in redistributing income is central to so many debates over economic policy, here we digress from economic science to consider a bit of political philosophy.

Utilitarianism

utilitarianism
the political philosophy according to which the government should choose policies to maximise the total utility of everyone in society

utility
a measure of happiness or satisfaction

A prominent school of thought in political philosophy is **utilitarianism**. The founders of utilitarianism are the English philosophers Jeremy Bentham (1748–1832) and John Stuart Mill (1806–73). To a large extent, the goal of utilitarians is to apply the logic of individual decision making to questions concerning morality and public policy.

The starting point of utilitarianism is the notion of **utility** – the level of happiness or satisfaction that people receive from their circumstances. Utility is a measure of wellbeing and, according to utilitarians, is the ultimate objective of all public and private actions. The proper goal of the government, they claim, is to maximise the sum of utility of everyone in society.

The utilitarian case for redistributing income is based on the assumption of *diminishing marginal utility*. It seems reasonable that an extra dollar of income to a poor person provides that person with more additional utility than does an extra dollar to a rich person. In other words, as a person's income rises, the extra wellbeing derived from an additional dollar of income falls. This plausible assumption, together with the utilitarian goal of maximising total utility, implies that the government should try to achieve a more equitable distribution of income.

The argument is simple. Imagine that Peter and Paul are the same, except that Peter earns $80 000 and Paul earns $20 000. In this case, taking a dollar from Peter to pay Paul will reduce Peter's utility and raise Paul's utility. But, because of diminishing marginal utility, Peter's utility falls by less than Paul's utility rises. Thus, this redistribution of income raises total utility, which is the utilitarian's objective.

At first, this utilitarian argument might seem to imply that the government should continue to redistribute income until everyone in society has exactly the same income. Indeed, that would be the case if the total amount of income – $100 000 in our example – were fixed. But, in fact, it is not. Utilitarians reject complete equalisation of incomes because they accept one of the *Ten Lessons from Economics* presented in chapter 1 – people respond to incentives.

To take from Peter to pay Paul, the government must pursue policies that redistribute income, such as the Australian income tax and social security system. Under these policies, people with high incomes pay high taxes and people with low incomes receive income transfers. Yet, as we have seen in chapters 8 and 12, taxes distort incentives and cause deadweight losses. If the government takes away additional income a person might earn through higher income taxes or reduced transfers, both Peter and Paul have less incentive to work hard. As they work less, society's income falls and so does total utility. The utilitarian government has to balance the gains from greater equality against the losses from distorted incentives. To maximise total utility, therefore, the government stops short of making society fully egalitarian.

A famous parable sheds light on the utilitarian's logic. Imagine that Peter and Paul are thirsty travellers trapped at different places in the desert. Peter's oasis has much water; Paul's has little. If the government could transfer water from one oasis to the other without cost, it would maximise total utility from water by equalising the amount in the two places. But suppose that the government has only a leaky bucket. As it tries to move water from one place to the other, some of the water is lost in transit. In this case, a utilitarian government might still try to move some water from Peter to Paul, depending on how thirsty Paul is and how leaky the bucket is. But, with only a leaky bucket at its disposal, a utilitarian government will not try to reach complete equality.

Liberalism

A second way of thinking about inequality might be called *liberalism*. American philosopher John Rawls develops this view in his book *A Theory of Justice*. This book was first published in 1971 and it quickly became a classic in political philosophy.

Rawls begins with the premise that a society's institutions, laws and policies should be just. He then takes up the natural question: How can we, the members of society, ever agree on what justice means? It might seem that every person's point of view is inevitably based on his or her particular circumstances – whether he or she is talented or less talented, diligent or lazy, educated or less educated, born to a wealthy family or a poor one. Could we ever objectively determine what a just society would be?

To answer this question, Rawls proposes the following thought experiment. Imagine that before any of us is born, we all get together for a meeting to design the rules that govern society. At this point, we are all ignorant about the station in life each of us will end up filling. In Rawls's words, we are sitting in an 'original position' behind a 'veil of ignorance'. In this original position, Rawls argued, we can choose a just set of rules for society because we must consider how those rules will affect every person. As Rawls puts it: 'Since all are similarly situated and no one is able to design principles to favor his particular conditions, the principles of justice are the result of fair agreement or bargain'. Designing public policies and institutions in this way allows us to be objective about what policies are just.

Rawls then considers what public policy designed behind this veil of ignorance would try to achieve. In particular, he considers what income distribution a person would consider just if that person did not know whether he or she would end up at the top, bottom or middle of the distribution. Rawls argues that a person in the original position would be especially concerned about the possibility of being at the bottom of the income distribution. In designing public policies, therefore, we should aim to raise the welfare of the worst-off person in society. That is, rather than maximising the sum of everyone's utility, as a utilitarian would do, Rawls would maximise the minimum utility. Rawls's rule is called the **maximin criterion**.

maximin criterion
the claim that the government should aim to maximise the wellbeing of the worst-off person in society

Because the maximin criterion emphasises the least fortunate person in society, it justifies public policies aimed at equalising the distribution of income. By transferring income from the rich to the poor, society raises the wellbeing of the least fortunate. The maximin criterion would not, however, lead to a completely egalitarian society. If the government promised to equalise incomes completely, people would have no incentive to work hard, society's total income would fall substantially and the least fortunate person would be worse off. Thus, the maximin criterion still allows disparities in income, because such disparities can improve incentives and thereby raise society's ability to help the poor. Nonetheless, because Rawls's philosophy puts weight on only the least fortunate members of society, it calls for more income redistribution than does utilitarianism.

Rawls's views are controversial, but the thought experiment he proposes has much appeal. In particular, this thought experiment allows us to consider the redistribution of income as a form of social insurance. That is, from the perspective of the original position behind the veil of ignorance, income redistribution is like an insurance policy. Homeowners insure their houses to protect themselves from the risk of their houses burning down. Similarly, when we as a society choose policies that tax the rich to supplement the incomes of the poor, we are all insuring ourselves against the possibility that we might have been a member of a poor family. Because people dislike risk, we should be happy to have been born into a society that provides us with this insurance.

It is not at all clear, however, that rational people behind the veil of ignorance would truly be so averse to risk as to follow the maximin criterion. Indeed, because a person in the original position might end up anywhere in the distribution of outcomes, he or she might treat all possible outcomes equally when designing public policies. In this case, the best policy behind the veil of ignorance would be to maximise the average utility of members of society and the resulting notion of justice would be more utilitarian than **Rawlsianism** suggests.

Rawlsianism
the political philosophy according to which the government should choose policies deemed to be just, as evaluated by an impartial observer behind a 'veil of ignorance'

Libertarianism

A third view of inequality is called **libertarianism**. The two views we have considered so far – utilitarianism and the maximin criterion – both view the total income of society as a shared resource that a social planner can freely redistribute to achieve some social goal. In contrast, libertarians argue that society itself earns no income – only individual members of society earn income. According to

libertarianism
the political philosophy according to which the government should punish crimes and enforce voluntary agreements but not redistribute income

libertarians, the government should not take from some individuals and give to others in order to achieve any particular distribution of income.

For instance, philosopher Robert Nozick writes the following in his famous 1974 book, *Anarchy, State and Utopia*:

> We are not in the position of children who have been given portions of pie by someone who now makes last minute adjustments to rectify careless cutting. There is no central distribution, no person or group entitled to control all the resources, jointly deciding how they are to be doled out. What each person gets, he gets from others who give to him in exchange for something, or as a gift. In a free society, diverse persons control different resources, and new holdings arise out of the voluntary exchanges and actions of persons.

Whereas utilitarians and supporters of Rawls try to judge what amount of inequality is desirable in a society, Nozick denies the validity of this very question.

The libertarian alternative to evaluating economic outcomes is to evaluate the process by which these outcomes arise. When the distribution of income is achieved unfairly – for instance, when one person steals from another – the government has the right and duty to remedy the problem. But, as long as the process determining the distribution of income is just, the resulting distribution is fair, no matter how unequal.

Nozick criticises Rawls's maximin criterion by drawing an analogy between the distribution of income in society and the distribution of marks in a course. Suppose you were asked to judge the fairness of the marks in the economics course you are now taking. Would you imagine yourself behind a veil of ignorance and choose a distribution without knowing the talents and efforts of each student? Or would you ensure that the process of assigning marks to students is fair without regard for whether the resulting distribution is equal or unequal? In the case of marks at least, the libertarian emphasis on process over outcomes is compelling.

Libertarians conclude that equality of opportunities is more important than equality of incomes. They believe that the government should enforce individual rights to ensure that everyone has the same opportunity to use their talents and achieve success. Once these rules of the game are established, the government has no reason to alter the resulting distribution of income.

Q

Pam earns more than Pauline. Someone proposes taxing Pam in order to supplement Pauline's income. How would a utilitarian, a supporter of Rawls and a libertarian evaluate this proposal?

Policies to reduce poverty

As we have just seen, political philosophers hold various views about what role the government should take in altering the distribution of income. Political debate among the larger population of voters reflects a similar disagreement. Despite these continuing debates, however, most people believe that, at the very least, the government should try to help those most in need. According to a popular metaphor, the government should provide a 'safety net' to prevent any citizen from falling too far.

Poverty is one of the most difficult problems that policymakers face. Poor families are more likely than the overall population to experience homelessness, drug dependency, domestic violence, health problems, teenage pregnancy, illiteracy, unemployment and low educational attainment. Members of poor families are both more likely to commit crimes and more likely to be victims of crimes.

Although it is hard to separate the causes of poverty from the effects, there is no doubt that poverty is associated with various economic and social ills.

Suppose that you were a policymaker in the government and your goal was to reduce the number of people living in poverty. How would you achieve this goal? Here we consider some of the policy options that you might consider. As we shall see, although each of these options does help some people escape poverty none of them is perfect and deciding which is best is not easy.

Minimum-wage laws

Laws setting a minimum or award wage that employers can pay workers are a perennial source of debate. Advocates view the minimum wage as a way of helping the working poor without any cost to the government. Critics view it as hurting those it is intended to help.

The minimum wage is easily understood using the tools of supply and demand, as we first saw in chapter 6. For workers with low levels of skill and experience, a high award wage forces the wage above the level that balances supply and demand. It therefore raises the cost of labour to firms and reduces the quantity of labour that those firms demand. The result is higher unemployment among those groups of workers affected by the award wage. Although those workers who remain employed benefit from a higher wage, those who might have been employed at a lower wage are worse off.

The magnitude of these effects depends crucially on the elasticity of demand. Advocates of a high minimum wage argue that the demand for unskilled labour is relatively inelastic, so that a high minimum wage depresses employment only slightly. Critics of the minimum wage argue that labour demand is more elastic, especially in the long run when firms can adjust employment and production more fully. They also note that many minimum-wage workers are teenagers from middle-class families so that a high minimum wage is imperfectly targeted as a policy for helping the poor. In Australia, several studies have shown that the typical minimum wage worker lives in a household in about the middle of the income distribution.

Social security

One way to raise the living standards of the poor is for the government to supplement their incomes. The primary way in which the government does this is through the social security system. **Social security** is a broad term that encompasses various government programs. It includes unemployment benefits, the aged pension, family assistance allowances and disability payments.

social security
government programs that supplement the incomes of the needy

A common criticism of social security programs is that they create incentives for people to become 'needy'. For example, some of these programs may encourage families to break up, for many families qualify for financial assistance only if one parent is absent. In the United States, critics of the US welfare system argue that some programs may encourage illegitimate births, for many poor, single women qualify for assistance only if they have children. Poor, single-parent households are an important part of the poverty problem in many developed countries. To the extent that some social security programs seem to raise the number of single-parent families, critics of the welfare system assert that these policies exacerbate the very problems they are supposed to cure.

How severe are these potential problems with the social security system? No one knows for sure. Proponents of the social security system point out that being a poor, single parent on unemployment or other benefits is a difficult existence at best and they are sceptical that many people would be encouraged to pursue such a life if it were not thrust upon them. Moreover, trends over time do not support the view that the decline of the two-parent family is a symptom of the social security system, as the system's critics sometimes claim. Since the early 1970s, benefits (adjusted for inflation) have declined, yet the percentage of children living with only one parent has risen.

Negative income tax

Whenever the government chooses a system to collect taxes, it affects the distribution of income. This is clearly true in the case of a progressive income tax, whereby high-income families pay a larger percentage of their income in taxes than do low-income families. As we discussed in chapter 12, equity across income groups is an important criterion in the design of a tax system.

Many economists have advocated supplementing the income of the poor using a **negative income tax**. It has been supported by economists generally identified with the political right, such as Milton Friedman in the United States, as well as economists associated with the political left, such as Nicholas Kaldor in the United Kingdom. According to this policy, every family would report its income to the government. High-income families would pay a tax based on their incomes. Low-income families would receive a subsidy. In other words, they would 'pay' a 'negative tax'.

negative income tax
a tax system that collects revenue from high-income households and gives transfers to low-income households

Search me!
▸ negative income tax

For example, suppose the government used the following formula to calculate the tax liability of a family:

$$\text{Taxes owed} = (1/3 \text{ of income}) - \$10\,000$$

In this case, a family that earned $60 000 would pay $10 000 in taxes and a family that earned $90 000 would pay $20 000 in taxes. A family that earned $30 000 would owe nothing. And a family that earned $15 000 would 'owe' –$5000. In other words, the government would send this family a cheque for $5000.

Under a negative income tax, poor families would receive financial assistance without having to demonstrate need. The only qualification required to receive assistance would be a low income. Depending on one's point of view, this feature can be either an advantage or a disadvantage. On the one hand, a negative income tax does not encourage illegitimate births and the break-up of families, as critics of the social security system believe current policy does. On the other hand, a negative income tax would subsidise those who are just lazy and, in some people's eyes, undeserving of government support.

IN THE NEWS . . .

THINKING INNOVATIVELY ABOUT INCOME REDISTRIBUTION

Housing is a big part of the problems facing families in poverty. But how do you provide housing assistance without creating poverty traps? Two of the authors of this textbook give their suggestion.

Housing lifelines would rescue many

by Joshua Gans and Stephen King

The announcement of a Productivity Commission inquiry into housing affordability should be welcomed by all. It is precisely because there is a 'blame game' surrounding what makes housing unaffordable that an independent inquiry is needed.

In that regard, media attention has focused on the plight of the first home buyer as housing

>>

prices rise. The image is of a young couple, likely contemplating children, with little savings, staring down the face of a debt burden for the rest of their lives. To them the issue is how to purchase a cheaper home. And, as a matter of simple economics, the only sustainable way to achieve that is to find a way of expanding the housing stock. Working out what governments can do in this regard is clearly worthwhile.

But, outside the gaze of media attention, there are other real affordability problems. One such class is for those households who have never been able to become homeowners. For them, the problem is as much low income as it is a lack of housing.

But affordability can be an issue for households who have already opted for a large mortgage. When incomes and house prices fluctuate, households with a temporary change in circumstances – such as income loss or the need to move cities to find work – find themselves in immediate housing stress. A primary income earner could lose their job or suffer illness and the danger would be that the whole household would have to sell up and move. The loss of income hopefully would only be temporary, but the effect on housing and lifestyle choices, credit rating and family stress would be longer term. Put simply, a short term loss of income could mean foreclosure or eviction, forcing the household to 'start again'. For those households, the issue is how to afford their current home.

Dealing with this type of affordability problem necessitates new thinking beyond issues of the housing stock per se. In our report to the Prime Minister, we proposed a housing lifeline to deal with this. The idea is that when there is a temporary loss of income the government would step into the breach and offer eligible households (with eligibility based on nothing more than an assets means test) a payment to their housing provider – be it a landlord or a lender – to tide them over the rough patch. When the household's income rose again, they would face a slightly higher marginal tax rate for as long as it took to repay the loan. This would operate in much the same way as the HECS system operates today for higher education.

The housing lifeline has several advantages over traditional social security. For one, its main benefit is the removal of anxiety. Even a household that never uses the lifeline knows that it is there and faces less risk as a result. Accessing the lifeline is a choice that rests with the household itself, so that the people best placed to judge the need for temporary assistance are the ones who choose whether or not to use the lifeline. Also, remember that the lifeline is not a handout – it is a debt that has to be repaid. But this avoids any stigma and uncertainty associated with working out eligibility or waiting for rent assistance and other programs aimed at long-term assistance. Only if a household has persistent difficulties is a more interventionist long-term approach desired. Under the housing lifeline, households are empowered by having the option to access temporary assistance that it can use if need be.

The hope is that a policy like the housing lifeline might actually prevent households from turning what was a short-run loss of income into a long-term social security liability. Income-based handouts can have undesirable outcomes, creating high levels of taxation for subsequent income earned. The housing lifeline, by being based on long-term lifetime income avoids such poverty and incentive traps. Thus, it should reduce the number of households who need to access basic social security and public housing programs.

For landlords and investors in housing, the existence of a lifeline changes the risk calculation when providing housing for those with low incomes and high risk. This will open up housing markets to households who are currently excluded due to income variations and risk. Ultimately, the lifeline will alleviate the problems of housing affordability for a wide range of the community.

Source: Joshua Gans & Stephen King/ *Australian Financial Review*, 6 August 2003.

In-kind transfers

Another way to help the poor is to provide them directly with some of the goods and services they need to raise their living standards. For example, charities provide the needy with food, shelter and toys at Christmas. Indeed, in the United States, the government itself is involved in direct provision of goods. For instance, it gives poor families food stamps, which are government vouchers that can be used to buy food at shops; the shops then redeem these vouchers for money.

Is it better to help the poor with these in-kind transfers or with direct cash payments? There is no clear answer.

Advocates of in-kind transfers argue that such transfers ensure that the poor get what they need most. Among the poorest members of society, alcohol and drug addiction is more common than it is in society as a whole. By providing the poor with food and shelter, society can be more confident that it is not helping to support such addictions. This is one reason that in-kind transfers are more politically popular than cash payments to the poor.

Advocates of cash payments argue that in-kind transfers are inefficient and disrespectful. The government does not know what goods and services the poor need most. Many of the poor are ordinary people down on their luck. Despite their misfortune, they are in the best position to decide how to raise their own living standards. Rather than giving the poor in-kind transfers of goods and services that they may not want, it may be better to give them cash and allow them to buy what they think they need most.

Anti-poverty programs and work incentives

Many policies aimed at helping the poor can have the unintended effect of discouraging the poor from escaping poverty on their own. To see why, consider the following example. Suppose that a family needs an income of \$15 000 to maintain a reasonable standard of living. And suppose that, out of concern for the poor, the government promises to guarantee every family that income. Whatever a family earns, the government makes up the difference between that income and \$15 000. What effect would you expect this policy to have?

The incentive effects of this policy are obvious – any person who would make under \$15 000 by working has no incentive to find and keep a job. For every dollar that the person would earn, the government would reduce the income supplement by a dollar. In effect, the government taxes

100 per cent of additional earnings. An effective marginal tax rate of 100 per cent is surely a policy with a large deadweight loss.

The adverse effects of this high effective tax rate can persist over time. People discouraged from working lose the on-the-job training that jobs might offer. In addition, their children miss the lessons learned by observing parents with a full-time job and this may adversely affect their own ability to find and hold a job.

Although the anti-poverty program we have been discussing is hypothetical, it is not as unrealistic as it might first appear. Unemployment benefits and other social security payments are tied to family income as are payments for health insurance through the government's Medicare program. As a family's income rises, the family becomes ineligible for these programs. When all the government programs are taken together, it is common for families to face effective marginal tax rates that are very high. Sometimes the effective marginal tax rates even exceed 100 per cent, so that poor families are worse off when they earn more. By trying to help the poor, the government discourages those families from working. According to critics of anti-poverty programs, these programs alter work attitudes and create a 'culture of poverty'.

It might seem that there is an easy solution to this problem – reduce benefits to poor families more gradually as their incomes rise. For example, if a poor family loses 30 cents of benefits for every dollar it earns, then it faces an effective marginal tax rate of 30 per cent. This effective tax reduces work effort to some extent, but it does not eliminate the incentive to work completely.

The problem with this solution is that it greatly increases the cost of programs to combat poverty. If benefits are phased out gradually as a poor family's income rises, then families just above the poverty level will also be eligible for substantial benefits. The more gradual the phase-out, the greater the number of eligible families and the greater the cost of the program. Thus, policymakers face a trade-off between burdening the poor with high effective marginal tax rates and burdening taxpayers with costly programs to reduce poverty.

Q

List three policies aimed at helping the poor and discuss the pros and cons of each.

Conclusion

People have long reflected on the distribution of income in society. The ancient Greek philosopher Plato concluded that in an ideal society the income of the richest person would be no more than four times the income of the poorest person. Although the measurement of inequality is difficult, it is clear that our society has much more inequality than Plato recommended.

One of the *Ten Lessons from Economics* discussed in chapter 1 is that governments can sometimes improve market outcomes. There is little consensus, however, about how this idea should be applied to the distribution of income. Philosophers and policymakers today do not agree on how much income inequality is desirable, or even whether public policy should aim to alter the distribution of income. Much of public debate reflects this disagreement. Whenever taxes are raised, for instance, lawmakers argue over how much of the tax hike should fall on the rich, the middle class and the poor.

Another of the *Ten Lessons from Economics* is that people face trade-offs. This lesson is important to keep in mind when thinking about economic inequality. Policies that penalise the successful and reward the unsuccessful may reduce the incentive to succeed. Thus, policymakers face a trade-off between equality and efficiency. As the pie is divided more equitably, the smaller it may become. This is the one lesson concerning the distribution of income about which almost everyone agrees.

IN THE NEWS . . .

SCHOOL VOUCHERS

One aim of universal education is to shrink the gap between rich and poor. But government-financed education does not require government-run schools.

The market can transform our schools

by Milton Friedman

The Supreme Court's voucher decision clears the way for a major expansion of parental school choice. Opponents of choice can no longer use the First Amendment's religious Establishment Clause to attack voucher programs, now that the Supreme Court has declared the Cleveland program constitutionally acceptable even though most voucher recipients went to parochial schools.

The state of Ohio provided vouchers worth up to $2250 to low-income parents in Cleveland who chose to send their children to private schools that charge them tuition of no more than $2500 per child. The voucher was offered as an alternative to government schooling costing nearly three times as much per student. Yet some 4000 low-income parents still found the private alternative preferable – enough so to pay 10 per cent of private school tuition out of their own pockets. What an indictment of government schools.

Most schools that accept vouchers are religious for a simple reason, and one that is easily corrected. That reason is the low value of the voucher. It is not easy, perhaps not possible, to provide a satisfactory education for $2500 per student. Most private schools spend more than that. But parochial schools are able to accept that low voucher amount because they are subsidized by their churches.

Raise the voucher amount to $7000 – the sum that Ohio state and local governments now spend per child in government schools – and make it available to all students, not simply to students from low-income families, and most private schools accepting vouchers would no longer be religious. A host of new nonprofit and for-profit schools would emerge. Voucher-bearing students would then be less dependent on low-tuition parochial schools.

Parents would then truly have a choice, and the quality of schooling – in both public and private schools – would soar as competition worked its magic. This has happened in Milwaukee, where the voucher program has evolved over the past 10 years. Since that program's creation, 37 new schools have opened, nearly two-thirds of them nonreligious.

Assumption of responsibility by government for educating all children does not require that schooling be delivered in government-run institutions – just as government food stamps need not be spent in government grocery stores.

Besides, an emphasis on school choice is not new, even in public programs. The G.I. Bill enacted at the end of World War II demonstrates how well choice can work. That program provided vouchers for higher education – for use in religious and nonreligious institutions – to millions of veterans; it transformed higher education and provided the educational leadership that has

>>

played a major role in political and economic change in the postwar period.

When the G.I. Bill was enacted, doubts were expressed that the colleges could expand rapidly enough to handle the flood of new students. Yet the number of students enrolled in colleges nearly doubled in the two years after the end of the war. The supply expanded to meet the surge in demand.

The market will respond as fully and rapidly to the increased demand for private schools generated by the expansion of vouchers for elementary and secondary education. Private voucher programs, financed by foundations and individuals, plus the limited government programs so far enacted have already brought forth a market response.

School vouchers can push elementary and secondary education out of the 19th century and into the 21st by introducing market competition on a broad scale, just as competition has made progress possible in every other area of economic and civic life.

The biggest winner from such an educational revolution would be American society as a whole. A better schooled work force promises higher productivity and more rapid economic growth. Even more important, improved education could help narrow the income gap between the less skilled and more skilled workers and would fend off the prospect of a society divided between the haves and have-nots, of a society in which an educated elite provides for a permanent class of unemployables.

Source: From *The New York Times*, 2 July 2002.

Summary

- Data on the distribution of income show wide disparity in our society. The richest fifth of families earns about 10 times as much income as the poorest fifth.
- Because the economic life cycle, transitory income and economic mobility are so important for understanding variation in income, it is difficult to gauge the degree of inequality in our society using data on the distribution of income in a single year. When these factors are taken into account, they tend to suggest that economic wellbeing is more evenly distributed than is annual income.
- Political philosophers differ in their views about the role of government in altering the distribution of income. Utilitarians (such as John Stuart Mill) would choose the distribution of income to maximise the sum of utility of everyone in society. Followers of John Rawls would determine the distribution of income as if we were behind a 'veil of ignorance' that prevented us from knowing our own stations in life. Libertarians (such as Robert Nozick) would have the government enforce individual rights to ensure a fair process but then not be concerned about inequality in the resulting distribution of income.
- Various policies aim to help the poor – minimum-wage laws/award wages, social security and negative income taxes. Although each of these policies helps some families escape poverty, they also have unintended side effects. Because financial assistance declines as income rises, the poor often face effective marginal tax rates that are very high. Such high effective tax rates discourage poor families from escaping poverty on their own.

Key concepts

libertarianism
life cycle
maximin criterion
negative income tax
permanent income
poverty line
poverty rate
Rawlsianism
social security
utilitarianism
utility

Questions for review

1 Does the richest fifth of the Australian population earn two, four or 10 times the income of the poorest fifth?
2 What groups in the population are most likely to live in poverty?
3 When gauging the amount of inequality, why do transitory and life cycle variations in income cause difficulties?
4 How would a utilitarian, a supporter of John Rawls and a libertarian determine how much income inequality is permissible?
5 What are the pros and cons of in-kind (rather than cash) transfers to the poor?

Problems and applications

1 Table 21.2 shows that income inequality in Australia has increased during the past 20 years. Some factors contributing to this increase were discussed in chapter 20. What are they?

2 Economists often view life cycle variation in income as one form of transitory variation in income around people's lifetime, or permanent, income. In this sense, how does your current income compare with your permanent income? Do you think your current income accurately reflects your standard of living?

3 The chapter suggests that people can use saving and borrowing to smooth out transitory variation in income in order to maintain steady consumption.
   a What obstacles might prevent such smoothing?
   b What does this tell you about whether it is appropriate to base measures of income inequality purely on permanent income?

4 Consider two communities. In one community, 10 families have incomes of $100 each and 10 families have incomes of $20 each. In the other community, 10 families have incomes of $200 each and 10 families have incomes of $22 each.
   a In which community is the distribution of income more inequitable? In which community is the problem of poverty likely to be worse?
   b Which distribution of income would Rawls prefer? Explain.
   c Which distribution of income do you prefer? Explain.

5 The chapter uses the analogy of a 'leaky bucket' to explain one constraint on the redistribution of income.
   a What elements of the Australian system for redistributing income create the leaks in the bucket? Be specific.
   b In your opinion, which political party, Liberal or Labor, generally has a stronger belief that the bucket used for redistributing income is leaky? How does that belief affect the party's views about the amount of income redistribution that the government should undertake?

6 Suppose there are two possible income distributions in a society of 10 people. In the first distribution, nine people have incomes of $30 000 and one person has an income of $10 000. In the second distribution, all 10 people have incomes of $25 000.
   a If the society had the first income distribution, what would be the utilitarian argument for redistributing income?
   b Which income distribution would Rawls consider more equitable? Explain.
   c Which income distribution would Nozick consider more equitable? Explain.

7 Do you think a person who believes that the government should help poor children but not poor adults would be more likely to advocate cash welfare payments or in-kind transfers?

8 Suppose that a family's tax liability equalled half its income minus $10 000. Under this system, some families would pay taxes to the government and some families would receive money from the government through a 'negative income tax'.
   a Consider families with pre-tax incomes of $0, $10 000, $20 000, $30 000 and $40 000. Draw up a table showing pre-tax income, taxes paid to the government or money received from the government, and after-tax income for each family.
   b What is the marginal tax rate in this system? (See chapter 12 if you need to review the definition of marginal tax rate.) What is the maximum amount of income at which a family receives money from the government?
   c Now suppose that the tax schedule is changed, so that a family's tax liability equals a quarter of its income minus $10 000. What is the marginal tax rate in this new system? What is the maximum amount of income at which a family receives money from the government?
   d What is the main advantage of each of the tax schedules discussed here?

9 John and Jeremy are both utilitarians. John believes that labour supply is highly elastic, whereas Jeremy believes that labour supply is quite inelastic. How do you suppose their views about income redistribution differ?

10 Consider each of the following statements. Do you agree or disagree? What do your views imply for public policies, such as taxes on inheritance?

a 'All parents have the right to work hard and save in order to give their children a better life.'

b 'Children should not be disadvantaged by the sloth or bad luck of their parents.'

Search me!

Search me!

When accessing information about microeconomics use the following keywords in any combinations you require:

- negative income tax
- poverty line

CourseMate

CourseMate

For more multimedia resources and activities on economics, visit the Economics CourseMate website.

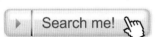

PART SEVEN
Topics for further study

22

The theory of consumer choice

Learning objectives

In this chapter you will:

- see how a budget constraint represents the choices a consumer can afford
- learn how indifference curves can be used to represent a consumer's preferences
- analyse how a consumer's optimum choices are determined
- see how a consumer responds to changes in income and changes in prices
- break down the impact of a price change into an income effect and a substitution effect
- apply the theory of consumer choice to four questions about household behaviour.

When you walk into a shop, you are confronted with thousands of goods that you might buy. Of course, because your financial resources are limited, you cannot buy everything that you want. You therefore consider the prices of the various goods being offered for sale and buy a bundle of goods that, given your resources, best suits your needs and desires.

In this chapter we develop the theory that describes how consumers make decisions about what to buy. So far throughout this book, we have summarised consumers' decisions with the demand curve. As we discussed in chapters 4 to 7, the demand curve for a good reflects consumers' willingness to pay for it. When the price of a good rises, consumers are willing to pay for fewer units, so the quantity demanded falls. We now look more deeply at the decisions that lie behind the demand curve. The theory of consumer choice presented in this chapter provides a more complete understanding of demand, just as the theory of the competitive firm in chapter 14 provides a more complete understanding of supply.

One of the *Ten Lessons from Economics* discussed in chapter 1 is that people face trade-offs. The theory of consumer choice examines the trade-offs that people face in their role as consumers. A consumer who buys more of one good can afford less of other goods. A consumer who spends more time enjoying leisure and less time working has a lower income and can afford less consumption. A consumer who spends more income in the present and saves less of it must accept a lower level of consumption in the future. The theory of consumer choice examines how consumers facing these trade-offs make decisions and how they respond to changes in their environment.

After developing the basic theory of consumer choice, we apply it to several questions about household decisions. In particular, we ask:

- Do all demand curves slope downwards?
- How do wages affect labour supply?
- How do interest rates affect household savings?
- Do the poor prefer to receive cash or in-kind transfers?

At first, these questions might seem unrelated. But, as we will see, we can use the theory of consumer choice to consider each of them.

The budget constraint: What the consumer can afford

Most people would like to increase the quantity or quality of the goods they consume – to take longer holidays, drive fancier cars or buy better clothes. People consume less than they desire because their spending is constrained, or limited, by their income. We begin our study of consumer choice by examining this link between income and spending.

To keep things simple, we examine the decision facing a consumer (Natalie) who buys only two goods – Pepsi and pizza. Of course, real people buy thousands of different kinds of goods. Yet assuming there are only two goods greatly simplifies the problem without altering the basic insights about consumer choice.

We first consider how Natalie's income constrains the amount she spends on Pepsi and pizza. Suppose that Natalie has an income of $1000 per month and spends that entire income each month on Pepsi and pizza. The price of a litre of Pepsi is $2 and the price of a pizza is $10.

Table 22.1 shows some of the many combinations of Pepsi and pizza that Natalie can buy. The first line in the table shows that if all income is spent on pizza, Natalie can eat 100 pizzas during the month, but would not be able to buy any Pepsi at all. The second line shows another possible

Table 22.1 The consumer's opportunities

Litres of Pepsi	Number of pizzas	Spending on Pepsi	Spending on pizza	Total spending
0	100	$0	$1000	$1000
50	90	100	900	1000
100	80	200	800	1000
150	70	300	700	1000
200	60	400	600	1000
250	50	500	500	1000
300	40	600	400	1000
350	30	700	300	1000
400	20	800	200	1000
450	10	900	100	1000
500	0	1000	0	1000

This table shows what our consumer, Natalie, can afford if income is $1000, the price of Pepsi is $2 and the price of a pizza is $10.

consumption bundle – 90 pizzas and 50 litres of Pepsi. And so on. Each consumption bundle in the table costs exactly $1000.

Figure 22.1 graphs the consumption bundles that Natalie can choose. The vertical axis measures the number of litres of Pepsi, and the horizontal axis measures the number of pizzas. Three points are marked on this figure. At point A, Natalie buys no Pepsi and consumes 100 pizzas. At point B, Natalie buys no pizzas and consumes 500 litres of Pepsi. At point C, Natalie buys 50 pizzas and 250 litres of Pepsi. Point C, which is exactly at the middle of the line from A to B, is the point at which Natalie spends an equal amount ($500) on Pepsi and pizza. Of course, these are only three of the many combinations of Pepsi and pizza that Natalie can choose. All the points on the line from A to B are possible. This line, which is called the **budget constraint**, shows the consumption bundles that Natalie can afford. In this case, it shows Natalie's trade-off between Pepsi and pizza.

budget constraint
the limit on the consumption bundles that a consumer can afford

The slope of the budget constraint measures the rate at which Natalie can trade one good for the other. Recall from the appendix to chapter 2 that the slope between two points is calculated as the change in the vertical distance divided by the change in the horizontal distance ('rise over run'). From point A to point B, the vertical distance is 500 litres and the horizontal distance is 100 pizzas. Thus, the slope is 5 litres per pizza. (Actually, because the budget constraint slopes downwards, the slope is a negative number. But for our purposes we can ignore the minus sign.)

Notice that the slope of the budget constraint equals the *relative price* of the two goods – the price of one good compared with the price of the other. A pizza costs five times as much as a litre of Pepsi.

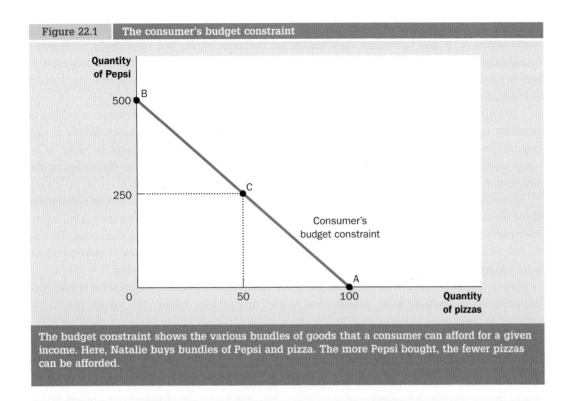

Figure 22.1 The consumer's budget constraint

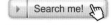

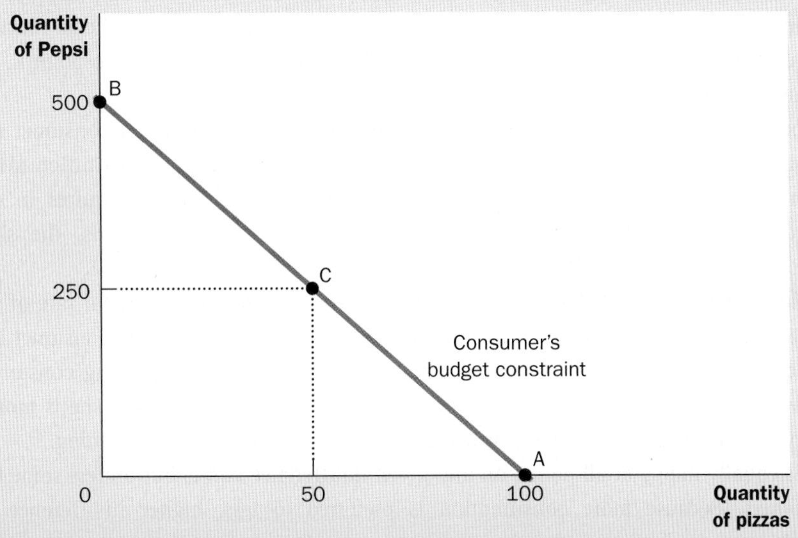

The budget constraint shows the various bundles of goods that a consumer can afford for a given income. Here, Natalie buys bundles of Pepsi and pizza. The more Pepsi bought, the fewer pizzas can be afforded.

Q

Draw the budget constraint for a person with an income of $1000 if the price of Pepsi is $5 and the price of a pizza is $10. What is the slope of this budget constraint?

Thus, the opportunity cost of a pizza is five litres of Pepsi. The budget constraint's slope of 5 reflects the trade-off the market is offering the consumer: 1 pizza for 5 litres of Pepsi.

Preferences: What the consumer wants

Our goal in this chapter is to see how consumers make choices. Budget constraints are one piece of the analysis – they show what combinations of goods consumers can afford given their incomes and the prices of the goods. Consumers' choices, however, depend not only on this budget constraint but also on their preferences for certain goods. Therefore, a consumer's preferences are the next piece of our analysis.

Representing preferences with indifference curves

Natalie's (the consumer's) preferences allow a choice among different bundles of Pepsi and pizza. If two different bundles are offered, Natalie chooses the bundle to best suit her tastes. If the two bundles suit her tastes equally well, we say that Natalie is *indifferent* between the two bundles.

Just as we have represented Natalie's budget constraint graphically, we can also represent her preferences graphically. We do this with indifference curves. An **indifference curve** shows the bundles of consumption that make a consumer equally happy. In this case, the indifference curves show the combinations of Pepsi and pizza with which Natalie is equally satisfied.

indifference curve
a curve that shows consumption bundles that give the consumer the same level of satisfaction

Search me!
▸ indifference curve

marginal rate of substitution
the rate at which a consumer is willing to trade one good for another

Figure 22.2 shows two of Natalie's many indifference curves. Natalie is indifferent among combinations A, B and C, because they are all on the same curve. Not surprisingly, if Natalie's consumption of pizza is reduced, say from point A to point B, consumption of Pepsi must increase to keep her equally happy. If consumption of pizza is reduced again, from point B to point C, the amount of Pepsi consumed must increase yet again.

The slope at any point on an indifference curve equals the rate at which a consumer is willing to substitute one good for the other. This rate is called the **marginal rate of substitution** (*MRS*). In this case, the marginal rate of substitution measures how much Pepsi Natalie requires in order to be compensated for a one-unit reduction in pizza consumption. In other words, the slope of the indifference curve shows the marginal rate *of* substitution of Pepsi *for* pizza.

Notice that, because the indifference curves are not straight lines, the marginal rate of substitution is not the same at all points on a given indifference curve. The rate at which a consumer is willing to trade one good for the other depends on the amounts of the goods already being consumed. That is, the rate at which Natalie is willing to trade Pepsi for pizza depends on whether she is more thirsty or more hungry, which in turn depends on how much Pepsi and pizza she is consuming.

Natalie is equally happy at all points on any given indifference curve, but prefers some indifference curves to others. Because more consumption is preferred to less, higher indifference curves are preferred to lower ones. In Figure 22.2, any point on curve I_2 is preferred to any point on curve I_1.

A consumer's set of indifference curves gives a complete ranking of the consumer's preferences. That is, we can use the indifference curves to rank any two bundles of goods. For example, the indifference curves tell us that point D is preferred to point A because point D is on a higher

Figure 22.2 The consumer's preferences

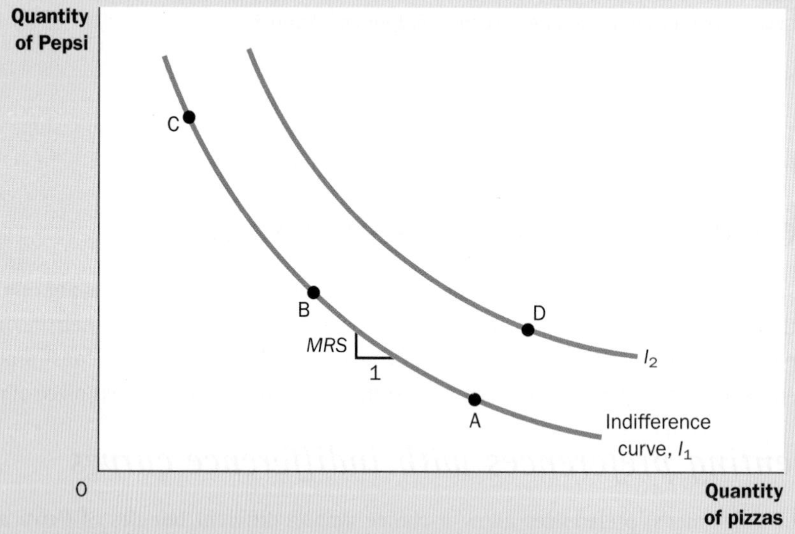

The consumer's preferences are represented with indifference curves, which show the combinations of Pepsi and pizza that make Natalie equally satisfied. Because Natalie prefers more of a good, points on a higher indifference curve (I_2 here) are preferred to points on a lower indifference curve (I_1). The marginal rate of substitution (*MRS*) shows the rate at which Natalie is willing to trade Pepsi for pizza.

indifference curve than point A. (That conclusion may be obvious, however, because point D offers Natalie both more pizza and more Pepsi.) The indifference curves also tell us that point D is preferred to point C because point D is on a higher indifference curve. Even though point D has less Pepsi than point C, it has more than enough extra pizza to make Natalie prefer it. By seeing which point is on the higher indifference curve, we can use the set of indifference curves to rank any combinations of Pepsi and pizza.

Four properties of indifference curves

Because indifference curves represent a consumer's preferences, they have certain properties that reflect those preferences. Here we consider four properties that describe most indifference curves.

- *Property 1: Higher indifference curves are preferred to lower ones.* A consumer usually prefers more of something to less of it. This preference for greater quantities is reflected in the indifference curves. As Figure 22.2 shows, higher indifference curves represent larger quantities of goods than lower indifference curves. Thus, a consumer prefers being on a higher indifference curve.
- *Property 2: Indifference curves are downward-sloping.* The slope of an indifference curve reflects the rate at which a consumer is willing to substitute one good for the other. In most cases, the consumer likes both goods. Therefore, if the quantity of one good is reduced, the quantity of the other good must increase in order for the consumer to be equally happy. For this reason, most indifference curves slope downwards.
- *Property 3: Indifference curves do not cross.* To see why this is true, suppose that two indifference curves did cross, as in Figure 22.3. Then, because point A is on the same indifference curve as point B, the two points would make the consumer (Natalie) equally happy. In addition, because point B is on the same indifference curve as point C, these two points would make Natalie equally

Figure 22.3 **The impossibility of intersecting indifference curves**

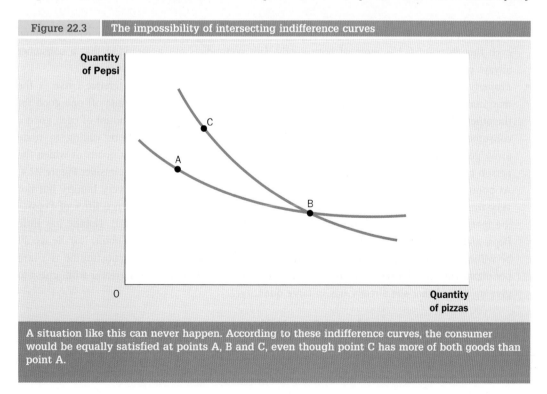

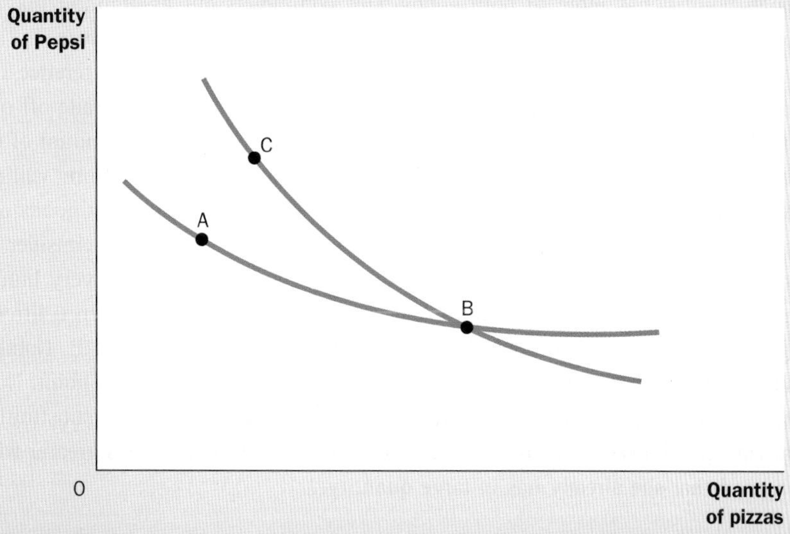

A situation like this can never happen. According to these indifference curves, the consumer would be equally satisfied at points A, B and C, even though point C has more of both goods than point A.

Figure 22.4 Bowed indifference curves

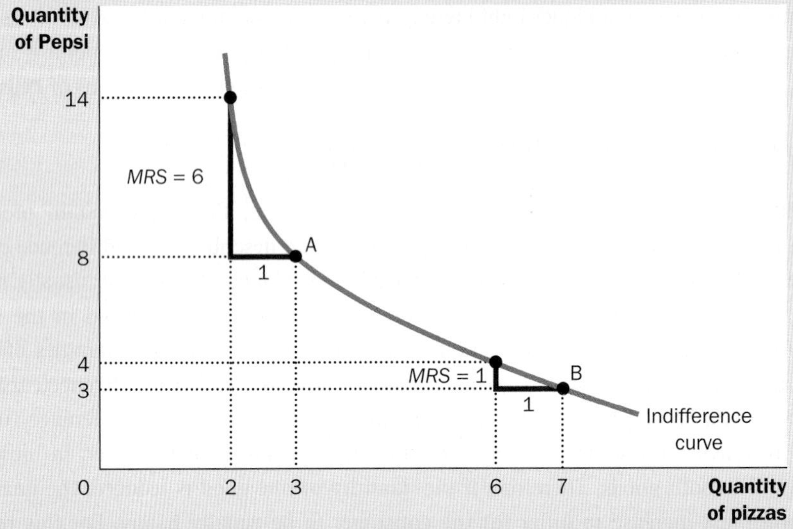

Indifference curves are usually bowed inwards. This shape implies that the marginal rate of substitution (*MRS*) depends on the quantity of the two goods the consumer is consuming. At point A, Natalie has little pizza and much Pepsi, and requires a lot of extra Pepsi in order to give up one of the pizzas – the marginal rate of substitution is 6 litres of Pepsi per pizza. At point B, Natalie has much pizza and little Pepsi, and requires only a little extra Pepsi to give up one of the pizzas – the marginal rate of substitution is 1 litre of Pepsi per pizza.

happy. But these conclusions imply that points A and C would also make Natalie equally happy, even though point C has more of both goods. This contradicts our assumption that a consumer always prefers more of both goods to less. Thus, indifference curves cannot cross.

- *Property 4: Indifference curves are bowed inwards.* The slope of an indifference curve is the marginal rate of substitution – the rate at which a consumer is willing to trade off one good for the other. The marginal rate of substitution (*MRS*) usually depends on the amount of each good a consumer is currently consuming. In particular, because a person is more willing to trade away goods that he or she has in abundance and less willing to trade away goods of which the person has little, the indifference curves are bowed inwards. As an example, consider Figure 22.4. At point A, Natalie has a lot of Pepsi and only a little pizza, making her very hungry but not very thirsty. To induce Natalie to give up one pizza, Natalie has to be given 6 litres of Pepsi – the marginal rate of substitution is 6 litres per pizza. In contrast, at point B, Natalie has little Pepsi and a lot of pizza, and so is very thirsty but not very hungry. At this point, Natalie would be willing to give up one pizza to get 1 litre of Pepsi – the marginal rate of substitution is 1 litre per pizza. Thus, the bowed shape of the indifference curve reflects Natalie's greater willingness to give up a good that she already has in large quantity.

Two extreme examples of indifference curves

The shape of an indifference curve tells us about a consumer's willingness to trade one good for the other. When the goods are easy to substitute for each other, the indifference curves are less bowed;

when the goods are hard to substitute, the indifference curves are very bowed. To see why this is true, let's consider the extreme cases.

Perfect substitutes

Suppose that someone offered you bundles of 10-cent and 20-cent coins. How would you rank the different bundles?

Most likely, you would care only about the total monetary value of each bundle. If so, you would judge a bundle based on the number of 20-cent coins plus twice the number of 10-cent coins. In other words, you would always be willing to trade one 20-cent coin for two 10-cent coins, regardless of the number of 10- and 20-cent coins in the bundle. Your marginal rate of substitution of 10-cent coins for 20-cent coins would be a fixed number – two.

We can represent your preferences regarding 10- and 20-cent coins with the indifference curves in panel (a) of Figure 22.5. Because the marginal rate of substitution is constant, the indifference curves are straight lines. In this extreme case of straight indifference curves, we say that the two goods are **perfect substitutes.**

perfect substitutes
two goods with straight-line indifference curves

Perfect complements

Suppose now that someone offered you bundles of shoes. Some of the shoes fit your left foot, others your right foot. How would you rank these different bundles?

In this case, you might care only about the number of pairs of shoes. In other words, you would judge a bundle based on the number of pairs you could assemble from it. A bundle of five left shoes and seven right shoes yields only five pairs. Getting one more right shoe has no value if there is no left shoe to go with it.

We can represent your preferences for right and left shoes with the indifference curves in panel (b) of Figure 22.5. In this case, a bundle with five left shoes and five right shoes is just as good as a

Figure 22.5 **Perfect substitutes and perfect complements**

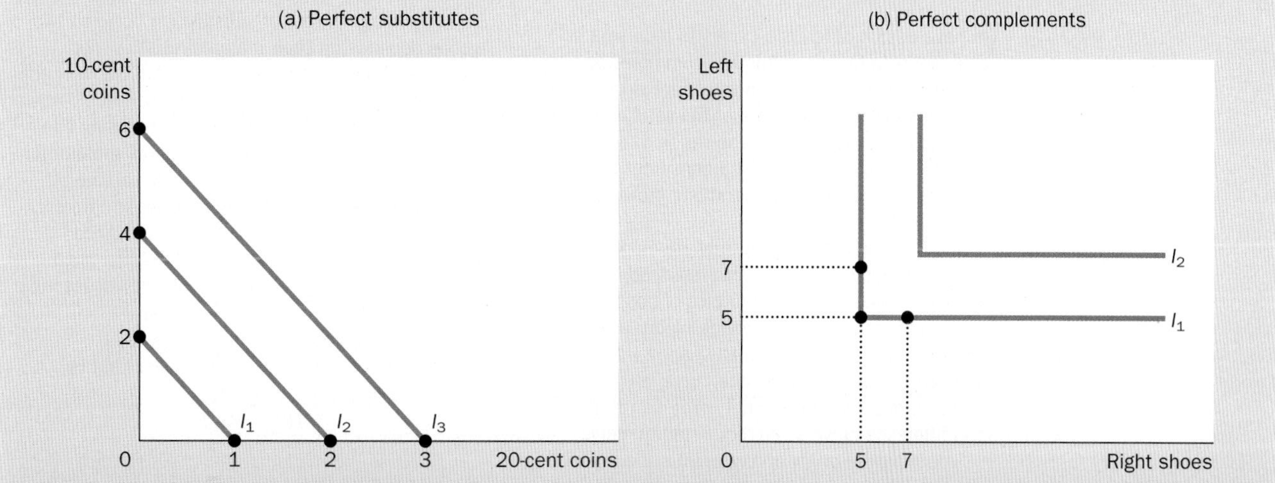

When two goods are easily substitutable, such as 10- and 20-cent coins, the indifference curves are straight lines, as shown in panel (a). When two goods are strongly complementary, such as left shoes and right shoes, the indifference curves are right angles, as shown in panel (b).

perfect complements
two goods with right-angle indifference curves

bundle with five left shoes and seven right shoes. It is also just as good as a bundle with seven left shoes and five right shoes. The indifference curves, therefore, are right angles. In this extreme case of right-angle indifference curves, we say that the two goods are **perfect complements.**

In the real world, of course, most goods are neither perfect substitutes (like 10- and 20-cent coins) nor perfect complements (like right shoes and left shoes). More typically, the indifference curves are bowed inwards, but not so bowed as to become right angles.

Q

Draw some indifference curves for Pepsi and pizza. Explain the four properties of these indifference curves.

Optimisation: What the consumer chooses

The goal of this chapter is to understand how a consumer makes choices. We have the two pieces necessary for this analysis – the consumer's budget constraint (how much she can *afford* to buy) and the consumer's preferences (what she would *like* to buy). Now we put these two pieces together and consider the consumer's decision about what to buy.

The consumer's optimum choices

Consider once again our Pepsi and pizza example. Our consumer, Natalie, would like to end up with the best possible combination of Pepsi and pizza – that is, the combination on the highest possible indifference curve. But Natalie must also end up on or below her budget constraint, which measures the total resources available to her.

fyi

Utility – an alternative way to describe preferences and optimisation

We have used indifference curves to represent a consumer's preferences. Another common way to represent preferences is with the concept of *utility*. Utility is an abstract measure of the satisfaction or happiness that a consumer receives from a bundle of goods. Economists say that a consumer prefers one bundle of goods to another if one provides more utility than the other.

Indifference curves and utility are closely related. Because the consumer prefers points on higher indifference curves, bundles of goods on higher indifference curves provide higher utility. Because the consumer is equally happy with all points on the same indifference curve, all these bundles provide the same utility. You can think of an indifference curve as an 'equal-utility' curve.

The *marginal utility* of any good is the increase in utility that the consumer gets from an additional unit of that good. Most goods are assumed to exhibit *diminishing marginal utility*. The more of the good the consumer already has, the lower the marginal utility provided by an extra unit of that good.

The marginal rate of substitution between two goods depends on their marginal utilities. For example, if the marginal utility of good *X* is twice the marginal utility of good *Y*, then a person would need two units of good *Y* to compensate for losing one unit of good *X* and the marginal rate of substitution equals two. More generally, the marginal rate of substitution (and thus the slope of the indifference curve) equals the marginal utility of one good divided by the marginal utility of the other good.

Utility analysis provides another way to describe consumer optimisation. Recall that at the consumer's optimum, the marginal rate of substitution equals the ratio of prices. That is:

$$MRS = P_X/P_Y$$

Because the marginal rate of substitution equals the ratio of marginal utilities, we can write this condition for optimisation as:

$$MU_X/MU_Y = P_X/P_Y$$

Now rearrange this expression to become:

$$MU_X/P_X = MU_Y/P_Y$$

This equation has a simple interpretation: At the optimum, the marginal utility per dollar spent on good X equals the marginal utility per dollar spent on good Y. (Why? If this equality did not hold, the consumer could increase utility by spending less on the good that provided lower marginal utility per dollar and more on the good that provided higher marginal utility per dollar.)

When economists discuss the theory of consumer choice, they might express the theory using different words. One economist might say that the goal of the consumer is to maximise utility. Another might say that the goal of the consumer is to end up on the highest possible indifference curve. The first economist would conclude that at the consumer's optimum, the marginal utility per dollar is the same for all goods, whereas the second would conclude that the indifference curve is tangent to the budget constraint. In essence, these are two ways of saying the same thing.

Figure 22.6 shows the budget constraint and three of Natalie's many indifference curves. The highest indifference curve that Natalie can reach (I_2 in the figure) is the one that just barely touches the budget constraint. The point at which this indifference curve and the budget constraint touch is called the *optimum*. Natalie would prefer point A, but cannot afford that point because it lies above the budget constraint. Natalie can afford point B, but that point is on a lower indifference curve and, therefore, provides Natalie less satisfaction. The optimum point represents the best combination of consumption of Pepsi and pizza available to Natalie.

Figure 22.6 **The consumer's optimum**

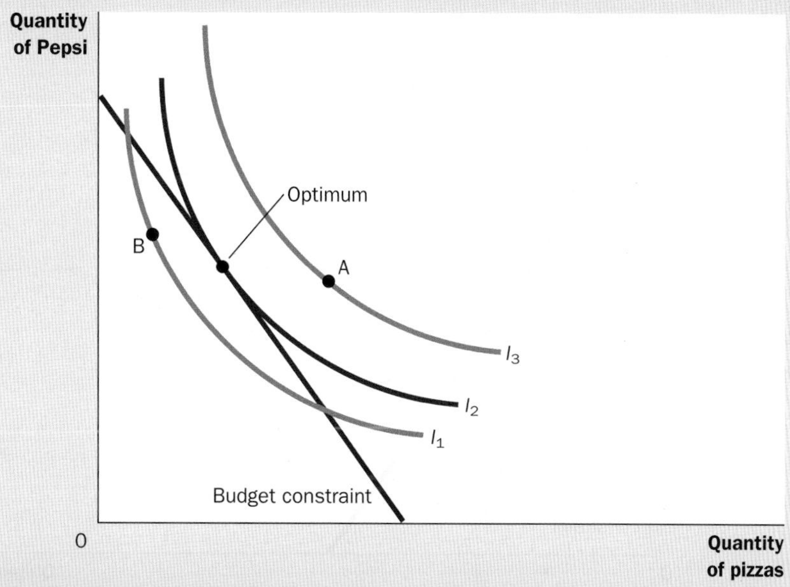

The consumer chooses the point on her budget constraint that lies on the highest indifference curve. At this point, called the optimum, the marginal rate of substitution equals the relative price of the two goods. Here the highest indifference curve Natalie can reach is I_2. Natalie prefers point A, which lies on indifference curve I_3, but cannot afford this bundle of Pepsi and pizza. In contrast, point B is affordable, but because it lies on a lower indifference curve, Natalie does not prefer it.

Notice that, at the optimum, the slope of the indifference curve equals the slope of the budget constraint. We say that the indifference curve is tangent to the budget constraint. The slope of the indifference curve is the marginal rate of substitution between Pepsi and pizza, and the slope of the budget constraint is the relative price of Pepsi and pizza. Thus, *a consumer chooses consumption of the two goods so that the marginal rate of substitution equals the relative price.*

In chapter 7 we saw how market prices reflect the marginal value that consumers place on goods. This analysis of consumer choice shows the same result in another way. In making consumption choices, a consumer takes as given the relative price of the two goods and then chooses an optimum at which the marginal rate of substitution equals this relative price. The relative price is the rate at which the *market* is willing to trade one good for the other, whereas the marginal rate of substitution is the rate at which a *consumer* is willing to trade one good for the other. At a consumer's optimum, the consumer's valuation of the two goods (as measured by the marginal rate of substitution) equals the market's valuation (as measured by the relative price). As a result of this consumer optimisation, market prices of different goods reflect the value that consumers place on those goods.

How changes in income affect a consumer's choices

Now that we have seen how a consumer makes the consumption decision, let's examine how consumption responds to changes in income. To be specific, suppose that income increases. With a higher income, Natalie can afford more of both goods. The increase in income, therefore, shifts the budget constraint outwards, as in Figure 22.7. Because the relative price of the two goods has not

Figure 22.7 An increase in income

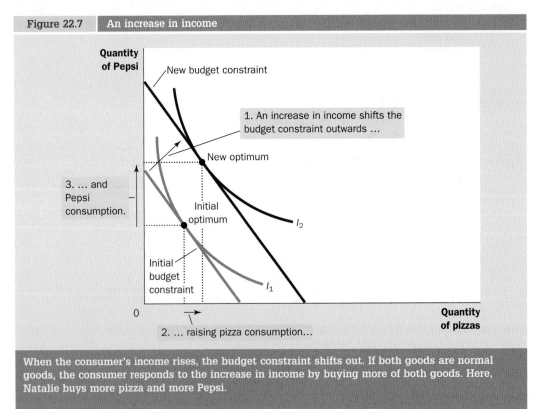

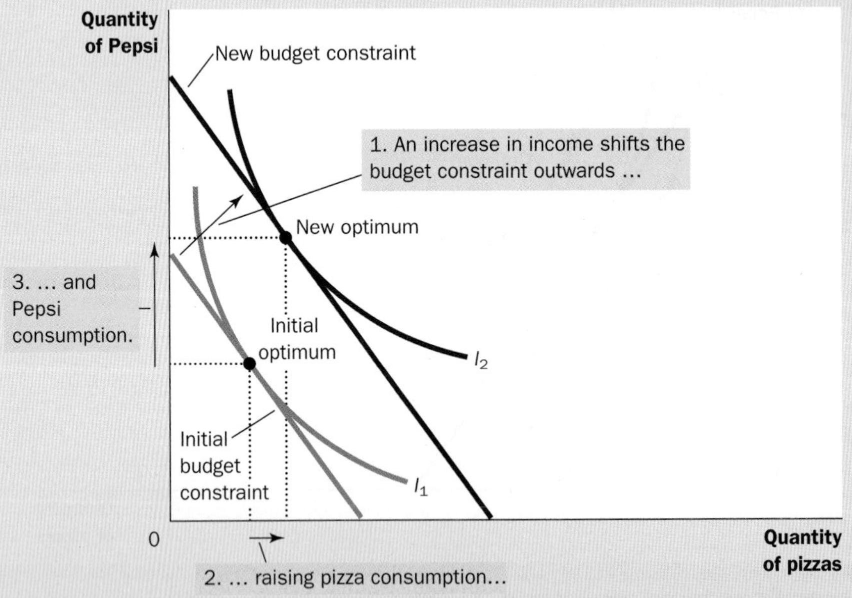

When the consumer's income rises, the budget constraint shifts out. If both goods are normal goods, the consumer responds to the increase in income by buying more of both goods. Here, Natalie buys more pizza and more Pepsi.

changed, the slope of the new budget constraint is the same as the slope of the initial budget constraint. That is, an increase in income leads to a parallel shift in the budget constraint.

The expanded budget constraint allows our consumer, Natalie, to choose a better combination of Pepsi and pizza. In other words, Natalie can now reach a higher indifference curve. Given the shift in the budget constraint and Natalie's preferences as represented by the indifference curves, Natalie's optimum moves from the point labelled 'initial optimum' to the point labelled 'new optimum'.

Notice that, in Figure 22.7, Natalie chooses to consume more Pepsi and more pizza. Although the logic of the model does not require increased consumption of both goods in response to increased income, this situation is the most common one. As you may recall from chapter 4, if consumers want more of a good when their incomes rise, economists call it a *normal good*. The indifference curves in Figure 22.7 are drawn under the assumption that both Pepsi and pizza are normal goods.

Figure 22.8 shows an example in which an increase in income induces our consumer, Natalie, to buy more pizzas but less Pepsi. If a consumer buys less of a good when income rises, economists call it an *inferior good*. Figure 22.8 is drawn under the assumption that pizza is a normal good and Pepsi is an inferior good.

Search me!
▸ inferior good

Although most goods are normal goods, there are some inferior goods in the world. One example is second-hand clothes. High-income consumers are more likely to buy new clothes and less likely to buy second-hand clothes than are low-income consumers. Second-hand clothes, therefore, are an inferior good.

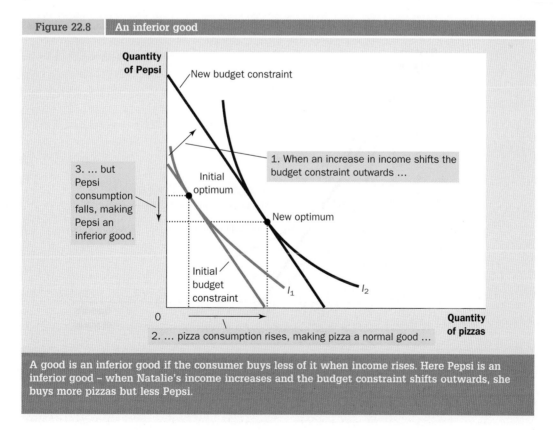

Figure 22.8 **An inferior good**

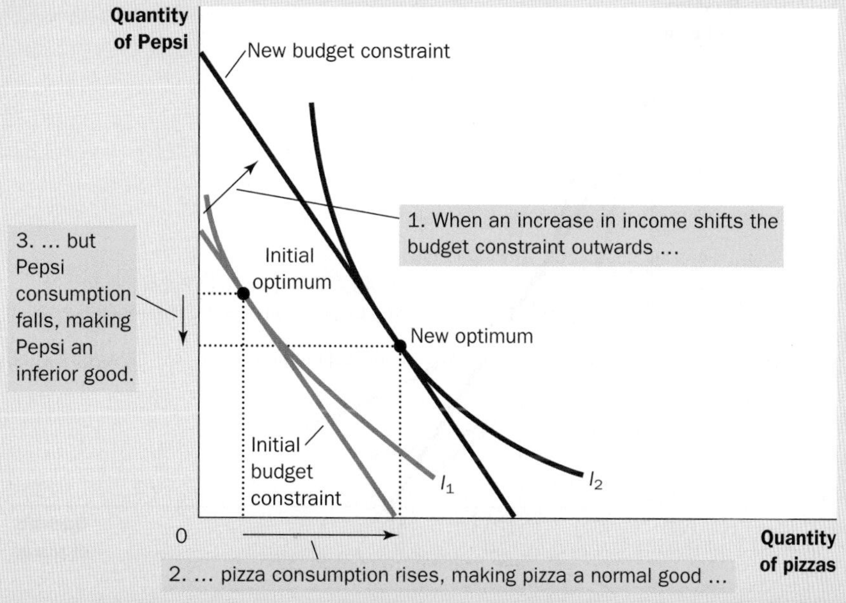

A good is an inferior good if the consumer buys less of it when income rises. Here Pepsi is an inferior good – when Natalie's income increases and the budget constraint shifts outwards, she buys more pizzas but less Pepsi.

How changes in prices affect a consumer's choices

Let's now use this model of consumer choice to consider how a change in the price of one of the goods alters a consumer's choices. Suppose, in particular, that the price of Pepsi falls from \$2 to \$1 a litre. It is no surprise that the lower price expands the consumer's set of buying opportunities. In other words, a fall in the price of any good shifts the budget constraint outwards.

Figure 22.9 considers more specifically how the fall in price affects the budget constraint. If our consumer, Natalie, spends the entire \$1000 income on pizza, then the price of Pepsi is irrelevant. Thus, point A in the figure stays the same. Yet Natalie, by spending the entire income of \$1000 on Pepsi, can now buy 1000 rather than only 500 litres. Thus, the end point of the budget constraint moves from point B to point D.

Notice that, in this case, the outward shift in the budget constraint changes the slope of the budget constraint. (This differs from what happened previously when prices stayed the same but the consumer's income changed.) As we have discussed, the slope of the budget constraint reflects the relative price of Pepsi and pizza. Because the price of Pepsi has fallen to \$1 from \$2 and the price of a pizza has remained \$10, our consumer can now trade a pizza for 10 rather than 5 litres of Pepsi. As a result, the new budget constraint is more steeply sloped.

How such a change in the budget constraint alters the consumption of both goods depends on a consumer's preferences. For the indifference curves drawn in this figure, Natalie buys more Pepsi and fewer pizzas.

Figure 22.9 **A change in price**

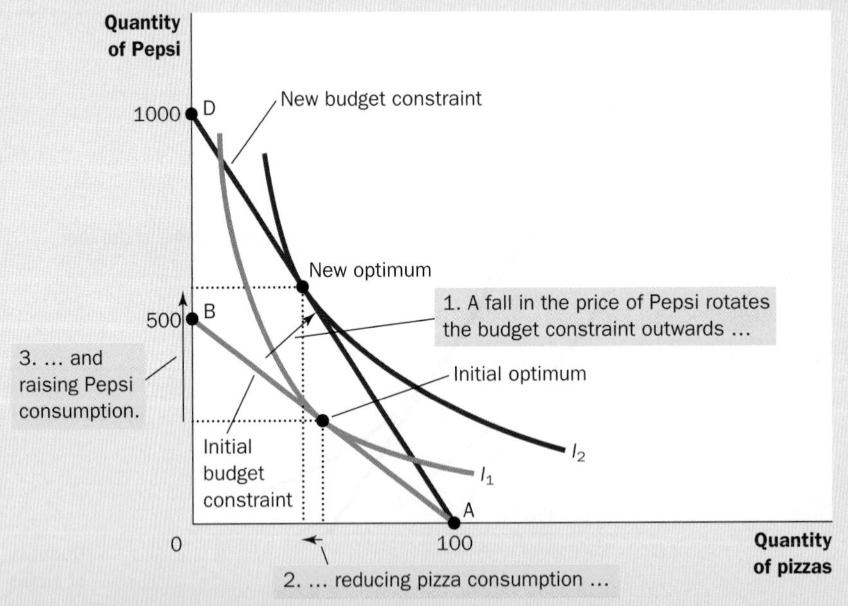

When the price of Pepsi falls, Natalie's budget constraint shifts outwards and changes slope. She moves from the initial optimum to the new optimum, which changes her purchases of both Pepsi and pizza. In this case, the quantity of Pepsi consumed rises and the quantity of pizza consumed falls.

Income and substitution effects

The impact of a change in the price of a good on consumption can be divided into two effects – an **income effect** and a **substitution effect**. To see what these two effects are, consider how our consumer might respond upon learning that the price of Pepsi has fallen. Natalie might reason in the following ways:

income effect
the change in consumption that results when a price change moves the consumer to a higher or lower indifference curve

substitution effect
the change in consumption that results when a price change moves the consumer along a given indifference curve to a point with a new marginal rate of substitution

- 'Great news! Now that Pepsi is cheaper, my income has greater purchasing power. I am, in effect, richer than I was. Because I am richer, I can buy both more Pepsi and more pizza.' (This is the income effect.)
- 'Now that the price of Pepsi has fallen, I get more litres of Pepsi for every pizza that I give up. Because pizza is now relatively more expensive, I should buy fewer pizzas and more Pepsi.' (This is the substitution effect.)

Which statement do you find more compelling?

In fact, both of these statements make sense. The decrease in the price of Pepsi makes Natalie better off. If Pepsi and pizza are both normal goods, Natalie will want to spread this improvement in purchasing power over both goods. This income effect tends to make Natalie buy more pizzas and more Pepsi. Yet, at the same time, consumption of Pepsi has become less expensive relative to consumption of pizzas. This substitution effect tends to make Natalie choose more Pepsi and fewer pizzas.

Now consider the end result of these two effects. Natalie certainly buys more Pepsi, because the income and substitution effects both act to raise purchases of Pepsi. But it is ambiguous whether Natalie buys more pizzas, because the income and substitution effects work in opposite directions. This conclusion is summarised in Table 22.2.

We can interpret the income and substitution effects using indifference curves. The income effect is the change in consumption that results from the movement to a higher indifference curve. The substitution effect is the change in consumption that results from being at a point on an indifference curve with a different marginal rate of substitution.

Figure 22.10 shows graphically how to divide the change in a consumer's decision into the income effect and the substitution effect. When the price of Pepsi falls, Natalie moves from the initial optimum, point A, to the new optimum, point C. We can view this change as occurring in two steps. First, Natalie moves along the initial indifference curve I_1 from point A to point B. Natalie is equally happy at these two points, but at point B, the marginal rate of substitution reflects the new relative price. Next, Natalie shifts to the higher indifference curve I_2 by moving from point B to point C. Even though point B and point C are on different indifference curves, they have the same marginal rate of substitution – that is, the slope of the indifference curve I_1 at point B equals the slope of the indifference curve I_2 at point C.

Table 22.2 Income and substitution effects when the price of Pepsi falls

Good	Income effect	Substitution effect	Total effect
Pepsi	Natalie is richer, so she buys more Pepsi	Pepsi is relatively cheaper, so Natalie buys more Pepsi	Income and substitution effects act in the same direction, so Natalie buys more Pepsi
Pizza	Natalie is richer, so she buys more pizza	Pizza is relatively more expensive, so Natalie buys fewer pizzas	Income and substitution effects act in opposite directions, so the total effect on pizza is ambiguous

Figure 22.10 Income and substitution effects

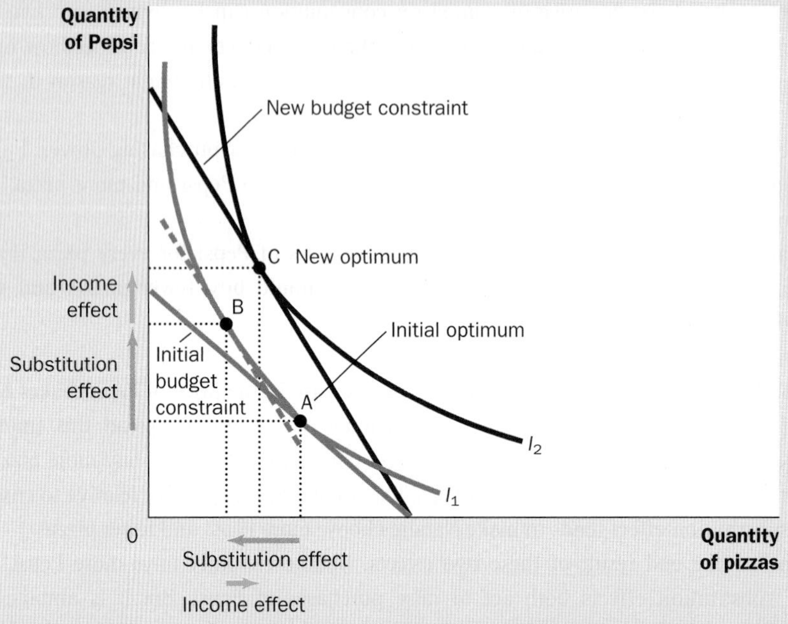

The effect of a change in price can be broken down into an income effect and a substitution effect. The substitution effect – the movement along an indifference curve to a point with a different marginal rate of substitution – is shown here as the change from point A to point B along indifference curve I_1. The income effect – the shift to a higher indifference curve – is shown here as the change from point B on indifference curve I_1 to point C on indifference curve I_2.

Although a consumer never actually chooses point B, this hypothetical point is useful to clarify the two effects that determine a consumer's decision. Notice that the change from point A to point B represents a pure change in the marginal rate of substitution without any change in the consumer's welfare. Similarly, the change from point B to point C represents a pure change in welfare without any change in the marginal rate of substitution. Thus, the movement from A to B shows the substitution effect and the movement from B to C shows the income effect.

Deriving the demand curve

We have just seen how changes in the price of a good alter a consumer's budget constraint and, therefore, the quantities of the two goods bought. The demand curve for any good reflects these consumption decisions. As you should recall, a demand curve shows how the price of a good affects the quantity demanded. We can view a consumer's demand curve as a summary of the optimum decisions that arise from the consumer's budget constraint and indifference curves.

For example, Figure 22.11 considers the demand for Pepsi. Panel (a) shows that when the price of a litre falls from \$2 to \$1, Natalie's budget constraint shifts outwards. Because of both income and substitution effects, Natalie increases purchases of Pepsi from 50 to 150 litres. Panel (b) shows the demand curve that results from Natalie's decisions. In this way, the theory of consumer choice provides the theoretical foundation for a consumer's demand curve.

Figure 22.11 Deriving the demand curve

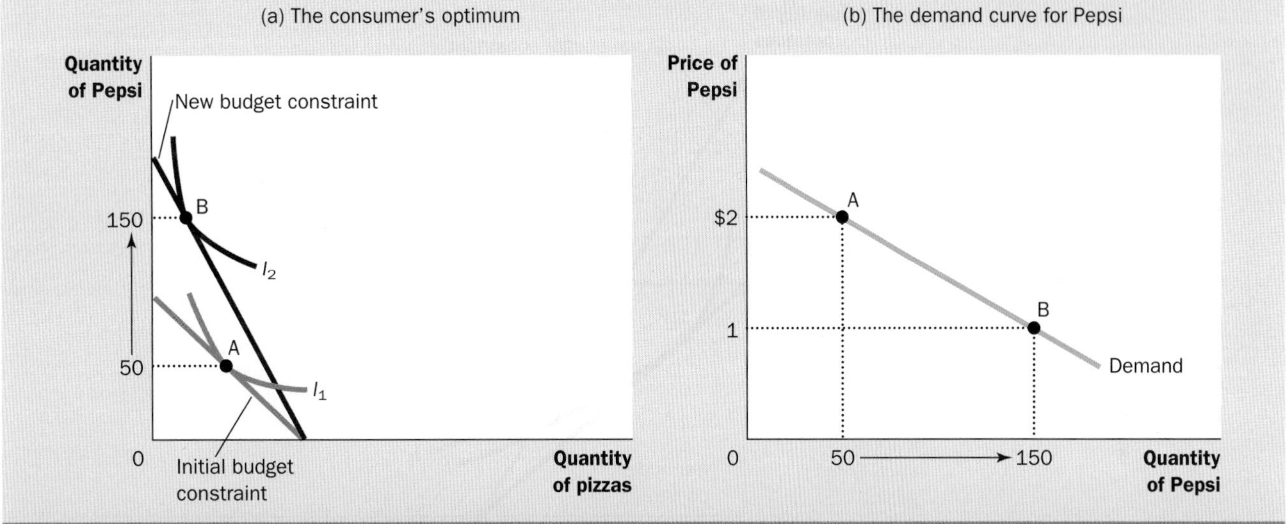

Panel (a) shows that when the price of Pepsi falls from \$2 to \$1, Natalie's optimum moves from point A to point B and the quantity of Pepsi consumed rises from 50 to 150 litres. The demand curve in panel (b) reflects this relationship between the price and the quantity demanded.

It may be comforting to know that the demand curve arises naturally from the theory of consumer choice, but this exercise by itself does not justify developing the theory. There is no need for a rigorous, analytic framework just to establish that people respond to changes in prices. The theory of consumer choice is, however, useful in studying the various decisions people make as they go about their lives, as we see in the next section.

Draw a budget constraint and indifference curves for Pepsi and pizza. Show what happens to the budget constraint and the consumer's optimum when the price of pizza rises. In your diagram, divide the change into an income effect and a substitution effect.

Four applications

Now that we have developed the basic theory of consumer choice, let's use it to shed light on four questions about how the economy works. These four questions might at first seem unrelated. But because each question involves household decision making, we can consider it using the model of consumer behaviour we have just developed.

Do all demand curves slope downwards?

Normally, when the price of a good rises, people buy less of it. Chapter 4 called this usual behaviour the *law of demand*. This law is reflected in the downward slope of the demand curve.

As a matter of economic theory, however, demand curves can sometimes slope upwards. In other words, consumers can sometimes violate the law of demand and buy *more* of a good when

Figure 22.12 A Giffen good

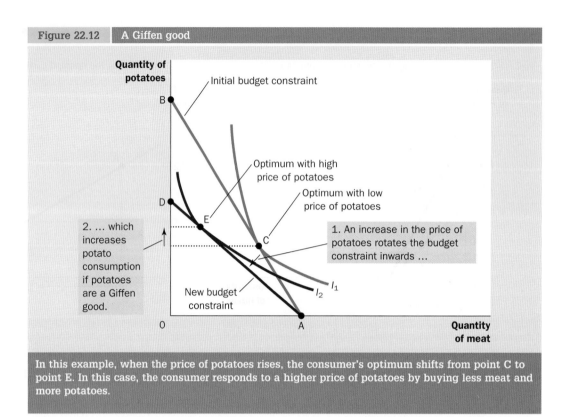

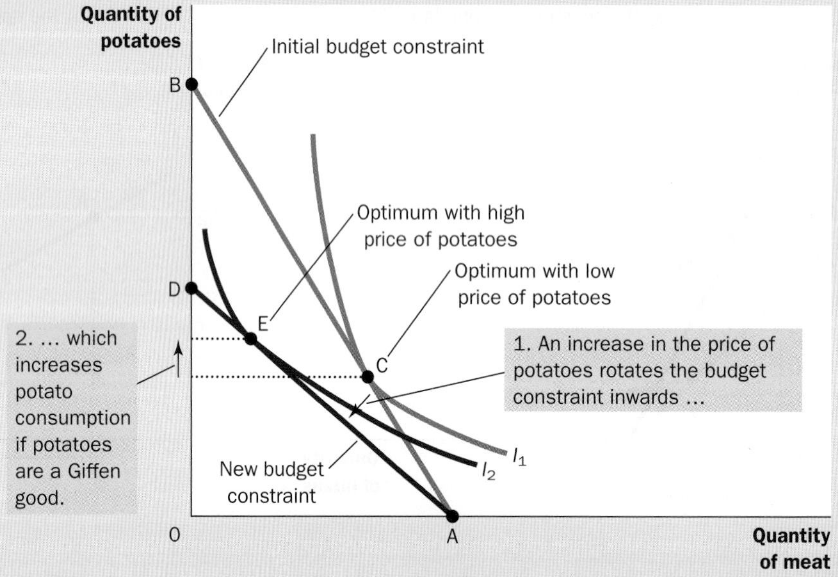

In this example, when the price of potatoes rises, the consumer's optimum shifts from point C to point E. In this case, the consumer responds to a higher price of potatoes by buying less meat and more potatoes.

the price rises. To see how this can happen, consider Figure 22.12. In this example, a consumer buys two goods – meat and potatoes. Initially, the consumer's budget constraint is the line from point A to point B. The optimum is point C. When the price of potatoes rises, the budget constraint shifts inwards and is now the line from point A to point D. The optimum is now point E. Notice that a rise in the price of potatoes has led the consumer to buy a larger quantity of potatoes.

Why is the consumer responding in a seemingly perverse way? The reason is that potatoes here are a strongly inferior good. When the price of potatoes rises, the consumer is poorer. The income effect makes the consumer want to buy less meat and more potatoes. At the same time, because potatoes have become more expensive relative to meat, the substitution effect makes the consumer want to buy more meat and less potatoes. In this particular case, however, the income effect is so strong that it exceeds the substitution effect. In the end, the consumer responds to the higher price of potatoes by buying less meat and more potatoes.

Giffen good
a good for which an increase in the price raises the quantity demanded

Economists use the term **Giffen good** to describe a good that violates the law of demand. (The term is named for economist Robert Giffen, who first noted this possibility.) In this example, potatoes are a Giffen good. Giffen goods are inferior goods for which the income effect dominates the substitution effect. Therefore, they have demand curves that slope upwards.

Have any actual Giffen goods ever been observed? Some historians suggest that potatoes were a Giffen good during the Irish potato famine of the nineteenth century. Potatoes were such a large part of people's diet that when the price of potatoes rose, it had a large income effect. People responded to their reduced living standard by cutting back on the luxury of meat and buying more of the staple food of potatoes. Thus, it is argued that a higher price of potatoes actually raised the quantity of potatoes demanded.

A recent study by Robert Jensen and Nolan Miller has produced similar but more concrete evidence for the existence of Giffen goods. These two economists conducted a field experiment for five months in the Chinese province of Hunan. They gave randomly selected households vouchers that subsidised the purchase of rice, a staple in local diets, and used surveys to measure how consumption of rice responded to changes in the price. They found strong evidence that poor households exhibited Giffen behavior. Lowering the price of rice with the subsidy voucher caused households to reduce their consumption of rice and removing the subsidy had the opposite effect. Jensen and Miller wrote, 'To the best of our knowledge, this is the first rigorous empirical evidence of Giffen behavior'.

Thus, the theory of consumer choice allows demand curves to slope upward and sometimes that strange phenomenon actually occurs. As a result, the law of demand we first saw in Chapter 4 is not completely reliable. It is safe to say, however, that Giffen goods are very rare.

How do wages affect labour supply?

So far we have used the theory of consumer choice to analyse how a person decides to allocate income between two goods. We can use the same theory to analyse how a person allocates time. People spend some of their time enjoying leisure and some of it working so they can afford to buy consumption goods. The essence of the time-allocation problem is the trade-off between leisure and consumption.

Consider the decision facing Sally, a freelance software designer. Sally is awake for 100 hours per week. She spends some of this time enjoying leisure – riding her bike, watching television, studying economics and so on. She spends the rest of this time at her computer developing software. For every hour she spends developing software, she earns $50, which she spends on consumption goods. Thus, her wage ($50) reflects the trade-off Sally faces between leisure and consumption. For every hour of leisure she gives up, she works one more hour and gets $50 of consumption.

Figure 22.13 shows Sally's budget constraint. If she spends all 100 hours enjoying leisure, she has no consumption. If she spends all 100 hours working, she earns a weekly consumption of $5000 but has no time for leisure. If she works 40 hours a week, she enjoys 60 hours of leisure and has weekly consumption of $2000.

Figure 22.13 uses indifference curves to represent Sally's preferences for consumption and leisure. Here consumption and leisure are the two 'goods' that Sally is choosing between. Because Sally always prefers more leisure and more consumption, she prefers points on higher indifference curves to points on lower ones. At a wage of $50 per hour, Sally chooses a combination of consumption and leisure represented by the point labelled 'optimum'. This is the point on the budget constraint that is on the highest possible indifference curve, which is curve I_2.

Now consider what happens when Sally's wage increases from $50 to $60 per hour. Figure 22.14 shows two possible outcomes. In each case, the budget constraint, shown in the left-hand graph, shifts outwards from BC_1 to BC_2. In the process, the budget constraint becomes steeper, reflecting the change in relative price – at the higher wage, Sally gets more consumption for every hour of leisure that she gives up.

Sally's preferences, as represented by her indifference curves, determine how her choice regarding consumption and leisure responds to the higher wage. In both panels, consumption rises. Yet the

Figure 22.13 The work–leisure decision

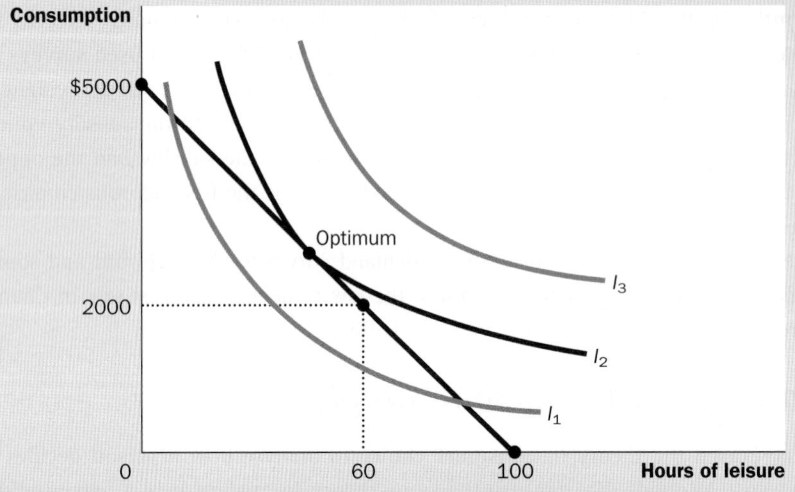

This figure shows Sally's budget constraint for deciding how much to work, her indifference curves for consumption and leisure and her optimum.

response of leisure to the change in the wage is different in the two cases. In panel (a), Sally responds to the higher wage by enjoying less leisure. In panel (b), Sally responds by enjoying more leisure.

Sally's decision between leisure and consumption determines her supply of labour, for the more leisure she enjoys the less time she has left to work. In each panel, the right-hand graph in Figure 22.14 shows the labour supply curve implied by Sally's decision. In panel (a), a higher wage induces Sally to enjoy less leisure and work more, so the labour supply curve slopes upwards. In panel (b), a higher wage induces Sally to enjoy more leisure and work less, so the labour supply curve slopes 'backward'.

At first, the backward-sloping labour supply curve is puzzling. Why would a person respond to a higher wage by working less? The answer comes from considering the income and substitution effects of a higher wage.

Consider first the substitution effect. When Sally's wage rises, leisure becomes more costly relative to consumption and this encourages Sally to substitute consumption for leisure. In other words, the substitution effect induces Sally to work harder in response to higher wages, which tends to make the labour supply curve slope upward.

Now consider the income effect. When Sally's wage rises, she moves to a higher indifference curve. She is now better off than she was. As long as consumption and leisure are both normal goods, she tends to want to use this increase in wellbeing to enjoy both higher consumption and greater leisure. In other words, the income effect induces her to work less, which tends to make the labour supply curve slope backward.

In the end, economic theory does not give a clear prediction about whether an increase in the wage induces Sally to work more or less. If the substitution effect is greater than the income effect for Sally, she works more. If the income effect is greater than the substitution effect, she works less. The labour supply curve, therefore, could be either upward- or backward-sloping.

Figure 22.14 An increase in the wage

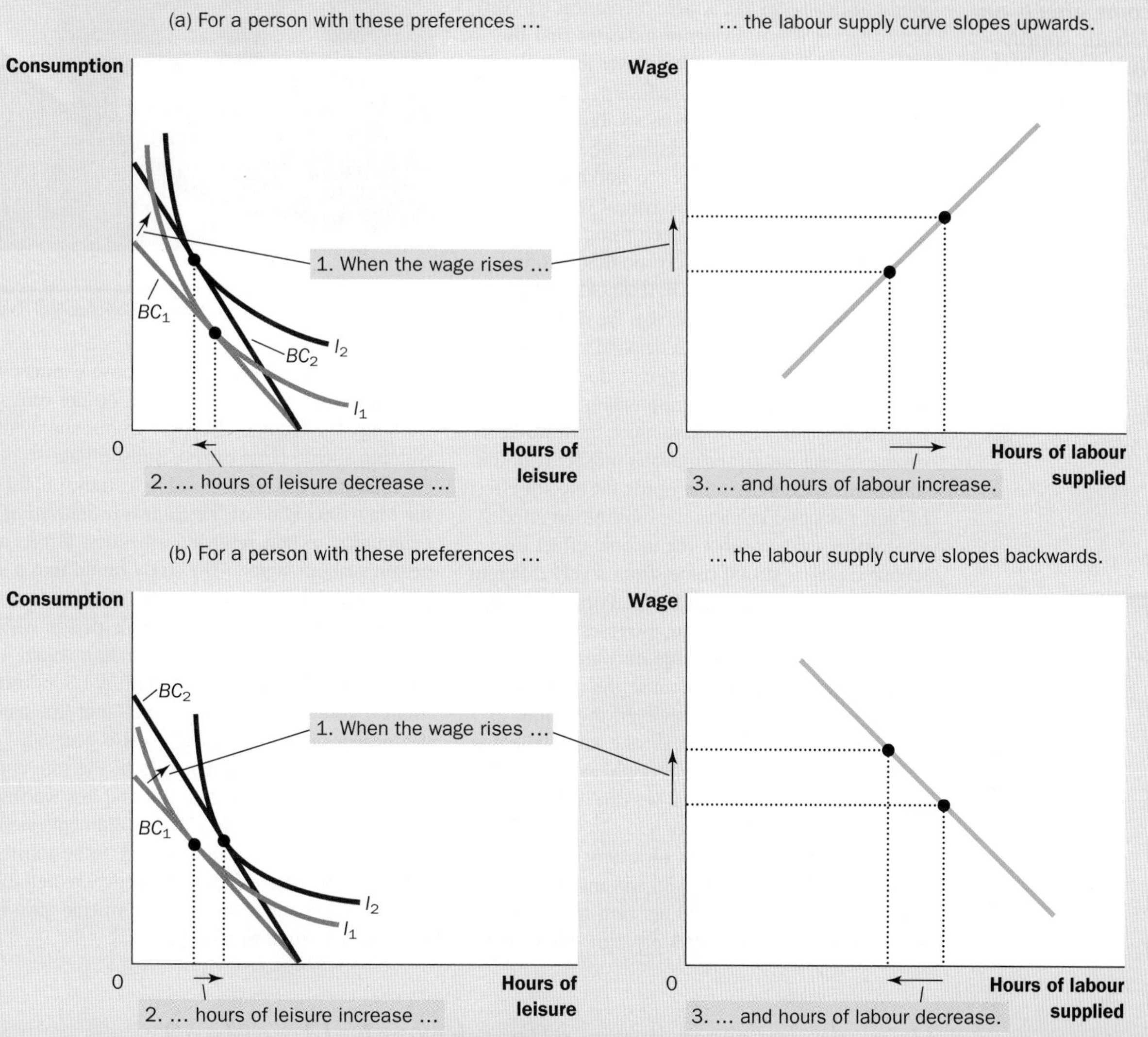
(a) For a person with these preferences ...
... the labour supply curve slopes upwards.
Consumption
Wage
1. When the wage rises ...
BC1
BC2
I2
I1
0
Hours of leisure
2. ... hours of leisure decrease ...
0
Hours of labour supplied
3. ... and hours of labour increase.
(b) For a person with these preferences ...
... the labour supply curve slopes backwards.
Consumption
Wage
BC2
1. When the wage rises ...
BC1
I2
I1
0
Hours of leisure
2. ... hours of leisure increase ...
0
Hours of labour supplied
3. ... and hours of labour decrease.

The two panels of this figure show how a person might respond to an increase in the wage. The graphs on the left show the consumer's initial budget constraint BC_1 and new budget constraint BC_2, as well as the consumer's optimum choices between consumption and leisure. The graphs on the right show the resulting labour supply curve. Because hours worked equal total hours available minus hours of leisure, any change in leisure implies an opposite change in the quantity of labour supplied. In panel (a), when the wage rises, consumption rises and leisure falls, resulting in a labour supply curve that slopes upwards. In panel (b), when the wage rises, both consumption and leisure rise, resulting in a labour supply curve that slopes backwards.

CASESTUDY

Income effects on labour supply – historical trends, lottery winners and the Carnegie conjecture

The idea of a backward-sloping labour supply curve might at first seem like a mere theoretical curiosity, but in fact it is not. Evidence indicates that the labour supply curve, considered over long periods of time, does in fact slope backwards. A hundred years ago many people worked six days a week. Today five-day working weeks are the norm. At the same time that the length of the working week has been falling, the wage of the typical worker (adjusted for inflation) has been rising.

Here is how economists explain this historical pattern. Over time, advances in technology raise workers' productivity and, thereby, the demand for labour. The increase in labour demand raises equilibrium wages. As wages rise, so does the reward for working. Yet rather than responding to this increased incentive by working more, most workers choose to take part of their greater prosperity in the form of more leisure. In other words, the income effect of higher wages dominates the substitution effect.

Further evidence that the income effect on labour supply is strong comes from a very different kind of data – winners of lotteries. Winners of large prizes in the lottery see large increases in their incomes and, as a result, large outward shifts in their budget constraints. Because the winners' wages have not changed, however, the slopes of their budget constraints remain the same. There is, therefore, no substitution effect. By examining the behaviour of lottery winners, we can isolate the income effect on labour supply.

The results from studies of lottery winners are striking. Of those winners who win more than a total of $50 000, almost 25 per cent quit working within a year, and another 9 per cent reduce the number of hours they work. Of those winners who win more than $1 million, almost 40 per cent stop working. The income effect on labour supply of winning such a large prize is substantial.

'No more 9 to 5 for me.'

Source: iStockphoto/Mark Evans.

Similar results were found in a study, published in the May 1993 issue of the *Quarterly Journal of Economics*, of how receiving a bequest affects a person's labour supply. The study found that a single person who inherits more than $150 000 is four times as likely to stop working as a single person who inherits less than $25 000. This finding would not have surprised the nineteenth-century US industrialist Andrew Carnegie. Carnegie warned that 'the parent who leaves his son enormous wealth generally deadens the talents and energies of the son, and tempts him to lead a less useful and less worthy life than he otherwise would'. That is, Carnegie viewed the income effect on labour supply to be substantial and, from his paternalistic perspective, regrettable. During his life and at his death, Carnegie gave much of his vast fortune to charity.

How do interest rates affect household saving?

An important decision that every person faces is how much income to consume today and how much to save for the future. We can use the theory of consumer choice to analyse how people make this decision and how the amount they save depends on the interest rate their savings will earn.

Consider the decision facing Sam, a worker planning ahead for retirement. To keep things simple, let's divide Sam's life into two periods. In the first period, Sam is young and working. In the second period, he is old and retired. When young, Sam earns $100 000. He divides this income between current consumption and saving. When he is old, Sam will consume what he has saved, including the interest that his savings have earned.

Suppose that the interest rate is 10 per cent. Then for every dollar that Sam saves when young, he can consume $1.10 when old. We can view 'consumption when young' and 'consumption when old' as the two goods that Sam must choose between. The interest rate determines the relative price of these two goods.

Figure 22.15 The consumption–saving decision

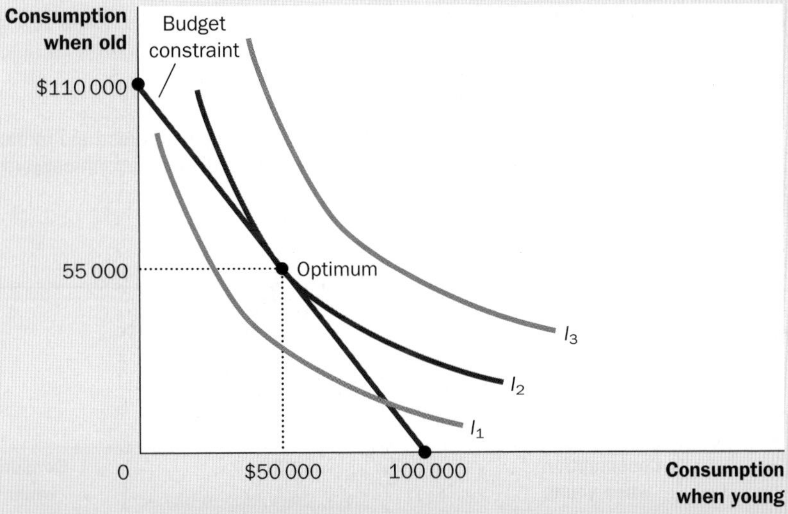

This figure shows the budget constraint for a person deciding how much to consume in the two periods of his life, the indifference curves representing his preferences and the optimum.

Figure 22.15 shows Sam's budget constraint. If he saves nothing, he consumes $100 000 when young and nothing when old. If he saves everything, he consumes nothing when young and $110 000 when old. The budget constraint shows these and all the intermediate possibilities.

Figure 22.15 uses indifference curves to represent Sam's preferences for consumption in the two periods. Because Sam prefers more consumption in both periods, he prefers points on higher indifference curves to points on lower ones. Given his preferences, Sam chooses the optimum combination of consumption in both periods of life, which is the point on the budget constraint that is on the highest possible indifference curve. At this optimum, Sam consumes $50 000 when young and $55 000 when old.

Now consider what happens when the interest rate increases from 10 per cent to 20 per cent. Figure 22.16 shows two possible outcomes. In both cases, the budget constraint shifts outwards and becomes steeper. At the new higher interest rate, Sam gets more consumption when old for every dollar of consumption that he gives up when young.

The two panels show different preferences for Sam and the resulting response to the higher interest rate. In both cases, consumption when old rises. Yet the response of consumption when young to the change in the interest rate is different in the two cases. In panel (a), Sam responds to the higher interest rate by consuming less when young. In panel (b), Sam responds by consuming more when young.

Sam's saving, of course, is his income when young minus the amount he consumes when young. In panel (a), consumption when young falls when the interest rate rises, so saving must rise. In panel (b), Sam consumes more when young, so saving must fall.

The case shown in panel (b) might at first seem odd – Sam responds to an increase in the return on savings by saving less. Yet this behaviour is not as peculiar as it might seem. We can understand it by considering the income and substitution effects of a higher interest rate.

Consider first the substitution effect. When the interest rate rises, consumption when old becomes less costly relative to consumption when young. Therefore, the substitution effect induces Sam to consume more when old and less when young. In other words, the substitution effect induces Sam to save more.

Figure 22.16 An increase in the interest rate

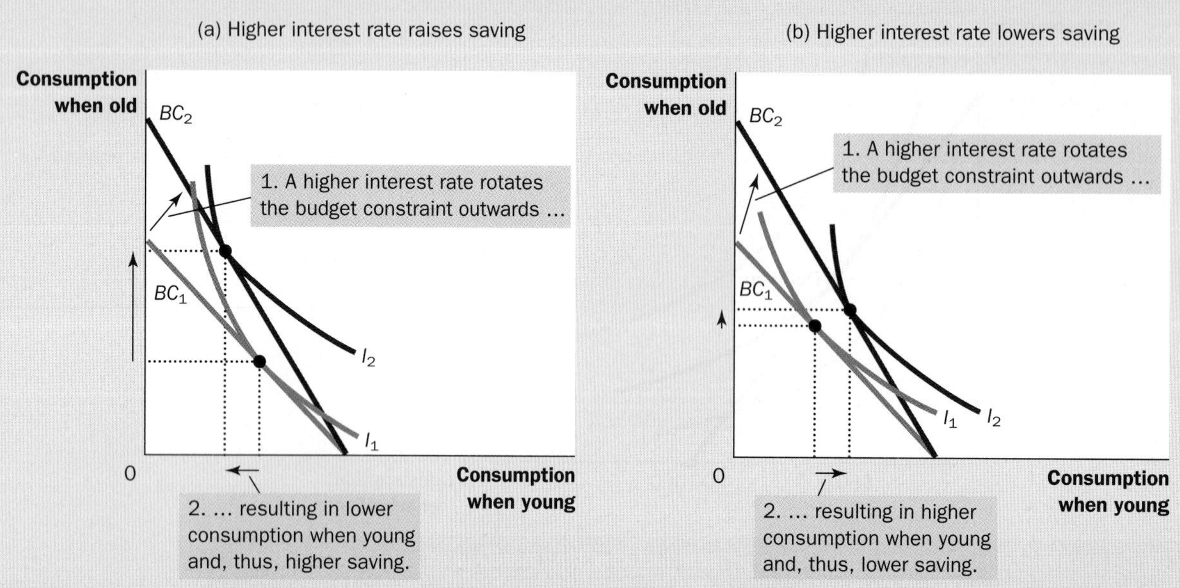
(a) Higher interest rate raises saving
Consumption when old
BC_2
1. A higher interest rate rotates the budget constraint outwards ...
BC_1
I_2
I_1
0
Consumption when young
2. ... resulting in lower consumption when young and, thus, higher saving.
(b) Higher interest rate lowers saving
Consumption when old
BC_2
1. A higher interest rate rotates the budget constraint outwards ...
BC_1
I_1
I_2
0
Consumption when young
2. ... resulting in higher consumption when young and, thus, lower saving.

In both panels, an increase in the interest rate shifts the budget constraint outwards. In panel (a), consumption when young falls, and consumption when old rises. The result is an increase in saving when young. In panel (b), consumption in both periods rises. The result is a decrease in saving when young.

Now consider the income effect. When the interest rate rises, Sam moves to a higher indifference curve. He is now better off than he was. As long as consumption in both periods consists of normal goods, he tends to want to use this increase in wellbeing to enjoy higher consumption in both periods. In other words, the income effect induces him to save less.

The end result, of course, depends on both the income and substitution effects. If the substitution effect of a higher interest rate is greater than the income effect, Sam saves more. If the income effect is greater than the substitution effect, Sam saves less. Thus, the theory of consumer choice says that an increase in the interest rate could either encourage or discourage saving.

Although this ambiguous result is interesting from the standpoint of economic theory, it is disappointing from the standpoint of economic policy. It turns out that an important issue in tax policy hinges in part on how saving responds to interest rates. Some economists have advocated reducing the tax on interest and other capital income, arguing that such a policy change would raise the after-tax interest rate that savers can earn and would thereby encourage people to save more. Other economists have argued that because of offsetting income and substitution effects, such a tax change might not increase saving and could even reduce it. Unfortunately, research has not led to a consensus about how interest rates affect saving. As a result, there remains disagreement among economists about whether changes in tax policy aimed to encourage saving would, in fact, have the intended effect.

Do the poor prefer to receive cash or in-kind transfers?

Paul is poor. Because of his low income, he has a meagre standard of living. The government wants to help. It can either give Paul $1000 worth of food or simply give him $1000 in cash.

What does the theory of consumer choice have to say about the comparison between these two policy options?

Figure 22.17 shows how the two options might work. If the government gives Paul cash, then the budget constraint shifts outwards. He can divide the extra cash between food and non-food consumption however he pleases. In contrast, if the government gives Paul an in-kind transfer of

Figure 22.17 **Cash versus in-kind transfers**

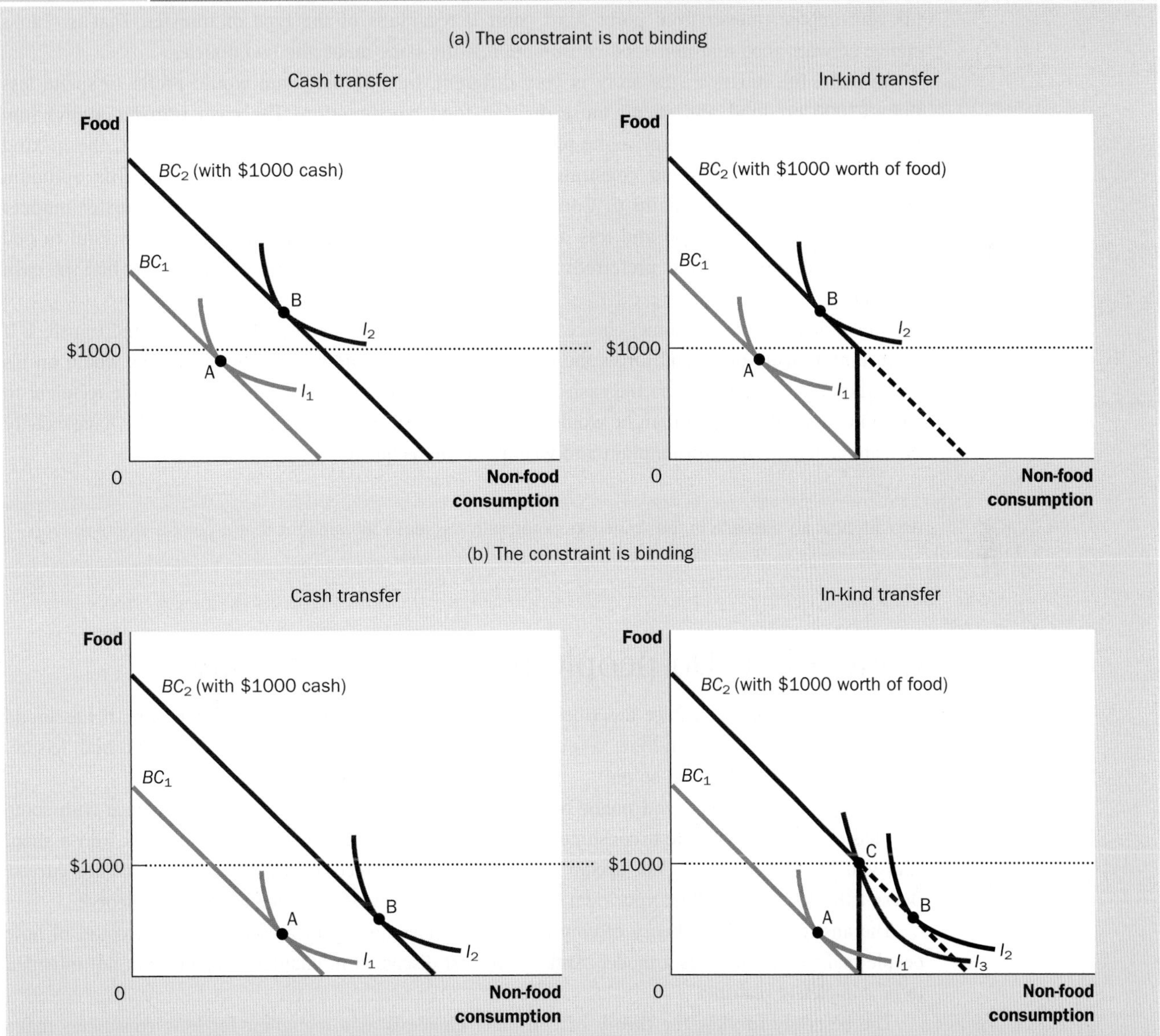

Both panels compare a cash transfer and a similar in-kind transfer of food. In panel (a), the in-kind transfer does not impose a binding constraint and the consumer ends up on the same indifference curve under the two policies. In panel (b), the in-kind transfer imposes a binding constraint and the consumer ends up on a lower indifference curve with the in-kind transfer than with the cash transfer.

food, then his new budget constraint is more complicated. The budget constraint has again shifted out. But now the budget constraint has a kink at $1000 of food, for Paul must consume at least that amount in food. That is, even if Paul spends all his money on non-food consumption, he still consumes $1000 in food.

The ultimate comparison between the cash transfer and in-kind transfer depends on Paul's preferences. In panel (a), Paul would choose to spend at least $1000 on food even if he receives a cash transfer. Therefore, the constraint imposed by the in-kind transfer is not binding. In this case, his consumption moves from point A to point B regardless of the type of transfer. That is, Paul's choice between food and non-food consumption is the same under the two policies.

In panel (b), however, the story is very different. In this case, Paul would prefer to spend less than $1000 on food and spend more on non-food consumption. The cash transfer allows him discretion to spend the money as he pleases and he consumes at point B. In contrast, the in-kind transfer imposes the binding constraint that he consume at least $1000 of food. His optimum allocation is at the kink, point C. Compared with the cash transfer, the in-kind transfer induces Paul to consume more food and less of other goods. The in-kind transfer also forces Paul to end up on a lower (and thus less preferred) indifference curve. Paul is worse off than if he had the cash transfer.

Thus, the theory of consumer choice teaches a simple lesson about cash versus in-kind transfers. If an in-kind transfer of a good forces the recipient to consume more of the good than he would on his own, then the recipient prefers the cash transfer. If the in-kind transfer does not force the recipient to consume more of the good than he would on his own, then the cash and in-kind transfer have exactly the same effect on the consumption and welfare of the recipient.

Q

Explain how an increase in the wage can potentially decrease the amount that a person wants to work.

Conclusion: Do people really think this way?

The theory of consumer choice describes how people make decisions. As we have seen, it has broad applicability. It can explain how a person chooses between Pepsi and pizza, work and leisure, consumption and saving and so on.

At this point, however, you might be tempted to treat the theory of consumer choice with some scepticism. After all, you are a consumer. You decide what to buy every time you walk into a shop. And you know that you do not decide by writing down budget constraints and indifference curves. Doesn't this knowledge about your own decision making provide evidence against the theory?

The answer is no. The theory of consumer choice does not try to present a literal account of how people make decisions. It is a model. And, as we first discussed in chapter 2, models are not intended to be completely realistic.

The best way to view the theory of consumer choice is as a metaphor for how consumers make decisions. No consumer (except an occasional economist) goes through the explicit optimisation envisioned in the theory. Yet consumers are aware that their choices are constrained by their financial resources. And, given those constraints, they do the best they can to achieve the highest level of satisfaction. The theory of consumer choice tries to describe this implicit psychological process in a way that permits explicit economic analysis.

The proof of the pudding is in the eating. And the test of a theory is in its applications. In the last section of this chapter we applied the theory of consumer choice to four practical issues about the economy. If you take more advanced courses in economics, you will see that this theory provides the framework for much additional analysis.

Summary

- A consumer's budget constraint shows the possible combinations of different goods that can be bought given his/her income and the prices of the goods. The slope of the budget constraint equals the relative price of the goods.
- A consumer's indifference curves represent his or her preferences. An indifference curve shows the various bundles of goods that make a consumer equally happy. Points on higher indifference curves are preferred to points on lower indifference curves. The slope of an indifference curve at any point is the consumer's marginal rate of substitution – the rate at which the consumer is willing to trade one good for the other.
- A consumer optimises by choosing the point on the budget constraint that lies on the highest indifference curve. At this point, the slope of the indifference curve (the marginal rate of substitution between the goods) equals the slope of the budget constraint (the relative price of the goods).
- When the price of a good falls, the impact on a consumer's choices can be broken down into an income effect and a substitution effect. The income effect is the change in consumption that arises because a lower price makes the consumer better off. The substitution effect is the change in consumption that arises because a price change encourages greater consumption of the good that has become relatively cheaper. The income effect is reflected in the movement from a lower to a higher indifference curve, whereas the substitution effect is reflected by a movement along an indifference curve to a point with a different slope.
- The theory of consumer choice can be applied in many situations. It can explain why demand curves can potentially slope upwards, why higher wages could either increase or decrease the quantity of labour supplied, why higher interest rates could either increase or decrease saving, and why the poor prefer cash to in-kind transfers.

Key concepts

budget constraint
Giffen good
income effect
indifference curve
marginal rate of substitution
perfect complements
perfect substitutes
substitution effect

Questions for review

1 A consumer has income of $3000. Wine costs $3 a glass and cheese costs $6 a kilogram. Draw the consumer's budget constraint. What is the slope of this budget constraint?

2 Draw a consumer's indifference curves for wine and cheese. Describe and explain four properties of these indifference curves.

3 Pick a point on an indifference curve for wine and cheese and show the marginal rate of substitution. What does the marginal rate of substitution tell us?

4 Show a consumer's budget constraint and indifference curves for wine and cheese. Show the optimum consumption choice. If the price of wine is $3 a glass and the price of cheese is $6 a kilogram, what is the marginal rate of substitution at this optimum?

5 A person who consumes wine and cheese gets a raise, so his income increases from $3000 to $4000. Show what happens if both wine and cheese are normal goods. Now show what happens if cheese is an inferior good.

6 The price of cheese rises from $6 to $10 a kilogram and the price of wine remains $3 a glass. For a consumer with a constant income of $3000, show what happens to consumption of wine and cheese. Divide the change into income and substitution effects.

7 Can an increase in the price of cheese possibly induce a consumer to buy more cheese? Explain.

Problems and applications

1 Jennifer divides her income between coffee and croissants. An early frost in Brazil causes a large increase in the price of coffee in Australia.
   a Show the effect of the frost on Jennifer's budget constraint.
   b Show the effect of the frost on Jennifer's optimum consumption bundle assuming that the substitution effect outweighs the income effect for croissants.
   c Show the effect of the frost on Jennifer's optimum consumption bundle assuming that the income effect outweighs the substitution effect for croissants.

2 Compare the following two pairs of goods:
   a Coke and Pepsi
   b skis and ski bindings.

   In which case do you expect the indifference curves to be fairly straight and in which case do you expect the indifference curves to be very bowed? In which case will the consumer respond more to a change in the relative price of the two goods?

3 Mario consumes only cheese and crackers.
   a Could cheese and crackers both be inferior goods for Mario? Explain.
   b Suppose that cheese is a normal good for Mario whereas crackers are an inferior good. If the price of cheese falls, what happens to Mario's consumption of crackers? What happens to his consumption of cheese? Explain.

4 Jim buys only milk and biscuits.
   a In 2004, Jim earns $100, milk costs $2 per litre and biscuits cost $4 per dozen. Draw Jim's budget constraint.
   b Now suppose that all prices increase by 10 per cent in the year 2005 and that Jim's salary increases by 10 per cent as well. Draw Jim's new budget constraint. How would Jim's optimum combination of milk and biscuits in 2005 compare with his optimum combination in 2004?

5 Consider your decision about how many hours to work.
   a Draw your budget constraint assuming that you pay no taxes on your income. On the same diagram, draw another budget constraint assuming that you pay a 15 per cent tax.
   b Show how the tax might lead to more hours of work, fewer hours or the same number of hours. Explain.

6 Sarah is awake for 100 hours per week. Using one diagram, show Sarah's budget constraints if she earns $6 per hour, $8 per hour and $10 per hour. Now draw indifference curves such that Sarah's labour supply curve is upward-sloping when the wage is between $6 and $8 per hour, and backward-sloping when the wage is between $8 and $10 per hour.

7 Draw the indifference curve for someone deciding how much to work. Suppose the wage increases. Is it possible that the person's consumption would fall? Is this plausible? Discuss. (*Hint:* Think about income and substitution effects.)

8 The labour force participation rate of married women has more than doubled over the past 50 years. One economic influence on this rate was the increase in women's wages over this period. Another economic influence was the increase in men's wages, which raised the standard of living for most married women.

a Using an indifference-curve diagram, show and then explain how a rise in the income of a husband can lead to a fall in the number of hours worked by his wife. What assumption do you need to make about leisure to get this result?

b Using another indifference-curve diagram, show and then explain how a rise in female wages affects a woman's decision about how many hours to work.

9 Suppose you take a job that pays $30 000 and set some of this income aside in a savings account that pays an annual interest rate of 5 per cent. Use a diagram with a budget constraint and indifference curves to show how your consumption changes in each of the following situations. To keep things simple, assume that you pay no taxes on your income.

a Your salary increases to $40 000.

b The interest rate on your bank account rises to 8 per cent.

10 As discussed in the text, we can divide an individual's life into two hypothetical periods – 'young' and 'old'. Suppose that the individual earns income only when young and saves some of that income to consume when old. If the interest rate on savings falls, can you tell what happens to consumption when young? Can you tell what happens to consumption when old? Explain.

11 Suppose that your state gives each town $5 million in aid per year. The way in which the money is spent is currently unrestricted, but the premier has proposed that towns be required to spend the entire $5 million on education. You can illustrate the effect of this proposal on your town's spending on education using a budget constraint and indifference-curve diagram. The two goods are education and non-education spending.

a Draw your town's budget constraint under the existing policy, assuming that your town's only source of revenue besides the state aid is a property tax that yields $10 million. On the same diagram, draw the budget constraint under the premier's proposal.

b Would your town spend more on education under the premier's proposal than under the existing policy? Explain.

c Now compare two towns – Youngton and Oldton – with the same revenue and the same state aid. Youngton has a large school-age population and Oldton has a large elderly population. In which town is the premier's proposal most likely to increase education spending? Explain.

12 (This problem is challenging.) The social security system provides income to some needy families. Typically, the maximum payment goes to families that earn no income; then, as families begin to earn income, the social security payment declines gradually and eventually disappears. Let's consider the possible effects of this program on a family's labour supply.

a Draw a budget constraint for a family assuming that the social security system did not exist. On the same diagram, draw a budget constraint that reflects the existence of the social security system.

b Adding indifference curves to your diagram, show how the social security system could reduce the number of hours worked by the family. Explain, with reference to both the income and substitution effects.

c Using your diagram from part (b), show the effect of the social security system on the wellbeing of the family.

13 (This problem is challenging.) Suppose that an individual owed no taxes on the first $10 000 she earned and 15 per cent of any income she earned over $10 000. Now suppose that the federal government is considering two ways to reduce the tax burden – a reduction in the tax rate and an increase in the amount on which no tax is owed.

a What effect would a reduction in the tax rate have on the individual's labour supply if she earned $30 000 to start? Explain in words using the income and substitution effects. You do not need to use a diagram.

b What effect would an increase in the amount on which no tax is owed have on the individual's labour supply? Again, explain in words using the income and substitution effects.

14 (This problem is challenging.) Consider a person deciding how much to consume and how much to save for retirement. This person has particular preferences – her lifetime utility depends on the lowest level of consumption during the two periods of her life. That is:

$$\text{Utility} = \text{Minimum}\ \{\text{consumption when young, consumption when old}\}$$

a Draw this person's indifference curves. (*Hint*: Recall that indifference curves show the combinations of consumption in the two periods that yield the same level of utility.)

b Draw the budget constraint and the optimum.

c When the interest rate increases, does this person save more or less? Explain your answer using income and substitution effects.

Search me!

Search me!

When accessing information about microeconomics use the following keywords in any combinations you require:

- indifference curve
- inferior good

CourseMate

CourseMate

For more multimedia resources and activities on economics, visit the Economics CourseMate website.

23

Frontiers of microeconomics

Learning objectives

In this chapter you will:

- consider what happens when economic agents have private information
- understand how political institutions impact on economic policymaking
- learn how economic agents really behave.

Economics is a study of the choices that people make and the resulting interactions they have with one another. This study has many facets, as we have seen in the preceding chapters. Yet it would be a mistake to think that all the facets we have seen make up a finished jewel, perfect and unchanging. Like all scientists, economists are always on the lookout for new areas to study and new phenomena to explain. This final chapter on microeconomics offers an assortment of three topics at the discipline's frontier to see how economists are trying to expand their understanding of human behaviour and society.

The first topic is the economics of *asymmetric information.* Many times in life, some people are better informed than others and this difference in information can affect the choices they make and how they deal with one another. Thinking about this asymmetry can shed light on many aspects of the world, from the market for used cars to the custom of gift giving.

The second topic we examine in this chapter is *political economy.* Throughout this book we have seen many examples where markets fail and government policy can potentially improve matters. But 'potentially' is a needed qualifier: Whether this potential is realised depends on how well our political institutions work. The field of political economy applies the tools of economics to understand the functioning of government.

The third topic in this chapter is *behavioural economics.* This field brings some of the insights from psychology into the study of economic issues. It offers a view of human behaviour that is more subtle and complex than that found in conventional economic theory, but this view may also be more realistic.

This chapter covers a great deal of ground. To do so, it offers not a full helping of these three topics but, instead, a taste of each. One goal is to show a few of the directions in which economists are heading in their effort to expand knowledge of how the economy works. Another goal is to whet your appetite for more courses in economics.

Asymmetric information

'I know something that you don't know.' This statement is a common taunt among children, but it also conveys a deep truth about how people sometimes interact with one another. Many times in life, one person knows more about what is going on than another. A difference in access to relevant knowledge is called an *information asymmetry.*

Examples abound. As we saw in chapter 20, workers know more than their employers about how much effort they put into their jobs. A seller of a used car knows more than the buyer about the car's condition. The first is an example of a *hidden action,* whereas the second is an example of a *hidden characteristic.* In each case, the party in the dark (the employer, the car buyer) would like to know the relevant information, but the informed party (the worker, the car seller) may have an incentive to conceal it.

Because asymmetric information is so prevalent, economists have devoted much effort in recent decades to studying its effects. And, indeed, the 2001 Nobel Prize in economics was awarded to three economists (George Akerlof, Michael Spence and Joseph Stiglitz) for their pioneering work on this topic. Let's discuss some of the insights that this study has revealed.

Hidden actions: Principals, agents and moral hazard

Moral hazard is a problem that arises when one person, called the **agent**, is performing some task on behalf of another person, called the **principal**. If the principal cannot perfectly monitor the agent's

moral hazard
the tendency of a person who is imperfectly monitored to engage in dishonest or otherwise undesirable behaviour

agent
a person who is performing an act for another person, called the principal

principal
a person for whom another person, called the agent, is performing some act

behaviour, the agent tends to undertake less effort than the principal considers desirable. The phrase *moral hazard* refers to the risk, or 'hazard', of inappropriate or otherwise 'immoral' behaviour by the agent. In such a situation, the principal tries various ways to encourage the agent to act more responsibly.

The employment relationship is the classic example. The employer is the principal and the worker is the agent. The moral-hazard problem is the temptation of imperfectly monitored workers to shirk their responsibilities. Employers can respond to this problem in various ways:

Search me!

▸ moral hazard

- *Better monitoring:* Parents hiring babysitters have been known to plant hidden video cameras in their homes to record the sitter's behaviour when the parents are away. The aim is to catch irresponsible behaviour.
- *Higher wages:* According to *efficiency-wage theories* (discussed in chapter 20), some employers may choose to pay their workers a wage that is above the level of equilibrium of supply and demand in the labour market. A worker who earns an above-equilibrium wage is less likely to shirk, because being caught and fired makes it very hard to find another high-paying job.
- *Delayed payment:* Firms can delay part of a worker's compensation, so if the worker is caught shirking and is fired, a larger penalty is suffered. One example of delayed compensation is the year-end bonus. Similarly, a firm may choose to pay its workers more later in their lives. Thus, the wage increases that workers get as they age may reflect not just the benefits of experience but also a response to moral hazard.
- *Employee stock ownership:* Firms can give worker's stocks or stock options that allow them to share in the profitability of the company directly. This is common in smaller firms but also in legal and accounting partnerships. The ownership stake aligns incentives so long as employees understand the impact of their actions on the firm as a whole.

These various mechanisms to reduce the problem of moral hazard need not be used alone. Employers can use a combination of them.

There are also many other examples of moral hazard beyond the workplace. A homeowner with fire insurance will likely buy too few fire extinguishers because the homeowner bears the cost of the extinguisher while the insurance company receives much of the benefit. A family may live near a river with a high risk of flooding because the family enjoys the scenic views, while the government bears the cost of disaster relief after a flood. Many regulations are aimed at addressing the problem: An insurance company may require homeowners to buy extinguishers and the government may prohibit building homes on land with high risk of flooding. But the insurance company does not have perfect information about how cautious homeowners are and the government does not have perfect information about the risk that families undertake when choosing where to live. As a result, the problem of moral hazard persists.

CASESTUDY

Corporate management

Much production in the modern economy takes place within corporations. Like other firms, corporations buy inputs in markets for the factors of production and sell their output in markets for goods and services. Also like other firms, they are guided in their decisions by the objective of profit maximisation. But a large corporation has to deal with some issues that do not arise in, say, a small family-owned business.

What is distinctive about a corporation? From a legal standpoint, a corporation is an organisation that is granted a charter recognising it as a separate legal entity, with its own rights and responsibilities distinct from those of its owners and employees. From an economic standpoint, the most important feature of the corporate form of organisation is the separation of ownership and control. One group of people, called the shareholders, own the corporation's resources.

The separation of ownership and control creates a principal–agent problem. In this case, the shareholders are the principals and the managers are the agents. The chief executive officer and other managers are in the best position to know how to maximise profit for the shareholders. But ensuring that they carry out this task is not always easy. The managers may have goals of their own, such as taking life easy, having a plush office and a private jet, throwing lavish parties or presiding over a large business empire. The managers' goals may not always coincide with the goal of profit maximisation.

The corporation's board of directors is responsible for hiring and firing the top management. The board monitors the managers' performance and it designs their compensation packages. These packages often include incentives aimed at aligning the interest of shareholders with the interest of management. Managers might be given bonuses based on performance or options to buy the company's stock, which are more valuable if the company performs well.

Note, however, that the directors are themselves agents of the shareholders. The existence of a board overseeing management only shifts the principal–agent problem. The issue then becomes how to ensure that the board of directors fulfils its own legal obligation of acting in the best interest of the shareholders. If the directors become too friendly with management, they may not provide the required oversight.

The corporation's principal–agent problem has been in the news in recent years. The top managers of several prominent companies, such as Enron, Tyco and WorldCom, were found to be engaging in activities that enriched themselves at the expense of their shareholders. In these cases, the actions were so extreme as to be criminal and the corporate managers were not just fired but also sent to prison. Some shareholders sued directors for failing to monitor management sufficiently.

Fortunately, criminal activity by corporate managers is rare. But in some ways, it is only the tip of the iceberg. Whenever ownership and control are separated, as they are in most large corporations, there is an inevitable tension between the interests of shareholders and the interests of management.

IN THE NEWS . . .

REAL ESTATE AGENTS ARE FREAKONOMISTS

Real estate agents know more about buying and selling houses than their customers. But how much more? This article documents a study by Steven Levitt and Chad Syverson that featured in the popular book *Freakonomics*. It turns out that when they come to selling their own houses, estate agents don't hold back.

Why a real estate agent may skip the extra mile

by Daniel Gross

As housing prices keep rising year after year, real estate has become a national obsession – and a more powerful economic engine. Sales of homes and condominiums totaled an estimated $2.17 trillion in 2004, said Lawrence Yun, senior economist at the National Association of Realtors.

The industry couldn't function without the armies of agents who help buyers and sellers reach mutually agreeable terms on those four-bedroom, center-hall colonials, and who generally collect hefty 6 per cent commissions for their trouble. But a recent study by two University of Chicago economists suggests that home sellers should regard agents with some caution. The study does not suggest that agents are inherently untrustworthy. Rather, it says, the housing market remains inefficient, and the incentives for agents to maximize profits for their clients aren't powerful enough.

The study was instigated by Steven D. Levitt, a self-described 'rogue economist' who has applied the analytical tools of his trade to everything from sumo wrestlers to drug-dealing

>>

gangs; his work is cataloged in the forthcoming book *Freakonomics*, written with Stephen J. Dubner.

Professor Levitt had fixed up and sold several houses in Oak Park, Ill., a suburb of Chicago. When working with real estate agents, he said, 'I got the impression they weren't working solely in their clients' best interest.'

Along with a colleague, Chad Syverson, Professor Levitt set out to prove it by comparing data on homes that agents sold on behalf of others with those that they owned and sold for themselves. They analyzed sales from 1992 to 2002 of 98 000 homes in suburban Chicago, of which 3300 were owned by real estate agents. When the economists constructed an analysis that controlled for amenities, location and the adjectives used to describe the houses, they found that agent-owned homes, on average, stayed on the market 9.5 days longer and commanded median prices that were 3.7 per cent higher than comparable homes owned by clients.

Of course, agents may just know how to position homes for sale better than other people do. It's their job, after all. And, being human, they may work harder selling their own homes, the way a dentist may take extra care cleaning her own child's teeth. But these explanations don't square with the data. 'If that were the case, you'd expect the clients' homes to stay on the market longer than the brokers' homes,' Professor Levitt said.

The two professors conclude that poorly designed incentives bear some of the blame. 'You have to keep in mind that the agent's incentives don't line up perfectly with your own,' Professor Syverson said.

Real estate agents have a better sense than others of the best price a home can command. But when they work for others, they don't have the financial incentive to pursue it. Most home sales generate a 6 per cent commission, split between the brokerage firms representing the buyer and seller. The agent generally receives half of the firm's draw, or 1.5 per cent of the sale. So if a home sells for $500 000, the agent personally receives $7500. Not bad for what may be just a few days of work. If the agent works for an additional week and urges the seller to hold out for $515 000, that's an extra $15 000 for the seller, but only an extra $225 for the agent. Because every additional dollar throws only a penny and a half into the pocket of the agent, the economists reason, the agent may push clients to accept lowball offers.

Of course, price is just one factor motivating sellers to accept offers. Many are in a hurry, may be because they are relocating for new jobs, or want to be in their new city by the time the next school year starts. So they may feel compelled to accept the first offer. Most agents who sell their own homes, by contrast, aren't leaving the area. 'The brokers may be in a situation where they can be more patient,' said Mr Yun of the National Association of Realtors.

Armed with this knowledge, what should home sellers do? 'You cannot completely trust the advice your broker gives you,' said Christopher J. Mayer, a professor of real estate at Columbia Business School. 'You have to become more educated as a buyer.'

In fact, the economists concluded that sellers, empowered by the Internet, are already eroding agents' advantage. Sites like Realtor.com and domania.com allow anyone to survey the market and check out neighborhood price histories. From 1992 to 1995, in the days before such sites existed, agents' homes commanded prices that were 4.9 per cent higher and stayed on the market more than 14 days longer than equivalent other homes. But from 2000 to 2002, a period when such sites came into popular use, the margins shrank to 2.9 per cent and 2.5 days.

'As consumers become more comfortable with the idea that they can price their own properties, times will get tougher and tougher for real estate agents,' Professor Levitt said.

Source: From *The New York Times*, 20 February 2005

Hidden characteristics: Adverse selection and the lemons problem

Adverse selection is a problem that arises in markets where the seller knows more about the attributes of the good being sold than the buyer does. As a result, the buyer runs the risk of being sold a good of low quality. That is, the 'selection' of goods being sold may be 'adverse' from the standpoint of the uninformed buyer.

adverse selection
the tendency for the mix of unobserved attributes to become undesirable from the standpoint of an uninformed party

Search me!
▸ adverse selection

The classic example of adverse selection is the market for used cars. Sellers of used cars know their vehicles' defects while buyers often do not. Because owners of the worst cars are more likely to sell them than are the owners of the best cars, buyers are apprehensive about getting a 'lemon'. As a result, many people avoid buying vehicles in the used car market. This lemons problem can explain why a used car only a few weeks old sells for thousands of dollars less than a new car of the same type. A buyer of the used car might surmise that the seller is getting rid of the car quickly because the seller knows something about it that the buyer does not.

A second example of adverse selection occurs in the labour market. According to another efficiency-wage theory, workers vary in their abilities and they may know their own abilities better than do the firms that hire them. When a firm cuts the wage it pays, the more talented workers are more likely to quit, knowing they are better able to find other employment. Conversely, a firm may choose to pay an above-equilibrium wage to attract a better mix of workers.

A third example of adverse selection occurs in markets for insurance. For example, buyers of health insurance know more about their own health problems than do insurance companies. Because people with greater hidden health problems are more likely to buy health insurance than are other people, the price of health insurance reflects the costs of a sicker-than-average person. As a result, people in average health may observe the high price of insurance and decide not to buy it.

When markets suffer from adverse selection, the invisible hand does not necessarily work its magic. In the used car market, owners of good cars may choose to keep them rather than sell them at the low price that sceptical buyers are willing to pay. In the labour market, wages may be stuck above the level that balances supply and demand, resulting in unemployment. In insurance markets, buyers with low risk may choose to remain uninsured, because the policies they are offered fail to reflect their true characteristics. Advocates of government-provided health insurance sometimes point to the problem of adverse selection as one reason not to trust the private market to provide the right amount of health insurance on its own.

Signalling to convey private information

Although asymmetric information is sometimes a motivation for public policy, it also motivates some individual behaviour that otherwise might be hard to explain. Markets respond to problems of asymmetric information in many ways. One of them is **signalling**, which refers to actions taken by an informed party for the sole purpose of credibly revealing their private information.

signalling
an action taken by an informed party to reveal private information to an uninformed party

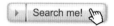

We have seen examples of signalling in previous chapters. As we saw in chapter 18, firms may spend money on advertising to signal to potential customers that they have high-quality products. As we saw in chapter 20, students may earn university and postgraduate degrees to signal to potential employers that they are high-ability individuals. Recall that the signalling theory of education contrasts with the human-capital theory, which asserts that education increases a person's productivity, rather than merely conveying information about innate talent. These two examples of signalling (advertising, education) may seem very different, but below the surface they are much the same: In both cases, the informed party (the firm, the student) is using the signal to convince the uninformed party (the customer, the employer) that the informed party is offering something of high quality.

What does it take for an action to be an effective signal? Obviously, it must be costly. If a signal were free, everyone would use it and it would convey no information. For the same reason, there is another requirement: The signal must be less costly, or more beneficial, to the person with the higher-quality product. Otherwise, everyone would have the same incentive to use the signal and the signal would reveal nothing.

Consider again our two examples. In the advertising case, a firm with a good product reaps a larger benefit from advertising because customers who try the product once are more likely to become repeat customers. Thus, it is rational for the firm with the good product to pay for the cost of the signal (advertising), and it is rational for the customer to use the signal as a piece of information about the product's quality. In the education case, a talented person can get through school more easily than a less talented one. Thus, it is rational for the talented person to pay for the cost of the signal (education) and it is rational for the employer to use the signal as a piece of information about the person's talent.

The world is replete with instances of signalling. Magazine ads sometimes include the phrase 'as seen on TV'. Why does a firm selling a product in a magazine choose to stress this fact? One possibility is that the firm is trying to convey its willingness to pay for an expensive signal (a spot on television) in the hope that you will infer that its product is of high quality. For the same reason, graduates of elite universities are always sure to put that fact on their résumés.

CASESTUDY

Gifts as signals

A man is debating what to give his girlfriend for her birthday. 'I know,' he says to himself, 'I'll give her cash. After all, I don't know her tastes as well as she does, and with cash, she can buy anything she wants'. But when he hands her the money, she is offended. Convinced he doesn't really love her, she breaks off the relationship.

'Now we'll see how much he loves me.'

Source: photos.com/Getty Images.

What's the economics behind this story?

In some ways, gift giving is a strange custom. As the man in our story suggests, people typically know their own preferences better than others do, so we might expect everyone to prefer cash to in-kind transfers. If your employer substituted merchandise for your pay cheque, you would likely object to the means of payment. But your reaction is very different when someone who (you hope) loves you does the same thing.

One interpretation of gift giving is that it reflects asymmetric information and signalling. The man in our story has private information that the girlfriend would like to know: Does he really love her? Choosing a good gift for her is a signal of his love. Certainly, picking out a gift has the right characteristics to be a signal. It is costly (it takes time), and its cost depends on the private information (how much he loves her). If he really loves her, choosing a good gift is easy because he is thinking about her all the time. If he doesn't love her, finding the right gift is more difficult. Thus, giving a gift that suits the girlfriend is one way for him to convey the private information of his love for her. Giving cash shows that he isn't even bothering to try.

The signalling theory of gift giving is consistent with another observation: People care most about the custom when the strength of affection is most in question. Thus, giving cash to a girlfriend or boyfriend is usually a bad move. But when college students receive a cheque from their parents, they are less often offended. The parents' love is less likely to be in doubt, so the recipient probably won't interpret the cash gift as a signal of lack of affection.

Screening to induce information revelation

When an informed party takes actions to reveal private information, the phenomenon is called signalling. When an uninformed party takes actions to induce the informed party to reveal private information, the phenomenon is called **screening**.

screening
an action taken by an uninformed party to induce an informed party to reveal information

Some screening is commonsense. A person buying a used car may ask that it be checked by a mechanic before the sale. A seller who refuses this request reveals his private information that the car is a lemon. The buyer may decide to offer a lower price or to look for another car.

Other examples of screening are more subtle. For example, consider a firm that sells car insurance. The firm would like to charge a low premium to safe drivers and a high premium to risky drivers. But how can it tell them apart? Drivers know whether they are safe or risky, but the risky ones won't admit to it. A driver's history is one piece of information (which insurance companies in fact use), but because of the intrinsic randomness of car accidents, history is an imperfect indicator of future risks.

The insurance company might be able to sort out the two kinds of drivers by offering different insurance policies that would induce them to separate themselves. One policy would have a high premium and cover the full cost of any accidents that occur. Another policy would have low premiums but would have, say, $1000 deductible. (That is, the driver would be responsible for the first $1000 of damage and the insurance company would cover the remaining risk.) Notice that the deductible is more of a burden for risky drivers because they are more likely to have an accident. Thus, with a large enough deductible, the low-premium policy with a deductible would attract the safe drivers, while the high-premium policy without a deductible would attract the risky drivers. Faced with these two policies, the two kinds of drivers would reveal their private information by choosing different insurance policies.

Asymmetric information and public policy

We have examined two kinds of asymmetric information – moral hazard and adverse selection. And we have seen how individuals may respond to the problem with signalling or screening. Now let's consider what the study of asymmetric information suggests about the proper scope of public policy.

The tension between market success and market failure is central in microeconomics. We learned in chapter 7 that the equilibrium of supply and demand is efficient in the sense that it maximises the total surplus that society can obtain in a market. Adam Smith's invisible hand seemed to reign supreme. This conclusion was then tempered with the study of externalities (chapter 10), public goods (chapter 11), imperfect competition (chapters 15 to 18) and poverty (chapter 21). These examples of market failure showed that government can sometimes improve market outcomes.

The study of asymmetric information gives us new reason to be wary of markets. When some people know more than others, the market may fail to put resources to their best use. People with high-quality used cars may have trouble selling them because buyers will be afraid of getting a lemon. People with few health problems may have trouble getting low-cost health insurance because insurance companies lump them together with those who have significant (but hidden) health problems.

Although asymmetric information may call for government action in some cases, three facts complicate the issue. First, as we have seen, the private market can sometimes deal with information asymmetries on its own using a combination of signalling and screening. Second, the government rarely has more information than the private parties. Even if the market's allocation of resources is not efficient, when there are information asymmetries, policymakers may find it hard to improve upon the market's admittedly imperfect outcome. Third, the government is itself an imperfect institution – a topic we take up in the next section.

Q

A person who buys a life insurance policy pays a certain amount per year and receives for their family a much larger payment in the event of their death. Would you expect buyers of life insurance to have higher or lower death rates than the average person? How might this be an example of moral hazard? Of adverse selection? How might a life insurance company deal with these problems?

Political economy

As we have seen, markets left on their own do not always reach a desirable allocation of resources. When we judge the markets' outcome to be either inefficient or inequitable, there may be a role for the government to step in and improve the situation. Yet before we embrace an activist government, we need to consider one more fact: The government is also an imperfect institution. The field of *political economy* (sometimes called the field of *public choice*) applies the methods of economics to study how government works.

The Condorcet voting paradox

Most advanced societies rely on democratic principles to set government policy. When a city is deciding between two locations to build a new park, for example, we have a simple way to choose – the majority gets its way. Yet, for most policy issues, the number of possible outcomes far exceeds two. A new park, for instance, could be placed in many possible locations. In this case, as the eighteenth-century French political theorist Marquis de Condorcet famously noted, democracy might run into some problems trying to choose one of the outcomes.

Condorcet paradox
the failure of majority rule to produce transitive preferences for society

To illustrate the **Condorcet paradox**, imagine that three people – Kirk, Spock and McCoy – are choosing what DVD – *Star Wars Episode V: The Empire Strikes Back*, *Harry Potter and the Order of the Phoenix* and *Police Academy 5: Assignment Miami Beach* – to watch. Their individual preferences are shown in Table 23.1.

Table 23.1 Individual preferences

Rank	Kirk's preferences	Spock's preferences	McCoy's preferences
1st choice	*Star Wars*	*Harry Potter*	*Police Academy*
2nd choice	*Harry Potter*	*Police Academy*	*Star Wars*
3rd choice	*Police Academy*	*Star Wars*	*Harry Potter*

They want to aggregate these individual preferences into preferences for society as a whole. How should they do it?

At first, they might try some pairwise votes. If they started with a comparison of *Star Wars* and *Harry Potter*, they would choose *Star Wars* (both Kirk and McCoy prefer this to *Harry Potter*). Then turning to *Star Wars* and *Police Academy*, they would choose *Police Academy* (Spock's and McCoy's preferences). As *Police Academy* beats *Star Wars*, and *Star Wars* beats *Harry Potter*, they appear to have a clear choice.

But wait, suppose instead that they had begun with *Star Wars* and *Police Academy* – choosing *Police Academy* – and then voted on *Harry Potter* and *Police Academy*, they would have chosen *Harry Potter*! (Kirk and Spock prefer *Harry Potter* to *Police Academy*.) Normally, we expect preferences to exhibit a property called *transitivity*: If A is preferred to B, and B is preferred to C, then we would expect A to be preferred to C. The Condorcet paradox is that democratic outcomes do not always obey this property. Pairwise voting might produce transitive preferences for a society, depending on the pattern of individual preferences, but as our example in the table shows, it cannot be counted on to do so.

One implication of the Condorcet paradox is that the order on which things are voted can affect the result. If they decide by choosing between *Star Wars* and *Harry Potter* and then compare the winner to *Police Academy*, they end up choosing *Police Academy*. But if the voters choose first between *Star Wars* and *Police Academy* and then compare the winner to *Harry Potter*, the town ends up with *Harry Potter*. And if the voters choose first between *Harry Potter* and *Police Academy* and then compare the winner to *Star Wars*, the trio ends up with *Star Wars*.

The Condorcet paradox has two lessons. The narrow lesson is that when there are more than two options, setting the agenda (that is, deciding the order in which items are voted) can have a powerful impact on the outcome of a democratic election. The broad lesson is that majority voting by itself does not tell us what outcome a society really wants.

Arrow's impossibility theorem

Since political theorists first noticed Condorcet's paradox, they have spent much energy studying voting systems and proposing new ones. For example, as an alternative to pairwise majority voting, each person could be asked to rank the possible outcomes – a preference system used as we do for elections in Australia. Of course, in this case, it would not be much help; there would be a three-way tie.

Is there a perfect voting system? Economist Kenneth Arrow took up this question in his 1951 book *Social Choice and Individual Values*. Arrow started by defining what a perfect voting system would be. He assumes that individuals in society have preferences over the various possible outcomes: A, B, C and so on. He then assumes that society wants a voting scheme to choose among these outcomes that satisfies several properties:

- *Unanimity*: If everyone prefers A to B, then A should beat B.
- *Transitivity*: If A beats B, and B beats C, then A should beat C.
- *Independence of irrelevant alternatives*: The ranking between any two outcomes A and B should not depend on whether some third outcome C is also available.
- *No dictators*: There is no person that always gets his way, regardless of everyone else's preferences.

Table 23.2 A Borda count

	Voter type		
	Type 1	Type 2	Type 3
% of electorate	35	45	20
1st choice	A	B	C
2nd choice	B	C	A
3rd choice	C	A	B

These all seem like desirable properties for a voting system to have. Yet Arrow proved, mathematically and incontrovertibly, that *no voting system can satisfy all of these properties.* This amazing result is called **Arrow's impossibility theorem.**

Arrow's impossibility theorem
a mathematical result showing that, under certain assumed conditions, there is no scheme for aggregating individual preferences into a valid set of social preferences

The mathematics needed to prove Arrow's theorem is beyond the scope of this book, but we can get some sense of why the theorem is true from a couple of examples. We have already seen the problem with the method of majority rule. The Condorcet paradox shows that majority rule fails to produce a ranking among the outcomes that always satisfies transitivity.

Consider a new situation. Suppose that a town is to vote on three possible locations for a new theatre: A, B or C. The preferences are in Table 23.2. Suppose that the mayor decides on the following voting: For each option, we could give one point for last place, two points for second to last, three points for third to last, and so on. The outcome that receives the most total points wins. With the preferences in the table, outcome B is the winner. (You can do the arithmetic yourself.) This voting method is called a *Borda count*, for the eighteenth-century French mathematician and political scientist who devised it. It is often used in polls that rank sports teams.

Notice that the Borda count fails to satisfy the independence of irrelevant alternatives. Recall that outcome B wins with a Borda count. But suppose that suddenly C disappears as an alternative. If the Borda count method is applied only to outcomes A and B, then A wins. (Once again, you can do the arithmetic on your own.) Thus, eliminating alternative C changes the ranking between A and B. The reason for this change is that the result of the Borda count depends on the number of points that A and B receive, and the number of points depends on whether the irrelevant alternative, C, is also available.

Arrow's impossibility theorem is a deep and disturbing result. It doesn't say that we should abandon democracy as a form of government. But it does say that, no matter what voting scheme society adopts for aggregating the preferences of its members, in some way it will be flawed as a mechanism for social choice.

The median voter is king

Despite Arrow's theorem, voting is how most societies choose their leaders and public policies, often by majority rule. The next step in studying government is to examine how governments run by majority

Figure 23.1 The median voter theorem: An example

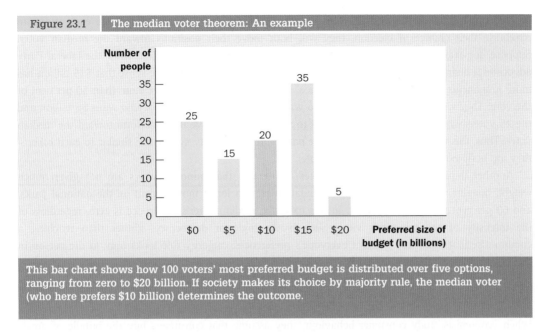

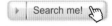

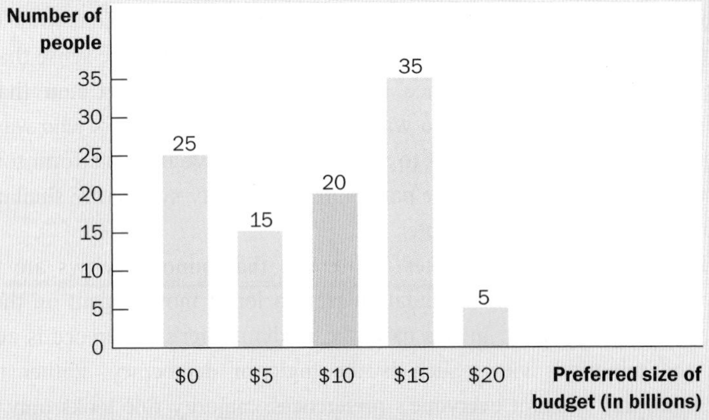

This bar chart shows how 100 voters' most preferred budget is distributed over five options, ranging from zero to $20 billion. If society makes its choice by majority rule, the median voter (who here prefers $10 billion) determines the outcome.

rule work. That is, in a democratic society, who determines what policy is chosen? In some cases, the theory of democratic government yields a surprisingly simple answer.

Let's consider an example. Imagine that society is deciding on how much money to spend on some public good, such as the army or the national parks. Each voter has his own most preferred budget and he always prefers outcomes closer to his most preferred value to outcomes further away. Thus, we can line up voters from those who prefer the smallest budget to those who prefer the largest. Figure 23.1 is an example. Here there are 100 voters and the budget size varies from zero to $20 billion. Given these preferences, what outcome would you expect democracy to produce?

According to a famous result called the **median voter theorem**, majority rule will produce the outcome most preferred by the median voter. The *median voter* is the voter exactly in the middle of the distribution. In this example, if you take the line of voters ordered by their preferred budgets and count 50 voters from either end of the line, you will find that the median voter wants a budget of $10 billion. By contrast, the average preferred outcome (calculated by adding the preferred outcomes and dividing by the number of voters) is $9 billion, and the modal outcome (the one preferred by the greatest number of voters) is $15 billion.

median voter theorem
a mathematical result showing that if voters are choosing a point along a line and each voter wants the point closest to their most preferred point, then majority rule will pick the most preferred point of the median voter

Search me!
▸ median voter theorem

The median voter rules the day because his or her preferred outcome beats any other proposal in a two-way race. In our example, more than half the voters want $10 billion or more, and more than half want $10 billion or less. If someone proposes, say, $8 billion instead of $10 billion, everyone who prefers $10 billion or more will vote with the median voter. Similarly, if someone proposes $12 billion instead of $10 billion, everyone who wants $10 billion or less will vote with the median voter. In either case, the median voter has more than half the voters on his or her side.

What about the Condorcet voting paradox? It turns out that when the voters are picking a point along a line and each voter aims for his or her own most preferred point, the Condorcet paradox cannot arise. The median voter's most preferred outcome beats all comers.

One implication of the median voter theorem is that if two political parties are each trying to maximise their chance of election, they will both move their positions toward the median voter. Suppose, for example, that the Labor Party advocates a budget of $15 billion, while the Liberal Party advocates a budget of $10 billion. The Labor position is more popular in the sense that $15 billion has more proponents than any other single choice. Nonetheless, the Liberals get more than 50 per cent of the vote: They will attract the 20 voters who want $10 billion, the 15 voters who want $5 billion and the 25 voters who want zero. If Labor want to win, they will move their platform toward the median voter. Thus, this theory can explain why the parties in a two-party system are similar to each other – they are both moving toward the median voter.

Another implication of the median voter theorem is that minority views are not given much weight. Imagine that 40 per cent of the population want a lot of money spent on the national parks, and 60 per cent want nothing spent. In this case, the median voter's preference is zero, regardless of the intensity of the minority's view. Such is the logic of democracy. Rather than reaching a compromise that takes into account everyone's preferences, majority rule looks only to the person in the exact middle of the distribution.

Politicians are people too

When economists study consumer behaviour, they assume that consumers buy the bundle of goods and services that gives them the greatest level of satisfaction. When economists study firm behaviour, they assume that firms produce the quantity of goods and services that yields the greatest level of profits. What should they assume when they study people involved in the practice of politics?

Politicians also have objectives. It would be nice to assume that political leaders are always looking out for the wellbeing of society as a whole, that they are aiming for an optimal combination of efficiency and equity. Nice, perhaps, but not realistic. Self-interest is as powerful a motive for political actors as it is for consumers and firm owners. Some politicians are motivated by desire for re-election and are willing to sacrifice the national interest when doing so solidifies their base of voters. Other politicians are motivated by simple greed. If you have any doubt, you should look at the world's poor nations, where corruption among government officials is a common impediment to economic development.

This book is not the place to develop a theory of political behaviour. That topic is best left to the political scientists. But when thinking about economic policy, remember that this policy is made not by a benevolent king, but by real people with their own all-too-human desires. Sometimes they are motivated to further the national interest, but sometimes they are motivated by their own political and financial ambitions. We shouldn't be surprised when economic policy fails to resemble the ideals derived in economics textbooks.

Q

A school council is voting on the school budget and the resulting student–teacher ratio. A poll finds that 35 per cent of the voters want a ratio of 9:1, 25 per cent want a ratio of 10:1 and 40 per cent want a ratio of 12:1. What outcome would you expect the school to end up with?

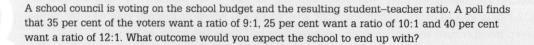

Behavioural economics

Economics is a study of human behaviour, but it is not the only field that can make that claim. The social science of psychology also sheds light on the choices that people make in their lives. The fields of economics and psychology usually proceed independently, in part because they address a different range of questions. But recently a field called *behavioural economics* has emerged in which economists are making use of basic psychological insights. Let's consider some of these insights here.

People aren't always rational

Economic theory is populated by a particular species of organism, sometimes called *homo economicus*. Members of this species are always rational. As firm managers, they maximise profits. As consumers, they maximise utility (or, equivalently, pick the point on the highest indifference curve). Given the constraints they face, they rationally weigh all the costs and benefits and always choose the best possible course of action.

Real people, however, are *homo sapiens*. Although in many ways they resemble the rational, calculating people assumed in economic theory, they are far more complex. They can be forgetful, impulsive, confused, emotional and shortsighted. These imperfections of human reasoning are the bread-and-butter of psychologists, but until recently, economists have neglected them.

Herbert Simon, one of the first social scientists to work at the boundary of economics and psychology, suggested that humans should be viewed not as rational maximisers but as *satisficers*. Rather than always choosing the best course of action, they make decisions that are merely good enough. Similarly, other economists have suggested that humans are only 'near rational' or that they exhibit 'bounded rationality'.

Studies of human decision making have tried to detect systematic mistakes that people make. Here are a few of the findings:

- *People are overconfident*: Imagine that you were asked some numerical questions, such as the number of African countries in the United Nations, the height of the tallest mountain in North America, and so on. Instead of being asked for a single estimate, however, you were asked to give a 90 per cent confidence interval – a range such that you were 90 per cent confident the true number falls within it. When psychologists run experiments like this, they find that most people give ranges that are too small: The true number falls within their intervals far less than 90 per cent of the time. That is, most people are too sure of their own abilities.
- *People give too much weight to a small number of vivid observations*: Imagine that you are thinking about buying a car of brand X. To learn about its reliability, you read *Consumer Reports*, which has surveyed 1000 owners of car X. Then you run into a friend who owns car X, and she tells you that her car is a lemon. How do you treat your friend's observation? If you think rationally, you will realise that she has only increased your sample size from 1000 to 1001, which does not provide much new information. But because your friend's story is so vivid, you may be tempted to give it more weight in your decision making than you should.
- *People are reluctant to change their minds*: People tend to interpret evidence to confirm beliefs they already hold. In one study, subjects were asked to read and evaluate a research report on whether capital punishment deters crime. After reading the report, those who initially favoured the death penalty said they were more sure in their view and those who initially opposed the

death penalty also said they were more sure in their view. The two groups interpreted the same evidence in exactly opposite ways.

Think about decisions you have made in your own life. Do you exhibit some of these traits?

A hotly debated issue is whether deviations from rationality are important for understanding economic phenomena. An intriguing example arises in the study of tax-advantaged retirement savings accounts that some firms in the United States offer their workers. In some firms, workers can choose to participate in the plan by filling out a simple form. In other firms, workers are automatically enrolled and can opt out of the plan by filling out a simple form. It turns out many more workers participate in the second case than in the first. If workers were perfectly rational maximisers, they would choose the optimal amount of retirement saving, regardless of the default offered by their employer. In fact, workers' behaviour appears to exhibit substantial inertia. Understanding their behaviour seems easier once we abandon the model of perfect rationality.

Why, you might ask, is economics built on the rationality assumption when psychology and commonsense cast doubt on it? One answer is that the assumption, even if not exactly true, is still a good approximation. For example, when we studied the differences between competitive and monopoly firms, the assumption that firms rationally maximise profit yielded many important and valid insights. Recall from chapter 2 that economic models are not meant to replicate reality but are supposed to show the essence of the problem at hand as an aid to understanding.

Another reason that economists so often assume rationality may be that economists are themselves not rational maximisers. Like most people they are overconfident and they are reluctant to change their minds. Their choice among alternative theories of human behaviour may exhibit excessive inertia. Moreover, economists may be content with a theory that is not perfect but is good enough. The model of rational man may be the theory of choice for a satisficing social scientist.

IN THE NEWS . . .

USE MONEY TO COMMIT TO A DIET

It is tough to commit to a diet. Even when you know it will pay off in the long term, behavioural economics has demonstrated that the short term looms. Two economists imagine bringing the pain forward in the form of money.

Skin in the game

by Ian Ayres and Barry Nalebuff

In 1519 Hernán Cortés scuttled his ships upon arrival in Veracruz, Mexico. Vastly outnumbered, his 600 soldiers decided that they would either defeat the Aztecs or perish trying. By making defeat worse, Cortés increased his chance of victory. And conquer he did.

While we can't all scuttle our ships, we can use this same type of commitment strategy to help us lose weight, stop smoking, exercise more or achieve just about any goal.

Imagine a Commitment Store that offered a financial incentive to lose weight. You promise to lose a pound a week for the next 20 weeks and then keep the 20 pounds off for the remainder of the year. You back up the promise with a $1000 weight-loss bond. Weigh-ins are biweekly. Every time you meet your goal, you get back $60. Over the course of the year you could earn back $1560. Of course, each time you miss, that costs you $60.

Here's a diet system that literally pays you to lose the weight. If you miss your goal weight one week, you still have an incentive to get back on track to collect the next payout. If $60 a weigh-in isn't enough to get your attention, then buy two or more bonds.

The 56 per cent interest rate might seem high, but the fact is that more than 95 per cent of dieters fail to keep their weight off for a year. Even if half the dieters succeed under this new regime, the store can still turn a healthy profit. Putting aside the interest it could earn on deposited funds (and the overhead costs), it would be taking in $2000 from a pair of dieters and paying out $1560 to one of them.

We're not the first to suggest the idea of financial incentives. This season's edition of NBC's *The Biggest Loser* will pay $250 000 to the person who loses the largest percentage of his or her body weight. We tried something like this ourselves with ABC's *Primetime*. Five volunteers were photographed in bikinis. Unless they lost 15 pounds in two months, those photographs would be splashed on *Primetime* and the Web. As one of the dieters, Cynthia Nacson-Schechter, explained, she knew all about the dangers of being overweight – the increased risk of diabetes, heart attack and death – and yet that wasn't enough to scare her into action. What she feared most was the possibility that her ex-boyfriend would see her hanging out of a bikini on national TV. She lost the weight and then some.

The stick is mightier than the carrot. People hate losing their own money even more than they love gaining a windfall of the same amount. Psychologists call this phenomenon loss aversion. The great thing about the weight-loss bonds is that the overweight investors have put their own skin in the game.

You might be worried that it's unethical to profit from people's failure to lose weight. But the Commitment Store would publish detailed statistics on the distribution of results. You'd know going in the chance of losing money. And you might rationally decide that getting halfway to your goal is not a bad outcome – you'd lose some of your principal but lose some pounds, too. Even if weight-loss bond buyers lose $200 on average, if the dieters lose 10 pounds this would be a bargain. And those buyers who lose the full 20 make out like bandits, earning interest rates that would make loan sharks proud.

Of course, financial incentives aren't for everyone. The idea of putting a dollar price on every morsel of food that you put in your mouth might ruin the pleasure of eating. (For some people that might be the point.) The store can serve people who react better to financial incentives than to other types of encouragement. Indeed, financial incentives have been shown to help drug addicts abstain. Prizes of cash, computers and even iPods are being used in Vacaville, Calif. and elsewhere to reward school attendance.

This needn't be a question of either financial incentives or nonfinancial weight-loss support. It can be both. Right now people spend about $10 a week to attend Weight Watchers weigh-ins. Weight Watchers should offer people the option of paying $1000 up front and then to be paid $15 a week for every time they come over the next year.

The commitment idea isn't just about weight loss. Any action that can be monitored can be subject to commitment contracts. The American Cancer Society should offer non-smoking bonds. You invest $10 000 and agree to have your hair tested for nicotine over the course of the year. If your hair is nicotine free, you get your money back with interest; if not, your money is forfeited to the charity. The Cancer Society is a winner either way.

People care about fairness

Another insight about human behaviour is best illustrated with an experiment called the *ultimatum game*. The game works like this: Two volunteers (who are otherwise strangers to each other) are told that they are going to play a game and could win a total of $100. Before they play, they learn the rules. The game begins with a coin flip, which is used to assign the volunteers to the roles of player A and player B. Player A's job is to propose a division of the $100 prize between himself and the other player. After player A makes his proposal, player B decides whether to accept or reject it.

If he accepts it, both players are paid according to the proposal. If player B rejects the proposal, both players walk away with nothing. In either case, the game then ends.

Before proceeding, stop and think about what you would do in this situation. If you were player A, what division of the $100 would you propose? If you were player B, what proposals would you accept?

Conventional economic theory assumes in this situation that people are rational wealth-maximisers. This assumption leads to a simple prediction: Player A should propose that he gets $99 and player B gets $1, and player B should accept the proposal. After all, once the proposal is made, player B is better off accepting it as long as he gets something out of it. Moreover, because player A knows that accepting the proposal is in player's B interest, player A has no reason to offer him more than $1. In the language of game theory (discussed in chapter 16), the 99–1 split is the Nash equilibrium.

Yet when experimental economists ask real people to play the ultimatum game, the results are very different from this prediction. People in the role of player B usually reject proposals that give them only $1 or a similarly small amount. Knowing this, people in the role of player A usually propose giving player B much more than $1. Some people will offer a 50–50 split, but it is more common for player A to propose giving player B an amount such as $30 or $40, keeping the larger share for himself. In this case, player B usually accepts the proposal.

What's going on here? The natural interpretation is that people are driven in part by some innate sense of fairness. A 99–1 split seems so wildly unfair to many people that they reject it, even to their own detriment. By contrast, a 70–30 split is still unfair, but it is not so unfair that it induces people to abandon their normal self-interest.

Throughout our study of household and firm behaviour, the innate sense of fairness has not played any role. But the results of the ultimatum game suggest that perhaps it should. For example, in chapters 19 and 20 we discussed how wages were determined by labour supply and labour demand. Some economists have suggested that the perceived fairness of what a firm pays its workers should also enter the picture. Thus, when a firm has an especially profitable year, workers (like player B) may expect to be paid a fair share of the prize, even if the standard equilibrium does not dictate it. The firm (like player A) might well decide to give workers more than the equilibrium wage for fear that the workers might otherwise try to punish the firm with reduced effort, strikes or even vandalism.

People are inconsistent over time

Imagine some dreary task, such as doing your laundry, mowing the lawn or filling out your income tax forms. Now consider the following questions:

1 Would you prefer (A) to spend 50 minutes doing the task immediately or (B) to spend 60 minutes doing the task tomorrow?
2 Would you prefer (A) to spend 50 minutes doing the task in 90 days or (B) to spend 60 minutes doing the task in 91 days?

When asked questions like these, many people choose B to question 1 and A to question 2. When looking ahead to the future (as in question 2), they minimise the amount of time spent on the dreary task. But faced with the prospect of doing the task immediately (as in question 1), they choose to put it off.

In some ways, this behaviour is not surprising – everyone procrastinates from time to time. But from the standpoint of the theory of rationality, it is puzzling. Suppose that, in response to question 2, a person chooses to spend 50 minutes in 90 days. Then, when the 90th day arrives, we allow them to change their mind. In effect, they then face question 1, so they opt for doing the task the next day. But why should the mere passage of time affect the choices made?

Many times in life, people make plans for themselves, but then they fail to follow through. Smokers promise themselves that they will quit, but within a few hours of smoking their last cigarette, they crave another and break their promise. People trying to lose weight promise that they will stop eating dessert, but when the waiter brings the dessert menu, the promise is forgotten. In both cases, the desire for instant gratification induces the decision maker to abandon their own past plans.

Some economists believe that the consumption–saving decision is an important instance where people exhibit this inconsistency over time. For many people, spending provides a type of instant gratification. Saving, like passing up the cigarette or the dessert, requires a sacrifice in the present for a reward in the distant future. And just as many smokers wish they could quit and many overweight individuals wish they ate less, many consumers wish they saved more. According to one survey, 76 per cent of Americans said they were not saving enough for retirement and figures for Australia and New Zealand are believed to be similar.

An implication of this inconsistency over time is that people should try to find ways to commit their future selves to following through on their plans. A smoker trying to quit may throw away his cigarettes and a person on a diet may put a lock on the refrigerator. What can a person who saves too little do? He should find some way to lock up his money before he spends it. Some retirement accounts, like superannuation, do exactly that. Workers can agree to have some money taken out of their pay cheque before they ever see it. The money is deposited in an account that can be used before retirement only with a tax penalty. In effect these plans protect people from their own desires for instant gratification.

Q

Describe at least three ways in which human decision making differs from that of the rational individual of conventional economic theory.

Conclusion

This chapter has examined the frontier of microeconomics. You may have noticed that we have sketched out ideas rather than fully developing them. This is no accident. One reason is that you might study these topics in more detail in advanced courses. Another reason is that these topics remain active areas of research and, therefore, are still being fleshed out.

To see how these topics fit into the broader picture, recall the *Ten Lessons from Economics* in chapter 1. One lesson states that markets are usually a good way to organise economic activity. Another lesson states that governments can sometimes improve market outcomes. As you study economics, you can more fully appreciate the truth of these principles as well as the caveats that go with them. The study of asymmetric information should make you more wary of market outcomes. The study of political economy should make you more wary of government solutions. And the study of behavioural economics should make you wary of any institution that relies on human decision making – including both the market and the government.

If there is a unifying theme to these topics, it is that life is messy. Information is imperfect, government is imperfect and people are imperfect. Of course, you knew this long before you started studying economics, but economists need to understand these imperfections as precisely as they can if they are to explain, and perhaps even improve, the world around them.

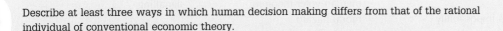

Summary

- In many economic transactions, information is asymmetric. When there are hidden actions, principals may be concerned that agents suffer from the problem of moral hazard. When there are hidden characteristics, buyers may be concerned about the problem of adverse selection among the sellers. Private markets sometimes deal with asymmetric information with signalling and screening.
- Although government policy can sometimes improve market outcomes, governments are themselves imperfect institutions. The Condorcet paradox shows that majority rule fails to produce transitive preferences for society and Arrow's impossibility theorem shows that no voting scheme will be perfect. In many situations, democratic institutions will produce the outcome desired by the median voter, regardless of the preferences of the rest of the electorate. Moreover, the individuals who set government policy may be motivated by self-interest rather than the national interest.
- The study of psychology and economics reveals that human decision making is more complex than is assumed in conventional economic theory. People are not always rational, they care about the fairness of economic outcomes (even to their own detriment) and they can be inconsistent over time.

Key concepts

adverse selection
agent
Arrow's impossibility theorem
Condorcet paradox
median voter theorem
moral hazard
principal
screening
signalling

Questions for review

1. What is moral hazard? List three things an employer might do to reduce the severity of this problem.
2. What is adverse selection? Give an example of a market in which adverse selection might be a problem.
3. Define *signalling* and *screening*, and give an example of each.
4. What unusual property of voting did Condorcet notice?
5. Explain why majority rule respects the preferences of the median voter rather than the average voter.
6. Describe the ultimatum game. What outcome from this game would conventional economic theory predict? Do experiments confirm this prediction? Explain.

Problems and applications

1. Each of the following situations involves moral hazard. In each case, identify the principal and the agent, and explain why there is asymmetric information. How does the action described reduce the problem of moral hazard?
   a. Landlords require tenants to pay security deposits.
   b. Firms compensate top executives with options to buy company stock at a given price in the future.
   c. Car insurance companies offer discounts to customers who install anti-theft devices in their cars.

2 Suppose that the Live-Long-and-Prosper Health Insurance Company charges $5000 annually for a family insurance policy. The company's president suggests that the company raise the annual price to $6000 in order to increase its profits. If the firm followed this suggestion, what economic problem might arise? Would the firm's pool of customers tend to become more or less healthy on average? Would the company's profits necessarily increase?

3 The case study in this chapter describes how a boyfriend can signal to a girlfriend that he loves her by giving an appropriate gift. Do you think saying 'I love you' can also serve as a signal? Why or why not?

4 Some AIDS activists believe that health insurance companies should not be allowed to ask applicants if they are infected with the HIV virus that causes AIDS. Would this rule help or hurt those who are HIV-positive? Would it help or hurt those who are not HIV-positive? Would it exacerbate or mitigate the problem of adverse selection in the market for health insurance? Do you think it would increase or decrease the number of people without health insurance? In your opinion, would this be a good policy?

5 The government is considering two ways to help the needy: giving them cash, or giving them free meals at soup kitchens. Give an argument for giving cash. Give an argument, based on asymmetric information, for why the soup kitchen may be better than the cash handout.

6 Ken walks into an ice-cream parlour.

Waiter: We have vanilla and chocolate today.
Ken: I'll take vanilla.
Waiter: I almost forgot. We also have strawberry.
Ken: In that case, I'll take chocolate.

What standard property of decision making is Ken violating? (*Hint:* Re-read the section on Arrow's impossibility theorem.)

7 Why might a political party in a two-party system choose not to move toward the median voter? (*Hint:* Think about abstentions from voting and political contributions.)

8 Two ice-cream stands are deciding where to locate along a 3-km beach. The people sitting on the beach buy exactly one ice-cream cone each per day from the stand nearest to them. Each ice-cream seller wants the maximum number of customers. Where along the beach will the two stands locate?

9 After a widely reported earthquake in California, many people call their insurance company to apply for earthquake insurance. Might this reaction reflect some deviation from rationality? Discuss.

Search me!

Search me!

When accessing information about microeconomics use the following keywords in any combinations you require:

- adverse selection
- moral hazard
- median voter theorem

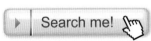

CourseMate

CourseMate

For more multimedia resources and activities on economics, visit the Economics CourseMate website.

Glossary

ability-to-pay principle
the idea that taxes should be levied on a person according to how well that person can shoulder the burden

absolute advantage
the comparison among producers of a good according to their productivity

adverse selection
the tendency for the mix of unobserved attributes to become undesirable from the standpoint of an uninformed party

agent
a person who is performing an act for another person, called the principal

Arrow's impossibility theorem
a mathematical result showing that, under certain assumed conditions, there is no scheme for aggregating individual preferences into a valid set of social preferences

average fixed cost
fixed costs divided by the quantity of output

average revenue
total revenue divided by the quantity sold

average tax rate
total taxes paid divided by total income

average total cost
total cost divided by the quantity of output

average variable cost
variable costs divided by the quantity of output

awards
the minimum wage rates that can be paid to particular workers in particular industries

benefits principle
the idea that people should pay taxes based on the benefits they receive from government services

bilateral monopoly
a market situation where there is both a single buyer and a single seller for a product

budget constraint
the limit on the consumption bundles that a consumer can afford

budget deficit
an excess of government spending over government receipts

budget surplus
an excess of government receipts over government spending

capital
the equipment and structures used to produce goods and services

cartel
a group of firms acting in unison

ceteris paribus
a Latin phrase, translated as 'other things being equal', used as a reminder that all variables other than the ones being studied are assumed to be constant

circular-flow diagram
a visual model of the economy that shows how dollars flow through markets among households and firms

club goods
goods that are excludable but not rival in consumption

Coase theorem
the proposition that if private parties can bargain without cost over the allocation of resources, they can solve the problem of externalities on their own

collective bargaining
the process by which unions and firms agree on the terms of employment

collusion
an agreement among firms in a market about quantities to produce or prices to charge

common resources
goods that are rival in consumption but not excludable

comparative advantage
the comparison among producers of a good according to their opportunity cost

compensating differential
a difference in wages that arises to offset the non-monetary characteristics of different jobs

Competition and Consumer Act
Australia's main competition laws (formerly the *Trade Practices Act*).

competition laws
laws that restrict the behaviour of firms with market power, such as monopolies or firms in a small oligopoly

competition policy
the laws and procedures that aim to improve social efficiency in oligopolistic and monopolistic markets

competitive market
a market in which there are many buyers and many sellers so that each has a negligible impact on the market price

complements
two goods for which a decrease in the price of one good leads to an increase in the demand for the other good

Condorcet paradox
the failure of majority rule to produce transitive preferences for society

constant returns to scale
the property whereby long-run average total cost stays the same as the quantity of output changes

consumer surplus
a buyer's willingness to pay minus the amount the buyer actually pays

corrective tax
a tax imposed to correct the effects of a negative externality

cost
the value of everything a seller must give up to produce a good

cost–benefit analysis
a study that compares the costs and benefits to society of providing a public good

cross-price elasticity of demand
a measure of how much the quantity demanded of one good responds to a change in the price of another good, computed as the percentage change in quantity demanded of the first good divided by the percentage change in the price of the second good

deadweight loss
the reduction in total surplus that results from a market distortion such as a tax or a monopoly price

demand curve
a graph of the relationship between the price of a good and the quantity demanded

demand schedule
a table that shows the relationship between the price of a good and the quantity demanded

diminishing marginal product
the property whereby the marginal product of an input declines as the quantity of the input increases

discrimination
the offering of different opportunities to similar individuals who differ only by race, ethnic group, sex, age or other personal characteristics

diseconomies of scale
the property whereby long-run average total cost rises as the quantity of output increases

dominant strategy
a strategy that is best for a player in a game regardless of the strategies chosen by the other players

economics
the study of how society manages its scarce resources

economies of scale
the property whereby long-run average total cost falls as the quantity of output increases

efficiency
the property of society getting the most it can from its scarce resources

efficiency wages
above-equilibrium wages paid by firms in order to increase worker productivity

efficient scale
the quantity of output that minimises average total cost

elasticity
a measure of the responsiveness of quantity demanded or quantity supplied to one of its determinants

equilibrium
a situation in which supply and demand have been brought into balance

equilibrium price
the price that balances supply and demand

equilibrium quantity
the quantity supplied and the quantity demanded when the price has adjusted to balance supply and demand

equity
the property of distributing economic prosperity fairly among the members of society

excludable
the property of a good whereby a person can be prevented from using it

exports
goods produced domestically and sold abroad

externality
the uncompensated impact of one person's actions on the wellbeing of a bystander. A positive externality makes the bystander better off. A negative externality makes the bystander worse off.

factors of production
the inputs used to produce goods and services

fixed costs
costs that do not vary with the quantity of output produced

free rider
a person who receives the benefit of a good but avoids paying for it

game theory
the study of how people behave in strategic situations

Giffen good
a good for which an increase in the price raises the quantity demanded

horizontal equity
the idea that taxpayers with similar abilities to pay taxes should pay the same amount

human capital
the accumulation of investments in people, such as education and on-the-job training

import quota
a limit on the quantity of a good produced abroad that can be sold domestically

imports
goods produced abroad and sold domestically

income effect
the change in consumption that results when a price change moves the consumer to a higher or lower indifference curve

income elasticity of demand
a measure of how much the quantity demanded of a good responds to a change in consumers' income, calculated as the percentage change in quantity demanded divided by the percentage change in income

indifference curve
a curve that shows consumption bundles that give the consumer the same level of satisfaction

inferior good
a good for which, other things being equal, an increase in income leads to a decrease in quantity demanded

inflation
an increase in the overall level of prices in the economy

internalising an externality
altering incentives so that people take into account the external effects of their actions

invisible hand
The idea that buyers and sellers freely interacting in a market economy will create an outcome that allocates goods and services to those people who value them most highly and makes the best use of our scarce resources

law of demand
the claim that, other things being equal, the quantity demanded of a good falls when the price of the good rises

law of supply
the claim that, other things being equal, the quantity supplied of a good rises when the price of the good rises

law of supply and demand
the claim that the price of any good adjusts to bring the supply and demand for that good into balance

libertarianism
the political philosophy according to which the government should punish crimes and enforce voluntary agreements but not redistribute income

life cycle
the regular pattern of income variation over a person's life

lump-sum tax
a tax that is the same amount for every person

macroeconomics
the study of economy-wide phenomena, including inflation, unemployment and economic growth

marginal change
a small incremental adjustment to a plan of action

marginal cost
the increase in total cost that arises from an extra unit of production

marginal product
the increase in output that arises from an additional unit of input

marginal product of labour
the increase in the amount of output from an additional unit of labour

marginal rate of substitution
the rate at which a consumer is willing to trade one good for another

marginal revenue
the change in total revenue from an additional unit sold

marginal tax rate
the extra taxes paid on an additional dollar of income

market
a group of buyers and sellers of a particular good or service

market economy
an economy that allocates resources through the decentralised decisions of many firms and households as they interact in markets for goods and services

market failure
a situation in which a market left on its own fails to allocate resources efficiently

market power
the ability of a single economic actor (or small group of actors) to have a substantial influence on market prices

maximin criterion
the claim that the government should aim to maximise the wellbeing of the worst-off person in society

median voter theorem
a mathematical result showing that if voters are choosing a point along a line and each voter wants the point closest to his most preferred point, then majority rule will pick the most preferred point of the median voter

microeconomics
the study of how households and firms make decisions and how they interact in markets

monopolistic competition
a market structure in which many firms sell products that are similar but not identical

monopoly
a firm that is the sole seller of a product without close substitutes

monopsony
a market situation where there is a single buyer for a product

moral hazard
the tendency of a person who is imperfectly monitored to engage in dishonest or otherwise undesirable behaviour

Nash equilibrium
a situation in which economic actors interacting with one another each choose their best strategy given the strategies that all the other actors have chosen

natural monopoly
a monopoly that arises because a single firm can supply a good or service to an entire market at a smaller cost than could two or more firms

negative income tax
a tax system that collects revenue from high-income households and gives transfers to low-income households

normal good
a good for which, other things being equal, an increase in income leads to an increase in quantity demanded

normative statements
claims that attempt to prescribe how the world should be

oligopoly
a market structure in which only a few sellers offer similar or identical products

opportunity cost
whatever must be given up to obtain some item

perfect complements
two goods with right-angle indifference curves

perfect substitutes
two goods with straight-line indifference curves

permanent income
a person's normal income

Phillips curve
the short-term trade-off between inflation and unemployment

positive statements
claims that attempt to describe the world as it is

possibilities frontier
a graph depicting all the outcomes that maximise the sum of profits plus wages to workers

poverty line
an absolute level of income set by the federal government for each family size below which a family is deemed to be in poverty

poverty rate
the percentage of the population whose family income falls below an absolute level called the poverty line

predatory pricing
when a firm sells its product at an artificially low price in order to drive out an efficient competitor and reduce long-run competition

price ceiling
a legal maximum on the price at which a good can be sold

price discrimination
the business practice of selling the same good at different prices to different customers

price elasticity of demand
a measure of how much the quantity demanded of a good responds to a change in the price of that good, calculated as the percentage change in quantity demanded divided by the percentage change in price

price elasticity of supply
a measure of how much the quantity supplied of a good responds to a change in the price of that good, calculated as the percentage change in quantity supplied divided by the percentage change in price

price floor
a legal minimum on the price at which a good can be sold

principal
a person for whom another person, called the agent, is performing some act

prisoners' dilemma
a particular 'game' between two captured prisoners that illustrates why cooperation is difficult to maintain even when it is mutually beneficial

private goods
goods that are both excludable and rival in consumption

privatisation
the sale of a government-owned business to private owners

producer surplus
the amount a seller is paid for a good minus the seller's cost

production function
the relationship between quantity of inputs used to make a good and the quantity of output of that good

production possibilities frontier
a graph that shows the various combinations of output that the economy can possibly produce given the available factors of production and the available production technology

productivity
the quantity of goods and services produced from each hour of a worker's time

profit
total revenue minus total cost

progressive tax
a tax for which high-income taxpayers pay a larger fraction of their income than do low-income taxpayers

proportional tax
a tax for which high-income and low-income taxpayers pay the same fraction of income

public goods
goods that are neither excludable nor rival in consumption

quantity demanded
the amount of a good that buyers are willing and able to purchase

quantity supplied
the amount of a good that sellers are willing and able to sell

Rawlsianism
the political philosophy according to which the government should choose policies deemed to be just, as evaluated by an impartial observer behind a 'veil of ignorance'

regressive tax
a tax for which high-income taxpayers pay a smaller fraction of their income than do low-income taxpayers

resale price maintenance
when a wholesaler requires that its retailers do not sell its products to their customers below a specified retail price

rival in consumption
the property of a good where one person's use diminishes other people's use

scarcity
the limited nature of society's resources

screening
an action taken by an uninformed party to induce an informed party to reveal information

shortage
a situation in which quantity demanded is greater than quantity supplied

signalling
an action taken by an informed party to reveal private information to an uninformed party

social security
government programs that supplement the incomes of the needy

strike
the organised withdrawal of labour from a firm by a union

substitutes
two goods for which a decrease in the price of one good leads to a decrease in the demand for the other good

substitution effect
the change in consumption that results when a price change moves the consumer along a given indifference curve to a point with a new marginal rate of substitution

supply curve
a graph of the relationship between the price of a good and the quantity supplied

supply schedule
a table that shows the relationship between the price of a good and the quantity supplied

surplus
a situation in which quantity supplied is greater than quantity demanded

tariff
a tax on goods produced abroad and sold domestically

tax incidence
the study of who bears the burden of taxation

total cost
the amount a firm pays to buy the inputs into production

total revenue (for a firm)
the amount a firm receives for the sale of its output

total revenue (in a market)
the amount paid by buyers and received by sellers of a good, calculated as the price of the good times the quantity sold

Trade Practices Act
see *Competition and Consumer Act*.

Tragedy of the Commons
a parable that illustrates why common resources get used more than is desirable from the standpoint of society as a whole

transaction costs
the costs that parties incur in the process of agreeing and following through on a bargain

tying
when a firm will only sell customers one product if they also buy another product

union
a worker association that bargains with employers over wages and working conditions

utilitarianism
the political philosophy according to which the government should choose policies to maximise the total utility of everyone in society

utility
a measure of happiness or satisfaction

value of the marginal product
the marginal product of an input times the price of the output

variable costs
costs that vary with the quantity of output produced

vertical equity
the idea that taxpayers with a greater ability to pay taxes should pay larger amounts

welfare economics
the study of how the allocation of resources affects economic wellbeing

willingness to pay
the maximum amount that a buyer will pay for a good

world price
the price of a good that prevails in the world market for that good

Suggestions for reading

If you enjoyed the economics course you have just finished, you might like reading more about economic issues in the following books.

- *Freakonomics: A Rogue Economist Explores the Hidden Side of Everything*, Steven D. Levitt and Stephen J. Dubner (New York: William Morrow, 2005). Economic principles and clever data analysis applied to a wide range of offbeat topics, including drug dealing, online dating and sumo wrestling.
- *The Undercover Economist: Exposing Why the Rich Are Rich, the Poor Are Poor and Why You Can Never Buy a Decent Used Car!*, Tim Harford (Oxford: Oxford University Press, 2006). An easy to read and thought-provoking introduction to the key economic issues of the day.
- *Supercrunchers: Why Thinking-by-Numbers Is the New Way to Be Smart*, Ian Ayres (New York: Bantam, 2007). What happens when you combine economics, statistics and large datasets? The answer is 'answers' and lots of them to issues that drive government and business.
- *Reinventing the Bazaar: A Natural History of Markets*, John McMillan (New York: Norton, 2002). The late, great New Zealand economist provides a deep and nuanced, yet still very readable, analysis of how society can make the best use of market mechanisms.
- *Thinking Strategically: A Competitive Edge in Business, Politics, and Everyday Life*, 2nd edn, Avinash Dixit and Barry Nalebuff (New York: Norton, 2008). This introduction to game theory discusses how all people – from corporate executives to arrested criminals – should and do make strategic decisions that affect themselves and others.
- *Micromotives and Macrobehavior*, rev. edn, Thomas Schelling (New York: Norton, 2006). The Nobel Prize winning game theorist explains how to construct models to explain how seemingly small and meaningless decisions have a big impact on the patterns of large groups.
- *Information Rules: A Strategic Guide to the Network Economy*, Carl Shapiro and Hal R. Varian (Boston: Harvard Business School Press, 1999). Two microeconomists explain how businesses succeed in the modern information-driven economy.
- *Co-opetition*, Adam M. Brandenburger and Barry J. Nalebuff (New York: Doubleday, 1996). This book explains the usefulness of game theory for business decision making in a competitive environment.
- *Capitalism and Freedom*, Milton Friedman (Chicago: University of Chicago Press, 1962). In this classic book, one of the most important economists of the twentieth century argues that society should rely less on the government and more on the free market.
- *The Worldly Philosophers*, Robert L. Heilbroner (New York: Touchstone, 1953). This classic book discusses the lives, times and ideas of the great economic thinkers, including Adam Smith, David Ricardo and John Maynard Keynes.
- *Murder at the Margin*, Marshall Jevons (Princeton, NJ: Princeton University Press, 1993), and *The Fatal Equilibrium*, Marshall Jevons (Cambridge, Mass.: MIT Press, 1985). In each of these two mystery novels, an economist-sleuth applies the principles of economics to figure out who did it. Yes, the books are corny, but they are also fun.

- *The Logic of Life,* Tim Harford (Random House, 2009). The best review of how economics can be used to explain aspects of everyday life.
- *The Limits of Organization*, Kenneth J. Arrow (New York: Norton, 1974). A Nobel laureate conducts a thoughtful examination of the foundations of economic decision making and the organisation of society.
- *Core Economics for Managers*, Joshua Gans (Melbourne: Cengage Learning, 2005). Take your economics one step further into bargaining and strategy with this text designed to teach economics to business students.

Pick of the Economics blogs

- *Marginal Revolution*: www.marginalrevolution.com. The most popular economics blog from two economists at George Mason University.
- *Freakonomics*: freakonomics.com. The two authors of Freakonomics extend their commentary of economics and everyday life.
- *Greg Mankiw*: gregmankiw.blogspot.com. One of the authors of this textbook takes a hard-headed look at macroeconomics and economic policy.
- *Brad DeLong's Semi-Daily Journal*: Delong.typepad.com. The oldest and one of the most influential economics blogs, from a Berkeley professor who grasps reality with both hands.
- *The Becker-Posner Blog*: www.becker-posner-blog.com. One Nobel laureate and a judge debate economic trends and policies.
- *Core Economics*: economics.com.au. Australian academic economists examine policy, economics and strategy.
- *John Quiggin*: johnquiggin.com. Australia's foremost economic commentator looks at the world from a social democratic perspective.

Index